JEEP | WAGONEER/COMANCHE/CHEROKEE
1984-01 REPAIR MANUAL

Covers all U.S. and Canadian models of Jeep
Cherokee, Grand Cherokee (1993 thru 1998)
Comanche, Wagoneer and
Grand Wagoneer (1993 only)

by **Matthew E. Frederick,** A.S.E., S.A.E.
and **Bob Henderson**

CHILTON *Automotive Books*

PUBLISHED BY **HAYNES NORTH AMERICA.** Inc.

AUTOMOTIVE
PARTS &
ACCESSORIES
ASSOCIATION MEMBER

Manufactured in USA
©1999, 2008 Haynes North America, Inc.
ISBN-13: 978-1-56392-710-2
ISBN-10: 1-56392-710-1
Library of Congress Control Number 2008923046

Haynes Publishing Group
Sparkford Nr Yeovil
Somerset BA22 7JJ England

Haynes North America, Inc
861 Lawrence Drive
Newbury Park
California 91320 USA

ABCDE
FGHIJ
KLMN

2

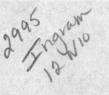

7N5

Contents

Contents

SAFETY NOTICE

Proper service and repair procedures are vital to the safe, reliable operation of all motor vehicles, as well as the personal safety of those performing repairs. This manual outlines procedures for servicing and repairing vehicles using safe, effective methods. The procedures contain many NOTES, CAUTIONS and WARNINGS which should be followed, along with standard procedures to eliminate the possibility of personal injury or improper service which could damage the vehicle or compromise its safety.

It is important to note that repair procedures and techniques, tools and parts for servicing motor vehicles, as well as the skill and experience of the individual performing the work vary widely. It is not possible to anticipate all of the conceivable ways or conditions under which vehicles may be serviced, or to provide cautions as to all possible hazards that may result. Standard and accepted safety precautions and equipment should be used when handling toxic or flammable fluids, and safety goggles or other protection should be used during cutting, grinding, chiseling, prying, or any other process that can cause material removal or projectiles.

Some procedures require the use of tools specially designed for a specific purpose. Before substituting another tool or procedure, you must be completely satisfied that neither your personal safety, nor the performance of the vehicle will be endangered.

Although information in this manual is based on industry sources and is complete as possible at the time of publication, the possibility exists that some car manufacturers made later changes which could not be included here. While striving for total accuracy, NP/Chilton cannot assume responsibility for any errors, changes or omissions that may occur in the compilation of this data.

PART NUMBERS

Part numbers listed in this reference are not recommendations by Haynes North America, Inc. for any product brand name. They are references that can be used with interchange manuals and aftermarket supplier catalogs to locate each brand supplier's discrete part number.

SPECIAL TOOLS

Special tools are recommended by the vehicle manufacturer to perform their specific job. Use has been kept to a minimum, but where absolutely necessary, they are referred to in the text by the part number of the tool manufacturer. These tools can be purchased, under the appropriate part number, from your local dealer or regional distributor, or an equivalent tool can be purchased locally from a tool supplier or parts outlet. Before substituting any tool for the one recommended, read the SAFETY NOTICE at the top of this page.

ACKNOWLEDGMENTS

The publisher expresses appreciation to Chrysler Corporation for their generous assistance.

1

GENERAL
INFORMATION
AND
MAINTENANCE

HOW TO USE THIS BOOK

Chilton's Total Car Care manual for the Wagoneer, Cherokee, Comanche and Grand Cherokee/Wagoneer models is intended to help you learn more about the inner workings of your vehicle while saving you money on its upkeep and operation.

The beginning of the book will likely be referred to the most, since that is where you will find information for maintenance and tune-up. The other sections deal with the more complex systems of your vehicle. Operating systems from engine through brakes are covered to the extent that the average do-it-yourselfer becomes mechanically involved. This book will not explain such things as rebuilding a differential for the simple reason that the expertise required and the investment in special tools make this task uneconomical. It will, however, give you detailed instructions to help you change your own brake pads and shoes, replace spark plugs, and perform many more jobs that can save you money, give you personal satisfaction and help you avoid expensive problems.

A secondary purpose of this book is a reference for owners who want to understand their vehicle and/or their mechanics better. In this case, no tools at all are required.

Where to Begin

Before removing any bolts, read through the entire procedure. This will give you the overall view of what tools and supplies will be required. There is nothing more frustrating than having to walk to the bus stop on Monday morning because you were short one bolt on Sunday afternoon. So read ahead and plan ahead. Each operation should be approached logically and all procedures thoroughly understood before attempting any work.

All sections contain adjustments, maintenance, removal and installation procedures, and in some cases, repair or overhaul procedures. When repair is not considered practical, we tell you how to remove the part and then how to install the new or rebuilt replacement. In this way, you at least save labor costs. "Backyard" repair of some components is just not practical.

Avoiding Trouble

Many procedures in this book require you to "label and disconnect . . ." a group of lines, hoses or wires. Don't be lulled into thinking you can remember where everything goes—you won't. If you hook up vacuum or fuel lines incorrectly, the vehicle may run poorly, if at all. If you hook up electrical wiring incorrectly, you may instantly learn a very expensive lesson.

You don't need to know the official or engineering name for each hose or line. A piece of masking tape on the hose and a piece on its fitting will allow you to assign your own label such as the letter A or a short name. As long as you remember your own code, the lines can be reconnected by matching similar letters or names. Do remember that tape will dissolve in gasoline or other fluids; if a component is to be washed or cleaned, use another method of identification. A permanent felt-tipped marker or a metal scribe can be very handy for marking metal parts. Remove any tape or paper labels after assembly.

Maintenance or Repair?

It's necessary to mention the difference between maintenance and repair. Maintenance includes routine inspections, adjustments, and replacement of parts which show signs of normal wear. Maintenance compensates for wear or deterioration. Repair implies that something has broken or is not working. A need for repair is often caused by lack of maintenance. Example: draining and refilling the automatic transmission fluid is maintenance recommended by the manufacturer at specific mileage intervals. Failure to do this can shorten the life of the transmission/transaxle, requiring very expensive repairs. While no maintenance program can prevent items from breaking or wearing out, a general rule can be stated: MAINTENANCE IS CHEAPER THAN REPAIR.

Two basic mechanic's rules should be mentioned here. First, whenever the left side of the vehicle or engine is referred to, it is meant to specify the driver's side. Conversely, the right side of the vehicle means the passenger's side. Second, screws and bolts are removed by turning counterclockwise, and tightened by turning clockwise unless specifically noted.

Safety is always the most important rule. Constantly be aware of the dangers involved in working on an automobile and take the proper precautions. See the information in this section regarding SERVICING YOUR VEHICLE SAFELY and the SAFETY NOTICE on the acknowledgment page.

Avoiding the Most Common Mistakes

Pay attention to the instructions provided. There are 3 common mistakes in mechanical work:

1. Incorrect order of assembly, disassembly or adjustment. When taking something apart or putting it together, performing steps in the wrong order usually just costs you extra time; however, it CAN break something. Read the entire procedure before beginning disassembly. Perform everything in the order in which the instructions say you should, even if you can't immediately see a reason for it. When you're taking apart something that is very intricate, you might want to draw a picture of how it looks when assembled at one point in order to make sure you get everything back in its proper position. We will supply exploded views whenever possible. When making adjustments, perform them in the proper order. One adjustment possibly will affect another.

2. Overtorquing (or undertorquing). While it is more common for overtorquing to cause damage, undertorquing may allow a fastener to vibrate loose causing serious damage. Especially when dealing with aluminum parts, pay attention to torque specifications and utilize a torque wrench in assembly. If a torque figure is not available, remember that if you are using the right tool to perform the job, you will probably not have to strain yourself to get a fastener tight enough. The pitch of most threads is so slight that the tension you put on the wrench will be multiplied many times in actual force on what you are tightening. A good example of how critical torque is can be seen in the case of spark plug installation, especially where you are putting the plug into an aluminum cylinder head. Too little torque can fail to crush the gasket, causing leakage of combustion gases and consequent overheating of the plug and engine parts. Too much torque can damage the threads or distort the plug, changing the spark gap.

There are many commercial products available for ensuring that fasteners won't come loose, even if they are not torqued just right (a very common brand is Loctite®). If you're worried about getting something together tight enough to hold, but loose enough to avoid mechanical damage during assembly, one of these products might offer substantial insurance. Before choosing a threadlocking compound, read the label on the package and make sure the product is compatible with the materials, fluids, etc. involved.

3. Crossthreading. This occurs when a part such as a bolt is screwed into a nut or casting at the wrong angle and forced. Crossthreading is more likely to occur if access is difficult. It helps to clean and lubricate fasteners, then to start threading the bolt, spark plug, etc. with your fingers. If you encounter resistance, unscrew the part and start over again at a different angle until it can be inserted and turned several times without much effort. Keep in mind that many parts, especially spark plugs, have tapered threads, so that gentle turning will automatically bring the part you're threading to the proper angle. Don't put a wrench on the part until it's been tightened a couple of turns by hand. If you suddenly encounter resistance, and the part has not seated fully, don't force it. Pull it back out to make sure it's clean and threading properly.

Be sure to take your time and be patient, and always plan ahead. Allow yourself ample time to perform repairs and maintenance. You may find maintaining your car a satisfying and enjoyable experience.

TOOLS AND EQUIPMENT

▶ **See Figures 1 thru 15**

Naturally, without the proper tools and equipment it is impossible to properly service your vehicle. It would also be virtually impossible to catalog every tool that you would need to perform all of the operations in this book. Of course, It would be unwise for the amateur to rush out and buy an expensive set of tools on the theory that he/she may need one or more of them at some time.

The best approach is to proceed slowly, gathering a good quality set of those tools that are used most frequently. Don't be misled by the low cost of

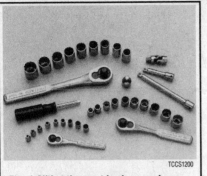

Fig. 1 All but the most basic procedures will require an assortment of ratchets and sockets

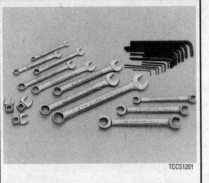

Fig. 2 In addition to ratchets, a good set of wrenches and hex keys will be necessary

Fig. 3 A hydraulic floor jack and a set of jackstands are essential for lifting and supporting the vehicle

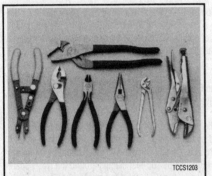

Fig. 4 An assortment of pliers, grippers and cutters will be handy for old rusted parts and stripped bolt heads

Fig. 5 Various drivers, chisels and prybars are great tools to have in your toolbox

Fig. 6 Many repairs will require the use of a torque wrench to assure the components are properly fastened

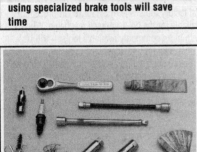

Fig. 7 Although not always necessary, using specialized brake tools will save time

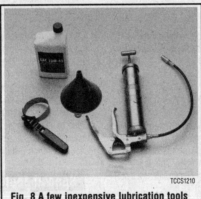

Fig. 8 A few inexpensive lubrication tools will make maintenance easier

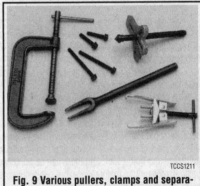

Fig. 9 Various pullers, clamps and separator tools are needed for many larger, more complicated repairs

Fig. 10 A variety of tools and gauges should be used for spark plug gapping and installation

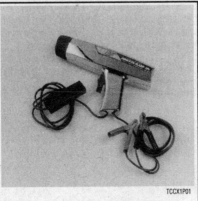

Fig. 11 Inductive type timing light

Fig. 12 A screw-in type compression gauge is recommended for compression testing

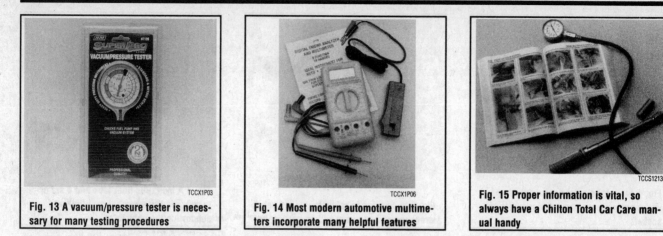

Fig. 13 A vacuum/pressure tester is necessary for many testing procedures

TCCX1P03

Fig. 14 Most modern automotive multimeters incorporate many helpful features

TCCX1P06

Fig. 15 Proper information is vital, so always have a Chilton Total Car Care manual handy

TCCS1213

bargain tools. It is far better to spend a little more for better quality. Forged wrenches, 6 or 12-point sockets and fine tooth ratchets are by far preferable to their less expensive counterparts. As any good mechanic can tell you, there are few worse experiences than trying to work on a vehicle with bad tools. Your monetary savings will be far outweighed by frustration and mangled knuckles.

Begin accumulating those tools that are used most frequently: those associated with routine maintenance and tune-up. In addition to the normal assortment of screwdrivers and pliers, you should have the following tools:

• Wrenches/sockets and combination open end/box end wrenches in sizes 3mm–19mm 13/16 in. or 5/8 in. spark plug socket (depending on plug type).

➡**If possible, buy various length socket drive extensions. Universal-joint and wobble extensions can be extremely useful, but be careful when using them, as they can change the amount of torque applied to the socket.**

• Jackstands for support.
• Oil filter wrench.
• Spout or funnel for pouring fluids.
• Grease gun for chassis lubrication (unless your vehicle is not equipped with any grease fittings—for details, please refer to information on Fluids and Lubricants, later in this section).
• Hydrometer for checking the battery (unless equipped with a sealed, maintenance-free battery).
• A container for draining oil and other fluids.
• Rags for wiping up the inevitable mess.

In addition to the above items there are several others that are not absolutely necessary, but handy to have around. These include Oil Dry® (or an equivalent oil absorbent gravel—such as cat litter) and the usual supply of lubricants, antifreeze and fluids, although these can be purchased as needed. This is a basic list for routine maintenance, but only your personal needs and desire can accurately determine your list of tools.

After performing a few projects on the vehicle, you'll be amazed at the other tools and non-tools on your workbench. Some useful household items are: a large turkey baster or siphon, empty coffee cans and ice trays (to store parts), ball of twine, electrical tape for wiring, small rolls of colored tape for tagging lines or hoses, markers and pens, a note pad, golf tees (for plugging vacuum lines), metal coat hangers or a roll of mechanic's wire (to hold things out of the way), dental pick or similar long, pointed probe, a strong magnet, and a small mirror (to see into recesses and under manifolds).

A more advanced set of tools, suitable for tune-up work, can be drawn up easily. While the tools are slightly more sophisticated, they need not be outrageously expensive. There are several inexpensive tach/dwell meters on the market that are every bit as good for the average mechanic as a professional model. Just be sure that it goes to a least 1200–1500 rpm on the tach scale and that it works on 4, 6 and 8-cylinder engines. The key to these purchases is to make them with an eye towards adaptability and wide range. A basic list of tune-up tools could include:

• Tach/dwell meter.
• Spark plug wrench and gapping tool.
• Feeler gauges for valve adjustment.
• Timing light.

The choice of a timing light should be made carefully. A light which works on the DC current supplied by the vehicle's battery is the best choice; it should have a xenon tube for brightness. On any vehicle with an electronic ignition system, a timing light with an inductive pickup that clamps around the No. 1 spark plug cable is preferred.

In addition to these basic tools, there are several other tools and gauges you may find useful. These include:

• Compression gauge. The screw-in type is slower to use, but eliminates the possibility of a faulty reading due to escaping pressure.
• Manifold vacuum gauge.
• 12V test light.
• A combination volt/ohmmeter
• Induction Ammeter. This is used for determining whether or not there is current in a wire. These are handy for use if a wire is broken somewhere in a wiring harness.

As a final note, you will probably find a torque wrench necessary for all but the most basic work. The beam type models are perfectly adequate, although the newer click types (breakaway) are easier to use. The click type torque wrenches tend to be more expensive. Also keep in mind that all types of torque wrenches should be periodically checked and/or recalibrated. You will have to decide for yourself which better fits your pocketbook, and purpose.

Special Tools

Normally, the use of special factory tools is avoided for repair procedures, since these are not readily available for the do-it-yourself mechanic. When it is possible to perform the job with more commonly available tools, it will be pointed out, but occasionally, a special tool was designed to perform a specific function and should be used. Before substituting another tool, you should be convinced that neither your safety nor the performance of the vehicle will be compromised.

Special tools can usually be purchased from an automotive parts store or from your dealer. In some cases special tools may be available directly from the tool manufacturer.

DIAGNOSTIC TEST EQUIPMENT

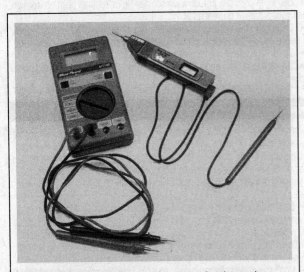

Digital multimeters come in a variety of styles and are a "must-have" for any serious home mechanic. Digital multimeters measure voltage (volts), resistance (ohms) and sometimes current (amperes). These versatile tools are used for checking all types of electrical or electronic components

Modern vehicles equipped with computer-controlled fuel, emission and ignition systems require modern electronic tools to diagnose problems. Many of these tools are designed solely for the professional mechanic and are too costly and difficult to use for the average do-it-yourselfer. However, various automotive aftermarket companies have introduced products that address the needs of the average home mechanic, providing sophisticated information at affordable cost. Consult your local auto parts store to determine what is available for your vehicle.

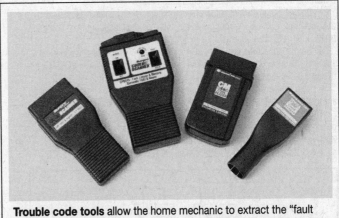

Trouble code tools allow the home mechanic to extract the "fault code" number from an on-board computer that has sensed a problem (usually indicated by a Check Engine light). Armed with this code, the home mechanic can focus attention on a suspect system or component

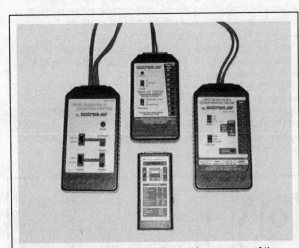

Sensor testers perform specific checks on many of the sensors and actuators used on today's computer-controlled vehicles. These testers can check sensors both on or off the vehicle, as well as test the accompanying electrical circuits

Hand-held scanners represent the most sophisticated of all do-it-yourself diagnostic tools. These tools do more than just access computer codes like the code readers above; they provide the user with an actual interface into the vehicle's computer. Comprehensive data on specific makes and models will come with the tool, either built-in or as a separate cartridge

SERVICING YOUR VEHICLE SAFELY

▶ **See Figures 16, 17, 18 and 19**

It is virtually impossible to anticipate all of the hazards involved with automotive maintenance and service, but care and common sense will prevent most accidents.

The rules of safety for mechanics range from "don't smoke around gasoline," to "use the proper tool(s) for the job." The trick to avoiding injuries is to develop safe work habits and to take every possible precaution.

Do's

- Do keep a fire extinguisher and first aid kit handy.
- Do wear safety glasses or goggles when cutting, drilling, grinding or prying, even if you have 20–20 vision. If you wear glasses for the sake of vision, wear safety goggles over your regular glasses.
- Do shield your eyes whenever you work around the battery. Batteries contain sulfuric acid. In case of contact with the eyes or skin, flush the area with water or a mixture of water and baking soda, then seek immediate medical attention.
- Do use safety stands (jackstands) for any undervehicle service. Jacks are for raising vehicles; jackstands are for making sure the vehicle stays raised until you want it to come down. Whenever the vehicle is raised, block the wheels remaining on the ground and set the parking brake.
- Do use adequate ventilation when working with any chemicals or hazardous materials. Like carbon monoxide, the asbestos dust resulting from some brake lining wear can be hazardous in sufficient quantities.
- Do disconnect the negative battery cable when working on the electrical system. The secondary ignition system contains EXTREMELY HIGH VOLTAGE. In some cases it can even exceed 50,000 volts.
- Do follow manufacturer's directions whenever working with potentially hazardous materials. Most chemicals and fluids are poisonous if taken internally.
- Do properly maintain your tools. Loose hammerheads, mushroomed punches and chisels, frayed or poorly grounded electrical cords, excessively worn screwdrivers, spread wrenches (open end), cracked sockets, slipping ratchets, or faulty droplight sockets can cause accidents.

- Likewise, keep your tools clean; a greasy wrench can slip off a bolt head, ruining the bolt and often harming your knuckles in the process.
- Do use the proper size and type of tool for the job at hand. Do select a wrench or socket that fits the nut or bolt. The wrench or socket should sit straight, not cocked.
- Do, when possible, pull on a wrench handle rather than push on it, and adjust your stance to prevent a fall.
- Do be sure that adjustable wrenches are tightly closed on the nut or bolt and pulled so that the force is on the side of the fixed jaw.
- Do strike squarely with a hammer; avoid glancing blows.
- Do set the parking brake and block the drive wheels if the work requires a running engine.

Don'ts

- Don't run the engine in a garage or anywhere else without proper ventilation—EVER! Carbon monoxide is poisonous; it takes a long time to leave the human body and you can build up a deadly supply of it in your system by simply breathing in a little every day. You may not realize you are slowly poisoning yourself. Always use power vents, windows, fans and/or open the garage door.
- Don't work around moving parts while wearing loose clothing. Short sleeves are much safer than long, loose sleeves. Hard-toed shoes with neoprene soles protect your toes and give a better grip on slippery surfaces. Jewelry such as watches, fancy belt buckles, beads or body adornment of any kind is not safe working around a vehicle. Long hair should be tied back under a hat or cap.
- Don't use pockets for toolboxes. A fall or bump can drive a screwdriver deep into your body. Even a rag hanging from your back pocket can wrap around a spinning shaft or fan.
- Don't smoke when working around gasoline, cleaning solvent or other flammable material.
- Don't smoke when working around the battery. When the battery is being charged, it gives off explosive hydrogen gas.
- Don't use gasoline to wash your hands; there are excellent soaps available. Gasoline contains dangerous additives which can enter the body through a cut or through your pores. Gasoline also removes all the natural oils from the skin so that bone dry hands will suck up oil and grease.
- Don't service the air conditioning system unless you are equipped with the necessary tools and training. When liquid or compressed gas refrigerant is released to atmospheric pressure it will absorb heat from whatever it contacts. This will chill or freeze anything it touches.
- Don't use screwdrivers for anything other than driving screws! A screwdriver used as an prying tool can snap when you least expect it, causing injuries. At the very least, you'll ruin a good screwdriver.
- Don't use an emergency jack (that little ratchet, scissors, or pantograph jack supplied with the vehicle) for anything other than changing a flat! These jacks are only intended for emergency use out on the road; they are NOT designed as a maintenance tool. If you are serious about maintaining your vehicle yourself, invest in a hydraulic floor jack of at least a 1 1/2 ton capacity, and at least two sturdy jackstands.

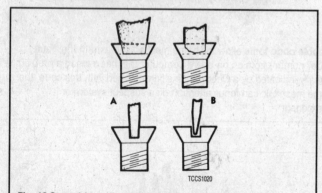

TCCS1020

Fig. 16 Screwdrivers should be kept in good condition to prevent injury or damage which could result if the blade slips from the screw

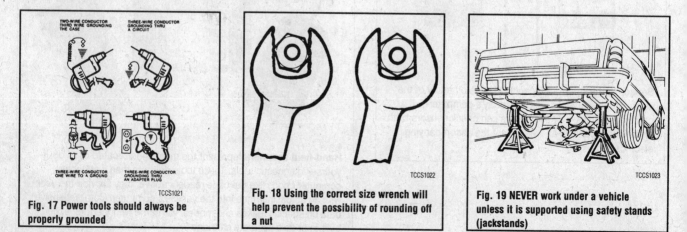

Fig. 17 Power tools should always be properly grounded

TCCS1021

Fig. 18 Using the correct size wrench will help prevent the possibility of rounding off a nut

TCCS1022

Fig. 19 NEVER work under a vehicle unless it is supported using safety stands (jackstands)

TCCS1023

FASTENERS, MEASUREMENTS AND CONVERSIONS

Bolts, Nuts and Other Threaded Retainers

▶ See Figures 20, 21, 22 and 23

Although there are a great variety of fasteners found in the modern car or truck, the most commonly used retainer is the threaded fastener (nuts, bolts, screws, studs, etc.). Most threaded retainers may be reused, provided that they are not damaged in use or during the repair. Some retainers (such as stretch bolts or torque prevailing nuts) are designed to deform when tightened or in use and should not be reinstalled.

Whenever possible, we will note any special retainers which should be replaced during a procedure. But you should always inspect the condition of a retainer when it is removed and replace any that show signs of damage. Check all threads for rust or corrosion which can increase the torque necessary to achieve the desired clamp load for which that fastener was originally selected. Additionally, be sure that the driver surface of the fastener has not been compromised by rounding or other damage. In some cases a driver surface may become only partially rounded, allowing the driver to catch in only one direction. In many of these occurrences, a fastener may be installed and tightened, but the driver would not be able to grip and loosen the fastener again. (This could lead to frustration down the line should that component ever need to be disassembled again).

If you must replace a fastener, whether due to design or damage, you must ALWAYS be sure to use the proper replacement. In all cases, a retainer of the same design, material and strength should be used. Markings on the heads of most bolts will help determine the proper strength of the fastener. The same material, thread and pitch must be selected to assure proper installation and safe operation of the vehicle afterwards.

Thread gauges are available to help measure a bolt or stud's thread. Most automotive and hardware stores keep gauges available to help you select the

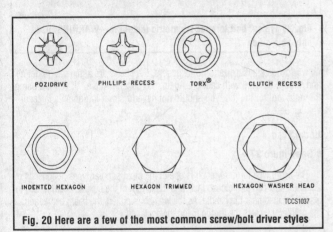

Fig. 20 Here are a few of the most common screw/bolt driver styles

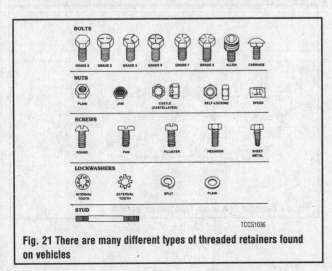

Fig. 21 There are many different types of threaded retainers found on vehicles

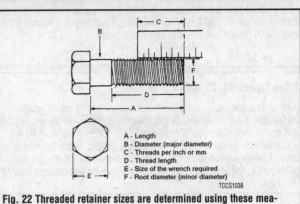

Fig. 22 Threaded retainer sizes are determined using these measurements

Fig. 23 Special fasteners such as these Torx® head bolts are used by manufacturers to discourage people from working on vehicles without the proper tools

proper size. In a pinch, you can use another nut or bolt for a thread gauge. If the bolt you are replacing is not too badly damaged, you can select a match by finding another bolt which will thread in its place. If you find a nut which threads properly onto the damaged bolt, then use that nut to help select the replacement bolt. If however, the bolt you are replacing is so badly damaged (broken or drilled out) that its threads cannot be used as a gauge, you might start by looking for another bolt (from the same assembly or a similar location on your vehicle) which will thread into the damaged bolt's mounting. If so, the other bolt can be used to select a nut; the nut can then be used to select the replacement bolt.

In all cases, be absolutely sure you have selected the proper replacement. Don't be shy, you can always ask the store clerk for help.

✳✳ WARNING

Be aware that when you find a bolt with damaged threads, you may also find the nut or drilled hole it was threaded into has also been damaged. If this is the case, you may have to drill and tap the hole, replace the nut or otherwise repair the threads. NEVER try to force a replacement bolt to fit into the damaged threads.

Torque

Torque is defined as the measurement of resistance to turning or rotating. It tends to twist a body about an axis of rotation. A common example of this would be tightening a threaded retainer such as a nut, bolt or screw. Measuring torque is one of the most common ways to help assure that a threaded retainer has been properly fastened.

When tightening a threaded fastener, torque is applied in three distinct areas, the head, the bearing surface and the clamp load. About 50 percent of the measured torque is used in overcoming bearing friction. This is the friction between the bearing surface of the bolt head, screw head or nut face and the base material or washer (the surface on which the fastener is rotating). Approximately 40 percent of the applied torque is used in overcoming thread friction. This leaves only about 10 percent of the applied torque to develop a useful clamp load (the force which holds a joint together). This means that friction can account for as much as 90 percent of the applied torque on a fastener.

TORQUE WRENCHES

▶ **See Figures 24, 25 and 26**

In most applications, a torque wrench can be used to assure proper installation of a fastener. Torque wrenches come in various designs and most automotive supply stores will carry a variety to suit your needs. A torque wrench should be used any time we supply a specific torque value for a fastener. A torque wrench can also be used if you are following the general guidelines in the accompanying charts. Keep in mind that because there is

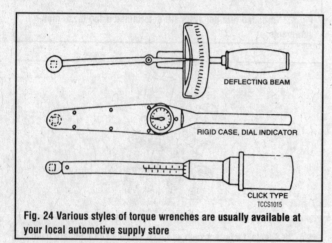

Fig. 24 Various styles of torque wrenches are usually available at your local automotive supply store

Class	Diameter mm	Pitch mm	Hexagon head bolt			Hexagon flange bolt		
			N·m	kgf·cm	ft-lbf	N·m	kgf·cm	ft-lbf
4T	6	1	5	55	48 in.·lbf	6	60	52 in.·lbf
	8	1.25	12.5	130	9	14	145	10
	10	1.25	26	260	19	29	290	21
	12	1.25	47	480	35	53	540	39
	14	1.5	74	760	55	84	850	61
	16	1.5	115	1,150	83			
5T	6	1	6.5	65	56 in.·lbf	7.5	75	65 in.·lbf
	8	1.25	15.5	160	12	17.5	175	13
	10	1.25	32	330	24	36	360	26
	12	1.25	59	600	43	65	670	48
	14	1.5	91	930	67	100	1,050	76
	16	1.5	140	1,400	101			
6T	6	1	8	80	69 in.·lbf	9	90	78 in.·lbf
	8	1.25	19	195	14	21	210	15
	10	1.25	39	400	29	44	440	32
	12	1.25	71	730	53	80	810	59
	14	1.5	110	1,100	80	125	1,250	90
	16	1.5	170	1,750	127	—	—	—
7T	6	1	10.5	110	8	12	120	9
	8	1.25	25	260	19	28	290	21
	10	1.25	52	530	38	58	590	43
	12	1.25	95	970	70	105	1,050	76
	14	1.5	145	1,500	108	165	1,700	123
	16	1.5	230	2,300	166	—	—	—
8T	8	1.25	29	300	22	33	330	24
	10	1.25	61	620	45	68	690	50
	12	1.25	110	1,100	80	120	1,250	90
9T	8	1.25	34	340	25	37	380	27
	10	1.25	70	710	51	78	790	57
	12	1.25	125	1,300	94	140	1,450	105
10T	8	1.25	38	390	28	42	430	31
	10	1.25	78	800	58	88	890	64
	12	1.25	140	1,450	105	155	1,600	116
11T	8	1.25	42	430	31	47	480	35
	10	1.25	87	890	64	97	990	72
	12	1.25	155	1,600	116	175	1,800	130

TCCS1241

Fig. 26 Typical bolt torques for metric fasteners—WARNING: use only as a guide

no worldwide standardization of fasteners, the charts are a general guideline and should be used with caution. Again, the general rule of "if you are using the right tool for the job, you should not have to strain to tighten a fastener" applies here.

Beam Type

▶ **See Figure 27**

The beam type torque wrench is one of the most popular types. It consists of a pointer attached to the head that runs the length of the flexible beam (shaft) to a scale located near the handle. As the wrench is pulled, the beam bends and the pointer indicates the torque using the scale.

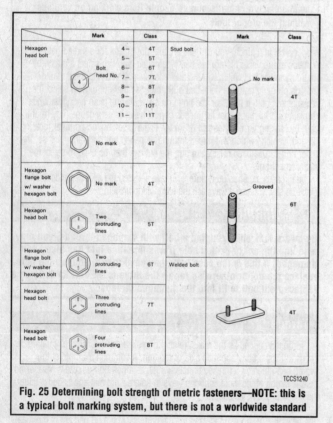

	Mark		Class		Mark	Class
Hexagon head bolt	Bolt head No.	4— 5— 6— 7— 8— 9— 10— 11—	4T 5T 6T 7T 8T 9T 10T 11T	Stud bolt	No mark	4T
	No mark		4T		Grooved	6T
Hexagon flange bolt w/ washer hexagon bolt	No mark		4T			
Hexagon head bolt	Two protruding lines		5T	Welded bolt		
Hexagon flange bolt w/ washer hexagon bolt	Two protruding lines		6T			4T
Hexagon head bolt	Three protruding lines		7T			
Hexagon head bolt	Four protruding lines		8T			

TCCS1240

Fig. 25 Determining bolt strength of metric fasteners—NOTE: this is a typical bolt marking system, but there is not a worldwide standard

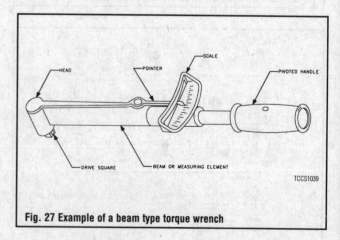

Fig. 27 Example of a beam type torque wrench

Click (Breakaway) Type

▶ See Figure 28

Another popular design of torque wrench is the click type. To use the click type wrench you pre-adjust it to a torque setting. Once the torque is reached, the wrench has a reflex signaling feature that causes a momentary breakaway of the torque wrench body, sending an impulse to the operator's hand.

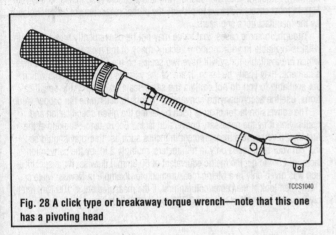

Fig. 28 A click type or breakaway torque wrench—note that this one has a pivoting head

Pivot Head Type

▶ See Figures 28 and 29

Some torque wrenches (usually of the click type) may be equipped with a pivot head which can allow it to be used in areas of limited access. BUT, it must be used properly. To hold a pivot head wrench, grasp the handle lightly, and as you pull on the handle, it should be floated on the pivot point. If the handle comes in contact with the yoke extension during the process of pulling, there is a very good chance the torque readings will be inaccurate because this could alter the wrench loading point. The design of the handle is usually such as to make it inconvenient to deliberately misuse the wrench.

➡ It should be mentioned that the use of any U-joint, wobble or extension will have an effect on the torque readings, no matter what type of wrench you are using. For the most accurate readings, install the socket directly on the wrench driver. If necessary, straight extensions (which hold a socket directly under the wrench driver) will have the least effect

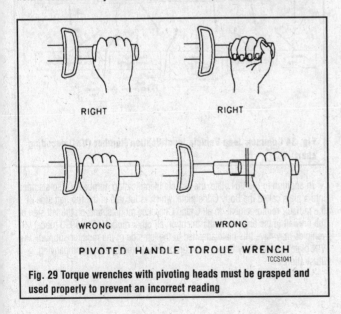

Fig. 29 Torque wrenches with pivoting heads must be grasped and used properly to prevent an incorrect reading

on the torque reading. Avoid any extension that alters the length of the wrench from the handle to the head/driving point (such as a crow's foot). U-joint or wobble extensions can greatly affect the readings; avoid their use at all times.

Rigid Case (Direct Reading)

▶ See Figure 30

A rigid case or direct reading torque wrench is equipped with a dial indicator to show torque values. One advantage of these wrenches is that they can be held at any position on the wrench without affecting accuracy. These wrenches are often preferred because they tend to be compact, easy to read and have a great degree of accuracy.

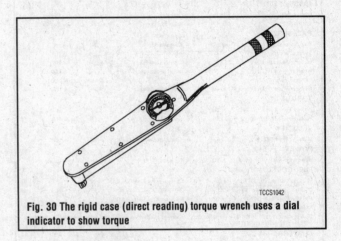

Fig. 30 The rigid case (direct reading) torque wrench uses a dial indicator to show torque

TORQUE ANGLE METERS

▶ See Figure 31

Because the frictional characteristics of each fastener or threaded hole will vary, clamp loads which are based strictly on torque will vary as well. In most applications, this variance is not significant enough to cause worry. But, in certain applications, a manufacturer's engineers may determine that more precise clamp loads are necessary (such is the case with many aluminum cylinder heads). In these cases, a torque angle method of installation would be specified. When installing fasteners which are torque angle tightened, a predetermined seating torque and standard torque wrench are usually used first to remove any compliance from the joint. The fastener is then tightened the specified additional portion of a turn measured in degrees. A torque angle gauge (mechanical protractor) is used for these applications.

Fig. 31 Some specifications require the use of a torque angle meter (mechanical protractor)

CONVERSION FACTORS

LENGTH–DISTANCE

Inches (in.)	x 25.4	= Millimeters (mm)	x .0394	= Inches
Feet (ft.)	x .305	= Meters (m)	x 3.281	= Feet
Miles	x 1.609	= Kilometers (km)	x .0621	= Miles

VOLUME

Cubic Inches (in3)	x 16.387	= Cubic Centimeters	x .061	= in3
IMP Pints (IMP pt.)	x .568	= Liters (L)	x 1.76	= IMP pt.
IMP Quarts (IMP qt.)	x 1.137	= Liters (L)	x .88	= IMP qt.
IMP Gallons (IMP gal.)	x 4.546	= Liters (L)	x .22	= IMP gal.
IMP Quarts (IMP qt.)	x 1.201	= US Quarts (US qt.)	x .833	= IMP qt.
IMP Gallons (IMP gal.)	x 1.201	= US Gallons (US gal.)	x .833	= IMP gal.
Fl. Ounces	x 29.573	= Milliliters	x .034	= Ounces
US Pints (US pt.)	x .473	= Liters (L)	x 2.113	= Pints
US Quarts (US qt.)	x .946	= Liters (L)	x 1.057	= Quarts
US Gallons (US gal.)	x 3.785	= Liters (L)	x .264	= Gallons

MASS–WEIGHT

Ounces (oz.)	x 28.35	= Grams (g)	x .035	= Ounces
Pounds (lb.)	x .454	= Kilograms (kg)	x 2.205	= Pounds

PRESSURE

Pounds Per Sq. In. (psi)	x 6.895	= Kilopascals (kPa)	x .145	= psi
Inches of Mercury (Hg)	x .4912	= psi	x 2.036	= Hg
Inches of Mercury (Hg)	x 3.377	= Kilopascals (kPa)	x .2961	= Hg
Inches of Water (H₂O)	x .07355	= Inches of Mercury	x 13.783	= H₂O
Inches of Water (H₂O)	x .03613	= psi	x 27.684	= H₂O
Inches of Water (H₂O)	x .248	= Kilopascals (kPa)	x 4.026	= H₂O

TORQUE

Pounds–Force Inches (in–lb)	x .113	= Newton Meters (N·m)	x 8.85	= in–lb
Pounds–Force Feet (ft–lb)	x 1.356	= Newton Meters (N·m)	x .738	= ft–lb

VELOCITY

Miles Per Hour (MPH)	x 1.609	= Kilometers Per Hour (KPH)	x .621	= MPH

POWER

Horsepower (Hp)	x .745	= Kilowatts	x 1.34	= Horsepower

FUEL CONSUMPTION*

Miles Per Gallon IMP (MPG)	x .354	= Kilometers Per Liter (Km/L)	
Kilometers Per Liter (Km/L)	x 2.352	= IMP MPG	
Miles Per Gallon US (MPG)	x .425	= Kilometers Per Liter (Km/L)	
Kilometers Per Liter (Km/L)	x 2.352	= US MPG	

*It is common to covert from miles per gallon (mpg) to liters/100 kilometers (1/100 km), where mpg (IMP) x 1/100 km = 282 and mpg (US) x 1/100 km = 235.

TEMPERATURE

Degree Fahrenheit (°F)	= (°C x 1.8) + 32
Degree Celsius (°C)	= (°F – 32) x .56

TCCS1044

Fig. 32 Standard and metric conversion factors chart

Standard and Metric Measurements

▶ **See Figure 32**

Throughout this manual, specifications are given to help you determine the condition of various components on your vehicle, or to assist you in their installation. Some of the most common measurements include length (in. or cm/mm), torque (ft. lbs., inch lbs. or Nm) and pressure (psi, in. Hg, kPa or mm Hg). In most cases, we strive to provide the proper measurement as determined by the manufacturer's engineers.

Though, in some cases, that value may not be conveniently measured with what is available in your toolbox. Luckily, many of the measuring devices which are available today will have two scales so the Standard or Metric measurements may easily be taken. If any of the various measuring tools which are available to you do not contain the same scale as listed in the specifications, use the accompanying conversion factors to determine the proper value.

The conversion factor chart is used by taking the given specification and multiplying it by the necessary conversion factor. For instance, looking at the first line, if you have a measurement in inches such as "free-play should be 2 in." but your ruler reads only in millimeters, multiply 2 in. by the conversion factor of 25.4 to get the metric equivalent of 50.8mm. Likewise, if the specification was given only in a Metric measurement, for example in Newton Meters (Nm), then look at the center column first. If the measurement is 100 Nm, multiply it by the conversion factor of 0.738 to get 73.8 ft. lbs.

SERIAL NUMBER IDENTIFICATION

Vehicle

▶ **See Figures 33 and 34**

The Vehicle Identification Number (VIN) is stamped into a metal plate that is located on the left side of the instrument panel pad, visible through the windshield.

86741P01

Fig. 33 The VIN plate is usually located on the left side of the instrument panel, visible through the windshield

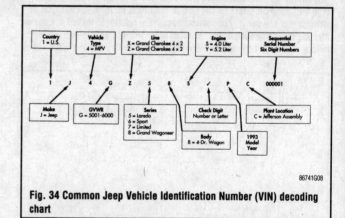

86741G08

Fig. 34 Common Jeep Vehicle Identification Number (VIN) decoding chart

In addition to the VIN plate, the vehicle identification number is also stamped into a plate called the Body Code plate, which is located at the top, left side of the radiator reinforcement on all Grand Cherokee models, and on the left side of the firewall in the engine compartment on all other models. Pre-1990 model vehicles may have this plate attached to the left side of the radiator support. The VIN plate and the Body Code plate can be interpreted by the accompanying illustrations.

VEHICLE IDENTIFICATION CHART

Engine Code						Model Year	
Code	Liters	Cu. In.	Cyl.	Fuel Sys.	Eng. Mfg.	Code	Year
B	2.1	126	4	Diesel	Renault	E	1984
U	2.5	150	4	1 bbl	AMC	F	1985
H	2.5	150	4	TBI	AMC	G	1986
W	2.8	173	6	2 bbl	Chevrolet	H	1987
M	4.0	243	6	MPI	Chrysler	J	1988
E	2.5	150	4	TBI	AMC	K	1989
L	4.0	243	6	MPI	Chrysler	L	1990
P	2.5	150	4	MPI	AMC	M	1991
S	4.0	243	6	MPI	Chrysler	N	1992
Y	5.2	318	8	MPI	Chrysler	P	1993
Z	5.9	360	8	MPI	Chrysler	R	1994
						S	1995
						T	1996
						V	1997
						W	1998
						X	1999
						Y	2000
						I	2001

TBI - Throttle Body Injection

MPI - Multi Port Injection

91071C01

Engine

2.1L TURBO DIESEL

▶ **See Figure 35**

The serial number for the Renault-built diesel is found on a machined pad located at the front of the block.

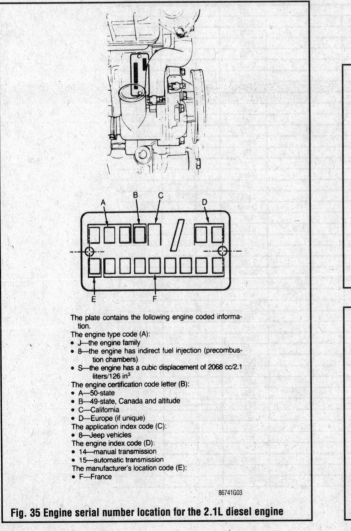

The plate contains the following engine coded information.
The engine type code (A):
- J—the engine family
- 8—the engine has indirect fuel injection (precombustion chambers)
- S—the engine has a cubic displacement of 2068 cc/2.1 liters/126 in³
The engine certification code letter (B):
- A—50-state
- B—49-state, Canada and altitude
- C—California
- D—Europe (if unique)
The application index code (C):
- 8—Jeep vehicles
The engine index code (D):
- 14—manual transmission
- 15—automatic transmission
The manufacturer's location code (E):
- F—France

86741G03

Fig. 35 Engine serial number location for the 2.1L diesel engine

2.5L ENGINE

▶ **See Figures 36 and 37**

The serial number for the American-Motors built 2.5L engine is located on a machined pad on the rear right side of the block, between cylinders number 3 and 4.

Also on the block, just above the oil filter, is the oversized/undersized component code. The codes are explained as follows:

- B: cylinder bores 0.010 in. over
- C: camshaft bearing bores 0.010 in. over
- M: main bearing journals 0.010 in. under
- P: connecting rod journals 0.010 in. under

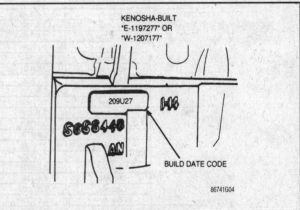

Fig. 36 Engine serial number location for the 2.5L engine

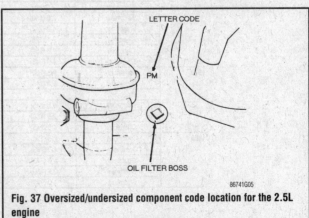

Fig. 37 Oversized/undersized component code location for the 2.5L engine

2.8L ENGINE

♦ See Figure 38

The serial number for the Chevrolet built 2.8L engine is located on an upward facing, machined surface on the right side of the block, just below the cylinder head and above the water pump.

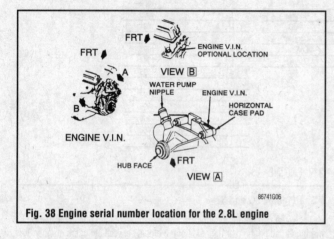

Fig. 38 Engine serial number location for the 2.8L engine

4.0L ENGINE

♦ See Figure 39

The serial number is found on a machined surface on the right side of the engine block between number 2 and 3 cylinders. For further identification, the displacement is cast into the side of the block. The letter in the code identifies the engine by displacement (cu. in.), carburetor type and compression ratio.

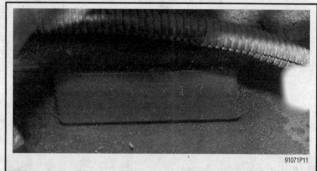

Fig. 39 Engine serial number location for the 4.0L engine can be found on the right side of the cylinder block between the number 2 and 3 cylinders

ENGINE IDENTIFICATION

Year	Model	Engine Displacement Liters (cu. in.)	Engine Series (ID/VIN)	Fuel System	No. of Cylinders	Engine Type
1984	Comanche	2.5 (150)	U	1 bbl	4	OHV
	Comanche	2.8 (173)	W	2 bbl	6	OHV
	Wagoneer	2.5 (150)	U	1 bbl	4	OHV
	Wagoneer	2.8 (173)	W	2 bbl	6	OHV
	Cherokee	2.5 (150)	U	1 bbl	4	OHV
	Cherokee	2.8 (173)	W	2 bbl	6	OHV
1985	Comanche	2.1 (126)	B	Diesel	4	OHC
	Comanche	2.5 (150)	H	TBI	4	OHV
	Comanche	2.8 (173)	W	2 bbl	6	OHV
	Wagoneer	2.1 (126)	B	Diesel	4	OHC
	Wagoneer	2.5 (150)	H	TBI	4	OHV
	Wagoneer	2.8 (173)	W	2 bbl	6	OHV
	Cherokee	2.1 (126)	B	Diesel	4	OHC
	Cherokee	2.5 (150)	H	TBI	4	OHV
	Cherokee	2.8 (173)	W	2 bbl	6	OHV
1986	Comanche	2.1 (126)	B	Diesel	4	OHC
	Comanche	2.5 (150)	H	TBI	4	OHV
	Comanche	2.8 (173)	W	2 bbl	6	OHV
	Wagoneer	2.1 (126)	B	Diesel	4	OHC
	Wagoneer	2.5 (150)	H	TBI	4	OHV
	Wagoneer	2.8 (173)	W	2 bbl	6	OHV
	Cherokee	2.1 (126)	B	Diesel	4	OHC
	Cherokee	2.5 (150)	H	TBI	4	OHV
	Cherokee	2.8 (173)	W	2 bbl	6	OHV
1987	Comanche	2.1 (126)	B	Diesel	4	OHC
	Comanche	2.5 (150)	H	TBI	4	OHV
	Comanche	4.0 (243)	M	MPI	6	OHV
	Wagoneer	2.1 (126)	B	Diesel	4	OHC
	Wagoneer	2.5 (150)	H	TBI	4	OHV
	Wagoneer	4.0 (243)	M	MPI	6	OHV
	Cherokee	2.1 (126)	B	Diesel	4	OHC
	Cherokee	2.5 (150)	H	TBI	4	OHV
	Cherokee	4.0 (243)	M	MPI	6	OHV
1988	Comanche	2.5 (150)	H	TBI	4	OHV
	Comanche	4.0 (243)	M	MPI	6	OHV
	Wagoneer	2.5 (150)	H	TBI	4	OHV
	Wagoneer	4.0 (243)	M	MPI	6	OHV
	Cherokee	2.5 (150)	H	TBI	4	OHV
	Cherokee	4.0 (243)	M	MPI	6	OHV
1989	Comanche	2.5 (150)	E	TBI	4	OHV
	Comanche	4.0 (243)	L	MPI	6	OHV
	Wagoneer	4.0 (243)	L	MPI	6	OHV
	Cherokee	2.5 (150)	E	TBI	4	OHV
	Cherokee	4.0 (243)	L	MPI	6	OHV

GENERAL ENGINE SPECIFICATIONS

Year	Engine ID/VIN	Engine Displacement Liters (cc)	Fuel System Type	Net Horsepower @ rpm	Net Torque @ rpm (ft. lbs.)	Bore x Stroke (in.)	Compression Ratio	Oil Pressure (psi) @ rpm
1984	U	2.5 (150)	1 bbl	83 @ 4200	116 @ 2600	3.88 x 3.19	9.2:1	40 @ 2000
1985	W	2.8 (173)	2 bbl	115 @ 4800	150 @ 3500	3.50 x 2.10	8.5:1	45 @ 2000
	B	2.1 (126)	Diesel	85 @ 3750	132 @ 2750	3.50 x 3.36	21.5:1	43 @ 2000
	H	2.5 (150)	TBI	117 @ 5000	135 @ 3000	3.88 x 3.19	9.2:1	40 @ 2000
1986	W	2.8 (173)	2 bbl	115 @ 4800	150 @ 3750	3.50 x 2.10	8.5:1	45 @ 2000
	B	2.1 (126)	Diesel	85 @ 3750	132 @ 2750	3.50 x 3.36	21.5:1	43 @ 2000
	H	2.5 (150)	TBI	117 @ 5000	135 @ 3000	3.88 x 3.19	9.2:1	40 @ 2000
1987	W	2.8 (173)	2 bbl	115 @ 4800	150 @ 3500	3.50 x 2.10	8.5:1	45 @ 2000
	B	2.1 (126)	Diesel	85 @ 3750	132 @ 2750	3.50 x 3.36	21.5:1	43 @ 2000
	H	2.5 (150)	TBI	117 @ 5000	135 @ 3000	3.88 x 3.19	9.2:1	40 @ 2000
1988	M	4.0 (243)	MPI	150 @ 4300	210 @ 2100	3.87 x 3.44	8.8:1	40 @ 2000
	H	2.5 (150)	TBI	117 @ 5000	135 @ 3000	3.88 x 3.19	9.2:1	40 @ 2000
1989	M	4.0 (243)	MPI	150 @ 4300	210 @ 2100	3.87 x 3.44	8.8:1	37 @ 1600
	E	2.5 (150)	TBI	121 @ 5250	141 @ 3250	3.88 x 3.19	9.2:1	37 @ 1600
1990	L	4.0 (243)	MPI	177 @ 4500	224 @ 2500	3.88 x 3.41	9.2:1	37 @ 1600
	E	2.5 (150)	TBI	121 @ 5250	141 @ 3250	3.88 x 3.19	9.2:1	37 @ 1600
1991	L	4.0 (243)	MPI	177 @ 4500	224 @ 2500	3.88 x 3.41	9.2:1	37 @ 1600
	P	2.5 (150)	MPI	128 @ 5250	147 @ 3000	3.88 x 3.19	9.2:1	37 @ 1600
1992	S	4.0 (243)	MPI	190 @ 4750	225 @ 4000	3.88 x 3.41	8.8:1	37 @ 1600
	P	2.5 (150)	MPI	130 @ 5250	149 @ 3000	3.88 x 3.19	9.2:1	37 @ 1600
1993	S	4.0 (243)	MPI	190 @ 4750	225 @ 4000	3.88 x 3.41	8.8:1	37 @ 1600
	P	2.5 (150)	MPI	130 @ 5250	149 @ 3000	3.88 x 3.19	9.2:1	37 @ 1600
	Y	5.2 (318)	MPI	220 @ 4800	285 @ 3600	3.91 x 3.31	9.1:1	30 @ 3000
1994	P	2.5 (150)	MPI	130 @ 5250	149 @ 3000	3.88 x 3.19	9.2:1	37 @ 1600
	S	4.0 (243)	MPI	190 @ 4750	225 @ 4000	3.88 x 3.41	8.8:1	37 @ 1600
	Y	5.2 (318)	MPI	220 @ 4800	285 @ 3600	3.91 x 3.31	9.1:1	30 @ 3000
1995	P	2.5 (150)	MPI	130 @ 5250	149 @ 3000	3.88 x 3.19	9.2:1	37 @ 1600
	S	4.0 (243)	MPI	190 @ 4750	225 @ 4000	3.88 x 3.41	8.8:1	37 @ 1600
	Y	5.2 (318)	MPI	220 @ 4800	285 @ 3600	3.91 x 3.31	9.1:1	30 @ 3000
1996	P	2.5 (150)	MPI	125 @ 5400	150 @ 3250	3.88 x 3.19	9.2:1	37 @ 1600
	S	4.0 (243)	MPI	190 @ 4600	225 @ 3000	3.88 x 3.41	8.8:1	37 @ 1600
	Y	5.2 (318)	MPI	220 @ 4400	300 @ 3200	3.91 x 3.31	9.1:1	30 @ 3000
1997	P	2.5 (150)	MPI	125 @ 5400	150 @ 3250	3.88 x 3.19	9.2:1	37 @ 1600
	S	4.0 (243)	MPI	190 @ 4600	225 @ 3000	3.88 x 3.41	8.8:1	37 @ 1600
	Y	5.2 (318)	MPI	220 @ 4400	300 @ 2800	3.91 x 3.31	9.1:1	30 @ 3000
	Z	5.9 (360)	MPI	245 @ 4000	345 @ 3200	4.00 x 3.58	8.7:1	30 @ 3000
1998 on	P	2.5 (150)	MPI	125 @ 5400	150 @ 3250	3.88 x 3.19	9.2:1	37 @ 1600
	S	4.0 (243)	MPI	190 @ 4600	225 @ 3000	3.88 x 3.41	8.8:1	37 @ 1600
	Y	5.2 (318)	MPI	220 @ 4400	300 @ 2800	3.91 x 3.31	9.1:1	30 @ 3000
	Z	5.9 (360)	MPI	245 @ 4000	345 @ 3200	4.00 x 3.58	8.7:1	30 @ 3000

MPI-Multi port injection
TBI-Throttle body injection

91071C08

ENGINE IDENTIFICATION

Year	Model	Engine Displacement Liters (cu. in.)	Engine Series (ID/VIN)	Fuel System	No. of Cylinders	Engine Type
1990	Comanche	2.5 (150)	E	TBI	4	OHV
	Comanche	4.0 (243)	L	MPI	6	OHV
	Wagoneer	4.0 (243)	L	MPI	6	OHV
	Cherokee	2.5 (150)	E	TBI	4	OHV
	Cherokee	4.0 (243)	L	MPI	6	OHV
1991	Comanche	2.5 (150)	P	MPI	4	OHV
	Comanche	4.0 (243)	S	MPI	6	OHV
	Cherokee	2.5 (150)	P	MPI	4	OHV
	Cherokee	4.0 (243)	S	MPI	6	OHV
1992	Comanche	2.5 (150)	P	MPI	4	OHV
	Cherokee	4.0 (243)	S	MPI	6	OHV
1993	Cherokee	2.5 (150)	P	MPI	4	OHV
	Grand Cherokee	4.0 (243)	S	MPI	6	OHV
	Grand Cherokee	5.2 (318)	Y	MPI	8	OHV
1994	Cherokee	2.5 (150)	P	MPI	4	OHV
	Cherokee	4.0 (243)	S	MPI	6	OHV
	Grand Cherokee	5.2 (318)	Y	MPI	8	OHV
1995	Cherokee	2.5 (150)	P	MPI	4	OHV
	Cherokee	4.0 (243)	S	MPI	6	OHV
	Grand Cherokee	5.2 (318)	Y	MPI	8	OHV
1996	Cherokee	2.5 (150)	P	MPI	4	OHV
	Cherokee	4.0 (243)	S	MPI	6	OHV
	Grand Cherokee	5.2 (318)	Y	MPI	8	OHV
1997	Cherokee	2.5 (150)	P	MPI	4	OHV
	Cherokee	4.0 (243)	S	MPI	6	OHV
	Grand Cherokee	5.2 (318)	Y	MPI	8	OHV
	Grand Cherokee	5.9 (360)	Z	MPI	8	OHV
1998 on	Cherokee	2.5 (150)	P	MPI	4	OHV
	Cherokee	4.0 (243)	S	MPI	6	OHV
	Grand Cherokee	5.2 (318)	Y	MPI	8	OHV
	Grand Cherokee	5.9 (360)	Z	MPI	8	OHV

TBI - Throttle Body Injection
MPI - Multi Port Injection
OHV - Over Head Valve
OHC - Over Head Camshaft

91071C03

The undersize/oversize bearing letter codes, located on the boss directly above the oil filter, are as follows:
- Letter B indicates 0.010 in. oversized cylinder bore
- Letter C indicates 0.010 in. oversized camshaft block bores
- Letter M indicates 0.010 in. undersized main bearings
- Letter P indicates 0.010 in. undersized connecting rod bearings

5.2L & 5.9L ENGINES

The serial number is found on a machined surface on the left, front corner of the cylinder block.

Transmission

MANUAL TRANSMISSIONS

Aisin AX4, AX5 and AX15 Transmissions

▶ See Figures 40 and 41

The AX4 is a 4-speed synchromesh manual transmission. The AX5 and AX15 are 5-speed synchromesh manual transmissions. The shift mechanism in all is integral and mounted in the shift tower portion of the housing. The transmission identification code for the Aisin AX4/5/15 transmissions is located on the bottom of the transmission case near the filler plug. The first three numbers identify the date of manufacture (for example, 902=1989, February). The next series of numbers is the serial number.

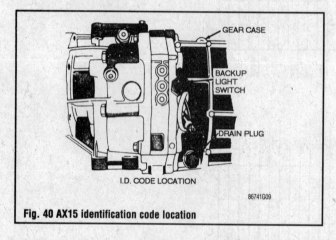

Fig. 40 AX15 identification code location

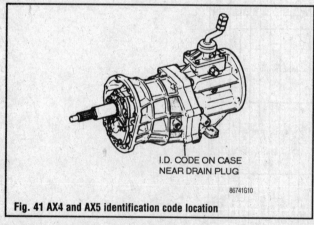

Fig. 41 AX4 and AX5 identification code location

BA10/5 Transmission

▶ See Figure 42

The BA10/5 is a 5-speed, synchromesh manual transmission. The shifter is mounted in the transmission's intermediate case. The BA10/5 identification code

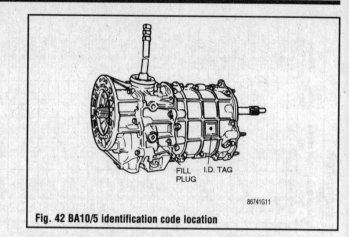

Fig. 42 BA10/5 identification code location

is located on a tag, riveted to the left side of the transmission. The plate provides build date, part number, and serial number identification.

AUTOMATIC TRANSMISSIONS

AW-4 Transmission

▶ See Figure 43

The AW-4 is a 4-speed, electronically controlled automatic transmission. The identification plate is attached to the right side of the transmission case.

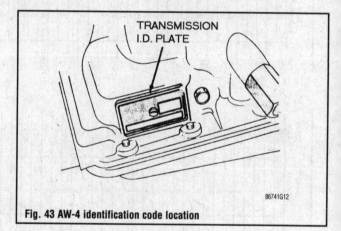

Fig. 43 AW-4 identification code location

42RE/44RE/46RE Transmission

▶ See Figure 44

The 42RE/44RE/46RE is a 4-speed fully automatic transmission with electronic governor. The ID numbers are stamped on the case's left side just above the oil pan.

Fig. 44 Common location of the identification code for the 42/44/46RE, 42/46RH and 30/32RH transmissions

42RH/46RH Transmission

The Chrysler 42RH/46RH automatic transmission is a 4-speed fully automatic unit with an overdrive 4th gear. The ID numbers are stamped on the case's left side just above the oil pan.

30RH/32RH Transmission

The Chrysler 30RH/32RH transmission is a 3-speed automatic transmission with a gear type oil pump. The ID numbers are stamped on case's left side just above the oil pan.

Drive Axles

DANA 30, 35, 44 & 8 1/4 IN. AXLE

▶ See Figure 45

Dana model 30 drive axles can be identified by an ID plate attached to the right side of the cover housing. The information tag includes ring and pinion gear, production date and manufacturer's ID.

Gear ratio for the Dana 30 axle can be computed by dividing the number of teeth on the ring gear (the larger number) by the number of teeth on the pinion gear. Both numbers are provided on the ID plate.

➡ If the ID plate cannot be located, the rear cover can be removed in order to count the teeth.

Dana model 35, 44 and 8 1/4in. drive axles can be identified by a tag located on the left side of the housing cover. The tag lists part number and gear ratio. The production date and manufacturer's ID are stamped into the right side axle shaft.

Fig. 45 Location of identification tag on a front and/or rear differential/axle assembly

AMC 7 9/16 IN.

▶ See Figure 46

The ID code for the AMC 7 9/16 in. axle is stamped in the right side axle tube boss. Code "S" indicates a 3.73:1 ratio. Code "T" indicates a 3.31:1 ratio. Code "SS" or "TT" indicates the rear axle has a Trac-Lok® differential.

181 FBI, 194 RBI & 216 RBA AXLE

181 Front Beam-design Iron (FBI), 194 Rear Beam-design Iron (RBI) and 216 Rear Beam-design Aluminum (RBA) drive axles can be identified by an ID tag attached to the differential housing cover by a cover bolt. The ID tag includes assembly part numbers and gear ratio information. Manufacturing date identification codes are stamped onto the differential cover side of the axle shaft tube.

All 4WD Cherokee and Grand Cherokee models for 1997 and later are equipped with the 181 FBI drive axle.

All 1997 and later Cherokee models are equipped with the 194 RBI drive axle.

Grand Cherokee models for 1997–98 are equipped with either the 194 RBI or 216 RBA drive axles.

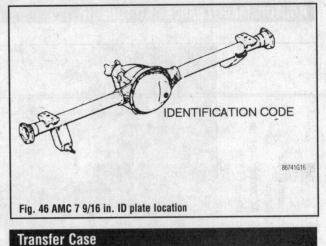

Fig. 46 AMC 7 9/16 in. ID plate location

Transfer Case

▶ See Figures 47 and 48

The ID plate for all New Process and New Venture transfer cases is a circular tag attached to the rear of the case. The ID plate provides model, assembly and serial numbers along with low range ratio. The serial number is also the build date (for example, 8-10-89 = August 10, 1989).

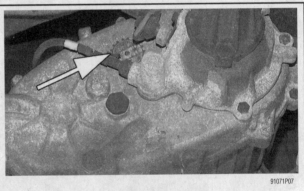

Fig. 47 Location of the identification tag on the transfer case (4x4 only)

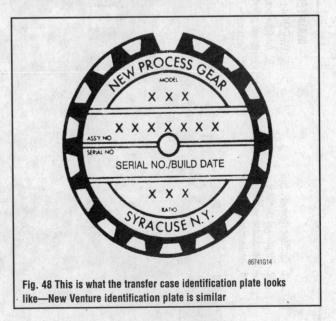

Fig. 48 This is what the transfer case identification plate looks like—New Venture identification plate is similar

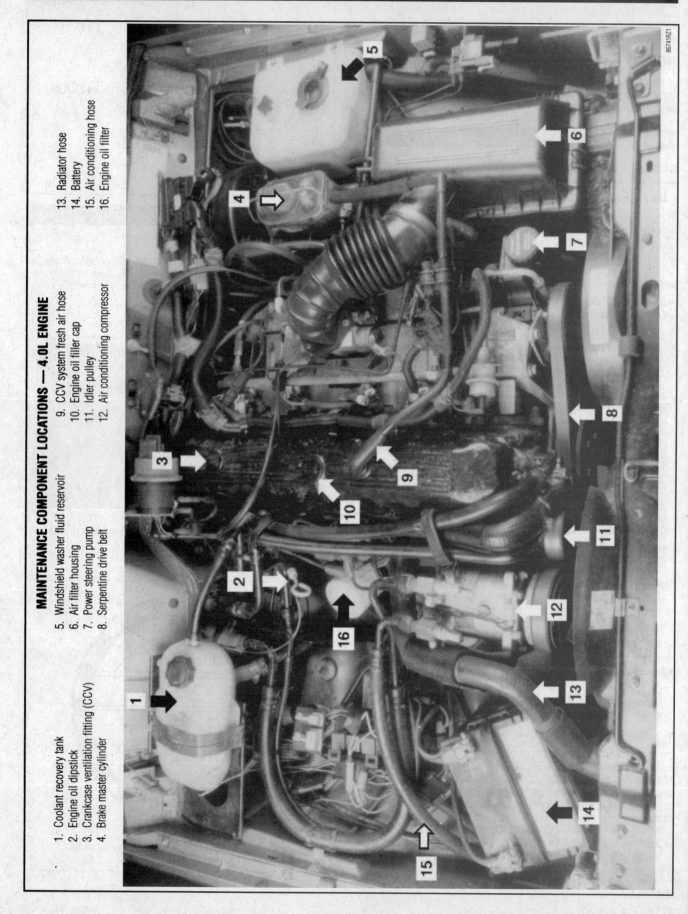

MAINTENANCE COMPONENT LOCATIONS — 4.0L ENGINE

1. Coolant recovery tank
2. Engine oil dipstick
3. Crankcase ventilation fitting (CCV)
4. Brake master cylinder
5. Windshield washer fluid reservoir
6. Air filter housing
7. Power steering pump
8. Serpentine drive belt
9. CCV system fresh air hose
10. Engine oil filler cap
11. Idler pulley
12. Air conditioning compressor
13. Radiator hose
14. Battery
15. Air conditioning hose
16. Engine oil filter

86741R21

MAINTENANCE COMPONENT LOCATIONS — 5.2L ENGINE

1. Coolant recovery tank
2. Engine oil filler cap
3. Air conditioning hose
4. Brake master cylinder reservoir
5. Brake booster
6. Windshield washer fluid reservoir
7. Power steering pump
8. Air filter housing
9. Radiator hose
10. Serpentine drive belt
11. Vehicle emission label
12. Air conditioning compressor
13. Alternator
14. Engine oil dipstick
15. Battery
16. Supplemental Restraint System label (SRS)
17. Serpentine belt routing label
18. Refrigerant label

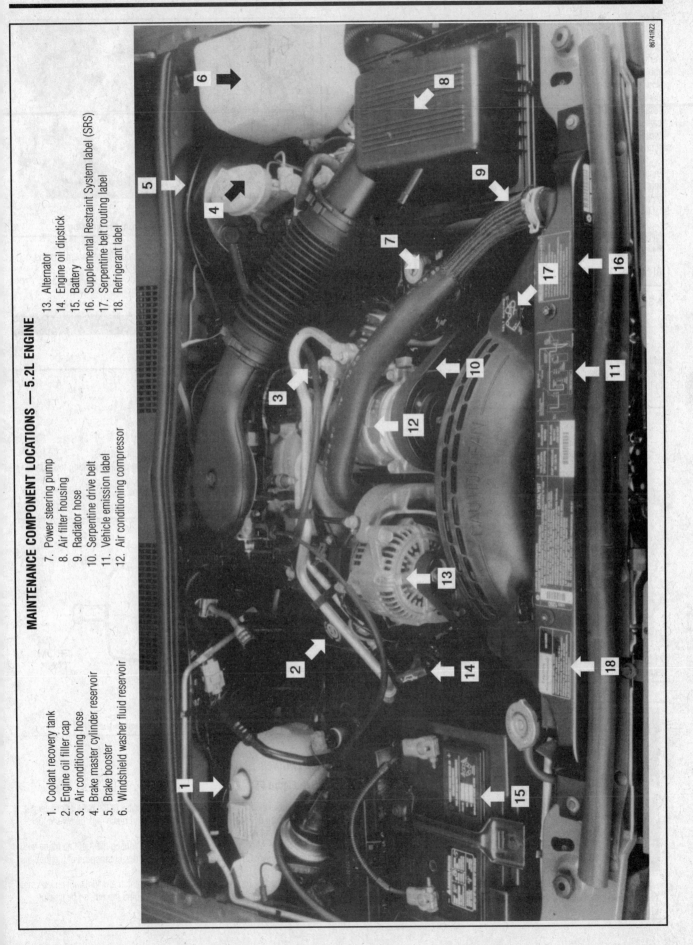

86741R22

Proper maintenance and tune-up is the key to long and trouble-free vehicle life, and the work can yield its own rewards. Studies have shown that a properly tuned and maintained vehicle can achieve better gas mileage than an out-of-tune vehicle. As a conscientious owner and driver, set aside a Saturday morning, say once a month, to check or replace items which could cause major problems later. Keep your own personal log to jot down which services you performed, how much the parts cost you, the date, and the exact odometer reading at the time. Keep all receipts for such items as engine oil and filters, so that they may be referred to in case of related problems or to determine operating expenses. As a do-it-yourselfer, these receipts are the only proof you have that the required maintenance was performed. In the event of a warranty problem, these receipts will be invaluable.

The literature provided with your vehicle when it was originally delivered includes the factory recommended maintenance schedule. If you no longer have this literature, replacement copies are usually available from the dealer. A maintenance schedule is provided later in this section, in case you do not have the factory literature.

Air Cleaner

REMOVAL & INSTALLATION

▶ See Figures 49, 50 and 51

1. Remove the air cleaner cover by disengaging the retaining screw or clips.
2. Remove the air filter element.
3. Clean the filter element by gently blowing trapped debris from the filter with compressed air. Direct the air in the opposite direction of normal flow. Keep the air nozzle at least two inches (50 mm) away from the filter to avoid damage to the filter.

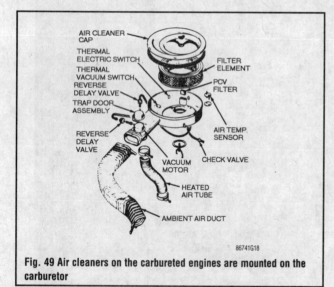

Fig. 49 Air cleaners on the carbureted engines are mounted on the carburetor

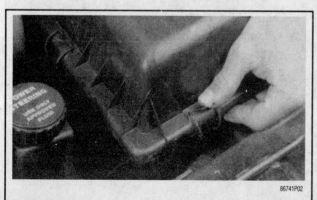

Fig. 50 Fuel injected engines use a remote mounted filter. Undo the clips . . .

Fig. 51 . . . then remove filter element from the housing

4. If the filter element has become saturated with oil, replace it and inspect the crankcase ventilating system for proper operation.
5. Clean the air cleaner cover and body.
6. Install the air cleaner element and cover.

Fuel Filter

REMOVAL & INSTALLATION

Carbureted Engines

2.5L ENGINES

▶ See Figure 52

1. Remove and discard the fuel filter, hoses and clamps.
2. Install the new fuel filter with arrows on the casing pointing toward the carburetor and fuel return nipple facing upward.
3. Secure the filter with new hoses and clamps.

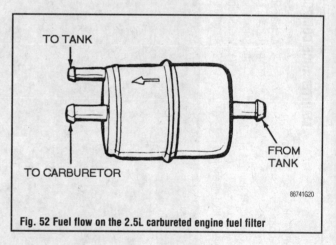

Fig. 52 Fuel flow on the 2.5L carbureted engine fuel filter

2.8L ENGINES

▶ See Figure 53

1. Remove the air cleaner assembly to gain access to the carburetor inlet nut.
2. Clean all debris away from the manifold and place rags below the fuel line and inlet nut to absorb any fuel spillage.
3. Hold the large inlet nut with a wrench and loosen the fuel line fitting with a flare nut wrench. (This wrench is designed to prevent stripping of the fuel line fitting).
4. Pull the fuel pipe from the carburetor and catch any fuel with a clean rag. Next, unscrew the large nut. There is a spring behind the nut, so be careful. Remove the spring and the old filter.

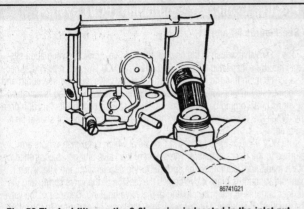

Fig. 53 The fuel filter on the 2.8L engine in located in the inlet nut

To install:

5. Install the new filter and, if you are at all in doubt about its condition, a new gasket behind the inlet nut.

6. Tighten the inlet nut carefully, because the carburetor is made of very soft metal and the threads could EASILY strip. Hold the inlet nut securely while tightening the fuel line fitting.

7. Start the vehicle and check for leaks.

Gasoline Fuel Injection Engines

EXCEPT 1997 AND LATER ENGINES

▶ See Figures 54 and 55

The fuel filter is located under the vehicle, mounted on the frame rail on the driver's side.

1. Disconnect the battery ground cable.

7. Place the new filter on the frame rail and tighten the strap bolt to 106 inch lbs. (12 Nm).

8. Install and securely clamp the hoses.

9. Lower the vehicle and connect the negative battery cable.

10. Start the vehicle and check for leaks.

1997 AND LATER ENGINES

▶ See Figures 56, 57 and 58

> ※ **CAUTION**
>
> Observe all applicable safety precautions when working around fuel. Whenever servicing the fuel system, always work in a well ventilated area. Do not allow fuel spray or vapors to come in contact with a spark or open flame. Keep a dry chemical fire extinguisher near the work area. Always keep fuel in a container specifically designed for fuel storage; also, always properly seal fuel containers to avoid the possibility of fire or explosion.

The fuel filter is an integral component of the fuel pressure regulator, which is mounted on top of the fuel pump module, located in the fuel tank. When the fuel filter/regulator assembly requires service, the fuel tank must be removed from the vehicle, however, the fuel pump module does not need to be removed.

1. Disconnect the battery ground cable.

2. Relieve the fuel system pressure. Refer to Section 5 for the proper procedure.

3. Remove the fuel tank assembly.

4. Clean the area around the fuel filter/regulator.

5. Disengage the retaining clamp from the top of the filter/regulator assembly. Discard the retaining clamp.

6. Using 2 small prying tools, pry the filter/regulator assembly out from the top of the fuel pump module. The filter/regulator assembly will unsnap from the fuel pump module.

7. Remove and discard the mounting gasket below the filter/regulator.

Fig. 54 Remove the hoses and clamps from the filter

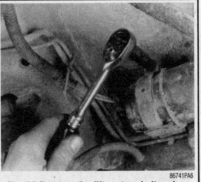

Fig. 55 Remove the filter strap bolt and then remove the filter

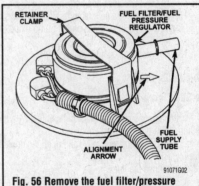

Fig. 56 Remove the fuel filter/pressure regulator retaining clip from the top of the assembly

2. Remove the fuel tank filler cap.

> ※ **CAUTION**
>
> Don't allow fuel to spray or spill on the engine or exhaust manifold! Place heavy shop towels under the pressure port to absorb any escaped fuel! Do not smoke while working near fuel vapors.

3. Relieve the fuel system pressure. Refer to Section 5 for the proper procedure.

4. Raise and safely support the rear end on jackstands.

5. Remove the hoses and clamps from the filter.

6. Remove the filter strap bolt and remove the filter.

To install:

➡The filter is marked for installation. IN goes towards the fuel tank OUT towards the engine.

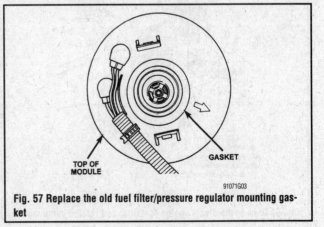

Fig. 57 Replace the old fuel filter/pressure regulator mounting gasket

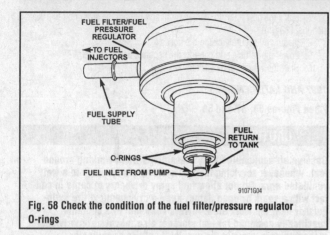

Fig. 58 Check the condition of the fuel filter/pressure regulator O-rings

8. Before discarding the fuel filter/pressure regulator assembly, inspect the assembly to verify that the O-rings are intact. If the smallest of the 2 O-rings cannot be found on the bottom of the filter/regulator, it may be necessary to remove it from the fuel inlet passage in the fuel pump module.

To install:

9. Clean the recessed area in the pump module where the filter/regulator assembly is to be installed.

10. Check the replacement filter/regulator assembly to make sure that the new O-rings are already installed on the assembly.

11. Apply a small amount of clean engine oil to the O-rings.

12. Install a new gasket on top of the fuel pump module.

13. Press the new fuel filter/pressure regulator assembly into the top of the fuel pump module until it snaps into position (a positive click must be heard or felt).

14. The arrow on top of the fuel pump module should be pointed towards the front of the vehicle (12 O'clock position).

15. Turn the filter/regulator assembly until the supply tube (fitting) is pointed to the 11 O'clock position.

16. Install new retainer clamp (the clamp snaps over the top of the filter/regulator and locks to the flanges on the pump module).

17. Install the fuel tank assembly.

18. Connect the negative battery cable.

Diesel Engines

▶ See Figure 59

1. Attach one end of a piece of flexible tubing to the filter draincock. Run the other end into a one quart container.

2. Open the filter vent valve and open the draincock. Drain the filter completely.

3. Remove the filter.

4. Discard the filter. Install the new filter, close the vent and drain cock.

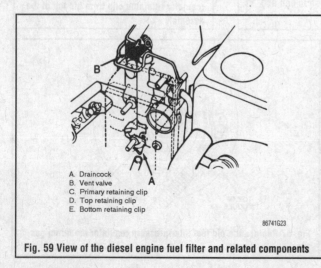

A. Draincock
B. Vent valve
C. Primary retaining clip
D. Top retaining clip
E. Bottom retaining clip

Fig. 59 View of the diesel engine fuel filter and related components

Positive Crankcase Ventilation (PCV) System

▶ See Figures 60 and 61

The PCV valve, which is the heart of the positive crankcase ventilation system, should be inspected every 60,000 miles (96,000 km) and replaced, if necessary. The main thing to keep in mind is that the valve must be free of dirt and residue to stay in working order. As long as the valve is clean and is not showing signs of becoming damaged or clogged, it should perform its function properly. When the valve becomes sticky and will not operate freely, it should be replaced.

The PCV valve is used to control the rate at which crankcase vapors are returned to the intake manifold. The action of the valve plunger is controlled by intake manifold vacuum and the spring. During deceleration and idle, when manifold vacuum is high, it overcomes the tension of the valve spring and the plunger bottoms in the manifold end of the valve housing. Because of the valve construction, it reduces, but does not stop, the passage of vapors to the intake manifold. When the engine is lightly accelerated, or operated at constant speed, spring tension matches intake manifold vacuum pull and the plunger takes a mid-position in the valve body, allowing more vapors to flow into the manifold.

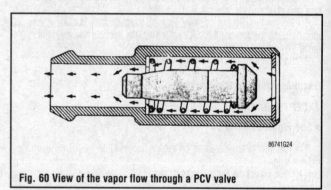

Fig. 60 View of the vapor flow through a PCV valve

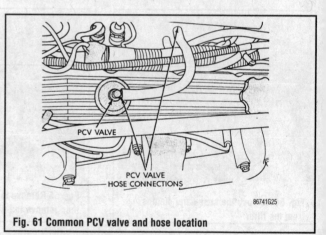

Fig. 61 Common PCV valve and hose location

REMOVAL & INSTALLATION

▶ See Figure 62

1. Remove the PCV valve from cylinder head.

2. Remove the PCV valve from PCV hose.

3. Installation is the reverse of removal.

Crankcase Ventilation (CCV) System

▶ See Figures 63 and 64

The Crankcase Ventilation (CCV) System performs the same function as the conventional PCV system, but without the use of a vacuum controlled valve. When in operation, fresh air enters the engine through an inlet and is mixed with crankcase vapors. Manifold vacuum draws the vapor/air mixture through a

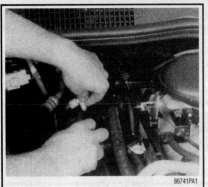

Fig. 62 Removing the PCV valve from the PCV hose

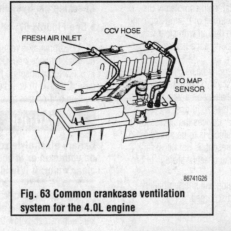

Fig. 63 Common crankcase ventilation system for the 4.0L engine

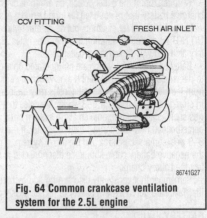

Fig. 64 Common crankcase ventilation system for the 2.5L engine

fixed size orifice and into the intake manifold. The vapors are then burned off during combustion.

There is no servicing to the CCV system unless one of the components gets clogged or fails.

Evaporative Canister

▶ See Figure 65

The function of the evaporative canister is to prevent gasoline vapors from the fuel tank from escaping into the atmosphere. Periodic maintenance is not required on any of the 1988 and later models (on all vehicles a sealed, maintenance-free, charcoal canister is used).

Some older model vehicles may have a removable air filter. The air filter in the bottom of the canister, if so equipped, should be replaced every 30,000 miles (48,000 km).

To determine if your vehicle has a canister filter, remove the canister from the vehicle and inspect the bottom of the canister for a filter.

In spite of the fact that this system requires no periodic maintenance, it is a good idea to quickly look over the hoses when servicing the PCV system. If any of these hoses is cracked, torn, or rotted, the result could be vacuum leaks and consequent poor engine operation, or an annoying smell of fuel vapor. If any of these hoses should require replacement, make sure to use a high quality replacement hose of a material approved for use in fuel bearing applications. Ordinary vacuum type rubber hose will not give satisfactory life or reliable performance.

The evaporative canister is mounted in the following locations:
• All Grand Cherokee models—below the left front headlamp
• All Left Hand Drive (LHD) 1984–97 models except Grand Cherokee—engine compartment on the right side frame rail
• All Right Hand Drive (RHD) 1984–97 models—engine compartment on the left side near the heater blower motor
• All 1998 and later Cherokee models—below the left side of the vehicle near the front of the rear axle

Battery

PRECAUTIONS

Always use caution when working on or near the battery. Never allow a tool to bridge the gap between the negative and positive battery terminals. Also, be careful not to allow a tool to provide a ground between the positive cable/terminal and any metal component on the vehicle. Either of these conditions will cause a short circuit, leading to sparks and possible personal injury.

Do not smoke, have an open flame or create sparks near a battery; the gases contained in the battery are very explosive and, if ignited, could cause severe injury or death.

All batteries, regardless of type, should be carefully secured by a battery hold-down device. If this is not done, the battery terminals or casing may crack from stress applied to the battery during vehicle operation. A battery which is not secured may allow acid to leak out, making it discharge faster; such leaking corrosive acid can also eat away at components under the hood.

Always visually inspect the battery case for cracks, leakage and corrosion. A white corrosive substance on the battery case or on nearby components would indicate a leaking or cracked battery. If the battery is cracked, it should be replaced immediately.

GENERAL MAINTENANCE

▶ See Figure 66

A battery that is not sealed must be checked periodically for electrolyte level. You cannot add water to a sealed maintenance-free battery (though not all maintenance-free batteries are sealed); however, a sealed battery must also be checked for proper electrolyte level, as indicated by the color of the built-in hydrometer "eye."

Always keep the battery cables and terminals free of corrosion. Check these components about once a year. Refer to the removal, installation and cleaning procedures outlined in this section.

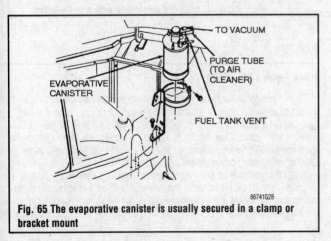

Fig. 65 The evaporative canister is usually secured in a clamp or bracket mount

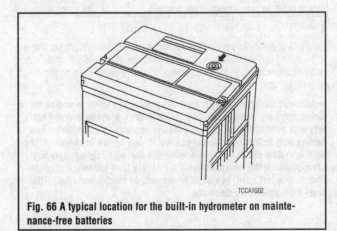

Fig. 66 A typical location for the built-in hydrometer on maintenance-free batteries

Keep the top of the battery clean, as a film of dirt can help completely discharge a battery that is not used for long periods. A solution of baking soda and water may be used for cleaning, but be careful to flush this off with clear water. DO NOT let any of the solution into the filler holes. Baking soda neutralizes battery acid and will de-activate a battery cell.

Batteries in vehicles which are not operated on a regular basis can fall victim to parasitic loads (small current drains which are constantly drawing current from the battery). Normal parasitic loads may drain a battery on a vehicle that is in storage and not used for 6–8 weeks. Vehicles that have additional accessories such as a cellular phone, an alarm system or other devices that increase parasitic load may discharge a battery sooner. If the vehicle is to be stored for 6–8 weeks in a secure area and the alarm system, if present, is not necessary, the negative battery cable should be disconnected at the onset of storage to protect the battery charge.

Remember that constantly discharging and recharging will shorten battery life. Take care not to allow a battery to be needlessly discharged.

BATTERY FLUID

Check the battery electrolyte level at least once a month, or more often in hot weather or during periods of extended vehicle operation. On non-sealed batteries, the level can be checked either through the case on translucent batteries or by removing the cell caps on opaque-cased types. The electrolyte level in each cell should be kept filled to the split ring inside each cell, or the line marked on the outside of the case.

If the level is low, add only distilled water through the opening until the level is correct. Each cell is separate from the others, so each must be checked and filled individually. Distilled water should be used, because the chemicals and minerals found in most drinking water are harmful to the battery and could significantly shorten its life.

If water is added in freezing weather, the vehicle should be driven several miles to allow the water to mix with the electrolyte. Otherwise, the battery could freeze.

Although some maintenance-free batteries have removable cell caps for access to the electrolyte, the electrolyte condition and level on all sealed maintenance-free batteries must be checked using the built-in hydrometer "eye." The

Checking the Specific Gravity

▶ See Figures 67, 68 and 69

A hydrometer is required to check the specific gravity on all batteries that are not maintenance-free. On batteries that are maintenance-free, the specific gravity is checked by observing the built-in hydrometer "eye" on the top of the battery case. Check with your battery's manufacturer for proper interpretation of its built-in hydrometer readings.

✳✳ CAUTION

Battery electrolyte contains sulfuric acid. If you should splash any on your skin or in your eyes, flush the affected area with plenty of clear water. If it lands in your eyes, get medical help immediately.

The fluid (sulfuric acid solution) contained in the battery cells will tell you many things about the condition of the battery. Because the cell plates must be kept submerged below the fluid level in order to operate, maintaining the fluid level is extremely important. And, because the specific gravity of the acid is an indication of electrical charge, testing the fluid can be an aid in determining if the battery must be replaced. A battery in a vehicle with a properly operating charging system should require little maintenance, but careful, periodic inspection should reveal problems before they leave you stranded.

As stated earlier, the specific gravity of a battery's electrolyte level can be used as an indication of battery charge. At least once a year, check the specific gravity of the battery. It should be between 1.20 and 1.26 on the gravity scale. Most auto supply stores carry a variety of inexpensive battery testing hydrometers. These can be used on any non-sealed battery to test the specific gravity in each cell.

The battery testing hydrometer has a squeeze bulb at one end and a nozzle at the other. Battery electrolyte is sucked into the hydrometer until the float is lifted from its seat. The specific gravity is then read by noting the position of the float. If gravity is low in one or more cells, the battery should be slowly charged and checked again to see if the gravity has come up. Generally, if after charging, the specific gravity between any two cells varies more than 50 points (0.50), the battery should be replaced, as it can no longer produce sufficient voltage to guarantee proper operation.

Fig. 67 On non-maintenance-free batteries, the fluid level can be checked through the case on translucent models; the cell caps must be removed on other models

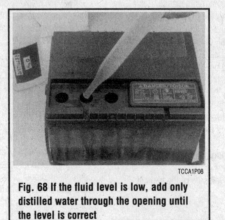

Fig. 68 If the fluid level is low, add only distilled water through the opening until the level is correct

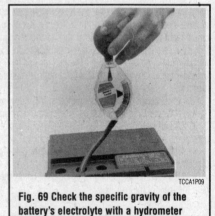

Fig. 69 Check the specific gravity of the battery's electrolyte with a hydrometer

exact type of eye varies between battery manufacturers, but most apply a sticker to the battery itself explaining the possible readings. When in doubt, refer to the battery manufacturer's instructions to interpret battery condition using the built-in hydrometer.

➡**Although the readings from built-in hydrometers found in sealed batteries may vary, a green eye usually indicates a properly charged battery with sufficient fluid level. A dark eye is normally an indicator of a battery with sufficient fluid, but one which may be low in charge. And a light or yellow eye is usually an indication that electrolyte supply has dropped below the necessary level for battery (and hydrometer) operation. In this last case, sealed batteries with an insufficient electrolyte level must usually be discarded.**

CABLES

▶ See Figures 70, 71, 72, 73 and 74

Once a year (or as necessary), the battery terminals and the cable clamps should be cleaned. Loosen the clamps and remove the cables, negative cable first. Use a 1/2 inch box wrench to loosen the clamps on a top post battery. On batteries with posts on top, the use of a puller specially made for this purpose is recommended. These are inexpensive and available in most auto parts stores. Side terminal battery cables are secured with a small bolt.

Clean the cable clamps and the battery terminal with a wire brush, until all corrosion, grease, etc., is removed and the metal is shiny. It is especially important to clean the inside of the clamp thoroughly (an old knife is useful here), since a small deposit of foreign material or oxidation there will prevent a sound

Fig. 70 Maintenance is performed with household items and with special tools like this post cleaner

Fig. 71 The underside of this special battery tool has a wire brush to clean post terminals

Fig. 72 Place the tool over the battery posts and twist to clean until the metal is shiny

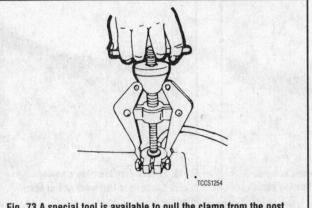

Fig. 73 A special tool is available to pull the clamp from the post

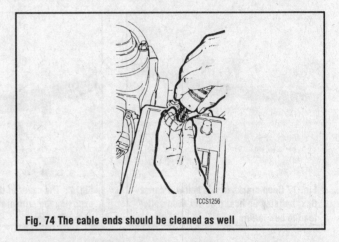

Fig. 74 The cable ends should be cleaned as well

electrical connection and inhibit either starting or charging. Special tools are available for cleaning these parts, one type for conventional top post batteries and another type for side terminal batteries. It is also a good idea to apply some dielectric grease to the terminal, as this will aid in the prevention of corrosion.

After the clamps and terminals are clean, reinstall the cables, negative cable last; DO NOT hammer the clamps onto battery posts. Tighten the clamps securely, but do not distort them. Give the clamps and terminals a thin external coating of grease after installation, to retard corrosion.

Check the cables at the same time that the terminals are cleaned. If the cable insulation is cracked or broken, or if the ends are frayed, the cable should be replaced with a new cable of the same length and gauge.

CHARGING

✳✳ CAUTION

The chemical reaction which takes place in all batteries generates explosive hydrogen gas. A spark can cause the battery to explode and splash acid. To avoid serious personal injury, be sure there is proper ventilation and take appropriate fire safety precautions when connecting, disconnecting, or charging a battery and when using jumper cables.

A battery should be charged at a slow rate to keep the plates inside from getting too hot. However, if some maintenance-free batteries are allowed to discharge until they are almost "dead," they may have to be charged at a high rate to bring them back to "life." Always follow the charger manufacturer's instructions on charging the battery.

REPLACEMENT

When it becomes necessary to replace the battery, select one with an amperage rating equal to or greater than the battery originally installed. Deterioration and just plain aging of the battery cables, starter motor, and associated wires

makes the battery's job harder in successive years. The slow increase in electrical resistance over time makes it prudent to install a new battery with a greater capacity than the old.

V-Belts

INSPECTION

▶ See Figures 75, 76, 77, 78 and 79

Inspect the belts for signs of glazing or cracking. A glazed belt will be perfectly smooth from slippage, while a good belt will have a slight texture of fabric visible. Cracks will usually start at the inner edge of the belt and run outward. All worn or damaged drive belts should be replaced immediately. It is best to replace all drive belts at one time, as a preventive maintenance measure, during this service operation.

ADJUSTMENTS

✳✳ CAUTION

On models equipped with an electric cooling fan, disconnect the negative battery cable or fan motor wiring harness connector before replacing or adjusting drive belts. Otherwise, the fan may come on, under certain circumstances, even though the ignition is off.

Alternator Belt

▶ See Figures 80 and 81

1. Position the ruler perpendicular to the drive belt at its longest straight run. Test the tightness of the belt by pressing it firmly with your thumb. The deflection should not exceed 1/4 inch (6mm).

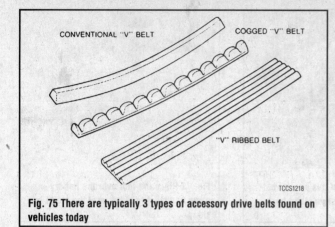

Fig. 75 There are typically 3 types of accessory drive belts found on vehicles today

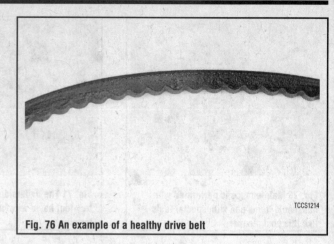

Fig. 76 An example of a healthy drive belt

Fig. 77 Deep cracks in this belt will cause flex, building up heat that will eventually lead to belt failure

Fig. 78 The cover of this belt is worn, exposing the critical reinforcing cords to excessive wear

Fig. 79 Installing too wide a belt can result in serious belt wear and/or breakage

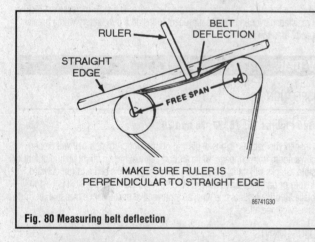

Fig. 80 Measuring belt deflection

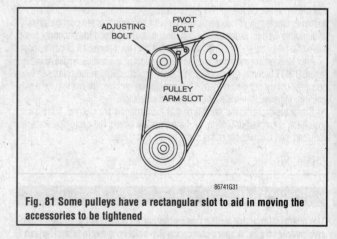

Fig. 81 Some pulleys have a rectangular slot to aid in moving the accessories to be tightened

2. If the deflection exceeds 1/4 inch (6mm), loosen the alternator mounting and adjusting arm bolts.

3. Place a 1 inch open-end or adjustable wrench on the adjusting ridge cast on the body, and pull on the wrench until the proper tension is achieved.

4. Holding the alternator in place to maintain tension, tighter the adjusting arm bolt. Recheck the belt tension. When the belt is properly tensioned, tighten the alternator mounting bolt.

Power Steering Belt

♦ See Figure 82

1. Hold a ruler perpendicular to the drive belt at its longest run. Test the tightness of the belt by pressing it firmly with you thumb. The deflection should not exceed 1/4 inch (6mm).

2. To adjust the belt tension, loosen the adjusting and mounting bolts on the front face of the steering pump cover plate (hub side).

3. Using a prybar or broom handle on the pump hub, move the power steering pump toward or away from the engine until the proper tension is reached. Do not pry against the reservoir as it is relatively soft and easily deformed.

4. Holding the pump in place, tighten the adjusting arm bolt and then recheck the belt tension. When the belt is properly tensioned, tighten the mounting bolts.

Air Conditioning Belt

1. Position a ruler perpendicular to the drive belt at its longest run. Test the tightness of the belt by pressing it firmly with your thumb. The deflection should not exceed 1/4 inch (6mm).

2. If the engine is equipped with an idler pulley, loosen the idler pulley

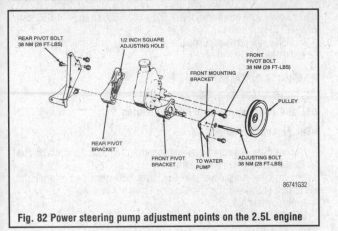

Fig. 82 Power steering pump adjustment points on the 2.5L engine

adjusting bolt, insert a prybar between the pulley and the engine (or in the idler pulley adjusting slot), and adjust the tension accordingly. If the engine is not equipped with an idler pulley, the alternator must be moved to accomplish this adjustment, as outlined under Alternator Belt.

3. When the proper tension is reached, tighten the idler pulley adjusting bolt (if so equipped) or the alternator adjusting and mounting bolts.

Air Pump Belt

1. Position a ruler perpendicular to the drive belt at its longest run. Test the tightness of the belt by pressing it firmly with your thumb. The deflection should be about 1/4 inch (6mm).
2. To adjust the belt tension, loosen the adjusting arm bolt slightly. If necessary, also loosen the mounting bolt slightly.
3. Using a prybar or broom handle, pry against the pump rear cover to move the pump toward or away from the engine as necessary.

✳✳ WARNING

Do not pry against the pump housing itself, as damage to the housing may result.

4. Holding the pump in place, tighten the adjusting arm bolt and recheck the tension. When the belt is properly tensioned tighten the mounting bolt.

REMOVAL & INSTALLATION

Alternator Belt

1. Loosen the alternator mounting and adjusting arm bolts.
2. Pivot the alternator inward and remove the belt from the vehicle.
To install:
3. Install a new belt.
4. Holding the alternator in place to maintain tension, tighten the alternator mounting and adjusting arm bolts.

Power Steering Belt

1. Loosen the adjusting and mounting bolts on the front face of the steering pump cover plate (hub side).
2. Pivot the power steering pump inward and remove the drive belt.
To install:
3. Install the drive belt.
4. Holding the pump in place, tighten the adjusting arm bolt and the mounting bolts.

Air Conditioning Compressor Belt

1. If the engine is equipped with an idler pulley, loosen the idler pulley adjusting bolt and remove the belt.
2. If not equipped with an idler pulley, loosen the adjusting and mounting bolts.
3. Pivot the air conditioning compressor inward and remove the drive belt.
4. Installation is the reverse of removal.

Air Pump Drive Belt

1. Loosen the adjusting arm bolt slightly. If necessary, also loosen the mounting bolt slightly and remove the drive belt.
To install:
2. Holding the pump in place, install the drive belt, then tighten the adjusting arm bolt and the mounting bolt.

Serpentine Belt

INSPECTION

When inspecting serpentine drive belts, small cracks that run across the ribbed surface of the belt from rib to rib are considered normal. If the the cracks are running along the rib (rather across), this is not normal and the belt(s) must be replaced.

ADJUSTMENT

It is not necessary to adjust belt tension on the 5.2L or 5.9L engines and on the 2.5L and 4.0L engines (without power steering). These engines are equipped with an automatic tensioner. The tensioner maintains correct tension at all times.

2.5L and 4.0L Engines With Power Steering

▶ See Figures 83, 84, 85 and 86

➡If the vehicle is not equipped with power steering, it will be equipped with an idler pulley. If equipped with an idler pulley, refer to and follow the 5.2L/5.9L belt removal and installation procedure.

1. Loosen the pump upper pivot bolt, lower locknut and pump adjusting bolt using a ratchet and 13mm socket or a 13mm box wrench.
2. Use a belt tension gauge placed in the middle of the belt being tested.

Fig. 83 Loosen the pivot bolt (1), then the locking bolt (2) to loosen the power steering pump from behind

Fig. 84 Use a ratchet and 13mm size socket to rotate the power steering pump

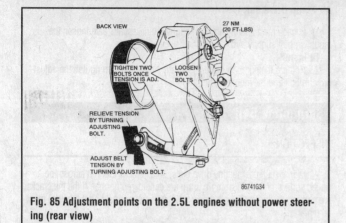

Fig. 85 Adjustment points on the 2.5L engines without power steering (rear view)

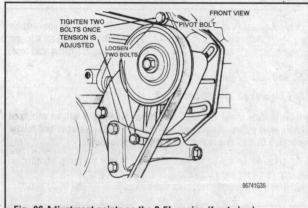

Fig. 86 Adjustment points on the 2.5L engine (front view)

Proper tension for a new belt is 180–200 lbs. (800–900 N) and 140–160 lbs. (623–712 N) for a used belt.

3. Tighten the pump adjusting bolt to achieve proper tension and recheck the belt tension.

REMOVAL & INSTALLATION

2.5L and 4.0L Engines With Power Steering

▶ **See Figures 87, 88 and 89**

1. Loosen the rear power steering pump mounting bolts using a ratchet and 13mm socket or a 13mm box wrench.

2. Loosen the pump upper pivot bolt, lower locknut and the pump adjusting bolt using a ratchet and 13mm socket or a 13mm box wrench.

3. Remove the belt.

To install:

4. Install the belt.

5. Tighten the pump adjusting bolt to achieve proper tension.

6. Install the pump rear mounting bolts, pivot bolt and locknut. Tighten the bolts to 20. ft. lbs. (27 Nm).

7. Check the belt for proper tension. If tension is incorrect, refer to the adjustment procedure in this section.

5.2L and 5.9L Engines

▶ **See Figures 90, 91 and 92**

1. Attach a socket or wrench to the pulley mounting bolt on the automatic tensioner and rotate the tensioner assembly clockwise until the tension has been removed from the belt.

2. Remove the belt from the idler pulley first and then from the vehicle.

To install:

➡ **The tensioner is equipped with an indexing arrow on the back of the tensioner and an indexing mark on the tensioner housing. If a new belt is being installed, ensure the arrow is within 1/8 inch (3mm) of the indexing mark.**

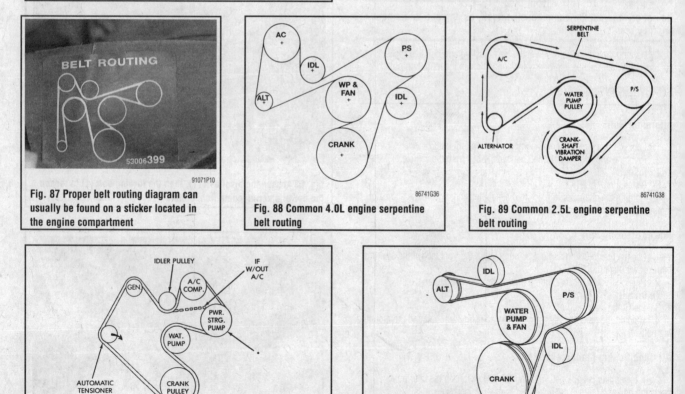

Fig. 87 Proper belt routing diagram can usually be found on a sticker located in the engine compartment

Fig. 88 Common 4.0L engine serpentine belt routing

Fig. 89 Common 2.5L engine serpentine belt routing

Fig. 90 1993–97 V-8 engine serpentine belt routing

Fig. 91 1998 V-8 engine serpentine belt routing

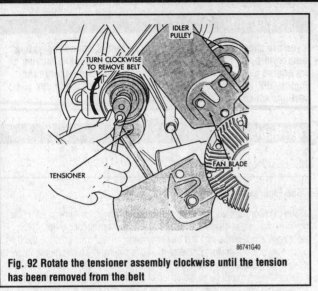

Fig. 92 Rotate the tensioner assembly clockwise until the tension has been removed from the belt

3. Position the belt over all the pulleys except the idler pulley.
4. Attach a socket or wrench to the pulley mounting bolt on the automatic tensioner and rotate the tensioner assembly clockwise and place the belt over the idler pulley.
5. Let the tensioner rotate back into place and remove the socket or wrench.
6. Ensure that the belt is properly seated.
7. Check the belt indexing marks.

Whether or not you decide to replace it, you would be wise to check it periodically to make sure it has not become damaged or worn. Generally speaking, a severely worn belt may cause engine performance to drop dramatically, but a damaged belt (which could give out suddenly) may not give as much warning. In general, any time the engine timing cover(s) is (are) removed you should inspect the belt for premature parting, severe cracks or missing teeth.

Hoses

INSPECTION

▶ See Figures 93, 94, 95 and 96

Upper and lower radiator hoses, along with the heater hoses, should be checked for deterioration, leaks and loose hose clamps at least every 7,500 miles (12,000 km). It is also wise to check the hoses periodically in early spring and at the beginning of the fall or winter when you are performing other maintenance. A quick visual inspection could discover a weakened hose which might have left you stranded if it had remained unrepaired.

Whenever you are checking the hoses, make sure the engine and cooling system are cold. Visually inspect for cracking, rotting or collapsed hoses, and replace as necessary. Run your hand along the length of the hose. If a weak or swollen spot is noted when squeezing the hose wall, the hose should be replaced.

REMOVAL & INSTALLATION

1. Remove the radiator pressure cap.

⁂ CAUTION

Never remove the pressure cap while the engine is running, or personal injury from scalding hot coolant or steam may result. If possi-

Fig. 93 The cracks developing along this hose are a result of age-related hardening

Fig. 94 A hose clamp that is too tight can cause older hoses to separate and tear on either side of the clamp

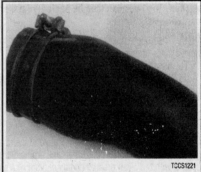

Fig. 95 A soft spongy hose (identifiable by the swollen section) will eventually burst and should be replaced

Timing Belts

SERVICING

The 2.1L turbo diesel engine utilizes a timing belt to drive the camshaft from the crankshaft's turning motion and to maintain proper valve timing. Some manufacturers schedule periodic timing belt replacement to assure optimum engine performance, to make sure the motorist is never stranded should the belt break (as the engine will stop instantly) and for some (manufacturers with interference motors) to prevent the possibility of severe internal engine damage should the belt break.

Although the 2.1L turbo diesel engine is not listed as an interference motor (it is not listed by the manufacturer as a motor whose valves might contact the pistons if the camshaft was rotated separately from the crankshaft) the first 2 reasons for periodic replacement still apply. Jeep recommends timing belt replacement at 55,000 miles.

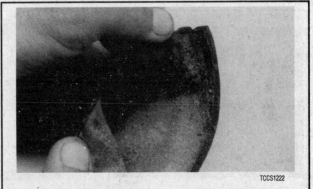

Fig. 96 Hoses are likely to deteriorate from the inside if the cooling system is not periodically flushed

ble, wait until the engine has cooled to remove the pressure cap. If this is not possible, wrap a thick cloth around the pressure cap and turn it slowly to the stop. Step back while the pressure is released from the cooling system. When you are sure all the pressure has been released, use the cloth to turn and remove the cap.

2. Position a clean container under the radiator and/or engine draincock or plug, then open the drain and allow the cooling system to drain to an appropriate level. For some upper hoses, only a little coolant must be drained. To remove hoses positioned lower on the engine, such as a lower radiator hose, the entire cooling system must be emptied.

✳✳ CAUTION

When draining coolant, keep in mind that cats and dogs are attracted by ethylene glycol antifreeze, and are quite likely to drink any that is left in an uncovered container or in puddles on the ground. This will prove fatal in sufficient quantity. Always drain coolant into a sealable container. Coolant may be reused unless it is contaminated or several years old.

3. Loosen the hose clamps at each end of the hose requiring replacement. Clamps are usually either of the spring tension type (which require pliers to squeeze the tabs and loosen) or of the screw tension type (which require screw or hex drivers to loosen). Pull the clamps back on the hose away from the connection.

4. Twist, pull and slide the hose off the fitting, taking care not to damage the neck of the component from which the hose is being removed.

➡**If the hose is stuck at the connection, do not try to insert a screwdriver or other sharp tool under the hose end in an effort to free it, as the connection and/or hose may become damaged. Heater connections especially may be easily damaged by such a procedure. If the hose is to be replaced, use a single-edged razor blade to make a slice along the portion of the hose which is stuck on the connection, perpendicular to the end of the hose. Do not cut deep so as to prevent damaging the connection. The hose can then be peeled from the connection and discarded.**

5. Clean both hose mounting connections. Inspect the condition of the hose clamps and replace them, if necessary.
To install:
6. Dip the ends of the new hose into clean engine coolant to ease installation.
7. Slide the clamps over the replacement hose, then slide the hose ends over the connections into position.
8. Position and secure the clamps at least 1/4 in. (6mm) from the ends of the hose. Make sure they are located beyond the raised bead of the connector.
9. Close the radiator and/or engine drains and properly refill the cooling system with the clean drained engine coolant or a suitable mixture of coolant and water.
10. If available, install a pressure tester and check for leaks. If a pressure tester is not available, run the engine until normal operating temperature is reached (allowing the system to naturally pressurize), then check for leaks.

✳✳ CAUTION

If you are checking for leaks with the system at normal operating temperature, BE EXTREMELY CAREFUL not to touch any moving or hot engine parts. Once temperature has been reached, shut the engine OFF, and check for leaks around the hose fittings and connections which were removed earlier.

CV-Boots

INSPECTION

▸ **See Figures 97 and 98**

The CV (Constant Velocity) boots should be checked for damage each time the oil is changed and any other time the vehicle is raised for service. These boots keep water, grime, dirt and other damaging matter from entering the CV-joints. Any of these could cause early CV-joint failure which can be expensive to repair. Heavy grease thrown around the inside of the front wheel(s) and on the brake caliper/drum can be an indication of a torn boot. Thoroughly check the boots for missing clamps and tears. If the boot is damaged, it should be replaced immediately. Please refer to Section 7 for procedures.

Spark Plugs

▸ **See Figure 99**

A typical spark plug consists of a metal shell surrounding a ceramic insulator. A metal electrode extends downward through the center of the insulator and protrudes a small distance. Located at the end of the plug and attached to the side of the outer metal shell is the side electrode. The side electrode bends in at a 90° angle so that its tip is just past and parallel to the tip of the center electrode. The distance between these two electrodes (measured in thousandths of an inch or hundredths of a millimeter) is called the spark plug gap.

The spark plug does not produce a spark but instead provides a gap across which the current can arc. The coil produces anywhere from 20,000 to 50,000 volts (depending on the type and application) which travels through the wires to the spark plugs. The current passes along the center electrode and jumps the gap to the side electrode, and in doing so, ignites the air/fuel mixture in the combustion chamber.

SPARK PLUG HEAT RANGE

▸ **See Figure 100**

Spark plug heat range is the ability of the plug to dissipate heat. The longer the insulator (or the farther it extends into the engine), the hotter the plug will operate; the shorter the insulator (the closer the electrode is to the block's cooling passages) the cooler it will operate. A plug that absorbs little heat and remains too cool will quickly accumulate deposits of oil and carbon since it is not hot enough to burn them off. This leads to plug fouling and consequently to misfiring. A plug that absorbs too much heat will have no deposits but, due to

Fig. 97 CV-boots must be inspected periodically for damage

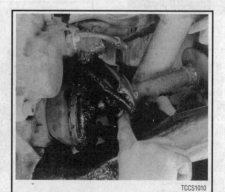

Fig. 98 A torn boot should be replaced immediately

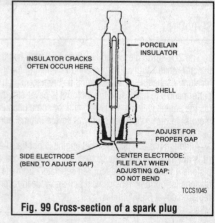

Fig. 99 Cross-section of a spark plug

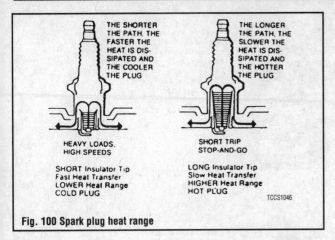

THE SHORTER THE PATH, THE FASTER THE HEAT IS DISSIPATED AND THE COOLER THE PLUG

THE LONGER THE PATH, THE SLOWER THE HEAT IS DISSIPATED AND THE HOTTER THE PLUG

HEAVY LOADS. HIGH SPEEDS

SHORT TRIP STOP-AND-GO

SHORT Insulator Tip
Fast Heat Transfer
LOWER Heat Range
COLD PLUG

LONG Insulator Tip
Slow Heat Transfer
HIGHER Heat Range
HOT PLUG

TCCS1046

Fig. 100 Spark plug heat range

the excessive heat, the electrodes will burn away quickly and might possibly lead to preignition or other ignition problems. Preignition takes place when plug tips get so hot that they glow sufficiently to ignite the air/fuel mixture before the actual spark occurs. This early ignition will usually cause a pinging during low speeds and heavy loads.

The general rule of thumb for choosing the correct heat range when picking a spark plug is: if most of your driving is long distance, high speed travel, use a colder plug; if most of your driving is stop and go, use a hotter plug. Original equipment plugs are generally a good compromise between the 2 styles and most people never have the need to change their plugs from the factory-recommended heat range.

REMOVAL & INSTALLATION

▶ **See Figures 101 and 102**

A set of spark plugs usually requires replacement after approximately 30,000 miles (48,000 km). In normal operation, plug gap increases about 0.001 in. (0.025mm) for every 2,500 miles (4000 km). As the gap increases, the plug's voltage requirement also increases. It requires a greater voltage to jump the wider gap and about two to three times as much voltage to fire the plug at high speeds than at idle. The improved air/fuel ratio control of modern fuel injection combined with the higher voltage output of modern ignition systems will often allow an engine to run significantly longer on a set of standard spark plugs, but keep in mind that efficiency will drop as the gap widens (along with fuel economy and power).

When you're removing spark plugs, work on one at a time. Don't start by removing the plug wires all at once, because, unless you number them, they may become mixed up. Take a minute before you begin and number the wires with tape.

1. If the vehicle has been run recently, allow the engine to thoroughly cool.
2. Carefully twist the spark plug wire boot to loosen it, then pull upward and remove the boot from the plug. Be sure to pull on the boot and not on the wire, otherwise the connector located inside the boot may become separated.

3. Using compressed air, blow any water or debris from the spark plug well to assure that no harmful contaminants are allowed to enter the combustion chamber when the spark plug is removed. If compressed air is not available, use a rag or a brush to clean the area.

➡Remove the spark plugs when the engine is cold, if possible, to prevent damage to the threads. If removal of the plugs is difficult, apply a few drops of penetrating oil or silicone spray to the area around the base of the plug, and allow it a few minutes to work.

4. Using a 5/8 inch spark plug socket that is equipped with a rubber insert to properly hold the plug, turn the spark plug counterclockwise to loosen and remove the spark plug from the bore.

✳✳ WARNING

Be sure not to use a flexible extension on the socket. Use of a flexible extension may allow a shear force to be applied to the plug. A shear force could break the plug off in the cylinder head, leading to costly and frustrating repairs.

To install:
5. Inspect the spark plug boot for tears or damage. If a damaged boot is found, the spark plug wire must be replaced.
6. Using a wire feeler gauge, check and adjust the spark plug gap.
7. Carefully thread the plug into the bore by hand. If resistance is felt before the plug is almost completely threaded, back the plug out and begin threading again. In small, hard to reach areas, an old spark plug wire and boot could be used as a threading tool. The boot will hold the plug while you twist the end of the wire and the wire is supple enough to twist before it would allow the plug to crossthread.

✳✳ WARNING

Do not use the spark plug socket to thread the plugs. Always carefully thread the plug by hand or using an old plug wire to prevent the possibility of crossthreading and damaging the cylinder head bore.

8. If the plug you are installing is equipped with a crush washer, seat the plug, then tighten about 1/4 turn to crush the washer. If you are installing a tapered seat plug, tighten the plug to 26–30 ft. lbs. (35–41 Nm).
9. Apply a small amount of silicone dielectric compound to the end of the spark plug or inside the spark plug boot to prevent sticking, then install the boot to the spark plug and push until it clicks into place. The click may be felt or heard, then gently pull back on the boot to assure proper contact.
10. Connect the negative battery cable.

INSPECTION & GAPPING

▶ **See Figures 103, 104, 105, 106 and 107**

Check the plugs for deposits and wear. If they are not going to be replaced, clean the plugs thoroughly. Remember that any kind of deposit will decrease the

86741P08

Fig. 101 Using a spark plug socket, remove the spark plug from the bore

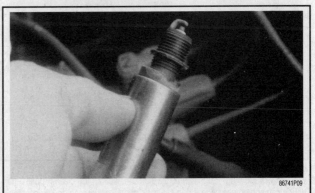

86741P09

Fig. 102 Inspect the spark plug for signs of damage, deposits and wear

 **A normally worn** spark plug should have light tan or gray deposits on the firing tip.

 **A carbon fouled** plug, identified by soft, sooty, black deposits, may indicate an improperly tuned vehicle. Check the air cleaner, ignition components and engine control system.

 This spark plug has been **left in the engine too long,** as evidenced by the extreme gap. Plugs with such an extreme gap can cause misfiring and stumbling accompanied by a noticeable lack of power.

 **An oil fouled** spark plug indicates an engine with worn poston rings and/or bad valve seals allowing excessive oil to enter the chamber.

 **A physically damaged** spark plug may be evidence of severe detonation in that cylinder. Watch that cylinder carefully between services, as a continued detonation will not only damage the plug, but could also damage the engine.

 **A bridged or almost bridged** spark plug, identified by a build-up between the electrodes caused by excessive carbon or oil build-up on the plug.

TCCA1P40

Fig. 103 Inspect the spark plug to determine engine running conditions

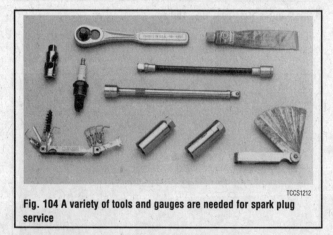

TCCS1212

Fig. 104 A variety of tools and gauges are needed for spark plug service

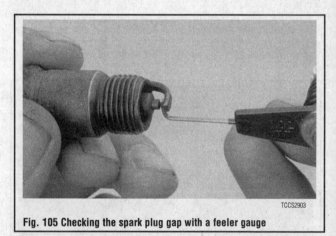

TCCS2903

Fig. 105 Checking the spark plug gap with a feeler gauge

efficiency of the plug. Plugs can be cleaned on a spark plug cleaning machine, which can sometimes be found in service stations, or you can do an acceptable job of cleaning with a stiff brush. If the plugs are cleaned, the electrodes must be filed flat. Use an ignition points file, not an emery board or the like, which will leave deposits. The electrodes must be filed perfectly flat with sharp edges; rounded edges reduce the spark plug voltage by as much as 50%.

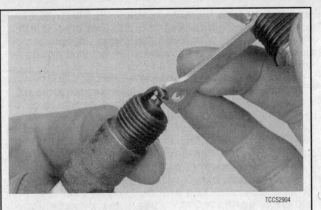

Fig. 106 Adjusting the spark plug gap

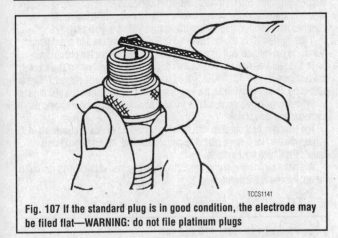

Fig. 107 If the standard plug is in good condition, the electrode may be filed flat—WARNING: do not file platinum plugs

Check spark plug gap before installation. The ground electrode (the L-shaped one connected to the body of the plug) must be parallel to the center electrode and the specified size wire gauge (please refer to the Tune-Up Specifications chart for details) must pass between the electrodes with a slight drag.

➡NEVER adjust the gap on a used platinum type spark plug.

Always check the gap on new plugs as they are not always set correctly at the factory. Do not use a flat feeler gauge when measuring the gap on a used plug, because the reading may be inaccurate. A round-wire type gapping tool is the best way to check the gap. The correct gauge should pass through the electrode gap with a slight drag. If you're in doubt, try one size smaller and one larger. The smaller gauge should go through easily, while the larger one shouldn't go through at all. Wire gapping tools usually have a bending tool attached. Use that to adjust the side electrode until the proper distance is obtained. Absolutely never attempt to bend the center electrode. Also, be careful not to bend the side electrode too far or too often as it may weaken and break off within the engine, requiring removal of the cylinder head to retrieve it.

Spark Plug Wires

TESTING

▶ See Figure 108

At every tune-up/inspection, visually check the spark plug cables for burns, cuts, or breaks in the insulation. Check the boots and nipples on the distributor cap and/or coil. Replace any damaged wiring.

Every 50,000 miles (80,000 Km) or 60 months, the resistance of the wires should be checked with an ohmmeter. Wires with excessive resistance will cause misfiring, and may make the engine difficult to start in damp weather.

To check resistance, measure the length of each wire with a ruler and then multiply the length by the figures given, in order to measure total resistance. Resistance must be 250–1,000 ohms per inch (25mm) or 3,000–12,000 ohms per foot (30.5mm).

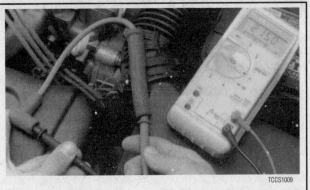

Fig. 108 Checking individual plug wire resistance with a digital ohmmeter

If you do not have an ohmmeter, you may want to take your car to a mechanic or diagnostic center with an oscilloscope type of diagnosis system. This unit will read the curve of ignition voltage and uncover problems with wires, or any other component, easily. You may also want to refer to the previous procedures on spark plug analysis, as looking at the plugs may help you to identify wire problems.

REMOVAL & INSTALLATION

▶ See Figure 109

1. Be sure to number all the spark plug wires to the correct terminal on the distributor cap before disconnecting them.
2. When removing spark plug wires, use great care. Grasp and twist the insulator back and forth on the spark plug to free the insulator. Do not pull on the wire directly as it may become separated from the connector inside the insulator. If necessary, use a spark plug wire removal tool.

To install:

➡Whenever a high tension wire is removed for any reason form a spark plug, coil or distributor terminal housing, silicone grease must be applied to the boot before it is reconnected. Using a small clean tool, coat the entire interior surface of the boot with silicone grease or an equivalent.

3. Install each wire on the proper terminal of the distributor cap. Be sure the terminal connector inside the insulator is fully seated. A snap should be felt when a good connection is made between the spark plug wire and distributor cap terminal.
4. If equipped, remove wire separators from old wire set and install them on new set in approximately same position. Be sure that all of the spark plug wires are properly routed, otherwise, ignition noise through the radio, cross ignition of the spark plugs or short circuiting of the wires to ground could result.
5. Connect wires to proper spark plugs. Be certain all wires are fully seated on the terminals.
6. Connect the negative battery cable.

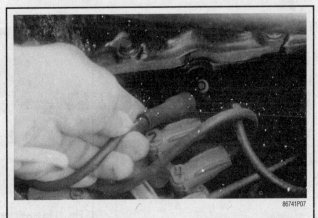

Fig. 109 Tag and disengage the spark plug wire from the spark plug

Distributor Cap and Rotor

REMOVAL & INSTALLATION

▸ **See Figures 110, 111, 112 and 113**

1. Disconnect the negative battery cable.
2. Unplug the distributor connector from the wiring harness connector.
3. Label, and if necessary, disconnect the spark plug wires from the distributor cap.
4. Using a phillips head screwdriver or a 9/32 inch nut driver tool, loosen the distributor cap retaining screws.
5. Lift the cap off of the distributor.
6. Note in which direction the distributor spark pick-up is pointing, then pull the rotor off of the distributor shaft.
7. Installation is the reverse of the removal procedures.

INSPECTION

Remove the distributor cap and inspect the inside for flashover, cracking of the carbon button, lack of spring tension on the carbon button, cracking of the cap, and burned, worn terminals. Also check for broken distributer cap towers. If any of these conditions are present, the distributor cap and/or cables should be replaced.

When replacing the distributor cap, transfer cables from the original cap to the new cap one at a time. Ensure that each cable is installed into the corresponding tower of the new cap. Fully seat the wires into the towers. If necessary, refer to the appropriate engine firing order diagram.

Light scaling of the terminals can be cleaned with a sharp knife. If the terminals are heavily scaled, replace the distributor cap.

A cap that is greasy, dirty or has a powder-like substance on the inside should be cleaned with a solution of warm water and mild detergent. Scrub the cap with a soft brush. Thoroughly rinse the cap and dry it with a clean soft cloth.

Replace the rotor with a new one if it is cracked, or if the tip is excessively burned or heavily scaled. If the spring terminal does not have adequate tension, replace the rotor with a new one.

Ignition Timing

➡**Timing is adjustable on 1984–86 vehicles only. On 1987 and later vehicles, the timing is controlled by the Powertrain Control Module (PCM) and is not adjustable.**

GENERAL INFORMATION

Ignition timing is the measurement, in degrees of crankshaft rotation, of the point at which the spark plugs fire in each of the cylinders. It is measured in degrees before or after Top Dead Center (TDC) of the compression stroke. Ignition timing is controlled by turning the distributor body in the engine.

Ideally, the air/fuel mixture in the cylinder will be ignited by the spark plug just as the piston passes TDC of the compression stroke. If this happens, the piston will be beginning its downward motion of the power stroke just as the compressed and ignited air/fuel mixture starts to expand. The expansion of the air/fuel mixture then forces the piston down on the power stroke and turns the crankshaft.

Because it takes a fraction of a second for the spark plug to ignite the mixture in the cylinder, the spark plug must fire a little before the piston reaches TDC. Otherwise, the mixture will not be completely ignited as the piston passes TDC and the full power of the explosion will not be used by the engine.

The timing measurement is given in degrees of crankshaft rotation before the piston reaches TDC (BTDC). If the setting for the ignition timing is 5° BTDC, the spark plug must fire 5° before each piston reaches TDC. This only holds true, however, when the engine is at idle speed.

As the engine speed increases, the pistons go faster. The spark plugs have to ignite the fuel even sooner if it is to be completely ignited when the piston reaches TDC. To do this, the distributor has a means to advance the timing of the spark as the engine speed increases. This is accomplished by input from the electronic ignition control module and other computer sources. If the distributor is equipped with a vacuum advance unit, it is necessary to disconnect the vacuum line from the diaphragm when the ignition timing is being set.

If the ignition is set too far advanced (BTDC), the ignition and expansion of the fuel in the cylinder will occur too soon and tend to force the piston down while it is still traveling up. This causes engine ping. If the ignition spark is set too far retarded, after TDC (ATDC), the piston will have already passed TDC and started on its way down when the fuel is ignited. This will cause the piston to be forced down for only a portion of its travel. This will result in poor engine performance and lack of power.

The timing is best checked with a timing light. This device is connected in series with the No. 1 spark plug. The current that fires the spark plug also causes the timing light to flash.

When the engine is running, the timing light is aimed at the timing marks on the engine and crankshaft pulley.

ADJUSTMENT

▸ **See Figures 114, 115, 116 and 117**

Timing is adjustable on 1984–86 vehicles only. On 1987 and later vehicles, the timing is controlled by the Powertrain Control Module (PCM) and is not adjustable.

On 1984–86 models, timing should be checked at each tune-up and any time components are replaced in the ignition system. The timing marks consist of a notch on the rim of the crankshaft pulley and a graduated scale attached to the engine front (timing) cover. A stroboscopic flash (dynamic) timing light must be used, as a static light is too inaccurate for emission controlled engines.

There are three basic types of timing lights available. The first is a simple neon bulb with two wire connections. One wire connects to the spark plug terminal and the other plugs into the end of the spark plug wire for the No. 1 cylinder, thus connecting the light in series with the spark plug. This type of light is pretty dim and must be held very close to the timing marks to be seen. Sometimes a dark corner has to be sought out to see the flash at all. This type of light is very inexpensive. The second type operates from the vehicle's battery—two alligator clips connect to the battery terminals, while an adapter enables a third

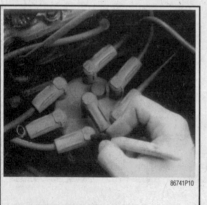

Fig. 110 Label the spark plug wires

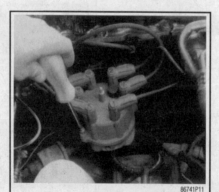

Fig. 111 Loosen the distributor retaining screws

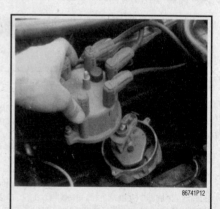

Fig. 112 Remove the distributor cap

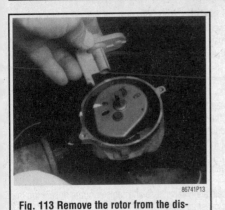

Fig. 113 Remove the rotor from the distributor shaft

Fig. 114 Common location of timing marks

Fig. 115 Using a timing light to adjust ignition timing

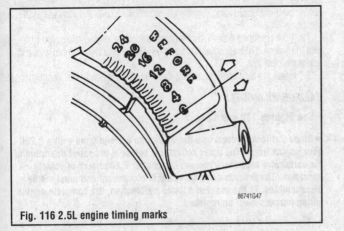

Fig. 116 2.5L engine timing marks

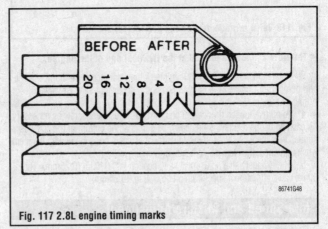

Fig. 117 2.8L engine timing marks

clip to be connected to the No. 1 spark plug and wire. This type provides a nice bright flash that you can see even in bright sunlight. It is the type most often seen in professional shops. The third type replaces the battery power source with 110 volt current.

1. Warm up the engine to normal operating temperature. Stop the engine and connect the timing light to the No. 1 spark plug wire and a tachometer to the Tach terminal on the distributor cap.

➡Most tachometers require a special clip to attach the meter to the distributor. This clip may or may not be included with the tachometer.

2. Clean off the timing marks and mark the pulley notch and timing scale with white chalk.

3. Disconnect and plug the vacuum hose from the vacuum advance unit (if equipped).

4. Start the engine and aim the timing light at the pointer marks. Be careful not to touch the fan, because it may appear to be standing still. If the pulley notch isn't aligned with the proper timing mark (refer to the Tune-Up Specifications chart), the timing will have to be adjusted.

5. Loosen the distributor clamp locknut. Turn the distributor slowly to adjust the timing, holding it by the base and not the cap. Turn it counterclockwise to advance timing (toward BTDC), and clockwise to retard (toward TDC or ATDC).

6. Tighten the locknut. Check the timing again, in case the distributor moved slightly as you tightened it.

7. Unplug and connect the distributor vacuum line if applicable, and correct the idle speed to that specified in the Tune-Up Specifications chart.

8. Stop the engine and disconnect the timing light.

Valve Lash

Valve adjustment determines how far the valves enter the cylinder and how long they stay open and closed.

If the valve clearance is too large, part of the lift of the camshaft will be used in removing the excessive clearance. Consequently, the valve will not be opening as far as it should. This condition has two effects: the valve train compo-

nents will emit a tapping sound as they take up the excessive clearance, and the engine will perform poorly because the valves don't open fully and allow the proper amount of gases to flow into and out of the engine.

If the valve clearance is too small, the intake valves and the exhaust valves will open too far and they will not fully seat on the cylinder head when they close. When a valve seats itself on the cylinder head, it does two things: it seals the combustion chamber so that none of the gases in the cylinder escape and it cools itself by transferring some of the heat it absorbs from the combustion in the cylinder to the cylinder head and to the engine's cooling system. If the valve clearance is too small, the engine will run poorly because of the gases escaping from the combustion chamber. The valves will also become overheated and will warp, since they cannot transfer heat unless they are touching the valve seat in the cylinder head.

✳✳ WARNING

While all valve adjustments must be made as accurately as possible, it is better to have the valve adjustment slightly loose than slightly tight, as a burned valve may result from overly tight adjustments.

ADJUSTMENT

2.1L Diesel Engine

♦ See Figure 118

➡The 2.1L Diesel engines have adjustable valves. All other engines have hydraulic valve lifters which maintain a zero clearance and cannot be adjusted.

1. Be sure that the engine is cold before adjusting the valves. Remove the valve cover.

2. Set the No. 1 cylinder to TDC on the compression stroke. Check the valve clearance of number one and number two intake, and number one and number three exhaust valves. Adjust as required.

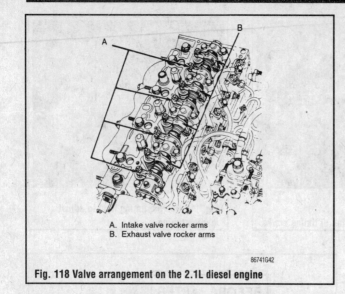

A. Intake valve rocker arms
B. Exhaust valve rocker arms

86741G42

Fig. 118 Valve arrangement on the 2.1L diesel engine

➡ **The No.1 cylinder is located at the flywheel end of the engine.**

3. Rotate the crankshaft 360°, then check the clearance of the number three and number four intake, and number two and number four exhaust valves. Adjust as required.

4. To adjust, loosen the locknut and turn the adjustment screw as necessary. As each adjustment screw is tightened, be sure that the bottom of the screw is aligned with the valve stem. If the adjustment screw is not aligned with the stem when tightened, the stem could bend. Tighten the locknut.

5. The exhaust valve adjustment specification is 0.010 in. (0.25mm). The intake valve adjustment specification is 0.008 in. (0.20mm)

Idle Speed and Mixture Adjustments

This section contains only tune-up adjustment procedures for fuel systems. Descriptions, adjustments, and replacement procedures for fuel system components can be found in Section 5.

1984–85 MODELS

2.5L Engine

1. Fully warm up the engine.
2. Check the choke fast idle adjustment: Disconnect and plug the EGR valve vacuum hose. Position the fast idle adjustment screw on the second step of the fast idle cam with the transmission in Neutral. Adjust the fast idle speed to 2,000 rpm for manual transmission models, or 2,300 rpm for automatic transmission models. Allow the throttle to return to normal curb idle and reconnect the EGR vacuum.
3. To adjust the Sol-Vac Vacuum Actuator: Remove the vacuum hose from the vacuum actuator and plug the hose. Connect an external vacuum source to the actuator and apply 10–15 in. Hg (68–103 kPa) of vacuum to the actuator. Shift the transmission to Neutral. Adjust the idle speed to the following rpm using the vacuum actuator adjustment screw on the throttle lever: 850 rpm for automatic transmission models, or 950 rpm for manual transmission models. The adjustment is made with all accessories turned off.

➡ **The curb idle should always be adjusted after vacuum actuator adjustment.**

4. To adjust the curb idle: Remove the vacuum hose from the Sol-Vac vacuum actuator and plug the hose. Shift the transmission into Neutral. Adjust the curb idle using the 1/4 in. hex head adjustment screw on the end of the Sol-Vac unit. Set the speed to 750 rpm for manual transmission models, or 700 rpm for automatic transmission models. Reconnect the vacuum hose to the vacuum actuator.

➡ **Engine speed will vary 10–30 rpm during this mode due to the closed loop fuel control.**

5. To adjust the TRC: The TRC screw is preset at the factory and should not require adjustment. However, to check adjustment, the screw should be 3/4 turn from the closed throttle position.

2.8L Engine

EXCEPT CALIFORNIA

1. Connect a tachometer to the ignition coil negative terminal or to the pigtail wire connector above the heater blower motor.
2. Disconnect and plug the vacuum hose at the distributor vacuum advance.
3. If necessary, adjust the ignition timing with the engine speed at or below specifications.
4. Unplug and reconnect the vacuum hose to the distributor vacuum advance unit.
5. Disconnect the deceleration valve hose and canister purge hose. Plug the hose and remove the air cleaner assembly.
6. If equipped with air conditioning, turn the control switch to the ON position and open the throttle momentarily to insure the solenoid armature is fully extended. Adjust the solenoid idle speed adjusting screw to obtain the specified engine curb idle speed rpm. Turn the air conditioning control switch to the OFF position.
7. If not equipped with air conditioning, adjust the engine idle speed rpm with the solenoid idle speed adjusting screw. Disconnect the solenoid wire and adjust the curb idle.
8. Install the air cleaner assembly. Connect all hoses and other connections.

CALIFORNIA MODELS

▶ **See Figures 119 and 120**

➡ **Some California Jeeps with the V6 engine are equipped with a 2,200 hour engine timer. The timer activates a solenoid to control operation of the carburetor secondary vacuum break after 2,200 hours of vehicle operation. The timer is not a serviceable component and must not be disassembled. In the event of a timer malfunction, the complete engine wiring harness must be replaced.**

1. Connect a tachometer to the ignition system. Start the engine and operate to normal operating temperature.
2. Turn off all accessories including the air conditioning system.
3. Put the manual transmission equipped vehicles in Neutral, and the automatic transmission equipped vehicles in Drive with the parking brake locked and the wheels chocked.
4. Adjust the curb idle speed adjusting screw to obtain the specified rpm of 700 for both manual and automatic transmission equipped vehicles.
5. Disconnect the vacuum hose from the idle kick actuator and connect an outside vacuum source to the actuator. Apply 15 in. Hg. (51 kPa) of vacuum to the actuator.
6. Adjust the actuator hex head adjustment screw for the specified 1,200 rpm with both types of transmissions in the Neutral position.
7. Stop the engine, remove the tachometer and vacuum pump. Install the vacuum hose to the actuator.

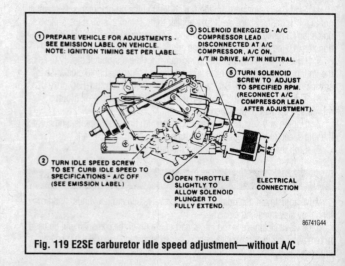

① PREPARE VEHICLE FOR ADJUSTMENTS - SEE EMISSION LABEL ON VEHICLE. NOTE: IGNITION TIMING SET PER LABEL.

③ SOLENOID ENERGIZED - A/C COMPRESSOR LEAD DISCONNECTED AT A/C COMPRESSOR, A/C ON, A/T IN DRIVE, M/T IN NEUTRAL.

⑤ TURN SOLENOID SCREW TO ADJUST TO SPECIFIED RPM. (RECONNECT A/C COMPRESSOR LEAD AFTER ADJUSTMENT).

② TURN IDLE SPEED SCREW TO SET CURB IDLE SPEED TO SPECIFICATIONS - A/C OFF (SEE EMISSION LABEL)

④ OPEN THROTTLE SLIGHTLY TO ALLOW SOLENOID PLUNGER TO FULLY EXTEND.

ELECTRICAL CONNECTION

86741G44

Fig. 119 E2SE carburetor idle speed adjustment—without A/C

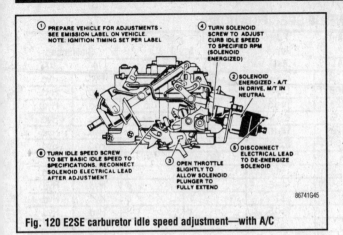

Fig. 120 E2SE carburetor idle speed adjustment—with A/C

1985–87 MODELS

2.1L Diesel Engine

♦ **See Figure 121**

1. Connect a tachometer to the ignition system. The idle speed is adjusted on the injection pump linkage.
2. Loosen the screw locknut, adjust the idle speed to 750–850 rpm with the adjusting screw and tighten the locknut.
3. Stop the engine and remove the tachometer.

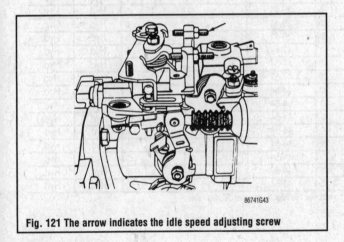

Fig. 121 The arrow indicates the idle speed adjusting screw

2.5L Engine

WITH YFA CARBURETOR

1. The Throttle Return Control TRC (anti-diesel) adjustment screw is statically set at 3/4 turn from the throttle valve closed position during factory assembly and does not normally require readjustment. Should this adjustment be required, turn the adjustment screw counterclockwise to the throttle plate closed position and then turn the screw clockwise 3/4 turn.
2. Connect a tachometer to the ignition coil TACH wire connector.
3. Place the transmission in Neutral and set the parking brake.
4. Start the engine and allow it to reach normal operating temperature.
5. Connect an external vacuum source to the Sol-Vac vacuum actuator and apply 10–15 in. Hg (34–51 kPa) of vacuum. Plug the engine vacuum hose.
6. Adjust the vacuum actuator until an engine speed of approximately 1,000 rpm is achieved.

➡ **Refer to the Vehicle Emission Control Information Label for the latest specifications for the particular engine being adjusted.**

7. Remove the vacuum source from the vacuum actuator and retain the plug in the vacuum hose from the engine.
8. Turn the hex-head curb idle speed adjustment screw until the speed of 500 rpm is obtained.

➡ **Refer to the Vehicle Emission Control Label for the latest specifications for the particular engine being adjusted.**

9. Stop the engine, then unplug and connect the engine vacuum hose to the vacuum actuator.
10. Remove the tachometer from the engine.

WITH THROTTLE BODY FUEL INJECTION

Adjustments are not possible on this unit, as all functions are computer controlled.

2.8L Engines

EXCEPT CALIFORNIA

1. Connect a tachometer to the ignition coil negative terminal or to the pigtail wire connector above the heater blower motor.
2. Disconnect and plug the vacuum hose at the distributor vacuum advance.
3. If necessary, adjust the ignition timing with the engine speed at or below specifications.
4. Unplug and reconnect the vacuum hose to the distributor vacuum advance unit.
5. Disconnect the deceleration valve hose and canister purge hose. Plug the hose and remove the air cleaner assembly.
6. If equipped with air conditioning, turn the control switch to the ON position and open the throttle momentarily to insure the solenoid armature is fully extended. Adjust the solenoid idle speed adjusting screw to obtain the specified engine curb idle speed rpm. Turn the air conditioning control switch to the OFF position.
7. If not equipped with air conditioning, adjust the engine idle speed rpm with the solenoid idle speed adjusting screw. Disconnect the solenoid wire and adjust the curb idle.
8. Install the air cleaner assembly. Connect all hoses and other connections.

CALIFORNIA MODELS

➡ **Some California Jeeps with the V6 engine are equipped with a 2,200 hour engine timer. The timer activates a solenoid to control operation of the carburetor secondary vacuum break after 2,200 hours of vehicle operation. The timer is not a serviceable component and must not be disassembled. In the event of a timer malfunction, the complete engine wiring harness must be replaced.**

1. Connect a tachometer to the ignition system. Start the engine and operate to normal operating temperature.
2. Turn off all accessories including the air conditioning system.
3. Put the manual transmission equipped vehicles in Neutral and the automatic transmission equipped vehicles in Drive with the parking brake set and the wheels chocked.
4. Adjust the curb idle speed adjusting screw to obtain the specified rpm of 700 for both manual and automatic transmission equipped vehicles.
5. Disconnect the vacuum hose from the idle kick actuator and connect an outside vacuum source to the actuator. Apply 15 in. Hg (68 kPa) of vacuum to the actuator.
6. Adjust the actuator hex head adjustment screw for the specified 1,200 rpm with both types of transmissions in the Neutral position.
7. Stop the engine, remove the tachometer and vacuum pump. Install the vacuum hose to the actuator.

1988 AND LATER MODELS

The 2.5L TBI, 2.5L MFI, 4.0L MFI, 5.2L MFI and 5.9L MFI are all fuel injected. Routine adjustments are computer controlled. No routine idle speed adjustments are possible.

GASOLINE ENGINE TUNE-UP SPECIFICATIONS

Year	Engine ID/VIN	Engine Displacement Liters (c.i.d)	Spark Plugs Gap (In.)	Ignition Timing (deg.) MT	AT	Fuel Pump (psi)	Idle Speed (rpm) MT	AT	Valve Clearance In.	Ex.
1984	U	2.5 (150)	0.035	12B	12B	6.5–8	750	750	Hyd.	Hyd.
	W	2.8 (173)	0.041	10B	10B	6.5–8	750	750	Hyd.	Hyd.
1985	H	2.5 (150)	0.035	12B	12B	14–15	750	750	Hyd.	Hyd.
	W	2.8 (173)	0.041	10B	10B	6.5–8	750	750	Hyd.	Hyd.
1986	H	2.5 (150)	0.035	12B	12B	14–15	750	750	Hyd.	Hyd.
	W	2.8 (173)	0.041	10B	10B	6.5–8	750	750	Hyd.	Hyd.
1987	H	2.5 (150)	0.035	①	①	14–15	750	750	Hyd.	Hyd.
	M	4.0 (242)	0.035	①	①	31	①	①	Hyd.	Hyd.
1988	H	2.5 (150)	0.035	①	①	14–15	①	①	Hyd.	Hyd.
	M	4.0 (242)	0.035	①	①	31	①	①	Hyd.	Hyd.
1989	E	2.5 (150)	0.035	①	①	14–15	①	①	Hyd.	Hyd.
	L	4.0 (242)	0.035	①	①	31	①	①	Hyd.	Hyd.
1990	E	2.5 (150)	0.035	①	①	14–15	①	①	Hyd.	Hyd.
	L	4.0 (242)	0.035	①	①	31	①	①	Hyd.	Hyd.
1991	P	2.5 (150)	0.035	①	①	39–41	①	①	Hyd.	Hyd.
	S	4.0 (242)	0.035	①	①	39–41	①	①	Hyd.	Hyd.
1992	P	2.5 (150)	0.035	①	①	39–41	①	①	Hyd.	Hyd.
	S	4.0 (242)	0.035	①	①	39–41	①	①	Hyd.	Hyd.
1993	P	2.5 (150)	0.035	①	①	39–41	①	①	Hyd.	Hyd.
	S	4.0 (242)	0.035	①	①	39–41	①	①	Hyd.	Hyd.
	Y	5.2 (5211)	0.035	①	①	39–41	①	①	Hyd.	Hyd.
1994	P	2.5 (150)	0.035	①	①	39–41	①	①	Hyd.	Hyd.
	S	4.0 (242)	0.035	①	①	39–41	①	①	Hyd.	Hyd.
	Y	5.2 (5211)	0.035	①	①	39–41	①	①	Hyd.	Hyd.
1995	P	2.5 (150)	0.035	①	①	39–41	①	①	Hyd.	Hyd.
	S	4.0 (242)	0.035	①	①	39–41	①	①	Hyd.	Hyd.
	Y	5.2 (5211)	0.035	①	①	39–41	①	①	Hyd.	Hyd.
1996	P	2.5 (150)	0.035	①	①	47–51	①	①	Hyd.	Hyd.
	S	4.0 (242)	0.035	①	①	47–51	①	①	Hyd.	Hyd.
	Y	5.2 (5211)	0.035	①	①	47–51	①	①	Hyd.	Hyd.
1997	P	2.5 (150)	0.035	①	①	44–54	①	①	Hyd.	Hyd.
	S	4.0 (242)	0.035	①	①	44–54	①	①	Hyd.	Hyd.
	Y	5.2 (5211)	0.040	①	①	44–54	①	①	Hyd.	Hyd.
	Z	5.9 (5899)	0.035	①	①	44–54	①	①	Hyd.	Hyd.
1998 -on	P	2.5 (150)	0.035	①	①	44–54	①	①	Hyd.	Hyd.
	S	4.0 (242)	0.035	①	①	44–54	①	①	Hyd.	Hyd.
	Y	5.2 (5211)	0.040	①	①	44–54	①	①	Hyd.	Hyd.
	Z	5.9 (5899)	0.040	①	①	44–54	①	①	Hyd.	Hyd.

NOTE: The Vehicle Emission Control Information label often reflects specification changes made during production. The label figures must be used if they differ from those in this chart.

① Not adjustable. Controlled by the PCM.

91071C04

DIESEL ENGINE TUNE-UP SPECIFICATIONS

Year	Engine ID/VIN	Engine Displacement Liters (cu. in.)	Valve Clearance Intake (In.)	Exhaust (In.)	Intake Valve Opens (deg.)	Injection Pump Setting (deg.)	Injection Nozzle Pressure (psi) New	Used	Idle Speed (rpm)	Cranking Compression Pressure (psi)
1985	B	2.1 (126)	0.008	0.010	14B	8B	1885	NA	800 ①	②
1986	B	2.1 (126)	0.008	0.010	14B	8B	1885	NA	800 ①	②
1987	B	2.1 (126)	0.008	0.010	14B	8B	1885	NA	800 ①	②

NOTE: The Vehicle Emission Control Information label often reflects specification changes made during production. The label figures must be used if they differ from those in this chart.

① Without solenoid. 1100 with solenoid
② Check all cylinders. The difference between cylinders should not be more than 25%.

91071C05

Air Conditioning System

SYSTEM SERVICE & REPAIR

▶ **See Figure 122**

➡ **It is recommended that the A/C system be serviced by an EPA Section 609 certified automotive technician utilizing a refrigerant recovery/recycling machine.**

The do-it-yourself should not service his/her own vehicle's A/C system for many reasons, including legal concerns, personal injury, environmental damage and cost. The following are some of the reasons why you may decide not to service your own vehicle's A/C system.

According to the U.S. Clean Air Act, it is a federal crime to service or repair (involving the refrigerant) a Motor Vehicle Air Conditioning (MVAC) system for money without being EPA certified. It is also illegal to vent R-12 and R-134a refrigerants into the atmosphere. Selling or distributing A/C system refrigerant (in a container which contains less than 20 pounds of refrigerant) to any person who is not EPA 609 certified is also not allowed by law.

State and/or local laws may be more strict than the federal regulations, so be sure to check with your state and/or local authorities for further information. For further federal information on the legality of servicing your A/C system, call the EPA Stratospheric Ozone Hotline.

➡ **Federal law dictates that a fine of up to $25,000 may be levied on people convicted of venting refrigerant into the atmosphere. Additionally, the EPA may pay up to $10,000 for information or services leading to a criminal conviction of the violation of these laws.**

When servicing an A/C system you run the risk of handling or coming in contact with refrigerant, which may result in skin or eye irritation or frostbite. Although low in toxicity (due to chemical stability), inhalation of concentrated refrigerant fumes is dangerous and can result in death; cases of fatal cardiac arrhythmia have been reported in people accidentally subjected to high levels of refrigerant. Some early symptoms include loss of concentration and drowsiness.

➡ **Generally, the limit for exposure is lower for R-134a than it is for R-12. Exceptional care must be practiced when handling R-134a.**

Also, refrigerants can decompose at high temperatures (near gas heaters or open flame), which may result in hydrofluoric acid, hydrochloric acid and phosgene (a fatal nerve gas).

R-12 refrigerant can damage the environment because it is a Chlorofluorocarbon (CFC), which has been proven to add to ozone layer depletion, leading to increasing levels of UV radiation. UV radiation has been linked with an increase in skin cancer, suppression of the human immune system, an increase in cataracts, damage to crops, damage to aquatic organisms, an increase in ground-level ozone, and increased global warming.

R-134a refrigerant is a greenhouse gas which, if allowed to vent into the atmosphere, will contribute to global warming (the Greenhouse Effect).

It is usually more economically feasible to have a certified MVAC automotive technician perform A/C system service on your vehicle. Some possible reasons for this are as follows:

- While it is illegal to service an A/C system without the proper equipment, the home mechanic would have to purchase an expensive refrigerant recovery/recycling machine to service his/her own vehicle.
- Since only a certified person may purchase refrigerant—according to the Clean Air Act, there are specific restrictions on selling or distributing A/C system refrigerant—it is legally impossible (unless certified) for the home mechanic to service his/her own vehicle. Procuring refrigerant in an illegal fashion exposes one to the risk of paying a $25,000 fine to the EPA.

R-12 Refrigerant Conversion

If your vehicle still uses R-12 refrigerant, one way to save A/C system costs down the road is to investigate the possibility of having your system converted to R-134a. The older R-12 systems can be easily converted to R-134a refrigerant by a certified automotive technician by installing a few new components and changing the system oil.

The cost of R-12 is steadily rising and will continue to increase, because it is no longer imported or manufactured in the United States. Therefore, it is often possible to have an R-12 system converted to R-134a and recharged for less than it would cost to just charge the system with R-12.

If you are interested in having your system converted, contact local automotive service stations for more details and information.

PREVENTIVE MAINTENANCE

▶ **See Figures 123 and 124**

Although the A/C system should not be serviced by the do-it-yourselfer, preventive maintenance can be practiced and A/C system inspections can be performed to help maintain the efficiency of the vehicle's A/C system. For preventive maintenance, perform the following:

- The easiest and most important preventive maintenance for your A/C system is to be sure that it is used on a regular basis. Running the system for five minutes each month (no matter what the season) will help ensure that the seals and all internal components remain lubricated.

➡ **Some newer vehicles automatically operate the A/C system compressor whenever the windshield defroster is activated. When running, the compressor lubricates the A/C system components; therefore, the A/C system would not need to be operated each month.**

- In order to prevent heater core freeze-up during A/C operation, it is necessary to maintain proper antifreeze protection. Use a hand-held coolant tester (hydrometer) to periodically check the condition of the antifreeze in your engine's cooling system.

➡ **Antifreeze should not be used longer than the manufacturer specifies.**

- For efficient operation of an air conditioned vehicle's cooling system, the radiator cap should have a holding pressure which meets manufacturer's specifications. A cap which fails to hold these pressures should be replaced.
- Any obstruction of or damage to the condenser configuration will restrict air flow which is essential to its efficient operation. It is, therefore, a good rule to keep this unit clean and in proper physical shape.

Fig. 122 Refrigerant charge information can sometimes be found on the compressor

91071P13

TCCS1233

Fig. 123 A coolant tester can be used to determine the freezing and boiling levels of the coolant in your vehicle

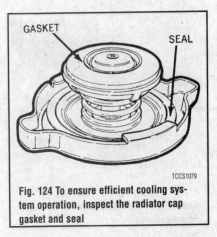

TCCS1079

Fig. 124 To ensure efficient cooling system operation, inspect the radiator cap gasket and seal

➡Bug screens which are mounted in front of the condenser (unless they are original equipment) are regarded as obstructions.

• The condensation drain tube expels any water which accumulates on the bottom of the evaporator housing into the engine compartment. If this tube is obstructed, the air conditioning performance can be restricted and condensation buildup can spill over onto the vehicle's floor.

SYSTEM INSPECTION

◢ See Figure 125

Although the A/C system should not be serviced by the do-it-yourselfer, preventive maintenance can be practiced and A/C system inspections can be performed to help maintain the efficiency of the vehicle's A/C system. For A/C system inspection, perform the following:

The easiest and often most important check for the air conditioning system consists of a visual inspection of the system components. Visually inspect the air conditioning system for refrigerant leaks, damaged compressor clutch, abnormal compressor drive belt tension and/or condition, plugged evaporator drain tube, blocked condenser fins, disconnected or broken wires, blown fuses, corroded connections and poor insulation.

A refrigerant leak will usually appear as an oily residue at the leakage point in the system. The oily residue soon picks up dust or dirt particles from the surrounding air and appears greasy. Through time, this will build up and appear to be a heavy dirt impregnated grease.

For a thorough visual and operational inspection, check the following:
• Check the surface of the radiator and condenser for dirt, leaves or other material which might block air flow.
• Check for kinks in hoses and lines. Check the system for leaks.
• Make sure the drive belt is properly tensioned. When the air conditioning is operating, make sure the drive belt is free of noise or slippage.
• Make sure the blower motor operates at all appropriate positions, then check for distribution of the air from all outlets with the blower on **HIGH** or **MAX**.

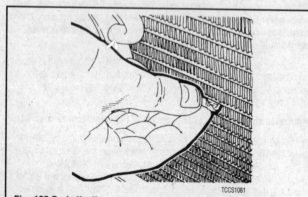

Fig. 125 Periodically remove any debris from the condenser and radiator fins

➡Keep in mind that under conditions of high humidity, air discharged from the A/C vents may not feel as cold as expected, even if the system is working properly. This is because vaporized moisture in humid air retains heat more effectively than dry air, thereby making humid air more difficult to cool.

• Make sure the air passage selection lever is operating correctly. Start the engine and warm it to normal operating temperature, then make sure the temperature selection lever is operating correctly.

Windshield Wipers

ELEMENT (REFILL) CARE & REPLACEMENT

◢ See Figures 126, 127 and 128

For maximum effectiveness and longest element life, the windshield and wiper blades should be kept clean. Dirt, tree sap, road tar and so on will cause streaking, smearing and blade deterioration if left on the glass. It is advisable to wash the windshield carefully with a commercial glass cleaner at least once a month. Wipe off the rubber blades with the wet rag afterwards. Do not attempt to move wipers across the windshield by hand; damage to the motor and drive mechanism will result.

To inspect and/or replace the wiper blade elements, place the wiper switch in the **LOW** speed position and the ignition switch in the **ACC** position. When the wiper blades are approximately vertical on the windshield, turn the ignition switch to **OFF**.

Examine the wiper blade elements. If they are found to be cracked, broken or torn, they should be replaced immediately. Replacement intervals will vary with usage, although ozone deterioration usually limits element life to about one year. If the wiper pattern is smeared or streaked, or if the blade chatters across the glass, the elements should be replaced. It is easiest and most sensible to replace the elements in pairs.

If your vehicle is equipped with aftermarket blades, there are several different types of refills and your vehicle might have any kind. Aftermarket blades and arms rarely use the exact same type blade or refill as the original equipment.

Regardless of the type of refill used, be sure to follow the part manufacturer's instructions closely. Make sure that all of the frame jaws are engaged as the refill is pushed into place and locked. If the metal blade holder and frame are allowed to touch the glass during wiper operation, the glass will be scratched.

Tires and Wheels

Common sense and good driving habits will afford maximum tire life. Fast starts, sudden stops and hard cornering are hard on tires and will shorten their useful life span. Make sure that you don't overload the vehicle or run with incorrect pressure in the tires. Both of these practices will increase tread wear.

➡For optimum tire life, keep the tires properly inflated, rotate them often and have the wheel alignment checked periodically.

Inspect your tires frequently. Be especially careful to watch for bubbles in the tread or sidewall, deep cuts or underinflation. Replace any tires with bubbles in

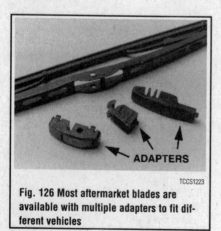

Fig. 126 Most aftermarket blades are available with multiple adapters to fit different vehicles

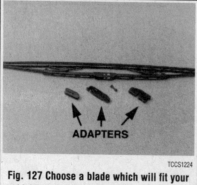

Fig. 127 Choose a blade which will fit your vehicle, and that will be readily available next time you need blades

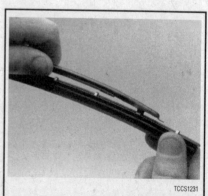

Fig. 128 When installed, be certain the blade is fully inserted into the backing

the sidewall. If cuts are so deep that they penetrate to the cords, discard the tire. Any cut in the sidewall of a radial tire renders it unsafe. Also look for uneven tread wear patterns that may indicate the front end is out of alignment or that the tires are out of balance.

TIRE ROTATION

▶ **See Figures 129 and 130**

Tires must be rotated periodically to equalize wear patterns that vary with a tire's position on the vehicle. Tires will also wear in an uneven way as the front steering/suspension system wears to the point where the alignment should be reset.

Rotating the tires will ensure maximum life for the tires as a set, so you will not have to discard a tire early due to wear on only part of the tread. Regular rotation is required to equalize wear.

When rotating "unidirectional tires," make sure that they always roll in the same direction. This means that a tire used on the left side of the vehicle must not be switched to the right side and vice-versa. Such tires should only be rotated front-to-rear or rear-to-front, while always remaining on the same side of the vehicle. These tires are marked on the sidewall as to the direction of rotation; observe the marks when reinstalling the tire(s).

Some styled or "mag" wheels may have different offsets front to rear. In these cases, the rear wheels must not be used up front and vice-versa. Furthermore, if these wheels are equipped with unidirectional tires, they cannot be rotated unless the tire is remounted for the proper direction of rotation.

➡ **The compact or space-saver spare is strictly for emergency use. It must never be included in the tire rotation or placed on the vehicle for everyday use.**

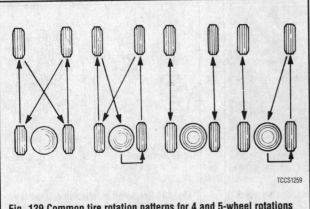

Fig. 129 Common tire rotation patterns for 4 and 5-wheel rotations

Fig. 130 Unidirectional tires are identifiable by sidewall arrows and/or the word "rotation"

TIRE DESIGN

▶ **See Figure 131**

For maximum satisfaction, tires should be used in sets of four. Mixing of different types (radial, bias-belted, fiberglass belted) must be avoided. In most cases, the vehicle manufacturer has designated a type of tire on which the vehicle will perform best. Your first choice when replacing tires should be to use the same type of tire that the manufacturer recommends.

When radial tires are used, tire sizes and wheel diameters should be selected to maintain ground clearance and tire load capacity equivalent to the original specified tire. Radial tires should always be used in sets of four.

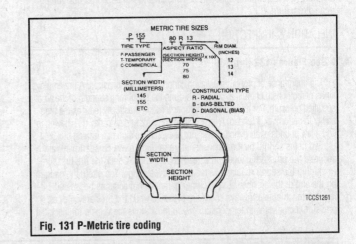

Fig. 131 P-Metric tire coding

✳✳ CAUTION

Radial tires should never be used on only the front axle.

When selecting tires, pay attention to the original size as marked on the tire. Most tires are described using an industry size code sometimes referred to as P-Metric. This allows the exact identification of the tire specifications, regardless of the manufacturer. If selecting a different tire size or brand, remember to check the installed tire for any sign of interference with the body or suspension while the vehicle is stopping, turning sharply or heavily loaded.

Snow Tires

Good radial tires can produce a big advantage in slippery weather, but in snow, a street radial tire does not have sufficient tread to provide traction and control. The small grooves of a street tire quickly pack with snow and the tire behaves like a billiard ball on a marble floor. The more open, chunky tread of a snow tire will self-clean as the tire turns, providing much better grip on snowy surfaces.

To satisfy municipalities requiring snow tires during weather emergencies, most snow tires carry either an M + S designation after the tire size stamped on the sidewall, or the designation "all-season." In general, no change in tire size is necessary when buying snow tires.

Most manufacturers strongly recommend the use of 4 snow tires on their vehicles for reasons of stability. If snow tires are fitted only to the drive wheels, the opposite end of the vehicle may become very unstable when braking or turning on slippery surfaces. This instability can lead to unpleasant endings if the driver can't counteract the slide in time.

Note that snow tires, whether 2 or 4, will affect vehicle handling in all non-snow situations. The stiffer, heavier snow tires will noticeably change the turning and braking characteristics of the vehicle. Once the snow tires are installed, you must re-learn the behavior of the vehicle and drive accordingly.

➡ **Consider buying extra wheels on which to mount the snow tires. Once done, the "snow wheels" can be installed and removed as needed. This** eliminates the potential damage to tires or wheels from seasonal removal and installation. Even if your vehicle has styled wheels, see if inexpensive steel wheels are available. Although the look of the vehicle will change, the expensive wheels will be protected from salt, curb hits and pothole damage.

TIRE STORAGE

If they are mounted on wheels, store the tires at proper inflation pressure. All tires should be kept in a cool, dry place. If they are stored in the garage or basement, do not let them stand on a concrete floor; set them on strips of wood, a mat or a large stack of newspaper. Keeping them away from direct moisture is of paramount importance. Tires should not be stored upright, but in a flat position.

INFLATION & INSPECTION

♦ **See Figures 132 thru 139**

The importance of proper tire inflation cannot be overemphasized. A tire employs air as part of its structure. It is designed around the supporting strength of the air at a specified pressure. For this reason, improper inflation drastically reduces the tire's ability to perform as intended. A tire will lose some air in day-to-day use; having to add a few pounds of air periodically is not necessarily a sign of a leaking tire.

Two items should be a permanent fixture in every glove compartment: an accurate tire pressure gauge and a tread depth gauge. Check the tire pressure (including the spare) regularly with a pocket type gauge. Too often, the gauge on the end of the air hose at your corner garage is not accurate because it suffers too much abuse. Always check tire pressure when the tires are cold, as pressure increases with temperature. If you must move the vehicle to check the

the cold pressure specification by more than 2 psi. A slightly softer tire pressure will give a softer ride but also yield lower fuel mileage. A slightly harder tire will give crisper dry road handling but can cause skidding on wet surfaces. Unless you're fully attuned to the vehicle, stick to the recommended inflation pressures.

All tires made since 1968 have built-in tread wear indicator bars that show up as 1/2 in. (13mm) wide smooth bands across the tire when 1/16 inch (1.5mm) of tread remains. The appearance of tread wear indicators means that the tires should be replaced. In fact, many states have laws prohibiting the use of tires with less than this amount of tread.

You can check your own tread depth with an inexpensive gauge or by using a Lincoln head penny. Slip the Lincoln penny (with Lincoln's head upside-down) into several tread grooves. If you can see the top of Lincoln's head in 2 adjacent grooves, the tire has less than 1/16 in. (1.5mm) tread left and should be replaced. You can measure snow tires in the same manner by using the "tails" side of the Lincoln penny. If you can see the top of the Lincoln memorial, it's time to replace the snow tire(s).

CARE OF SPECIAL WHEELS

If you have invested money in magnesium, aluminum alloy or sport wheels, special precautions should be taken to make sure your investment is not wasted and that your special wheels look good for the life of the vehicle.

Special wheels are easily damaged and/or scratched. Occasionally check the rims for cracking, impact damage or air leaks. If any of these are found, replace the wheel. But in order to prevent this type of damage and the costly replacement of a special wheel, observe the following precautions:

• Use extra care not to damage the wheels during removal, installation, balancing, etc. After removal of the wheels from the vehicle, place them on a mat or other protective surface. If they are to be stored for any length of time, support

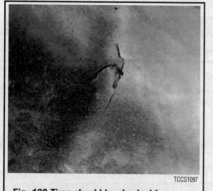

Fig. 132 Tires should be checked frequently for any sign of puncture or damage

Fig. 133 Tires with deep cuts, or cuts which bulge, should be replaced immediately

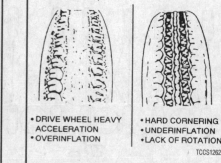

• DRIVE WHEEL HEAVY
ACCELERATION
• OVERINFLATION

• HARD CORNERING
• UNDERINFLATION
• LACK OF ROTATION

TCCS1262

Fig. 134 Examples of inflation-related tire wear patterns

tire inflation, do not drive more than a mile before checking. A cold tire is generally one that has not been driven for more than three hours.

A plate or sticker is normally provided somewhere in the vehicle (door post, hood, tailgate or trunk lid) which shows the proper pressure for the tires. Never counteract excessive pressure build-up by bleeding off air pressure (letting some air out). This will cause the tire to run hotter and wear quicker.

> **⁂ CAUTION**
>
> **Never exceed the maximum tire pressure embossed on the tire! This is the pressure to be used when the tire is at maximum loading, but it is rarely the correct pressure for everyday driving. Consult the owner's manual or the tire pressure sticker for the correct tire pressure.**

Once you've maintained the correct tire pressures for several weeks, you'll be familiar with the vehicle's braking and handling personality. Slight adjustments in tire pressures can fine-tune these characteristics, but never change

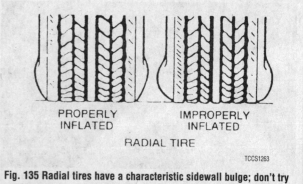

PROPERLY
INFLATED

IMPROPERLY
INFLATED

RADIAL TIRE

TCCS1263

Fig. 135 Radial tires have a characteristic sidewall bulge; don't try to measure pressure by looking at the tire. Use a quality air pressure gauge

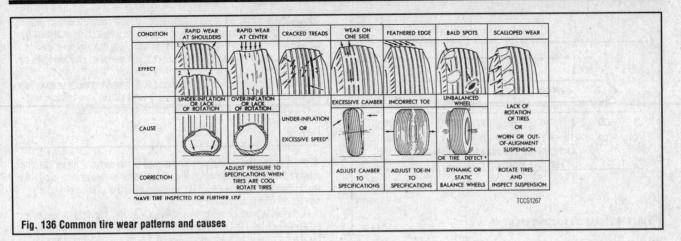

Fig. 136 Common tire wear patterns and causes

Fig. 137 Tread wear indicators will appear when the tire is worn

Fig. 138 Accurate tread depth indicators are inexpensive and handy

Fig. 139 A penny works well for a quick check of tread depth

them on strips of wood. Never store tires and wheels upright; the tread may develop flat spots.

• When driving, watch for hazards; it doesn't take much to crack a wheel.

• When washing, use a mild soap or non-abrasive dish detergent (keeping in mind that detergent tends to remove wax). Avoid cleansers with abrasives or the use of hard brushes. There are many cleaners and polishes for special wheels.

• If possible, remove the wheels during the winter. Salt and sand used for snow removal can severely damage the finish of a wheel.

• Make certain the recommended lug nut torque is never exceeded or the wheel may crack. Never use snow chains on special wheels; severe scratching will occur.

FLUIDS AND LUBRICANTS

Fluid Disposal

Used fluids such as engine oil, transmission fluid, antifreeze and brake fluid are hazardous wastes and must be disposed of properly. Before draining any fluids, consult with your local authorities; in many areas, waste oil, antifreeze, etc. is being accepted as a part of recycling programs. A number of service stations and auto parts stores are also accepting waste fluids for recycling.

Be sure of the recycling center's policies before draining any fluids, as many will not accept different fluids that have been mixed together.

Oil and Fuel Recommendations

OIL

♦ See Figures 140 and 141

Jeep recommends the use of what are called "multigrade" oils. These are specially formulated to change their viscosity with a change in temperature, unlike straight grade oils. The oils are designated by the use of two numbers, the first referring to the thickness of the oil, relative to straight mineral oils, at a low temperature such as 0°F (-18°C). The second number refers to the thickness, also relative to straight mineral oils, at high temperatures typical of highway driving (200°F 93°C). These numbers are preceded by the designation SAE, representing the Society of Automotive Engineers which sets the viscosity standards. For example, use of an SAE 10W–40 oil would give nearly ideal engine operation under almost all operating conditions. The oil would be as thin as a straight 10 weight oil at cold cranking temperatures, and as thick as a straight 40 weight oil at hot running conditions.

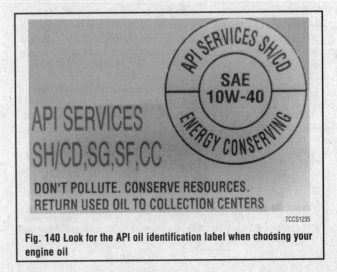

API SERVICES SH/CD,SG,SF,CC

DON'T POLLUTE. CONSERVE RESOURCES. RETURN USED OIL TO COLLECTION CENTERS

Fig. 140 Look for the API oil identification label when choosing your engine oil

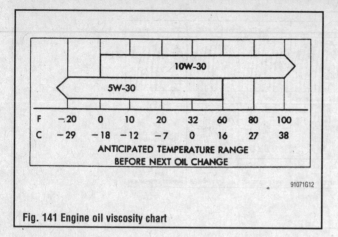

Fig. 141 Engine oil viscosity chart

SYNTHETIC OIL

There are excellent synthetic and fuel-efficient oils available that, under the right circumstances, can help provide better fuel mileage and better engine protection. However, these advantages come at a price, which can be more than the cost per quart of conventional motor oils.

Before pouring any synthetic oils into your vehicle's engine, you should consider the condition of the engine and the type of driving you do. Also, check the manufacturer's warranty conditions regarding the use of synthetics.

Generally, it is best to avoid the use of synthetic oil in both brand new and older, high mileage engines. New engines require a proper break-in, and the synthetics are so slippery that they can hinder this. Most manufacturers recommend that you wait at least 5,000 miles (8,000 km) before switching to a synthetic oil. Conversely, older engines are looser and tend to use more oil. Synthetics will slip past worn parts more readily than regular oil. If your truck already leaks oil (due to worn parts and bad seals or gaskets), it will leak more with a slippery synthetic inside.

Consider your type of driving. If most of your accumulated mileage is on the highway at higher, steadier speeds, a synthetic oil will reduce friction and probably help deliver better fuel mileage. Under such ideal highway conditions, the oil change interval can be extended, as long as the oil filter will operate effectively for the extended life of the oil. If the filter can't do its job for this extended period, dirt and sludge will build up in your engine's crankcase, sump, oil pump and lines, no matter what type of oil is used. If using synthetic oil in this manner, you should continue to change the oil filter at the recommended intervals.

Vehicles used under harder, stop-and-go, short hop circumstances should always be serviced more frequently, and for these vehicles, synthetic oil may not be a wise investment. Because of the necessary shorter change interval needed for this type of driving, you cannot take advantage of the long recommended change interval of most synthetic oils.

GASOLINE

A prime requirement for gasoline is the use of unleaded fuel only. All the vehicles covered in this manual require the use of unleaded fuel exclusively, to protect the catalytic converter. Failure to follow this recommendation will result in failure of the catalyst and consequent failure to pass the emission test many states now require. The use of unleaded fuel also prolongs the life of spark plugs, the engine as a whole, and the exhaust system.

Fuels of the same octane rating have varying anti-knock qualities. Thus, if your engine knocks or pings, try switching brands of gasoline before trying a more expensive higher octane fuel. Fuel should be selected for the brand and octane which performs without pinging.

Your engine's fuel requirements can change with time, due to carbon buildup which changes the compression ratio. If switching brands or grades of gas doesn't work, check the ignition timing. If it is necessary to retard timing from specifications, don't change it more than about 4°. Retarded timing will reduce power output and fuel mileage, and will also increase engine temperature.

Basic engine octane requirements, to be used in your initial choice of fuel, are 87 octane, unleaded. This rating is an average of Research and Motor methods of determination: (R+M)/2. For increased vehicle performance and gas mileage, use a premium unleaded fuel, that is, one with a rating of at least 91 octane. More octane results in better performance and economy in these engines because the ignition system will compensate for its characteristics by advancing the timing.

Gasohol consisting of 10% ethanol and 90% gasoline may be used in your vehicle, but gasolines containing methanol (wood alcohol) are not approved. They can damage fuel system parts and cause operating problems.

DIESEL

The diesel engine in your Jeep is designed to run on No. 2 diesel fuel with a cetane rating of 40. For operation when the outdoor air temperature is consistently below freezing, the use of No.1 diesel fuel or the addition of a cold weather additive is recommended.

Fuel makers produce two grades of diesel fuel, No. 1 and No. 2, for use in automotive diesel engines. Generally speaking, No. 2 fuel is recommended over No. 1 for driving in temperatures above 20°F (-7°C). In fact, in many areas, No. 2 diesel is the only fuel available. By comparison, No. 2 diesel fuel is less volatile than No. 1 fuel, and gives better fuel economy. No. 2 fuel is also a better injection pump lubricant.

Two important characteristics of diesel fuel are its cetane number and its viscosity.

The cetane number of a diesel fuel refers to the ease with which a diesel fuel ignites. High cetane numbers mean that the fuel will ignite with relative ease or that it ignites well at low temperatures. Naturally, the lower the cetane number, the higher the temperature must be to ignite the fuel. Most commercial fuels have cetane numbers that range from 35 to 65. No. 1 diesel fuel generally has a higher cetane rating than No. 2 fuel.

Viscosity is the ability of a liquid, in this case diesel fuel, to flow. Using straight No. 2 diesel fuel below 20°F (-7°C) can cause problems, because this fuel tends to become cloudy, meaning wax crystals begin forming in the fuel. 20°F (-7°C) is often called the cloud point for No. 2 fuel. In extremely cold weather No. 2 fuel can stop flowing altogether. In either case, fuel flow is restricted, which can result in a no-start condition or poor engine performance. Fuel manufacturers often winterize No. 2 diesel fuel by using various fuel additives and blends (No. 1 diesel fuel, kerosene, etc.) to lower its wintertime viscosity. Generally speaking, though, No. 1 diesel fuel is more satisfactory in extremely cold weather.

➡**No. 1 and No. 2 diesel fuels will mix and burn with no ill effects, although the engine manufacturer will undoubtedly recommend one or the other. Consult the owner's manual for information.**

Depending on local climate, most fuel manufacturers make winterized No. 2 fuel available seasonally.

Many automobile manufacturers publish pamphlets giving the locations of diesel fuel stations nationwide. Contact the local dealer for information.

Do not substitute home heating oil for automotive diesel fuel. While in some cases, home heating oil refinement levels equal those of diesel fuel, many times they are far below diesel engine requirements. The result of using dirty home heating oil will be a clogged fuel system, in which case the entire system may have to be dismantled and cleaned.

One more word on diesel fuels. Don't thin diesel fuel with gasoline in cold weather. The lighter gasoline, which is more explosive, will cause rough running at the very least, and may cause extensive damage to the fuel system if enough is used.

Engine

✳✳ CAUTION

The EPA warns that prolonged contact with used engine oil may cause a number of skin disorders, including cancer! You should make every effort to minimize your exposure to used engine oil. Protective gloves should be worn when changing the oil. Wash your hands and any other exposed skin areas as soon as possible after exposure to used engine oil. Soap and water, or waterless hand cleaner, should be used.

OIL LEVEL CHECK

▶ **See Figures 142, 143 and 144**

1. With the engine **OFF**. Park your vehicle is on a level surface to ensure an accurate reading.
2. Let the engine cool for a few moments to allow the oil to drain into the crankcase.
3. Raise the hood and position the hold-up rod, if so equipped.
4. Remove the oil dipstick from the right rear side of 4-cylinder engines, left side of 6-cylinder engines or right front of V-8 engines and wipe it clean.
5. Reinstall the dipstick until it is firmly seated in the tube.
6. Remove the dipstick and take the oil level reading.
7. Add oil through the valve cover filler hole if the oil level is below the add mark on the dipstick.
8. Allow sufficient time for all the oil to drain into the crankcase after you have added it and recheck the oil level.

OIL & FILTER CHANGE

▶ **See Figures 145 thru 150**

✳✳ CAUTION

The EPA warns that prolonged contact with used engine oil may cause a number of skin disorders, including cancer! You should make every effort to minimize your exposure to used engine oil. Protective gloves should be worn when changing the oil. Wash your hands and any other exposed skin areas as soon as possible after exposure to used engine oil. Soap and water, or waterless hand cleaner should be used.

The manufacturer's recommended oil change interval is 7,500 miles (12,000 km) under normal operating conditions. We recommend an oil change interval of 3,000–3,500 miles (4,800–5,600 km) under normal conditions; more frequently under severe conditions such as when the average trip is less than 4 miles (6 km), the engine is operated for extended periods at idle or low speed, when towing a trailer or operating in dusty areas.

In addition, we recommend that the filter be replaced EVERY time the oil is changed.

➡ **Please be considerate of the environment. Dispose of waste oil properly by taking it to a service station, municipal facility or recycling center.**

1. Before draining the oil, run the engine until it reaches normal operating temperature. Hot oil will hold more impurities in suspension and will flow better, allowing it to remove more oil and dirt. Then turn the engine **OFF**.
2. Remove the oil filler cap.
3. Raise and safely support the front of the vehicle using jackstands.
4. Slide a drain pan of at least 5 quarts (4.7 liters) capacity under the oil pan. Wipe the drain plug and surrounding area clean using an old rag.
5. Loosen the drain plug using a 16mm socket or box wrench.
6. Unscrew the plug by hand, using a rag to shield your fingers from the hot oil. By keeping an inward pressure on the plug as you unscrew it, oil won't escape past the threads and you can remove it without being burned by hot oil. Quickly withdraw the plug and move your hands out of the way, but be careful not to drop the plug into the drain pan, as fishing it out can be an unpleasant mess. Allow the oil to drain completely.
7. Examine the condition of the drain plug for thread damage or stretching, then examine the plug gasket for cracks or wear. Replace the drain plug, gasket or both if damaged.
8. After the oil has completely drained from the oil pan, install the drain plug and gasket. Be careful to not overtighten the plug.

➡ **Be careful when removing the oil filter, because the filter contains about 1 quart of hot, dirty oil.**

9. Move the drain pan under the oil filter. Use a strap-type or end cap-type wrench to loosen the oil filter. Cover your hand with a rag and spin the filter off by hand, but turn it slowly. Keep in mind that it's holding about one quart of dirty, hot oil.

Fig. 142 Remove the engine oil dipstick

86741P16

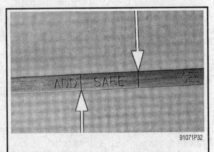

91071P32

Fig. 143 After removing the dipstick, check the oil level. The markings on the dipstick indicate that the oil level should be topped off when it is near or below the ADD line

86741P18

Fig. 144 If needed, add the proper amount and grade of oil

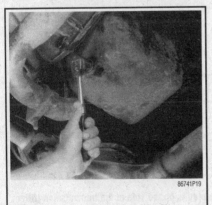

86741P19

Fig. 145 Loosen the oil pan drain plug

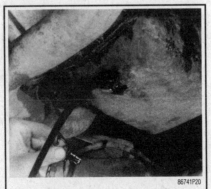

86741P20

Fig. 146 Remove the oil pan drain plug and let the engine oil completely drain

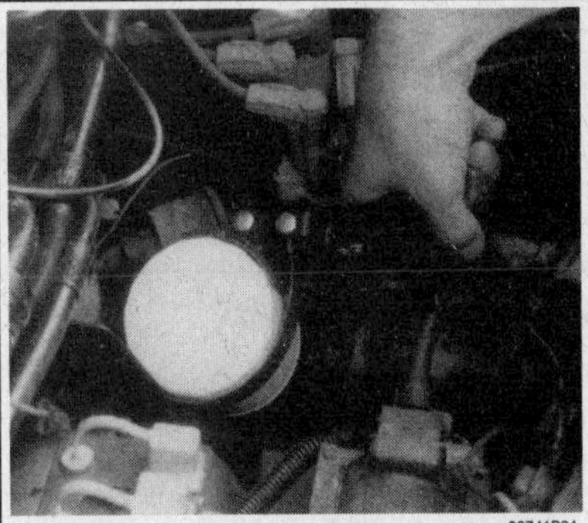

Fig. 147 Remove the old oil filter using a suitable oil filter wrench

86741P21

Fig. 148 Before installing a new oil filter, lightly coat the rubber gasket with clean oil

Fig. 149 Pour some fresh oil into the new filter before installation to lubricate the engine quicker during initial start-up

Fig. 150 Fill the crankcase with proper amount and grade of engine oil

➡**When using a band type oil filter wrench to remove an oil filter, place the wrench as high up on the filter as possible (closest to the filter mounting pad). This will reduce the chance of crushing the oil filter and making it very difficult to remove.**

10. Empty the old oil filter into the drain pan, then properly dispose of the filter.
To install:
11. Using a clean shop towel, wipe off the filter adapter on the engine block. Be sure the towel does not leave any lint which could clog an oil passage
12. Before you install the new filter, smear a small amount of clean oil on the oil filter gasket with your finger, just enough to coat the entire surface where it comes in contact with the mounting pad.
13. Pour some fresh oil into the new filter before installation; this will lubricate the engine quicker during initial startup.
14. Spin the filter onto the adapter by hand until it contacts the mounting surface, then hand-tighten the filter one full turn. Do NOT overtighten the filter.
15. Carefully lower the vehicle.
16. Refill the crankcase with the correct amount of fresh engine oil. Please refer to the Capacities chart later in this section as a guide.
17. Install the oil filler cap.
18. Check the oil level on the dipstick. It is normal for the level to be a bit above the full mark until the engine is run and the new filter is filled with oil. Start the engine and allow it to idle for a few minutes.
19. Shut off the engine and allow the oil to flow back to the crankcase for a minute, then recheck the oil level. Check around the filter and drain plug for any leaks, and correct as necessary.
When you have finished this job, you will notice that you now possess four or five quarts of dirty oil. The best thing to do is to pour it into plastic jugs, such as milk or old antifreeze containers. Then, locate a service station or automotive parts store where you can pour it into their used oil tank for recycling.

➡**Improperly disposing of used motor oil not only pollutes the environment, it violates federal law. Dispose of waste oil properly.**

Manual Transmissions

FLUID RECOMMENDATIONS

Recommended lubricant for AX4/5/15 and BA10/5 manual transmissions is SAE 75W-90, API Grade GL-3 gear lubricant. Warner T4 & T5 manual transmissions use DEXRON®II automatic transmission fluid.

LEVEL CHECK

▶ **See Figures 151 and 152**

The level of lubricant in the transmission should be maintained at the filler hole on all manual transmissions. This hole may be located on either side of the transmission case.
1. Raise and safely support the vehicle using jackstands.
2. Remove the filler hole plug.
3. Being careful of sharp edges, insert your finger into the filler hole. The lube should be within 1/4 in. (6mm) of the bottom edge of the hole.

4. After checking the level, make sure to reinstall the filler hole plug. Tighten the filler hole plug to 27–33 ft. lbs (37–44 Nm).
5. Lower the vehicle.

DRAIN & REFILL

The lubricant in the manual transmission should be changed every 30,000 miles (48,000 km).
1. Raise the vehicle and safely support it with jackstands.
2. Remove the filler hole plug from the transmission case.
3. Place a container to collect the fluid under the drain hole.

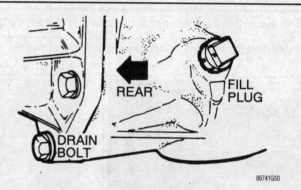

Fig. 151 On some models, the drain plug is on the back of the transmisson

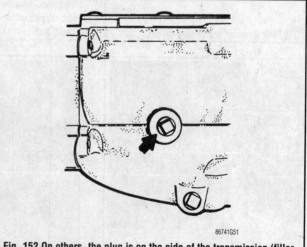

Fig. 152 On others, the plug is on the side of the transmission (filler plug shown with arrow)

4. Remove the drain plug which is located at the bottom of the transmission or on either side near the bottom, and allow all the fluid to drain into the container.

5. Reinstall the drain plug. Tighten the drain plug to 27–33 ft. lbs (37–44 Nm).

6. Refill the transmission with the recommended lubricant added in small amounts through the filler hole.

7. After the proper fluid level has been reached, install the filler hole plug. Tighten the filler hole plug to 27–33 ft. lbs (37–44 Nm).

8. Lower the vehicle.

Automatic Transmission

FLUID RECOMMENDATIONS

Use only Dexron®IIE/Mercon Automatic Transmission Fluid (ATF) on all AW-4 transmissions and ATF Plus 3/Type 7176 on all automatic transmissions except the AW-4 (or their superceding fluid types).

LEVEL CHECK

▶ **See Figures 153, 154 and 155**

The fluid level in automatic transmissions is checked with a dipstick located in the filler pipe at the right rear of the engine. The fluid level should be maintained between the ADD and FULL marks on the end of the dipstick, with the automatic transmission fluid at normal operating temperature. To raise the level from the ADD mark to the FULL mark requires the addition of one pint of fluid. The fluid level with the fluid at room temperature (75°F or 24°C) should be approximately 4 1/4 in. (10.8cm) below the ADD mark.

➡**In checking the automatic transmission fluid, insert the dipstick in the filler tube with the markings toward the center of the truck. Also, remember that the FULL mark on the dipstick is the indication of the** level of the automatic transmission fluid when it is at operating temperature. This temperature is only obtained after at least 15 miles of expressway driving or the equivalent of city driving.

To check the automatic transmission fluid level, follow the procedure given below. This procedure is applicable either when the fluid is at room temperature or at operating temperature.

1. With the transmission in Park, the engine running at idle speed, the foot brake applied and the vehicle resting on level ground, move the transmission gear selector through each of the gear positions, including Reverse, allowing time for the transmission to engage.

2. Return the shift selector to the Park position and apply the parking brake. Do not turn the engine off, but leave it running at idle speed.

3. Clean all dirt from around the transmission dipstick cap and the end of the filler tube.

4. Pull the dipstick out of the tube, wipe it off with a clean cloth, and push it back into the tube all the way, making sure that it seats completely.

5. Pull the dipstick out of the tube again and read the level of the fluid.

6. The level should be between the ADD and FULL marks. Do not overfill the transmission because this will cause foaming, loss of fluid through the vent and malfunctioning of the transmission.

➡**Transmission fluid should be light red and free of foreign material. If the fluid is dark brown or black in color and smells burnt, the fluid has been overheated and should be replaced.**

FLUID & FILTER CHANGE

▶ **See Figures 156 thru 163**

The fluid should be drained immediately after the vehicle has been driven for at least 20 minutes at expressway speeds or the equivalent of city driving, before it has had the chance to cool. Follow the procedure given below:

1. Raise and safely support the vehicle with jackstands.

2. Place a large pan under the transmission.

3. If the transmission pan has a drain plug, use a ratchet and 14mm socket

Fig. 153 Remove the automatic transmission dipstick

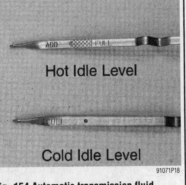

Fig. 154 Automatic transmission fluid level dipstick readings

Fig. 155 If necessary, add the proper type and amount of transmission fluid

Fig. 156 Using a 14mm size socket and ratchet tool, loosen the automatic transmission oil pan drain bolt (if equipped)

Fig. 157 After loosening the drain plug, unscrew the plug but hold it close to the pan so that it does not spill . . .

Fig. 158 . . . then carefully pull the drain plug away, allowing the fluid to drain into a container

Fig. 159 Remove the bolts, then remove the transmission pan

Fig. 160 Remove the filter retaining bolts . . .

Fig. 161 . . . then remove the filter from the transmission

Fig. 162 Clean the pan thoroughly with solvent and dry it with a clean rag

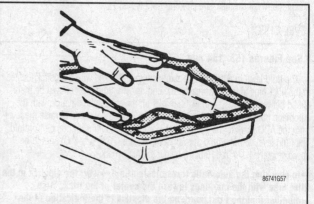

Fig. 163 Position a new gasket on the pan mating surface

to remove the plug. After draining the fluid completely, install and tighten the drain plug, then proceed with the pan removal.

4. Using a ratchet and 10mm socket, remove all the front and side retaining fasteners. Loosen the rear retainers about four turns. Pry or tap the pan loose and let any fluid drain out.

5. Remove the rear retainers, the pan and also the gasket. Clean the pan thoroughly with solvent and dry it with a clean rag. Be very careful not to get any lint from rags in the pan.

6. Remove the transmission oil filter screws and the oil filter. Discard the old filter.

7. If equipped, remove the O-ring seal from the pickup pipe and discard it.

To install:

8. If equipped, install a new O-ring seal on the pickup pipe.

9. Install the new oil filter and tighten the retaining screws to 35 inch lbs. (4 Nm).

10. Position a new gasket on the pan mating surface. Install the pan and secure it with the retaining fasteners. Tighten the retainers to 150 inch lbs. (17 Nm).

11. Lower the vehicle and remove the transmission dipstick.

12. Insert a clean transmission fluid funnel in the transmission dipstick tube.

13. Pour approximately 4 quarts (3.8L) of automatic transmission fluid in the filler pipe.

14. Start the engine. Do not race it. Allow the engine to idle for a few minutes.

15. Move the transmission gear selector through each of the gear positions, including Reverse, allowing time for the transmission to engage.

16. Return the shift selector to the Park position and apply the parking brake. Do not turn the engine off, but leave it running at idle speed.

17. Insert the dipstick into the tube.

18. Pull the dipstick out of the tube again and read the level of the fluid on the stick.

19. Add fluid as necessary. Do not overfill the transmission.

20. Drive the vehicle long enough to thoroughly warm up the transmission. Recheck the fluid level and add fluid as necessary.

Transfer Case

FLUID RECOMMENDATION

All transfer cases covered by this manual use Dexron®II or ATF Plus/Type 7176 automatic transmission fluid (or their superceding fluid type).

LEVEL CHECK

▶ **See Figure 164**

Fluid should be maintained at the level of the filler plug hole. When you check the lubricant, make sure that the vehicle is level so that you get a true reading.

1. Raise and safely support the vehicle with jackstands.
2. Place a large pan under the transfer case.

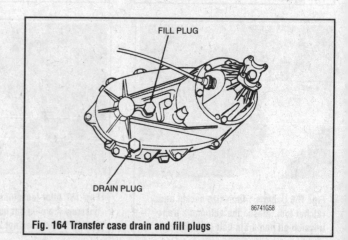

FILL PLUG

DRAIN PLUG

Fig. 164 Transfer case drain and fill plugs

3. Using a ratchet with a 30mm socket, or a 30mm box wrench, remove the filler plug from the transfer case. Lubricant should run out of the hole.

4. If there is lubricant present at the hole, it means that the case is filled to the proper level. Replace the plug quickly for a minimum loss of lubricant.

5. If lubricant does not run out of the hole when the plug is removed, lubricant should be added.

6. Replace the plug as soon as the lubricant reaches the level of the hole.

DRAIN & REFILL

▶ **See Figures 165 and 166**

All transfer cases are to be serviced at the same time and in the same manner as the manual transmissions.

1. Raise the vehicle and safely support it with jackstands.
2. Place a large pan under the transfer case and remove the transfer case

Fig. 165 Remove the transfer case drain plug and let the fluid completely drain

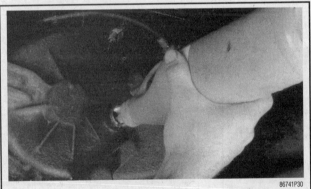

Fig. 166 Fill the transfer case with the proper type and amount of fluid

drain plug using a ratchet with a 30mm socket, or a 30mm box wrench.

3. Let all of the fluid drain completely from the transfer case, then install the drain plug.

4. Using a ratchet with a 30mm socket, or a 30mm box wrench, remove the fill plug and fill the transfer case with the proper type and amount of fluid.

5. Install the fill plug.

Front and Rear Axle

FLUID RECOMMENDATIONS

The standard front and rear axle differentials use SAE 80W/90, API grade GL 5 hypoid gear lubricant. SAE 75W-140 API grade GL 5 hypoid gear lubricant is recommended when trailer towing. With Trac-Lok® (limited slip) differentials, add a container of Trac-Lok® lubricant additive.

FLUID LEVEL CHECK

▶ **See Figures 167 thru 175**

Check the level of the oil in the differential housing every 7,500 miles (12,000 km) under normal driving conditions, and every 3,000 miles (4,800 km) if the vehicle is used in severe driving conditions. The level should be up to the filler hole. When you remove the filler plug, the oil should start to run out. If it does not, add fluid to obtain an acceptable level.

➡ **The differential housing fill hole plug may be a hexagonal plug that is removable using the appropriate sized box wrench or socket, a plug with a square drive hole in it suitable for a 3/8 inch drive ratchet or a rubber plug that can be removed simply by using a small, flat bladed tool.**

DRAIN & REFILL

▶ **See Figures 176 thru 181**

The lubricant should be changed every 30,000 miles (48,000 km). Under severe conditions, the lubricant should be changed every 12,000 miles (19,000 km). If running in deep water, change the lubricant daily.

Follow the procedure given below for changing the lubricant in the front and rear axle differentials:

1. Raise the vehicle and safely support it with jackstands.
2. Place a large pan under the diferential housing.
3. Using a ratchet with a 30mm socket, remove the axle differential housing cover bolts and allow the lubricant to completely drain out.
4. Utilizing a flat scraper tool, clean the axle housing-to-cover mating surface of all old gasket material.
5. Thoroughly clean the axle housing cover, especially the gasket sealing surface.
6. After thoroughly cleaning the axle cover, apply gasket sealer around the mating surface of the cover and on the inner portion of the mounting bolt holes.
7. Install the differential housing cover with a new gasket.

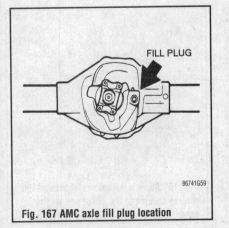

Fig. 167 AMC axle fill plug location

Fig. 168 Loosen the front axle drain plug

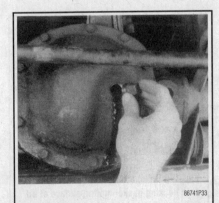

Fig. 169 Remove the front axle drain plug

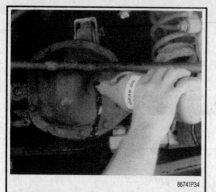

Fig. 170 If necessary, add the proper amount of gear oil

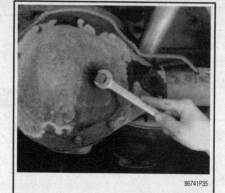

Fig. 171 Loosen the rear axle drain plug

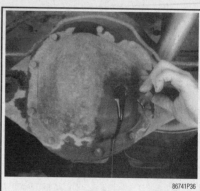

Fig. 172 Remove the rear axle drain plug, the oil should start to run out

Fig. 173 If the rear axle housing uses a rubber drain plug, remove it by simply prying it out using a flat bladed prying tool . . .

Fig. 174 . . . then remove it from the housing cover

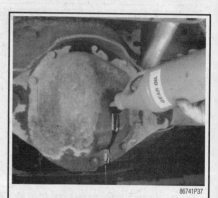

Fig. 175 If necessary, add the proper amount of gear oil

Fig. 176 Clean the axle housing cover perimeter using a wire brush

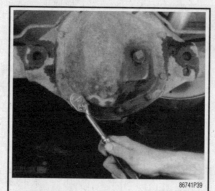

Fig. 177 Remove the axle housing cover bolts

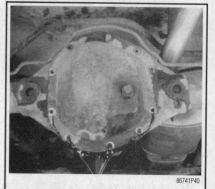

Fig. 178 Let the fluid drain completely from the axle

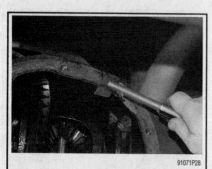

Fig. 179 Using a flat scraper, clean the axle housing gasket mating surface of all old gasket material before installing the hoiusing cover

Fig. 180 Thoroughly clean the axle housing cover, especially the gasket sealing surface

Fig. 181 Apply a gasket sealer around the mating surface of the cover and on the inner portion of the mounting bolt holes

➡Some rear axle covers are not equipped with a gasket. If a gasket is not used, seal the cover using RTV sealant.

8. Tighten the cover attaching bolts to 15–25 ft. lbs. (20–33 Nm).

➡The differential housing fill hole plug may be a hexagonal plug that is removable using the appropriate sized box wrench or socket, a plug with a square drive hole in it suitable for a 3/8 inch drive ratchet or a rubber plug that can be removed simply by using a small, flat bladed tool.

9. Remove the fill plug and add new lubricant to the fill hole level.
10. Replace the fill plug.
11. Lower the vehicle.

➡Trac-Lok® (limited-slip) differentials may be cleaned only by disassembling the unit and wiping with clean, lint-free rags. Use no chemical solvents or compressed air

Cooling Systems

FLUID RECOMMENDATIONS

▶ **See Figures 182 and 183**

The cooling system was filled at the factory with a high quality coolant solution that is good for year-round operation, which protects the system from freezing. If coolant is needed, a 50/50 mix of ethylene glycol or other suitable antifreeze and water should be used. Alcohol or methanol base coolants are specifically not recommended. Antifreeze solution should be used all year, even in summer, to prevent rust and to take advantage of the solution's higher boiling point compared to plain water. This is imperative on air conditioned models; the heater core can freeze if it isn't protected.

LEVEL CHECK

▶ **See Figures 184 and 185**

The coolant should be checked at each fuel stop, to prevent the possibility of overheating and serious engine damage. To check the coolant level simply look into the expansion tank.

> ❋❋ **CAUTION**
>
> The radiator coolant is under pressure when hot. To avoid the danger of physical injury, coolant should be checked or replenished only when cool. To remove the cap, slowly rotate it counterclockwise to the stop, but do not press down. Wait until all pressure is released (indicated when the hissing sound stops), then press down on the cap while continuing to rotate it counterclockwise. Wear eye protection and use a glove or a thick rag to prevent burns.

> ❋❋ **WARNING**
>
> Never add large quantities of cold coolant to a hot engine. A cracked engine block may result. If it is absolutely necessary to add coolant to a hot engine, do so only with the engine idling and add only small quantities at a time.

If the level is low, simply add coolant mixture to the tank until the upper level line is reached. If the system shows signs of overheating and, possibly, a small leak, you may want to check the level in the radiator when the engine is **cold**.

Each year, the cooling system should be serviced as follows:
1. Wash the radiator cap and filler neck with clean water.
2. Check the coolant for proper level and freeze protection.
3. Pressure test the cooling system using a cooling system pressure tester

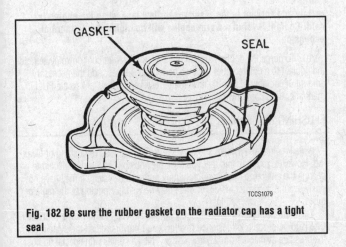

Fig. 182 Be sure the rubber gasket on the radiator cap has a tight seal

Fig. 184 After the engine has cooled, remove the radiator cap to check the coolant level

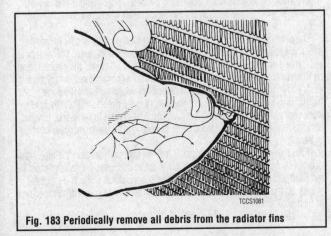

Fig. 183 Periodically remove all debris from the radiator fins

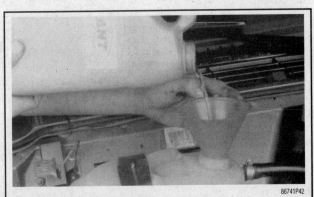

Fig. 185 Coolant may be added to the coolant recovery tank or to the radiator

and follow the tool manufacturers instructions. If a replacement cap is installed, be sure that it conforms to the original specifications.

4. Tighten the hose clamps and inspect all hoses. Replace hoses that are swollen, cracked or otherwise deteriorated.

5. Clean the frontal area of the radiator core, and the air conditioning condenser, if so equipped.

DRAIN & REFILL

▶ **See Figures 186, 187 and 188**

✳✳ CAUTION

Never open, service or drain the radiator or cooling system when hot; serious burns can occur from the steam and hot coolant. Also, when draining engine coolant, keep in mind that cats and dogs are attracted to ethylene glycol antifreeze and could drink any that is left in an uncovered container or in puddles on the ground. This will prove fatal in sufficient quantities. Always drain coolant into a sealable container. Coolant should be reused unless it is contaminated or is several years old.

Every 3 years or 45,000 miles (72,000 km) whichever comes first, the system should be serviced as follows:

1. On Cherokee, Comanche and Wagoneer models, remove the front grille assembly.

2. With the engine turned off and sufficiently cooled down, remove the radiator cap.

3. Place a drain pan underneath the radiator, then open the draincock which is found in the following locations:
- 4- and 6-cylinder engines—right, lower side of the radiator
- V-8 engines—left, lower side of the radiator facing the rear of the vehicle

4. If necessary, remove the cylinder block drain plug(s), found in the following locations:

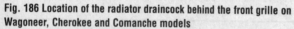

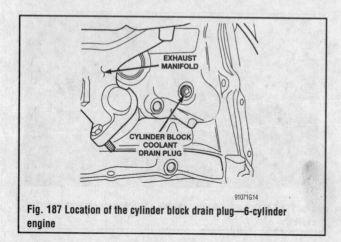

Fig. 186 Location of the radiator draincock behind the front grille on Wagoneer, Cherokee and Comanche models

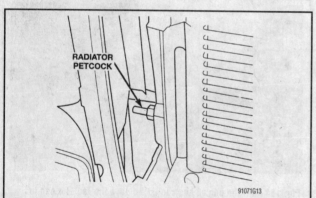

Fig. 187 Location of the cylinder block drain plug—6-cylinder engine

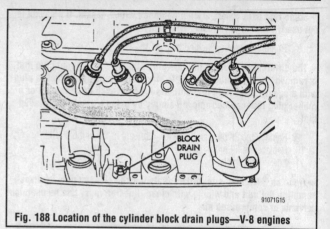

Fig. 188 Location of the cylinder block drain plugs—V-8 engines

- 4- and 6-cylinder engines—lower left side of the engine block
- V-8 engines—each side of the cylinder block above the oil pan rail

5. Completely drain the coolant, close the draincock and install/tighten the drain plug(s), if removed.

6. Add sufficient coolant to provide the required freezing and corrosion protection (at least a 50% solution of antifreeze and water). Fill the radiator to the top and install the radiator cap. Fill the reserve/overflow tank to the FULL cold level.

7. Place the heater control unit in the HEAT position and run the engine with the radiator cap in place.

8. After the engine reaches normal operating temperature, turn the engine off and allow it to cool. While the engine is cooling down, coolant will be drawn into the radiator from the reserve/overflow tank.

9. Add coolant to the reserve/overflow tank as necessary.

➡**Only add coolant to the reserve/overflow tank when the engine is cold. Coolant level in a warm engine will be higher due to thermal expansion.**

10. To purge the cooling system of all air, the heat up/cool down cycle (adding coolant to a cold engine) must be performed 3 times. Add the necessary amount of coolant to raise the level in the reserve/overflow tank to the FULL mark after each cool down period.

FLUSHING & CLEANING THE SYSTEM

A well maintained system should never require aggressive flushing or cleaning. However, you may find that you (or a previous owner) have neglected to change the antifreeze often enough to fully protect the system. It may have obviously accumulated rust inside, or there may be visible clogging of the radiator tubes.

There are two basic means of rectifying this situation for the do-it-yourselfer. One is to purchase a kit designed to allow you to reverse-flush the system with the pressure available from a garden hose. This kit comes with special fittings which allow you to force water downward inside the engine block and upward (or in reverse of normal flow) in the radiator. The kit will have complete instructions.

The other means is to purchase a chemical cleaner. The cleaner is installed after the system is flushed and filled with fresh water, and cleans the system as you drive a short distance or idle the engine hot. In all cases, the cleaner must be flushed completely from the system after use. In some cases, it may be necessary to follow up with the use of a neutralizer. Make sure to follow the instructions very carefully. These cleaners are quite potent, chemically, and work very well; because of that fact, you must be careful to flush and, if necessary, neutralize the effect of the cleaner to keep it from damaging your cooling system.

If the radiator is severely clogged, it may be necessary to have the tubes rodded out by a professional radiator repair shop. In this case, the radiator must be removed and taken to the shop for this highly specialized work. You can save money on the job by removing and replacing the radiator yourself, as described in Section 3.

Brake Master Cylinder

FLUID RECOMMENDATIONS

The only brake fluid recommended for Jeep vehicles with standard or anti-lock brakes is a fluid meeting DOT 3 specifications.

FLUID LEVEL CHECK

▶ See Figures 189, 190, 191 and 192

The master cylinder reservoir is located under the hood, on the left side of the firewall.

1. Before removing the master cylinder reservoir cap, make sure the vehicle is resting on level ground and clean all dirt away from the top of the master cylinder.

2. If equipped with a 1 piece, cast master cylinder/reservoir, pry off the retaining clip and remove the cover. The fluid level should be within 1/4 in. (6mm) of the top of the reservoir.

3. If equipped with a plastic, see-through brake fluid reservoir, the fluid level should be at the MAX (or FULL) mark on the side of either single or dual reservoir master cylinders. If below the MAX (or FULL) mark, unscrew and remove the brake fluid reservoir cap.

4. If the level is low, add clean, fresh brake fluid to the proper level of the reservoir.

5. Replace the reservoir cover, or cap, after the system has been replenished.

✳✳ WARNING

Do not overfill the fluid reservoir. Overfilling could cause fluid overflow and , on some ABS-equipped vehicles, possible reservoir damage when the pump begins cycling.

➡If the level of the fluid is less than half the volume of the reservoir, it is advised that you check the brake system for leaks. Leak in a hydraulic brake system most commonly occur at the wheel cylinders. Leaks may also occur in brake lines running down the frame.

There is a rubber diaphragm in the top of the master cylinder cover/cap. As the fluid level lowers in the reservoir due to normal brake shoe wear or leakage, the diaphragm takes up the space. This acts to prevent the loss of brake fluid out of the vented cover/cap and to prevent contamination of the brake fluid by dirt. After filling the master cylinder to the proper level with brake fluid, but before replacing the cover/cap, fold the rubber diaphragm up into the cover/cap, then install.

✳✳ WARNING

Do not allow brake fluid to come in contact with painted components on the vehicle. If left on any painted surface, it will dissolve the paint.

Clutch Master Cylinder

FLUID RECOMMENDATIONS

The only fluid recommended for Jeep vehicles with a clutch master cylinder is a fluid meeting DOT 3 specifications.

FLUID LEVEL CHECK

▶ See Figure 193

The clutch master cylinder reservoir is located under the hood, on the left side of the firewall.

1. Before removing the clutch master cylinder reservoir cap, make sure the vehicle is resting on level ground and clean all dirt away from the top of the master cylinder.

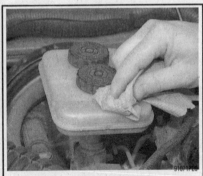

Fig. 189 Wipe the top of the brake fluid reservoir of any dirt or grime before removing the cap to add fluid

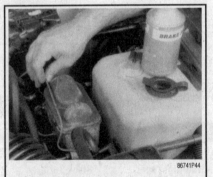

Fig. 190 Pry off the retaining clip from the master cylinder cover—1-piece, cast master cylinder/fluid reservoir shown

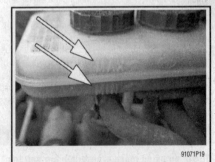

Fig. 191 On the plastic see-through brake fluid reservoir, the MAX (top arrow) and MIN (bottom arrow) fluid level marks are visible on the side of the reservoir

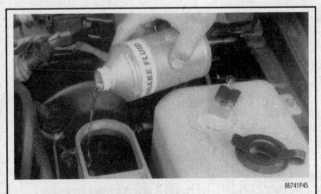

Fig. 192 After removing the reservoir cover, add the necessary amount of brake fluid until it reaches the correct level

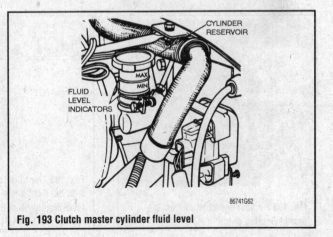

Fig. 193 Clutch master cylinder fluid level

2. Remove the reservoir cap. The fluid level should be within 1/4 in. (6mm) of the top of the reservoir or to the top indicator line (MAX) on the reservoir. Do not allow the fluid level to go below the MIN line.

3. Use new brake fluid only when adding fluid to the reservoir.

4. Add the fluid and bring it to the proper level.

✳✳ WARNING

Do not allow brake fluid to come in contact with painted components on the vehicle. If left on any painted surface, it will dissolve the paint.

Power Steering Pump

FLUID RECOMMENDATIONS

Use only Mopar® Power Steering Fluid, or its equivalent.

LEVEL CHECK

▶ **See Figures 194, 195 and 196**

On models with power steering, check the fluid in the power steering pump every 7,500 miles. (12,000 km). The fluid level can be checked with the fluid either hot or cold. Fluid level should be at the correct point (FULL HOT or FULL COLD) on the dipstick attached to the inside of the lid of the power steering pump. Fill the unit with power steering fluid to the proper level. To avoid spills, always use a funnel. If the pump is low on fluid, check all the power steering hoses and connections, and the hydraulic cylinder for possible leaks.

Chassis Greasing

▶ **See Figure 197**

The lubrication chart indicates where the grease fittings are located. The vehicle should be greased according to the intervals in the Preventive Maintenance Schedule at the end of this section.

Water resistant EP chassis lubricant (grease) should be used for all chassis grease points.

Every year or 7,500 miles (12,000 km), the front suspension ball joints, both upper and lower on each side of the vehicle, must be greased. Many vehicles covered in this manual are equipped with grease nipples on the ball joints, although some may have plugs which must be removed and nipples fitted. Some late model vehicles have lifetime lubricated chassis components which cannot be serviced.

✳✳ WARNING

Do not pump so much grease into the ball joint that excess grease squeezes out of the rubber boot. This destroys the watertight seal.

Jack up the front end of the vehicle and safely support it with jackstands. Block the rear wheels and firmly apply the parking brake. If the vehicle has been parked in temperatures below 20°F (−7°C) for any length of time, park it in a heated garage for an hour or so until the ball joints loosen up enough to accept the grease.

Depending on which front wheel you work on first, turn the wheel and tire outward, either full-lock right or full-lock left. You will then have the ends of the upper and lower suspension control arms in front of you, with the grease nipples visible. The upper ball joint nipples point up (top ball joint) and the lower ball joint nipples point down, through the end of each control arm. If the nipples are not accessible enough, remove the wheel and tire. Wipe all debris from the nipples or from around the plugs (if installed). If plugs are on the vehicle, remove them and install grease nipples in the holes (nipples are available in various thread sizes at most auto parts stores). Using a hand operated, low pressure grease gun loaded with a quality chassis grease, grease the ball joint only until the rubber joint boot begins to swell out.

STEERING LINKAGE

▶ **See Figures 198 and 199**

The steering linkage should be greased at the same interval as the ball joints. Grease nipples are installed on the steering tie rod ends on most models. Wipe all dirt from around the fittings at each tie rod end. Using a hand operated, low pressure grease gun loaded with a suitable chassis grease, grease the linkage until the old grease begins to squeeze out around the tie rod ends. Wipe off the nipples and any excess grease. Also grease the nipples on the steering idler arms.

DRIVESHAFTS & UNIVERSAL JOINTS

▶ **See Figures 200 and 201**

Use chassis grease on the front (4x4 only) and rear driveshafts and all drivehshaft universal joints.

PARKING BRAKE LINKAGE

Use chassis grease on the parking brake cable where it contacts the cable guides, levers and linkage.

AUTOMATIC TRANSMISSION LINKAGE

Apply a small amount of clean engine oil to the kickdown and shift linkage points at 7,500 mile (12,077 km) intervals.

Body Lubrication and Maintenance

CARE OF YOUR VEHICLE

Glass Surfaces

All glass surfaces should be kept clean at all times for safe driving. Use the same type of cleaner you use on windows in your home. Never use abrasive cleaners, as they will scratch the window surfaces.

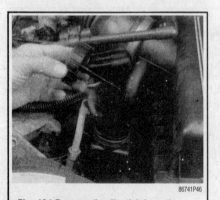

Fig. 194 Remove the dipstick from the power steering pump

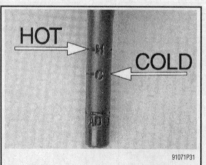

Fig. 195 The fluid level can be checked with the fluid either hot or cold. Fluid level should be at the correct point (FULL HOT or FULL COLD) on the dipstick

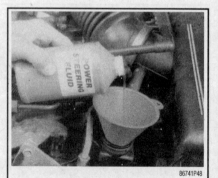

Fig. 196 If necessary, add the proper amount of power steering fluid and replace the dipstick

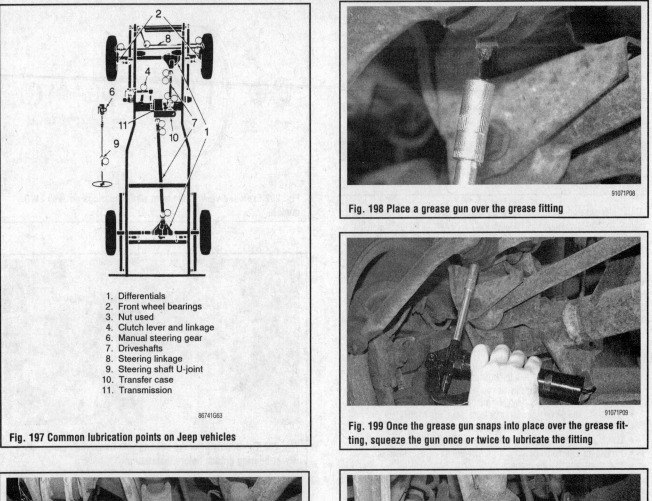

1. Differentials
2. Front wheel bearings
3. Nut used
4. Clutch lever and linkage
6. Manual steering gear
7. Driveshafts
8. Steering linkage
9. Steering shaft U-joint
10. Transfer case
11. Transmission

86741G63

Fig. 197 Common lubrication points on Jeep vehicles

91071P08

Fig. 198 Place a grease gun over the grease fitting

91071P09

Fig. 199 Once the grease gun snaps into place over the grease fitting, squeeze the gun once or twice to lubricate the fitting

91071P22

Fig. 200 Lubricating the front drive shaft (4x4 only)

91071P23

Fig. 201 Lubricating the the driveshaft universal joint (4x4 front driveshaft shown)

Exterior Care

Your vehicle is exposed to all kinds of corrosive effects from nature and chemicals. Some of these are road salt, oils, rain, hail and sleet, just to name a few. To protect not only the paint and trim, but also the many exposed mounts and fixtures, it is important to wash your vehicle often and thoroughly. After washing, allow all surfaces to drain and dry before parking in a closed garage. Washing may not clean all deposits off your vehicle, so you may need additional cleaners. When using professional cleaners, make sure they are suitable for enamel/acrylic painted surfaces, chrome, tires etc. These supplies can be purchased in your local auto parts store. You also should wax and polish your vehicle every few months to keep the paint in good shape.

LOCK CYLINDERS

Apply graphite lubricant sparingly through the key slot. Insert the key and operate the lock several times to be sure that the lubricant is worked into the lock cylinder.

DOOR HINGES & HINGE CHECKS

Spray a white lubricant on the hinge pivot points to eliminate any binding conditions. Open and close the door several times to be sure that the lubricant is evenly and thoroughly distributed.

TAILGATE

Spray a white lubricant on all of the pivot and friction surfaces to eliminate any squeaks or binds. Work the tailgate to distribute the lubricant.

BODY DRAIN HOLES

Be sure that the drain holes in the doors and rocker panels are open. A small screwdriver can be used to clear them of any debris.

Wheel Bearings

REPACKING

This procedure only applies to 1984–92 Jeep vehicles. The 1993 and later Jeep vehicles are equipped with wheel bearings that are an integral component of the wheel hub and therefore, cannot be serviced separately. If the wheel bearings on these models need servicing, the wheel hub and bearing assembly must be replaced.

➡**Sodium-based grease is not compatible with lithium-based grease. Read the package labels and be careful not to mix the two types. If there is any doubt as to the type of grease used, completely clean the old grease from the bearing and hub before replacing.**

Before handling the bearings, there are a few things that you should remember to do and not to do.
Remember to DO the following:
- Remove all outside dirt from the housing before exposing the bearing.
- Treat a used bearing as gently as you would a new one.
- Work with clean tools in clean surroundings.
- Use clean, dry canvas gloves, or at least clean, dry hands.
- Clean solvents and flushing fluids are a must.
- Use clean paper when laying out the bearings to dry.
- Protect disassembled bearings from rust and dirt. Cover them up.
- Use clean rags to wipe bearings.
- Keep the bearings in oil-proof paper when they are to be stored or are not in use.
- Clean the inside of the housing before replacing the bearing.

Do NOT do the following:
- Don't work in dirty surroundings.
- Don't use dirty, chipped or damaged tools.
- Try not to work on wooden work benches or use wooden mallets.
- Don't handle bearings with dirty or moist hands.
- Do not use gasoline for cleaning; use a safe solvent.
- Do not spin-dry bearings with compressed air. They will be damaged.
- Do not spin dirty bearings.
- Avoid using cotton waste or dirty cloths to wipe bearings.
- Try not to scratch or nick bearing surfaces.
- Do not allow the bearing to come in contact with dirt or rust at any time.

2-Wheel Drive

▶ **See Figures 202 and 203**

1. Remove the wheel bearing(s) from the vehicle.
2. If the old parts are retained, thoroughly clean them in a safe solvent and allow them to dry on a clean towel. Never spin them dry with compressed air.
3. Pack the inside of the hub with EP wheel bearing grease. Add grease to the hub until it is flush with the inside diameter of the bearing cup.
4. Pack the bearing with the same grease. A needle-shaped wheel bearing packer is best for this operation. If one is not available, place a large amount of grease in the palm of your hand and slide the edge of the bearing cage through the grease to pick up as much as possible, then work the grease in as best you can with your fingers.

4-Wheel Drive

▶ **See Figure 204**

1. Remove the wheel bearing(s) from the vehicle.
2. Thoroughly pack the new outer bearing with wheel bearing grease. Make sure that the bearing is fully packed.
3. Coat the race with wheel bearing grease and place the bearing in the bore.

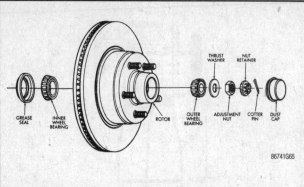

Fig. 202 Exploded view of the front wheel bearings on Jeep 2WD models

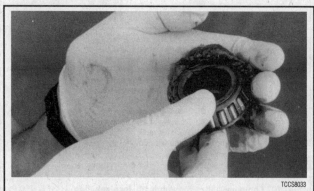

Fig. 203 Thoroughly pack the bearing with fresh, high temperature wheel-bearing grease before installation

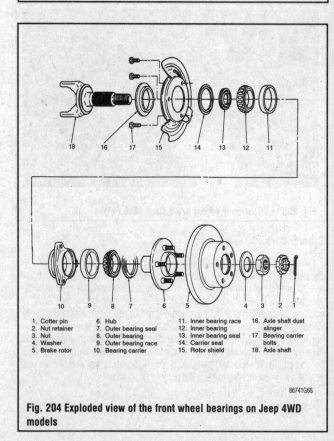

1. Cotter pin	6. Hub	11. Inner bearing race	16. Axle shaft dust
2. Nut retainer	7. Outer bearing seal	12. Inner bearing	slinger
3. Nut	8. Outer bearing	13. Inner bearing seal	17. Bearing carrier
4. Washer	9. Outer bearing race	14. Carrier seal	bolts
5. Brake rotor	10. Bearing carrier	15. Rotor shield	18. Axle shaft

Fig. 204 Exploded view of the front wheel bearings on Jeep 4WD models

TRAILER TOWING

Jeep vehicles have long been popular as trailer towing vehicles. Their strong construction, 4-wheel drive and wide range of engine transmission combinations make them ideal for towing campers boat trailers and utility trailers.

Factory trailer towing packages are available on most Jeep vehicles. However, if you are installing a trailer hitch and wiring on your Jeep, there are a few things that you ought to know.

General Recommendations

Your vehicle was primarily designed to carry passengers and cargo. It is important to remember that towing a trailer will place additional loads on your vehicles engine, drive train, steering, braking and other systems. However, if you decide to tow a trailer, using the prior equipment is a must.

Local laws may require specific equipment such as trailer brakes or fender mounted mirrors. Check your local laws.

Trailer Weight

The weight of the trailer is the most important factor. A good weight-to-horsepower ratio is about 35:1, 35 lbs. of Gross Combined Weight (GCW) for every horsepower your engine develops. Multiply the engine's rated horsepower by 35 and subtract the weight of the vehicle passengers and luggage. The number remaining is the approximate ideal maximum weight you should tow, although a numerically higher axle ratio can help compensate for heavier weight.

Hitch (Tongue) Weight

▶ **See Figure 205**

Calculate the hitch weight in order to select a proper hitch. The weight of the hitch is usually 9–11% of the trailer gross weight and should be measured with the trailer loaded. Hitches fall into various categories: those that mount on the frame and rear bumper, the bolt-on type, or the weld-on distribution type used for larger trailers. Axle mounted or clamp-on bumper hitches should never be used.

Check the gross weight rating of your trailer. Tongue weight is usually figured as 10% of gross trailer weight. Therefore, a trailer with a maximum gross weight of 2000 lbs. will have a maximum tongue weight of 200 lbs. Class I trailers fall into this category. Class II trailers are those with a gross weight rating of 2000–3000 lbs., while Class III trailers fall into the 3500–6000 lbs. category. Class IV trailers are those over 6000 lbs. and are for use with fifth wheel trucks, only.

When you've determined the hitch that you'll need, follow the manufacturer's installation instructions, exactly, especially when it comes to fastener torques. The hitch will subjected to a lot of stress and good hitches come with hardened bolts. Never substitute an inferior bolt for a hardened bolt.

Engine

One of the most common, if not THE most common, problems associated with trailer towing is engine overheating. If you have a cooling system without an expansion tank, you'll definitely need to get an aftermarket expansion tank kit, preferably one with at least a 2 quart capacity. These kits are easily installed on the radiator's overflow hose, and come with a pressure cap designed for expansion tanks.

Aftermarket engine oil coolers are helpful for prolonging engine oil life and reducing overall engine temperatures. Both of these factors increase engine life. While not absolutely necessary in towing Class I and some Class II trailers, they are recommended for heavier Class II and all Class III towing. Engine oil cooler systems usually consist of an adapter, screwed on in place of the oil filter, a remote filter mounting and a multi-tube, finned heat exchanger, which is mounted in front of the radiator or air conditioning condenser.

Transmission

An automatic transmission is usually recommended for trailer towing. Modern automatics have proven reliable and, of course, easy to operate, in trailer towing. The increased load of a trailer, however, causes an increase in the temperature of the automatic transmission fluid. Heat is the worst enemy of an automatic transmission. As the temperature of the fluid increases, the life of the fluid decreases.

It is essential, therefore, that you install an automatic transmission cooler. The cooler, which consists of a multi-tube, finned heat exchanger, is usually installed in front of the radiator or air conditioning compressor, and hooked in-line with the transmission cooler tank inlet line. Follow the cooler manufacturer's installation instructions.

Select a cooler of at least adequate capacity, based upon the combined gross weights of the vehicle and trailer.

Cooler manufacturers recommend that you use an aftermarket cooler in addition to, and not instead of, the present cooling tank in your radiator. If you do want to use it in place of the radiator cooling tank, get a cooler at least two sizes larger than normally necessary.

➡ **A transmission cooler can, sometimes, cause slow or harsh shifting in the transmission during cold weather, until the fluid has a chance to come up to normal operating temperature. Some coolers can be purchased with or retrofitted with a temperature bypass valve which will allow fluid flow through the cooler only when the fluid has reached above a certain operating temperature.**

Handling a Trailer

Towing a trailer with ease and safety requires a certain amount of experience. It's a good idea to learn the feel of a trailer by practicing turning, stopping and backing in an open area such as an empty parking lot.

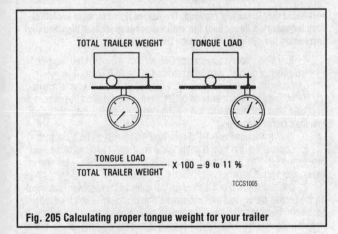

Fig. 205 Calculating proper tongue weight for your trailer

TOWING THE VEHICLE

▶ **See Figure 206**

If your Jeep has to be towed by a tow vehicle, it can be towed forward for any distance, as long as it is done fairly slowly. If your Jeep has to be towed backward, remove the front axle drive flanges to prevent the front differential from rotating. If the drive flanges are removed, improvise a cover to keep out dust and dirt.

➡ **When towing a 4WD-equipped vehicle with a Sling Type or Wheel Lift Tow Truck, utilize tow dollies under the opposite end of the vehicle.**

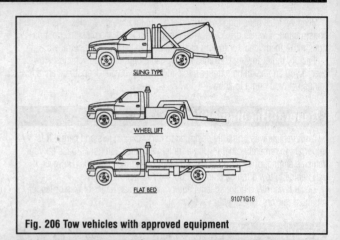

Fig. 206 Tow vehicles with approved equipment

JUMP STARTING A DEAD BATTERY

▶ **See Figure 207**

Whenever a vehicle is jump started, precautions must be followed in order to prevent the possibility of personal injury. Remember that batteries contain a small amount of explosive hydrogen gas which is a by-product of battery charging. Sparks should always be avoided when working around batteries, especially when attaching jumper cables. To minimize the possibility of accidental sparks, follow the procedure carefully.

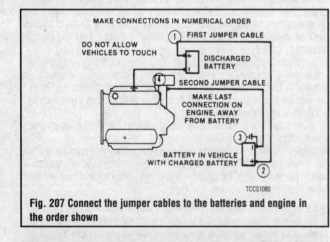

Fig. 207 Connect the jumper cables to the batteries and engine in the order shown

✳ CAUTION

NEVER hook the batteries up in a series circuit or the entire electrical system will go up in smoke, including the starter!

Vehicles equipped with a diesel engine may utilize two 12 volt batteries. If so, the batteries are connected in a parallel circuit (positive terminal to positive terminal, negative terminal to negative terminal). Hooking the batteries up in parallel circuit increases battery cranking power without increasing total battery voltage output. Output remains at 12 volts. On the other hand, hooking two 12 volt batteries up in a series circuit (positive terminal to negative terminal, positive terminal to negative terminal) increases total battery output to 24 volts (12 volts plus 12 volts).

Jump Starting Precautions

• Be sure that both batteries are of the same voltage. Vehicles covered by this manual and most vehicles on the road today utilize a 12 volt charging system.

• Be sure that both batteries are of the same polarity (have the same terminal, in most cases NEGATIVE grounded).

• Be sure that the vehicles are not touching or a short could occur.

• On serviceable batteries, be sure the vent cap holes are not obstructed.

• Do not smoke or allow sparks anywhere near the batteries.

• In cold weather, make sure the battery electrolyte is not frozen. This can occur more readily in a battery that has been in a state of discharge.

• Do not allow electrolyte to contact your skin or clothing.

Jump Starting Procedure

SINGLE BATTERY GASOLINE ENGINE MODELS

1. Make sure that the voltages of the 2 batteries are the same. Most batteries and charging systems are of the 12 volt variety.

2. Pull the jumping vehicle (with the good battery) into a position so the jumper cables can reach the dead battery and that vehicle's engine. Make sure that the vehicles do NOT touch.

3. Place the transmissions of both vehicles in **Neutral** (MT) or **P** (AT), as applicable, then firmly set their parking brakes.

➡ **If necessary for safety reasons, the hazard lights on both vehicles may be operated throughout the entire procedure without significantly increasing the difficulty of jumping the dead battery.**

4. Turn all lights and accessories OFF on both vehicles. Make sure the ignition switches on both vehicles are turned to the **OFF** position.

5. Cover the battery cell caps with a rag, but do not cover the terminals.

6. Make sure the terminals on both batteries are clean and free of corrosion or proper electrical connection will be impeded. If necessary, clean the battery terminals before proceeding.

7. Identify the positive (+) and negative (-) terminals on both batteries.

8. Connect the first jumper cable to the positive (+) terminal of the dead battery, then connect the other end of that cable to the positive (+) terminal of the booster (good) battery.

9. Connect one end of the other jumper cable to the negative (-) terminal on the booster battery and the final cable clamp to an engine bolt head, alternator bracket or other solid, metallic point on the engine with the dead battery. Try to pick a ground on the engine that is positioned away from the battery in order to minimize the possibility of the 2 clamps touching should one loosen during the procedure. DO NOT connect this clamp to the negative (-) terminal of the bad battery.

✳ CAUTION

Be very careful to keep the jumper cables away from moving parts (cooling fan, belts, etc.) on both engines.

10. Check to make sure that the cables are routed away from any moving parts, then start the donor vehicle's engine. Run the engine at moderate speed

for several minutes to allow the dead battery a chance to receive some initial charge.

11. With the donor vehicle's engine still running slightly above idle, try to start the vehicle with the dead battery. Crank the engine for no more than 10 seconds at a time and let the starter cool for at least 20 seconds between tries. If the vehicle does not start in 3 tries, it is likely that something else is also wrong or that the battery needs additional time to charge.

12. Once the vehicle is started, allow it to run at idle for a few seconds to make sure that it is operating properly.

13. Turn ON the headlights, heater blower and, if equipped, the rear defroster of both vehicles in order to reduce the severity of voltage spikes and subsequent risk of damage to the vehicles' electrical systems when the cables are disconnected. This step is especially important to any vehicle equipped with computer control modules.

14. Carefully disconnect the cables in the reverse order of connection. Start with the negative cable that is attached to the engine ground, then the negative cable on the donor battery. Disconnect the positive cable from the donor battery and finally, disconnect the positive cable from the formerly dead battery. Be careful when disconnecting the cables from the positive terminals not to allow the alligator clips to touch any metal on either vehicle or a short and sparks will occur.

DUAL BATTERY DIESEL MODELS

▶ See Figure 208

Some diesel model vehicles utilize two 12 volt batteries, one on either side of the engine compartment. The batteries are connected in a parallel circuit (positive terminal to positive terminal and negative terminal to negative terminal). Hooking the batteries up in a parallel circuit increases battery cranking power without increasing total battery voltage output. The output will remain at 12 volts. On the other hand, hooking two 12 volt batteries in a series circuit (positive terminal to negative terminal and negative terminal to positive terminal) increases the total battery output to 24 volts (12 volts plus 12 volts).

✳✳ WARNING

Never hook the batteries up in a series circuit or the entire electrical system will be damaged, including the starter motor.

In the event that a dual battery vehicle needs to be jump started, use the following procedure:

1. Turn the heater blower motor **ON** to help protect the electrical system from voltage surges when the jumper cables are connected and disconnected.
2. Turn all lights and other switches **OFF**.

➡The battery cables connected to one of the diesel vehicle's batteries may be thicker than those connected to its other battery. (The passenger

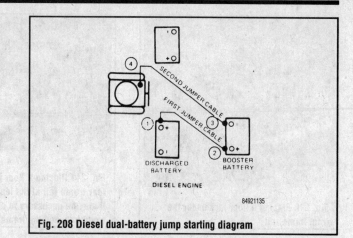

Fig. 208 Diesel dual-battery jump starting diagram

side battery often has thicker cables.) This set-up allows relatively high jump starting current to pass without damage. If so, be sure to connect the positive jumper cable to the appropriate battery in the disabled vehicle. If there is no difference in cable thickness, connect the jumper cable to either battery's positive terminal. Similarly, if the donor vehicle also utilizes two batteries, the jumper cable connections should be made to the battery with the thicker cables; if there is no difference in thickness, the connections can be made to either donor battery.

3. Connect the end of a jumper cable to one of the disabled diesel's positive (+) battery terminals, then connect the clamp at the other end of the same cable to the positive terminal (+) on the jumper battery.
4. Connect one end of the other jumper cable to the negative battery terminal (-) on the jumper battery, then connect the other cable clamp to an engine bolt head, alternator bracket or other solid, metallic point on the disabled vehicle's engine. DO NOT connect this clamp to the negative terminal (-) of the disabled vehicle's battery.

✳✳ CAUTION

Be careful to keep the jumper cables away from moving parts (cooling fan, belts, etc.) on both engines.

5. Start the engine on the vehicle with the good battery and run it at a moderate speed.
6. Start the engine of the vehicle with the discharged battery.
7. When the engine starts on the vehicle with the discharged battery, remove the cable from the engine block before disconnecting the cable from the positive terminal.

JACKING

▶ See Figures 209, 210, 211, 212 and 213

Your Jeep was supplied with a jack for emergency road repairs. This jack is fine for changing a flat tire or other short-term procedures not requiring you to go beneath the vehicle. If it is used in an emergency situation, carefully follow the instructions provided either with the jack or in your owner's manual. Do not attempt to use the jack on any portions of the vehicle other than specified by the vehicle manufacturer. Always block the diagonally opposite wheel when using a jack.

A more convenient way of jacking is the use of a garage or floor jack. You may use the floor jack at the specified points in following the illustrations.

Never place the jack under the radiator, engine or transmission components. Severe and expensive damage will result when the jack is raised. Additionally, never jack under the floorpan or bodywork; the metal will deform.

Whenever you plan to work under the vehicle, you must support it on jackstands or ramps. Never use cinder blocks or stacks of wood to support the vehicle, even if you're only going to be under it for a few minutes. Never crawl under the vehicle when it is supported only by the tire-changing jack or other floor jack.

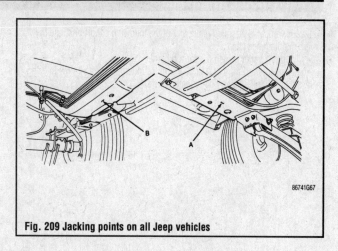

Fig. 209 Jacking points on all Jeep vehicles

Fig. 210 Placing a floor jack under the front frame rail

Fig. 211 Placing a floor jack under the rear frame rail at the leaf spring shackle. It may be necessary to place a block of wood between the frame rail and the jack

Fig. 212 Supporting the front of the vehicle with jack stands placed under each frame rail

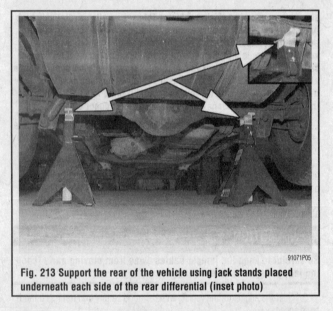

Fig. 213 Support the rear of the vehicle using jack stands placed underneath each side of the rear differential (inset photo)

➡Whenever necessary, position a block of wood or small rubber pad on top of the jack or jackstand to protect the lifting point's finish when lifting or supporting the vehicle.

Small hydraulic, screw, or scissors jacks are satisfactory for raising the vehicle. Drive-on trestles or ramps are also a handy and safe way to both raise and support the vehicle. Be careful though, some ramps may be too steep to drive your vehicle onto without scraping the front bottom panels. Never support the vehicle on any suspension member (unless specifically instructed to do so by a repair manual) or by an underbody panel.

Jacking Precautions

The following safety points cannot be overemphasized:
• Always block the opposite wheel or wheels to keep the vehicle from rolling off the jack.
• When raising the front of the vehicle, firmly apply the parking brake.
• When the drive wheels are to remain on the ground, leave the vehicle in gear to help prevent it from rolling.
• Always use jackstands to support the vehicle when you are working underneath. Place the stands beneath the vehicle's jacking brackets. Before climbing underneath, rock the vehicle a bit to make sure it is firmly supported.

Jacking Procedure

▶ See Figure 209

Scissors jacks or hydraulic jacks are recommended for all Jeep vehicles. To change a tire, place the jack beneath the correct jacking location point as illustrated, near the wheel to be changed.

Make sure that you are on level ground, that the transmission is in Reverse with manual transmissions (or in Park with automatic transmissions), the parking brake is set, and the tire diagonally opposite to the one to be changed is blocked so that it will not roll. Using the wrench supplied with the vehicle, or a 19mm deep well socket and breaker bar, loosen the lug nuts before you jack the wheel to be changed completely free of the ground.

MAINTENANCE INTERVALS

If your vehicle is operated under any of the following conditions, use the severe maintenance chart:
• Towing a trailer or using a car top carrier
• Repeated short trips of less than 5 miles in temperatures below freezing, or less than 10 miles in any other temperature

• Extensive idling or low-speed operation for long distances
• Operation on rough, muddy or salt covered roads
• Operation on unpaved or dusty roads
• Driving in extremely hot (over 90°) conditions

NORMAL MAINTENANCE INTERVALS

TO BE SERVICED	TYPE OF SERVICE	7.5	15	22.5	30	37.5	45	52.5	60	67.5	75	82.5	90	97.5	105	112.5	120
		VEHICLE MILEAGE INTERVAL (x1000)															
Change engine oil	R	✓	✓	✓	✓	✓	✓	✓	✓	✓	✓	✓	✓	✓	✓	✓	✓
Replace engine oil filter	R	✓	✓	✓	✓	✓	✓	✓	✓	✓	✓	✓	✓	✓	✓	✓	✓
Lubricate steering linkage	L	✓	✓	✓	✓	✓	✓	✓	✓	✓	✓	✓	✓	✓	✓	✓	✓
Inspect brake pads/linings	S/I						✓			✓							✓
Replace air cleaner element	R				✓				✓				✓				✓
Replace spark plugs	R				✓				✓				✓				✓
Inspect drive belt, adjust tension as necessary	S/I, A		✓		✓		✓		✓		✓		✓		✓		✓
Drain & refill automatic transmission fluid	R		✓		✓				✓				✓				✓
Drain & refill transfer case fluid	R				✓				✓				✓				✓
Flush & replace the coolant (at 36 mos. regardless of mileage)	R						✓						✓				
Clean and repack wheel bearings	C			✓			✓			✓			✓			✓	
Inspect PCV valve (if equipped)	S/I				✓				✓				✓				✓
Inspect all fluid levels and add, if necessary	S/I	✓	✓	✓	✓	✓	✓	✓	✓	✓	✓	✓	✓	✓	✓	✓	✓
Replace spark plug wires, distributor cap and rotor	R				✓				✓				✓				✓
Inspect exhaust system	S/I	✓	✓	✓	✓	✓	✓	✓	✓	✓	✓	✓	✓	✓	✓	✓	✓
Inspect brake hoses	S/I	✓	✓	✓	✓	✓	✓	✓	✓	✓	✓	✓	✓	✓	✓	✓	✓
Inspect coolant level, hoses & clamps	S/I	✓	✓	✓	✓	✓	✓	✓	✓	✓	✓	✓	✓	✓	✓	✓	✓
Lubricate ball joints	S/I	✓	✓	✓	✓	✓	✓	✓	✓	✓	✓	✓	✓	✓	✓	✓	✓

R - Replace   S/I - Inspect and service, if needed   L - Lubricate   A - Adjust   C - Clean

SEVERE MAINTENANCE INTERVALS

TO BE SERVICED	TYPE OF SERVICE	3	6	9	12	15	18	21	24	27	30	33	36	39	42	45	48	51	54	57	60
		VEHICLE MILEAGE INTERVAL (x1000)																			
Change engine oil	R	✓	✓	✓	✓	✓	✓	✓	✓	✓	✓	✓	✓	✓	✓	✓	✓	✓	✓	✓	✓
Replace engine oil filter	R	✓	✓	✓	✓	✓	✓	✓	✓	✓	✓	✓	✓	✓	✓	✓	✓	✓	✓	✓	✓
Inspect the front brake pads - nd rear brake pads/linings	S/I				✓				✓				✓				✓				✓
Accessory drive belt(s)	S/I, A, R								✓							✓					
Inspect the air cleaner element and replace if necessary	S/I, R					✓					✓					✓					✓
Change the automatic transaxle fluid and filter	R							✓							✓						
Check and replace, if necessary, the PCV valve (if equipped)	S/I								✓								✓				
Lubricate ball joints	L	✓	✓	✓	✓	✓	✓	✓	✓	✓	✓	✓	✓	✓	✓	✓	✓	✓	✓	✓	✓
Lubricate steering linkage	L		✓		✓		✓		✓		✓		✓		✓		✓		✓		✓
Replace spark plugs	R										✓										✓
Flush and replace the coolant	R												✓								
Drain and refill transfer case fluid	R										✓										✓
Replace ignition cables	R												✓								
Replace fuel filter	R												✓								
Drain, and refill front/rear differential housing fluid	R								✓								✓				
Inspect coolant level, hoses and clamps	S/I	✓	✓	✓	✓	✓	✓	✓	✓	✓	✓	✓	✓	✓	✓	✓	✓	✓	✓	✓	✓
Inspect brake hoses	S/I	✓	✓	✓	✓	✓	✓	✓	✓	✓	✓	✓	✓	✓	✓	✓	✓	✓	✓	✓	✓
Inspect exhaust system	S/I	✓	✓	✓	✓	✓	✓	✓	✓	✓	✓	✓	✓	✓	✓	✓	✓	✓	✓	✓	✓
Replace engine timing belt ①	R																				✓

① Replace the engine timing belt at approximately 55,000 miles (87,000km).

R - Replace   S/I - Inspect and service, if needed   L - Lubricate   A - Adjust   C - Clean

FREQUENT OPERATION MAINTENANCE (SEVERE SERVICE)

If a vehicle is operated under any of the following conditions it is considered severe service, and you should use this chart:

- Towing a trailer or using a camper or car-top carrier.
- Repeated short trips of less than 5 miles in temperatures below freezing, or trips of less than 10 miles in any temperature.
- Extensive idling or low-speed driving for long distances as in heavy commercial use, such as delivery, taxi or police cars.
- Operating on rough, muddy or salt-covered roads.
- Operating on unpaved or dusty roads.
- Driving in extremely hot (over 90°) conditions.

91071C09

91071C10

CAPACITIES

Year	Model	Engine ID/VIN	Engine Displacement Liters (cu. in.)	Engine Oil with Filter (qts.)	Transmission (pts.) 4-Spd	5-Spd	Auto.	Drive Axle (pts.)	Fuel Tank (gal.)	Cooling System (qts.)
1991	Comanche	P	2.5 (150)	4	7	7.4	17	2.5①	18.5	10
	Comanche	S	4.0 (243)	6	7	6.7	17	2.5①	18.5	12
	Cherokee	P	2.5 (150)	4	-	7.4	17	2.5①	20	10
	Cherokee	S	4.0 (243)	6	-	6.7	17	2.5①	20	12
1992	Comanche	P	2.5 (150)	4	7	7.4	17	2.5①	18.5	10
	Comanche	S	4.0 (243)	6	7	6.7	17	2.5①	18.5	12
	Cherokee	P	2.5 (150)	4	-	7.4	17	2.5①	20	10
	Cherokee	S	4.0 (243)	6	-	6.7	17	2.5①	20	12
1993	Cherokee	P	2.5 (150)	4	-	7.4	17	2.5①	20	10
	Cherokee	S	4.0 (243)	6	-	6.7	17	2.5①	20	12
	Grand Cherokee	S	4.0 (243)	6	-	6.5	17	3.4	23	9.3
	Grand Cherokee	Y	5.2 (318)	5	-	6.5	17	3.4	23	14.9
	Grand Wagoneer	Y	5.2 (318)	5	-	-	17	3.4	23	14.9
1994	Cherokee	P	2.5 (150)	4	-	7.4	17	2.5①	20	10
	Cherokee	S	4.0 (243)	6	-	6.7	17	2.5①	20	9.3
	Grand Cherokee	S	4.0 (243)	6	-	6.5	17	3.4	23	14.9
	Grand Cherokee	Y	5.2 (318)	5	-	-	17	3.4	23	10
1995	Cherokee	P	2.5 (150)	4	-	7.4	17	2.5①	20	10
	Cherokee	S	4.0 (243)	6	-	6.7	17	2.5①	20	12
	Grand Cherokee	S	4.0 (243)	6	-	6.5	17	3.4	23	12
	Grand Cherokee	Y	5.2 (318)	5	-	-	17	3.4	23	14.9
1996	Cherokee	P	2.5 (150)	4	-	7.4	17	2.5①	20	10
	Cherokee	S	4.0 (243)	6	-	6.6	17	2.5①	20	12
	Grand Cherokee	S	4.0 (243)	6	-	-	17-22	3.4	23	12
	Grand Cherokee	Y	5.2 (318)	5	-	-	17-22	3.4	23	14.9
1997	Cherokee	P	2.5 (150)	4	-	6.6⑥	17	2.5①	20	10
	Cherokee	S	4.0 (243)	6	-	-	17	2.5①	20	12
	Grand Cherokee	S	4.0 (243)	6	-	-	17-22	3.4	23	12
	Grand Cherokee	Y	5.2 (318)	5	-	-	17-22	3.4	23	14.9
	Grand Cherokee	Z	5.9 (360)	5	-	-	17-22	3.4	23	14.9
1998 and later	Cherokee	P	2.5 (150)	4	-	-	17	2.5①	20	10
	Cherokee	S	4.0 (243)	6	-	6.6⑥	17	2.5①	20	12
	Grand Cherokee	S	4.0 (243)	6	-	-	⑧	3.4	23	12
	Grand Cherokee	Y	5.2 (318)	5	-	-	⑧	3.4	23	12
	Grand Cherokee	Z	5.9 (360)	5	-	-	⑧	3.4	23	14.9

① Aisin Warner Transmission 7.4 pts.
② Optional 20 gallon tank available
③ Heavy Duty: 3 pts.
④ 8 1/4 axle: 4.4 pts. When equipped with TRAC-LOK, add 2 oz. of friction modifier
⑤ Rear wheel drive 7.4 pts.
⑥ 4WD 7.0 pts.
⑥ 42/44RE Transmission 19.5-22 pts.
⑦ 46RE Transmission 19.5-28 pts.
⑧ 2001 = 8 pts.

91071C07

CAPACITIES

Year	Model	Engine ID/VIN	Engine Displacement Liters (cu. in.)	Engine Oil with Filter (qts.)	Transmission (pts.) 4-Spd	5-Spd	Auto.	Drive Axle (pts.)	Fuel Tank (gal.)	Cooling System (qts.)
1984	Comanche	U	2.5 (150)	4	4①	4.5	15.8	2.5③	13.5⑤	9
	Comanche	W	2.8 (173)	5	4①	4.5	15.8	2.5③	13.5⑤	9
	Wagoneer	U	2.5 (150)	4	4①	4.5	15.8	2.5③	13.5⑤	9
	Wagoneer	W	2.8 (173)	5	4①	4.5	15.8	2.5③	13.5⑤	9
	Cherokee	U	2.5 (150)	4	4①	4.5	15.8	2.5③	13.5⑤	9
	Cherokee	W	2.8 (173)	5	4①	4.5	15.8	2.5③	13.5⑤	9
1985	Comanche	B	2.1 (126)	6.3	4①	4.5	15.8	2.5③	13.5⑤	9
	Comanche	H	2.5 (150)	4	4①	4.5	15.8	2.5③	13.5⑤	9
	Comanche	W	2.8 (173)	5	4①	4.5	15.8	2.5③	13.5⑤	9
	Wagoneer	B	2.1 (126)	6.3	4①	4.5	15.8	2.5③	13.5⑤	9
	Wagoneer	H	2.5 (150)	4	4①	4.5	15.8	2.5③	13.5⑤	9
	Wagoneer	W	2.8 (173)	5	4①	4.5	15.8	2.5③	13.5⑤	9
	Cherokee	B	2.1 (126)	6.3	4①	4.5	15.8	2.5③	13.5⑤	9
	Cherokee	H	2.5 (150)	4	4①	4.5	15.8	2.5③	13.5⑤	9
	Cherokee	W	2.8 (173)	5	4①	4.5	15.8	2.5③	13.5⑤	9
1986	Comanche	B	2.1 (126)	6.3	4①	4.5	15.8	2.5③	13.5⑤	9
	Comanche	H	2.5 (150)	4	4①	4.5	15.8	2.5③	13.5⑤	9
	Comanche	W	2.8 (173)	5	4①	4.5	15.8	2.5③	13.5⑤	9
	Wagoneer	B	2.1 (126)	6.3	4①	4.5	15.8	2.5③	13.5⑤	9
	Wagoneer	H	2.5 (150)	4	4①	4.5	15.8	2.5③	13.5⑤	9
	Wagoneer	W	2.8 (173)	5	4①	4.5	15.8	2.5③	13.5⑤	9
	Cherokee	B	2.1 (126)	6.3	4①	4.5	15.8	2.5③	13.5⑤	9
	Cherokee	H	2.5 (150)	4	4①	4.5	15.8	2.5③	13.5⑤	9
	Cherokee	W	2.8 (173)	5	4①	4.5	15.8	2.5③	13.5⑤	9
1987	Comanche	B	2.1 (126)	6.3	4①	4.5	15.8	2.5③	13.5⑤	9
	Comanche	H	2.5 (150)	4	3.9①	4.5	15.8	2.5③	13.5⑤	9
	Comanche	M	4.0 (243)	6	4①	4.5	15.8	2.5③	13.5⑤	12
	Wagoneer	B	2.1 (126)	6.3	4①	4.5	15.8	2.5③	13.5⑤	9
	Wagoneer	H	2.5 (150)	4	4①	4.5	15.8	2.5③	13.5⑤	9
	Wagoneer	M	4.0 (243)	6	3.9①	4.5	15.8	2.5③	13.5⑤	12
	Cherokee	B	2.1 (126)	6.3	4①	4.5	15.8	2.5③	13.5⑤	9
	Cherokee	H	2.5 (150)	4	3.9①	4.5	15.8	2.5③	13.5⑤	9
	Cherokee	M	4.0 (243)	6	4①	4.5	15.8	2.5③	13.5⑤	12
1988	Comanche	H	2.5 (150)	4	4①	4.5	17	2.5③	13.5⑤	9
	Wagoneer	M	4.0 (243)	6	4①	4.9	17	2.5③	13.5⑤	12
	Cherokee	H	2.5 (150)	4	4①	4.9	17	2.5③	13.5⑤	9
	Cherokee	M	4.0 (243)	6	4①	4.9	17	2.5③	13.5⑤	12
1989	Comanche	E	2.5 (150)	4	4①	4.9	17	2.5③	18.5	9
	Comanche	L	4.0 (243)	6	4①	4.9	17	2.5③	18.5	12
	Wagoneer	L	4.0 (243)	6	4①	4.9	17	2.5③	20	12
	Cherokee	E	2.5 (150)	4	4①	4.9	17	2.5③	20	9
	Cherokee	L	4.0 (243)	6	4①	4.9	17	2.5③	20	12
1990	Comanche	E	2.5 (150)	4	4①	4.9	17	2.5③	18.5	9
	Comanche	L	4.0 (243)	6	4①	4.9	17	2.5③	18.5	12
	Cherokee	E	2.5 (150)	4	4①	4.9	17	2.5③	20	9
	Cherokee	L	4.0 (243)	6	4①	4.9	17	2.5③	20	12

91071C06

2

ENGINE
ELECTRICAL

HIGH ENERGY IGNITION (HEI) SYSTEM

→For information on understanding electricity and troubleshooting electrical circuits, please refer to Section 6 of this manual.

Description And Operation

The HEI system, used on 2.5L, 2.8L and 4.0L engines, is a pulse-triggered, transistorized controlled, inductive discharge ignition system. The entire HEI system (except for the ignition coil on fuel injected engines) is contained within the distributor cap.

The distributor, in addition to housing the mechanical and vacuum advance mechanisms, contains the electronic control module, and the magnetic triggering device. The magnetic pick-up assembly contains a permanent magnet, a pole piece with internal teeth, and a pick-up coil (not to be confused with the ignition coil).

In the HEI system, as in other electronic ignition systems, the breaker points have been replaced with an electronic switch—a transistor—which is located within the control module. This switching transistor performs the same function the points did in an conventional ignition system. It simply turns coil primary current on and off at the correct time. Essentially then, electronic and conventional ignition systems operate on the same principle.

The module which houses the switching transistor is controlled (turned on and off) by a magnetically generated impulse induced in the pick-up coil. When the teeth of the rotating timer align with the teeth of the pole piece, the induced voltage in the pick-up coil signals the electronic module to open the coil primary circuit. The primary current then decreases, and a high voltage is induced in the ignition coil secondary windings which is then directed through the rotor and high voltage leads (spark plug wires) to fire the spark plugs.

In essence then, the pick-up coil module system simply replaces the conventional breaker points and condenser. The condenser found within the distributor is for radio suppression purposes only and has nothing to do with the ignition process. The module automatically controls the dwell period, increasing it with increasing engine speed. Since dwell is automatically controlled, it cannot be adjusted. The module itself is non-adjustable and non-repairable and must be replaced if found defective.

HEI SYSTEM PRECAUTIONS

Before going on to troubleshooting, it might be a good idea to take note of the following precautions:

Timing Light Use

Inductive pick-up timing lights are the best kind to use if your Jeep is equipped with HEI. Timing lights which connect between the spark plug and the spark plug wire occasionally (not always) give false readings.

Spark Plug Wires

The plug wires used with HEI systems are of a different construction than conventional wires. When replacing them, make sure you get the correct wires, since conventional wires won't carry the voltage. Also, handle them carefully to avoid cracking or splitting them and never pierce them.

Tachometer Use

Not all tachometers will operate or indicate correctly when used on an HEI system. While some tachometers may give a reading, this does not necessarily mean the reading is correct. In addition, some tachometers hook up differently from others. If you can't figure out whether or not your tachometer will work on your Jeep, check with the tachometer manufacturer.

HEI System Testers

♦ See Figure 1

Instruments designed specifically for testing HEI systems are available from several tool manufacturers. Some of these will even test the module itself. However, the tests given in the following section will require only an ohmmeter and a voltmeter.

Diagnosis and Testing

♦ See Figures 2, 3 and 4

The symptoms of a defective component within the HEI system are exactly the same as those you would encounter in a conventional system. Some of these symptoms are:

- Hard or no Starting
- Rough Idle
- Fuel Poor Economy
- Engine misses under load or while accelerating

If you suspect a problem in the ignition system, there are certain preliminary checks which you should carry out before you begin to check the electronic portions of the system. First, it is extremely important to make sure the vehicle battery is in a good state of charge. A defective or poorly charged battery will cause the various components of the ignition system to read incorrectly when they are being tested. Second, make sure all wiring connections are clean and tight, not only at the battery, but also at the distributor cap, ignition coil, and at the electronic control module.

SECONDARY SPARK TEST

Since the only change between electronic and conventional ignition systems is in the distributor component area, it is imperative to check the secondary ignition circuit first. If the secondary circuit checks out properly, then the engine condition is probably not the fault of the ignition system. To check the second-

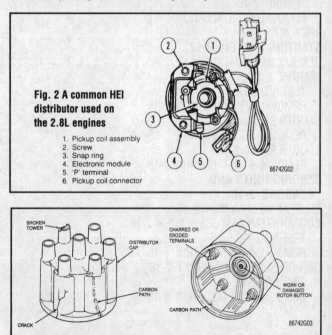

Fig. 2 A common HEI distributor used on the 2.8L engines

1. Pickup coil assembly
2. Screw
3. Snap ring
4. Electronic module
5. 'P' terminal
6. Pickup coil connector

86742G02

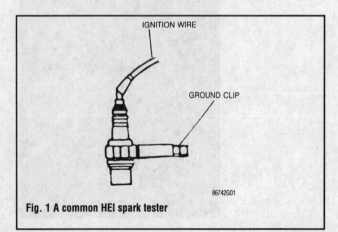

IGNITION WIRE

GROUND CLIP

86742G01

Fig. 1 A common HEI spark tester

BROKEN TOWER

DISTRIBUTOR CAP

CHARRED OR ERODED TERMINALS

CARBON PATH

CARBON PATH

CRACK

WORN OR DAMAGED ROTOR BUTTON

86742G03

Fig. 3 Check the distributor cap for cracking and carbon tracking

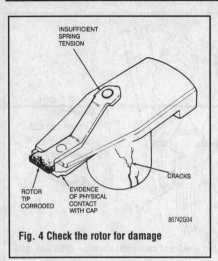

Fig. 4 Check the rotor for damage

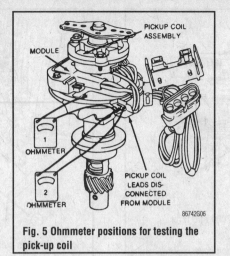

Fig. 5 Ohmmeter positions for testing the pick-up coil

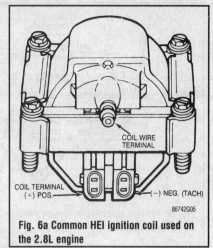

Fig. 6a Common HEI ignition coil used on the 2.8L engine

ary ignition system, perform a simple spark test.

1. Remove one of the plug wires and insert some sort of extension in the plug socket. An old spark plug with the ground electrode removed makes a good extension.

※ CAUTION:

Because of the ignition system design on 2000 and later six-cylinder models, a special set of spark plug wire must be obtained or fabricated before the ignition system check can be performed. A test set can be fabricated from bulk spark plug wires and terminals available at most auto parts stores. As an alternative, individual jumper wires can be used to ground the spark plug terminals not being tested. Whichever method you choose, make sure all the spark plug terminals are either connected to a spark plug or grounded to the engine block before cranking the engine or damage to the ignition coils may result.

2. Hold the wire and extension about 1/4 in. (6mm) away from the block and crank the engine. If a normal spark occurs, then the problem is most likely not in the ignition system.

3. Check for fuel system problems, or fouled spark plugs.

4. If, however, there is no spark or a weak spark, then further ignition system testing will have to be done. Troubleshooting techniques fall into two categories, depending on the nature of the problem. The categories are (1) Engine cranks, but won't start or (2) Engine runs, but runs rough or cuts out.

Engine Fails to Start

1. If the engine won't start, perform a spark test as described earlier. If no spark occurs, check for the presence of normal battery voltage at the battery (**BAT**) terminal in the distributor cap. The ignition switch must be in the **ON** position for this test.

2. If battery voltage is not present, this indicates an open circuit in the ignition primary wiring leading to the distributor. In this case, you will have to check wiring continuity back to the ignition switch using a test light.

3. If there is battery voltage at the **BAT** terminal, but no spark at the plugs, then the problem lies within the distributor assembly. Go on to test the ignition coil.

Engine Runs, but Runs Roughly or Cuts Out

1. Make sure the plug wires are in good shape first. There should be no obvious cracks or breaks. You can check the plug wires with an ohmmeter, but do not pierce the wires with a probe.

2. If the plug wires are OK, remove the cap assembly, and check for moisture, cracks, chips, or carbon tracks, or any other high voltage leaks or failures.

3. Replace the cap if you find any defects. Make sure the timer wheel rotates when the engine is cranked. If everything is all right so far, go on to test the ignition coil.

PICK-UP COIL

▶ See Figure 5

1. To test the pick-up coil, first disconnect the white and green module

leads. Set the ohmmeter on the high scale and connect it between a ground and either the white or green lead. Any resistance measurement less than infinity requires replacement of the pick-up coil.

2. Pick-up coil continuity is tested by connecting the ohmmeter (on low range) between the white and green leads. Normal resistance is between 500 and 1500 ohms. Move the vacuum advance arm while performing this test. This will detect any break in coil continuity. Such a condition can cause intermittent misfiring. Replace the pick-up coil if the reading is outside the specified limits.

3. If no defects have been found at this time, and you still have a problem, then the module will have to be checked. If you do not have access to a module tester, the only possible alternative is a substitution test. If the module fails the substitution test, replace it.

Ignition Coil

TESTING

Carbureted Engines

▶ See Figure 6a

1. Connect an ohmmeter between the **TACH** and **BAT** terminals in the distributor cap. The primary coil resistance should be less than one ohm (zero or nearly zero).

2. To check the coil secondary resistance, connect an ohmmeter between the rotor button and the **BAT** terminal. Then connect the ohmmeter between the ground terminal and the rotor button. The resistance in both cases should be between 6000 and 30,000 ohms.

3. Replace the coil only if the readings in Step 1 and 2 are infinite.

➡These resistance checks will not disclose shorted coil windings. This condition can be detected only with scope analysis or a suitably designed coil tester. If these instruments are unavailable, replace the coil with a known good coil as a final coil test.

Fuel Injected Engines - All Except 2000 and Later Inline Six-cylinder Engines

The ignition coil is designed to operate without an external ballast resistor. Inspect the coil for arcing. Test the coil primary and secondary resistance.

Measure the primary resistance as follows:

1. Connect an ohmmeter between the positive (+) and negative (-) terminals (the terminals which are connected to the engine wiring harness) on the coil.

2. To test the secondary resistance, connect an ohmmeter between the positive (+) coil terminal and the high voltage cable terminal on the coil, then, measure the resistance between the positive (+) coil terminal and the coil case; the resistance for the case should exhibit infinite resistance.

3. For coils manufactured by Diamond, the primary resistance at 70–80°F (21–27°C) should be 0.97–1.18 ohms and the secondary resistance should be 11,300–15,300 ohms.

4. Coils built by the Toyodenso company should exhibit a primary resistance at 70–80°F (21–27°C) of 0.95–1.20 ohms and a secondary resistance of 11,300–13,300 ohms.

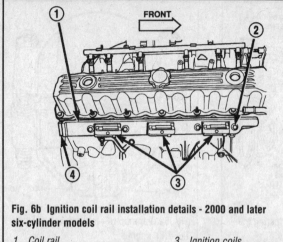

Fig. 6b Ignition coil rail installation details - 2000 and later six-cylinder models

1	Coil rail	3	Ignition coils
2	Mounting bolts (1 of 4)	4	Electrical connector

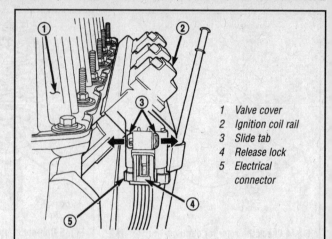

1 Valve cover
2 Ignition coil rail
3 Slide tab
4 Release lock
5 Electrical connector

Fig. 6c Ignition coil rail electrical connector details - 2000 and later six-cylinder models

5. Replace any coil with a new one if it does not meet the specifications.

6. If the ignition coil is replaced with a new one due to a burned tower, carbon tracking, arcing at the tower, or damage to the terminal or boot on the coil end of the secondary cable, the cable must also be replaced with a new one. Arcing at the tower will carbonize the nipple which, if it is connected to a new coil, will cause the coil to fail.

7. If a secondary cable shows any signs of damage, the cable should be replaced with a new cable and new terminal. Carbon tracking on the old cable can cause arcing and the failure of a new coil.

Fuel Injected Engines - 2000 and Later Inline Six-Cylinder Models

1 Remove the ignition coil rail assembly.

2 Clean the three outer cases and check for cracks or other damage. Clean the coil primary terminals and check the springs and spark plug boots for damage. If either the springs or spark plug boots are damaged, the coil rail assembly must be replaced.

3 Check the coil primary resistance. Connect an ohmmeter to terminals no. 2 and 1; 2 and 3; 2 and 4; of the coil connector. Each measurement is the primary resistance of one of the three coils in the coil rail assembly.

4 The coil resistance should be 0.97 to 1.18 ohms resistance for the primary side and 11,300 to 15,300 ohms for the secondary side. If either measured resistance value is not as specified, replace the ignition coil rail assembly.

➡The entire ignition coil rail assembly must be replaced if only one coil is defective.

REMOVAL & INSTALLATION

Carbureted Engines

1. Disconnect the feed and module wire terminal connectors from the distributor cap.

2. Remove the ignition set retainer.

3. Remove the coil cover-to-distributor cap screws and coil cover.

4. Remove the 4 coil-to-distributor cap screws.

5. Using a blunt drift, press the coil wire spade terminals up out of distribu-

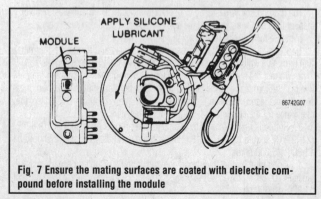

Fig. 7 Ensure the mating surfaces are coated with dielectric compound before installing the module

tor cap.

6. Lift the coil up out of the distributor cap.

7. Remove and clean the coil spring, rubber seal washer and coil cavity of the distributor cap.

8. Coat the rubber seal with a dielectric lubricant furnished in the replacement ignition coil package.

9. Reverse the above procedures to install.

Fuel Injected Engines - All Except 2000 and Later Inline Six-Cylinder Engines

1. Make sure that the ignition switch is in the **OFF** position.

2. Tag and disconnect the coil wire and the connector on the side of the coil.

3. Remove the nuts holding the coil and bracket assembly to the engine and lift out the coil. The coil may be riveted to the bracket, to remove it will require drilling the rivets and punching them out.

4. Position the coil on the engine and tighten the nuts.

5. Engage the coil wire and electrical connectors.

Fuel Injected Engines - 2000 and Later Inline Six-Cylinder Models

◆ See Figures 6b and 6c

➡The ignition coil rail assembly consists of the three ignition coils, spark plug boots, springs, electrical connector and internal wiring. None of the components are serviced separately. The entire assembly is removed and replaced as a unit.

1 Remove the ignition coil rail assembly mounting bolts.

2 Carefully work the spark plug boots off the spark plugs by alternately prying at one end of the coil rail, then the other. If difficulty is encountered, twist the spark plug boots with a spark plug boot removal tool to loosen the seal.

3 Position the coil rail to access the electrical connection. Disconnect the electrical connector from the coil rail by first pushing the slide tab up, then press the release lock and pull the connector off.

4 Remove the ignition coil rail assembly.

5 When installing the ignition coil rail, position all of the spark plug boots over the spark plugs and press the ignition coil rail down until the boots are completely seated.

6 Install the mounting bolts and tighten them in stages until secure.

7 Connect the electrical connector and slide the tab down until locked in place.

Ignition Module

REMOVAL & INSTALLATION

◆ See Figure 7

1. Remove the distributor cap and rotor.

2. Disconnect the harness connector and pick-up coil spade connectors from the module. Be careful not to damage the wires when removing the connector.

3. Remove the two screws and module from the distributor housing.

4. Coat the bottom of the new module with dielectric silicone lubricant. This is usually supplied with the new module. Reverse the above procedure to install.

Distributor

REMOVAL

1. Remove the high-tension wires from the distributor cap terminal towers, noting their positions to assure correct reassembly.

2. Remove the primary lead from the terminal post at the side of the distributor.

3. Disconnect the vacuum line if equipped.

4. Remove the distributor cap retaining hooks or screws and remove the distributor cap.

5. Note the position of the rotor in relation to the base. Scribe a mark on the base of the distributor and on the engine to facilitate reinstallation. Align the marks with the direction the metal tip of the rotor is pointing.

6. Remove the bolt that hold the distributor to the engine.

7. Lift the distributor assembly from the engine.

INSTALLATION

2.8L Engine

ENGINE NOT ROTATED

1. Insert the distributor shaft and assembly into the engine. Line up the mark on the distributor and the one on the engine with the metal tip of the rotor. Make sure that the vacuum advance diaphragm is pointed in the same direction as it was pointed originally. This will be done automatically if the marks on the engine and the distributor are line up with the rotor.

2. Install the distributor hold-down bolt and clamp. Leave the screw loose enough so that you can move the distributor with heavy hand pressure.

3. Connect the primary wire to the distributor side of the coil. Install the distributor cap on the distributor housing. Secure the distributor cap with the spring clips or the screw type retainers, whichever is used.

4. Install the spark plug wires. Make sure that the wires are pressed all of the way into the top of the distributor cap and firmly onto the spark plugs.

➡**Design of the V6 engine requires a special form of distributor cam. The distributor may be serviced in the regular way and should cause no more problems than any other distributor, if the firing plan is thoroughly understood. The distributor cam is not ground to standard 6-cylinder indexing intervals. This particular form requires that the original pattern of spark plug wiring be used. The engine will not run in balance if No. 1 spark plug wire is inserted into No. 6 distributor cap tower, even though each wire in the firing sequence is advanced to the next distributor tower. There is a difference between the firing intervals of each succeeding cylinder through the 720° engine cycle.**

5. Set the ignition timing.

ENGINE ROTATED

➡**If the engine has been turned while the distributor has been removed, or if the marks were not drawn, it will be necessary to initially time the engine.**

1. If the engine has been rotated while the distributor was out, you'll have to first put the engine at Top Dead Center firing position on No. 1 cylinder. You can either remove the valve cover or No. 1 spark plug to determine engine position. Rotate the engine with a socket wrench on the nut at the center of the front pulley in the normal direction of rotation. Either feel for air being expelled forcefully through the spark plug hole or watch for the engine to rotate up to the Top Center mark without the valves moving (both valves will be closed). If the valves are moving as you approach TDC or there is no air being expelled through the plug hole, turn the engine another full turn until you get the appropriate indication as the engine approaches TDC position.

2. Start the distributor into the engine with the matchmarks between the distributor body and the engine lined up. Turn the rotor slightly until the matchmarks on the bottom of the distributor body and the bottom of the distributor shaft near the gear are aligned. Then, insert the distributor all the way into the engine. If you have trouble getting the distributor and camshaft gears to mesh, turn the rotor back and forth very slightly until the distributor can be inserted easily. If the rotor is not now lined up with the position of No. 1 plug terminal, you'll have to pull the distributor back out slightly, shift the position of the rotor appropriately, and then reinstall it.

3. Align the matchmarks between the distributor and engine. Install the distributor mounting bolt and tighten it finger-tight. Reconnect the vacuum advance line and distributor wiring connector, and reinstall the cap. Reconnect the negative battery cable. Adjust the ignition timing as described in Section 1. Then, tighten the distributor mounting bolt securely.

2.5L and 4.0L

ENGINE NOT ROTATED

1. Clean the mounting area of the cylinder block and install a new distributor mounting gasket.

➡**On some models there is a fork on the distributor housing. The slot in the fork aligns with the distributor hold-down bolt hole in the engine block. The distributor is correctly installed when the rotor is correctly positioned and the slot is aligned with the hold-down bolt hole. On these computer controlled distributors, initial ignition timing is not adjustable.**

2. Align the rotor tip with the scribe mark on the distributor housing during removal, then turn the rotor approximately 1/8 turn counterclockwise past the scribe mark.

3. Slide the distributor shaft down into the engine. It may be necessary to move the rotor and shaft slightly to engage the distributor shaft with the oil pump slot. Align the scribe mark on the distributor housing with the mark on the cylinder block.

➡**Ensure that the distributor is fully seated against the cylinder block. It may be necessary to slightly rotate (bump) the engine while applying light downward force to fully engage the distributor shaft with the oil pump drive gear shaft.**

4. Install the distributor shaft hold-down and bolt. Tighten the bolt to 17 ft. lbs. (23 Nm).

5. Install distributor cap and ignition wires. Insure that the wires are routed correctly before attempting to start engine.

ENGINE ROTATED

1. Rotate the engine until the No.1 piston is at TDC compression.

2. Using a flat-bladed screwdriver, in the distributor hole, rotate the oil pump gear so that the slot in the oil pump shaft is in the correct position (see illustration).

3. With the distributor cap removed, install the distributor so that the rotor is positioned correctly (see illustration). Insure that the distributor is fully seated against the cylinder block. If not, remove the distributor and perform the entire procedure again.

4. Tighten the hold-down bolt.

5. Install distributor cap and ignition wires. Insure that the wires are routed correctly before attempting to start engine.

ELECTRONIC DISTRIBUTOR IGNITION SYSTEM

General Information

The ignition system consists of:
- an ignition coil
- an ignition control module (1987–90 models only)
- an ignition distributor containing a rotor and camshaft position sensor
- The Electronic Control Unit (ECU), also known as the Powertrain Control Module (PCM)
- Crankshaft position, throttle position and MAP sensors

The amount of spark advance provided by the engine controller is based on five input factors. The factors are coolant temperature, manifold absolute pressure, engine speed, manifold air temperature and throttle position.

Base ignition timing is not adjustable. The controller opens and closes the ignition coil ground circuit to adjust ignition timing for changing engine operating conditions.

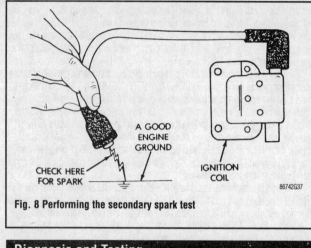

Fig. 8 Performing the secondary spark test

Diagnosis and Testing

SECONDARY SPARK TEST

▶ See Figure 8

Since the only change between electronic and conventional ignition systems is in the distributor component area, it is imperative to check the secondary ignition circuit first. If the secondary circuit checks out properly, then the engine condition is probably not the fault of the ignition system. To check the secondary ignition system, perform a simple spark test.

1. Remove one of the plug wires and insert some sort of extension in the plug socket. An old spark plug with the ground electrode removed makes a good extension.

2. Hold the wire and extension about 1/4 in. (6mm) away from the block and crank the engine. If a normal spark occurs, then the problem is most likely not in the ignition system. Check for fuel system problems, or fouled spark plugs.

VACUUM ADVANCE

➡This is used on carbureted models only

1. Bring the engine to operating temperature.
2. Disconnect the three-wire connector to the vacuum input switches, and disconnect and plug the vacuum hose from the distributor vacuum advance.
3. Connect a vacuum pump (available through local tool distributors) to the vacuum advance unit.
4. Connect a timing light to the No. 1 spark plug wire, and a tachometer to the negative terminal on the coil.
5. Start engine and increase engine speed.
6. While observing the timing degree scale with a timing light, apply vacuum to the distributor vacuum advance unit. If timing advances, the unit is func-

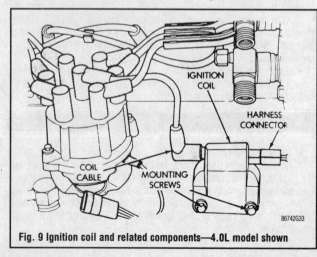

Fig. 9 Ignition coil and related components—4.0L model shown

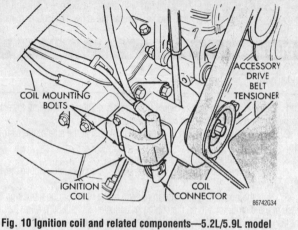

Fig. 10 Ignition coil and related components—5.2L/5.9L model shown

tioning properly. If timing does not advance, replace the vacuum advance unit.

7. Stop engine, remove all test equipment, replace the three-wire connector and vacuum advance hose.

CENTRIFUGAL ADVANCE

➡This is used on carbureted models only

1. Bring the engine to operating temperature.
2. Disconnect the three-wire connector to the vacuum input switches, and disconnect and plug the vacuum hose from the distributor vacuum advance.
3. Connect a timing light to the No. 1 spark plug wire.
4. With the engine idling, slowly increase the speed and observe the timing mark. Timing should advance smoothly as engine speed increases. If timing advances unevenly, check and repair the centrifugal advance unit.
5. Stop engine, remove all test equipment, replace the three-wire connector and vacuum advance hose.

Ignition Coil

TESTING

▶ See Figures 9 and 10

The ignition coil is designed to operate without an external ballast resistor. Inspect the coil for arcing. Test the coil primary and secondary resistance.

Measure the primary resistance as follows:

1. Connect an ohmmeter between the positive (+) and negative (-) terminals (the terminals which are connected to the engine wiring harness) on the coil.

2. To test the secondary resistance, connect an ohmmeter between the positive (+) coil terminal and the high voltage cable terminal on the coil, then measure the resistance between the positive (+) coil terminal and the coil case; the resistance for the case should exhibit infinite resistance.

3. For coils manufactured by Diamond, the primary resistance at 70–80°F

Fig. 11 Disconnect the coil wire from the ignition coil tower

Fig. 12 Disconnect the wiring harness from the side of the ignition coil

Fig. 13 Remove the left ignition coil bracket mounting stud and wiring harness retaining loop nut

Fig. 14 After removing the wiring harness nut, remove the ignition coil mounting bracket stud . . .

Fig. 15 . . . then remove the assembly from the vehicle

Fig. 16 After removing the ignition coil assembly, the coil can be separated from the bracket

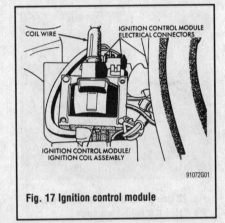

Fig. 17 Ignition control module

(21–27°C) should be 0.97–1.18 ohms and the secondary resistance should be 11,300–15,300 ohms.

4. Coils built by the Toyodenso company should exhibit a primary resistance at 70–80°F (21–27°C) of 0.95–1.20 ohms and a secondary resistance of 11,300–13,300 ohms.

5. Replace any coil with a new one if it does not meet the specifications.

REMOVAL & INSTALLATION

▶ See Figures 11 thru 16

1. Make sure that the ignition switch is in the OFF position.
2. Disengage the negative battery cable.
3. Tag (if necessary) and disengage all electrical connections from the ignition coil.
4. Remove the fasteners holding the coil and bracket assembly (if equipped) to the engine and lift out the coil. The coil may be riveted to the bracket, to remove it will require drilling the rivets and punching them out. If necessary, separate the coil from the bracket.

To install:

5. Install the coil onto the mounting bracket and tighten the retainers to 50 inch. lbs. (6 Nm).
6. Position the coil on the engine and tighten the nuts.
7. Engage the coil wire and electrical connector(s).
8. Connect the negative battery cable.

Ignition Control Module

▶ See Figure 17

1991 and later Jeep vehicles are not equipped with an ignition control module. However, the functions of the ignition control module are performed by the Electronic Control Unit (ECU), also known as the Powertrain Control Module (PCM).

The ignition control module on all Jeep models, except 1991 and later vehicles, is mounted together with the ignition coil. It is removed from the vehicle using the same procedure as the ignition coil removal and installation, but can be serviced separately.

Distributor

REMOVAL

2.5L and 4.0L Engines

▶ See Figures 18 thru 24

1. Disconnect the negative battery cable.
2. Tag and disconnect the spark plug wires from the distributor cap and coil
3. Remove the distributor cap retaining hooks or screws and remove the

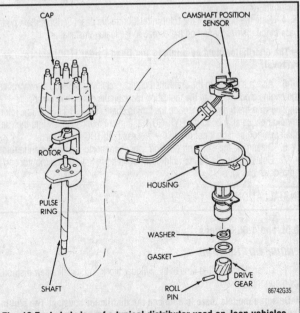

Fig. 18 Exploded view of a typical distributor used on Jeep vehicles

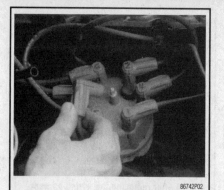

Fig. 19 Tag and disconnect the spark plug wires

Fig. 20 Tag and disengage any distributor electrical connections

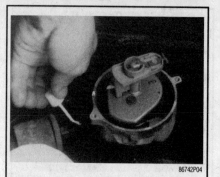

Fig. 21 Scribe a mark on the base of the distributor and on the engine to facilitate reinstallation

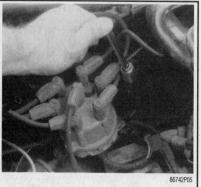

Fig. 22 Using a distributor wrench, loosen the distributor hold-down bolt

Fig. 23 Remove the distributor hold-down bolt and clamp

Fig. 24 Remove the distributor from the vehicle

distributor cap.

4. Note the position of the rotor in relation to the base. Scribe a mark on the base of the distributor and on the engine to facilitate reinstallation. Align the marks with the direction the metal tip of the rotor is pointing.

5. Remove the bolt that holds the distributor to the engine.

6. Lift the distributor assembly from the engine.

5.2L and 5.9L Engines

1. Disconnect the negative battery cable.

2. Tag and disconnect the spark plug wires from the distributor cap and coil

3. Remove the distributor cap retaining hooks or screws and remove the distributor cap.

4. Note the position of the rotor in relation to the base. Scribe a mark on the base of the distributor and on the engine to facilitate reinstallation.

➡**The distributor must be bright to Top Dead Center (TDC) before removal.**

5. Attach a socket to the crankshaft damper retaining bolt and slowly rotate the engine clockwise until the indicating mark on the crankshaft damper is aligned with the 0 degree mark on the timing chain cover. The distributor rotor should now be aligned to the CYL. NO 1 alignment mark stamped into the camshaft position sensor. If not repeat the process until TDC is achieved.

6. Disengage the camshaft position sensor connector and remove the rotor.

7. Unfasten the distributor hold-down bolt and remove the distributor and hold-down clamp.

INSTALLATION

2.5L and 4.0L Engines

ENGINE NOT ROTATED

1. Clean the mounting area of the cylinder block and install a new distributor mounting gasket.

➡**On some models there is a fork on the distributor housing. The slot in the fork aligns with the distributor hold-down bolt hole in the engine**

block. The distributor is correctly installed when the rotor is correctly positioned and the slot is aligned with the hold-down bolt hole. On these computer controlled distributors, initial ignition timing is not adjustable.

2. Align the rotor tip with the scribe mark on the distributor housing during removal, then turn the rotor approximately 1/8 turn counterclockwise past the scribe mark.

3. Slide the distributor shaft down into the engine. It may be necessary to move the rotor and shaft slightly to engage the distributor shaft with the oil pump slot. Align the scribe mark on the distributor housing with the mark on the cylinder block.

➡**Ensure that the distributor is fully seated against the cylinder block. It may be necessary to slightly rotate (bump) the engine while applying light downward force to fully engage the distributor shaft with the oil pump drive gear shaft.**

4. Install the distributor shaft hold-down and bolt. Tighten the bolt to 17 ft. lbs. (23 Nm).

5. Install distributor cap and ignition wires. Insure that the wires are routed correctly before attempting to start engine.

ENGINE ROTATED

1. Remove the No. 1 cylinder spark plug. Turn the engine using a socket wrench on the large bolt on the front of the crankshaft pulley. Place a finger near the No. 1 spark plug hole and turn the crankshaft until the piston reaches Top Dead Center (TDC). As the engine approaches TDC, you will feel air being expelled by the No. 1 cylinder. If the position is not being met, turn the engine another full turn (360 degree). Once the engine's position is correct, install the spark plug.

2. Using a flat-bladed screwdriver, in the distributor hole, rotate the oil pump gear so that the slot in the oil pump shaft is in the correct position.

3. With the distributor cap removed, install the distributor so that the rotor is positioned correctly. Insure that the distributor is fully seated against the cylinder block. If not, remove the distributor and perform the entire procedure again.

4. Tighten the hold-down bolt to 17 ft. lbs. (23 Nm).

5. Install distributor cap and ignition wires. Insure that the wires are routed correctly before attempting to start engine.

5.2L and 5.9L Engines

ENGINE NOT ROTATED

1. Clean the mounting area of the cylinder block and install a new distributor mounting gasket.
2. Lightly oil the O-ring seal on the distributor housing and install the rotor.
3. Slide the distributor shaft down into the engine. It may be necessary to move the rotor and shaft slightly to engage the distributor shaft with the oil pump slot. Ensure the rotor is aligned with the CYL. NO. 1 alignment mark on the camshaft position sensor.

➡Ensure that the distributor is fully seated against the cylinder block. It may be necessary to slightly rotate (bump) the engine while applying light downward force to fully engage the distributor shaft with the oil pump drive gear shaft.

4. Install the distributor shaft hold-down and bolt. Tighten the bolt to 200 inch. lbs. (22.5 Nm)
5. Install distributor cap and engage all electrical wires and connections. Insure that the wires are routed correctly before attempting to start the vehicle.

ENGINE ROTATED

1. Remove the No. 1 cylinder spark plug. Turn the engine using a socket wrench on the large bolt on the front of the crankshaft pulley. Place a finger near the No. 1 spark plug hole and turn the crankshaft until the piston reaches Top Dead Center (TDC). As the engine approaches TDC, you will feel air being expelled by the No. 1 cylinder. If the position is not being met, turn the engine another full turn (360 degree). Once the engine's position is correct, install the spark plug.

2. Using a flat-bladed screwdriver, in the distributor hole, rotate the oil pump gear so that the slot in the oil pump shaft is in the correct position.
3. Clean the mounting area of the cylinder block and install a new distributor mounting gasket.
4. Lightly oil the O-ring seal on the distributor housing and install the rotor.
5. Slide the distributor shaft down into the engine. It may be necessary to move the rotor and shaft slightly to engage the distributor shaft with the oil pump slot. Ensure the rotor is aligned with the CYL. NO. 1 alignment mark on the camshaft position sensor.

➡Ensure that the distributor is fully seated against the cylinder block. It may be necessary to slightly rotate (bump) the engine while applying light downward force to fully engage the distributor shaft with the oil pump drive gear shaft.

6. Install the distributor shaft hold-down and bolt. Tighten the bolt to 200 inch. lbs. (22.5 Nm)
7. Install distributor cap and engage all electrical wires and connections. Insure that the wires are routed correctly before attempting to start the vehicle.

Crankshaft and Camshaft Position Sensors

Refer to Section 4 under Electronic Engine Controls for removal, installation and testing of these sensors.

FIRING ORDERS

▶ **See Figures 25 thru 30**

➡To avoid confusion, tag and remove the spark plug wires one at a time, for replacement.

If a distributor is not keyed for installation with only one orientation, it could have been removed previously and rewired. The resultant wiring would hold the

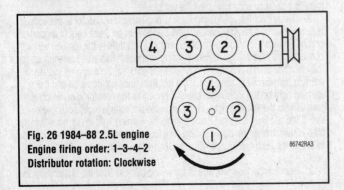

Fig. 25 The firing order can usually be found cast onto the intake manifold

Fig. 26 1984–88 2.5L engine
Engine firing order: 1–3–4–2
Distributor rotation: Clockwise

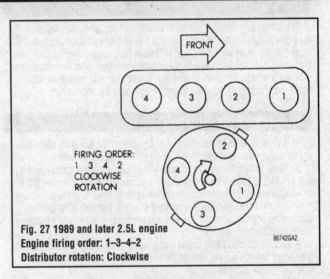

Fig. 27 1989 and later 2.5L engine
Engine firing order: 1–3–4–2
Distributor rotation: Clockwise

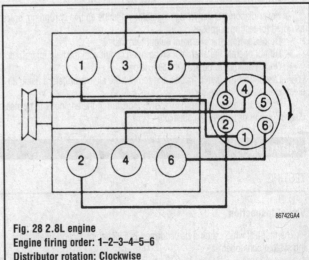

Fig. 28 2.8L engine
Engine firing order: 1–2–3–4–5–6
Distributor rotation: Clockwise

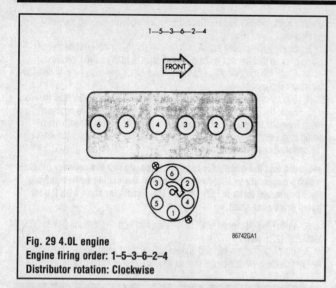

Fig. 29 4.0L engine
Engine firing order: 1–5–3–6–2–4
Distributor rotation: Clockwise

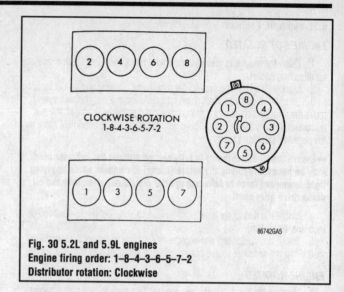

Fig. 30 5.2L and 5.9L engines
Engine firing order: 1–8–4–3–6–5–7–2
Distributor rotation: Clockwise

correct firing order, but could change the relative placement of the plug towers in relation to the engine. For this reason it is imperative that you label all wires before disconnecting any of them. Also, before removal, compare the current

wiring with the accompanying illustrations. If the current wiring does not match, make notes in your book to reflect how your engine is wired.

CHARGING SYSTEM

General Information

The automobile charging system provides electrical power for operation of the vehicle's ignition and starting systems and all the electrical accessories. The battery serves as an electrical surge or storage tank, storing (in chemical form) the energy originally produced by the engine driven generator. The system also provides a means of regulating generator output to protect the battery from being overcharged and to avoid excessive voltage to the accessories.

Alternator Precautions

To prevent damage to the alternator and regulator, the following precautionary measures must be taken when working with the electrical system.

• Never reverse the battery connections. Always check the battery polarity visually. This is to be done before any connections are made to ensure that all of the connections correspond to the battery ground polarity of the car

• Booster batteries must be connected properly. Make sure the positive cable of the booster battery is connected to the positive terminal of the battery which is getting the boost

• Disconnect the battery cables before using a fast charger; the charger has a tendency to force current through the diodes in the opposite direction for which they were designed.

• Never use a fast charger as a booster for starting the vehicle

• Never disconnect the voltage regulator while the engine is running, unless as noted for testing purposes.

• Do not ground the alternator output terminal

• Do not operate the alternator on an open circuit with the field energized

• Do not attempt to polarize the alternator

• Disconnect the battery cables and remove the alternator before using an electric arc welder on the car

• Protect the alternator from excessive moisture. If the engine is to be steam cleaned, cover or remove the alternator

Alternator

TESTING

Visual Inspection

The first test which should be performed is a visual inspection of all charging system components.

1. Inspect the condition of the battery cable terminals, battery posts, connections at the engine block, starter motor solenoid and relay. All connections should be clean and tight. All wire casings should be intact. If corrosion is evident, it can be easily cleaned by using a paste made from a mixture of baking soda and water.

2. Inspect all fuses in the fuse block for tightness in their receptacles. Replace any loose or blown fuses.

3. Check the electrolyte level in the battery. This can be done using a hydrometer. Add water to the battery and recharge if necessary.

4. Inspect alternator mounting bolts for tightness. Bolts should be torqued to 23–30 ft. lbs. (31–40 Nm).

5. Inspect the alternator drive belt condition and tension. Adjust and/or replace as necessary. Drive belt should be torqued to 140–160 ft. lbs.. if used, and 180–200 ft. lbs.. if new.

6. Inspect the connection at the alternator BAT terminal (usually located on the back side of the alternator). This is the alternator output to the battery. Assure that it rnator). This is the alternator output to the battery. Assure that it is clean and tight.

Electrical Test

After the visual inspection is complete, perform the following alternator and battery tests until the problem is found.

1. Turn off all electrical components on the vehicle. Make sure the doors of the car are closed. If the vehicle is equipped with a clock, disconnect the clock by removing the lead wire from the rear of the clock. Disconnect the positive battery cable from the battery and connect the ground wire on a test light to the disconnected positive battery cable. Touch the probe end of the test light to the positive battery post. The test light should not light. If the test light does light, there is a short or open circuit on the vehicle.

2. Disconnect the voltage regulator wiring harness connector at the voltage regulator. Turn on the ignition key. Connect the wire on a test light to a good ground (engine bolt). Touch the probe end of a test light to the ignition wire connector into the voltage regulator wiring connector. This wire corresponds to the I terminal on the regulator. If the test light goes on, the charging system warning light circuit is complete. If the test light does not come on and the warning light on the instrument panel is on, either the resistor wire, which is parallel with the warning light, or the wiring to the voltage regulator, is defective. If the test light does not come on and the warning light is not on, either the bulb is defective or the power supply wire from the battery through the ignition switch to the bulb has an open circuit. Connect the wiring harness to the regulator.

3. Examine the fuse link wire in the wiring harness from the starter relay to

the alternator. If the insulation on the wire is cracked or split, the fuse link may be melted. Connect a test light to the fuse link by attaching the ground wire on the test light to an engine bolt and touching the probe end of the light to the bottom of the fuse link wire where it splices into the alternator output wire. If the bulb in the test light does not light, the fuse link is melted.

4. Start the engine and place a current indicator on the positive battery cable. Turn off all electrical accessories and make sure the doors are closed. If the charging system is working properly, the gauge will show a draw of less than 5 amps. If the system is not working properly, the gauge will show a draw of more than 5 amps. A charge moves the needle toward the battery, a draw moves the needle away from the battery. Turn the engine **OFF**.

➡ **In order for the current indicator to give a valid reading, the car must be equipped with battery cables which are of the same gauge size and quality as original equipment battery cables.**

5. Disconnect the wiring harness from the voltage regulator at the regulator. Connect a male spade terminal (solderless connector) to each end of a jumper wire. Insert one end of the wire into the wiring harness connector which corresponds to the A terminal on the regulator. Insert the other end of the wire into the wiring harness connector which corresponds to the F terminal on the regulator. Position the connector with the jumper wire installed so that it cannot contact any metal surface under the hood. Position a current indicator gauge on the positive battery cable. Have an assistant start the engine. Observe the reading on the current indicator. Have your assistant slowly raise the speed of the engine to about 2000 rpm or until the current indicator needle stops moving, whichever comes first. Do not run the engine for more than a short period of time in this condition. If the wiring harness connector or jumper wire becomes excessively hot during this test turn off the engine and check for a grounded wire in the regulator wiring harness. If the current indicator shows a charge of about three amps less than the output of the alternator, the alternator is working properly. If the previous tests showed a draw, the voltage regulator is defective. If the gauge does not show the proper charging rate, the alternator is defective.

Once the determination is made that the alternator is at fault, off vehicle testing can be used to determine the defective component inside the alternator.

REMOVAL & INSTALLATION

◆ **See Figures 31 thru 41**

1. Disconnect the negative battery cable.
2. Remove the drive belt.
3. If necessary, remove any splash shielding for easier access to the alternator.
4. Tag and disengage the alternator wiring.

➡ **It may be necessary to remove the alternator and mounting bracket from the vehicle as an assembly.**

5. If equipped, remove the front alternator assembly mounting plate.
6. Unfasten the alternator mounting and pivot bolts and remove the alternator.
7. If installing the original alternator assembly, push out the pivot bushing as illustrated.
   To install:
8. Mount the alternator to the brackets with the nuts and bolts. Tighten the two mounting bolts and nuts to 40 ft. lbs. (54 Nm).
9. If the alternator and mounting bracket were removed as an assembly, install the assembly into the vehicle.
10. If removed, install the front mounting plate.
11. Engage the alternator electrical connections.
12. If removed, install the splash shield.
13. Install the drive belt and attach the negative battery cable.

Regulator

Regulators used with Jeep alternators are transistorized (they are either internally mounted in the alternator or the ECU/PCM) and cannot be serviced. If one of these units proves defective, the alternator or ECU/PCM must be replaced.

Fig. 31 For easiest access to the alternator assembly, first remove the splash shield mounting fasteners . . .

Fig. 32 . . . then swing it out of the way for access to the alternator assembly

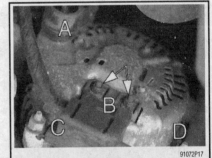

Fig. 33 View of the alternator electrical connections—(A) battery positive, (B) field terminals, (C) wire harness hold down, (D) ground terminal

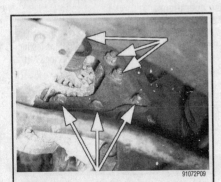

Fig. 34 Remove the six nuts and bolts that secure the front mounting plate to the alternator assembly

Fig. 35 Remove the front alternator assembly mounting plate from below the vehicle

Fig. 36 After removing the alternator assembly front mounting plate, remove the front engine-to-alternator bracket mounting stud

Fig. 37 Remove the two alternator bracket-to-engine mounting bolts

Fig. 38 Remove the alternator and mounting bracket assembly from the vehicle

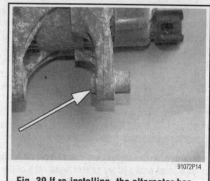

Fig. 39 If re-installing, the alternator has a pivot bushing on the pivot arm that should be pushed out before installation

Fig. 40 Mount a C-clamp and 18mm socket on the alternator pivot bushing . . .

Fig. 41 . . . then compress the C-clamp until it pushes the alternator pivot bushing out

STARTING SYSTEM

General Information

The starting system consists of an ignition switch, starter relay, neutral safety switch, wiring harness, battery, and a starter motor with an integral solenoid. These components form two separate circuits: a high amperage circuit that feeds the starter motor up to 300 or more amps, and a control circuit that operates on less than 20 amps.

Starter

TESTING

Testing Preparation

Before commencing with the starting system diagnostics, verify:
- The battery top posts, and terminals are clean.
- The alternator drive belt tension and condition is correct.
- The battery state-of-charge is correct.
- The battery cable connections at the starter and engine block are clean and free from corrosion.
- The wiring harness connectors and terminals are clean and free from corrosion.
- Proper circuit grounding.

Starter Feed Circuit

❊❊ CAUTION

The ignition system must be disabled to prevent engine start while performing the following tests.

1. Connect a volt-ampere tester (multimeter) to the battery terminals.
2. Disable the ignition system.
3. Verify that all lights and accessories are Off, and the transaxle shift selector is in Park (automatic) or Neutral (manual). Set the parking brake.
4. Rotate and hold the ignition switch in the **START** position. Observe the volt-ampere tester:
- If the voltage reads above 9.6 volts, and the amperage draw reads above 250 amps, go to the starter feed circuit resistance test (following this test).
- If the voltage reads 12.4 volts or greater and the amperage reads 0–10 amps, refer to the starter solenoid and relay tests.

❊❊ WARNING

Do not overheat the starter motor or draw the battery voltage below 9.6 volts during cranking operations.

5. After the starting system problems have been corrected, verify the battery state of charge and charge the battery if necessary. Disconnect all of the testing equipment and connect the ignition coil cable or ignition coil connector. Start the vehicle several times to assure the problem was corrected.

Starter Feed Circuit Resistance

Before proceeding with this test, refer to the battery tests and starter feed circuit test. The following test will require a voltmeter, which is capable of accuracy to 0.1 volt.

❊❊ CAUTION

The ignition system must be disabled to prevent engine start while performing the following tests.

1. Disable the ignition system.
2. With all wiring harnesses and components (except for the coils) properly connected, perform the following:

a. Connect the negative (-) lead of the voltmeter to the negative battery post, and the positive (+) lead to the negative (-) battery cable clamp. Rotate and hold the ignition switch in the **START** position. Observe the voltmeter. If the voltage is detected, correct the poor contact between the cable clamp and post.

b. Connect the positive (+) lead of the voltmeter to the positive battery post, and the negative (-) to the positive battery cable clamp. Rotate and hold the ignition switch key in the **START** position. Observe the voltmeter. If voltage is detected, correct the poor contact between the cable clamp and post.

c. Connect the negative lead of the voltmeter to the negative (-) battery terminal, and positive lead to the engine block near the battery cable attaching point. Rotate and hold the ignition switch in the **START** position. If the voltage reads above 0.2 volt, correct the poor contact at ground cable attaching point. If the voltage reading is still above 0.2 volt after correcting the poor contact, replace the negative ground cable with a new one.

3. Remove the heater shield. Refer to removal and installation procedures to gain access to the starter motor and solenoid connections. Perform the following steps:

a. Connect the positive (+) voltmeter lead to the starter motor housing and the negative (-) lead to the negative battery terminal. Hold the ignition switch key in the **START** position. If the voltage reads above 0.2 volt, correct the poor starter to engine ground.

b. Connect the positive (+) voltmeter lead to the positive battery terminal, and the negative lead to the battery cable terminal on the starter solenoid. Rotate and hold the ignition key in the **START** position. If the voltage reads above 0.2 volt, correct poor contact at the battery cable to the solenoid connection. If the reading is still above 0.2 volt after correcting the poor contacts, replace the positive battery cable with a new one.

c. If the resistance tests did not detect feed circuit failures, refer to the starter solenoid test.

Starter Solenoid

ON VEHICLE

1. Before testing, assure the parking brake is set, the transmission is in Park (automatic) or Neutral (manual), and the battery is fully charged and in good condition.
2. Connect a voltmeter from the (S) terminal on the solenoid to ground. Turn the ignition switch to the **START** position and test for battery voltage. If battery voltage is not found, inspect the ignition switch circuit. If battery voltage is found, proceed to next step.
3. Connect an ohmmeter between the battery negative post and the starter solenoid mounting plate (manual) or the ground terminal (automatic). Turn the ignition switch to the **START** position. The ohmmeter should read zero (0). If not, repair the faulty ground.
4. If both tests are performed and the solenoid still does not energize, replace the solenoid.

BENCH TEST

▶ **See Figures 42 and 43**

1. Remove the starter from the vehicle.
2. Disconnect the field coil wire from the field coil terminal.
3. Check for continuity between the solenoid terminal and field coil terminal with a continuity tester. Continuity (resistance) should be present.
4. Check for continuity between the solenoid terminal and solenoid housing. Continuity should be detected. If continuity is detected, the solenoid is good.
5. If continuity is not detected in either test, the solenoid has an open circuit and is defective and must be replaced.

Starter/Ground Cable Test

When performing these tests, it is important that the voltmeter be connected to the terminals, not the cables themselves.

Before testing, assure that the ignition control module (if equipped) is disconnected, the parking brake is set, the transmission is in Park (automatic) or Neutral (manual), and the battery is fully charged and in good condition.

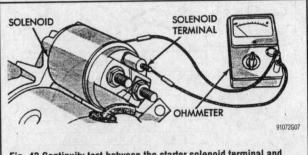

Fig. 42 Continuity test between the starter solenoid and field coil terminals

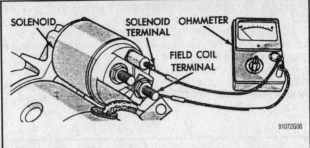

Fig. 43 Continuity test between the starter solenoid terminal and solenoid housing

1. Check voltage between the positive battery post and the center of the B + terminal on the starter solenoid stud.
2. Check voltage between the negative battery post and the engine block.
3. Disconnect the ignition coil wire from the distributor cap and connect a suitable jumper wire between the coil cable and a good body ground.
4. Have an assistant crank the engine and measure voltage again. Voltage drop should not exceed 0.5 volts.
5. If voltage drop is greater than 0.5 volts, clean metal surfaces. Apply a thick layer of silicone grease. Install a new cadmium plated bolt and star washer on the battery terminal and a new brass nut on the starter solenoid. Retest and replace cable not within specifications.

Starter Relay

1984–90 VEHICLES

▶ **See Figure 44**

1. Insure that the transmission is in Park (automatic) or Neutral (manual) and that the parking brake is applied.
2. Turn the ignition switch to the **START** position and listen for the starter

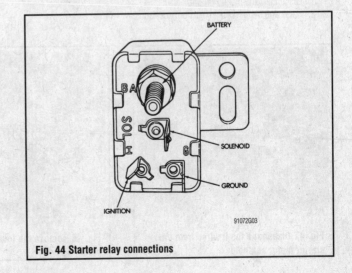

Fig. 44 Starter relay connections

relay to click. If a click is heard, the relay functioning correctly. If not, go to next step.

3. Connect a jumper wire from pin G on the relay to ground. Turn the ignition switch to **START** and listen for a click. If a click is heard, repair the short to ground. If not, go to next step.

4. With starter solenoid terminal (S) disconnected (prevent terminal from touching metal parts), test for battery voltage. If battery voltage is found, replace the relay. If battery voltage is not found, repair the short to the relay terminal (SOL).

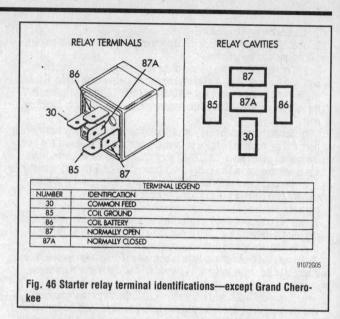

TERMINAL LEGEND	
NUMBER	IDENTIFICATION
30	COMMON FEED
85	COIL GROUND
86	COIL BATTERY
87	NORMALLY OPEN
87A	NORMALLY CLOSED

Fig. 46 Starter relay terminal identifications—except Grand Cherokee

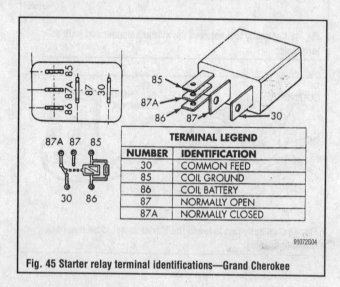

TERMINAL LEGEND	
NUMBER	IDENTIFICATION
30	COMMON FEED
85	COIL GROUND
86	COIL BATTERY
87	NORMALLY OPEN
87A	NORMALLY CLOSED

Fig. 45 Starter relay terminal identifications—Grand Cherokee

1991 AND LATER VEHICLES

♦ See Figures 45 and 46

1. Remove the relay from the power distribution center, located near the coolant overflow tank in the engine compartment.
2. Check continuity between terminals 87A and 30. If an open circuit is found, replace the relay.
3. Check resistance between terminals 85 and 86. If resistance is not 70–80 ohms, replace the relay.
4. Check continuity between terminals 30 and 87 with a battery connected between terminals 85 and 86. If an open circuit is found, replace the relay.

REMOVAL & INSTALLATION

Except 2.1L Diesel

♦ See Figures 47 thru 53

1. Disconnect the battery ground.
2. Raise and support the vehicle on jackstands.

3. On 1989–91 models equipped with a 2.5L engine, it is necessary to remove the exhaust clamp and bracket, and the transmission brace rod before removing the starter.
4. Remove all wires from the starter and tag them for installation.

➡It may be easier to remove the solenoid wires after lowering the starter. Support the starter before removing the wires. DO NOT LET THE STARTER HANG BY THE WIRES.

5. On 4.0L, 5.2L and 5.9L engines, it may be necessary to remove the oil cooler line bracket and the exhaust brace.
6. Remove all but one attaching bolt, support the starter (it's heavier than it looks) and remove the last bolt.
7. Lower the starter from the engine.
8. If installing the original starter, inspect the pinion gear for damage or excessive wear.
9. Inspect the flywheel gear teeth for damage through the starter mounting hole.

To install:

10. Install the starter in the engine and hand-tighten the retaining bolts.
11. Engage any electrical connections that were removed from the starter.
12. Tighten the retaining bolts and engage any cooler lines, braces and brackets that were removed. Lower the vehicle.
13. Connect the negative battery cable and check for proper starter operation.

2.1L Diesel

♦ See Figures 52 and 53

1. Disconnect the battery ground.
2. Remove all wires from the starter and tag them for installation.

Fig. 47 Disengage the 2 wires from the starter motor solenoid

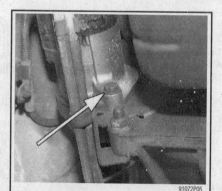

Fig. 48 Remove the lower starter motor mounting bolt

Fig. 49 Remove the upper starter motor mounting bolt located behind the starter

Fig. 50 Removing the starter motor from below the vehicle

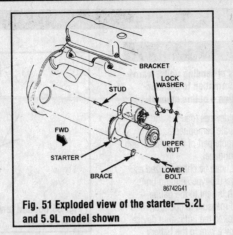

Fig. 51 Exploded view of the starter—5.2L and 5.9L model shown

Fig. 52 If installing the original starter, inspect the pinion gear of the motor for damage to the teeth

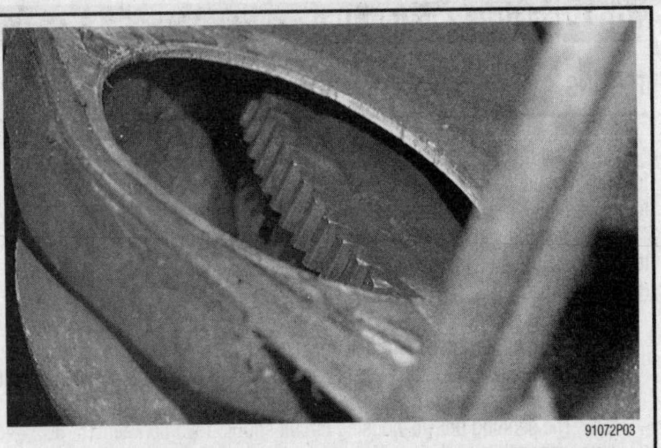

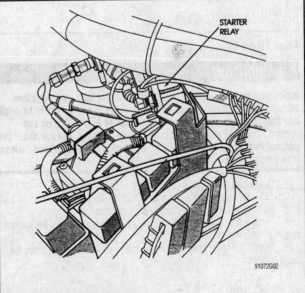

Fig. 53 Inspect the flywheel gear teeth for any damage after removing the starter motor

3. Raise and support the vehicle on jackstands.

4. Remove the starter upper bracket.

5. Take up the weight of the engine with a floor jack and remove the left side engine mount.

6. Remove the starter lower support bracket.

7. Support the starter (it's heavier than it looks) and remove the attaching bolts. Remove the starter.

8. If installing the original starter, inspect the pinion gear for damage or excessive wear.

9. Inspect the flywheel gear teeth for damage through the starter mounting hole.

To install:

10. Install the starter and HAND-TIGHTEN ONLY, the attaching bolts. Insure locating dowel is properly seated in hole.

11. Install the upper and lower support bracket, hand tighten only.

12. Tighten the starter attaching bolts to 37 ft. lbs. (50 Nm). Tighten the upper bracket bolts to 37 ft. lbs. (50 Nm), and then the lower bracket bolts to 37 ft. lbs. (50 Nm).

13. Install the engine mount. Tighten the engine mount-to-block bolt to 40 ft. lbs. (54 Nm), the engine mount-to-frame bolt to 48 ft. lbs. (65 Nm), the engine mount-to-bell housing bolt to 35 ft. lbs. (47 Nm).

14. Connect all wires and lower the vehicle.

Starter Solenoid

REMOVAL & INSTALLATION

Remotely Mounted

1. Disconnect negative battery cable.

2. Label and remove all wires from the solenoid. Remove the solenoid mounting screws.

3. Installation is the reverse of removal. Assure mounting surface is clean to provide a good ground.

Starter Mounted

The starter solenoid is an integral component of the starter motor assembly and therefore, cannot be serviced separately. If the starter solenoid requires service, the entire starter motor assembly must be replaced.

Starter Relay

REMOVAL & INSTALLATION

1984–90 Models

▶ **See Figure 54**

1. Disconnect the negative battery cable.

2. Identify, tag and disconnect relay wires. Remove relay attaching screws.

3. Replace the relay and reconnect all wires.

4. Replace negative battery cable and test relay operation.

1991 and Later Models

1. Remove the relay from the power distribution center, located in the engine compartment.

2. Installation is the reverse of removal.

Fig. 54 Starter relay location

SENDING UNITS AND SENSORS

General Information

➡This section describes the operating principles of sending units, warning lights and gauges. Sensors which provide information to the Electronic Control Module (ECM) are covered in Section 4 of this manual.

Instrument panels contain a number of indicating devices (gauges and warning lights). These devices are composed of two separate components. One is the sending unit, mounted on the engine or other remote part of the vehicle, and the other is the actual gauge or light in the instrument panel.

Several types of sending units exist, however most can be characterized as being either a pressure type or a resistance type. Pressure type sending units convert liquid pressure into an electrical signal which is sent to the gauge. Resistance type sending units are most often used to measure temperature and use variable resistance to control the current flow back to the indicating device. Both types of sending units are connected in series by a wire to the battery (through the ignition switch). When the ignition is turned **ON**, current flows from the battery through the indicating device and on to the sending unit.

Coolant Temperature Sender

TESTING

Perform this test on a cold or cool engine.
1. Disconnect the negative (-) battery cable.
2. Unplug the electrical wiring from the sending unit.
3. Using an ohmmeter, measure the resistance between the terminal and the sending unit's metal body
    a. Infinite resistance or zero resistance: the sending unit is bad, replace the sender with a new one.
    b. Other than infinite or zero resistance: continue test.
4. Remove the temperature sender from the engine.
5. Position the sending unit so the metal shaft (opposite end from the electrical connectors) is in a pot of water. Make sure that the electrical connector is not submerged and only the tip of the sending unit's body is in the water.
6. Heat the pot of water at a medium rate. While the water is warming, continue to measure the resistance of the terminal and the metal body of the sending unit:
    a. As the water warms up, the resistance goes down in a steady manner: the sending unit is good.
    b. As the water warms up, the resistance does not change or changes in erratic jumps: the sender is bad, replace it with a new one.
7. Install the good or new sending unit into the engine, then connect the negative battery cable.

REMOVAL & INSTALLATION

▶ **See Figure 55**

❊❊ **CAUTION**

When draining the coolant, keep in mind that cats and dogs are attracted by ethylene glycol antifreeze, and are quite likely to drink any that is left in an uncovered container or in puddles on the ground. This will prove fatal in sufficient quantity. Always drain the coolant into a sealable container. Coolant should be reused unless it is contaminated or several years old.

1. Disconnect the negative battery cable.
2. Drain the cooling system to a level is below the sensor.
3. Detach the electrical connector from the sensor.
4. Remove the sensor from the engine. On some applications, the coolant sensor threads into the thermostat housing.
5. Installation is the reverse of the removal procedure. Fill and bleed the cooling system.

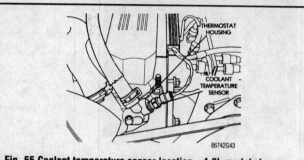

Fig. 55 Coolant temperature sensor location—4.0L model shown, others similar

Oil Pressure Sending Unit

TESTING

1. To test the normally closed oil lamp circuit, disengage the locking connector and measure the resistance between the switch terminal (terminal for the wire to the warning lamp) and the metal housing. The ohmmeter should read 0 ohms.
2. To test the sending unit, measure the resistance between the sending unit terminal and the metal housing. The ohmmeter should read an open circuit (infinite resistance).
3. Start the engine.
4. Once again, test each terminal against the metal housing:
    a. The oil switch terminal-to-housing circuit should read an open circuit if there is oil pressure present.
    b. The sending unit-to-housing circuit should read between 15–80 ohms, depending on the engine speed, oil temperature and oil viscosity.
5. To test the oil pressure sender only, rev the engine and watch the ohms reading, which should fluctuate slightly (within the range of 15–80 ohms) as rpm increases.
6. If the above results were not obtained, replace the sending unit/switch with a new one.

REMOVAL & INSTALLATION

▶ **See Figure 56**

1. Disconnect the negative battery cable from the battery.
2. Unplug the oil pressure sending unit wiring harness connector from the sending unit.
3. Unscrew the sending unit from the engine block.
To install:
4. Install and tighten the new sending unit.
5. Plug the electrical wiring harness into the sending unit.
6. Attach the negative battery cable.

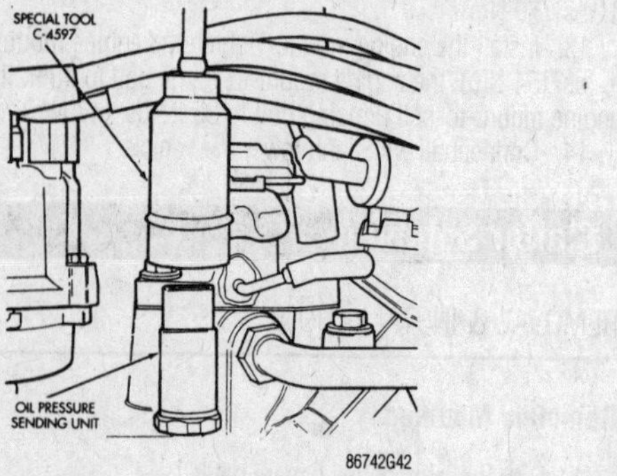

Fig. 56 View of the oil pressure sending unit removal

3

ENGINE AND ENGINE OVERHAUL

ENGINE MECHANICAL

Engine

REMOVAL & INSTALLATION

▶ **See Figure 1**

In the process of removing the engine, you will come across a number of steps which call for the removal of a separate component or system, such as "disconnect the exhaust system" or "remove the radiator." In most instances, a detailed removal procedure can be found elsewhere in this manual.

It is virtually impossible to list each individual wire and hose which must be disconnected, simply because so many different model and engine combinations have been manufactured. Careful observation and common sense are the best possible approaches to any repair procedure.

Removal and installation of the engine can be made easier if you follow these basic points:

• If you have to drain any of the fluids, use a suitable container.

• Always tag any wires or hoses and, if possible, the components they came from before disconnecting them.

• Because there are so many bolts and fasteners involved, store and label the retainers from components separately in muffin pans, jars or coffee cans. This will prevent confusion during installation.

• After unbolting the transmission or transaxle, always make sure it is properly supported.

• If it is necessary to disconnect the air conditioning system, have this service performed by a qualified technician using a recovery/recycling station. If the system does not have to be disconnected, unbolt the compressor and set it aside.

• When unbolting the engine mounts, always make sure the engine is properly supported. When removing the engine, make sure that any lifting devices are properly attached to the engine. It is recommended that if your engine is supplied with lifting hooks, your lifting apparatus be attached to them.

• Lift the engine from its compartment slowly, checking that no hoses, wires or other components are still connected.

• After the engine is clear of the compartment, place it on an engine stand or workbench.

• After the engine has been removed, you can perform a partial or full teardown of the engine using the procedures outlined in this manual.

1. Disconnect the battery cables (negative cable first) and remove the battery. Remove the hood.

❋❋ CAUTION

Observe all applicable safety precautions when working around fuel. Whenever servicing the fuel system, always work in a well ventilated area. Do not allow fuel spray or vapors to come in contact with a spark or open flame. Keep a dry chemical fire extinguisher near the work area. Always keep fuel in a container specifically designed for fuel storage; also, always properly seal fuel containers to avoid the possibility of fire or explosion.

2. On fuel injected engines only, relieve the fuel system pressure.
3. Remove the air cleaner assembly.

❋❋ CAUTION

Never open, service or drain the radiator or cooling system when hot; serious burns can occur from the steam and hot coolant. Also, when draining engine coolant, keep in mind that cats and dogs are attracted to ethylene glycol antifreeze and could drink any that is left in an uncovered container or in puddles on the ground. This will prove fatal in sufficient quantities. Always drain coolant into a sealable container. Coolant should be reused unless it is contaminated or is several years old.

4. Drain the coolant and engine oil.

➡**If your vehicle is equipped with air conditioning, refer to Section 1 for information regarding the implications of servicing your A/C system yourself. Only an MVAC-trained, EPA-certified, automotive technician should service the A/C system or its components.**

5. On models equipped with air conditioning, have the system discharged and evacuated by an MVAC, EPA-certified, automotive technician. Have the A/C compressor removed from the engine.

6. Remove the radiator assembly. If equipped with air conditioning, remove the condenser assembly.

7. Remove the engine cooling fan and install a 5/16 x 1/5 inch capscrew through the fan pulley into the water pump flange. This will maintain the pulley and water pump in alignment when the crankshaft is rotated.

8. Remove the heater hoses from the engine.

9. Tag and disconnect all hoses, wires, cables and linkages connected to the engine.

10. If necessary, remove the power brake vacuum check valve from the booster, if equipped.

11. If necessary, remove the distributor cap and wiring.

12. If necessary, remove the throttle body assembly.

13. If equipped with A/C, disconnect the hoses, then cap the compressor ports and hose openings.

14. Disconnect and plug the fuel lines at the fuel pump (diesel or carbureted engines) or at the fuel rail (on fuel injected engines).

15. If equipped, disconnect and drain the power steering hoses at the power steering pump or steering gear, whichever is the most convenient. Plug the hose openings to prevent system contamination.

16. If necessary, remove the power steering pump.

17. Raise and support the vehicle safely.

18. Remove the starter.

19. Remove the alternator.

20. Disconnect the exhaust pipe(s) from the manifold(s).

21. If necessary, remove the oil filter.

22. Remove the flywheel/converter housing access cover.

23. On vehicles equipped with an automatic transmission, matchmark the torque converter to the driveplate and remove the bolts.

24. If necessary, attach a C-clamp to the bottom of the torque converter housing to prevent the torque converter from coming out.

25. Remove the upper transmission housing-to-engine bolts and loosen the bottom bolts.

26. Lower the vehicle.

27. Attach a lifting device to the engine.

❋❋ WARNING

Do not lift the engine by the intake manifold.

28. Take up the weight of the engine with the lifting device.

29. Remove the engine mount bolts.

30. Raise the engine off the mounts.

31. Place a support jack under the transmission housing.

32. Remove the remaining engine-to-flywheel housing bolts.

33. On diesel models only, remove the reference pressure regulator from the dash panel.

34. Move the engine forward to clear the transmission, and carefully lift it out of the engine compartment.

35. Once the engine is removed from the vehicle, mount it on a suitable workstand.

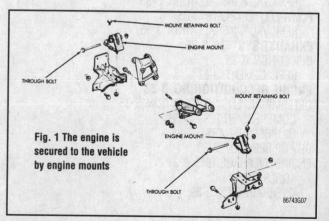

Fig. 1 The engine is secured to the vehicle by engine mounts

MOUNT RETAINING BOLT
ENGINE MOUNT
THROUGH BOLT
MOUNT RETAINING BOLT
ENGINE MOUNT
THROUGH BOLT

86743G07

36. If removed earlier, install the oil filter to keep foreign material out of the engine.

To install:

➡️**Lightly oil all bolts and stud threads, except those specifying special sealant, prior to installation.**

37. Using the hoist or engine crane, slowly and carefully position the engine in the vehicle. Make sure the exhaust manifolds are properly aligned with the exhaust pipes.

➡️**It may be easier to align the engine and transmission if you remove the engine mount cushions from the brackets.**

38. Align the engine to the transmission and install two engine-to-transmission bolts.

39. Install any engine mount cushions previously removed. Lower the engine onto the front engine mount cushions/insulators. Tighten the engine mount cushion nuts/bolts to the following values:
- All, except 5.2L/5.9L engines: 30 ft. lbs. (41 Nm)
- 5.2L/5.9L Engines: 65 ft. lbs. (88 Nm)

40. Detach the engine crane or hoist from the engine.

41. Remove the floor jack from beneath the transmission.

42. Tighten the two installed engine-to-transmission bolts, then raise and securely support the vehicle on jackstands.

43. Install and tighten the remaining engine-to-transmission bolts to the following values:
- 2.1L Engine: 30 ft. lbs. (41 Nm)
- 2.5L Engine: upper bolts—27 ft. lbs. (37 Nm), lower bolts—43 ft. lbs. (58 Nm)
- 2.8L Engine: 40 ft. lbs. (54 Nm)
- 4.0L Engine (Cherokee/Comanche): 40 ft. lbs. (54 Nm)
- 4.0L, 5.2L/5.9L Engines (Grand Cherokee): 30 ft. lbs. (41 Nm)

44. If equipped with automatic transmission, tighten the torque converter-to-drive plate bolts to the following values:
- 2.1L Engine: 40 ft. lbs. (54 Nm)
- 2.5L Engine: 40 ft. lbs. (54 Nm)
- 2.8L Engine: 25 ft. lbs. (34 Nm)
- 4.0L Engine (Cherokee/Comanche): 28 ft. lbs. (38 Nm)
- 4.0L, 5.2L/5.9L Engines (Grand Cherokee): 23 ft. lbs. (31 Nm)

45. Install and tighten the front engine mount through-bolts to the following values:
- 2.1L Engine: 48 ft. lbs. (65 Nm)
- 2.5L Engine: 48 ft. lbs. (65 Nm)
- 2.8L Engine: 92 ft. lbs. (125 Nm)
- 4.0L Engine (Cherokee/Comanche): 48 ft. lbs. (65 Nm)
- 4.0L Engine (Grand Cherokee): 89 ft. lbs. (121 Nm)
- 5.2L/5.9L Engines: 60 ft. lbs. (81 Nm)

46. The remainder of installation is the reverse of the removal procedure. Be sure to tighten the fasteners to the values presented in the torque specification chart. Torque specifications not found in this section can be found in other sections covering those specific components.

✳✳ WARNING

Do NOT start the engine without first filling it with the proper type and amount of clean engine oil, and installing a new oil filter. Oth-

erwise, severe engine damage will result.

47. Fill the crankcase with the proper type and quantity of engine oil. If necessary, adjust the transmission and/or throttle linkage.

48. Check to make sure that all electrical wiring harnesses, linkages, ground wires, hoses, vacuum and fuel lines have been properly connected.

49. Check to make sure that all components have been installed properly.

50. Check to make sure that all adjustments have been performed, as well as all fasteners tightened properly.

51. Install the air intake duct assembly.

52. Install the battery into the vehicle. Connect the positive battery cable first, then connect the negative battery cable.

53. Fill and bleed the cooling system.

54. Start the engine and allow it to reach normal operating temperature, then check for leaks and proper operation.

55. Stop the engine and check all fluid levels.

56. Install the hood, aligning the marks that were made during removal.

57. If equipped, have the A/C system properly leak-tested, evacuated and charged by a MVAC-trained, EPA-certified, automotive technician.

58. Road test the vehicle.

Rocker Arm (Valve) Cover

REMOVAL & INSTALLATION

2.1L Diesel Engine

1. Disconnect the negative battery cable

2. Disconnect vacuum and oil breather hoses that route over the rocker arm cover.

3. Remove the rocker arm cover retaining bolts. Remove the cover.

4. Remove the cover gasket, clean the mating surfaces and install the new gasket.

5. Install the retaining bolts and tighten them to 35 inch lbs. (4 Nm). Reconnect vacuum and oil breather hoses that were disconnected during removal.

2.5L Engine

▶ **See Figures 2 thru 7**

1. Remove the air cleaner and the PCV valve molded hose.

2. Disconnect the fuel line at the fuel pump and swivel to allow removal of the rocker arm cover (carbureted engines).

3. Disconnect or remove any vacuum or air hoses to provide access to the rocker arm cover.

➡️**To avoid damaging the rocker arm cover, DO NOT pry the cover upward until the RTV seal has been broken.**

4. Remove the rocker arm cover retaining bolts. Break the RTV seal by gently tapping the cover.

5. Thoroughly clean old sealer from head and cover. Examine rocker arm cover for cracks or bent rails.

To install:

6. Apply a 1/8 in. (3mm) bead of RTV sealant along the entire length of the

Fig. 2 Disconnect the PCV hose from the cover

Fig. 3 Unplug the fresh air hose from the valve cover

Fig. 4 Remove the bolts securing the cover to the head

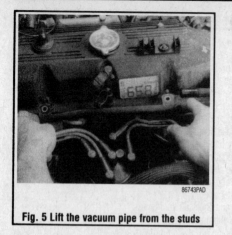

Fig. 5 Lift the vacuum pipe from the studs

Fig. 6 Remove the valve cover from the head

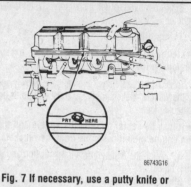

Fig. 7 If necessary, use a putty knife or razor blade to break the seal. Pry only where indicated

rocker arm cover rail. Allow the sealant to set-up for a few seconds.

7. While the sealant is still fluid, install the rocker arm cover on the cylinder head. Take care not to get any sealant on the rocker arms or valve train components.

8. Install rocker arm cover retaining bolts and tighten to 115 inch lbs. (13 Nm).

9. Reposition and connect all previously disconnected vacuum and air hoses. Install the PCV valve and hose. Install the air cleaner.

2.8L Engine

♦ See Figure 8

LEFT SIDE

1. Disconnect the battery cables.

2. Disconnect the hoses, wire connectors and pipe bracket Remove the spark plug wires and clips from the retaining stud.

3. Remove the rocker arm cover retaining bolts. Break the RTV seal by gently tapping the cover.

4. Thoroughly clean old sealer from head and cover. Examine rocker arm cover for cracks or bent rails.

To install:

5. Apply a 1/8 in. (3mm) bead of RTV sealant along the entire length of the rocker arm cover rail. Allow the sealant to set-up for a few seconds.

6. While the sealant is still fluid, install the rocker arm cover on the cylinder head. Take care not to get any sealant on the rocker arms or valve train components.

7. Install rocker arm cover retaining bolts and tighten to 8 ft. lbs. (11 Nm).

8. Connect all previously disconnected wires, hoses and brackets. Reconnect the battery cables.

RIGHT SIDE

1. Disconnect the battery cables.

2. Remove the air cleaner, air injection diverter and coil bracket.

3. Disconnect the air hose from the air injection manifold, wire connectors

and vacuum hoses.

4. Remove the spark plug wires and clip from the retaining stud.

5. Disconnect the carburetor controls and remove from the bracket.

6. Remove the rocker arm cover retaining bolts. Break the RTV seal by gently tapping on the cover.

7. Thoroughly clean old sealer from head and cover. Examine rocker arm cover for cracks or bent rails.

To install:

8. Apply a 1/8 in. (3mm) bead of RTV sealant along the entire length of the rocker arm cover rail. Allow the sealant to set-up for a few seconds.

9. While the sealant is still fluid, install the rocker arm cover on the cylinder head. Take care not to get any sealant on the rocker arms or valve train components.

10. Install rocker arm cover retaining bolts and tighten to 8 ft. lbs. (11 Nm).

11. Connect all previously disconnected wires, hoses and brackets. Reconnect the carburetor controls, air injection diverter valve and coil bracket. Install the air cleaner and reconnect the battery cables.

4.0L Engine

1. Remove the hoses and cruise control servo (if equipped).

2. Remove the rocker arm cover retaining bolts. Break the RTV seal by gently tapping on the cover.

3. Thoroughly clean old sealer from head and cover. Examine rocker arm cover for cracks or bent rails.

To install:

4. Apply a 1/8 in. (3mm) bead of RTV sealant along the entire length of the rocker arm cover rail. Allow the sealant to set-up for a few seconds.

5. While the sealant is still fluid, install the rocker arm cover on the cylinder head. Take care not to get any sealant on the rocker arms or valve train components.

6. Install rocker arm cover retaining bolts and tighten to 85 inch lbs. (10 Nm).

7. Install the PCV molded hoses and cruise control servo (if equipped).

5.2L and 5.9L Engines

1. Disconnect the negative battery cable.

2. Label and disconnect any and all necessary hoses from the cylinder head cover.

3. If removing the left cylinder head cover, remove the coolant tube bracket.

4. Remove the spark plug wires from the holders and disconnect them from the spark plugs.

5. Loosen the bolts, then remove the cylinder head cover and gasket. The steel backed silicon gasket can be used again if not damaged.

To install:

6. Install the cylinder head cover and gasket. On the left cover, install the coolant tube bracket. Tighten the cylinder head cover retaining bolts to 95 inch lbs. (11 Nm).

7. Connect the spark plug wires to the spark plugs and install the wires in the holders.

8. Connect all hoses that were disconnected during the removal procedure.

9. Connect the negative battery cable.

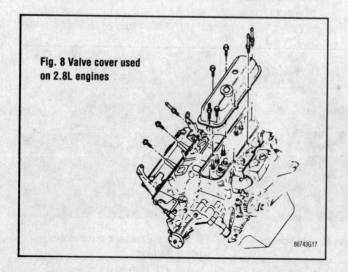

Fig. 8 Valve cover used on 2.8L engines

Fig. 9 Loosen and capscrews at each bridge and pivot assembly

Fig. 10 Remove the pivot assembly . . .

Fig. 11 . . . then the rocker arms

Rocker Arms/Shafts

REMOVAL & INSTALLATION

2.1L Diesel Engine

1. Disconnect the negative battery cable. Remove the rocker arm cover and gasket.
2. Remove the rocker shaft retaining bolts. Remove the rocker arm shaft assembly from the vehicle.
3. Installation is the reverse of the removal procedure. Be sure to use new gaskets and adjust the valves as required. Tighten the bolts to 20 ft. lbs. (27 Nm).

2.5L and 4.0L Engines

▶ **See Figures 9, 10 and 11**

1. Remove the rocker arm cover.
2. Remove the two capscrews at each bridge and pivot assembly. Alternately loosen the bolts one turn at a time to avoid damaging the bridges.
3. Remove the bridges, pivots and rocker arms. Keep them in order.
4. While the rocker arm is removed, inspect the pivot surface area. Replace any rocker arms that are scuffed, pitted or excessively worn.
5. Inspect the valve stem tip contact surface. Replace any rocker arm that is pitted or excessively worn.
6. Installation is the reverse of removal. Loosely install the capscrews then alternately tighten to 19 ft. lbs. (26 Nm).
7. Install the rocker arm cover.

2.8L Engines

▶ **See Figure 12**

1. Remove the rocker arm cover.
2. Remove the rocker arm hold-down nuts, pivots and rocker arms. Keep them in order.
   To install:
3. Installation is the reverse of removal. Apply a thin coat of Molykote®, or equivalent, to the bearing surfaces of the rocker arms and pivots. Tighten the rocker arm nut until it just touches the valve stem.
4. Rotate the engine until the No. 1 piston is at TDC of the compression stroke. The **0** mark on the timing scale should be aligned with the timing pointer and the rotor should be at the No. 1 spark plug tower of the distributor cap. The following valves can be adjusted:
   - Exhaust—1, 2, 3
   - Intake—1, 5, 6
5. Turn the adjusting nut until it backs off of the stem slightly, then tighten it until it just touches the stem. Then, turn the nut 1 1/8 turns more to center the tappet plunger.
6. Rotate the engine one complete revolution more. This will bring No. 4 piston to TDC compression. At this point, the following valves may be adjusted:
   - Exhaust—4, 5, 6
   - Intake—2, 3, 4
7. Install rocker arm covers. Start engine and check ignition timing and idle speed.

Fig. 12 2.8L valve-train components

1. Rocker arm nuts
2. Rocker arms
3. Pushrods
4. Pushrod guides

86743G19

5.2L and 5.9L Engines

▶ **See Figure 13**

1. Disconnect the negative battery cable.
2. Remove the cylinder head cover and gasket.
3. Remove the rocker arm bolts and remove the rocker arm pivots and rocker arms. Keep the rocker arm assemblies in order so they can be reinstalled in their original locations.
4. Remove the pushrods, keeping them in order so they can be reinstalled in their original locations.
   To install:
5. Rotate the crankshaft until the **V8** mark lines up with the TDC mark on the timing chain cover (located 147° ATDC from the No. 1 firing mark).

✴✴ WARNING

Do not rotate or crank the engine during or immediately after rocker arm installation. Allow about 5 minutes for the hydraulic lifters to bleed down.

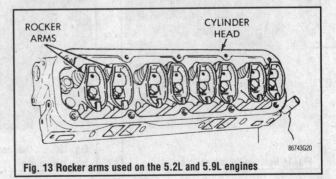

Fig. 13 Rocker arms used on the 5.2L and 5.9L engines

86743G20

6. Install the pushrods in their original locations. Make sure they are seated in the lifters.

7. Lubricate the pushrod tips, rocker arm bearing surfaces and rocker arm pivots with clean engine oil.

8. Install the rocker arm and pivot assemblies in their original locations. Tighten the bolts to 21 ft. lbs. (28 Nm).

9. Install the cylinder head cover and gasket.

10. Connect the negative battery cable.

Thermostat

REMOVAL & INSTALLATION

▶ **See Figures 14, 15 and 16**

1. Disconnect the negative battery cable.
2. If necessary, disconnect the coolant temperature sensor electrical connector.
3. Disconnect the upper radiator hose from the thermostat housing.
4. Remove the attaching bolts and lift the housing from the engine.
5. Remove the thermostat and gasket.

To install:

6. Clean all gasket surfaces thoroughly.
7. Place the thermostat in the housing with the spring inside the engine.
8. Install a new gasket with a small amount of sealing compound applied to both sides.
9. Install the water outlet and tighten the mounting bolts to 200 inch lbs. (23 Nm) on V-8 engines and 15 ft. lbs. (20 Nm) on non-8 cylinder engines.
10. Install the upper radiator hose to the housing and tighten the hose clamp.
11. Connect the coolant temperature sensor connector to the housing.
12. Refill the cooling system.

Intake Manifold

REMOVAL & INSTALLATION

2.1L Diesel Engine

▶ **See Figure 17**

1. Disconnect the negative battery cable. Disconnect the air inlet hose at the intake manifold.
2. Tag and remove all hoses and/or wires as necessary in order to gain access to the intake manifold retaining bolts.
3. Tag and remove all vacuum hoses and electrical connections that are attached to the intake manifold.
4. Remove the intake manifold retaining bolts. Remove the assembly from the vehicle. Discard the intake manifold gaskets.

To install:

5. Clean mating surfaces of all gasket material. Install new gasket.
6. Installation is the reverse of removal. Tighten bolts from center to outside of manifold in steps to 20 ft. lbs. (27 Nm).

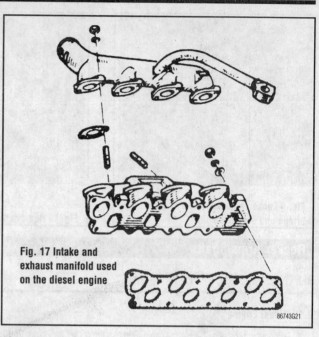

Fig. 17 Intake and exhaust manifold used on the diesel engine

86743G21

2.5L Engine

CARBURETED

▶ **See Figures 18 and 19**

➡ It may be necessary to remove the carburetor from the intake manifold before the manifold is removed.

1. Disconnect the negative battery cable. Drain the radiator.

✳✳ CAUTION

When draining the coolant, keep in mind that cats and dogs are attracted by ethylene glycol antifreeze, and are quite likely to drink any that is left in an uncovered container or in puddles on the ground. This will prove fatal in sufficient quantity. Always drain the coolant into a sealable container. Coolant should be reused unless it is contaminated or several years old.

2. Remove the air cleaner. Disconnect the fuel pipe. Remove the carburetor.
3. Disconnect the coolant hoses from the intake manifold.
4. Disconnect the throttle cable from the bellcrank.
5. Disconnect the PCV valve vacuum hose from the intake manifold.
6. If equipped, remove the vacuum advance CTO valve vacuum hoses.
7. Disconnect the system coolant temperature sender wire connector (located on the intake manifold). Disconnect the air temperature sensor wire, if equipped.
8. Disconnect the vacuum hose from the EGR valve.
9. On vehicles equipped with power steering remove the power steering pump and its mounting bracket. Do not detach the power steering pump hoses.

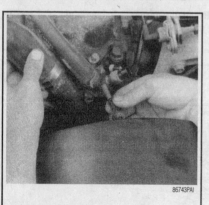

86743PAI

Fig. 14 Remove the attaching bolts . . .

86743PAJ

Fig. 15 . . . then remove the housing from the engine

86743PAK

Fig. 16 Remove the thermostat from the engine

10. Disconnect the intake manifold electric heater wire connector, as required.

11. Disconnect the throttle valve linkage, if equipped with automatic transmission.

12. Disconnect the EGR valve tube from the intake manifold.

13. Remove the intake manifold attaching screws, nuts and clamps. Remove the intake manifold. Discard the gasket.

14. Clean the mating surfaces of the manifold and cylinder head.

➡If the manifold is being replaced, ensure all fittings, etc., are transferred to the replacement manifold.

To install:

15. Clean the mating surfaces of the manifold and cylinder head.

16. Install the intake manifold, with a new gasket. Install intake manifold attaching screws, nuts and clamps. Using the sequence shown in the illustration, tighten the bolts in steps to 23 ft. lbs. (31 Nm).

17. Connect the EGR valve tube.

18. Connect the throttle valve linkage, if equipped with automatic transmission.

19. Connect the intake manifold electric heater wire connector, as required.

20. On vehicles equipped with power steering install the power steering pump and its mounting bracket.

21. Connect the vacuum hose to the EGR valve.

22. Connect the system coolant temperature sender wire connector (located on the intake manifold).

23. Connect the air temperature sensor wire, if equipped.

24. If equipped, install the vacuum advance CTO valve vacuum hoses.

25. Connect the PCV valve vacuum hose at the intake manifold.

26. Connect the throttle cable at the bellcrank.

27. Connect the coolant hoses at the intake manifold.

28. Install the carburetor and working in a crisscross pattern, tighten the nuts to 14 ft. lbs. (19 Nm).

29. Connect the fuel pipe.

30. Install the air cleaner.

31. Connect the negative battery cable.

32. Fill the cooling system.

FUEL INJECTED

▸ See Figures 20 thru 26

1. Disconnect negative battery cable.

2. Remove the air cleaner inlet hose.

3. Loosen the accessory drive belt tension and remove the drive belt.

4. Remove the power steering pump and brackets. Support them from the radiator support with wire.

5. Remove the fuel tank filler cap to relieve the fuel tank pressure. Relieve the fuel system pressure.

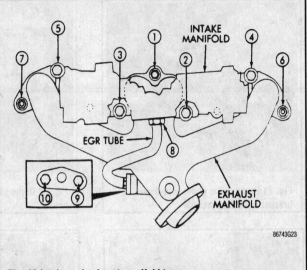

Fig. 19 Intake and exhaust manifold torque sequence

6. Disconnect the fuel supply tube from the fuel rail by squeezing the tabs of the quick connector and pulling. When disconnected, the retainer will stay on the fuel tube and the O-rings and spacer will remain in the connector. Use an "L" shaped paper clip to remove the O-rings and spacer.

➡Whenever a fuel system disconnect fitting is disconnected the O-rings, spacer and retainer must be replaced.

7. Follow the instructions on the O-ring replacement kit package to install the new O-rings and spacer.

8. Disconnect the accelerator cable from the throttle body and hold-down bracket. Disconnect the cruise control connector (if equipped) by loosening it with your hands. DO NOT attempt to pry off.

9. Disconnect all necessary electrical connectors:
- The throttle position sensor
- Idle speed motor
- Coolant temperature sensor at the thermostat
- Manifold air temperature sensor at the intake manifold
- Fuel injectors
- Oxygen sensor

10. Disconnect the crankcase ventilation vacuum hose and manifold absolute pressure sensor vacuum hose at the intake manifold. Disconnect the crankcase ventilation hose on the rocker arm cover.

11. Disconnect the vacuum hose at the EGR transducer and solenoid (if necessary).

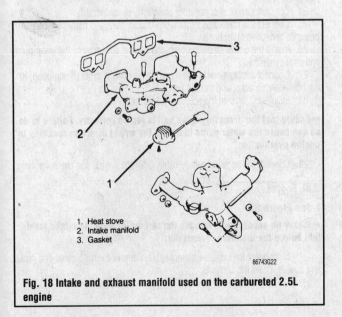

1. Heat stove
2. Intake manifold
3. Gasket

Fig. 18 Intake and exhaust manifold used on the carbureted 2.5L engine

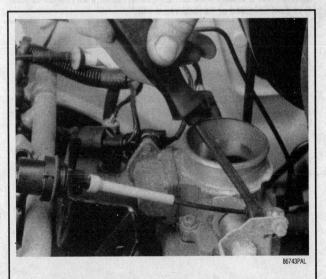

Fig. 20 Disengage the accelerator cable from the throttle body

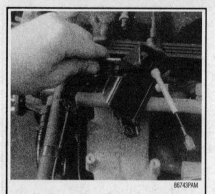

Fig. 21 Remove the cable hold-down bracket from the manifold

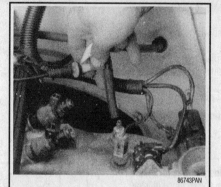

Fig. 22 Unplug the necessary vacuum hoses . . .

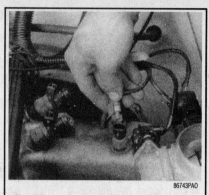

Fig. 23 . . . and electrical connectors from the manifold

Fig. 24 Remove the manifold retaining hardware . . .

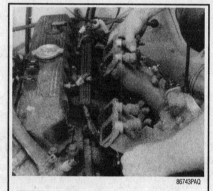

Fig. 25 . . . then remove the manifold from the engine

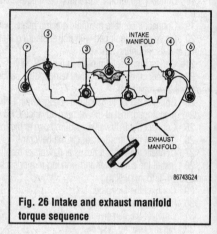

Fig. 26 Intake and exhaust manifold torque sequence

12. Disconnect the molded vacuum harness.

13. Loosen the EGR tube nut and remove the bolts securing the tube to the exhaust manifold (if necessary).

14. Drain the cooling system.

✳✳ CAUTION

When draining the coolant, keep in mind that cats and dogs are attracted by ethylene glycol antifreeze, and are quite likely to drink any that is left in an uncovered container or in puddles on the ground. This will prove fatal in sufficient quantity. Always drain the coolant into a sealable container. Coolant should be reused unless it is contaminated or several years old.

15. Disconnect the vacuum brake booster hose at the intake manifold.

16. Remove bolts number 2 through 5 securing the intake manifold. Loosen bolt 1 and nuts 6 and 7.

17. Remove the intake manifold.

To install:

18. Clean the intake manifold and cylinder head mating surfaces. DO NOT allow foreign material to enter the intake manifold or cylinder head ports. Install the new intake manifold gasket over the locating dowels.

19. Position the intake manifold in place and finger-tighten bolts.

20. Use a new EGR tube gasket and attach the EGR tube to the exhaust manifold. Finger-tighten bolts 9 and 10. Leave the EGR tube nut at the intake manifold finger-tight.

21. Tighten the fasteners in sequence and to the specified torque.

1985–90 Models
- Fasteners 1, 6, 7, and 8: 30 ft. lbs. (41 Nm)
- Fasteners 2, 3, 4, and 5: 23 ft. lbs. (31 Nm)
- Fasteners 9 and 10: 14 ft. lbs. (19 Nm)

1991 and Later Models
- Fastener 1: 30 ft. lbs. (41 Nm)
- Fasteners 2–7: 23 ft. lbs. (31 Nm)

22. Connect the fuel return and supply tube to the connector next to the fuel rail. Don't forget to install the new O-rings. Push them into the fitting until a click is heard. Verify correct installation by first ensuring only the retainer tabs protrude from the connectors and second by pulling out on the fuel tubes to ensure they are locked in place.

23. Attach heater hoses to manifold (if necessary), connect the molded vacuum hoses to the intake manifold, the EGR transducer, the EGR solenoid and the rocker arm cover.

24. Connect electrical connectors previously disconnected.

25. Connect the crankcase ventilation vacuum hose and manifold absolute pressure sensor vacuum hose.

26. Install the power steering pump and bracket assembly to the water pump and intake manifold.

27. Connect the accelerator cable and cruise control cable (if equipped) to the hold-down bracket and throttle arm.

28. Install and tension the accessory drive belt.

➥**Ensure that the accessory drive belt is routed correctly. Failure to do so can cause the water pump to turn in the wrong direction resulting in engine overheating.**

29. Connect the negative battery cable. Start the engine and check for leaks.

2.8L Engine

♦ See Figure 27

➥**It may be necessary to remove the carburetor from the intake manifold before the manifold is removed.**

1. Disconnect the negative battery cable. Remove the air cleaner and rocker arm covers. Drain the coolant.

2. If equipped with air conditioning disconnect the compressor and move it to one side. Disconnect the spark plugs wires at the spark plugs. Disconnect the wires at the ignition coil.

3. If equipped, remove the air pump and bracket.

4. Remove the distributor cap. Mark the position of the ignition rotor in relation to the distributor body and remove the distributor. Do not crank the engine with the distributor removed.

5. Remove the EGR valve. Remove the air hose. Disconnect the charcoal canister hoses. Remove the pipe bracket from the left cylinder head, if equipped.

6. Remove the diverter valve. Remove the power brake vacuum hose. Remove the heater and radiator hoses from the intake manifold.

7. Disconnect and label the vacuum hoses. If equipped, remove the EFE pipe from the rear of the manifold. Disconnect the coolant temperature switches.

8. Remove the carburetor linkage. Disconnect and plug the fuel line.

9. Remove the manifold retaining bolts and nuts.

10. Remove the intake manifold. Remove and discard the gaskets, and scrape off the old silicone seal from the front and rear ridges.

To install:

11. The gaskets are marked for right and left side installation; do not interchange them. Clean the sealing surface of the engine block, and apply a 0.19 in. (5mm) wide bead of silicone sealer to each ridge.

12. Install the new gaskets onto the heads. The gaskets will have to be cut slightly to fit past the center pushrods. Do not cut any more material than necessary. Hold the gaskets in place by extending the ridge bead of sealer 1/4 in. (6mm) onto the gasket ends.

13. Install the intake manifold. The area between the ridges and the manifold should be completely sealed.

14. Install the retaining bolts and nuts, and tighten in sequence to 23 ft. lbs. (31 Nm). Do not overtighten the manifold. It is made of aluminum, and can be warped or cracked with excessive force.

15. Connect the fuel line.

16. Install the carburetor linkage.

17. Connect the vacuum hoses.

18. Install the EFE pipe at the rear of the manifold.

19. Connect the coolant temperature switches.

20. Install the diverter valve.

21. Install the power brake vacuum hose.

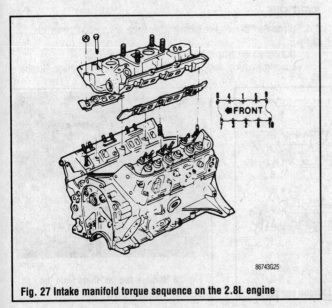

Fig. 27 Intake manifold torque sequence on the 2.8L engine

22. Install the heater and radiator hoses.

23. Install the EGR valve.

24. Install the air hose.

25. Connect the charcoal canister hoses.

26. Install the pipe bracket at the left cylinder head, if equipped.

27. Install the distributor.

28. Install the distributor cap.

29. Install the air pump and bracket.

30. Connect the air conditioning compressor.

31. Install the rocker arm covers.

32. Connect the spark plugs wires at the spark plugs.

33. Connect the wires at the ignition coil.

34. Connect the negative battery cable.

35. Install the air cleaner.

36. Fill the cooling system.

4.0L Engine

The intake and exhaust manifold are mounted externally on the left side of the engine and are attached to the cylinder head. They are removed as a unit. Please refer to the combination manifold procedure.

5.2L and 5.9L Engines

▶ **See Figures 28 and 29**

1. Disconnect the negative battery cable.

2. Properly relieve the fuel system pressure.

3. Drain the cooling system.

4. Remove the air cleaner.

5. Remove the alternator.

6. Remove the fuel lines and fuel rail.

7. Disconnect the accelerator linkage and, if equipped, the cruise control and transmission kickdown cables.

8. Remove the return spring.

9. Remove the distributor cap and wires.

10. Disconnect the coil wires.

11. Disconnect the heat indicator sending unit wire.

12. Disconnect the heater and bypass hoses.

13. Disconnect the PCV and EVAP lines.

14. If equipped with A/C, remove the compressor and position it aside with the lines attached.

15. Remove the support bracket from the mounting bracket and intake manifold.

16. Remove the intake manifold and discard the gaskets.

17. Remove the throttle body and discard the gasket.

18. Turn the intake manifold upside down and support it. Remove the bolts and lift the plenum pan off the manifold. Discard the gasket.

19. Clean all gasket mating surfaces. Clean the intake manifold with solvent and blow dry with compressed air. The plenum pan rail must be clean, dry and free of all foreign material.

To install:

20. Place a new plenum pan gasket onto the seal rail of the intake manifold.

21. Position the pan over the gasket and align the holes. Hand-tighten the bolts.

22. Tighten the bolts as follows:

   a. Tighten all bolts, in sequence, to 24 inch lbs. (3 Nm).

   b. Tighten all bolts, in sequence, to 48 inch lbs. (5.5 Nm).

   c. Tighten all bolts, in sequence, to 84 inch lbs. (10 Nm).

   d. Repeat Step c to ensure proper torque.

23. Using a new gasket, install the throttle body onto the intake manifold. Tighten the bolts to 200 inch lbs. (23 Nm).

24. Place the 4 plastic locator dowels into the holes in the block.

25. Apply Mopar rubber adhesive sealant or equivalent, to the 4 corner joints.

➡ **An excessive amount of sealant is not required to ensure a leak proof seal, however, and excessive amount of sealant may reduce the effectiveness of the flange gasket. The sealant should be slightly higher than the crossover gaskets (approximately 0.2 inch).**

26. Install the front and rear crossover gaskets onto the dowels.

27. Install the flange gaskets. Ensure the vertical port alignment tab is resting on the deck face of the block. Also, the horizontal mating alignment tabs

must be in position with the mating cylinder head gasket tabs. The words MANIFOLD SIDE should be visible on the center of each flange gasket.

28. Carefully lower the intake manifold into place. Use the alignment dowels in the crossover gaskets to position the manifold. Once in place ensure the gaskets are still in position.

29. Tighten the manifold bolts in sequence to the following specifications:

  a. Bolts 1–4—72 inch lbs. (8 Nm). Tighten in alternating steps to 12 inch lbs. (1.5 Nm)

  b. Bolts 5–12—72 inch lbs. (8 Nm)

  c. Repeat Steps a and b to ensure proper torque.

  d. All bolts—12 ft. lbs. (16 Nm)

  e. Repeat Step d to ensure proper torque.

30. Connect the PCV and EVAP lines.

31. Install the coil wires.

32. Connect the heat indicator sending unit wire.

33. Connect the heater and bypass hoses.

34. Install the distributor cap and wires.

35. Hook up the return spring.

36. Connect the accelerator linkage and, if equipped, cruise control and transmission kick down cables.

37. Install the fuel lines and fuel rail.

38. Install the support bracket.

39. Install the alternator and drive belt.

40. If equipped with A/C, install the compressor.

41. Install the air cleaner.

42. Fill the cooling system.

43. Connect the negative battery cable.

44. Start the engine and check for leaks.

Exhaust Manifold

REMOVAL & INSTALLATION

2.1L Diesel Engine

▶ See Figure 17

1. Disconnect the negative battery cable. Remove the intake manifold.

2. Disconnect the exhaust pipe from the adapter.

3. Remove the oil supply pipe and the oil return hose from the turbocharger assembly.

4. Disconnect the turbocharger air inlet and outlet hoses.

5. Remove the turbocharger retaining bolts. Remove the turbocharger from the vehicle.

6. Remove the exhaust manifold retaining bolts. Remove the exhaust manifold and gasket. Discard the gasket.

To install:

7. Position the exhaust manifold and gasket on the head.

8. Install the exhaust manifold retaining bolts and tighten them to 31 ft. lbs. (42 Nm).

9. Install the turbocharger.

10. Connect the turbocharger air inlet and outlet hoses.

11. Install the oil supply pipe and the oil return hose at the turbocharger assembly.

12. Connect the exhaust pipe at the adapter.

13. Install the intake manifold.

14. Connect the negative battery cable.

2.5L Engine

▶ See Figures 18, 19, 26, 30 and 31

1. Disconnect the negative battery cable.

2. Remove the intake manifold.

3. Disconnect the exhaust pipe at the manifold.

4. Remove the fasteners and exhaust manifold.

To install:

5. Clean the intake manifold and cylinder head mating surfaces.

6. Using a new intake manifold gasket, position the intake and exhaust manifolds on the cylinder head and place spacers over the end studs to center the exhaust manifold. Install the end stud nuts and washer clamps but do not tighten.

7. Install washer clamp and bolt at position 1 and tighten to 30 ft. lbs. (41 Nm).

8. Install bolts and washers at positions 2–5 and tighten to 23 ft. lbs. (31 Nm).

9. Tighten end stud nuts (positions 6 and 7) to 23 ft. lbs. (31 Nm).

10. Install all components removed from the intake manifold.

11. Connect the exhaust pipe and tighten the bolts to 23 ft. lbs. (31 Nm).

12. Lower the vehicle.

13. Connect the negative battery cable.

14. Start the engine and inspect it for leaks.

2.8L Engine

▶ See Figure 32

LEFT SIDE

1. Disconnect the negative battery cable. Remove the air cleaner.

2. Remove the air injection hose and manifold (if equipped).

3. Remove the power steering bracket.

4. Raise and support the vehicle safely. Unbolt and remove the exhaust pipe at the manifold.

5. Unbolt and remove the manifold.

To install:

6. Clean the mating surfaces of the cylinder head and manifold. Install the manifold onto the head, and install the retaining bolts finger-tight.

7. Tighten the manifold bolts in a circular pattern, working from the center to the ends, to 25 ft. lbs. (34 Nm) in two stages.

8. Connect the exhaust pipe to the manifold.

9. The remainder of installation is the reverse of removal.

RIGHT SIDE

1. Disconnect the negative battery cable. Raise and support the vehicle safely.

2. Disconnect the exhaust pipe from the exhaust manifold.

3. Lower the vehicle. Remove the spark plug wires from the plugs. Number

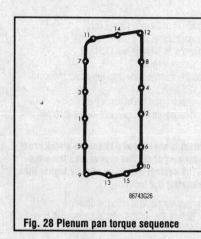

Fig. 28 Plenum pan torque sequence

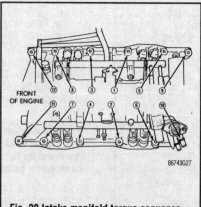

Fig. 29 Intake manifold torque sequence

Fig. 30 Remove the fasteners from the exhaust manifold . . .

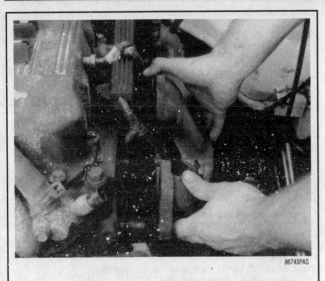

Fig. 31 . . . then remove the manifold from the engine

them first if they are not already labeled. Remove the cruise control servo from the right inner fender panel, if equipped.

4. Remove the air supply pipes from the manifold. Remove the Pulsair bracket bolt from the rocker cover, on models so equipped, then remove the pipe assembly.

5. Remove the manifold retaining bolts and remove the manifold.

To install:

6. Clean the mating surfaces of the cylinder head and manifold. Position the manifold against the head and install the retaining bolts finger-tight.

7. Tighten the bolts in a circular pattern, working from the center to the ends, to 25 ft. lbs. (34 Nm) in two stages.

8. Install the air supply system. Install the spark plug wires. If equipped install the cruise control servo.

9. Raise and support the vehicle safely. Connect the exhaust pipe to the manifold.

4.0L Engine

The intake and exhaust manifolds of the 4.0L must be removed together. Please refer to the combination manifold procedure in this section.

5.2L and 5.9L Engines

♦ **See Figure 33**

1. Disconnect the negative battery cable.

2. Remove the exhaust manifold heat shields.

3. Remove the spark plug wire loom and cables from the mounting stud at the rear of the valve cover and position the cables at the top of the valve cover.

4. Label and disconnect the 2 hoses from the EGR valve.

5. Disconnect the electrical connector and hoses from the EGR transducer.

6. Remove the EGR valve and discard the gasket.

7. Disconnect the oil pressure sending unit electrical connector.

8. Using oil pressure sending unit remover C-4597 or equivalent, remove the sending unit.

9. Loosen the EGR mounting nut from the intake manifold.

10. Remove the mounting bolts and EGR tube. Discard the gasket.

11. Raise and safely support the vehicle.

12. Disconnect the exhaust pipes from the manifolds.

13. Lower the vehicle.

14. Remove the fasteners and exhaust manifold.

To install:

➡If the manifold mounting studs came out with the fasteners, replace the studs.

15. Position the manifold and install the conical washers on the studs.

16. Install new bolt and washer assemblies into the remaining holes. Working from the center outward, tighten the fasteners to 20 ft. lbs. (27 Nm).

17. Raise and support the vehicle safely.

18. Connect the exhaust pipes to the manifolds and tighten the fasteners to 23 ft. lbs. (31 Nm).

19. Lower the vehicle.

20. Clean the EGR and tube gasket mating surfaces.

21. Install a new gasket onto the exhaust manifold ends of the EGR tube and install the tube. Tighten the tube nut to the intake manifold and tighten the tube-to-exhaust manifold bolts to 204 inch lbs. (14 Nm).

22. Coat the threads of the oil pressure sending unit with sealer taking care not to apply sealant to the opening.Install the sending unit and tighten it to 130 inch lbs. (14 Nm) and connect the electrical connector.

23. Install the EGR valve and new gasket to the intake manifold and tighten the bolts to 200 inch lbs. (23 Nm).

24. Position the EGR transducer and connect the vacuum lines and electrical connector.

25. Position the spark plug cables and loom into place and connect the cables.

26. Install the exhaust heat shields and tighten the bolts to 20 ft. lbs. (27 Nm).

27. Connect the negative battery cable.

Combination Manifold

REMOVAL & INSTALLATION

♦ **See Figures 34, 35a and 35b**

➡This procedure applies only to the 4.0L engine. The intake and exhaust manifold are mounted externally on the left side of the engine and are attached to the cylinder head. They are removed as a unit.

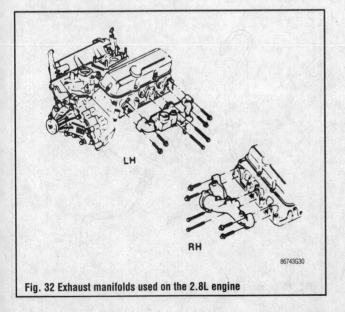

Fig. 32 Exhaust manifolds used on the 2.8L engine

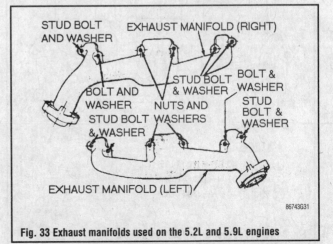

Fig. 33 Exhaust manifolds used on the 5.2L and 5.9L engines

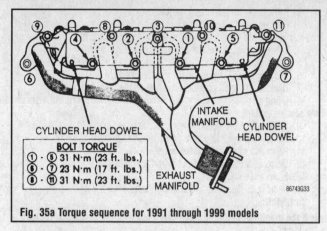

Fig. 35a Torque sequence for 1991 through 1999 models

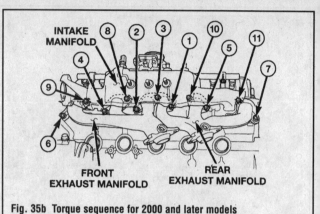

Fig. 35b Torque sequence for 2000 and later models

1. Disconnect the negative battery cable.
2. Remove the air cleaner assembly.
3. Disconnect the accelerator cable, cruise control cable, if equipped and transmission line pressure cable.
4. Disconnect all electrical connectors on the intake manifold.
5. Disconnect and remove the fuel supply and return lines from the fuel rail assembly.
6. Remove the fuel rail and injectors.
7. Loosen the accessory drive belts.
8. Remove the power steering pump.
9. Disconnect the exhaust pipe from the manifold and discard the seal.
10. Remove the intake and exhaust manifold attaching nuts and bolts.
11. Remove the manifold assembly and gasket.

To install:
12. Clean the gasket mating surfaces thoroughly. Install a new gasket over the alignment dowels and position the exhaust manifold to the cylinder head. Install bolt No. 3 finger-tight.
13. Install the intake manifold and the remaining bolts and washers.
14. On 1987–90 models, tighten bolts, in sequence, to the following torque specifications:
   a. Bolt 1—30 ft. lbs. (40.5 Nm)
   b. Bolts 2–11—23 ft. lbs. (31 Nm)
   c. Bolts 12 and 13—30 ft. lbs. (40.5 Nm)
15. On 1991 and later models, tighten bolts, in sequence, to the following torque specifications:
   a. Bolts 1–5—23 ft. lbs. (31 Nm)
   b. Bolts 6 and 7—17 ft. lbs. (23 Nm)
   c. Bolts 8–11—23 ft. lbs. (31 Nm)
16. Install the fuel rail and injectors.
17. Install the power steering pump and tension the accessory belt to specification.

18. Using new O-rings, install the fuel supply and return lines.
19. Connect all electrical connectors, vacuum connectors, throttle cable, cruise control cable and transmission lines pressure cable.
20. Install the air cleaner assembly.
21. Using a new seal, connect the exhaust pipe to the manifold and tighten the bolts to 23 ft. lbs. (31 Nm).
22. Connect the negative battery cable.
23. Start the engine and check for leaks.

Turbocharger

REMOVAL & INSTALLATION

▶ **See Figures 36 and 37**

➡ **This procedure applies to the 2.1L diesel engine only.**

1. Disconnect the negative battery cable.
2. Remove all the necessary components in order to gain access to the turbocharger retaining bolts.
3. Disconnect the exhaust pipe flange. Remove the oil supply pipe. Remove the oil return hose.
4. Remove the turbocharger retaining bolts. Remove the turbocharger from the vehicle.

To install:
5. Position the turbocharger on the manifold.
6. Install the turbocharger retaining bolts. Tighten the bolts to 31 ft. lbs. (42 Nm).
7. Install the oil return hose.
8. Install the oil supply pipe.

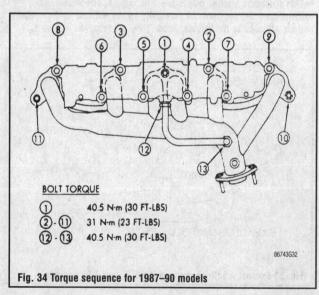

Fig. 34 Torque sequence for 1987–90 models

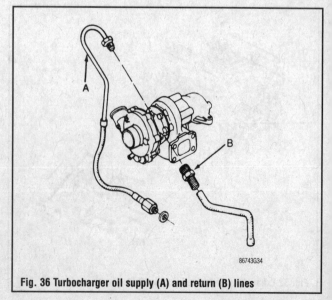

Fig. 36 Turbocharger oil supply (A) and return (B) lines

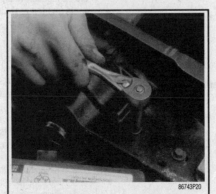

Fig. 37 Turbocharger mounting bolts (C)

9. Connect the exhaust pipe flange.
10. Install any removed components.
11. Connect the negative battery cable.

Radiator

REMOVAL & INSTALLATION

Except Grand Cherokee

▶ See Figures 38 thru 45

1. Disconnect the negative battery cable.
2. Remove the grille reinforcement panel/crossmember, as necessary.
3. Drain the cooling system.
4. Remove the radiator upper and lower hoses.
5. If equipped, remove the transmission cooler lines.

6. Unplug any electrical connections.
7. Remove the fan shroud mounting bolts and pull the fan shroud back to the engine.
8. If equipped, remove the alignment dowel E-clips from the lower radiator mounting bracket.
9. Disconnect the overflow tube from the radiator.
10. Remove all attaching bolts and screws that secure the radiator to the radiator support.
11. Remove the condenser-to-radiator mounting bolts and pull the radiator out of the vehicle.

➡Take care not to damage the radiator fins.

12. Empty the remaining coolant in the radiator.

To install:
13. Slide the radiator into position behind the condenser, if equipped.
14. Align the dowel pins with the bottom mounting bracket and install the E-clips (if equipped).
15. Tighten the condenser-to-radiator bolts to 55 inch lbs. (6 Nm).
16. Install and tighten the radiator mounting bolts.
17. Install the grille reinforcement panel/crossmember.
18. Connect the transmission cooler lines, if equipped.
19. Install the fan shroud.
20. Plug in all electrical connections.
21. Connect the radiator hoses.
22. Connect the negative battery cable.
23. Fill the cooling system to the correct level.

Grand Cherokee

▶ See Figures 46, 47 and 48

1. Disconnect the negative battery cable.
2. Open the radiator valve and drain the cooling system.
3. Remove the fan and shroud assembly.
4. If equipped, disconnect the automatic transmission cooling line quick-fit connections.

Fig. 38 Remove the bolts securing the grille reinforcement panel . . .

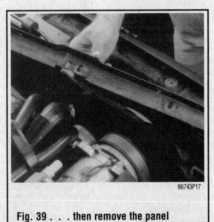

Fig. 39 . . . then remove the panel

Fig. 40 Disconnect the transmission cooler lines . . .

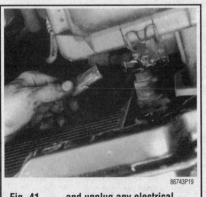

Fig. 41 . . . and unplug any electrical connections

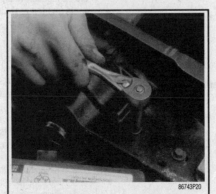

Fig. 42 Remove the radiator support bolts . . .

Fig. 43 . . . then remove the support

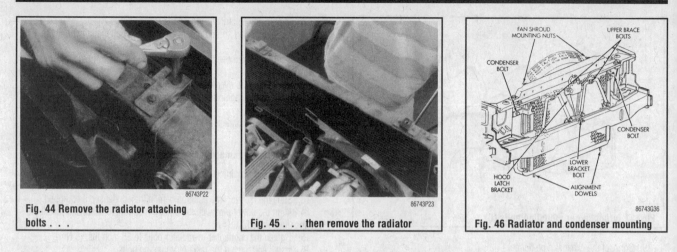

Fig. 44 Remove the radiator attaching bolts . . .

Fig. 45 . . . then remove the radiator

Fig. 46 Radiator and condenser mounting

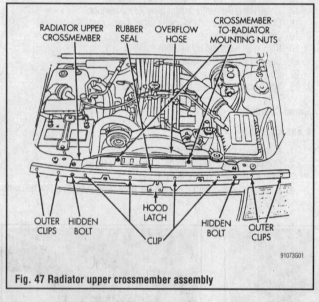

Fig. 47 Radiator upper crossmember assembly

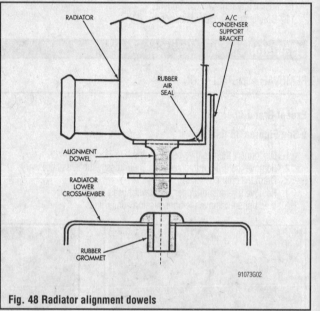

Fig. 48 Radiator alignment dowels

5. Matchmark the upper radiator crossmember and adjust the crossmember to the left or right.

6. Eight clips are used to retain a rubber seal to the body. Gently pry up the outboard clips (2 per side) until the rubber seal can be removed. Do not remove the seals entirely. Fold back the seal on both sides to access the grille opening reinforcement mounting bolts and remove the bolts.

7. Remove the grille.

8. Remove the upper brace bolt from each of the 2 radiator braces.

9. Remove the crossmember-to-radiator mounting nuts.

10. Working through the grille opening, remove the lower bracket bolt securing the lower part of the hood latch or hood latch cable from the crossmember.

11. Lift the crossmember straight up and position it aside.

12. If equipped with A/C, remove the 2 A/C condenser-to-radiator mounting bolts which also retain the side mounted rubber air seals.

13. If not equipped with A/C, remove the bolts retaining the side mounted rubber air seals compressed between the radiator and crossmember.

➡Note the location of the air seals. To prevent overheating, they must be installed in their original position.

14. Disconnect the coolant reservoir/overflow tank hose from the radiator.

15. Disconnect the upper hose from the radiator.

16. Carefully lift the radiator a slight amount and disconnect the lower hose from the radiator.

17. Lift the radiator up and out of the engine compartment, take care not to scrape the fins or disturb the A/C condenser if equipped.

➡If equipped with an auxiliary automatic transmission oil cooler, use caution during radiator removal. The oil cooler lines are routed through

a rubber air seal on the left side of the radiator. Do not cut or tear this seal.

To install:

18. Lower the radiator into the vehicle. Guide the alignment dowels into the hoses in the rubber air seals and then through the A/C support brackets, if equipped. Continue to guide the radiator through the rubber grommets located in the lower crossmember.

➡If equipped with A/C, the L-shaped brackets, located on the bottom of the condenser, must be positioned between the bottom of the rubber air seals and top of rubber grommets.

19. Connect the lower radiator hose to the radiator.

20. Connect the upper radiator hose to the radiator.

21. If equipped with A/C, install the bolts condenser-to-radiator mounting bolts.

22. If not equipped with A/C, install the rubber air seal retaining bolts.

23. Connect the reservoir/overflow tank hose to the radiator.

24. If the radiator-to-upper crossmember rubber insulators were removed, install them.

25. Install the hood latch support bracket-to-lower frame crossmember bolt.

26. Install the bolts securing the upper radiator crossmember to the body.

27. Install the radiator-to-upper crossmember nuts.

28. Install a bolt to each upper radiator brace.

29. Install the grille.

30. Position the rubber seal and push down on the clips until seated.

31. If equipped, connect the transmission cooling lines.

32. Install the fan shroud with the fan.

Fig. 49 Remove the fan shroud

Fig. 50 Remove the fan flange-to-pulley mounting nuts . . .

Fig. 51 . . . then remove the fan assembly

Fig. 52 Unplug the electrical connection

Fig. 53 Remove the shroud attaching bolts . . .

Fig. 54 . . . then remove the fan assembly

33. Install the fan and shroud.
34. Rotate the fan blades and ensure they do not interfere with the shroud and at least 1 inch (25mm) of clearance is allowed. Correct as necessary.
35. Fill the cooling system.

Engine Fan

REMOVAL & INSTALLATION

Except 5.2L Engines

VISCOUS DRIVE FAN

▶ See Figures 49, 50 and 51

1. Remove the upper fan shroud bolts and lift the shroud from its lower securing tabs.
2. Remove the accessory drive belts.
3. Remove the fan flange-to-pulley mounting nuts.
4. Remove the fan and viscous drive as an assembly.
5. Remove the fan blade-to-viscous drive bolts and separate the assembly.

To install:

6. Position the fan on the viscous drive. Install the bolts and tighten them to 187 inch lbs. (24 Nm).
7. Position the mounting flange of the viscous drive assembly onto the pulley. Install the nuts and tighten them to 18 ft. lbs. (24 Nm).
8. Install the accessory drive belts.
9. Insert the shroud into its retaining tabs and install the upper bolts.

ELECTRIC FAN

▶ See Figures 52, 53 and 54

1. Disconnect the negative battery cable.

2. If necessary to remove the fan assembly, partially drain the engine coolant enough to allow upper radiator hose removal.
3. Disconnect the electrical connector.
4. If necessary, disconnect the upper radiator hose from the radiator and secure the hose out of the way.
5. Remove the upper fan shroud bolts.
6. Lift the fan assembly up and out of the engine compartment.

To install:

7. Insert the shroud into its retaining tabs. Install and tighten the upper bolts.
8. Connect the upper hose to the radiator, if disconnected during removal.
9. Connect the electrical connector.
10. Fill the cooling system to the correct level.
11. Connect the negative battery cable.

5.2L Engines

▶ See Figure 55

1. Disconnect the negative battery cable.
2. The viscous fan drive and blade assembly is threaded into the water pump hub shaft. Remove the fan drive and blade assembly from the water pump by turning the mounting nut counterclockwise as viewed from the front while securing the water pump pulley. Do not remove or unbolt the fan drive and blade at this time.

➡ The threads on the viscous fan drive are right hand threaded.

3. Remove the 2 fan shroud-to-upper crossmember nuts.
4. Remove the fan drive, blade and shroud as an assembly.

✳✳ WARNING

Do not place the viscous fan drive in a horizontal position. If stored horizontally, silicone fluid in the viscous fan drive could drain into its bearing assembly and the assembly would have to be replaced.

⁂ CAUTION

Do not remove the water pump pulley-to-water pump bolts. The pulley is under spring tension.

5. Remove the 4 bolts securing the fan blade assembly to the viscous fan drive.

To install:

6. Install the fan blade on the viscous drive. Install the bolts and tighten them to 17 ft. lbs. (23 Nm).

7. Position the fan shroud, viscous fan and blade into the engine compartment as an assembly.

8. Position the fan shroud to the radiator. Insert the lower slots of the shroud into the crossmember. Install the upper attaching nuts.

➡**Ensure the upper and lower portions of the fan shroud are firmly connected. All air must flow through the radiator.**

9. Install the fan drive and blade assembly to the water pump shaft and tighten the nut.

➡**Ensure there is at least 1 inch (25mm) between the tips of the fan blades and shroud.**

10. Connect the negative battery cable.

Water Pump

REMOVAL & INSTALLATION

2.1L Diesel Engine

▶ See Figures 56 and 57

1. Disconnect the negative battery cable. Drain the engine coolant.

⁂ CAUTION

When draining the coolant, keep in mind that cats and dogs are attracted by ethylene glycol antifreeze, and are quite likely to drink any that is left in an uncovered container or in puddles on the ground. This will prove fatal in sufficient quantity. Always drain the coolant into a sealable container. Coolant should be reused unless it is contaminated or several years old.

2. Remove the coolant hose from the water pump.
3. Remove the drive belts.
4. Remove the fan and hub assembly.
5. It is not necessary to remove the timing belt tensioner. Use a long strap and clip in order to retain the timing belt tensioner plunger in place.
6. Remove the water pump retaining bolts. Remove the water pump assembly from the vehicle.

To install:

7. Clean the mating surfaces of all gasket material.
8. Do not use sealer on the new gasket. Position the gasket and pump on

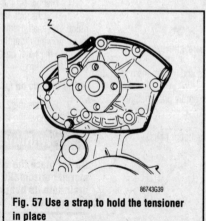
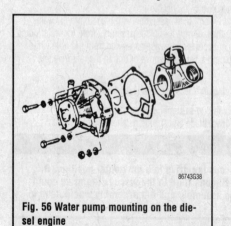

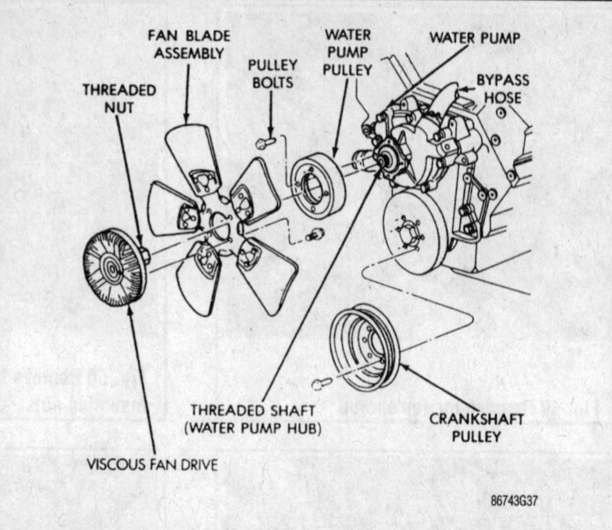

Fig. 55 Fan blade and viscous drive

the engine and install the bolts. Tighten the bolts to 15 ft. lbs. (20 Nm).

9. Re-tension the timing belt.
10. Install the fan and hub, drive belts and coolant hoses.
11. Fill the cooling system.
12. Connect the battery.

2.5L, 2.8L and 4.0L Engines

▶ See Figures 58, 59 and 60

➡**Some vehicles use a serpentine drive belt and have a reverse rotating water pump coupled with a viscous fan drive assembly. The components are identified by the words REVERSE stamped on the cover of the viscous drive and on the inner side of the fan. The word REV is also cast into the body of the water pump.**

1. Disconnect the negative battery cable.
2. Drain the cooling system.
3. Disconnect the hoses at the pump.
4. Remove the drive belts.
5. Remove the power steering pump bracket.
6. Remove the fan and shroud.
7. If equipped, remove the idler pulley to gain clearance for pump removal.
8. Unbolt and remove the pump.

To install:

9. Clean the mating surfaces thoroughly.
10. Using a new gasket, install the pump and tighten the bolts to 13 ft. lbs. (18 Nm).
11. If removed, install the idler pulley.
12. Reconnect the hoses at the pump and install accessory drive belt.
13. Install the power steering pump bracket. Install the fan and shroud.

Fig. 56 Water pump mounting on the diesel engine

Fig. 57 Use a strap to hold the tensioner in place

Fig. 58 Remove the power steering pump and bracket, then move it aside

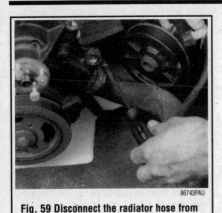

Fig. 59 Disconnect the radiator hose from the water pump

Fig. 60 Remove the bolts securing the pump, then remove it from the engine

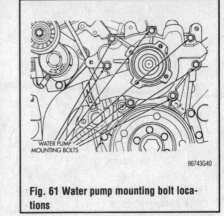

Fig. 61 Water pump mounting bolt locations

14. Adjust the belt tension and fill the cooling system to the correct level.

15. Operate the engine with the heater control valve in the **HEAT** position until the thermostat opens to purge air from the system. Check coolant level and fill as required.

5.2L and 5.9L Engines

▶ See Figure 61

1. Disconnect the negative battery cable.
2. Open the radiator valve and drain the cooling system.
3. Remove the cooling fan and shroud as an assembly.
4. Remove the accessory drive belt.
5. Remove the water pump pulley from the hub.
6. Disconnect the hoses from the water pump.
7. Loosen the heater hose coolant return tube mounting bolt and nut and remove the tube. Discard the O-ring.
8. Remove the water pump mounting bolts.
9. Loosen the clamp at the water pump end of the bypass hose. Slip the bypass hose from the water pump while removing the pump from the engine. Discard the gasket.

To install:

10. Clean all gasket mating surfaces.
11. Guide the water pump and new gasket into position while connecting the bypass hose to the pump. Tighten the water pump bolts to 30 ft. lbs. (40 Nm).
12. Install the bypass hose clamp.
13. Spin the water pump to ensure the pump impeller does not rub against the timing chain cover.
14. Coat a new O-ring with coolant and install it to the heater hose coolant return tube.
15. Install the coolant return tube to the engine. Ensure the slot in the tube bracket is bottomed to the mounting bolt. This will properly position the return tube.
16. Connect the radiator hose to the water pump.
17. Connect the heater hose and clamp to the return tube.
18. Install the water pump pulley and tighten the bolts to 20 ft. lbs. (27 Nm).
19. Install the accessory drive belt.

20. Install the cooling fan and shroud.
21. Fill the cooling system.
22. Connect the negative battery cable.
23. Start the engine and check for leaks.

Cylinder Head

REMOVAL & INSTALLATION

➡It is important to note that each engine has its own head bolt torque sequence and tightening specification. Incorrect tightening procedure may cause head warpage and compression loss.

2.1L Diesel Engine

▶ See Figures 62 thru 68

1. Disconnect the negative battery cable.
2. Remove the intake manifold. Remove the exhaust manifold.
3. Remove the rocker arm cover. Drain the engine coolant. Remove the timing belt cover.

✳✳ CAUTION

When draining the coolant, keep in mind that cats and dogs are attracted by ethylene glycol antifreeze, and are quite likely to drink any that is left in an uncovered container or in puddles on the ground. This will prove fatal in sufficient quantity. Always drain the coolant into a sealable container. Coolant should be reused unless it is contaminated or several years old.

4. Install sprocket holding tool MOT-854 or equivalent and remove the camshaft sprocket retaining bolt. Remove the special tool.
5. Loosen the bolts and move the tensioner away from the timing belt. Retighten the tensioner bolts.
6. Remove the timing belt from the sprockets.

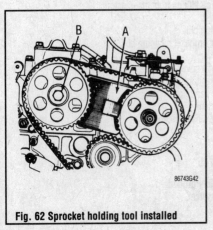

Fig. 62 Sprocket holding tool installed

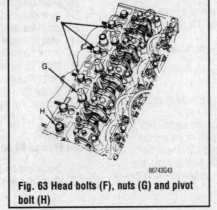

Fig. 63 Head bolts (F), nuts (G) and pivot bolt (H)

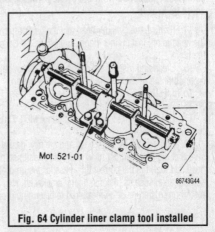

Fig. 64 Cylinder liner clamp tool installed

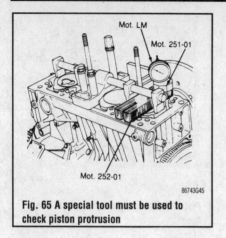

Fig. 65 A special tool must be used to check piston protrusion

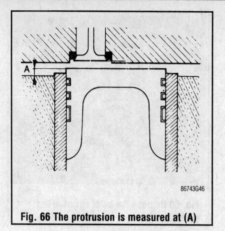

Fig. 66 The protrusion is measured at (A)

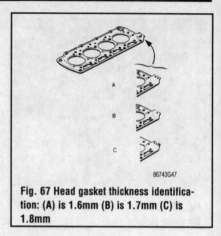

Fig. 67 Head gasket thickness identification: (A) is 1.6mm (B) is 1.7mm (C) is 1.8mm

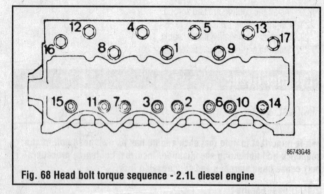

Fig. 68 Head bolt torque sequence - 2.1L diesel engine

➡️If it is necessary to remove the fuel injection pump sprocket use special tool BVI-28-01 or BVI-859 to accomplish this procedure.

7. Disconnect the fuel pipe fittings from the injectors. Plug them in order to prevent dirt from entering the system.

8. Disconnect the fuel pipe fittings from the fuel injection pump. Plug them in order to prevent dirt from entering the system.

9. Remove the fuel pipes from their mountings on the engine. Remove all hoses and connectors from the fuel injection pump.

10. Remove the injection pump retaining bolts. Remove the fuel injection pump and its mounting brackets, as an assembly, from the vehicle.

11. Remove the retaining bolts and nuts from the cylinder head. Loosen pivot bolt but do not remove it. Remove the remaining cylinder head bolts.

12. Place a block of wood against the cylinder head and tap it with a hammer in order to loosen the cylinder head gasket. The pivot movement will be minimal due to the small clearance between the studs and the cylinder head. Remove the pivot bolt from the cylinder head.

13. Remove the retaining bolts and the rocker arm shaft assembly from the cylinder head.

➡️Do not lift the cylinder head from the cylinder block until the gasket is completely loosened from the cylinder liners. Otherwise, the liner seals could be broken.

14. Remove the cylinder head and the gasket from the engine block. While the head is off, install liner clamp tool MOT 521-01 to hold the liners in place in the block.

15. Clean and inspect the cylinder head thoroughly. Refer to the engine reconditioning portion outlined later in this section.

To install:

16. Remove liner clamp tool MOT 521-01.

17. Position cylinder head locating tool MOT 720 on the block to insure proper alignment.

18. Position the cylinder head and the new gasket from the engine block. Be sure that the new cylinder head gasket is positioned properly on the cylinder head and that it is the correct thickness for piston protrusion. Whenever major components, such as pistons, liners, crankshaft, etc., have been replaced, the piston protrusion must be measured to determine proper replacement head gas-

ket thickness. Measure the protrusion as follows:

a. Rotate the crankshaft one complete revolution clockwise and bring No. 1 piston to a point just below and before TDC.

b. Place thrust plate tool MOT 252-01 on top of the piston.

c. Assemble a dial indicator in the block gauge MOT 25101 and place this assembly on one side of the thrust plate.

d. Zero the indicator with the stem on the cylinder block face.

e. Place the stem on the top of the piston and rotate the crankshaft clockwise to TDC of the piston. Record the piston travel.

f. Repeat the procedure with the dial indicator on the opposite side of the block. Record the piston travel.

g. Add the two figures together and divide by two. Repeat the protrusion measurement for the three remaining pistons. The piston with the greatest protrusion should be the basis for determining gasket thickness. For example, if the amount of greatest piston protrusion is:

• Less than 0.96mm, use a gasket 1.6mm thick
• Between 0.96mm and 1.04mm, use a 1.7mm thick gasket
• More than 1.04mm, use a 1.8mm thick gasket

19. Install the head bolts. Tighten the cylinder head retaining bolts to 22 ft. lbs. (30 Nm), then to 37 ft. lbs. (50 Nm), then to 70–77 ft. lbs. (95–104 Nm). Once all the bolts are tightened, recheck the torque.

➡️The cylinder head bolts must be retightened after the cylinder head is installed in the vehicle. Operate the engine for a minimum of twenty minutes. Allow the engine to cool for a minimum of two and one half hours. Loosen each cylinder head bolt in sequence about 1/8 turn. Then retighten in the proper sequence and tighten to 70–77 ft. lbs. (95–104 Nm). For the final tightening, tighten the bolts again, in sequence, without loosening them to 70–77 ft. lbs. (95–104 Nm).

20. Remove tool MOT 720.

21. Install the rocker arm shaft assembly.

22. Install the fuel injection pump and its mounting brackets, as an assembly. See Section 5.

23. Install the fuel pipes on their mountings on the engine. Install all hoses and connectors on the fuel injection pump.

24. Connect the fuel pipe fittings to the fuel injection pump.

25. Connect the fuel pipe fittings from the injectors.

26. Install the timing belt.

27. Re-tension the timing belt.

28. Install the camshaft sprocket retaining bolt.

29. Install the valve cover.

30. Install the timing belt cover.

31. Install the intake manifold.

32. Install the exhaust manifold.

33. Fill the cooling system.

34. Connect the negative battery cable.

2.5L Engine

▶ See Figures 69 thru 76b

1. Disconnect the battery ground.
2. Drain the cooling system.

✳✳ CAUTION

When draining the coolant, keep in mind that cats and dogs are attracted by ethylene glycol antifreeze, and are quite likely to drink any that is left in an uncovered container or in puddles on the ground. This will prove fatal in sufficient quantity. Always drain the coolant into a sealable container. Coolant should be reused unless it is contaminated or several years old.

---

3. Loosen the accessory drive belt and remove.

4. Without discharging the air conditioning system, remove the compressor and mounting bracket and stow to the side of the engine compartment.

5. Remove the power steering pump bracket and suspend out of the way.

6. Disconnect the hoses at the thermostat housing.

7. Remove the rocker arm cover.

8. Remove the rocker arms, bridges, pivots and pushrods. Keep them in the order they were removed!

9. Remove the intake and exhaust manifolds.

10. Remove the head bolts.

11. Lift the head off the engine and place it on a clean workbench.

12. Remove the head gasket.

13. Clean and inspect the cylinder head thoroughly. Refer to the engine reconditioning portion outlined later in this section.

To install:

14. Install the head gasket. Apply sealer to both sides of the new gasket; never to the head or block surfaces!

➡ **1989 and later cylinder head gaskets used on the 2.5L are a composition gasket. The gasket is to be installed DRY. DO NOT use sealing compound.**

15. Fabricate two cylinder head alignment dowels from used head bolts. Use the longest head bolts. Cut the bolt off below the hex head. Next cut a slot in the top of the dowel to allow easier removal.

16. Install cylinder head alignment dowels. Install head gasket (manufacturer number up) and cylinder head.

➡ **Cylinder head bolts should be reused only once. Replace head bolts which were previously used or are marked with paint. If head bolts are to be reused, mark each head with paint for later reference.**

17. Install cylinder head bolts replacing alignment dowels with cylinder head bolts as you go. Coat cylinder head bolt 8 (1984–88) or bolt 7 (1989 and later) with Permatex® No. 2 sealant, or equivalent, and install.

18. Tighten cylinder head bolts in the correct sequence, to the following torque specifications:

• On 1984–88 models, using three steps, tighten all bolts in sequence (except bolt 8) to 85 ft. lbs. (115 Nm); tighten bolt 8 to 75 ft. lbs. (101 Nm)

• On 1989 and later models, using three steps, tighten bolts 1 through 10 in sequence to 22 ft. lbs. (30 Nm), then tighten bolts 1 through 10 in sequence to 45 ft. lbs. (61 Nm). Check (in sequence) to verify that all of the head bolts are tightened to 45 ft. lbs. (61 Nm). Next, tighten bolts 1 through 6 in sequence to 110 ft. lbs. (150 Nm), bolt 7 to 100 ft. lbs. (136 Nm), and bolts 8 through 10 in sequence to 110 ft. lbs. (150 Nm). Check (in sequence) to verify that all of the head bolts are tightened to the correct torque.

19. If not alraedy done, clean and mark each head bolt with a dab of paint after the final tightening sequence.

➡ **Some head bolts used on the spark plug side of the 1984 2.5L were improperly hardened and may break under the head during service or at head installation while torquing the bolts. Engines with the defective bolts are serial numbers 310U06 through 310U14. Whenever a broken bolt is found, replace all bolts on the spark plug side of the head with bolt number 400 6593.**

20. Install the rocker arm cover.

21. Install the intake and exhaust manifolds.

22. Connect the hoses at the thermostat housing.

23. Install power steering pump bracket and pump.

24. Install air conditioning compressor mounting bracket. Tighten to 30 ft. lbs. (41 Nm). Install compressor and tighten to 20 ft. lbs. (27 Nm).

25. Install the accessory drive belt.

➡ **The accessory drive belt must be routed correctly. Incorrect routing**

Fig. 69 Remove the pushrods. Remember to keep them in order

Fig. 70 Disconnect the coolant hoses from the head

Fig. 71 Remove the bolts securing the head. A breaker bar will be necessary to loosen them

Fig. 72 Carefully lift the head from the block . . .

Fig. 73 . . . then remove and discard the old gasket

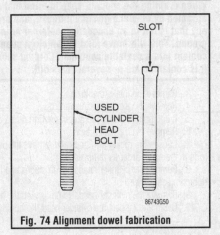

Fig. 74 Alignment dowel fabrication

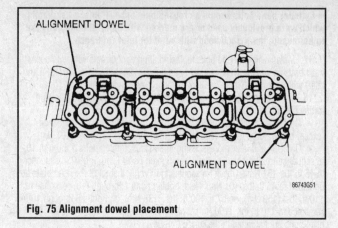

Fig. 75 Alignment dowel placement

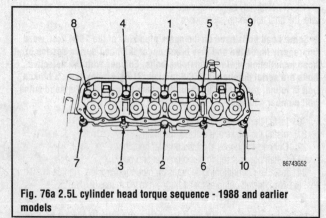

Fig. 76a 2.5L cylinder head torque sequence - 1988 and earlier models

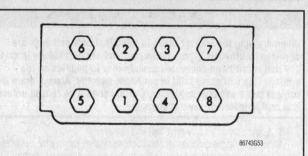

Fig. 77 Cylinder head torque sequence on 2.8L engines

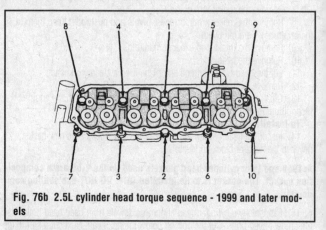

Fig. 76b 2.5L cylinder head torque sequence - 1999 and later models

can cause the water pump to turn in the opposite direction causing the engine to overheat.

26. Check to be sure that any disconnected wiring harnesses for this procedure have been connected properly.
27. Fill the cooling system.
28. Connect the battery ground.

2.8L Engines

▶ See Figure 77

LEFT SIDE

1. Disconnect the negative battery cable. Raise and support the vehicle safely. Disconnect the exhaust pipe from the exhaust manifold.
2. Drain the coolant from the block and lower the vehicle.

✳✳ CAUTION

When draining the coolant, keep in mind that cats and dogs are attracted by ethylene glycol antifreeze, and are quite likely to drink any that is left in an uncovered container or in puddles on the ground. This will prove fatal in sufficient quantity. Always drain the coolant into a sealable container. Coolant should be reused unless it is contaminated or several years old.

3. Remove the intake manifold.
4. Remove the exhaust manifold.
5. If equipped, remove the power steering pump and bracket.
6. Remove the dipstick tube.
7. Loosen the rocker arm bolts and remove the pushrods. Keep the pushrods in the same order as removed.
8. Remove the cylinder head bolts in stages and in the reverse order of the tightening sequence.
9. Remove the cylinder head. Do not pry on the head to loosen.
10. Clean and inspect the cylinder head thoroughly. Refer to the engine reconditioning portion outlined later in this section.

To install:
11. Thoroughly clean the head-to-block mating surface. All bolt holes must be free of foreign material.
12. Place a new head gasket on the block with the words "This Side Up" facing upward.
13. Position the cylinder head on the block.
14. Coat the cylinder head bolts with RTV silicone sealant and install them. Tighten the bolts, in sequence, in three equal stages. The final stage should be 70 ft. lbs. (95 Nm).
15. Install the pushrods, keeping them in the same order as removed.
16. Install the rocker arms.
17. Install the dipstick tube.
18. Install the power steering pump and bracket.
19. Install the exhaust manifold.
20. Install the intake manifold.
21. Connect the exhaust pipe from the exhaust manifold.
22. Fill the cooling system.
23. Connect the negative battery cable.
24. Adjust the valves.

RIGHT SIDE

1. Disconnect the negative battery cable. Raise and support the vehicle safely. Drain the coolant from the block.

✳✳ CAUTION

When draining the coolant, keep in mind that cats and dogs are attracted by ethylene glycol antifreeze, and are quite likely to drink any that is left in an uncovered container or in puddles on the ground. This will prove fatal in sufficient quantity. Always drain the coolant into a sealable container. Coolant should be reused unless it is contaminated or several years old.

2. Disconnect the exhaust pipe and lower the vehicle.
3. If equipped, remove the cruise control servo bracket.
4. Remove the alternator and air pump bracket assembly.
5. Remove the intake manifold.

6. Loosen the rocker arm nuts and remove the pushrods. Keep the pushrods in the order in which they were removed.

7. Remove the cylinder head bolts in stages and in the reverse order of the tightening sequence.

8. Remove the cylinder head. Do not pry on the cylinder head to loosen it.

9. Clean and inspect the cylinder head thoroughly. Refer to the engine reconditioning portion outlined later in this section.

To install:

10. Thoroughly clean the head-to-block mating surface. All bolt holes must be free of foreign material.

11. Place a new head gasket on the block with the words "This Side Up" facing upward.

12. Position the cylinder head on the block.

13. Coat the cylinder head bolts with RTV silicone sealant and install them. Tighten the bolts, in sequence, in three equal stages. The final stage should be 70 ft. lbs. (95 Nm).

14. Install the pushrods, keeping them in the same order as removed.

15. Install the rocker arms.

16. Install the exhaust manifold.

17. Install the intake manifold.

18. Connect the exhaust pipe from the exhaust manifold.

19. Fill the cooling system.

20. Connect the negative battery cable.

21. Adjust the valve lash.

4.0L Engines

▶ See Figure 78

1. Disconnect the negative battery cable.
2. Drain the cooling system.
3. Disconnect the hoses at the thermostat housing.
4. Properly relieve the fuel system pressure.
5. Remove the cylinder head cover.
6. Loosen the rocker arms.
7. Remove the pushrods.

➡**The valvetrain components must be replaced in their original positions.**

8. Remove the intake and exhaust manifold from the cylinder head.

9. Disconnect the spark plug wires and remove the spark plugs.

10. Disconnect the temperature sending unit wire, ignition coil and bracket assembly from the engine.

11. Remove the accessory drive belt(s).

12. Unbolt and set aside the power steering pump and bracket. Do not disconnect the hoses.

13. Remove the intake and exhaust manifold assembly.

14. If equipped with A/C, perform the following:
    a. Remove the compressor and position it aside with the lines attached.
    b. Remove the compressor bracket bolts from the cylinder head.
    c. Loosen the through bolt at the bottom of the bracket.

15. Remove the alternator.

16. Remove the cylinder head bolts, the cylinder head and gasket from the block.

➡**Bolt No. 14 cannot be removed until the head is moved forward. Pull the bolt out as far as it will go and suspend in place by wrapping with tape.**

17. Discard the gasket. Thoroughly clean the head-to-block mating surface.

18. Clean and inspect the cylinder head thoroughly. Refer to the engine reconditioning portion outlined later in this section.

To install:

19. Coat a new head gasket with suitable sealing compound and place it on the block. Most replacement gaskets will have the word **TOP** stamped on them.

➡**Apply sealing compound only to the cylinder head gasket. Do not allow sealing compound to enter the cylinder bore.**

➡**The 1991 and later cylinder head gaskets used on the 4.0L are a composition gasket. The gasket is to be installed DRY. DO NOT use sealing compound.**

20. Install the cylinder head and bolts. The threads of bolt No. 11 must be coated with Loctite® 592 sealant before installation. Tighten the bolts in 3 steps, using the correct sequence:
    a. Tighten all bolts to 22 ft. lbs. (30 Nm).
    b. Tighten all bolts to 45 ft. lbs. (61 Nm).
    c. Retighten all bolts to 45 ft. lbs. (61 Nm).
    d. Tighten bolts 1 through 10 in sequence to 110 ft. lbs. (150 Nm).
    e. Tighten bolt 11 to 100 ft. lbs. (136 Nm)
    f. Tighten bolts 12 through 14 to 110 ft. lbs. (150 Nm)

➡**Cylinder head bolts should be reused only once. Replace the head bolts which were previously used or are marked with paint. If head bolts are to be reused, mark each head bolt with paint for future reference. Head bolts should be installed using sealer.**

21. Install the ignition coil.

22. Install the air conditioning compressor.

23. Install the alternator.

24. Install the intake and exhaust manifold assembly.

25. Install the power steering pump and bracket.

26. Install the accessory drive belt(s).

27. Connect the temperature sending unit wire, ignition coil and bracket.

28. Install the spark plugs and wires.

29. Install the pushrods, rocker arm assembly, gasket and cylinder head cover.

30. Connect the hoses at the thermostat housing.

31. Fill the cooling system.

32. Connect the negative battery cable.

33. Run the engine to normal operating temperature and check for leaks.

5.2L and 5.9L Engines

▶ See Figures 79, 80 and 81

1. Disconnect the negative battery cable.
2. Properly relieve the fuel system pressure.
3. Drain the cooling system.
4. Remove the alternator.

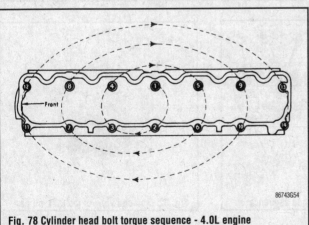

Fig. 78 Cylinder head bolt torque sequence - 4.0L engine

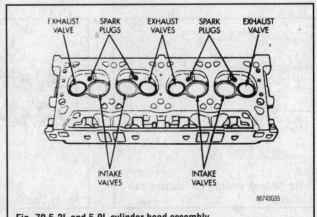

Fig. 79 5.2L and 5.9L cylinder head assembly

5. Disconnect the PCV valve.
6. Disconnect the EVAP fuel lines.
7. Remove the air cleaner and disconnect the fuel lines.
8. Disconnect the accelerator linkage, speed control cable, if equipped, and transmission kickdown cables.
9. Remove the return spring.
10. Remove the distributor cap and wires.
11. Disconnect the coil wires.
12. Disconnect the heat indicator sending unit wire.
13. Disconnect the heater and bypass hoses.
14. Remove the cylinder head covers, discard the gaskets.
15. Remove the intake manifold and throttle body.
16. Remove the exhaust manifolds.
17. Remove the rocker arm assemblies and pushrods.

➡**Identify the rocker arms and pushrods for installation purposes.**

18. Remove the spark plugs.
19. Remove the cylinder head bolts.
20. Remove the heads and discard the gaskets.
21. Thoroughly clean the gasket mating surfaces.
22. Clean and inspect the cylinder head thoroughly. Refer to the engine reconditioning portion outlined later in this section.

To install:
23. Apply Perfect Sealer No. 5 or equivalent, to the inner corners of the new head gaskets.
24. Position the head gaskets onto the block.
25. Position the cylinder heads onto the cylinder block.
26. Install the cylinder head bolts as follows:
   a. Tighten all bolts, in sequence, to 50 ft. lbs. (68 Nm).
   b. Tighten all bolts, in sequence, to 105 ft. lbs. (143 Nm).
   c. Repeat Step b to ensure the torque is correct.
27. Install the pushrods and rocker arms to their original positions.
28. Install the intake and exhaust manifolds.
29. Install the spark plugs.
30. Install the coil wires.
31. Connect the heat indicating sending unit wire.
32. Connect the heater and bypass hoses.
33. Install the distributor cap and wires.
34. Hook up the return spring.
35. Connect the accelerator linkage, speed control cable, if equipped and transmission kickdown cables.
36. Install the fuel lines.
37. Install the alternator.
38. Install the intake manifold-to-alternator bracket support rod.
39. Place new cylinder head cover gaskets into position and install the cylinder head covers.
40. Install the PCV valve.
41. Connect the EVAP lines.
42. Install the air cleaner.
43. Fill the cooling system.
44. Connect the negative battery cable. Start the engine and check for leaks.

Oil Pan

REMOVAL & INSTALLATION

2.1L Diesel Engine

▶ **See Figure 82**

1. Disconnect the negative battery cable. Raise and support the vehicle safely. Remove the converter housing shield as required.
2. Drain the engine oil. This engine has two oil drain plugs both must be opened.

✳✳ CAUTION

The EPA warns that prolonged contact with used engine oil may cause a number of skin disorders, including cancer! You should make every effort to minimize your exposure to used engine oil. Protective gloves should be worn when changing the oil. Wash your hands and any other exposed skin areas as soon as possible after exposure to used engine oil. Soap and water, or waterless hand cleaner should be used.

3. Remove all the necessary components in order to gain access to the oil pan retaining bolts.
4. Remove the oil pan retaining bolts. Remove the oil pan from the engine.

To install:
5. Clean all gasket surfaces thoroughly. Be careful to avoid bending the oil pan mating flanges.
6. If the oil pan was assembled with RTV gasket material, run a 0.23 inch (6mm) bead of new sealer around the oil pan flanges, outboard of the mounting holes. The sealer sets in 15 minutes, so work quickly! If a gasket was used, coat the oil pan flanges with gasket sealer and place the gasket on the pan. Coat the engine block mounting surfaces with sealer.
7. Position the pan on the block and install the bolts. Tighten the bolts to 79 inch lbs. (9 Nm).
8. Install the drain plugs, fill the crankcase, run the engine and check for leaks.

2.5L Engine

▶ **See Figure 83**

1. Disconnect the battery ground.
2. Raise and support the vehicle safely.
3. Drain the oil

✳✳ CAUTION

The EPA warns that prolonged contact with used engine oil may cause a number of skin disorders, including cancer! You should make every effort to minimize exposure to used engine oil. Protective gloves should be worn when changing the oil. Wash your hands and any other exposed skin areas as soon as possible after exposure to used engine oil. Soap and water, or waterless hand cleaner should be used.

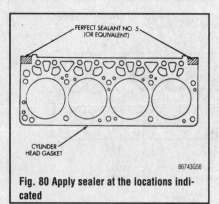

Fig. 80 Apply sealer at the locations indicated

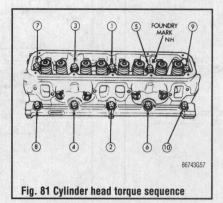

Fig. 81 Cylinder head torque sequence

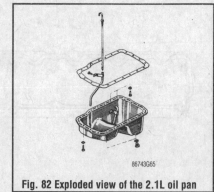

Fig. 82 Exploded view of the 2.1L oil pan

4. Disconnect the exhaust pipe at the manifold and the exhaust hanger at the catalytic converter. Lower the exhaust.

5. If necessary, disconnect the exhaust pipe from the exhaust manifold, then disconnect the exhaust hanger at the catalytic converter to lower the pipe.

6. Remove the starter.

7. Remove the bellhousing access plate.

8. If necessary, remove the engine mount and raise the engine to gain clearance.

9. Unbolt and remove the oil pan.

To install:

10. Clean the gasket surfaces thoroughly. Remove all sludge and dirt from the oil pan sump.

11. Install a replacement seal at the bottom of the timing case cover and at the rear bearing cap.

12. Using new gaskets coated with sealer, install the oil pan and tighten the 1/4 inch bolts to 80 inch lbs. (9 Nm); the 5/16 inch bolts to 11 ft. lbs. (15 Nm).

13. Lower the engine until it is properly located on the engine mounts. Tighten engine mount bolts to 48 ft. lbs. (65 Nm).

14. Tighten oil pan drain plug to 25 ft. lbs. (34 Nm).

15. Install the bellhousing access plate.

16. Install the starter.

17. Connect the exhaust pipe at the manifold and the exhaust hanger at the catalytic converter.

18. Fill the crankcase.

19. Connect the battery ground.

20. Start engine and inspect for leaks.

2.8L Engine

▶ See Figure 84

1. Disconnect the battery ground.
2. Raise the support the vehicle safely.
3. Drain the oil.

✳✳ CAUTION

The EPA warns that prolonged contact with used engine oil may cause a number of skin disorders, including cancer! You should make every effort to minimize your exposure to used engine oil. Protective gloves should be worn when changing the oil. Wash your hands and any other exposed skin areas as soon as possible after exposure to used engine oil. Soap and water, or waterless hand cleaner should be used.

4. Remove the bellhousing access cover.

5. Disconnect the exhaust pipes at the manifold.

6. Remove the starter.

7. Disconnect the exhaust pipe at the converter flange and lower the exhaust so that the "Y" portion rests on the axle upper control arms.

8. Unbolt and remove the pan.

To install:

9. Remove all RTV gasket material. Remove all sludge and dirt from the oil pan sump.

10. Install a new rear pan seal.

11. Apply a 1/8 inch (3mm) bead of RTV gasket material all the way around the pan sealing surface.

12. Install the pan and tighten the bolts to 12 ft. lbs. (16 Nm).

13. Connect the exhaust pipe at the converter flange.

14. Install the starter.

15. Connect the exhaust pipes at the manifold.

16. Install the bellhousing access cover.

17. Fill the crankcase.

18. Connect the battery ground.

4.0L Engine

▶ See Figures 85, 86 and 87

1. Disconnect the battery ground.
2. Raise and support the vehicle safely.
3. Drain the oil.

✳✳ CAUTION

The EPA warns that prolonged contact with used engine oil may cause a number of skin disorders, including cancer! You should make every effort to minimize your exposure to used engine oil. Protective gloves should be worn when changing the oil. Wash your hands and any other exposed skin areas as soon as possible after exposure to used engine oil. Soap and water, or waterless hand cleaner should be used.

4. Disconnect the exhaust pipe at the manifold and the exhaust hanger at the catalytic converter. Lower the exhaust.

5. Remove the starter.

6. Remove the bellhousing access plate.

7. If necessary, remove the engine mount and raise the engine to gain clearance.

8. Unbolt and remove the oil pan.

To install:

9. Clean the gasket surfaces thoroughly. Remove all sludge and dirt from the oil pan sump.

10. When installing the front oil pan seal to the timing chain cover, apply a generous amount of Permatex® No. 2 or equivalent sealer to the end tabs. Also, cement the oil pan side gaskets to the mating surface on the bottom of the engine block. Coat the inside curved surface of the new oil pan rear seal with soap and apply a generous amount of Permatex® No. 2 or equivalent to the gasket contacting surface of the seal end tabs.

11. Install the seal in the recess of the rear main bearing cap, making certain that it is fully seated.

12. Apply engine oil to the oil pan contacting surface of the front and rear oil pan seals.

13. Install the oil pan. Tighten the 1/4 inch bolts to 80 inch lbs. (9 Nm); the 5/16 inch bolts to 11 ft. lbs. (15 Nm); the oil pan drain plug to 30 ft. lbs. (41 Nm).

14. Lower the engine and install the engine mount.

15. Install the bellhousing access plate.

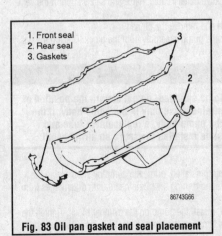

1. Front seal
2. Rear seal
3. Gaskets

86743G66

Fig. 83 Oil pan gasket and seal placement

86743G67

Fig. 84 Exploded view of the 2.8L engine oil pan mounting

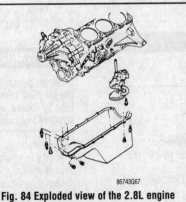

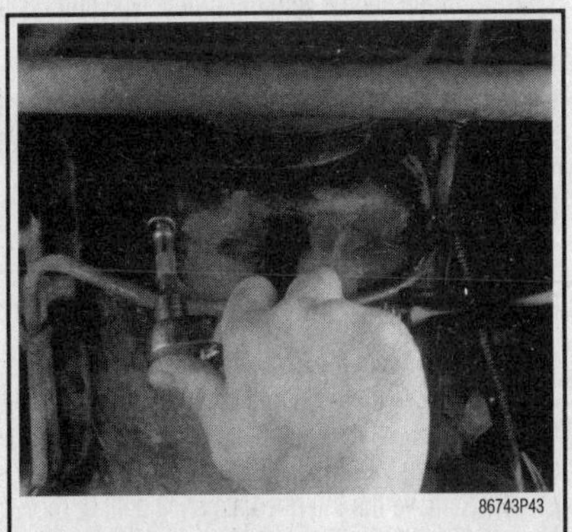

86743P43

Fig. 85 Use an extension to access the retaining bolts

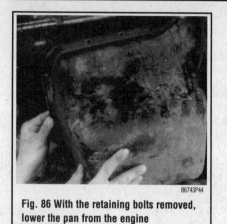

Fig. 86 With the retaining bolts removed, lower the pan from the engine

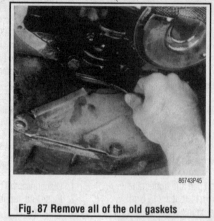

Fig. 87 Remove all of the old gaskets

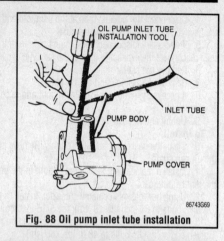

Fig. 88 Oil pump inlet tube installation

16. Install the starter.

17. Connect the exhaust pipe at the manifold and the exhaust hanger at the catalytic converter.

18. Fill the crankcase.

19. Connect the battery ground.

5.2L and 5.9L Engines

1. Disconnect the negative battery cable.
2. Raise and safely support the vehicle.
3. Remove the oil pan drain plug and drain the engine oil.
4. Remove the oil filter.
5. Remove the starter.
6. If equipped, disconnect the oil level sensor.
7. Position the oil cooler lines out of the way.
8. Disconnect the oxygen sensor and remove the exhaust pipe.
9. Remove the oil pan bolts and carefully slide the oil pan to the rear. If equipped, be careful not to damage the oil level sensor.
10. Clean all sealant and old gasket material from the oil pan and cylinder block mating surfaces. Thoroughly clean the oil pan.

To install:

11. Fabricate 4 alignment dowels from 1 1/2 x 5/16 inch bolts. Cut the heads off the bolts and cut a slot in the dowel to allow installation/removal with a screwdriver.

12. Install the dowels in the cylinder block. Apply a small amount of silicone sealant in the corner of the cap and cylinder block.

13. Slide the one-piece gasket over the dowels and onto the block. Position the oil pan over the dowels and onto the gasket. If equipped, be careful not to damage the oil level sensor.

14. Install the oil pan bolts and tighten to 18 ft. lbs. (24 Nm). Remove the dowels and install the remaining bolts. Tighten to 18 ft. lbs. (24 Nm).

15. Install the drain plug and tighten to 25 ft. lbs. (34 Nm).

16. Install the exhaust pipe and connect the oxygen sensor.

17. Install the oil filter. If equipped, connect the oil level sensor.

18. Install the starter. Move the oil cooler lines back into position.

19. Lower the vehicle and connect the negative battery cable.

20. Fill the engine with the proper type and quantity of oil. Start the engine and check for leaks.

Oil Pump

REMOVAL & INSTALLATION

2.1L Diesel Engine

1. Disconnect the negative battery cable.
2. Remove the vacuum pump along with the oil pump drive gear.
3. Remove the timing belt cover. Loosen the intermediate shaft drive sprocket using tool MOT 855 or equivalent.
4. Remove the intermediate shaft bolt, sprocket, cover, clamp plate and intermediate shaft.
5. Raise and support the vehicle safely. Drain the engine oil. Remove the oil pan.

✳✳ CAUTION

The EPA warns that prolonged contact with used engine oil may cause a number of skin disorders, including cancer! You should make every effort to minimize your exposure to used engine oil. Protective gloves should be worn when changing the oil. Wash your hands and any other exposed skin areas as soon as possible after exposure to used engine oil. Soap and water, or waterless hand cleaner should be used.

6. Remove the piston skirt cooling oil jet assembly to oil pump pipe.
7. Remove the oil pump retaining bolts. Remove the oil pump.
8. Be sure that the oil pump locating dowels are in place on the pump.
9. Inspect the gears for abnormal wear, chips, looseness on the shafts, galling, and scoring.
10. Inspect the cover and cavity for breaks, cracks, distortion, and abnormal wear.

To install:

11. Install the gears into the pump cavity, and with the use of a straight edge and feeler gauge, check the gear to housing clearance.

12. Repair or replace defective components as required.

13. Install the oil pump and retaining bolts. Use a new gasket. Tighten the bolts to 33 ft. lbs. (45 Nm).

14. Install the piston skirt cooling oil jet assembly on oil pump pipe.

15. Install the oil pan.

16. Install the intermediate shaft and sprocket.

17. Install the timing belt cover.

18. Install the vacuum pump and oil pump drive gear.

19. Connect the negative battery cable.

20. Fill the crankcase.

2.5L and 4.0L Engines

▶ See Figure 88

1. Disconnect the negative battery cable. Raise and safely support the vehicle.
2. Drain the engine oil and remove the oil pan.
3. Unbolt and remove the pump assembly from the block. Discard the gasket.

✳✳ WARNING

If the oil pump is not to be serviced, do not disturb the position of the oil inlet tube and strainer assembly in the pump body. If the tube is moved within the pump body, a replacement tube and strainer assembly must be installed to assure an airtight seal.

To install:

4. If a new pump is being installed, prime the pump by submerging the strainer in clean engine oil and turning the pump gears until oil emerges from the pump feed hole.

5. Using a new gasket, install the pump on the cylinder block. Tighten the short bolt to 10 ft. lbs. (14 Nm) and the long bolt to 17 ft. lbs. (23 Nm).

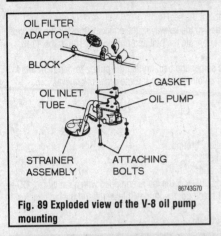

Fig. 89 Exploded view of the V-8 oil pump mounting

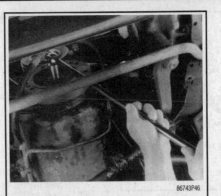

Fig. 90 Use a long breaker bar to loosen the bolt . . .

Fig. 91 . . . then remove it from the crankshaft

Fig. 92 A puller must be used to extract the damper from the engine

6. Install the oil pan and lower the vehicle.
7. Fill the engine with the proper type and quantity of oil.
8. Connect the negative battery cable. Start the engine and check for proper oil pressure.

2.8L Engine

1. Remove the oil pan.

➡Do not disturb the position of the oil pick-up tube and screen assembly in the pump body. If the tube is moved within the pump body, a new assembly must be installed to assure an airtight seal. Apply a thin film of Permatex® No. 2 sealant or equivalent around the end of the tube prior to assembly.

2. Unbolt and remove the pump assembly from the block. Discard any gaskets.
To install:
3. Install the pump on the block, using a new gasket (if one was removed).
4. Tighten the bolt to 25–30 ft. lbs. (34–41 Nm).
5. Install the pan.

5.2L and 5.9L Engines

♦ **See Figure 89**

1. Disconnect the negative battery cable.
2. Raise and safely support the vehicle.
3. Drain the engine oil and remove the oil pan.
4. Unbolt and remove the pump assembly from the rear main bearing cap.

To install:
5. If a new pump is being installed, prime the pump by submerging the pickup in clean engine oil and turning the pump gears until oil emerges from the pump feed hole.
6. Install the oil pump. During installation, slowly rotate the pump body to ensure driveshaft-to-pump rotor shaft engagement.
7. Hold the oil pump base flush against the mating surface of the rear main bearing cap and finger-tighten the pump mounting bolts. Tighten the mounting bolts to 30 ft. lbs. (41 Nm).
8. Install the oil pan and lower the vehicle. Fill the engine with the proper type and quantity of oil.
9. Connect the negative battery cable. Start the engine and check for proper oil pressure.

Crankshaft Pulley (Vibration Damper)

REMOVAL & INSTALLATION

♦ **See Figures 90, 91 and 92**

1. Remove the fan shroud, as required.
2. On those engines with a separate pulley, remove the retaining bolts and separate the pulley from the vibration damper.
3. Remove the vibration damper/pulley retaining bolt from the crankshaft end.
4. Using a puller, remove the damper/pulley from the crankshaft.
To install:
5. Inspect the damper shaft and remove any burrs. Inspect for oil leakage from the timing chain seal. If leakage is present it may be caused by an undersized damper shaft. Install a damper shaft collar to restore correct outside diameter.
6. Place a small amount of grease on the damper shaft to ease installation. Align the key slot of the damper with the key in the crankshaft and push damper on. The damper bolt is tightened to 80 ft. lbs. (108 Nm), except on 5.2L and 5.9L engines. On 5.2L and 5.9L engines, tighten to 135 ft. lbs. (183 Nm).
7. Install pulley and tighten bolts to 20 ft. lbs. (27 Nm).
8. Install drive belt and adjust to the specified tension.

Timing Belt Cover

REMOVAL & INSTALLATION

♦ **See Figure 93**

➡This applies to 2.1L diesel engines only.

1. Disconnect the negative battery cable.
2. Remove all necessary components in order to gain access to the timing belt cover bolts.
3. Remove the timing belt cover retaining bolts. Remove the timing belt cover from the engine.
4. Installation is the reverse of removal.

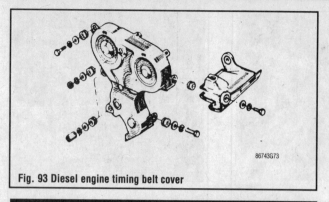

Fig. 93 Diesel engine timing belt cover

Timing Chain Cover and Seal

2.5L Engine

♦ See Figures 94, 95 and 96

1. Disconnect the battery ground.
2. Remove the drive belts and fan shroud.
3. Unscrew the vibration damper bolts and washer.
4. Using a puller, remove the vibration damper.
5. Remove the fan assembly. If the fan is equipped with a fan clutch DO NOT LAY IT DOWN! If you lay it down, the fluid will leak out of the clutch and irreversibly damage the fan.
6. Remove the air conditioning compressor/alternator bracket assembly and lay it out of the way. DO NOT DISCONNECT THE REFRIGERANT LINES!
7. Unbolt the cover from the block and oil pan. Remove the cover and front seal.
8. Cut off the oil pan side gasket end tabs and oil pan front seal tabs.
9. Clean all gasket mating surfaces thoroughly.
10. Remove the seal from the cover.

To install:

11. Apply sealer to both sides of the new case cover gasket and position it on the block.
12. Cut the end tabs off the new oil pan side gaskets corresponding to those cut off the original gasket and attach the tabs to the oil pan with gasket cement.
13. Coat the front cover seal end tab recesses generously with RTV sealant and position the side seal in the cover.
14. Apply engine oil to the seal-to-pan contact surface.
15. Position the cover on the block.
16. Insert alignment tool J-22248 into the crankshaft opening in the cover.
17. Install the cover bolts. Tighten the cover-to-block bolts to 5 ft. lbs. (7 Nm); the cover-to-pan bolts to 11 ft. lbs. (15 Nm).
18. Remove the alignment tool and position the new front seal on the tool with the seal lip facing outward. Apply a light film of sealer to the outside diameter of the seal. Lightly coat the crankshaft with clean engine oil.
19. Position the tool and seal over the end of the crankshaft and insert the Draw Screw J-9163-2 into the installation tool.
20. Tighten the nut until the tool just contacts the cover.
21. Remove the tools and apply a light film of engine oil on the vibration

damper hub contact surface of the seal.

22. With the key inserted in the keyway in the crankshaft install the vibration damper, washer and bolt. Lubricate the bolt and tighten it to 108 ft. lbs. (146 Nm).
23. If equipped with a serpentine belt, tighten the pulley-to-damper bolts to 20 ft. lbs. (27 Nm). Install all other parts in reverse order of removal.

2.8L Engine

♦ See Figure 97

1. Disconnect the battery ground.
2. Remove the drive belts.
3. Remove the fan shroud.
4. Remove the fan and pulley. If the fan is equipped with a fan clutch, DO NOT LAY IT ON ITS SIDE! If you do, the fluid will leak out and the fan clutch will have to be replaced.
5. Drain the cooling system.

❊❊ CAUTION

When draining the coolant, keep in mind that cats and dogs are attracted by ethylene glycol antifreeze, and are quite likely to drink any that is left in an uncovered container or in puddles on the ground. This will prove fatal in sufficient quantity. Always drain the coolant into a sealable container. Coolant should be reused unless it is contaminated or several years old.

6. Remove the air conditioning compressor and mounting bracket and position them out of the way. DO NOT DISCONNECT THE REFRIGERANT LINES!
7. Remove the water pump.
8. Remove the vibration damper retaining bolt and, using a puller, remove the damper.

➡ **On some vehicles the outer ring (weight) of the harmonic balancer is bonded to the hub with rubber. The balancer must be removed with a puller which acts on the inner hub only. Pulling on the outer portion of the balancer will break the rubber bond or destroy the tuning of the torsional damper.**

9. Disconnect the lower radiator hose.
10. Unbolt and remove the cover. Pry out the seal.

To install:

11. Thoroughly remove all traces of gasket material from the mating surfaces.
12. Position a new seal in the cover with the open end of the seal facing outward.
13. Apply a 3/32 in. (2.5mm) bead of RTV silicone gasket material to the mating surfaces of the cover and block. Place the cover on the block and install the bolts. Tighten the M8 x 1.25 bolts to 18 ft. lbs. (24 Nm); the M10 x 1.5 bolts to 30 ft. lbs. (41 Nm). Tighten the bolts within five minutes, as the sealer will begin to set.
14. Install all other parts in reverse order of removal.

➡ **Breakage may occur if the balancer is hammered back onto the crankshaft. A press or special installation tool is necessary.**

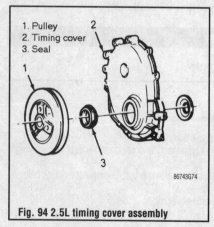

1. Pulley
2. Timing cover
3. Seal

Fig. 94 2.5L timing cover assembly

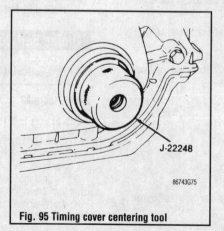

Fig. 95 Timing cover centering tool

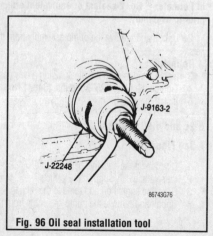

Fig. 96 Oil seal installation tool

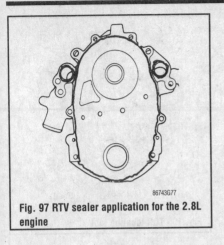

Fig. 97 RTV sealer application for the 2.8L engine

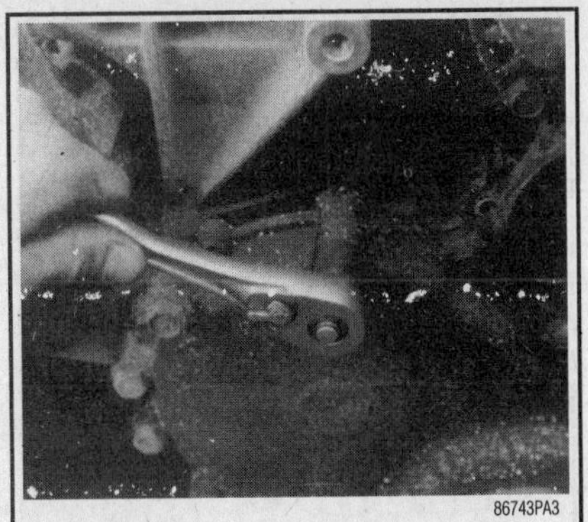

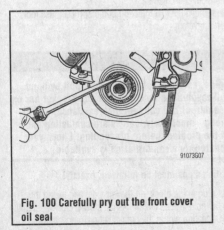

Fig. 98 Remove the bolts securing the cover to the block

Fig. 99 Carefully remove the cover from the engine

4.0L Engine

▶ See Figures 98 and 99

1. Remove the drive belts, engine fan and hub assembly, the accessory pulley and vibration damper.
2. Remove the air conditioning compressor and alternator bracket assembly and set it aside. Don't disconnect the refrigerant lines.
3. Remove the oil pan to timing chain cover screws and the screws that attach the cover to the block.
4. Raise the timing chain cover just high enough to detach the retaining nibs of the oil pan neoprene seal from the bottom side of the cover. This must be done to prevent pulling the seal end tabs away from the tongues of the oil pan gaskets, which would cause a leak.
5. Remove the timing chain cover and gasket from the engine. Make sure the timing chain tensioner spring and thrust pin do not fall out of the preload bolt.
6. Use a razor blade to cut off the oil pan seal end tabs flush with the front face of the cylinder block and remove the seal. Clean the timing chain cover, oil pan, and cylinder block surfaces.
7. Remove the crankshaft oil seal from the timing chain cover. Thoroughly clean the mating surfaces.

To install:

8. Apply RTV gasket material to both sides of the new gasket and position the gasket on the block.
9. Cut the end tabs off of the replacement oil pan side gaskets, corresponding to those cut off of the original gasket. Cement the end tabs to the oil pan.
10. Coat the front cover end tab recesses with a generous amount of RTV gasket sealant and position the seal on the timing case cover. Apply a coat of clean engine oil to the seal-to-pan contact surfaces.
11. Make sure the tension spring and thrust pin are in place in the preload bolt. Position the case cover on the block.
12. Place cover alignment tool (J-22248) in the crankshaft opening of the cover.

13. Install the cover-to-block bolts and the oil pan-to-cover bolts. Tighten the cover-to-block bolts to 62 inch lbs. (7 Nm); the cover-to-pan bolts to 11 ft. lbs. (15 Nm).
14. Remove the alignment tool and position the seal on the tool with the lip facing outward.
15. Apply a light coat of sealer on the outside diameter of the seal.
16. Lightly coat the crankshaft with clean engine oil.
17. Position the tool and seal over the end of the crankshaft and insert a screw tool into the seal installation tool.
18. Tighten the nut against the tool until it contacts the cover.
19. Remove the tools and apply a light coating of engine oil on the vibration damper hub contact surface of the seal.
20. Install the damper.
21. Install all other parts in reverse order of removal. tighten the damper pulley bolts to 20 ft.lbs.

5.2L and 5.9L Engines

▶ See Figures 100, 101, 102 and 103

1. Disconnect the negative battery cable.
2. Properly relieve the fuel system pressure.
3. Drain the cooling system.
4. Remove the serpentine belt.
5. Remove the cooling fan shroud and position it on the engine.
6. Remove the water pump.
7. Remove the power steering pump.
8. Remove the vibration damper using puller C-3688 or equivalent.
9. Disconnect the fuel lines.
10. Loosen the oil pan bolts and remove the front bolt at each side.
11. Remove the timing chain cover bolts. Remove the chain cover and gasket using extreme caution to avoid damaging the oil pan gasket.
12. Place a suitable tool behind the lips of the oil seal and pry the seal outward, being careful not to damage the crankshaft seal surface of the front cover.

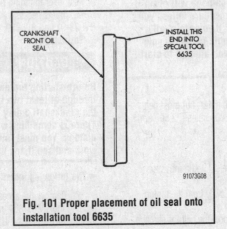

Fig. 100 Carefully pry out the front cover oil seal

Fig. 101 Proper placement of oil seal onto installation tool 6635

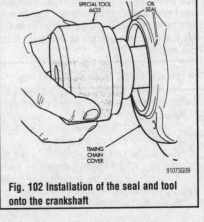

Fig. 102 Installation of the seal and tool onto the crankshaft

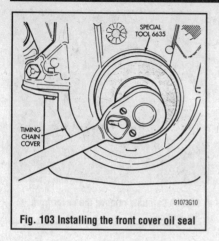

Fig. 103 Installing the front cover oil seal

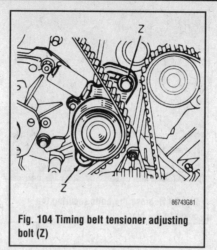

Fig. 104 Timing belt tensioner adjusting bolt (Z)

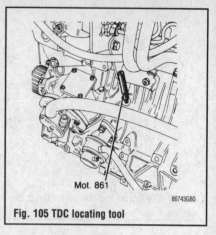

Fig. 105 TDC locating tool

To install:

13. Install a new timing chain cover gasket to the chain cover. Apply a small amount of Mopar silicone rubber adhesive sealant or equivalent, at the joint where the chain cover and oil pan gasket meet.

14. Install the timing chain cover taking care not to damage to oil pan. Finger tighten the cover bolts at this time.

15. Position the smaller diameter of the oil seal on top of seal installation tool 6635. Seat the oil seal in the groove of the tool and then position both onto the crankshaft.

16. Tighten the 4 lower cover bolts to 10 ft. lbs. (13 Nm) to prevent the cover from tipping during seal installation.

17. Using the vibration damper bolt, tighten the bolt to draw the seal into position.

18. Loosen the 4 cover bolts to allow the timing chain cover to be realigned.

19. Tighten the timing chain cover bolts to 30 ft. lbs. (41 Nm) and oil pan bolts to 215 inch lbs. (24 Nm).

20. Remove the vibration damper bolt and the seal installation tool.

21. Install the vibration damper.

22. Connect the fuel lines.

23. Install the water pump.

24. Install the power steering pump.

25. Install the serpentine belt.

26. Install the cooling fan shroud.

27. Fill the cooling system.

28. Connect the negative battery cable.

Timing Belt

REMOVAL & INSTALLATION

▶ See Figures 104, 105, 106 and 107

❊❊❊ CAUTION:

The timing system is complex. Severe engine damage will occur if you make any mistakes. Do not attempt this procedure unless you are highly experienced with this type of repair. If you are at all unsure of your abilities, consult an expert. Double-check all your work and be sure everything is correct before you attempt to start the engine.

➡This applies to 2.1L diesel engines only.

Jeep recommends timing belt replacement at 55,000 miles, but most belt manufacturers recommend intervals anywhere from 45,000 miles (72,500 km) to 90,000 miles (145,000 km).

1. Disconnect the negative battery cable.
2. Remove the timing belt cover.
3. Install sprocket holding tool MOT 854 or equivalent and remove the camshaft sprocket retaining bolt. Remove the special tool.
4. Loosen the bolts and move the chain tensioner away from the timing belt. Tighten the tensioner bolts.
5. Remove the timing belt from the sprockets. Inspect the belt for damage

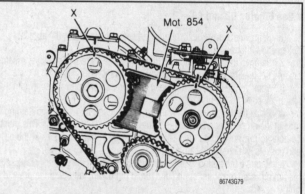

Fig. 106 Camshaft and injection pump timing marks aligned

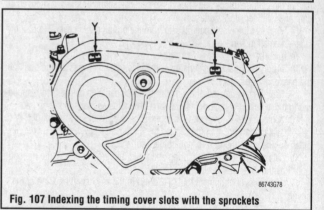

Fig. 107 Indexing the timing cover slots with the sprockets

or wear, refer to timing belt inspection below.

6. If it is necessary to remove the fuel injection pump sprocket, use tools BVI 28-01 and BVI 859, or equivalent.

To install:

❊❊❊ CAUTION:

Before starting the engine, carefully rotate the crankshaft by hand through at least two full revolutions (use a socket and breaker bar on the crankshaft pulley centerbolt). If you feel any resistance, STOP! There is something wrong - most likely, valves are contacting the pistons. You must find the problem before proceeding. Check your work and see if any updated repair information is available.

➡The following installation steps must be followed, exactly!

7. Remove the access plug in the block, on the left side, and install the holding tool, MOT 861 in the hole. Rotate the crankshaft slowly, clockwise, until the tool drops into the TDC locating slot in the crankshaft counterweight.

➡**Don't use this tool as a crankshaft holding tool. When tightening or loosening geartrain fasteners, use a flywheel holding tool, such as tool MOT 582.**

8. Install sprocket holding tool, MOT 854 to retain the camshaft and injection pump sprockets. Make sure that the timing marks are positioned as shown.

9. Install the timing belt. There should be a total of 19 belt teeth between the camshaft and injection pump timing marks.

10. Temporarily position the timing cover over the sprockets. The camshaft and injection pump timing marks must index with the pointers in the cover's timing slots.

11. Remove the cover.

12. Remove the holding tool, MOT 854.

13. Make sure that the timing belt tensioner bolts are 1/2 turn loose, maximum.

14. The tensioner should, automatically, bear against the belt giving the proper belt tension. Tighten the tensioner bolts.

15. Remove the TDC locating tool and install the plug.

16. Rotate the crankshaft, slowly, CLOCKWISE, two complete revolutions.

➡**NEVER rotate the crankshaft counterclockwise while adjusting belt tension.**

17. Loosen the tensioner bolts 1/8 turn, maximum, then tighten them again.

18. Check the belt deflection at a point midway between the camshaft and injection pump sprockets. The belt should deflect 1.37 inches (35mm).

19. Install the timing belt cover.

Timing Chain and Gears

REMOVAL & INSTALLATION

2.5L Engine

▶ **See Figures 108 and 109**

1. Disconnect the negative battery cable.

2. Remove the fan and shroud, the accessory drive belts, vibration damper and pulley.

3. Remove the timing case cover.

4. Rotate the crankshaft so that the timing marks on the cam and crank sprockets align next to each other.

5. Remove the oil slinger from the crankshaft.

6. Remove the cam sprocket retaining bolt and remove the sprocket and chain. The crank sprocket may also be removed at this time. If the tensioner is to be removed, the oil pan must be removed first.

To install:

7. Prior to installation, turn the tensioner lever to the unlock (down) position.

8. Pull the tensioner block toward the tensioner to compress the spring. Hold the block and turn the tensioner lever to the lock (up) position.

9. Install the camshaft/crankshaft sprocket and timing chain together, as a

unit. Ensure timing marks are aligned properly. The camshaft sprocket bolt should be tightened to 50 ft. lbs. (68 Nm) on 1984–88 models or 80 ft. lbs. (108 Nm) on 1989 and later models.

10. Install all other components in the reverse order of removal.

2.8L Engine

1. Disconnect the negative battery cable.

2. Remove the timing cover.

3. Turn the crankshaft to bring the No. 1 piston to TDC of its compression stroke. The timing marks on the crankshaft and camshaft sprockets should be aligned as shown with the No. 4 cylinder in firing position.

4. Remove the camshaft sprocket and chain. If the sprocket is stuck, you can remove it by tapping it lightly with a plastic or wood mallet.

5. Lubricate the chain and sprockets with Molykote®, or equivalent. Install the cam sprocket and chain, with the timing marks aligned and the dowel in the camshaft aligned with the hole in the sprocket.

6. Install the sprocket on the camshaft and tighten the cam sprocket bolts to 20 ft. lbs. (27 Nm).

7. Install the timing cover. Reconnect the negative battery cable.

4.0L Engine

▶ **See Figures 110 thru 114**

1. Remove the drive belts, engine fan and hub assembly, accessory pulley, vibration damper and timing chain cover.

2. Remove the tension spring and thrust pin from the preload bolt, if equipped.

3. Remove the oil seal from the timing chain cover.

4. Remove the camshaft sprocket retaining bolt and washer.

5. Rotate the crankshaft until the timing mark on the crankshaft sprocket is closest to and in a center line with the timing pointer of the camshaft sprocket.

6. Remove the camshaft sprocket and timing chain as an assembly. Disassemble the chain and sprockets. If necessary, remove the crankshaft sprocket.

To install:

7. Assemble the timing chain, crankshaft sprocket and camshaft sprocket with the timing marks aligned.

8. Install the assembly to the crankshaft and the camshaft. Install the camshaft sprocket retaining bolt and washer and tighten to 80 ft. lbs. (108 Nm).

9. Check the alignment of the chain and sprockets.

10. Lubricate the tension spring, thrust pin and pin bore with MOPAR engine oil supplement, or equivalent, and install.

11. Install the timing chain cover and a new oil seal.

12. Install the vibration damper, accessory pulley, engine fan and hub assembly and drive belts.

5.2L and 5.9L Engines

▶ **See Figures 116 and 117**

1. Disconnect the negative battery cable.

2. Remove the timing chain cover.

3. Place a scale next to the timing chain so any movement of the chain can be measured.

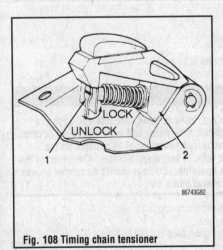

Fig. 108 Timing chain tensioner

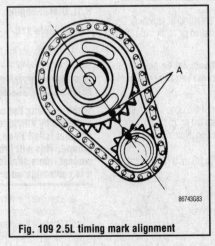

Fig. 109 2.5L timing mark alignment

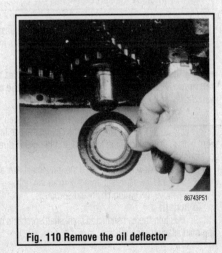

Fig. 110 Remove the oil deflector

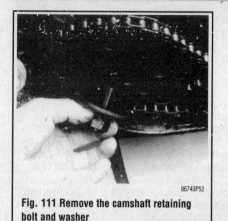

Fig. 111 Remove the camshaft retaining bolt and washer

Fig. 112 Be careful not to lose the thrust pin and spring

Fig. 113 Remove the camshaft sprocket and chain

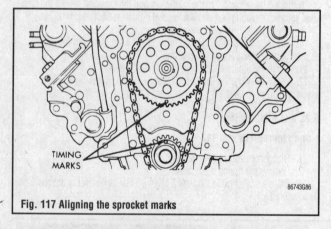

Fig. 114 It may be necessary to use a puller to extract the crankshaft sprocket

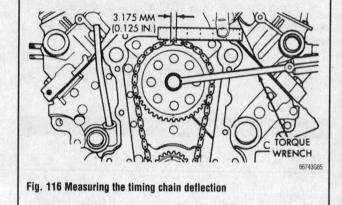

Fig. 116 Measuring the timing chain deflection

Fig. 117 Aligning the sprocket marks

4. Place a torque wrench and socket over the camshaft sprocket attaching bolt. Apply 30 ft. lbs. (41 Nm) with the cylinder heads installed or 15 ft. lbs. (20 Nm) with the cylinder heads removed.

➠With the torque applied the crankshaft sprocket should not be permitted to move, but it may be necessary to block the crankshaft to prevent rotation.

5. Hold the scale with the dimension reading even with the edge of a chain link. Apply 30 ft. lbs. (41 Nm) with the cylinder heads installed or 15 ft. lbs. (20 Nm) with the cylinder heads removed, in the reverse direction. Note the amount of chain movement.
6. Install a new timing chain if the movement exceeds 1/8 inch (3.175mm).
7. Remove the camshaft sprocket retaining bolt.
8. Remove the timing chain and sprockets.

To install:
9. Position the camshaft and crankshaft sprockets on a bench with the timing marks facing each other.

10. Position the timing chain onto the sprockets.
11. Turn the crankshaft and camshaft to align with the keyway location in the crankshaft and camshaft sprockets.
12. Keeping tension on the chain, slide the sprocket and chain assembly onto the engine.
13. Ensure the timing marks are still aligned by using a straight-edge.
14. Install the camshaft bolt and tighten it to 50 ft. lbs. (68 Nm).
15. Install the timing chain cover.
16. Connect the negative battery cable.

Camshaft and Bearings

REMOVAL & INSTALLATION

2.1L Diesel Engine

◆ See Figure 118

1. Disconnect the negative battery cable.
2. Drain the cooling system.

❊❊ CAUTION

When draining the coolant, keep in mind that cats and dogs are attracted by ethylene glycol antifreeze, and are quite likely to drink any that is left in an uncovered container or in puddles on the ground, This will prove fatal in sufficient quantity. Always drain the coolant into a sealable container. Coolant should be reused unless it is contaminated or several years old.

3. Remove the valve cover and timing belt cover.
4. Remove the cylinder head.
5. Remove the camshaft gear using tool BVI 28-01.

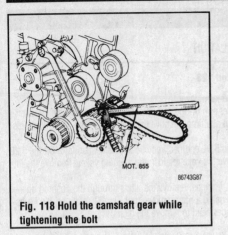

Fig. 118 Hold the camshaft gear while tightening the bolt

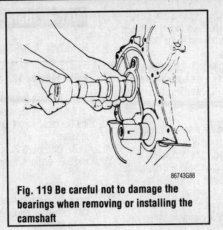

Fig. 119 Be careful not to damage the bearings when removing or installing the camshaft

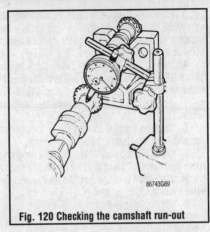

Fig. 120 Checking the camshaft run-out

6. Remove the oil seal from the cylinder head by prying it out using a suitable tool.

7. Remove the camshaft from the cylinder head.

To install:

8. Coat the camshaft with an engine oil supplement.

9. Carefully install the camshaft in the cylinder head.

10. Install the oil seal in the cylinder.

11. Install the camshaft gear. Hold the sprocket with tool MOT 855 while tightening to 37 ft. lbs. (50 Nm).

12. Install the cylinder head.

13. Install the valve cover and timing belt cover.

14. Fill the cooling system.

15. Connect the negative battery cable.

Except 2.1L Diesel Engine

▶ **See Figure 119**

1. Disconnect the battery ground.

2. Drain the cooling system.

✳✳ CAUTION

When draining the coolant, keep in mind that cats and dogs are attracted by ethylene glycol antifreeze, and are quite likely to drink any that is left in an uncovered container or in puddles on the ground. This will prove fatal in sufficient quantity. Always drain the coolant into a sealable container. Coolant should be reused unless it is contaminated or several years old.

➡ **The air conditioning system must be discharged using an approved recovery/recycling machine only. Please refer to Section 1 for more information.**

3. Discharge the air conditioning system, remove the radiator and air conditioning condenser.

4. On carbureted engines, remove the fuel pump.

5. Matchmark the distributor and engine for installation. Note the rotor position by marking it on the distributor body. Unbolt and remove the distributor and wires.

6. Remove the rocker arm cover.

7. Remove the rocker arm assemblies.

8. Remove the pushrods.

➡ **Keep everything in order for installation. If a replacement camshaft is to be installed, replace hydraulic lifters to ensure durability of camshaft lobes and lifter bottoms.**

9. Using a tool J-21884, or equivalent, remove the hydraulic lifters.

10. Remove the vibration damper and timing chain cover.

➡ **If the camshaft sprocket appears to have been rubbing against the cover, check the oil pressure relief holes in the rear cam journal for debris.**

11. Remove the timing chain and sprockets.

12. Slide the camshaft from the engine. If necessary, remove front bumper and/or grille to allow removal of camshaft through front of vehicle.

13. Inspect the cam lobes, bearing journals, bearings and distributor drive gear for wear. Replace if necessary.

To install:

14. Lubricate all moving parts with engine oil supplement prior to installation.

15. Install camshaft and tighten camshaft sprocket retaining bolts.

16. Remainder of installation procedure is reverse of removal.

➡ **Run engine for at least 30 minutes at varying rpm's (between 1000–2000 rpm) to allow camshaft and lifters to break-in. Change oil and filter immediately after break-in period.**

INSPECTION

Run-Out

▶ **See Figure 120**

1. Check camshaft for straightness. Place the camshaft in two V-blocks. Install a dial indicator so that the actuating point of the indicator rests on a camshaft bearing journal. Spin the camshaft and note the runout. If run-out exceeds 0.0009 in. (0.023mm) on any bearing journal, replace the camshaft.

Camshaft Lobe Lift

▶ **See Figure 121**

Check the lift of each lobe in consecutive order and make a note of the reading.

1. Remove valve rocker arm cover(s).

2. Remove the rocker arm assemblies.

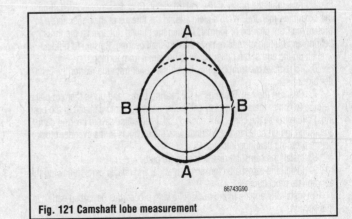

Fig. 121 Camshaft lobe measurement

3. Make sure the pushrod is in the valve lifter socket. Install a dial indicator so that the actuating point of the indicator is in the pushrod socket (or the indicator ball socket adaptor is on the end of the pushrod) and in the same plane as the push rod movement.

4. Install an auxiliary starter switch Crank the engine with the ignition switch **OFF**. Turn the crankshaft over until the tappet is on the base circle of the camshaft lobe. At this position, the pushrod will be in its lowest position.

5. Zero the dial indicator. Continue to rotate the crankshaft slowly until the pushrod is in the fully raised position.

6. Compare the total lift recorded on the dial indicator with the specification shown on the Camshaft Specification chart.

7. Check the accuracy of the original indicator reading by continuing to rotate the crankshaft and noting the highest lift recorded on the dial indicator. If the lift on any lobe is below specified wear limits listed, the camshaft and the valve lifters must be replaced.

8. Remove the dial indicator and auxiliary starter switch.

9. Install the rocker arm assemblies. Check the valve clearance. Adjust if required (refer to procedure in this section).

10. Install the rocker arm cover(s).

Camshaft End-Play

➡ **On engines with an aluminum or nylon camshaft sprocket, prying against the sprocket, with the valve train load on the camshaft, can break or damage the sprocket. Therefore, the rocker arm adjusting nuts must be backed off, or the rocker arm and shaft assembly must be loosened sufficiently to free the camshaft. After checking the camshaft end-play, check the valve clearance. Adjust if required (refer to procedure in this section).**

1. Push the camshaft toward the rear of the engine. Install a dial indicator so that the indicator point is on the camshaft sprocket attaching screw.

2. Zero the dial indicator. Position a prybar between the camshaft gear and the block. Pull the camshaft forward and release it. Compare the dial indicator reading with the specifications.

3. If the end play is excessive, check the spacer for correct installation before it is removed. If the spacer is correctly installed, replace the thrust plate.

4. Remove the dial indicator.

BEARING REPLACEMENT

1. Remove the engine following the procedures in this section and install it on an engine stand.

2. Remove the camshaft, flywheel and crankshaft, following the appropriate procedures. Push the pistons to the top of the cylinder.

3. Remove the camshaft rear bearing bore plug. Remove the camshaft bearings with a bearing removal tool.

4. Select the proper size expanding collet and back-up nut and assemble on the mandrel. With the expanding collet collapsed, install the collet assembly in the camshaft bearing and tighten the back-up nut on the expanding mandrel until the collet fits the camshaft bearing.

5. Assemble the puller screw and extension (if necessary) and install on the expanding mandrel. Wrap a cloth around the threads of the puller screw to protect the front bearing or journal. Tighten the pulling nut against the thrust bearing and pulling plate to remove the camshaft bearing. Be sure to hold a wrench on the end of the puller screw to prevent it from turning.

6. To remove the front bearing, install the puller from the rear of the cylinder block.

7. Position the new bearings at the bearing bores, and press them in place. Be sure to center the pulling plate and puller screw to avoid damage to the bearing. Failure to use the correct expanding collet can cause severe bearing damage. Align the oil holes in the bearings with the oil holes in the cylinder block before pressing bearings into place.

8. Install the camshaft rear bearing bore plug.

9. Install the camshaft, crankshaft, flywheel and related parts, following the appropriate procedures.

10. Install the engine in the truck, following procedures described earlier in this section.

REMOVAL & INSTALLATION

◆ **See Figures 122 and 123**

1. Remove the rocker arm cover.

2. Remove the rocker arm bridge and pivot assembly by alternately loosening the capscrews 1 turn at a time. Remove the pushrods. Keep all components in order.

3. On 2.8L, 5.2L and 5.9L engines, remove the intake manifold. On the 5.2L and 5.9L engines, remove the yoke retainer and aligning yokes. Remove the lifters.

4. On 2.1L and 2.5L engines, remove the lifters through the pushrod opening in the cylinder head using a lifter removal tool. On 4.0L engines, it's necessary to remove the cylinder head to remove the lifters.

To install:

5. Dip each lifter in MOPAR engine oil supplement and install into lifter bore using lifter tool.

6. Install all components (in their original positions) in reverse order of removal. On 5.2L and 5.9L engines, install the yoke retainers and tighten the bolts to 200 inch lbs. (23 Nm).

7. Pour remaining engine oil supplement in engine. The engine oil supplement must remain in the engine for at least 1000 miles but need not be drained until the next scheduled oil change.

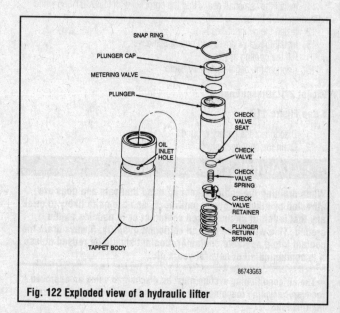

Fig. 122 Exploded view of a hydraulic lifter

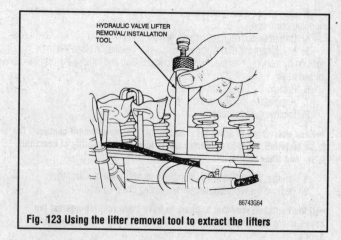

Fig. 123 Using the lifter removal tool to extract the lifters

Crankshaft Main Oil Seal

REMOVAL & INSTALLATION

2.1L Diesel Engine

If the end seals are being replaced, remove the engine and place it on an engine stand. If the side seals are being replaced, remove the oil pan. It is advisable to replace the end seals if the side seals are leaking.

FRONT END MAIN SEAL

▶ See Figure 124

1. Remove the engine.
2. Remove the timing belt and sprockets.
3. Using a sharp awl, punch a hole in the seal and pry it out of its bore.
4. Thoroughly clean the bore.
5. Coat the outer edge of the new seal with sealer and the inner sealing surface with clean engine oil.
6. Using a seal driver, drive the new seal into place.
7. Install the timing belt and sprockets, and all other related parts.
8. Install the engine.

REAR END MAIN SEAL

▶ See Figure 125

1. Remove the engine.
2. Remove the flywheel.
3. Using a sharp awl, punch a hole in the seal and pry it out of its bore.
4. Thoroughly clean the bore.
5. Coat the outer edge of the new seal with sealer and the inner sealing surface with clean engine oil.
6. Using a seal driver, drive the new seal into place.
7. Install the flywheel.
8. Install the engine.

SIDE SEALS

▶ See Figures 126 and 127

➡Depending on working clearance, it may be necessary to remove the engine.

1. Remove the oil pan.
2. Remove the main bearing cap.
3. Remove the side seals.
4. Thoroughly clean the seal surfaces in the block and cap.
5. Install the cap.
6. Measure the width of the seal bore.
7. If the seal bore is 0.196 in. (5mm) or less, use a 0.20 in. (5.1mm) thick seal; if it is more than 0.196 in. (5mm), use a 0.25 in. (5.4mm) thick seal.
8. Remove the bearing cap.
9. Insert the proper side seals in the cap grooves with the grooves in the

seals facing outward. Each seal should stick out from the cap about 0.007 in. (0.2mm).
10. Lightly coat the seals with clean engine oil.
11. Cover the length of each seal with a strip of aluminum foil and install the cap and seals in the block. Don't install the cap bolts. Remove the foil.
12. Measure the side seal protrusion above the cap. Protrusion should be greater than 0.027 in. (0.7mm).
13. Tighten the bearing cap bolts to 72 ft. lbs. (98 Nm).
14. Cut the side seals to within 0.019–0.027 in. (0.5–0.7mm) protrusion.
15. Install the oil pan.

2.5L Engine

▶ See Figure 128

1. Remove the transmission.
2. Remove the flywheel.
3. Pry out the seal from around the crankshaft flange.
To install:
4. Coat the inner lip of the new seal with clean engine oil.
5. Gently tap the new seal into place, flush with the block, using a rear main seal installer tool.

➡The felt lip must be located inside the flywheel mounting surface. If the lip is not positioned correctly, the flywheel could damage the seal.

6. Install all parts in reverse order of removal.

2.8L Engine

The General Motors built 2.8L will have one of two different rear main seal assemblies: either a 1-piece or 2-piece seal. The 2-piece type requires removal of the rear main bearing cap for servicing. The wide, 1-piece seal, used on later model engines, requires the removal of the transmission and flywheel.

2-PIECE

▶ See Figures 129 and 130

1. Remove the oil pan and pump.
2. Remove the rear main bearing cap.
3. Gently pack the upper seal into the groove approximate 1/4 in. (6mm) on each side.
4. Measure the amount the seal was driven in on one side and add 1/16 in. (1.5mm). Cut this length from the old lower cap seal. Be sure to get a sharp cut. Repeat for the other side.
5. Place the piece of cut seal into the groove and pack the seal into the block. Do this for each side.

➡GM makes a guide tool (J-29114-1) which bolts to the block via an oil pan bolt hole, and a packing tool (J29114-2) which are machined to provide a built-in stop for the installation of the short cut pieces. Using the packing tool, work the short pieces of seal onto the guide tool, then pack them into the block with the packing tool.

6. Install a new lower seal in the rear main cap.

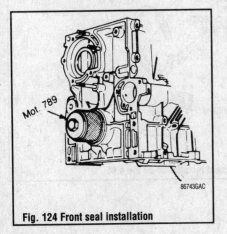

Fig. 124 Front seal installation

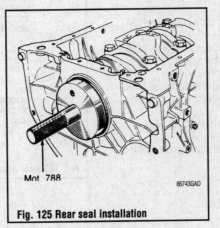

Fig. 125 Rear seal installation

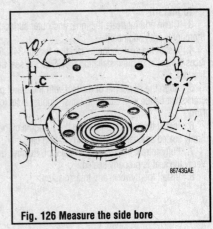

Fig. 126 Measure the side bore

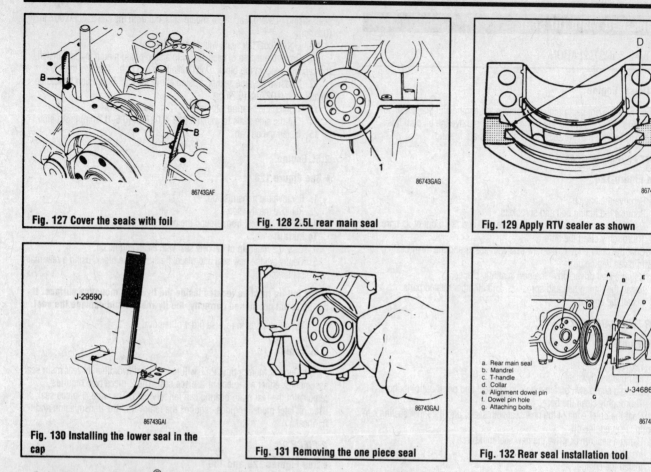

Fig. 127 Cover the seals with foil

Fig. 128 2.5L rear main seal

Fig. 129 Apply RTV sealer as shown

Fig. 130 Installing the lower seal in the cap

Fig. 131 Removing the one piece seal

a. Rear main seal
b. Mandrel
c. T-handle
d. Collar
e. Alignment dowel pin
f. Dowel pin hole
g. Attaching bolts

Fig. 132 Rear seal installation tool

7. Install a piece of Plastigage® or the equivalent on the bearing journal. Install the rear cap and tighten to 70 ft. lbs. (95 Nm). Remove the cap and check the gauge for bearing clearance. If out of specification, the ends of the seal may be frayed or not flush, preventing the cap from proper sealing. Correct as required.

8. Clean the journal, and apply a thin film of RTV silicone sealer to the mating surfaces of the cap and block. Do not allow any sealer to get onto the journal or bearing. Install the bearing cap and tighten to 70 ft. lbs. (95 Nm). Install the pan and pump.

1-PIECE

▶ See Figures 131 and 132

1. Remove transmission and flywheel.
2. Using an appropriate tool, pry the seal from around the crankshaft flange. Insert the prytool under the seal dust lip and pry up and out.

➡ **DO NOT allow the prytool to contact the crankshaft journal surface.**

To install:

3. Clean and lubricate the inner and outer surfaces of the replacement seal thoroughly with engine oil.
4. Install the seal on the installation tool (J-34686). Ensure the seal dust lip faces the collar of the installation tool. Seat the seal firmly against the collar of the tool.
5. Align the dowel pin of the tool with the dowel pin hole and tighten tool to crankshaft flange with attaching bolts. Tighten bolts to 24–36 ft. lbs. (33–49 Nm).
6. Install the seal by tightening the T-handle of the tool until the seal is firmly seated against the block and bearing cap.
7. Fully retract the T-handle of the tool. Remove the attaching bolts and tool. Verify the seal is properly seated.
8. Install the flywheel and transmission.

4.0L Engine

▶ See Figure 133

1. Remove the transmission.
2. Remove the flywheel or flexplate.
3. Pry the seal out from around the crankshaft flange.
4. Remove the rear main bearing cap and wipe clean the cap and crankshaft seal surfaces.

To install:

5. Apply a thin coat of engine oil to the seal surfaces of the cap and crankshaft.
6. Coat the lip of each seal half with clean engine oil.
7. Position the upper seal half in the block. The lip of the seal faces the front of the engine.

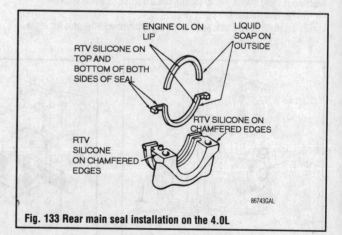

ENGINE OIL ON LIP

LIQUID SOAP ON OUTSIDE

RTV SILICONE ON TOP AND BOTTOM OF BOTH SIDES OF SEAL

RTV SILICONE ON CHAMFERED EDGES

RTV SILICONE ON CHAMFERED EDGES

Fig. 133 Rear main seal installation on the 4.0L

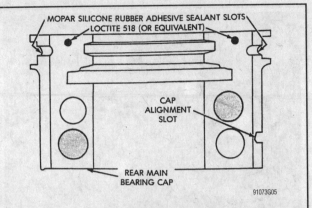

Fig. 134 Sealant application to the bearing cap

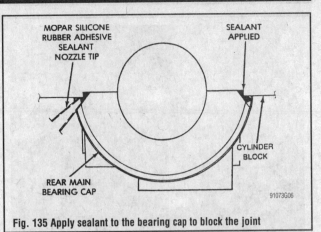

Fig. 135 Apply sealant to the bearing cap to block the joint

8. Coat both side of the lower seal's end tabs with RTV silicone gasket material. Don't get any on the seal lip.

9. Coat the outer, curved surface of the lower seal with soap.

10. Seat the lower seal firmly in the bearing cap recess.

11. Coat both chamfered edges of the bearing cap with RTV silicone gasket material.

✳✳ WARNING

Be careful to avoid getting and RTV material on the bearing cap-to-block mating surfaces! Doing so would change the bearing clearance!

12. Install the bearing cap.

13. Tighten all the main bearing caps to 80 ft. lbs. (108 Nm).

5.2L and 5.9L Engines

◆ See Figures 134 and 135

1. Remove the oil pan.

2. Remove the oil pump.

3. Remove the rear bearing cap. Remove and discard the old lower seal.

4. Carefully remove and discard the the upper seal.

5. Lightly oil the new upper seal lips with engine oil. To allow ease of installation of the seal, loosen at least 2 main bearing caps.

6. Rotate the new upper seal into the cylinder block being careful not to shave or cut the outer surface of the seal. Install the new seal with the yellow paint facing towards the rear of the engine.

7. Install the new lower seal with the yellow paint facing the rear of the engine.

8. Apply a 0.20 in. (5mm) drop of Loctite® 518 or equivalent on each side of the rear main bearing cap. Do not allow sealant to contact the seal. Assemble the cap immediately.

9. Install the cap with cleaned and oiled bolts. Alternately tighten all cap bolts to 85 ft. lbs. (115 Nm).

10. Install the oil pump.

11. Install the oil pan.

Flywheel/Flexplate

REMOVAL & INSTALLATION

1. Remove the transmission and transfer case.

2. Remove the clutch or torque converter, from the flywheel. The flywheel bolts should be loosened a little at a time in a cross pattern to avoid warping the flywheel. On vehicles with manual transmission, replace the pilot bearing in the end of the crankshaft if removing the flywheel.

3. The flywheel should be checked for cracks and glazing. It can be resurfaced by a machine shop.

4. Installation is the reverse of removal. Tighten the bolts a little at a time in a cross pattern, to the following torque specifications:

- 2.1L Engine (diesel)—44 ft. lbs. (60 Nm)
- 2.5L Engine (1984–93)—50 ft. lbs. (68 Nm), plus an additional 60°
- 2.5L Engine (1994 and later)—105 ft. lbs. (142 Nm)
- 2.8L Engine—44–55 ft. lbs. (60–75 Nm)
- 4.0L Engine—105 ft. lbs. (142 Nm)
- 5.2L Engine—55 ft. lbs. (75 Nm)
- 5.9L Engine—55 ft. lbs. (75 Nm)

EXHAUST SYSTEM

Inspection

◆ See Figures 136 thru 142

➡Safety glasses should be worn at all times when working on or near the exhaust system. Older exhaust systems will almost always be covered with loose rust particles which will shower you when disturbed. These particles are more than a nuisance and could injure your eye.

✳✳ CAUTION

DO NOT perform exhaust repairs or inspection with the engine or exhaust hot. Allow the system to cool completely before attempting any work. Exhaust systems are noted for sharp edges, flaking metal and rusted bolts. Gloves and eye protection are required. A healthy supply of penetrating oil and rags is highly recommended.

Your vehicle must be raised and supported safely to inspect the exhaust system properly. By placing 4 safety stands under the vehicle for support should provide enough room for you to slide under the vehicle and inspect the system completely. Start the inspection at the exhaust manifold or turbocharger pipe where the header pipe is attached and work your way to the back of the vehicle. On dual exhaust systems, remember to inspect both sides of the vehicle. Check the complete exhaust system for open seams, holes loose connections, or other deterioration which could permit exhaust fumes to seep into the passenger compartment. Inspect all mounting brackets and hangers for deterioration, some models may have rubber O-rings that can be overstretched and non-supportive. These components will need to be replaced if found. It has always been a practice to use a pointed tool to poke up into the exhaust system where the deterioration spots are to see whether or not they crumble. Some models may have heat shield covering certain parts of the exhaust system , it will be necessary to remove these shields to have the exhaust visible for inspection also.

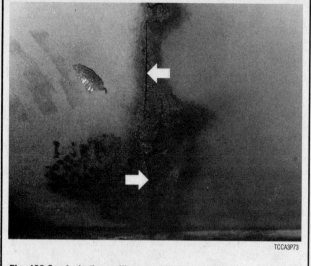

Fig. 136 Cracks in the muffler are a guaranteed leak

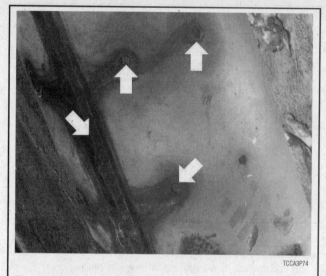

Fig. 137 Check the muffler for rotted spot welds and seams

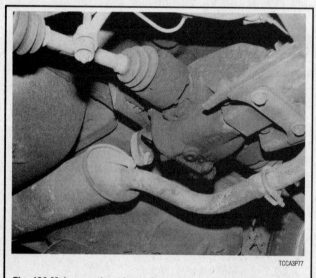

Fig. 138 Make sure the exhaust does contact the body or suspension

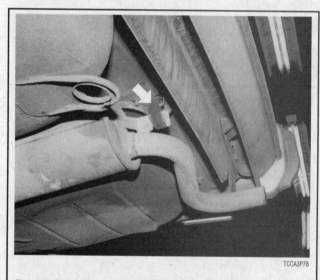

Fig. 139 Check for overstretched or torn exhaust hangers

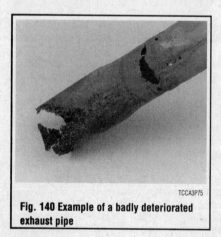

Fig. 140 Example of a badly deteriorated exhaust pipe

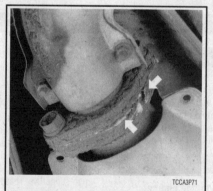

Fig. 141 Inspect flanges for gaskets that have deteriorated and need replacement

Fig. 142 Some systems, like this one, use large O-rings (donuts) in between the flanges

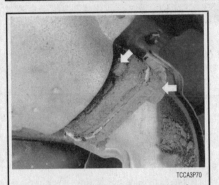

Fig. 143 Nuts and bolts will be extremely difficult to remove when deteriorated with rust

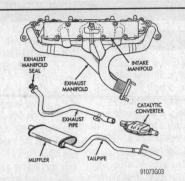

Fig. 144 Exhaust system found on in-line 6-cylinder engines covered in this manual—4-cylinder engines similar

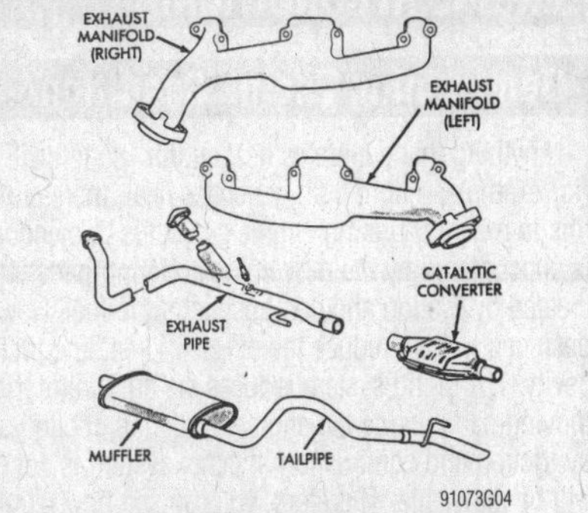

Fig. 145 Exhaust system found on V-8 engines covered in this manual—V-6 engine similar

REPLACEMENT

▶ See Figures 143, 144 and 145

There are basically two types of exhaust systems. One is the flange type where the component ends are attached with bolts and a gasket in-between. The other exhaust system is the slip joint type. These components slip into one another using clamps to retain them together.

✳✳ CAUTION

Allow the exhaust system to cool sufficiently before spraying a solvent exhaust fasteners. Some solvents are highly flammable and could ignite when sprayed on hot exhaust components.

Before removing any component of the exhaust system, ALWAYS squirt a liquid rust dissolving agent onto the fasteners for ease of removal. A lot of knuckle skin will be saved by following this rule. It may even be wise to spray the fasteners and allow them to sit overnight.

Flange Type

▶ See Figure 146

✳✳ CAUTION

Do NOT perform exhaust repairs or inspection with the engine or exhaust hot. Allow the system to cool completely before attempting any work. Exhaust systems are noted for sharp edges, flaking metal and rusted bolts. Gloves and eye protection are required. A healthy supply of penetrating oil and rags is highly recommended. Never spray liquid rust dissolving agent onto a hot exhaust component.

Before removing any component on a flange type system, ALWAYS squirt a liquid rust dissolving agent onto the fasteners for ease of removal. Start by unbolting the exhaust piece at both ends (if required). When unbolting the headpipe from the manifold, make sure that the bolts are free before trying to remove them. if you snap a stud in the exhaust manifold, the stud will have to be removed with a bolt extractor, which often means removal of the manifold itself. Next, disconnect the component from the mounting; slight twisting and turning may be required to remove the component completely from the vehicle. You may need to tap on the component with a rubber mallet to loosen the component. If all else fails, use a hacksaw to separate the parts. An oxy-acetylene cutting torch may be faster but the sparks are DANGEROUS near the fuel tank, and at the very least, accidents could happen, resulting in damage to the under-car parts, not to mention yourself.

Slip Joint Type

▶ See Figure 147

Before removing any component on the slip joint type exhaust system, ALWAYS squirt a liquid rust dissolving agent onto the fasteners for ease of removal. Start by unbolting the exhaust piece at both ends (if required). When unbolting the headpipe from the manifold, make sure that the bolts are free before trying to remove them. if you snap a stud in the exhaust manifold, the stud will have to be removed with a bolt extractor, which often means removal of the manifold itself. Next, remove the mounting U-bolts from around the exhaust pipe you are extracting from the vehicle. Don't be surprised if the U-bolts break while removing the nuts. Loosen the exhaust pipe from any mounting brackets retaining it to the floor pan and separate the components.

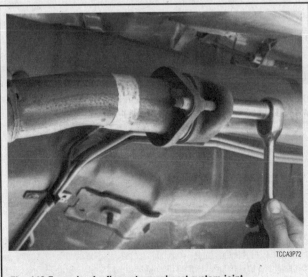

Fig. 146 Example of a flange type exhaust system joint

Fig. 147 Example of a common slip joint type system

ENGINE RECONDITIONING

Determining Engine Condition

Anything that generates heat and/or friction will eventually burn or wear out (for example, a light bulb generates heat, therefore its life span is limited). With this in mind, a running engine generates tremendous amounts of both; friction is encountered by the moving and rotating parts inside the engine and heat is created by friction and combustion of the fuel. However, the engine has systems designed to help reduce the effects of heat and friction and provide added longevity. The oiling system reduces the amount of friction encountered by the moving parts inside the engine, while the cooling system reduces heat created by friction and combustion. If either system is not maintained, a break-down will be inevitable. Therefore, you can see how regular maintenance can affect the service life of your vehicle. If you do not drain, flush and refill your cooling system at the proper intervals, deposits will begin to accumulate in the radiator, thereby reducing the amount of heat it can extract from the coolant. The same applies to your oil and filter; if it is not changed often enough it becomes laden with contaminates and is unable to properly lubricate the engine. This increases friction and wear.

There are a number of methods for evaluating the condition of your engine. A compression test can reveal the condition of your pistons, piston rings, cylinder bores, head gasket(s), valves and valve seats. An oil pressure test can warn you of possible engine bearing, or oil pump failures. Excessive oil consumption, evidence of oil in the engine air intake area and/or bluish smoke from the tailpipe may indicate worn piston rings, worn valve guides and/or valve seals. As a general rule, an engine that uses no more than one quart of oil every 1000 miles is in good condition. Engines that use one quart of oil or more in less than 1000 miles should first be checked for oil leaks. If any oil leaks are present, have them fixed before determining how much oil is consumed by the engine, especially if blue smoke is not visible at the tailpipe.

COMPRESSION TEST

A noticeable lack of engine power, excessive oil consumption and/or poor fuel mileage measured over an extended period are all indicators of internal engine wear. Worn piston rings, scored or worn cylinder bores, blown head gaskets, sticking or burnt valves, and worn valve seats are all possible culprits. A check of each cylinder's compression will help locate the problem.

Gasoline Engines

▶ **See Figure 148**

➡**A screw-in type compression gauge is more accurate than the type you simply hold against the spark plug hole. Although it takes slightly longer to use, it's worth the effort to obtain a more accurate reading.**

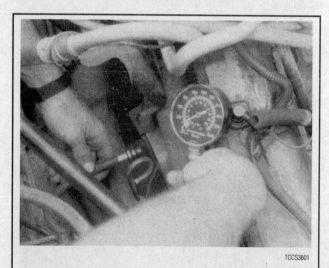

TCCS3801

Fig. 148 A screw-in type compression gauge is more accurate and easier to use without an assistant

1. Make sure that the proper amount and viscosity of engine oil is in the crankcase, then ensure the battery is fully charged.
2. Warm-up the engine to normal operating temperature, then shut the engine **OFF**.
3. Disable the ignition system.
4. Label and disconnect all of the spark plug wires from the plugs.
5. Thoroughly clean the cylinder head area around the spark plug ports, then remove the spark plugs.
6. Set the throttle plate to the fully open (wide-open throttle) position. You can block the accelerator linkage open for this, or you can have an assistant fully depress the accelerator pedal.
7. Install a screw-in type compression gauge into the No. 1 spark plug hole until the fitting is snug.

✳✳ WARNING

Be careful not to crossthread the spark plug hole.

8. According to the tool manufacturer's instructions, connect a remote starting switch to the starting circuit.
9. With the ignition switch in the **OFF** position, use the remote starting switch to crank the engine through at least five compression strokes (approximately 5 seconds of cranking) and record the highest reading on the gauge.
10. Repeat the test on each cylinder, cranking the engine approximately the same number of compression strokes and/or time as the first.
11. Compare the highest readings from each cylinder to that of the others. The indicated compression pressures are considered within specifications if the lowest reading cylinder is within 75 percent of the pressure recorded for the highest reading cylinder. For example, if your highest reading cylinder pressure was 150 psi (1034 kPa), then 75 percent of that would be 113 psi (779 kPa). So the lowest reading cylinder should be no less than 113 psi (779 kPa).
12. If a cylinder exhibits an unusually low compression reading, pour a tablespoon of clean engine oil into the cylinder through the spark plug hole and repeat the compression test. If the compression rises after adding oil, it means that the cylinder's piston rings and/or cylinder bore are damaged or worn. If the pressure remains low, the valves may not be seating properly (a valve job is needed), or the head gasket may be blown near that cylinder. If compression in any two adjacent cylinders is low, and if the addition of oil doesn't help raise compression, there is leakage past the head gasket. Oil and coolant in the combustion chamber, combined with blue or constant white smoke from the tailpipe, are symptoms of this problem. However, don't be alarmed by the normal white smoke emitted from the tailpipe during engine warm-up or from cold weather driving. There may be evidence of water droplets on the engine dipstick and/or oil droplets in the cooling system if a head gasket is blown.

Diesel Engines

Checking cylinder compression on diesel engines is basically the same procedure as on gasoline engines except for the following:
1. A special compression gauge adapter suitable for diesel engines (because these engines have much greater compression pressures) must be used.
2. Remove the injector tubes and remove the injectors from each cylinder.

✳✳ WARNING

Do not forget to remove the washer underneath each injector. Otherwise, it may get lost when the engine is cranked.

3. When fitting the compression gauge adapter to the cylinder head, make sure the bleeder of the gauge (if equipped) is closed.
4. When reinstalling the injector assemblies, install new washers underneath each injector.

OIL PRESSURE TEST

Check for proper oil pressure at the sending unit passage with an externally mounted mechanical oil pressure gauge (as opposed to relying on a factory installed dash-mounted gauge). A tachometer may also be needed, as some specifications may require running the engine at a specific rpm.

1. With the engine cold, locate and remove the oil pressure sending unit.

2. Following the manufacturer's instructions, connect a mechanical oil pressure gauge and, if necessary, a tachometer to the engine.

3. Start the engine and allow it to idle.

4. Check the oil pressure reading when cold and record the number. You may need to run the engine at a specified rpm, so check the specifications.

5. Run the engine until normal operating temperature is reached (upper radiator hose will feel warm).

6. Check the oil pressure reading again with the engine hot and record the number. Turn the engine **OFF**.

7. Compare your hot oil pressure reading to that given in the chart. If the reading is low, check the cold pressure reading against the chart. If the cold pressure is well above the specification, and the hot reading was lower than the specification, you may have the wrong viscosity oil in the engine. Change the oil, making sure to use the proper grade and quantity, then repeat the test.

Low oil pressure readings could be attributed to internal component wear, pump related problems, a low oil level, or oil viscosity that is too low. High oil pressure readings could be caused by an overfilled crankcase, too high of an oil viscosity or a faulty pressure relief valve.

Buy or Rebuild?

Now that you have determined that your engine is worn out, you must make some decisions. The question of whether or not an engine is worth rebuilding is largely a subjective matter and one of personal worth. Is the engine a popular one, or is it an obsolete model? Are parts available? Will it get acceptable gas mileage once it is rebuilt? Is the car it's being put into worth keeping? Would it be less expensive to buy a new engine, have your engine rebuilt by a pro, rebuild it yourself or buy a used engine from a salvage yard? Or would it be simpler and less expensive to buy another car? If you have considered all these matters and more, and have still decided to rebuild the engine, then it is time to decide how you will rebuild it.

➡**The editors at Chilton feel that most engine machining should be performed by a professional machine shop. Don't think of it as wasting money, rather, as an assurance that the job has been done right the first time. There are many expensive and specialized tools required to perform such tasks as boring and honing an engine block or having a valve job done on a cylinder head. Even inspecting the parts requires expensive micrometers and gauges to properly measure wear and clearances. Also, a machine shop can deliver to you clean, and ready to assemble parts, saving you time and aggravation. Your maximum savings will come from performing the removal, disassembly, assembly and installation of the engine and purchasing or renting only the tools required to perform the above tasks. Depending on the particular circumstances, you may save 40 to 60 percent of the cost doing these yourself.**

A complete rebuild or overhaul of an engine involves replacing all of the moving parts (pistons, rods, crankshaft, camshaft, etc.) with new ones and machining the non-moving wearing surfaces of the block and heads. Unfortunately, this may not be cost effective. For instance, your crankshaft may have been damaged or worn, but it can be machined undersize for a minimal fee.

So, as you can see, you can replace everything inside the engine, but, it is wiser to replace only those parts which are really needed, and, if possible, repair the more expensive ones. Later in this section, we will break the engine down into its two main components: the cylinder head and the engine block. We will discuss each component, and the recommended parts to replace during a rebuild on each.

Engine Overhaul Tips

Most engine overhaul procedures are fairly standard. In addition to specific parts replacement procedures and specifications for your individual engine, this section is also a guide to acceptable rebuilding procedures. Examples of standard rebuilding practice are given and should be used along with specific details concerning your particular engine.

Competent and accurate machine shop services will ensure maximum performance, reliability and engine life. In most instances it is more profitable for the do-it-yourself mechanic to remove, clean and inspect the component, buy the necessary parts and deliver these to a shop for actual machine work.

Much of the assembly work (crankshaft, bearings, piston rods, and other

components) is well within the scope of the do-it-yourself mechanic's tools and abilities. You will have to decide for yourself the depth of involvement you desire in an engine repair or rebuild.

TOOLS

The tools required for an engine overhaul or parts replacement will depend on the depth of your involvement. With a few exceptions, they will be the tools found in a mechanic's tool kit (see Section 1 of this manual). More in-depth work will require some or all of the following:

- A dial indicator (reading in thousandths) mounted on a universal base
- Micrometers and telescope gauges
- Jaw and screw-type pullers
- Scraper
- Valve spring compressor
- Ring groove cleaner
- Piston ring expander and compressor
- Ridge reamer
- Cylinder hone or glaze breaker
- Plastigage®
- Engine stand

The use of most of these tools is illustrated in this section. Many can be rented for a one-time use from a local parts jobber or tool supply house specializing in automotive work.

Occasionally, the use of special tools is called for. See the information on Special Tools and the Safety Notice in the front of this book before substituting another tool.

OVERHAUL TIPS

Aluminum has become extremely popular for use in engines, due to its low weight. Observe the following precautions when handling aluminum parts:

- Never hot tank aluminum parts (the caustic hot tank solution will eat the aluminum.
- Remove all aluminum parts (identification tag, etc.) from engine parts prior to the tanking.
- Always coat threads lightly with engine oil or anti-seize compounds before installation, to prevent seizure.
- Never overtighten bolts or spark plugs especially in aluminum threads.

When assembling the engine, any parts that will be exposed to frictional contact must be prelubed to provide lubrication at initial start-up. Any product specifically formulated for this purpose can be used, but engine oil is not recommended as a prelube in most cases.

When semi-permanent (locked, but removable) installation of bolts or nuts is desired, threads should be cleaned and coated with Loctite® or another similar, commercial non-hardening sealant.

CLEANING

◆ **See Figures 149, 150, 151 and 152**

Before the engine and its components are inspected, they must be thoroughly cleaned. You will need to remove any engine varnish, oil sludge and/or carbon deposits from all of the components to insure an accurate inspection. A crack in the engine block or cylinder head can easily become overlooked if hidden by a layer of sludge or carbon.

Most of the cleaning process can be carried out with common hand tools and readily available solvents or solutions. Carbon deposits can be chipped away using a hammer and a hard wooden chisel. Old gasket material and varnish or sludge can usually be removed using a scraper and/or cleaning solvent. Extremely stubborn deposits may require the use of a power drill with a wire brush. If using a wire brush, use extreme care around any critical machined surfaces (such as the gasket surfaces, bearing saddles, cylinder bores, etc.). USE OF A WIRE BRUSH IS NOT RECOMMENDED ON ANY ALUMINUM COMPONENTS. Always follow any safety recommendations given by the manufacturer of the tool and/or solvent. You should always wear eye protection during any cleaning process involving scraping, chipping or spraying of solvents.

An alternative to the mess and hassle of cleaning the parts yourself is to drop them off at a local garage or machine shop. They will, more than likely, have the necessary equipment to properly clean all of the parts for a nominal fee.

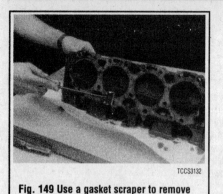

Fig. 149 Use a gasket scraper to remove the old gasket material from the mating surfaces

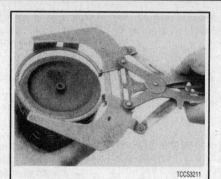

Fig. 150 Use a ring expander tool to remove the piston rings

Fig. 151 Clean the piston ring grooves using a ring groove cleaner tool, or . . .

✳✳ CAUTION

Always wear eye protection during any cleaning process involving scraping, chipping or spraying of solvents.

Remove any oil galley plugs, freeze plugs and/or pressed-in bearings and carefully wash and degrease all of the engine components including the fasteners and bolts. Small parts such as the valves, springs, etc., should be placed in a metal basket and allowed to soak. Use pipe cleaner type brushes, and clean all passageways in the components. Use a ring expander and remove the rings from the pistons. Clean the piston ring grooves with a special tool or a piece of broken ring. Scrape the carbon off of the top of the piston. You should never use a wire brush on the pistons. After preparing all of the piston assemblies in this manner, wash and degrease them again.

✳✳ WARNING

Use extreme care when cleaning around the cylinder head valve seats. A mistake or slip may cost you a new seat.

When cleaning the cylinder head, remove carbon from the combustion chamber with the valves installed. This will avoid damaging the valve seats.

REPAIRING DAMAGED THREADS

▶ **See Figures 153, 154, 155, 156 and 157**

Several methods of repairing damaged threads are available. Heli-Coil (shown here), Keenserts, and Microdot are among the most widely used. All involve basically the same principle—drilling out stripped threads, tapping the

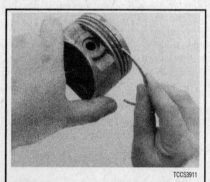

Fig. 152 . . . use a piece of an old ring to clean the grooves. Be careful, the ring can be quite sharp

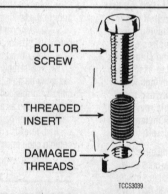

Fig. 153 Damaged bolt hole threads can be replaced with thread repair inserts

Fig. 154 Standard thread repair insert (left), and spark plug thread insert

Fig. 155 Drill out the damaged threads with the specified size bit. Be sure to drill completely through the hole or to the bottom of a blind hole

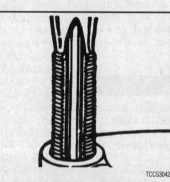

Fig. 156 Using the kit, tap the hole in order to receive the thread insert. Keep the tap well oiled and back it out frequently to avoid clogging the threads

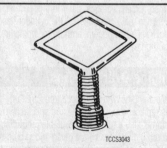

Fig. 157 Screw the insert onto the installer tool until the tang engages the slot. Thread the insert into the hole until it is 1/4-1/2 turn below the top surface, then remove the tool and break off the tang using a punch

hole and installing a prewound insert—making welding, plugging and oversize fasteners unnecessary.

Two types of thread repair inserts are usually supplied: a standard type for most inch coarse, inch fine, metric course and metric fine thread sizes and a spark lug type to fit most spark plug port sizes. Consult the individual tool manufacturer's catalog to determine exact applications. Typical thread repair kits will contain a selection of prewound threaded inserts, a tap (corresponding to the outside diameter threads of the insert) and an installation tool. Spark plug inserts usually differ because they require a tap equipped with pilot threads and a combined reamer/tap section. Most manufacturers also supply blister-packed thread repair inserts separately in addition to a master kit containing a variety of taps and inserts plus installation tools.

Before attempting to repair a threaded hole, remove any snapped, broken or damaged bolts or studs. Penetrating oil can be used to free frozen threads. The offending item can usually be removed with locking pliers or using a screw/stud extractor. After the hole is clear, the thread can be repaired; as shown in the series of accompanying illustrations and in the kit manufacturer's instructions.

Engine Preparation

To properly rebuild an engine, you must first remove it from the vehicle, then disassemble and diagnose it. Ideally you should place your engine on an engine stand. This affords you the best access to the engine components. Follow the manufacturer's directions for using the stand with your particular engine. Remove the flywheel or flexplate before installing the engine to the stand.

Now that you have the engine on a stand, and assuming that you have drained the oil and coolant from the engine, it's time to strip it of all but the necessary components. Before you start disassembling the engine, you may want to take a moment to draw some pictures, or fabricate some labels or containers to mark the locations of various components and the bolts and/or studs which fasten them. Modern day engines use a lot of little brackets and clips which hold wiring harnesses and such, and these holders are often mounted on studs and/or bolts that can be easily mixed up. The manufacturer spent a lot of time and money designing your vehicle, and they wouldn't have wasted any of it by haphazardly placing brackets, clips or fasteners on the vehicle. If it's present when you disassemble it, put it back when you assemble, you will regret not remembering that little bracket which holds a wire harness out of the path of a rotating part.

You should begin by unbolting any accessories still attached to the engine, such as the water pump, power steering pump, alternator, etc. Then, unfasten any manifolds (intake or exhaust) which were not removed during the engine removal procedure. Finally, remove any covers remaining on the engine such as the rocker arm, front or timing cover and oil pan. Some front covers may require the vibration damper and/or crank pulley to be removed beforehand. The idea is to reduce the engine to the bare necessities (cylinder head(s), valve train, engine block, crankshaft, pistons and connecting rods), plus any other `in block' components such as oil pumps, balance shafts and auxiliary shafts.

Finally, remove the cylinder head(s) from the engine block and carefully place on a bench. Disassembly instructions for each component follow later in this section.

Cylinder Head

There are two basic types of cylinder heads used on today's automobiles: the Overhead Valve (OHV) and the Overhead Camshaft (OHC). The latter can also be broken down into two subgroups: the Single Overhead Camshaft (SOHC) and the Dual Overhead Camshaft (DOHC). Generally, if there is only a single camshaft on a head, it is just referred to as an OHC head. Also, an engine with an OHV cylinder head is also known as a pushrod engine.

Most cylinder heads these days are made of an aluminum alloy due to its light weight, durability and heat transfer qualities. However, cast iron was the material of choice in the past, and is still used on many vehicles today. Whether made from aluminum or iron, all cylinder heads have valves and seats. Some use two valves per cylinder, while the more hi-tech engines will utilize a multi-valve configuration using 3, 4 and even 5 valves per cylinder. When the valve contacts the seat, it does so on precision machined surfaces, which seals the combustion chamber. All cylinder heads have a valve guide for each valve. The guide centers the valve to the seat and allows it to move up and down within it. The clearance between the valve and guide can be critical. Too much clearance and the engine may consume oil, lose vacuum and/or damage the seat. Too little, and the valve can stick in the guide causing the engine to run poorly if at all, and possibly causing severe damage. The last component all cylinder heads have are valve springs. The spring holds the valve against its seat. It also returns the valve to this position when the valve has been opened by the valve train or camshaft. The spring is fastened to the valve by a retainer and valve locks (sometimes called keepers). Aluminum heads will also have a valve spring shim to keep the spring from wearing away the aluminum.

An ideal method of rebuilding the cylinder head would involve replacing all of the valves, guides, seats, springs, etc. with new ones. However, depending on how the engine was maintained, often this is not necessary. A major cause of valve, guide and seat wear is an improperly tuned engine. An engine that is running too rich, will often wash the lubricating oil out of the guide with gasoline, causing it to wear rapidly. Conversely, an engine which is running too lean will place higher combustion temperatures on the valves and seats allowing them to wear or even burn. Springs fall victim to the driving habits of the individual. A driver who often runs the engine rpm to the redline will wear out or break the springs faster then one that stays well below it. Unfortunately, mileage takes it toll on all of the parts. Generally, the valves, guides, springs and seats in a cylinder head can be machined and re-used, saving you money. However, if a valve is burnt, it may be wise to replace all of the valves, since they were all operating in the same environment. The same goes for any other component on the cylinder head. Think of it as an insurance policy against future problems related to that component.

Unfortunately, the only way to find out which components need replacing, is to disassemble and carefully check each piece. After the cylinder head(s) are disassembled, thoroughly clean all of the components.

DISASSEMBLY

OHV Heads

◆ See Figures 158 thru 163

Before disassembling the cylinder head, you may want to fabricate some containers to hold the various parts, as some of them can be quite small (such as keepers) and easily lost. Also keeping yourself and the components organized will aid in assembly and reduce confusion. Where possible, try to maintain a components original location; this is especially important if there is not going to be any machine work performed on the components.

Fig. 158 When removing an OHV valve spring, use a compressor tool to relieve the tension from the retainer

Fig. 159 A small magnet will help in removal of the valve locks

Fig. 160 Be careful not to lose the small valve locks (keepers)

Fig. 161 Remove the valve seal from the valve stem—O-ring type seal shown

Fig. 162 Removing an umbrella/positive type seal

Fig. 163 Invert the cylinder head and withdraw the valve from the valve guide bore

1. If you haven't already removed the rocker arms and/or shafts, do so now.
2. Position the head so that the springs are easily accessed.
3. Use a valve spring compressor tool, and relieve spring tension from the retainer.

➡**Due to engine varnish, the retainer may stick to the valve locks. A gentle tap with a hammer may help to break it loose.**

4. Remove the valve locks from the valve tip and/or retainer. A small magnet may help in removing the locks.
5. Lift the valve spring, tool and all, off of the valve stem.
6. If equipped, remove the valve seal. If the seal is difficult to remove with the valve in place, try removing the valve first, then the seal. Follow the steps below for valve removal.
7. Position the head to allow access for withdrawing the valve.

➡**Cylinder heads that have seen a lot of miles and/or abuse may have mushroomed the valve lock grove and/or tip, causing difficulty in removal of the valve. If this has happened, use a metal file to carefully remove the high spots around the lock grooves and/or tip. Only file it enough to allow removal.**

8. Remove the valve from the cylinder head.
9. If equipped, remove the valve spring shim. A small magnetic tool or screwdriver will aid in removal.
10. Repeat Steps 3 though 9 until all of the valves have been removed.

OHC Heads

▶ **See Figures 164 and 165**

Whether it is a single or dual overhead camshaft cylinder head, the disassembly procedure is relatively unchanged. One aspect to pay attention to is careful labeling of the parts on the dual camshaft cylinder head. There will be an intake camshaft and followers as well as an exhaust camshaft and followers and they must be labeled as such. In some cases, the components are identical and could easily be installed incorrectly. DO NOT MIX THEM UP! Determining which is which is very simple; the intake camshaft and components are on the same side of the head as was the intake manifold. Conversely, the exhaust camshaft and components are on the same side of the head as was the exhaust manifold.

Fig. 164 Exploded view of a valve, seal, spring, retainer and locks from an OHC cylinder head

Fig. 165 Example of a multi-valve cylinder head. Note how it has 2 intake and 2 exhaust valve ports

CUP TYPE CAMSHAFT FOLLOWERS

▶ See Figures 166, 167 and 168

Most cylinder heads with cup type camshaft followers will have the valve spring, retainer and locks recessed within the follower's bore. You will need a C-clamp style valve spring compressor tool, an OHC spring removal tool (or equivalent) and a small magnet to disassemble the head.

1. If not already removed, remove the camshaft(s) and/or followers. Mark their positions for assembly.
2. Position the cylinder head to allow use of a C-clamp style valve spring compressor tool.

➡ It is preferred to position the cylinder head gasket surface facing you with the valve springs facing the opposite direction and the head laying horizontal.

3. With the OHC spring removal adapter tool positioned inside of the follower bore, compress the valve spring using the C-clamp style valve spring compressor.
4. Remove the valve locks. A small magnetic tool or screwdriver will aid in removal.
5. Release the compressor tool and remove the spring assembly.
6. Withdraw the valve from the cylinder head.
7. If equipped, remove the valve seal.

➡ Special valve seal removal tools are available. Regular or needle-nose type pliers, if used with care, will work just as well. If using ordinary pliers, be sure not to damage the follower bore. The follower and its bore are machined to close tolerances and any damage to the bore will effect this relationship.

Fig. 168 Position the OHC spring tool in the follower bore, then compress the spring with a C-clamp type tool

8. If equipped, remove the valve spring shim. A small magnetic tool or screwdriver will aid in removal.
9. Repeat Steps 3 through 8 until all of the valves have been removed.

ROCKER ARM TYPE CAMSHAFT FOLLOWERS

▶ See Figures 169 thru 177

Most cylinder heads with rocker arm-type camshaft followers are easily disassembled using a standard valve spring compressor. However, certain models

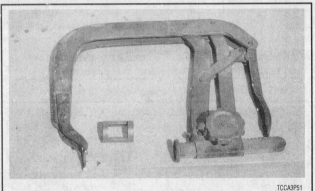

Fig. 166 C-clamp type spring compressor and an OHC spring removal tool (center) for cup type followers

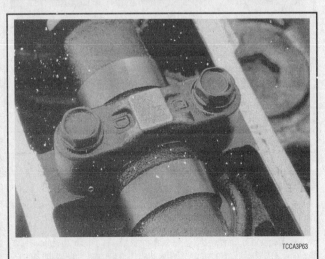

Fig. 167 Most cup type follower cylinder heads retain the camshaft using bolt-on bearing caps

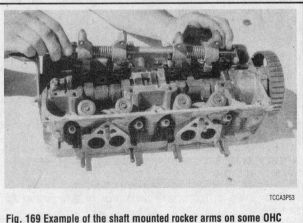

Fig. 169 Example of the shaft mounted rocker arms on some OHC heads

Fig. 170 Another example of the rocker arm type OHC head. This model uses a follower under the camshaft

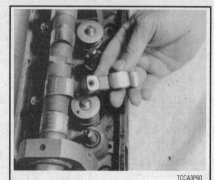

Fig. 171 Before the camshaft can be removed, all of the followers must first be removed . . .

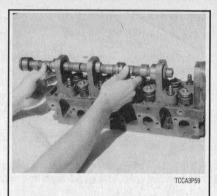

Fig. 172 . . . then the camshaft can be removed by sliding it out (shown), or unbolting a bearing cap (not shown)

Fig. 173 Compress the valve spring . . .

Fig. 174 . . . then remove the valve locks from the valve stem and spring retainer

Fig. 175 Remove the valve spring and retainer from the cylinder head

Fig. 176 Remove the valve seal from the guide. Some gentle prying or pliers may help to remove stubborn ones

Fig. 177 All aluminum and some cast iron heads will have these valve spring shims. Remove all of them as well

may not have enough open space around the spring for the standard tool and may require you to use a C-clamp style compressor tool instead.

1. If not already removed, remove the rocker arms and/or shafts and the camshaft. If applicable, also remove the hydraulic lash adjusters. Mark their positions for assembly.

2. Position the cylinder head to allow access to the valve spring.

3. Use a valve spring compressor tool to relieve the spring tension from the retainer.

➡Due to engine varnish, the retainer may stick to the valve locks. A gentle tap with a hammer may help to break it loose.

4. Remove the valve locks from the valve tip and/or retainer. A small magnet may help in removing the small locks.

5. Lift the valve spring, tool and all, off of the valve stem.

6. If equipped, remove the valve seal. If the seal is difficult to remove with the valve in place, try removing the valve first, then the seal. Follow the steps below for valve removal.

7. Position the head to allow access for withdrawing the valve.

➡**Cylinder heads that have seen a lot of miles and/or abuse may have mushroomed the valve lock grove and/or tip, causing difficulty in removal of the valve. If this has happened, use a metal file to carefully remove the high spots around the lock grooves and/or tip. Only file it enough to allow removal.**

8. Remove the valve from the cylinder head.

TCCA3P52

9. If equipped, remove the valve spring shim. A small magnetic tool or screwdriver will aid in removal.

10. Repeat Steps 3 though 9 until all of the valves have been removed.

INSPECTION

Now that all of the cylinder head components are clean, it's time to inspect them for wear and/or damage. To accurately inspect them, you will need some specialized tools:

- A 0–1 in. micrometer for the valves
- A dial indicator or inside diameter gauge for the valve guides
- A spring pressure test gauge

If you do not have access to the proper tools, you may want to bring the components to a shop that does.

Valves

▶ **See Figures 178 and 179**

The first thing to inspect are the valve heads. Look closely at the head, margin and face for any cracks, excessive wear or burning. The margin is the best

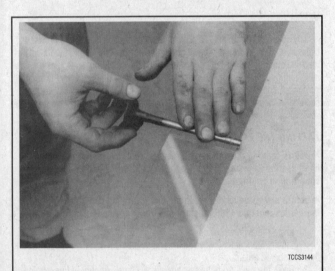

TCCS3144

Fig. 178 Valve stems may be rolled on a flat surface to check for bends

place to look for burning. It should have a squared edge with an even width all around the diameter. When a valve burns, the margin will look melted and the edges rounded. Also inspect the valve head for any signs of tulipping. This will show as a lifting of the edges or dishing in the center of the head and will usually not occur to all of the valves. All of the heads should look the same, any that seem dished more than others are probably bad. Next, inspect the valve lock grooves and valve tips. Check for any burrs around the lock grooves, especially if you had to file them to remove the valve. Valve tips should appear flat, although slight rounding with high mileage engines is normal. Slightly worn valve tips will need to be machined flat. Last, measure the valve stem diameter with the micrometer. Measure the area that rides within the guide, especially towards the tip where most of the wear occurs. Take several measurements along its length and compare them to each other. Wear should be even along the length with little to no taper. If no minimum diameter is given in the specifications, then the stem should not read more than 0.001 in. (0.025mm) below the unworn area of the valve stem. Any valves that fail these inspections should be replaced.

Springs, Retainers and Valve Locks

▶ **See Figures 180 and 181**

The first thing to check is the most obvious, broken springs. Next check the free length and squareness of each spring. If applicable, insure to distinguish between intake and exhaust springs. Use a ruler and/or carpenter's square to measure the length. A carpenter's square should be used to check the springs for squareness. If a spring pressure test gauge is available, check each springs rating and compare to the specifications chart. Check the readings against the specifications given. Any springs that fail these inspections should be replaced.

The spring retainers rarely need replacing, however they should still be checked as a precaution. Inspect the spring mating surface and the valve lock retention area for any signs of excessive wear. Also check for any signs of cracking. Replace any retainers that are questionable.

Valve locks should be inspected for excessive wear on the outside contact area as well as on the inner notched surface. Any locks which appear worn or broken and its respective valve should be replaced.

Cylinder Head

There are several things to check on the cylinder head: valve guides, seats, cylinder head surface flatness, cracks and physical damage.

VALVE GUIDES

▶ **See Figure 182**

Now that you know the valves are good, you can use them to check the guides, although a new valve, if available, is preferred. Before you measure anything, look at the guides carefully and inspect them for any cracks, chips or breakage. Also if the guide is a removable style (as in most aluminum heads), check them for any looseness or evidence of movement. All of the guides should appear to be at the same height from the spring seat. If any seem lower (or higher) from another, the guide has moved. Mount a dial indicator onto the spring side of the cylinder head. Lightly oil the valve stem and insert it into the cylinder head. Position the dial indicator against the valve stem near the tip and

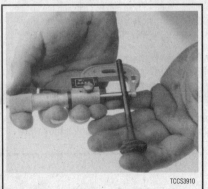

TCCS3910

Fig. 179 Use a micrometer to check the valve stem diameter

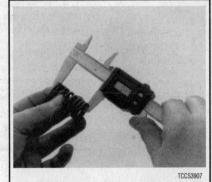

TCCS3907

Fig. 180 Use a caliper to check the valve spring free-length

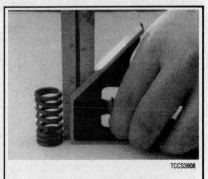

TCCS3908

Fig. 181 Check the valve spring for squareness on a flat surface; a carpenter's square can be used

Fig. 182 A dial gauge may be used to check valve stem-to-guide clearance; read the gauge while moving the valve stem

TCCS3142

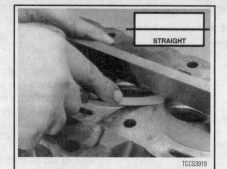

Fig. 183 Check the head for flatness across the center of the head surface using a straightedge and feeler gauge

TCCS3919

Fig. 184 Checks should also be made along both diagonals of the head surface

TCCS3918

zero the gauge. Grasp the valve stem and wiggle towards and away from the dial indicator and observe the readings. Mount the dial indicator 90 degrees from the initial point and zero the gauge and again take a reading. Compare the two readings for a out of round condition. Check the readings against the specifications given. An Inside Diameter (I.D.) gauge designed for valve guides will give you an accurate valve guide bore measurement. If the I.D. gauge is used, compare the readings with the specifications given. Any guides that fail these inspections should be replaced or machined.

VALVE SEATS

A visual inspection of the valve seats should show a slightly worn and pitted surface where the valve face contacts the seat. Inspect the seat carefully for severe pitting or cracks. Also, a seat that is badly worn will be recessed into the cylinder head. A severely worn or recessed seat may need to be replaced. All cracked seats must be replaced. A seat concentricity gauge, if available, should be used to check the seat run-out. If run-out exceeds specifications the seat must be machined (if no specification is given use 0.002 in. or 0.051mm).

CYLINDER HEAD SURFACE FLATNESS

▶ See Figures 183 and 184

After you have cleaned the gasket surface of the cylinder head of any old gasket material, check the head for flatness.

Place a straightedge across the gasket surface. Using feeler gauges, determine the clearance at the center of the straightedge and across the cylinder head at several points. Check along the centerline and diagonally on the head surface. If the warpage exceeds 0.003 in. (0.076mm) within a 6.0 in. (15.2cm) span, or 0.006 in. (0.152mm) over the total length of the head, the cylinder head must be resurfaced. After resurfacing the heads of a V-type engine, the intake manifold flange surface should be checked, and if necessary, milled proportionally to allow for the change in its mounting position.

CRACKS AND PHYSICAL DAMAGE

Generally, cracks are limited to the combustion chamber, however, it is not uncommon for the head to crack in a spark plug hole, port, outside of the head or in the valve spring/rocker arm area. The first area to inspect is always the hottest: the exhaust seat/port area.

A visual inspection should be performed, but just because you don't see a crack does not mean it is not there. Some more reliable methods for inspecting for cracks include Magnaflux®, a magnetic process or Zyglo®, a dye penetrant. Magnaflux® is used only on ferrous metal (cast iron) heads. Zyglo® uses a spray on fluorescent mixture along with a black light to reveal the cracks. It is strongly recommended to have your cylinder head checked professionally for cracks, especially if the engine was known to have overheated and/or leaked or consumed coolant. Contact a local shop for availability and pricing of these services.

Physical damage is usually very evident. For example, a broken mounting ear from dropping the head or a bent or broken stud and/or bolt. All of these defects should be fixed or, if unrepairable, the head should be replaced.

Camshaft and Followers

Inspect the camshaft(s) and followers as described earlier in this section.

REFINISHING & REPAIRING

Many of the procedures given for refinishing and repairing the cylinder head components must be performed by a machine shop. Certain steps, if the inspected part is not worn, can be performed yourself inexpensively. However, you spent a lot of time and effort so far, why risk trying to save a couple bucks if you might have to do it all over again?

Valves

Any valves that were not replaced should be refaced and the tips ground flat. Unless you have access to a valve grinding machine, this should be done by a machine shop. If the valves are in extremely good condition, as well as the valve seats and guides, they may be lapped in without performing machine work.

It is a recommended practice to lap the valves even after machine work has been performed and/or new valves have been purchased. This insures a positive seal between the valve and seat.

LAPPING THE VALVES

➡Before lapping the valves to the seats, read the rest of the cylinder head section to insure that any related parts are in acceptable enough condition to continue.

➡Before any valve seat machining and/or lapping can be performed, the guides must be within factory recommended specifications.

1. Invert the cylinder head.
2. Lightly lubricate the valve stems and insert them into the cylinder head in their numbered order.
3. Raise the valve from the seat and apply a small amount of fine lapping compound to the seat.
4. Moisten the suction head of a hand-lapping tool and attach it to the head of the valve.
5. Rotate the tool between the palms of both hands, changing the position of the valve on the valve seat and lifting the tool often to prevent grooving.
6. Lap the valve until a smooth, polished circle is evident on the valve and seat.
7. Remove the tool and the valve. Wipe away all traces of the grinding compound and store the valve to maintain its lapped location.

✳✳ WARNING

Do not get the valves out of order after they have been lapped. They must be put back with the same valve seat with which they were lapped.

Springs, Retainers and Valve Locks

There is no repair or refinishing possible with the springs, retainers and valve locks. If they are found to be worn or defective, they must be replaced with new (or known good) parts.

Cylinder Head

Most refinishing procedures dealing with the cylinder head must be performed by a machine shop. Read the sections below and review your inspection data to determine whether or not machining is necessary.

VALVE GUIDE

➡If any machining or replacements are made to the valve guides, the seats must be machined.

Unless the valve guides need machining or replacing, the only service to perform is to thoroughly clean them of any dirt or oil residue.

There are only two types of valve guides used on automobile engines: the replaceable-type (all aluminum heads) and the cast-in integral-type (most cast iron heads). There are four recommended methods for repairing worn guides.

- Knurling
- Inserts
- Reaming oversize
- Replacing

Knurling is a process in which metal is displaced and raised, thereby reducing clearance, giving a true center, and providing oil control. It is the least expensive way of repairing the valve guides. However, it is not necessarily the best, and in some cases, a knurled valve guide will not stand up for more than a short time. It requires a special knurlizer and precision reaming tools to obtain proper clearances. It would not be cost effective to purchase these tools, unless you plan on rebuilding several of the same cylinder head.

Installing a guide insert involves machining the guide to accept a bronze insert. One style is the coil-type which is installed into a threaded guide. Another is the thin-walled insert where the guide is reamed oversize to accept a split-sleeve insert. After the insert is installed, a special tool is then run through the guide to expand the insert, locking it to the guide. The insert is then reamed to the standard size for proper valve clearance.

Reaming for oversize valves restores normal clearances and provides a true valve seat. Most cast-in type guides can be reamed to accept an valve with an oversize stem. The cost factor for this can become quite high as you will need to purchase the reamer and new, oversize stem valves for all guides which were reamed. Oversizes are generally 0.003 to 0.030 in. (0.076 to 0.762mm), with 0.015 in. (0.381mm) being the most common.

To replace cast-in type valve guides, they must be drilled out, then reamed to accept replacement guides. This must be done on a fixture which will allow centering and leveling off of the original valve seat or guide, otherwise a serious guide-to-seat misalignment may occur making it impossible to properly machine the seat.

Replaceable-type guides are pressed into the cylinder head. A hammer and a stepped drift or punch may be used to install and remove the guides. Before removing the guides, measure the protrusion on the spring side of the head and record it for installation. Use the stepped drift to hammer out the old guide from the combustion chamber side of the head. When installing, determine whether or not the guide also seals a water jacket in the head, and if it does, use the recommended sealing agent. If there is no water jacket, grease the valve guide and its bore. Use the stepped drift, and hammer the new guide into the cylinder head from the spring side of the cylinder head. A stack of washers the same thickness as the measured protrusion may help the installation process.

VALVE SEATS

➡Before any valve seat machining can be performed, the guides must be within factory recommended specifications.

➡If any machining or replacements were made to the valve guides, the seats must be machined.

If the seats are in good condition, the valves can be lapped to the seats, and the cylinder head assembled. See the valves section for instructions on lapping.

If the valve seats are worn, cracked or damaged, they must be serviced by a machine shop. The valve seat must be perfectly centered to the valve guide, which requires very accurate machining.

CYLINDER HEAD SURFACE

If the cylinder head is warped, it must be machined flat. If the warpage is extremely severe, the head may need to be replaced. In some instances, it may be possible to straighten a warped head enough to allow machining. In either case, contact a professional machine shop for service.

➡Any OHC cylinder head that shows excessive warpage should have the camshaft bearing journals align bored after the cylinder head has been resurfaced.

✳✳ WARNING

Failure to align bore the camshaft bearing journals could result in severe engine damage including but not limited to: valve and piston damage, connecting rod damage, camshaft and/or crankshaft breakage.

CRACKS AND PHYSICAL DAMAGE

Certain cracks can be repaired in both cast iron and aluminum heads. For cast iron, a tapered threaded insert is installed along the length of the crack. Aluminum can also use the tapered inserts, however welding is the preferred method. Some physical damage can be repaired through brazing or welding. Contact a machine shop to get expert advice for your particular dilemma.

ASSEMBLY

The first step for any assembly job is to have a clean area in which to work. Next, thoroughly clean all of the parts and components that are to be assembled. Finally, place all of the components onto a suitable work space and, if necessary, arrange the parts to their respective positions.

OHV Engines

1. Lightly lubricate the valve stems and insert all of the valves into the cylinder head. If possible, maintain their original locations.
2. If equipped, install any valve spring shims which were removed.
3. If equipped, install the new valve seals, keeping the following in mind:
- If the valve seal presses over the guide, lightly lubricate the outer guide surfaces.
- If the seal is an O-ring type, it is installed just after compressing the spring but before the valve locks.
4. Place the valve spring and retainer over the stem.
5. Position the spring compressor tool and compress the spring.
6. Assemble the valve locks to the stem.
7. Relieve the spring pressure slowly and insure that neither valve lock becomes dislodged by the retainer.
8. Remove the spring compressor tool.
9. Repeat Steps 2 through 8 until all of the springs have been installed.

OHC Engines

◆ See Figure 185

CUP TYPE CAMSHAFT FOLLOWERS

To install the springs, retainers and valve locks on heads which have these components recessed into the camshaft follower's bore, you will need a small screwdriver-type tool, some clean white grease and a lot of patience. You will also need the C-clamp style spring compressor and the OHC tool used to disassemble the head.

1. Lightly lubricate the valve stems and insert all of the valves into the cylinder head. If possible, maintain their original locations.
2. If equipped, install any valve spring shims which were removed.
3. If equipped, install the new valve seals, keeping the following in mind:
- If the valve seal presses over the guide, lightly lubricate the outer guide surfaces.
- If the seal is an O-ring type, it is installed just after compressing the spring but before the valve locks.
4. Place the valve spring and retainer over the stem.
5. Position the spring compressor and the OHC tool, then compress the spring.

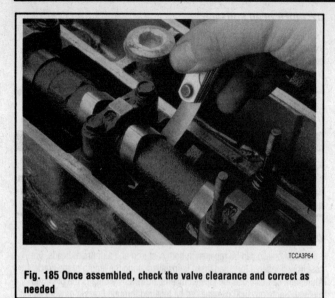

Fig. 185 Once assembled, check the valve clearance and correct as needed

6. Using a small screwdriver as a spatula, fill the valve stem side of the lock with white grease. Use the excess grease on the screwdriver to fasten the lock to the driver.

7. Carefully install the valve lock, which is stuck to the end of the screwdriver, to the valve stem then press on it with the screwdriver until the grease squeezes out. The valve lock should now be stuck to the stem.

8. Repeat Steps 6 and 7 for the remaining valve lock.

9. Relieve the spring pressure slowly and insure that neither valve lock becomes dislodged by the retainer.

10. Remove the spring compressor tool.

11. Repeat Steps 2 through 10 until all of the springs have been installed.

12. Install the followers, camshaft(s) and any other components that were removed for disassembly.

ROCKER ARM TYPE CAMSHAFT FOLLOWERS

1. Lightly lubricate the valve stems and insert all of the valves into the cylinder head. If possible, maintain their original locations.

2. If equipped, install any valve spring shims which were removed.

3. If equipped, install the new valve seals, keeping the following in mind:

• If the valve seal presses over the guide, lightly lubricate the outer guide surfaces.

• If the seal is an O-ring type, it is installed just after compressing the spring but before the valve locks.

4. Place the valve spring and retainer over the stem.

5. Position the spring compressor tool and compress the spring.

6. Assemble the valve locks to the stem.

7. Relieve the spring pressure slowly and insure that neither valve lock becomes dislodged by the retainer.

8. Remove the spring compressor tool.

9. Repeat Steps 2 through 8 until all of the springs have been installed.

10. Install the camshaft(s), rockers, shafts and any other components that were removed for disassembly.

Engine Block

GENERAL INFORMATION

A thorough overhaul or rebuild of an engine block would include replacing the pistons, rings, bearings, timing belt/chain assembly and oil pump. For OHV engines also include a new camshaft and lifters. The block would then have the cylinders bored and honed oversize (or if using removable cylinder sleeves, new sleeves installed) and the crankshaft would be cut undersize to provide new wearing surfaces and perfect clearances. However, your particular engine may not have everything worn out. What if only the piston rings have worn out and the clearances on everything else are still within factory specifications? Well, you could just replace the rings and put it back together, but this would be a

very rare example. Chances are, if one component in your engine is worn, other components are sure to follow, and soon. At the very least, you should always replace the rings, bearings and oil pump. This is what is commonly called a "freshen up".

Cylinder Ridge Removal

Because the top piston ring does not travel to the very top of the cylinder, a ridge is built up between the end of the travel and the top of the cylinder bore.

Pushing the piston and connecting rod assembly past the ridge can be difficult, and damage to the piston ring lands could occur. If the ridge is not removed before installing a new piston or not removed at all, piston ring breakage and piston damage may occur.

➡**It is always recommended that you remove any cylinder ridges before removing the piston and connecting rod assemblies. If you know that new pistons are going to be installed and the engine block will be bored oversize, you may be able to forego this step. However, some ridges may actually prevent the assemblies from being removed, necessitating its removal.**

There are several different types of ridge reamers on the market, none of which are inexpensive. Unless a great deal of engine rebuilding is anticipated, borrow or rent a reamer.

1. Turn the crankshaft until the piston is at the bottom of its travel.

2. Cover the head of the piston with a rag.

3. Follow the tool manufacturers instructions and cut away the ridge, exercising extreme care to avoid cutting too deeply.

4. Remove the ridge reamer, the rag and as many of the cuttings as possible. Continue until all of the cylinder ridges have been removed.

DISASSEMBLY

▶ **See Figures 186 and 187**

The engine disassembly instructions following assume that you have the engine mounted on an engine stand. If not, it is easiest to disassemble the engine on a bench or the floor with it resting on the bell housing or transmission mounting surface. You must be able to access the connecting rod fasteners and turn the crankshaft during disassembly. Also, all engine covers (timing, front, side, oil pan, whatever) should have already been removed. Engines which are seized or locked up may not be able to be completely disassembled, and a core (salvage yard) engine should be purchased.

Fig. 186 Place rubber hose over the connecting rod studs to protect the crankshaft and cylinder bores from damage

Pushrod Engines

If not done during the cylinder head removal, remove the pushrods and lifters, keeping them in order for assembly. Remove the timing gears and/or timing chain assembly, then remove the oil pump drive assembly and withdraw the camshaft from the engine block. Remove the oil pick-up and pump assembly. If equipped, remove any balance or auxiliary shafts. If necessary, remove the cylinder ridge from the top of the bore. See the cylinder ridge removal procedure earlier in this section.

OHC Engines

If not done during the cylinder head removal, remove the timing chain/belt and/or gear/sprocket assembly. Remove the oil pick-up and pump assembly and, if necessary, the pump drive. If equipped, remove any balance or auxiliary shafts. If necessary, remove the cylinder ridge from the top of the bore. See the cylinder ridge removal procedure earlier in this section.

All Engines

Rotate the engine over so that the crankshaft is exposed. Use a number punch or scribe and mark each connecting rod with its respective cylinder number. The cylinder closest to the front of the engine is always number 1. However, depending on the engine placement, the front of the engine could either be the flywheel or damper/pulley end. Generally the front of the engine faces the front of the vehicle. Use a number punch or scribe and also mark the main bearing caps from front to rear with the front most cap being number 1 (if there are five caps, mark them 1 through 5, front to rear).

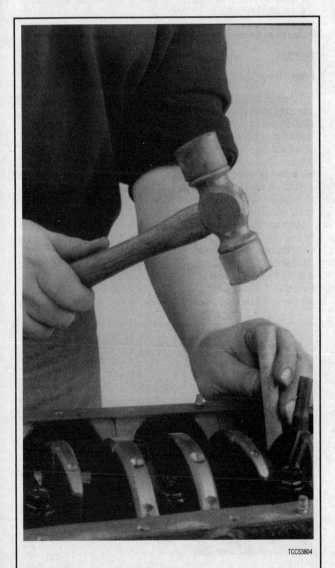

TCCS3804

Fig. 187 Carefully tap the piston out of the bore using a wooden dowel

⁕⁕ WARNING

Take special care when pushing the connecting rod up from the crankshaft because the sharp threads of the rod bolts/studs will score the crankshaft journal. Insure that special plastic caps are installed over them, or cut two pieces of rubber hose to do the same.

Again, rotate the engine, this time to position the number one cylinder bore (head surface) up. Turn the crankshaft until the number one piston is at the bottom of its travel, this should allow the maximum access to its connecting rod. Remove the number one connecting rods fasteners and cap and place two lengths of rubber hose over the rod bolts/studs to protect the crankshaft from damage. Using a sturdy wooden dowel and a hammer, push the connecting rod up about 1 in. (25mm) from the crankshaft and remove the upper bearing insert. Continue pushing or tapping the connecting rod up until the piston rings are out of the cylinder bore. Remove the piston and rod by hand, put the upper half of the bearing insert back into the rod, install the cap with its bearing insert installed, and hand-tighten the cap fasteners. If the parts are kept in order in this manner, they will not get lost and you will be able to tell which bearings came form what cylinder if any problems are discovered and diagnosis is necessary. Remove all the other piston assemblies in the same manner. On V-style engines, remove all of the pistons from one bank, then reposition the engine with the other cylinder bank head surface up, and remove that banks piston assemblies.

The only remaining component in the engine block should now be the crankshaft. Loosen the main bearing caps evenly until the fasteners can be turned by hand, then remove them and the caps. Remove the crankshaft from the engine block. Thoroughly clean all of the components.

INSPECTION

Now that the engine block and all of its components are clean, it's time to inspect them for wear and/or damage. To accurately inspect them, you will need some specialized tools:

- Two or three separate micrometers to measure the pistons and crankshaft journals
- A dial indicator
- Telescoping gauges for the cylinder bores
- A rod alignment fixture to check for bent connecting rods

If you do not have access to the proper tools, you may want to bring the components to a shop that does.

Generally, you shouldn't expect cracks in the engine block or its components unless it was known to leak, consume or mix engine fluids, it was severely overheated, or there was evidence of bad bearings and/or crankshaft damage. A visual inspection should be performed on all of the components, but just because you don't see a crack does not mean it is not there. Some more reliable methods for inspecting for cracks include Magnaflux®, a magnetic process or Zyglo®, a dye penetrant. Magnaflux® is used only on ferrous metal (cast iron). Zyglo® uses a spray on fluorescent mixture along with a black light to reveal the cracks. It is strongly recommended to have your engine block checked professionally for cracks, especially if the engine was known to have overheated and/or leaked or consumed coolant. Contact a local shop for availability and pricing of these services.

Engine Block

ENGINE BLOCK BEARING ALIGNMENT

Remove the main bearing caps and, if still installed, the main bearing inserts. Inspect all of the main bearing saddles and caps for damage, burrs or high spots. If damage is found, and it is caused from a spun main bearing, the block will need to be align-bored or, if severe enough, replacement. Any burrs or high spots should be carefully removed with a metal file.

Place a straightedge on the bearing saddles, in the engine block, along the centerline of the crankshaft. If any clearance exists between the straightedge and the saddles, the block must be align-bored.

Align-boring consists of machining the main bearing saddles and caps by means of a flycutter that runs through the bearing saddles.

DECK FLATNESS

The top of the engine block where the cylinder head mounts is called the deck. Insure that the deck surface is clean of dirt, carbon deposits and old gasket material. Place a straightedge across the surface of the deck along its centerline and, using feeler gauges, check the clearance along several points. Repeat the checking procedure with the straightedge placed along both diagonals of the deck surface. If the reading exceeds 0.003 in. (0.076mm) within a 6.0 in. (15.2cm) span, or 0.006 in. (0.152mm) over the total length of the deck, it must be machined.

CYLINDER BORES

▶ **See Figure 188**

The cylinder bores house the pistons and are slightly larger than the pistons themselves. A common piston-to-bore clearance is 0.0015–0.0025 in. (0.0381mm–0.0635mm). Inspect and measure the cylinder bores. The bore should be checked for out-of-roundness, taper and size. The results of this inspection will determine whether the cylinder can be used in its existing size and condition, or a rebore to the next oversize is required (or in the case of removable sleeves, have replacements installed).

The amount of cylinder wall wear is always greater at the top of the cylinder than at the bottom. This wear is known as taper. Any cylinder that has a taper of 0.0012 in. (0.305mm) or more, must be rebored. Measurements are taken at a number of positions in each cylinder: at the top, middle and bottom and at two points at each position; that is, at a point 90 degrees from the crankshaft centerline, as well as a point parallel to the crankshaft centerline. The measurements are made with either a special dial indicator or a telescopic gauge and micrometer. If the necessary precision tools to check the bore are not available, take the block to a machine shop and have them mike it. Also if you don't have the tools to check the cylinder bores, chances are you will not have the necessary devices to check the pistons, connecting rods and crankshaft. Take these components with you and save yourself an extra trip.

For our procedures, we will use a telescopic gauge and a micrometer. You will need one of each, with a measuring range which covers your cylinder bore size.

1. Position the telescopic gauge in the cylinder bore, loosen the gauges lock and allow it to expand.

➡ **Your first two readings will be at the top of the cylinder bore, then proceed to the middle and finally the bottom, making a total of six measurements.**

2. Hold the gauge square in the bore, 90 degrees from the crankshaft centerline, and gently tighten the lock. Tilt the gauge back to remove it from the bore.
3. Measure the gauge with the micrometer and record the reading.
4. Again, hold the gauge square in the bore, this time parallel to the crankshaft centerline, and gently tighten the lock. Again, you will tilt the gauge back to remove it from the bore.
5. Measure the gauge with the micrometer and record this reading. The difference between these two readings is the out-of-round measurement of the cylinder.
6. Repeat steps 1 through 5, each time going to the next lower position, until you reach the bottom of the cylinder. Then go to the next cylinder, and continue until all of the cylinders have been measured.

The difference between these measurements will tell you all about the wear in your cylinders. The measurements which were taken 90 degrees from the crankshaft centerline will always reflect the most wear. That is because at this position is where the engine power presses the piston against the cylinder bore the hardest. This is known as thrust wear. Take your top, 90 degree measurement and compare it to your bottom, 90 degree measurement. The difference between them is the taper. When you measure your pistons, you will compare these readings to your piston sizes and determine piston-to-wall clearance.

Crankshaft

Inspect the crankshaft for visible signs of wear or damage. All of the journals should be perfectly round and smooth. Slight scores are normal for a used crankshaft, but you should hardly feel them with your fingernail. When measuring the crankshaft with a micrometer, you will take readings at the front and rear of each journal, then turn the micrometer 90 degrees and take two more readings, front and rear. The difference between the front-to-rear readings is the journal taper and the first-to-90 degree reading is the out-of-round measurement. Generally, there should be no taper or out-of-roundness found, however, up to 0.0005 in. (0.0127mm) for either can be overlooked. Also, the readings should fall within the factory specifications for journal diameters.

If the crankshaft journals fall within specifications, it is recommended that it be polished before being returned to service. Polishing the crankshaft insures that any minor burrs or high spots are smoothed, thereby reducing the chance of scoring the new bearings.

Pistons and Connecting Rods

PISTONS

▶ **See Figure 189**

The piston should be visually inspected for any signs of cracking or burning (caused by hot spots or detonation), and scuffing or excessive wear on the skirts. The wrist pin attaches the piston to the connecting rod. The piston should move freely on the wrist pin, both sliding and pivoting. Grasp the connecting rod securely, or mount it in a vise, and try to rock the piston back and forth along the centerline of the wrist pin. There should not be any excessive play evident between the piston and the pin. If there are C-clips retaining the pin in the piston then you have wrist pin bushings in the rods. There should not be any excessive play between the wrist pin and the rod bushing. Normal clearance for the wrist pin is approx. 0.001–0.002 in. (0.025mm–0.051mm).

Use a micrometer and measure the diameter of the piston, perpendicular to the wrist pin, on the skirt. Compare the reading to its original cylinder measurement obtained earlier. The difference between the two readings is the piston-to-wall clearance. If the clearance is within specifications, the piston may be used as is. If the piston is out of specification, but the bore is not, you will need a new piston. If both are out of specification, you will need the cylinder rebored and oversize pistons installed. Generally if two or more pistons/bores are out of

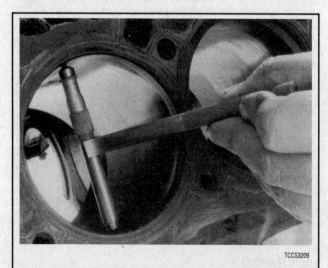

Fig. 188 Use a telescoping gauge to measure the cylinder bore diameter—take several readings within the same bore

TCCS3209

Fig. 189 Measure the piston's outer diameter, perpendicular to the wrist pin, with a micrometer

TCCS3210

specification, it is best to rebore the entire block and purchase a complete set of oversize pistons.

CONNECTING ROD

You should have the connecting rod checked for straightness at a machine shop. If the connecting rod is bent, it will unevenly wear the bearing and piston, as well as place greater stress on these components. Any bent or twisted connecting rods must be replaced. If the rods are straight and the wrist pin clearance is within specifications, then only the bearing end of the rod need be checked. Place the connecting rod into a vice, with the bearing inserts in place, install the cap to the rod and torque the fasteners to specifications. Use a telescoping gauge and carefully measure the inside diameter of the bearings. Compare this reading to the rods original crankshaft journal diameter measurement. The difference is the oil clearance. If the oil clearance is not within specifications, install new bearings in the rod and take another measurement. If the clearance is still out of specifications, and the crankshaft is not, the rod will need to be reconditioned by a machine shop.

➡You can also use Plastigage® to check the bearing clearances. The assembling section has complete instructions on its use.

Camshaft

Inspect the camshaft and lifters/followers as described earlier in this section.

Bearings

All of the engine bearings should be visually inspected for wear and/or damage. The bearing should look evenly worn all around with no deep scores or pits. If the bearing is severely worn, scored, pitted or heat blued, then the bearing, and the components that use it, should be brought to a machine shop for inspection. Full-circle bearings (used on most camshafts, auxiliary shafts, balance shafts, etc.) require specialized tools for removal and installation, and should be brought to a machine shop for service.

Oil Pump

➡The oil pump is responsible for providing constant lubrication to the whole engine and so it is recommended that a new oil pump be installed when rebuilding the engine.

Completely disassemble the oil pump and thoroughly clean all of the components. Inspect the oil pump gears and housing for wear and/or damage. Insure that the pressure relief valve operates properly and there is no binding or sticking due to varnish or debris. If all of the parts are in proper working condition, lubricate the gears and relief valve, and assemble the pump.

REFINISHING

◆ See Figure 190

Almost all engine block refinishing must be performed by a machine shop. If the cylinders are not to be rebored, then the cylinder glaze can be removed with a ball hone. When removing cylinder glaze with a ball hone, use a light or penetrating type oil to lubricate the hone. Do not allow the hone to run dry as this may cause excessive scoring of the cylinder bores and wear on the hone. If new pistons are required, they will need to be installed to the connecting rods. This should be performed by a machine shop as the pistons must be installed in the correct relationship to the rod or engine damage can occur.

Pistons and Connecting Rods

◆ See Figure 191

Only pistons with the wrist pin retained by C-clips are serviceable by the home-mechanic. Press fit pistons require special presses and/or heaters to remove/install the connecting rod and should only be performed by a machine shop.

All pistons will have a mark indicating the direction to the front of the engine and the must be installed into the engine in that manner. Usually it is a notch or

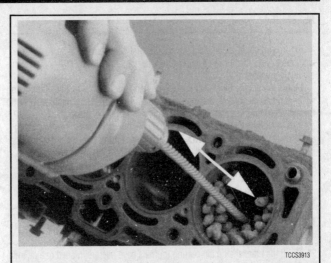

TCCS3913

Fig. 190 Use a ball type cylinder hone to remove any glaze and provide a new surface for seating the piston rings

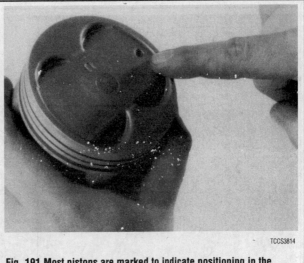

TCCS3814

Fig. 191 Most pistons are marked to indicate positioning in the engine (usually a mark means the side facing the front)

arrow on the top of the piston, or it may be the letter F cast or stamped into the piston.

C-CLIP TYPE PISTONS

1. Note the location of the forward mark on the piston and mark the connecting rod in relation.
2. Remove the C-clips from the piston and withdraw the wrist pin.

➡Varnish build-up or C-clip groove burrs may increase the difficulty of removing the wrist pin. If necessary, use a punch or drift to carefully tap the wrist pin out.

3. Insure that the wrist pin bushing in the connecting rod is usable, and lubricate it with assembly lube.
4. Remove the wrist pin from the new piston and lubricate the pin bores on the piston.
5. Align the forward marks on the piston and the connecting rod and install the wrist pin.
6. The new C-clips will have a flat and a rounded side to them. Install both C-clips with the flat side facing out.
7. Repeat all of the steps for each piston being replaced.

ASSEMBLY

Before you begin assembling the engine, first give yourself a clean, dirt free work area. Next, clean every engine component again. The key to a good assembly is cleanliness.

Mount the engine block into the engine stand and wash it one last time using water and detergent (dishwashing detergent works well). While washing it, scrub the cylinder bores with a soft bristle brush and thoroughly clean all of the oil passages. Completely dry the engine and spray the entire assembly down with an anti-rust solution such as WD-40® or similar product. Take a clean lint-free rag and wipe up any excess anti-rust solution from the bores, bearing saddles, etc. Repeat the final cleaning process on the crankshaft. Replace any freeze or oil galley plugs which were removed during disassembly.

Crankshaft

▶ **See Figures 192, 193, 194 and 195**

1. Remove the main bearing inserts from the block and bearing caps.
2. If the crankshaft main bearing journals have been refinished to a definite undersize, install the correct undersize bearing. Be sure that the bearing inserts and bearing bores are clean. Foreign material under inserts will distort bearing and cause failure.
3. Place the upper main bearing inserts in bores with tang in slot.

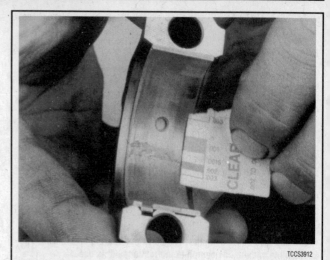

Fig. 193 After the cap is removed again, use the scale supplied with the gauging material to check the clearance

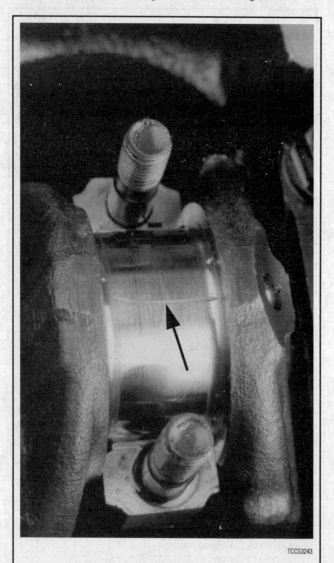

Fig. 192 Apply a strip of gauging material to the bearing journal, then install and torque the cap

Fig. 194 A dial gauge may be used to check crankshaft end-play

Fig. 195 Carefully pry the crankshaft back and forth while reading the dial gauge for end-play

➡ **The oil holes in the bearing inserts must be aligned with the oil holes in the cylinder block.**

4. Install the lower main bearing inserts in bearing caps.
5. Clean the mating surfaces of block and rear main bearing cap.
6. Carefully lower the crankshaft into place. Be careful not to damage bearing surfaces.
7. Check the clearance of each main bearing by using the following procedure:

   a. Place a piece of Plastigage® or its equivalent, on bearing surface across full width of bearing cap and about 1/4 in. off center.

   b. Install cap and tighten bolts to specifications. Do not turn crankshaft while Plastigage® is in place.

   c. Remove the cap. Using the supplied Plastigage® scale, check width of Plastigage® at widest point to get maximum clearance. Difference between readings is taper of journal.

   d. If clearance exceeds specified limits, try a 0.001 in. or 0.002 in. undersize bearing in combination with the standard bearing. Bearing clearance must be within specified limits. If standard and 0.002 in. undersize bearing does not bring clearance within desired limits, refinish crankshaft journal, then install undersize bearings.

8. After the bearings have been fitted, apply a light coat of engine oil to the journals and bearings. Install the rear main bearing cap. Install all bearing caps except the thrust bearing cap. Be sure that main bearing caps are installed in original locations. Tighten the bearing cap bolts to specifications.
9. Install the thrust bearing cap with bolts finger-tight.
10. Pry the crankshaft forward against the thrust surface of upper half of bearing.
11. Hold the crankshaft forward and pry the thrust bearing cap to the rear. This aligns the thrust surfaces of both halves of the bearing.
12. Retain the forward pressure on the crankshaft. Tighten the cap bolts to specifications.
13. Install the rear main seal.
14. Measure the crankshaft end-play as follows:

   a. Mount a dial gauge to the engine block and position the tip of the gauge to read from the crankshaft end.

   b. Carefully pry the crankshaft toward the rear of the engine and hold it there while you zero the gauge.

   c. Carefully pry the crankshaft toward the front of the engine and read the gauge.

   d. Confirm that the reading is within specifications. If not, install a new thrust bearing and repeat the procedure. If the reading is still out of specifications with a new bearing, have a machine shop inspect the thrust surfaces of the crankshaft, and if possible, repair it.

15. Rotate the crankshaft so as to position the first rod journal to the bottom of its stroke.

Pistons and Connecting Rods

◆ **See Figures 196, 197, 198 and 199**

1. Before installing the piston/connecting rod assembly, oil the pistons, piston rings and the cylinder walls with light engine oil. Install connecting rod bolt protectors or rubber hose onto the connecting rod bolts/studs. Also perform the following:

   a. Select the proper ring set for the size cylinder bore.

   b. Position the ring in the bore in which it is going to be used.

   c. Push the ring down into the bore area where normal ring wear is not encountered.

   d. Use the head of the piston to position the ring in the bore so that the ring is square with the cylinder wall. Use caution to avoid damage to the ring or cylinder bore.

   e. Measure the gap between the ends of the ring with a feeler gauge. Ring gap in a worn cylinder is normally greater than specification. If the ring gap is greater than the specified limits, try an oversize ring set.

   f. Check the ring side clearance of the compression rings with a feeler gauge inserted between the ring and its lower land according to specification. The gauge should slide freely around the entire ring circumference without binding. Any wear that occurs will form a step at the inner portion of the lower land. If the lower lands have high steps, the piston should be replaced.

2. Unless new pistons are installed, be sure to install the pistons in the cylinders from which they were removed. The numbers on the connecting rod and bearing cap must be on the same side when installed in the cylinder bore. If a connecting rod is ever transposed from one engine or cylinder to another, new bearings should be fitted and the connecting rod should be numbered to correspond with the new cylinder number. The notch on the piston head goes toward the front of the engine.
3. Install all of the rod bearing inserts into the rods and caps.
4. Install the rings to the pistons. Install the oil control ring first, then the second compression ring and finally the top compression ring. Use a piston ring expander tool to aid in installation and to help reduce the chance of breakage.
5. Make sure the ring gaps are properly spaced around the circumference of the piston. Fit a piston ring compressor around the piston and slide the piston and connecting rod assembly down into the cylinder bore, pushing it in with the wooden hammer handle. Push the piston down until it is only slightly below the top of the cylinder bore. Guide the connecting rod onto the crankshaft bearing journal carefully, to avoid damaging the crankshaft.
6. Check the bearing clearance of all the rod bearings, fitting them to the crankshaft bearing journals. Follow the procedure in the crankshaft installation above.
7. After the bearings have been fitted, apply a light coating of assembly oil to the journals and bearings.
8. Turn the crankshaft until the appropriate bearing journal is at the bottom of its stroke, then push the piston assembly all the way down until the connecting rod bearing seats on the crankshaft journal. Be careful not to allow the bearing cap screws to strike the crankshaft bearing journals and damage them.
9. After the piston and connecting rod assemblies have been installed, check the connecting rod side clearance on each crankshaft journal.
10. Prime and install the oil pump and the oil pump intake tube.
11. On all engines, except the 2.1L OHC diesel engine, perform the following:

   a. Install the camshaft.

   b. Install the lifters/followers into their bores.

   c. Install the timing gears/chain assembly.

   d. Install the cylinder head(s) using new gaskets.

   e. Assemble the rest of the valve train (pushrods and rocker arms and/or shafts).

Fig. 196 Checking the piston ring-to-ring groove side clearance using the ring and a feeler gauge

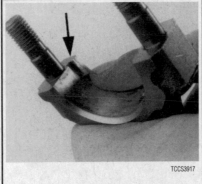

Fig. 197 The notch on the side of the bearing cap matches the tang on the bearing insert

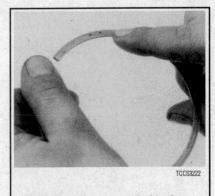

Fig. 198 Most rings are marked to show which side of the ring should face up when installed to the piston

Fig. 199 Install the piston and rod assembly into the block using a ring compressor and the handle of a hammer

12. On the 2.1L OHC diesel engine, perform the following:
   a. Install the cylinder head(s) using new gaskets.
   b. Install the timing sprockets/gears and the belt/chain assemblies.

Engine Covers and Components

Install the timing cover(s) and oil pan. Refer to your notes and drawings made prior to disassembly and install all of the components that were removed. Install the engine into the vehicle.

Engine Start-up and Break-in

STARTING THE ENGINE

Now that the engine is installed and every wire and hose is properly connected, go back and double check that all coolant and vacuum hoses are connected. Check that your oil drain plug is installed and properly tightened. If not already done, install a new oil filter onto the engine. Fill the crankcase with the proper amount and grade of engine oil. Fill the cooling system with a 50/50 mixture of coolant/water.

1. Connect the vehicle battery.
2. Start the engine. Keep your eye on your oil pressure indicator; if it does not indicate oil pressure within 10 seconds of starting, turn the vehicle off.

✳ WARNING

Damage to the engine can result if it is allowed to run with no oil pressure. Check the engine oil level to make sure that it is full. Check for any leaks and if found, repair the leaks before continuing. If there is still no indication of oil pressure, you may need to prime the system.

3. Confirm that there are no fluid leaks (oil or other).
4. Allow the engine to reach normal operating temperature (the upper radiator hose will be hot to the touch).
5. At this point you can perform any necessary checks or adjustments, such as checking the ignition timing.
6. Install any remaining components or body panels which were removed.

BREAKING IT IN

Make the first miles on the new engine, easy ones. Vary the speed but do not accelerate hard. Most importantly, do not lug the engine, and avoid sustained high speeds until at least 100 miles. Check the engine oil and coolant levels frequently. Expect the engine to use a little oil until the rings seat. Change the oil and filter at 500 miles, 1500 miles, then every 3000 miles past that.

KEEP IT MAINTAINED

Now that you have just gone through all of that hard work, keep yourself from doing it all over again by thoroughly maintaining it. Not that you may not have maintained it before, heck you could have had one to two hundred thousand miles on it before doing this. However, you may have bought the vehicle used, and the previous owner did not keep up on maintenance. Which is why you just went through all of that hard work. See?

4

DRIVEABILITY AND EMISSION CONTROLS

EMISSION CONTROLS

Crankcase Ventilation System (PCV/CCV)

OPERATION

▶ **See Figure 1**

Crankcase emission control equipment is separated into two different systems: Positive Crankcase Ventilation (PVC) and Crankcase Ventilation System (CCV). The systems perform the same function, differing only in the way the exhaust gases are metered. The PVC system uses a valve, containing spring loaded plunger, which meters the amount of crankcase vapors routed to the combustion chamber based on manifold vacuum. The CCV system contains a metered orifice of a calibrated size which meters the amount of crankcase vapors drawn from the engine based on manifold vacuum.

COMPONENT TESTING

PCV Valve

▶ **See Figure 2**

To inspect the PCV valve, remove the valve from the rocker arm cover hose, then shake it. If the valve rattles, it is probably fine; if there is no sound, it must be replaced and the PCV hose cleaned by spraying solvent (such as a carburetor cleaner type of solvent) through it.

If the valve rattles, you should still check the PCV valve with the engine idling. Pull it out of the vent module and place your finger or thumb over the end to stop air flow. You should feel some suction, and the engine speed should drop slightly. If there is no suction, or if the engine idle speeds up and smooths out considerably, replace the valve. Remove the PCV hose from the engine, then inspect it and, if the inside is coated with gum and varnish, clean it by spraying

solvent through it.

Check the vacuum at the PCV inlet (from the rocker arm cover to the air cleaner) tube, as well. Disconnect this tube from the air cleaner and loosely hold a piece of paper over the tube. After a few seconds (10–15 seconds), enough vacuum should build up to cause the paper to be sucked against the opening with a noticeable amount of force. This test proves whether or not the suction side of the system is clear.

CCV Fitting

▶ **See Figures 3 and 4**

1. With the engine running, remove the CCV fitting.

   a. If the fitting is not plugged, a hissing noise will be heard as air passes through the valve. A strong vacuum should also be felt when a finger is placed over the fitting.

   b. Install the CCV fitting.

   c. Remove the fresh air hose from the air cleaner assembly and loosely hold a piece of paper over the open end of the hose. After allowing about one minute for the crankcase pressure to reduce, the paper should be sucked against the opening with a noticeable amount of force.

2. Turn the engine **OFF**. Remove the metered orifice fitting, and check for a plugged condition. A clicking noise should be heard to indicate that the valve mechanism is free.

3. If the crankcase ventilation system meets the tests in Steps 1 and 2 above, no further service is required. If not, the CCV fitting must be cleaned and the system checked again.

4. If Step 1c fails when the CCV fitting is cleaned, it will be necessary to replace the molded vacuum hose with a new one, and to clean the metered orifice port.

5. Clean or replace the engine air cleaner filter element with a new

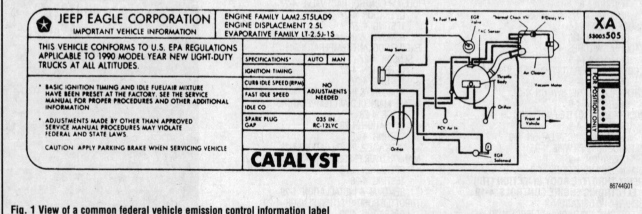

Fig. 1 View of a common federal vehicle emission control information label

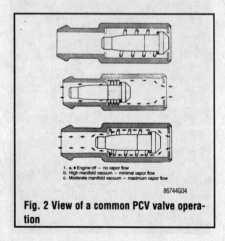

Fig. 2 View of a common PCV valve operation

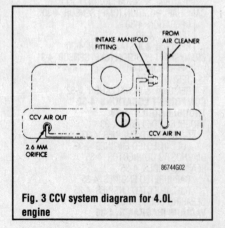

Fig. 3 CCV system diagram for 4.0L engine

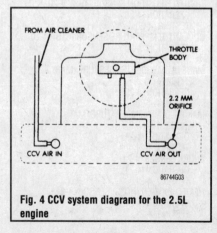

Fig. 4 CCV system diagram for the 2.5L engine

one—for more details, refer to the air cleaner procedure located in Section 1.

REMOVAL & INSTALLATION

Refer to Section 1 for the PCV valve removal/installation procedure.

Evaporative Emission Control System

OPERATION

The evaporative emission control system prevents the release of unburned hydrocarbons, from gasoline or gasoline vapor, into the atmosphere. When pressure in the fuel tank is below 3 psi (20 kPa), the pressure relief/rollover valves open allowing fuel vapors to flow to the evaporative canister where they are absorbed by a charcoal mixture. This prevents excessive pressure build-up in the fuel system. Most canisters are equipped with a calibrated orifice at the inlet to the canister.

The evaporative canister is mounted to the passenger side frame rail. Inlet ports on the canister are connected to the rollover/pressure relief valves, the air cleaner, and the fuel tank vent through hoses and tubes.

Canister purge operation is activated by the purge shutoff switch. An air cleaner venturi provides the vacuum to open the switch which allows vapors collected in the canister to be drawn into the airstream. The vapors then pass through the intake manifold and are burned in the combustion process.

The fuel tanks of all vehicles are equipped with two pressure relief/rollover valves. The valves relieve fuel tank pressure and prevent fuel flow through the fuel tank vent hoses in the event of vehicle rollover.

The valves consist of a plunger, spring, orifice and guide plate. The valve is normally open allowing fuel vapor to vent to the canister. If the bottom of the plunger is contacted by sloshing fuel, the plunger seats in the guide plate preventing fuel from reaching the canister.

If the vehicle should roll over, the valve is inverted and the plunger is forced against the guideplate, preventing fuel from flowing through the vent tube.

REMOVAL & INSTALLATION

Evaporative Canister

EXCEPT 1996 AND LATER GRAND CHEROKEE AND 1998 AND LATER CHEROKEE

▶ See Figure 5

1. Tag and disconnect the vacuum lines from the canister.
2. Remove the canister strap bolt and remove the canister from the vehicle.
3. Installation is the reverse of removal. Tighten the bolt to 45 inch. lbs. (5 Nm).

1996–98 GRAND CHEROKEE

▶ See Figures 6 and 7

1. Remove the grille and the front bumper/fascia assembly as outlined in Section 10.
2. Tag and disconnect the vacuum lines from the canister.
3. Unfasten the canister retaining nuts and remove the canister through the bottom of the vehicle.

To install:
4. Install the canister and tighten the retaining nuts to 80 inch. lbs. (9 Nm).
5. Connect the vacuum lines.
6. Install the front bumper/fascia assembly and the grille as outlined in Section 10.

1998 AND LATER CHEROKEE

The EVAP canister is located below the left side of the vehicle near the front of the rear axle.
1. Tag and disconnect the vacuum lines from the canister.
2. Unfasten the canister mounting bracket retaining nuts and remove the canister/bracket assembly from the vehicle.
3. Installation is the reverse of the removal procedures.

Purge Solenoid

▶ See Figure 8

1. Disengage the solenoid electrical connection.
2. Tag and disconnect the solenoid vacuum lines.

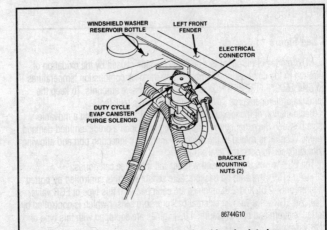

Fig. 8 Common EVAP canister purge solenoid and related components

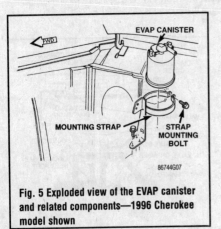

Fig. 5 Exploded view of the EVAP canister and related components—1996 Cherokee model shown

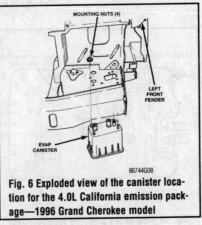

Fig. 6 Exploded view of the canister location for the 4.0L California emission package—1996 Grand Cherokee model

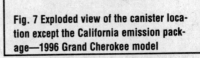

Fig. 7 Exploded view of the canister location except the California emission package—1996 Grand Cherokee model

3. Unfasten the solenoid retaining nuts and remove the solenoid.

4. Installation is the reverse of removal. Tighten the retaining fasteners to 45 inch. lbs. (5 Nm).

Pressure Relief/Rollover Valve

◆ **See Figures 9 and 10**

1. Disconnect the battery negative cable.
2. Relieve the fuel system as outlined in Section 5.

➡**DO NOT allow fuel to spill on the intake or exhaust manifolds. Use shop rags to absorb any spilled fuel.**

3. Drain the fuel tank dry using a siphon pump.
4. Raise and support the vehicle with jackstands.
5. Remove the fuel tank. See appropriate procedure in Section 5.
6. If equipped, remove the vapor hose at the valve.
7. The rollover valve is seated in a grommet. Pry one side of the valve up and twist to remove the grommet from the tank.

To install:

8. Start one side of the grommet into the fuel tank opening and using finger pressure only, press the valve grommet into position.
9. Engage the vapor hose, if equipped.
10. Install the tank as outlined in Section 5.
11. Fill the tank and connect the negative battery cable.
12. Start the vehicle and check for leaks.

Exhaust Gas Recirculation (EGR) System

OPERATION

◆ **See Figure 11**

NOx (oxides of nitrogen) is a tailpipe emission caused by the oxidation of nitrogen in the combustion chamber. When the peak combustion temperatures go over 2500°F (1371°C) NOx is formed in excessive amounts. To keep the combustion temperatures down, exhaust gas is recirculated.

Recirculation of the exhaust gases is accomplished by having a movable valve between the exhaust and intake manifolds. Upon a predetermined demand, engine vacuum is routed to the valve, opening the connecting port and allowing exhaust gases to enter the intake tract.

The EGR valves used on Jeep vehicles fall into three categories:
• An EGR valve with no backpressure sensor which is controlled by ported vacuum only. 2.5L and 2.8L engines are equipped with this type of EGR valve.
• An EGR valve with an external backpressure sensor which is controlled by ported vacuum and backpressure. 4.0L engines are equipped with this type of EGR valve.
• An EGR valve with an electric EGR transducer is found on 5.2L engines.

Thermal vacuum switches, which control the amount of vacuum available to the EGR valve based on air or water temperature, are used to disable the EGR system before the vehicle reaches operating temperature.

COMPONENT TESTING

EGR Solenoid

1. Start engine and bring to normal operating temperature. Allow engine to idle while performing tests.
2. Check vacuum at solenoid vacuum source hose. Disconnect the hose and attach a vacuum gauge.
3. Vacuum should be 15 in. Hg. (103 kPa), If low, check for leaks, loose fittings or kinks in the line.
4. Check vacuum at solenoid port. Disconnect the line and attach a vacuum gauge.
5. If vacuum reading is zero, go to Step 6. If vacuum is present, check solenoid operation with the Diagnostic Readout Box (DRB II) service tester and repair as necessary.
6. Disengage electrical connector at solenoid. If vacuum is present, proceed to EGR valve test. If not, replace the solenoid.

EGR Valve

1. Leave solenoid electrical connector disengaged. Bypass the vacuum transducer, if equipped, and connect EGR valve solenoid output hose directly to the nipple on the EGR valve.
2. The engine should run roughly or stall. If this occurs, the valve is good. Proceed to the transducer test, for 4.0L engines. If engine rpm does not change, disconnect hose from EGR and connect a hand vacuum pump.
3. Apply 12 in. Hg (82 kPa) of vacuum. If engine runs rough or stalls, inspect vacuum lines in EGR system for leaks and repair as necessary. If no leaks are found, go to transducer test for the 4.0L engine; Step 4 for the other engines.
4. If engine idle still does not change, remove the EGR valve and inspect for a blockage in the intake manifold passage. Repair as necessary. If no blockage is found, replace the EGR valve.

Vacuum Transducer

◆ **See Figures 12, 13 and 14**

➡**This is used on 4.0L engines only.**

1. Disconnect all transducer lines and remove transducer.
2. Plug transducer output port. Apply 1–2 pounds air pressure to transducer backpressure port (used compressed air adjusted to correct pressure). Apply a minimum of 12 in. Hg (kPa) of vacuum to transducer input port.
3. Replace transducer if it will not hold vacuum.

Coolant Temperature Override (CTO) Switch

◆ **See Figure 15**

1. Check vacuum lines for leaks and proper routing.
2. Disconnect vacuum line from EGR valve and connect a vacuum gauge.
3. Start engine and ensure that coolant is below 100°F (38°C).

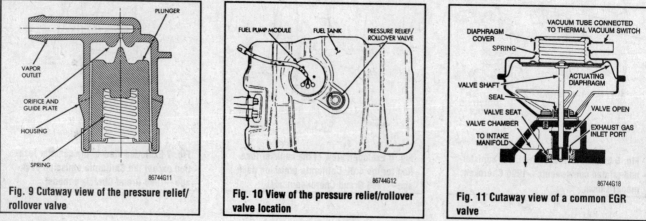

Fig. 9 Cutaway view of the pressure relief/rollover valve

Fig. 10 View of the pressure relief/rollover valve location

Fig. 11 Cutaway view of a common EGR valve

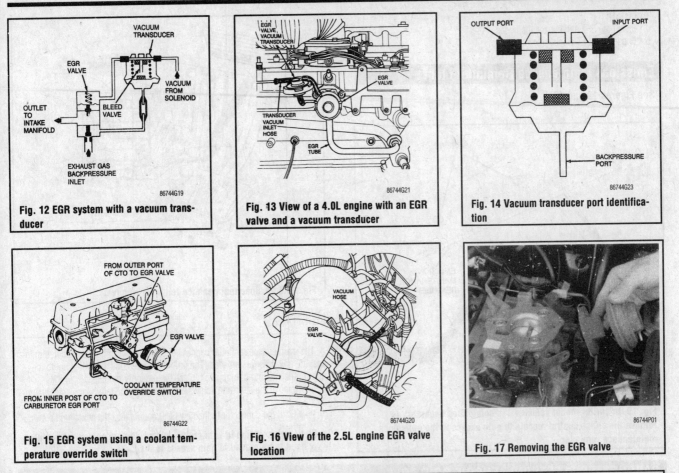

Fig. 12 EGR system with a vacuum transducer

Fig. 13 View of a 4.0L engine with an EGR valve and a vacuum transducer

Fig. 14 Vacuum transducer port identification

Fig. 15 EGR system using a coolant temperature override switch

Fig. 16 View of the 2.5L engine EGR valve location

Fig. 17 Removing the EGR valve

4. Operate engine a 1,500 rpm. There should be no vacuum. If vacuum is present, replace the CTO switch.

5. Allow engine to idle until coolant temperature exceeds 115°F (46°C).

6. Operate the engine at 1,500 rpm. Vacuum should be present. If not, replace the CTO switch.

Thermal Vacuum Switch (TVS)

1. With the engine cold and ambient air temperature in the air cleaner below 40°F (4°C), disconnect the vacuum hoses from the TVS (located on the air cleaner).

2. Connect a hand vacuum pump to the inner port and apply vacuum.

3. Vacuum should be maintained at air cleaner intake temperatures below 40°F (4°C). If vacuum is not held, check to see that temperature is below 40°F (4°C). If so, replace the TVS.

4. Start the engine and warm to normal operating temperature. With an air cleaner intake temperature above 55°F (13°C), the switch should not hold vacuum. If vacuum is held, check to see that temperatures are above 55°F (13°C). If so, replace the TVS.

➡Temperatures are nominal values and the actual switching temperature may vary.

REMOVAL & INSTALLATION

EGR Valve

▶ See Figures 16, 17 and 18

1. Tag and disengage the vacuum hoses to the EGR valve and the valve control.

2. Remove the EGR retaining bolts, then the valve and gasket.

To install:

3. Clean both mating surfaces and install a new gasket.

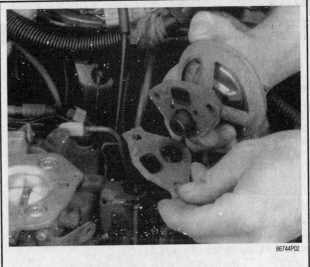

Fig. 18 Remove and discard the old EGR valve gasket

4. Install the EGR valve and tighten the retaining bolts to 200 inch. lbs. (23 Nm).

5. Engage the vacuum hoses.

Electric EGR Transducer (EET)

1. Disengage the EET electrical connector.

2. Tag and disengage the hoses to the EET.

3. Remove the EET from the engine.

To install:

4. Install the EET and engage the hoses.
5. Engage the EET electrical connections.

Emissions Maintenance Reminder Light

♦ **See Figures 19 and 20**

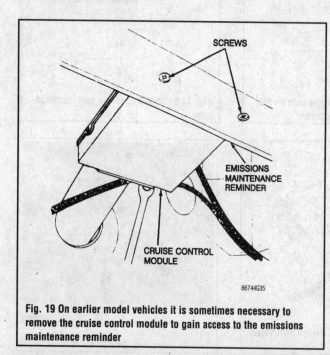

Fig. 19 On earlier model vehicles it is sometimes necessary to remove the cruise control module to gain access to the emissions maintenance reminder

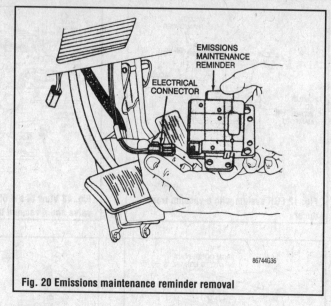

Fig. 20 Emissions maintenance reminder removal

RESETTING

The maintenance reminder cannot be reset after reaching the specified mileage, the unit must be replaced. The unit is mounted on the dash panel to the right of the steering column. To replace the reminder module:

1. Remove the attaching screws and disengage the reminder electrical connector.
2. Install the connector to the new EMR and replace the attaching screws.

➡ **On vehicles equipped with cruise control, the cruise control module may need to be moved to gain access to the EMR.**

CARBURETED ELECTRONIC ENGINE CONTROLS

General Information

There are two primary modes of operation of the Computerized Emission Control (CEC) feedback system: open loop and closed loop. The system will be in the open loop mode of operation (or a variation of it) whenever the engine operating conditions do not meet the programmed criteria for closed loop operation. During open loop operation, the air/fuel mixture is maintained at a programmed ratio that is dependent on the type of engine operation involved. The oxygen sensor data is not accepted by the system during this mode of operation.

When all input data meets the programmed criteria for closed loop operation, the exhaust gas oxygen content signal from the oxygen sensor is accepted by the computer. This results in an air/fuel mixture that will be optimum for the engine operating condition and also will correct any pre-existing mixture condition which is too lean or too rich.

➡ **A high oxygen content in the exhaust gas indicates a lean air/fuel mixture. A low oxygen content indicates a rich air/fuel mixture. The optimum air/fuel mixture ratio is 14.7:1.**

Micro Computer Unit (MCU)

OPERATION

The Micro Computer Unit, or MCU, is the heart of the electronic control system. The MCU receives signals from various engine sensors to constantly monitor the engine operating conditions, then it uses this information to make adjustments in order to achieve the optimum performance and economy with a minimum of engine emissions. The MCU monitors the oxygen sensor voltage and, based upon the mode of operation, generates an output control signal for the carburetor stepper motor or mixture control solenoid. If the system is in the closed loop mode of operation, the air/fuel mixture will vary according to the oxygen content in the exhaust gas and engine operating conditions. If the system is in the open loop mode of operation, the air/fuel mixture will be based on a predetermined ratio that is dependent on engine rpm.

Throttle Position Sensor

OPERATION

The Throttle Position Sensor (TPS) is located inside the carburetor. It is a potentiometer with one wire connected to 5 volts from the ECU and the other to ground. A third wire is connected to the ECU to measure the voltage from the TPS.

As the accelerator pedal is moved, the output of the TPS also changes. At a closed throttle position, the output of the TPS is low (approximately 0.5 volts). As the throttle valve opens, the output increases so that, at wide-open throttle, the output voltage should be approximately 4.5 volts.

By monitoring the output voltage from the TPS, the ECU can determine fuel delivery based on throttle valve angle (driver demand).

REMOVAL & INSTALLATION

1. Remove the upper and lower bonnet assemblies.
2. Remove the throttle body assembly from the vehicle.
3. Remove the two Torx® head retaining screws holding the TPS assembly to the throttle body.
4. Remove the throttle position sensor from the throttle shaft lever.
5. Installation is the reverse of removal. Adjust the sensor.

❋❋ WARNING

Make sure that the sensor arm is installed UNDERNEATH the arm of the throttle valve shaft!

ADJUSTMENT

▶ **See Figure 21**

A tamper-resistant plug covers the TPS adjustment screw. This plug should not be removed unless diagnosis indicates the TPS sensor is not adjusted properly or it is necessary to replace the air horn assembly, float bowl, TPS sensor or TPS adjustment screw. This is a critical adjustment that must be performed accurately and carefully to ensure proper engine performance and emission control. If TPS adjustment is indicated, proceed as follows:

1. Use a 5/64 in. (2mm) drill bit to drill a hole in the steel cup plug covering the TPS adjustment screw. Use care in drilling to prevent damage to the adjustment screw head.

2. Use a small slide hammer to remove the steel plug from the air horn.

3. Unplug the TPS connector and use jumper wires to connect all three terminals.

4. Connect a digital voltmeter between the TPS connector center terminal B and the bottom terminal C (ground).

5. With the ignition **ON** (engine **OFF**), turn the TPS adjustment screw to obtain 0.26 volts (260 mv) at the curb idle throttle position with the A/C off.

6. After all adjustments are complete, a new tamper-proof plug (supplied in service kits) or silicone RTV rubber sealant must be inserted into the TPS adjustment screw hole to seal the adjustment. If a plug is used, it should be installed with the cup facing outward and flush with the top of the casting.

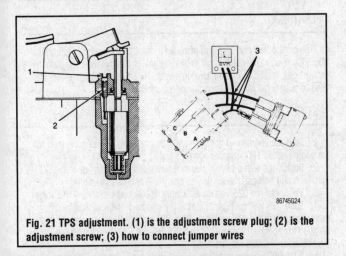

Fig. 21 TPS adjustment. (1) is the adjustment screw plug; (2) is the adjustment screw; (3) how to connect jumper wires

Mixture Control Solenoid

OPERATION

On engines with the Carter YFA or Rochester E2SE carburetors, a Mixture Control (MC) solenoid is used to regulate the air/fuel mixture. During open loop operation, the MC solenoid supplies a preprogrammed amount of air to the carburetor idle circuit and main metering circuit where it mixes with the fuel. During closed loop operation, the MCU operates the MC solenoid to provide additional or less air to the fuel mixture, depending on the engine operating conditions as monitored by the various engine sensors.

TESTING

E2SE Carburetor

▶ **See Figure 22**

If the mixture control solenoid is suspected of either sticking, binding or leaking, test it using the following procedure:

1. Connect one end of a jumper wire to either terminal of the solenoid wire connector and the other end to the positive (+) terminal of a 12 volt battery.

2. Connect one end of another jumper wire to the other terminal of the solenoid wire connector and the other end to the negative (-) terminal of the battery.

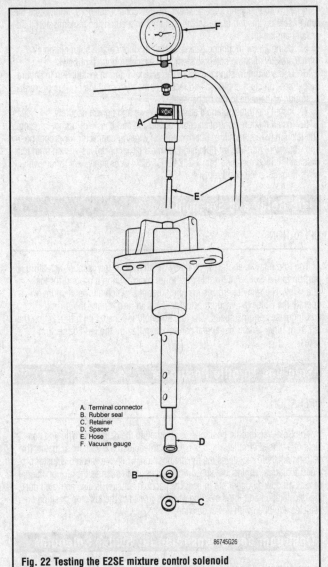

A. Terminal connector
B. Rubber seal
C. Retainer
D. Spacer
E. Hose
F. Vacuum gauge

Fig. 22 Testing the E2SE mixture control solenoid

3. With the rubber seal, retainer and spacer removed from the end of the solenoid stem, attach a hose from a hand vacuum pump.

4. With the solenoid fully energized (lean position), apply at least 25 in. Hg (172 kPa) of vacuum and time the leak-down rate from 20-to-15 in. Hg (137–103 kPa). The leak-down rate should not exceed 5 in. Hg (34 kPa) in 5 seconds. If the leak-down rate exceeds that amount, replace the solenoid.

5. To test the solenoid for sticking in the down (de-energized) position, remove the jumper wire to the 12 volt battery and observe the hand vacuum pump gauge. It should move to zero in less than one second.

REMOVAL & INSTALLATION

1. Remove three (3) mixture control solenoid screws in the horn, then using a slight twisting motion, carefully lift solenoid out of air horn. Remove and discard solenoid gasket.

2. Remove seal retainer and rubber seal from end of solenoid stem being careful not to damage or nick end of solenoid stem. Discared seal and retainer.

To install:

3. Install spacer and new rubber seal on new mixture control solenoid stem making sure seal is up against the spacer. Then, using a suitable socket and hammer, carefully drive retainer on stem. Drive retainer on stem only far enough to retain rubber seal on stem leaving a slight clearance between the retainer and seal to allow for seal expansion.

4. Prior to installing a replacement mixture control solenoid, lightly coat the rubber seal on the end of the solenoid stem with a automatic transmission fluid or light engine oil.

5. Using a new mounting gasket, install mixture control solenoid on air horn, carefully aligning solenoid stem with recess in bottom of bowl.

6. Use a slight twisting motion of the solenoid during installation to ensure rubber seal on stem is guided into recess in the bottom of the bowl to prevent distortion or damage to the rubber seal.

7. Install the three solenoid attaching screws and tighten securely.

8. Install mixture control solenoid connector, and check for proper latching. The latch may require filing. Check colors of wires in connector for proper position. Pink wire must be on right hand terminal of connector, as viewed from harness end. If incorrect, use Tool J-28742, BT 8234-A or equivalent to remove wires from connector and replace.

Idle Relay and Solenoid

OPERATION

The idle relay is energized by the MCU to control the vacuum actuator portion of the Sole-Vac throttle positioner by providing a ground for the idle relay. The relay energizes the idle solenoid, which allows vacuum to operate the Sole-Vac vacuum actuator. This, in turn, opens the throttle and increases engine speed. The idle solenoid is located on a bracket on the left front inner fender panel and can be identified by the red connecting wires.

Sole-Vac Throttle Positioner

OPERATION

The Sole-Vac throttle positioner is attached to the carburetor. The unit consists of a closed throttle switch, a holding solenoid and a vacuum actuator. The holding solenoid maintains the throttle position, while the vacuum actuator provides additional engine idle speed when accessories such as the air conditioner or rear window defogger are in use. The vacuum actuator is also activated during deceleration and if the steering wheel is turned to the full stop position on vehicles equipped with power steering.

Upstream and Downstream Air Switch Solenoids

OPERATION

The upstream and downstream solenoids of the pulse air system distribute air to the exhaust pipe and catalytic converter. Both solenoids are energized by the MCU to route air into the the exhaust pipe at a point after the oxygen sensor. When energized, the downstream solenoid routes air into the second bed of the dual-bed catalytic converter. This additional air reacts with the exhaust gases to reduce engine emissions.

The solenoids are located on a bracket attached to the left inner front fender panel. The idle solenoid is also located on this same bracket.

PCV Shutoff Solenoid

OPERATION

The positive crankcase ventilation shutoff solenoid is installed in the PCV valve hose and is energized by the MCU to turn off the crankcase ventilation system when the engine is at idle speed. An anti-diesel relay system on 4-cylinder engines, consisting of an anti-diesel relay and a delay relay, prevents engine run-on when the ignition is switched off by momentarily energizing the PCV valve solenoid when the ignition is switched **OFF** to prevent air entering below the throttle plate.

Bowl Vent Solenoid

OPERATION

The bowl vent solenoid is located in the hose between the carburetor bowl vent and the canister. The bowl vent solenoid is closed and allows no fuel vapor to flow when the engine is operating. When the engine is not operating, the solenoid is open and allows vapor to flow to the charcoal canister to control hydrocarbon emissions from the carburetor float bowl. The bowl vent solenoid is electrically energized when the ignition is switched **ON** and is not controlled by the MCU.

Intake Manifold Heater Switch

OPERATION

The intake manifold heater switch is located in the intake manifold and is controlled by the temperature of the engine coolant. Below 160°F (71°C) the manifold heater switch activates the intake manifold heater to improve fuel vaporization. The switch is not controlled by the MCU and does not provide input information to it.

Oxygen Sensor

OPERATION

This component of the system provides a variable voltage (millivolts) for the Micro Computer Unit (MCU) that is proportional to the oxygen content in the exhaust gas. In addition to the oxygen sensor, the following data senders are used to supply the MCU with engine operation data.

TESTING

1. Start the engine and bring it to normal operating temperature, then run the engine above 1200 rpm for two minutes.

2. Backprobe with a high impedance averaging voltmeter (set to the DC voltage scale) between the oxygen sensor (02S) and battery ground.

3. Verify that the 02S voltage fluctuates rapidly between 0.40–0.60 volts.

4. If the 02S voltage is stabilized at the middle of the specified range (approximately 0.45–0.55 volts) or if the 02S voltage fluctuates very slowly between the specified range (02S signal crosses 0.5 volts less than 5 times in ten seconds), the 02S may be faulty.

5. If the 02S voltage stabilizes at either end of the specified range, the ECM is probably not able to compensate for a mechanical problem such as a vacuum leak or a high float level. These types of mechanical problems will cause the 02S to sense a constant lean or constant rich mixture. The mechanical problem will first have to be repaired and then the 02S test repeated.

6. Pull a vacuum hose located after the throttle plate. Voltage should drop to approximately 0.12 volts (while still fluctuating rapidly). This tests the ability of the 02S to detect a lean mixture condition. Reattach the vacuum hose.

7. Richen the mixture using a propane enrichment tool. Voltage should rise to approximately 0.90 volts (while still fluctuating rapidly). This tests the ability of the 02S to detect a rich mixture condition.

8. If the 02S voltage is above or below the specified range, the 02S and/or the 02S wiring may be faulty. Check the wiring for any breaks, repair as necessary and repeat the test.

REMOVAL & INSTALLATION

❄ WARNING

The sensor uses a permanently attached pigtail and connector. This pigtail should not be removed from the sensor. Damage or removal of the pigtail or connector could affect the proper operation of the sensor. Keep the electrical connector and louvered end of the sensor clean and free of grease. NEVER use cleaning solvents of any

type on the sensor!

➡The oxygen sensor may be difficult to remove when the temperature of the engine is below 120°F (49°C). Excessive force may damage the threads in the exhaust manifold or exhaust pipe.

1. Unplug the electrical connector and any attaching hardware.
2. Remove the sensor using an appropriate sized wrench or special socket.

To install:

3. Coat the threads of the sensor with an anti-seize compound before installation. New sensors are usually precoated with this compound.

➡DO NOT use a conventional anti-seize paste. The use of a regular paste may electrically insulate the sensor, rendering it useless. The threads MUST be coated with the proper electrically conductive anti-seize compound.

4. Install the sensor and tighten to 30 ft. lbs. (40 Nm). Use care in making sure the silicone boot is in the correct position to avoid melting it during operation.
5. Engage the electrical connector and attaching hardware if used.

Knock Sensor

OPERATION

The knock sensor is a tuned piezoelectric crystal transducer that is located in the cylinder head. The knock sensor provides the MCU with an electrical signal that is created by vibrations that correspond to its center frequency (5550 Hz). Vibrations from engine knock (detonation) cause the crystal inside the sensor to vibrate and produce an electrical signal that is used by the MCU to selectively retard the ignition timing of any single cylinder or combination of cylinders to eliminate the knock condition.

Vacuum Switches

OPERATION

Two vacuum-operated electrical switches (ported and manifold) are used to detect and send throttle position data to the MCU for idle (closed), partial and Wide Open Throttle (WOT). These switches are located together in a bracket attached to the dash panel in the engine compartment. The 4 in. Hg (27 kPa) vacuum switch can be identified by its natural (beige) color, while the 10 in. Hg (68 kPa) vacuum switch is green in color. The 4 in. Hg (27 kPa) switch is controlled by ported vacuum and its electrical contact is normally in the open position when the vacuum level is less than 4 in. Hg (27 kPa). When the vacuum exceeds 4 in. Hg (27 kPa), the switch closes. The 4 in. Hg (27 kPa) vacuum switch tells the MCU when either a closed or deep throttle condition exists.

The 10 in. Hg (68 kPa) vacuum switch is controlled by manifold vacuum. Its electrical contact is normally closed when the vacuum level is less than 10 in. Hg (68 kPa); if the vacuum level exceeds 10 in. Hg (68 kPa), the switch opens. This switch tells the MCU that either a partial or medium throttle condition exists.

Coolant Temperature Switch

OPERATION

The temperature switch supplies engine coolant temperature data to the MCU. Until the engine is sufficiently warmed (above 135°F/57°C), the system remains in the open loop mode of operation (i.e., a fixed air/fuel mixture based upon engine rpm).

Thermal Electric Switch

OPERATION

The thermal electric switch is located inside the air cleaner to sense the incoming air temperature and indicate a cold weather start-up condition to the MCU when the air temperature is below 50°F (10°C). Above 65°F (18°C), the switch opens to indicate a normal engine start-up condition to the MCU.

Wide Open Throttle (WOT) Switch

OPERATION

The wide open throttle switch is attached to the base of the carburetor by a mounting bracket. It is a mechanically operated electrical switch that is controlled by the position of the throttle. When the throttle is placed in the wide-open position, a cam on the throttle shaft actuates the switch about 15 degrees before the wide-open position to indicate a full-throttle demand to the MCU.

REMOVAL & INSTALLATION

1. Remove the air cleaner assembly.
2. Disconnect the throttle return spring.
3. Disconnect the throttle cable.
4. Disengage the wire harness connector to the WOT switch.
5. Remove the two WOT switch-to-bracket mounting screws.
6. Remove the WOT switch.

To install:

7. Install the WOT switch and tighten the retainers.
8. Engage the wire harness connector to the switch.
9. Connect the throttle cable and the throttle return spring.
10. Install the air cleaner assembly.

Altitude Jumper Wire

OPERATION

The altitude jumper wire connector is located next to the MCU. The jumper wire provides the MCU with an indication of whether the vehicle is being operated above or below a 4000 ft. elevation (high altitude operation). The connector normally has no jumper wire installed. If a vehicle is to be operated in a designated high altitude area, a jumper wire must be installed.

Diagnosis and Testing

▶ **See Figures 23 thru 56**

➡The CEC system should be considered as a possible source of trouble only after normal tests, that would apply to a vehicle without the system, have been performed.

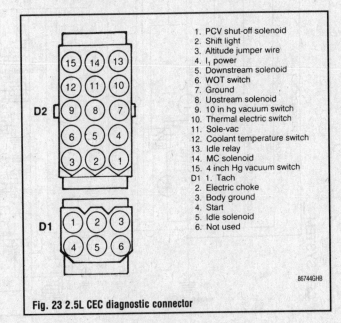

1. PCV shut-off solenoid
2. Shift light
3. Altitude jumper wire
4. I, power
5. Downstream solenoid
6. WOT switch
7. Ground
8. Uostream solenoid
9. 10 in hg vacuum switch
10. Thermal electric switch
11. Sole-vac
12. Coolant temperature switch
13. Idle relay
14. MC solenoid
15. 4 inch Hg vacuum switch
D1 1. Tach
2. Electric choke
3. Body ground
4. Start
5. Idle solenoid
6. Not used

86744GHB

Fig. 23 2.5L CEC diagnostic connector

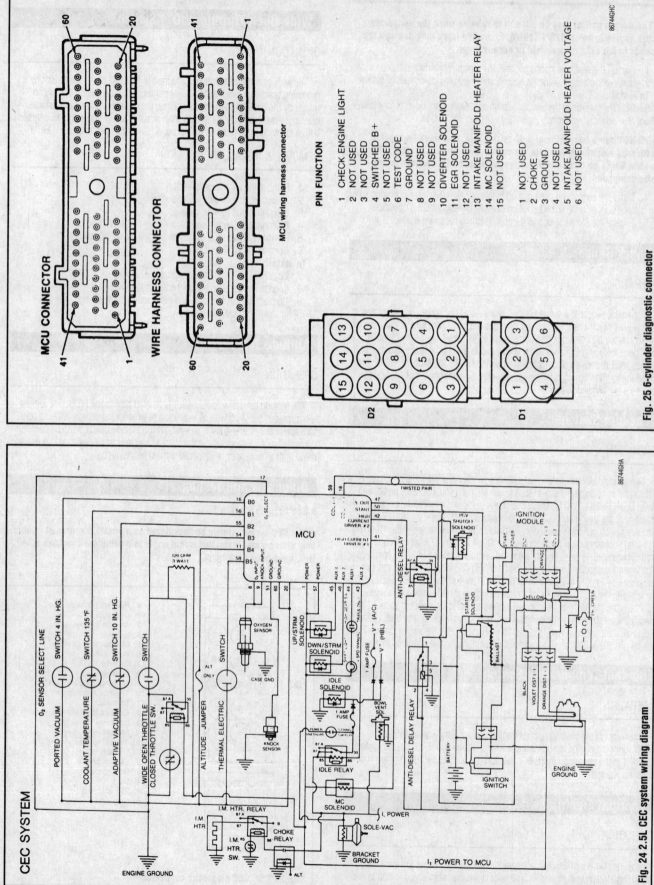

PIN FUNCTION

1. CHECK ENGINE LIGHT
2. NOT USED
3. NOT USED
4. SWITCHED B+
5. NOT USED
6. TEST CODE
7. GROUND
8. NOT USED
9. NOT USED
10. DIVERTER SOLENOID
11. EGR SOLENOID
12. NOT USED
13. INTAKE MANIFOLD HEATER RELAY
14. MC SOLENOID
15. NOT USED

1. NOT USED
2. CHOKE
3. GROUND
4. NOT USED
5. INTAKE MANIFOLD HEATER VOLTAGE
6. NOT USED

MCU CONNECTOR

WIRE HARNESS CONNECTOR

MCU wiring harness connector

Fig. 25 6-cylinder diagnostic connector

Fig. 24 2.5L CEC system wiring diagram

The CEC Fuel Feedback System incorporates a diagnostic connector to provide a means for systematic evaluation of each component that could cause an operational failure. Electronic Fuel Feedback testers, ET-501-82 and ET-501-84 or equivalent, are available to aid in the system diagnosis. When a tester is not available, other test equipment can be substituted.

The equipment required to perform the checks and tests includes a tachometer, a hand vacuum pump and a digital volt-ohmmeter (DVOM) with a minimum ohms per volt of 10 megaohms.

⁂ WARNING

The use of a voltmeter with less than 10 megaohms per volt input impedance can destroy the oxygen sensor. Since it is necessary to look inside the carburetor with the engine running, observe the following precautions.

Before performing the Diagnostic Tests, other engine associated systems that can affect air/fuel mixture, combustion efficiency or exhaust gas composition should be tested for faults. These systems include:

1. Basic carburetor adjustments.
2. Mechanical engine operation (spark plugs, valves, rings, etc.).
3. Ignition system components and operation.
4. Gaskets (intake manifold, carburetor or base plate); loose vacuum hoses or fittings, or loose electrical connections.

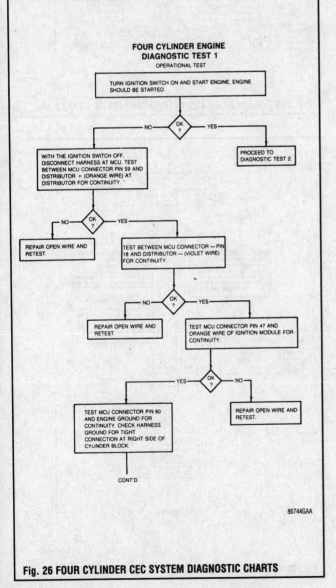

Fig. 26 FOUR CYLINDER CEC SYSTEM DIAGNOSTIC CHARTS

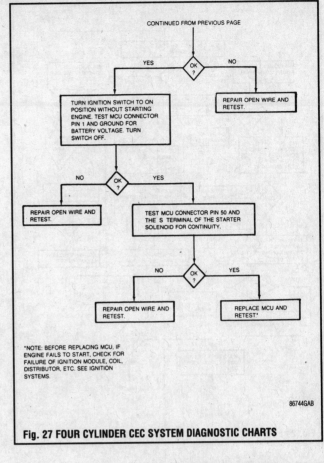

Fig. 27 FOUR CYLINDER CEC SYSTEM DIAGNOSTIC CHARTS

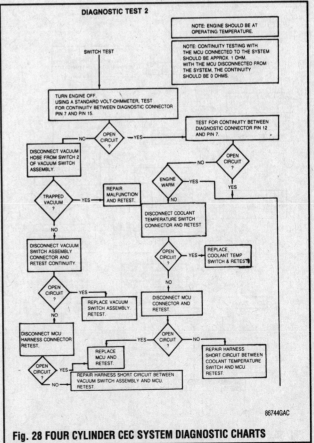

Fig. 28 FOUR CYLINDER CEC SYSTEM DIAGNOSTIC CHARTS

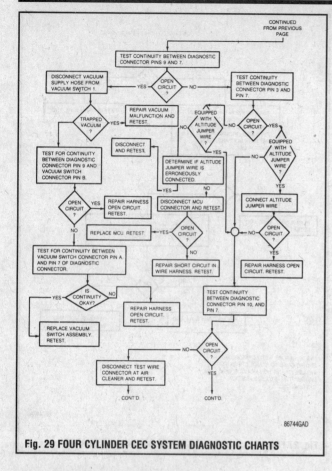

Fig. 29 FOUR CYLINDER CEC SYSTEM DIAGNOSTIC CHARTS

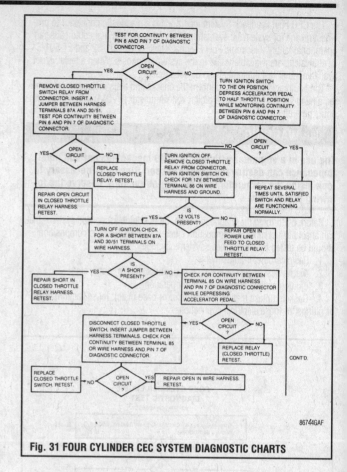

Fig. 31 FOUR CYLINDER CEC SYSTEM DIAGNOSTIC CHARTS

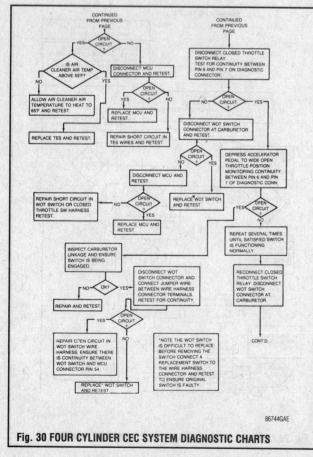

Fig. 30 FOUR CYLINDER CEC SYSTEM DIAGNOSTIC CHARTS

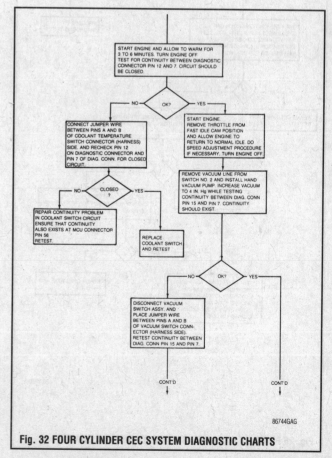

Fig. 32 FOUR CYLINDER CEC SYSTEM DIAGNOSTIC CHARTS

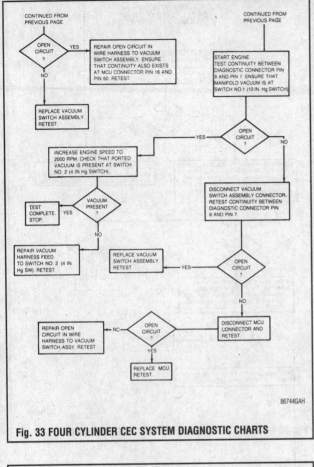

Fig. 33 FOUR CYLINDER CEC SYSTEM DIAGNOSTIC CHARTS

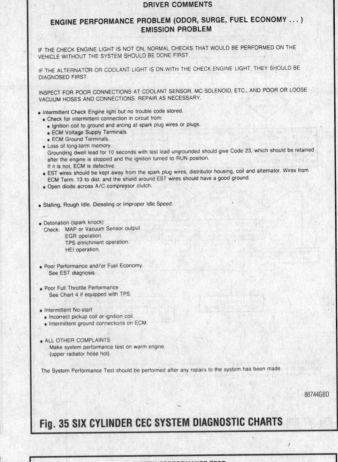

Fig. 35 SIX CYLINDER CEC SYSTEM DIAGNOSTIC CHARTS

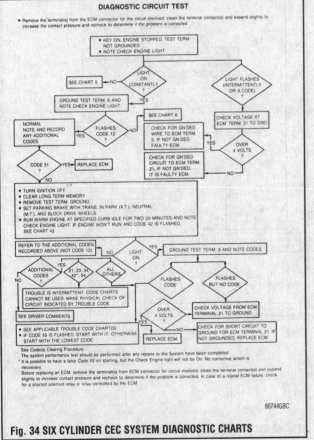

Fig. 34 SIX CYLINDER CEC SYSTEM DIAGNOSTIC CHARTS

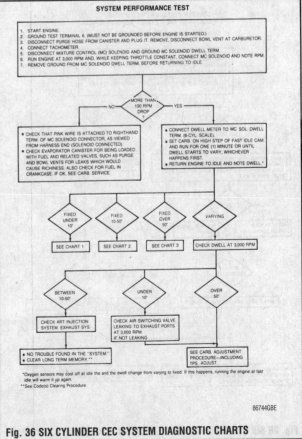

Fig. 36 SIX CYLINDER CEC SYSTEM DIAGNOSTIC CHARTS

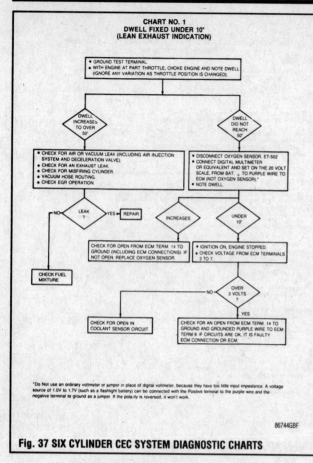

Fig. 37 SIX CYLINDER CEC SYSTEM DIAGNOSTIC CHARTS

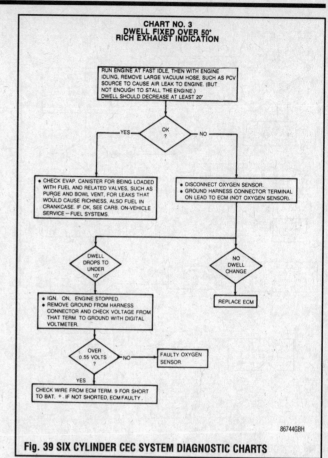

Fig. 39 SIX CYLINDER CEC SYSTEM DIAGNOSTIC CHARTS

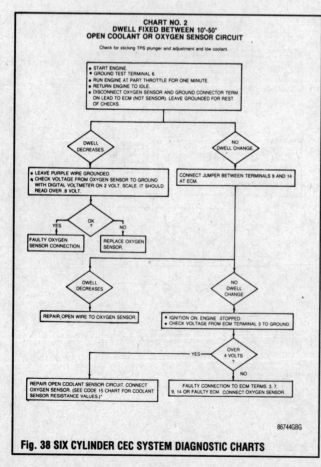

Fig. 38 SIX CYLINDER CEC SYSTEM DIAGNOSTIC CHARTS

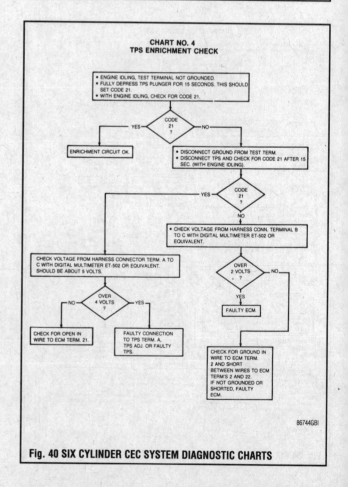

Fig. 40 SIX CYLINDER CEC SYSTEM DIAGNOSTIC CHARTS

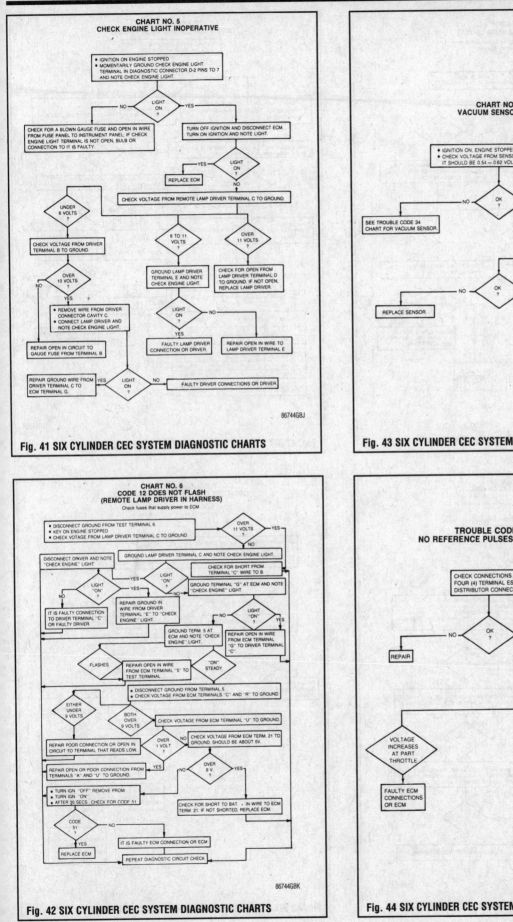

CHART NO. 5
CHECK ENGINE LIGHT INOPERATIVE

Fig. 41 SIX CYLINDER CEC SYSTEM DIAGNOSTIC CHARTS

CHART NO. 6
CODE 12 DOES NOT FLASH
(REMOTE LAMP DRIVER IN HARNESS)

Fig. 42 SIX CYLINDER CEC SYSTEM DIAGNOSTIC CHARTS

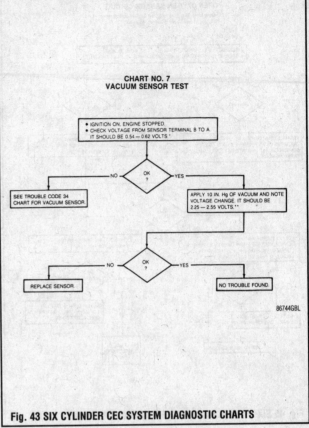

CHART NO. 7
VACUUM SENSOR TEST

Fig. 43 SIX CYLINDER CEC SYSTEM DIAGNOSTIC CHARTS

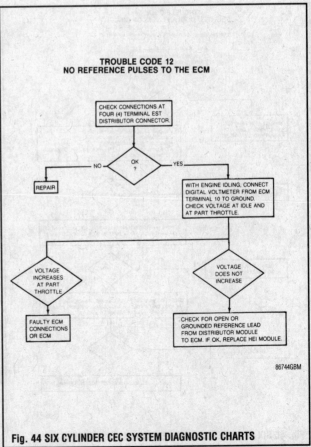

TROUBLE CODE 12
NO REFERENCE PULSES TO THE ECM

Fig. 44 SIX CYLINDER CEC SYSTEM DIAGNOSTIC CHARTS

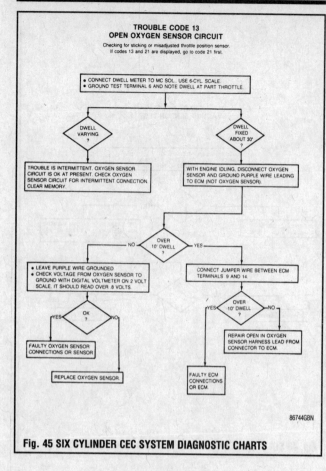

TROUBLE CODE 13
OPEN OXYGEN SENSOR CIRCUIT

Checking for sticking or misadjusted throttle position sensor.
If codes 13 and 21 are displayed, go to code 21 first.

- CONNECT DWELL METER TO MC SOL., USE 6-CYL. SCALE.
- GROUND TEST TERMINAL 6 AND NOTE DWELL AT PART THROTTLE.

DWELL VARYING?

TROUBLE IS INTERMITTENT. OXYGEN SENSOR CIRCUIT IS OK AT PRESENT. CHECK OXYGEN SENSOR CIRCUIT FOR INTERMITTENT CONNECTION. CLEAR MEMORY.

DWELL FIXED ABOUT 30°?

WITH ENGINE IDLING, DISCONNECT OXYGEN SENSOR AND GROUND PURPLE WIRE LEADING TO ECM (NOT OXYGEN SENSOR).

OVER 10° DWELL?

NO

- LEAVE PURPLE WIRE GROUNDED.
- CHECK VOLTAGE FROM OXYGEN SENSOR TO GROUND WITH DIGITAL VOLTMETER ON 2 VOLT SCALE. IT SHOULD READ OVER .8 VOLTS.

YES

CONNECT JUMPER WIRE BETWEEN ECM TERMINALS 9 AND 14.

OK?

YES / NO

FAULTY OXYGEN SENSOR CONNECTIONS OR SENSOR.

REPLACE OXYGEN SENSOR.

OVER 10° DWELL?

YES / NO

REPAIR OPEN IN OXYGEN SENSOR HARNESS LEAD FROM CONNECTOR TO ECM.

FAULTY ECM CONNECTIONS OR ECM.

86744GBN

Fig. 45 SIX CYLINDER CEC SYSTEM DIAGNOSTIC CHARTS

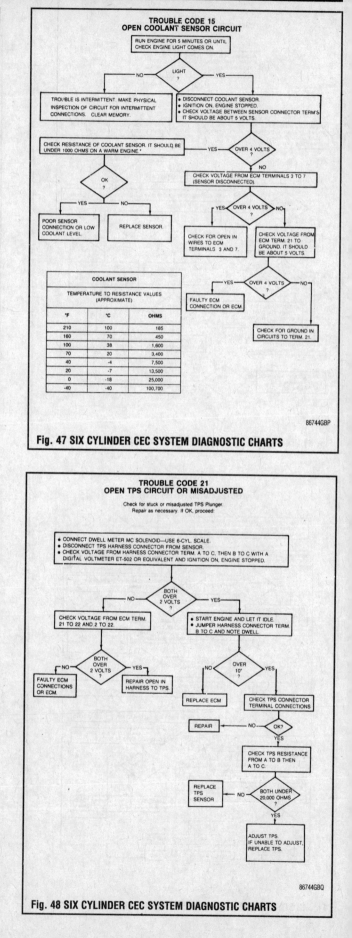

TROUBLE CODE 15
OPEN COOLANT SENSOR CIRCUIT

RUN ENGINE FOR 5 MINUTES OR UNTIL CHECK ENGINE LIGHT COMES ON.

LIGHT?

NO

TROUBLE IS INTERMITTENT. MAKE PHYSICAL INSPECTION OF CIRCUIT FOR INTERMITTENT CONNECTIONS. CLEAR MEMORY.

YES

- DISCONNECT COOLANT SENSOR.
- IGNITION ON, ENGINE STOPPED.
- CHECK VOLTAGE BETWEEN SENSOR CONNECTOR TERM'S IT SHOULD BE ABOUT 5 VOLTS.

CHECK RESISTANCE OF COOLANT SENSOR. IT SHOULD BE UNDER 1000 OHMS ON A WARM ENGINE.*

YES

OVER 4 VOLTS?

NO

CHECK VOLTAGE FROM ECM TERMINALS 3 TO 7 (SENSOR DISCONNECTED).

OK?

YES / NO

POOR SENSOR CONNECTION OR LOW COOLANT LEVEL.

REPLACE SENSOR.

OVER 4 VOLTS?

YES / NO

CHECK FOR OPEN IN WIRES TO ECM TERMINALS 3 AND 7.

CHECK VOLTAGE FROM ECM TERM. 21 TO GROUND. IT SHOULD BE ABOUT 5 VOLTS.

OVER 4 VOLTS?

YES / NO

FAULTY ECM CONNECTION OR ECM.

CHECK FOR GROUND IN CIRCUITS TO TERM. 21.

COOLANT SENSOR		
TEMPERATURE TO RESISTANCE VALUES (APPROXIMATE)		
°F	°C	OHMS
210	100	185
160	70	450
100	38	1,600
70	20	3,400
40	-4	7,500
20	-7	13,500
0	-18	25,000
-40	-40	100,700

86744GBP

Fig. 47 SIX CYLINDER CEC SYSTEM DIAGNOSTIC CHARTS

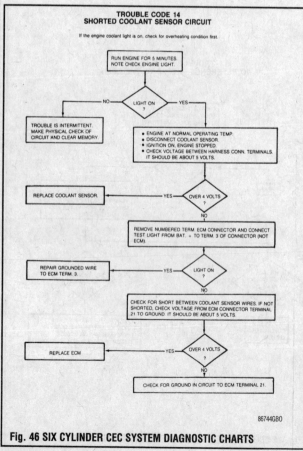

TROUBLE CODE 14
SHORTED COOLANT SENSOR CIRCUIT

If the engine coolant light is on, check for overheating condition first.

RUN ENGINE FOR 5 MINUTES. NOTE CHECK ENGINE LIGHT.

LIGHT ON?

NO

TROUBLE IS INTERMITTENT. MAKE PHYSICAL CHECK OF CIRCUIT AND CLEAR MEMORY.

YES

- ENGINE AT NORMAL OPERATING TEMP.
- DISCONNECT COOLANT SENSOR.
- IGNITION ON, ENGINE STOPPED.
- CHECK VOLTAGE BETWEEN HARNESS CONN. TERMINALS. IT SHOULD BE ABOUT 5 VOLTS.

REPLACE COOLANT SENSOR.

YES

OVER 4 VOLTS?

NO

REMOVE NUMBERED TERM. ECM CONNECTOR AND CONNECT TEST LIGHT FROM BAT. + TO TERM. 3 OF CONNECTOR (NOT ECM).

REPAIR GROUNDED WIRE TO ECM TERM. 3.

YES

LIGHT ON?

NO

CHECK FOR SHORT BETWEEN COOLANT SENSOR WIRES. IF NOT SHORTED, CHECK VOLTAGE FROM ECM CONNECTOR TERMINAL 21 TO GROUND. IT SHOULD BE ABOUT 5 VOLTS.

REPLACE ECM

YES

OVER 4 VOLTS?

NO

CHECK FOR GROUND IN CIRCUIT TO ECM TERMINAL 21.

86744GBO

Fig. 46 SIX CYLINDER CEC SYSTEM DIAGNOSTIC CHARTS

TROUBLE CODE 21
OPEN TPS CIRCUIT OR MISADJUSTED

Check for stuck or misadjusted TPS Plunger.
Repair as necessary. If OK, proceed:

- CONNECT DWELL METER MC SOLENOID—USE 6-CYL. SCALE.
- DISCONNECT TPS HARNESS CONNECTOR FROM SENSOR.
- CHECK VOLTAGE FROM HARNESS CONNECTOR TERM. A TO C. THEN B TO C WITH A DIGITAL VOLTMETER ET-502 OR EQUIVALENT AND IGNITION ON, ENGINE STOPPED.

BOTH OVER 2 VOLTS?

NO

CHECK VOLTAGE FROM ECM TERM. 21 TO 22 AND 2 TO 22.

YES

- START ENGINE AND LET IT IDLE.
- JUMPER HARNESS CONNECTOR TERM. B TO C AND NOTE DWELL.

BOTH OVER 2 VOLTS?

NO / YES

FAULTY ECM CONNECTIONS OR ECM.

REPAIR OPEN IN HARNESS TO TPS.

OVER 10°?

NO / YES

REPLACE ECM

CHECK TPS CONNECTOR TERMINAL CONNECTIONS

REPAIR

NO

OK?

YES

CHECK TPS RESISTANCE FROM A TO B THEN A TO C.

REPLACE TPS SENSOR

NO

BOTH UNDER 20,000 OHMS?

YES

ADJUST TPS. IF UNABLE TO ADJUST, REPLACE TPS.

86744GBQ

Fig. 48 SIX CYLINDER CEC SYSTEM DIAGNOSTIC CHARTS

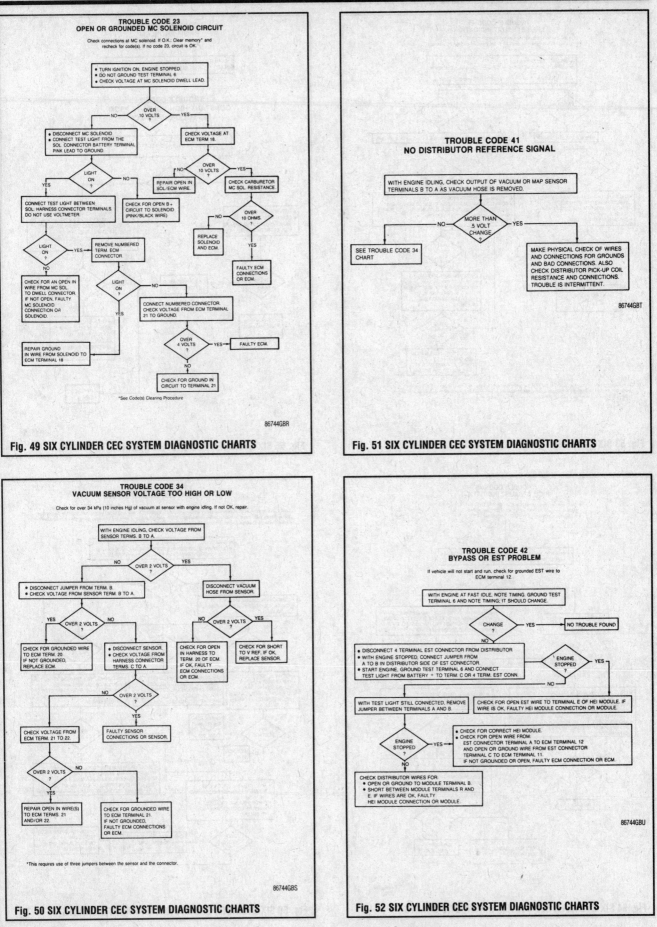

Fig. 49 SIX CYLINDER CEC SYSTEM DIAGNOSTIC CHARTS

Fig. 50 SIX CYLINDER CEC SYSTEM DIAGNOSTIC CHARTS

Fig. 51 SIX CYLINDER CEC SYSTEM DIAGNOSTIC CHARTS

Fig. 52 SIX CYLINDER CEC SYSTEM DIAGNOSTIC CHARTS

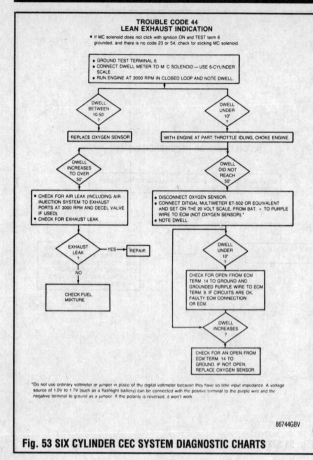

Fig. 53 SIX CYLINDER CEC SYSTEM DIAGNOSTIC CHARTS

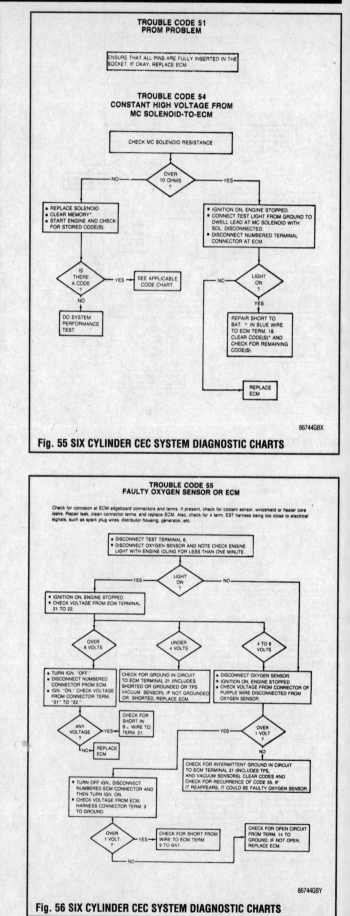

Fig. 55 SIX CYLINDER CEC SYSTEM DIAGNOSTIC CHARTS

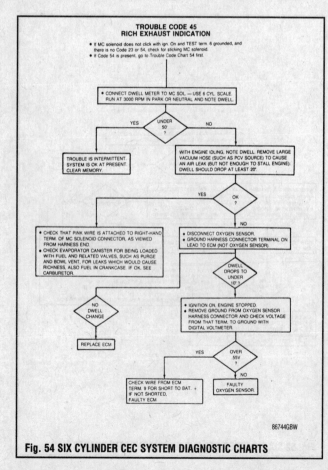

Fig. 54 SIX CYLINDER CEC SYSTEM DIAGNOSTIC CHARTS

Fig. 56 SIX CYLINDER CEC SYSTEM DIAGNOSTIC CHARTS

RENIX THROTTLE BODY INJECTION (TBI) ELECTRONIC ENGINE CONTROLS

General Information

▶ **See Figures 57, 58, 59, 60 and 61**

The Renix throttle body fuel injection system is a ìpulse time" system that uses a single solenoid-type injector to meter fuel into the throttle body above the throttle blade. Fuel is metered to the engine by an Electronic Control Unit (ECU), which controls the amount of fuel delivery according to input from various engine sensors that monitor exhaust gas oxygen content, coolant temperature, manifold absolute pressure, crankshaft position and throttle position. These sensors provide an electronic signal by varying resistance within the sensor itself. By reading the difference in resistance, the ECU can determine engine operating conditions and calculate the correct air/fuel mixture, and ignition timing under varying engine loads and temperatures. In addition, the ECU controls idle speed, emission control and fuel pump operation, the upshift indicator lamp and the A/C compressor clutch.

Renix TBI fuel injection has two main subsystems; a fuel subsystem and a control subsystem. The fuel subsystem consists of an electric fuel pump (mounted in the fuel tank), a fuel filter, a pressure regulator and the fuel injector.

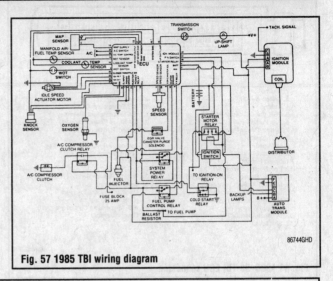

Fig. 57 1985 TBI wiring diagram

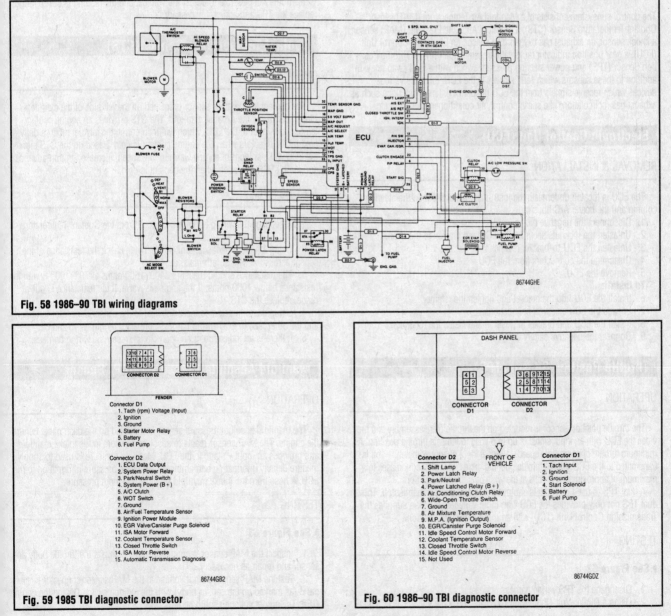

Fig. 58 1986–90 TBI wiring diagrams

FENDER

Connector D1
1. Tach (rpm) Voltage (Input)
2. Ignition
3. Ground
4. Starter Motor Relay
5. Battery
6. Fuel Pump

Connector D2
1. ECU Data Output
2. System Power Relay
3. Park/Neutral Switch
4. System Power (B+)
5. A/C Clutch
6. WOT Switch
7. Ground
8. Air/Fuel Temperature Sensor
9. Ignition Power Module
10. EGR Valve/Canister Purge Solenoid
11. ISA Motor Forward
12. Coolant Temperature Sensor
13. Closed Throttle Switch
14. ISA Motor Reverse
15. Automatic Transmission Diagnosis

Fig. 59 1985 TBI diagnostic connector

DASH PANEL

FRONT OF VEHICLE

Connector D2
1. Shift Lamp
2. Power Latch Relay
3. Park/Neutral
4. Power Latched Relay (B+)
5. Air Conditioning Clutch Relay
6. Wide-Open Throttle Switch
7. Ground
8. Air Mixture Temperature
9. M.P.A. (Ignition Output)
10. EGR/Canister Purge Solenoid
11. Idle Speed Control Motor Forward
12. Coolant Temperature Sensor
13. Closed Throttle Switch
14. Idle Speed Control Motor Reverse
15. Not Used

Connector D1
1. Tach Input
2. Ignition
3. Ground
4. Start Solenoid
5. Battery
6. Fuel Pump

Fig. 60 1986–90 TBI diagnostic connector

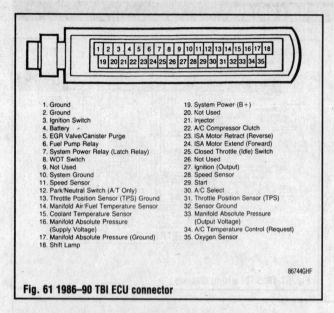

1. Ground
2. Ground
3. Ignition Switch
4. Battery
5. EGR Valve/Canister Purge
6. Fuel Pump Relay
7. System Power Relay (Latch Relay)
8. WOT Switch
9. Not Used
10. System Ground
11. Speed Sensor
12. Park/Neutral Switch (A/T Only)
13. Throttle Position Sensor (TPS) Ground
14. Manifold Air/Fuel Temperature Sensor
15. Coolant Temperature Sensor
16. Manifold Absolute Pressure (Supply Voltage)
17. Manifold Absolute Pressure (Ground)
18. Shift Lamp

19. System Power (B+)
20. Not Used
21. Injector
22. A/C Compressor Clutch
23. ISA Motor Retract (Reverse)
24. ISA Motor Extend (Forward)
25. Closed Throttle (Idle) Switch
26. Not Used
27. Ignition (Output)
28. Speed Sensor
29. Start
30. A/C Select
31. Throttle Position Sensor (TPS)
32. Sensor Ground
33. Manifold Absolute Pressure (Output Voltage)
34. A/C Temperature Control (Request)
35. Oxygen Sensor

86744GHF

Fig. 61 1986–90 TBI ECU connector

The control subsystem consists of a Manifold Air Temperature (MAT) sensor, a Coolant Temperature Sensor (CTS), a Manifold Absolute Pressure (MAP) sensor, a knock sensor, an exhaust gas oxygen (O_2) sensor, an Electronic Control Unit (ECU), a gear position indicator (automatic transmission only), a Throttle Position Sensor (TPS) and power steering pressure switch with a load swap relay. In addition to these sensors which send signals to the ECU, there are various devices which receive signals from the ECU to control different functions such as exhaust gas recirculation, idle speed control, air conditioner operation, etc.

Electronic Control Unit (ECU)

REMOVAL & INSTALLATION

The ECU is located underneath the instrument panel between the steering column and the heater A/C housing.

1. Disconnect the negative battery cable.
2. Unfasten the locknuts securing the ECU and bracket to the dash.
3. Unfasten the ECU-to-bracket retainer.
4. Disengage the connectors from the ECU.
5. Remove the ECU.

To install:

6. Install the ECU into the bracket and tighten the retainer.
7. Engage the ECU electrical connections.
8. Install the ECU and bracket in position and fasten the retainers.
9. Connect the negative battery cable.

Throttle Position Sensor (TPS)

OPERATION

The throttle position sensor is mounted on the throttle plate assembly and provides the ECU with an input signal of up to 5 volts to indicate throttle position. At minimum throttle opening (idle speed), a signal input of approximately 1 volt is transmitted to the ECU. As the throttle opening increases, voltage increases to a maximum of approximately 5 volts at the wide open throttle position.

A dual TPS is used on models equipped with automatic transmission. This dual TPS not only provides the ECU with input voltages, but also supplies the Transmission Control Unit (TCU) with an input of throttle position.

TESTING

▶ See Figure 62

1. Disengage the TPS wiring harness connector.
2. Using a Digital-Volt-Ohm-Meter (DVOM), check the voltage at TPS con-

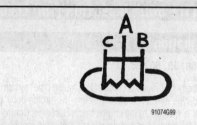

91074G99

Fig. 62 Throttle position sensor connector terminal identifications

nector pins B (ground) and C (5 volt supply) with the ignition key in the îONî position. It should read approximately 5 volts..

3. Plug in the TPS wiring harness connector to the TPS.
4. Check the voltage by carefully inserting the DVOM test leads through the back of the wiring harness connector to make contact with the sensor terminals A (+) and B (ground).
5. With the ignition key in the îONî position and the throttle plate held at the Wide Open Throttle (WOT) position, the output voltage should read 4.6–4.7 volts. If the reading is out of range, adjust the voltage by loosening the TPS mounting screws while at WOT and carefully turn the sensor until the correct voltage reading is achieved, afterwards, just tighten down the retaining screws.
6. If it is not possible to adjust the voltage, and the reading is out of range, replace the TPS and adjust if necessary.

Coolant Temperature Sensor (CTS)

OPERATION

The coolant temperature sensor is located on the left side of the cylinder block, just below the exhaust manifold. The CTS provides an engine coolant temperature input to the ECU, which will then enrich the air/fuel mixture delivered by the injectors when the engine coolant is cold. Based on the CTS signal, the ECU will also control engine warmup idle speed, increase ignition advance and inhibit EGR operation when the coolant is cold.

TESTING

1. Disengage the wiring harness connector from the Coolant Temperature Sensor (CTS).
2. Using a high impedance, digital ohmmeter, check the resistance of the sensor across the sensor terminals.
3. The resistance should measure 3400–1600 ohms at 70°–100° F, with the resistance below 1000 ohms, if the engine is warm. If the resistance is out of range, replace the CTS.
4. Using the ohmmeter, connect one lead to the sensor connector terminal, and the other lead to ECU wiring harness connector terminals 15 and 32.
5. If there is an indication of an open circuit, repair the wiring harness.

Manifold Absolute Pressure (MAP) Sensor

OPERATION

The manifold absolute pressure sensor is mounted on the dash panel behind the engine. The MAP sensor reacts to absolute pressure in the intake manifold and provides an input voltage to the ECU. Manifold pressure is used to supply mixture density information and ambient barometric pressure information to the ECU. A hose from the intake manifold provides the input pressure.

TESTING

▶ See Figure 63

1. Inspect the MAP sensor vacuum hose connection at the throttle body and sensor and repair as necessary.
2. Test the MAP sensor output voltage at the MAP sensor connector terminal B (as marked on the sensor body) with the ignition switch **ON** and the engine **OFF**. The output voltage should be 4–5 volts.

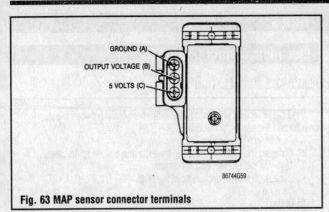

GROUND (A)
OUTPUT VOLTAGE (B)
5 VOLTS (C)

86744G59

Fig. 63 MAP sensor connector terminals

➡**The voltage should drop to 0.5–1.5 volts with a hot, neutral idle speed condition.**

3. Test ECU terminal pin 33 for the same voltage as in Step 2 to verify the wire harness condition and repair as necessary.

4. Test the MAP sensor supply voltage at the sensor connector terminal C with the ignition **ON**. The voltage should be 4.5–5.5 volts. The same voltage should be present at terminal pin 16 of the ECU wire harness connector. Repair or replace the wire harness as necessary.

5. Test the MAP sensor ground circuit at the sensor connector terminal A and ECU connector pin 17. Repair the wire harness as necessary.

6. Test the MAP sensor ground circuit at the ECU connector between terminal pin 17 and terminal pin 2 with an ohmmeter. If the ohmmeter indicates an open circuit, check for a defective sensor ground connection located on the flywheel housing near the starter motor. If the ground connection is good, replace the ECU.

➡**If terminal pin 17 has a short circuit to 12 volts, correct this condition before replacing the ECU.**

Manifold Air Temperature (MAT) Sensor

OPERATION

The manifold air temperature sensor is located in the intake manifold. The MAT sensor reacts to the temperature of the air in the intake manifold and provides an input to the ECU to allow it to compensate for air density changes during high temperature operation.

TESTING

◆ **See Figure 64**

1. Disengage the wire harness connector from the MAT.
2. Measure the resistance of the sensor with a high input impedance (digital) volt-ohmmeter. The resistance should be less than 1000 ohms with the engine warm. Refer to the resistance chart and replace the sensor if it is not within the range of resistance specified in the chart.

Temperature-to-Resistance Values (Approximate)		
°F	°C	Ohms
212	100	185
160	70	450
100	38	1,600
70	20	3,400
40	4	7,500
20	-7	13,500
0	-18	25,000
-40	-40	100,700

86744G58

Fig. 64 MAT sensor resistance test chart

3. Measure the resistance of the wire harness between ECU wire harness connector terminal 32 and the sensor connector terminal, and terminal 14 to the sensor connector terminal.
4. Repair the wire harness if the resistance is greater than 1 ohm.

Knock Sensor

OPERATION

The knock sensor is located on the lower left side of the cylinder block, just above the oil pan. The knock sensor provides and input to the ECU that indicates detonation (knock) during engine operation. When detonation occurs, the ECU retards the ignition timing advance to eliminate the detonation at the applicable cylinder.

TESTING

1. Using a DRB, or equivalent, scan tool, proceed to display the test mode.
2. Start the engine and note the knock unit value.
3. Using the tip of a screwdriver, or similar tool, gently tap on the engine block near the knock sensor and note the knock value.
4. The knock value should increase while tapping on the engine block.
5. If the knock value does not increase while tapping on the engine block, inspect the wiring harness for a proper connection.
6. If the connection is good, replace the knock sensor.

Heated Oxygen (HO2S) Sensor

OPERATION

The heated oxygen sensor, or HO2S sensor is located at the exhaust system, usually near the catalytic converter. It produces a voltage signal of 0.1–1.0 volts based on the amount of oxygen in the exhaust gas. When a low amount of oxygen is present (caused by a rich air/fuel mixture), the sensor produces a low voltage. When a high amount of oxygen is present (caused by a lean air/fuel mixture), the sensor produces a high voltage. Because an accurate voltage signal is only produced if the sensor temperature is above approximately 600°F, a fast acting heating element is built into its body.

The ECU uses the HO2S sensor voltage signal to constantly adjust the amount of fuel injected which keeps the engine at its peek efficiency.

TESTING

1. Start the engine and bring it to normal operating temperature, then run the engine above 1200 rpm for two minutes.
2. Backprobe with a high impedance averaging voltmeter (set to the DC voltage scale) between the HO2S sensor signal wire and battery ground.
3. Verify that the sensor voltage fluctuates rapidly between 0.40–0.60 volts.
4. If the sensor voltage is stabilized at the middle of the specified range (approximately 0.45–0.55 volts) or if the voltage fluctuates very slowly between the specified range (HO2S signal crosses 0.5 volts less than 5 times in ten seconds), the sensor may be faulty.
5. If the sensor voltage stabilizes at either end of the specified range, the ECU is probably not able to compensate for a mechanical problem such as a vacuum leak. These types of mechanical problems will cause the sensor to report a constant lean or constant rich mixture. The mechanical problem will first have to be repaired and then the HO2S sensor test repeated.
6. Pull a vacuum hose located after the throttle plate. Voltage should drop to approximately 0.12 volts (while still fluctuating rapidly). This tests the ability of the sensor to detect a lean mixture condition. Reattach the vacuum hose.
7. Richen the mixture using a propane enrichment tool. Sensor voltage should rise to approximately 0.90 volts (while still fluctuating rapidly). This tests the ability of the sensor to detect a rich mixture condition.
8. If the sensor voltage is above or below the specified range, the sensor and/or the sensor wiring may be faulty. Check the wiring for any breaks, repair as necessary and repeat the test.
9. Further sensor operational testing requires the use of a special tester M.S.1700, or equivalent.

RENIX MULTI-POINT INJECTION ELECTRONIC ENGINE CONTROLS

General Information

▶ **See Figures 65, 66 and 67**

The Renix Multi-Point Fuel Injection (MPI) system, used on 4.0L engines through 1990, is controlled by a digital microprocessor called the Electronic Control Unit, or ECU. The ECU receives information from various input sensors. Based on this information, the ECU is programmed to provide a precise amount of fuel and the correct ignition timing to meet existing engine speed and load conditions.

The ECU also calculates ignition timing and operates the ignition control module. Ignition timing is modified by the ECU to meet any engine operating condition. Information such as air temperature, engine coolant temperature, engine speed, absolute pressure in the intake manifold, or the presence of spark knock is used by the ECU when calculating the correct ignition timing.

The ECU controls the engine by receiving input signals from the Manifold Absolute Pressure (MAP) sensor, the Crankshaft Position Sensor (CKP), knock sensor, oxygen sensor, Throttle Position Sensor (TPS), Coolant Temperature Sensor (CTS), Manifold Air Temperature (MAT) sensor and battery voltage. Based on the information received from the input sensors, the ECU then sends control (output) signals to the fuel pump relay, fuel injectors, idle speed control solenoid, ignition control module and the EGR valve.

As input signals to the ECU change, the ECU adjusts its signals to the output devices. For example, the ECU must calculate a different injector pulse width and ignition timing for idle than it calculates for Wide Open Throttle (WOT).

Electronic Control Unit (ECU)

REMOVAL & INSTALLATION

The ECU is located underneath the instrument panel between the steering column and the heater A/C housing.
1. Disconnect the negative battery cable.
2. Unfasten the locknuts securing the ECU and bracket to the dash.
3. Unfasten the ECU-to-bracket retainer.
4. Disengage the connectors from the ECU.
5. Remove the ECU.

To install:
6. Install the ECU into the bracket and tighten the retainer.
7. Engage the ECU electrical connections.
8. Install the ECU and bracket in position and fasten the retainers.
9. Connect the negative battery cable.

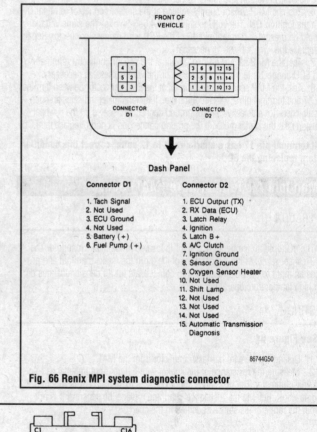

Connector D1	Connector D2
1. Tach Signal	1. ECU Output (TX)
2. Not Used	2. RX Data (ECU)
3. ECU Ground	3. Latch Relay
4. Not Used	4. Ignition
5. Battery (+)	5. Latch B +
6. Fuel Pump (+)	6. A/C Clutch
	7. Ignition Ground
	8. Sensor Ground
	9. Oxygen Sensor Heater
	10. Not Used
	11. Shift Lamp
	12. Not Used
	13. Not Used
	14. Not Used
	15. Automatic Transmission Diagnosis

86744G50

Fig. 66 Renix MPI system diagnostic connector

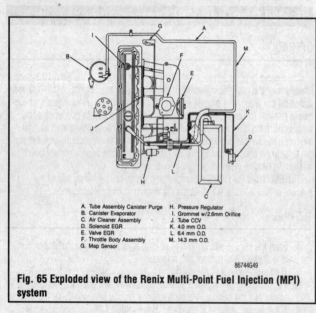

A.	Tube Assembly Canister Purge	H.	Pressure Regulator
B.	Canister Evaporator	I.	Grommet w/2.6mm Orifice
C.	Air Cleaner Assembly	J.	Tube CCV
D.	Solenoid EGR	K.	4.0 mm O.D.
E.	Valve EGR	L.	6.4 mm O.D.
F.	Throttle Body Assembly	M.	14.3 mm O.D.
G.	Map Sensor		

86744G49

Fig. 65 Exploded view of the Renix Multi-Point Fuel Injection (MPI) system

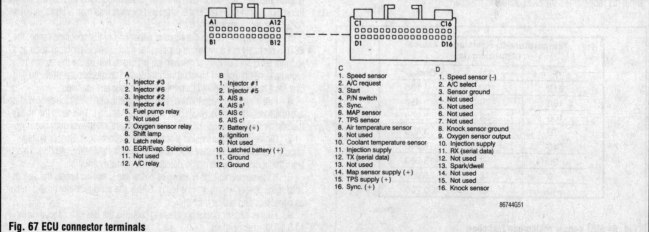

A	B
1. Injector #3	1. Injector #1
2. Injector #6	2. Injector #5
3. Injector #2	3. AIS a
4. Injector #4	4. AIS a¹
5. Fuel pump relay	5. AIS c
6. Not used	6. AIS c¹
7. Oxygen sensor relay	7. Battery (+)
8. Shift lamp	8. Ignition
9. Latch relay	9. Not used
10. EGR/Evap. Solenoid	10. Latched battery (+)
11. Not used	11. Ground
12. A/C relay	12. Ground

C	D
1. Speed sensor	1. Speed sensor (–)
2. A/C request	2. A/C select
3. Start	3. Sensor ground
4. P/N switch	4. Not used
5. Sync.	5. Not used
6. MAP sensor	6. Not used
7. TPS sensor	7. Not used
8. Air temperature sensor	8. Knock sensor ground
9. Not used	9. Oxygen sensor output
10. Coolant temperature sensor	10. Injection supply
11. Injection supply	11. RX (serial data)
12. TX (serial data)	12. Not used
13. Not used	13. Spark/dwell
14. Map sensor supply (+)	14. Not used
15. TPS supply (+)	15. Not used
16. Sync. (+)	16. Knock sensor

86744G51

Fig. 67 ECU connector terminals

Heated Oxygen (HO2S) Sensor

OPERATION

▶ **See Figure 68**

The heated oxygen sensor, or HO2S sensor is located at the exhaust system, usually near the catalytic converter. It produces a voltage signal of 0.1–1.0 volts based on the amount of oxygen in the exhaust gas. When a low amount of oxygen is present (caused by a rich air/fuel mixture), the sensor produces a low voltage. When a high amount of oxygen is present (caused by a lean air/fuel mixture), the sensor produces a high voltage. Because an accurate voltage signal is only produced if the sensor temperature is above approximately 600°F, a fast acting heating element is built into its body.

The ECU uses the HO2S sensor voltage signal to constantly adjust the amount of fuel injected which keeps the engine at its peek efficiency.

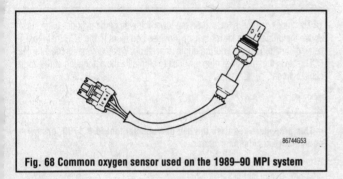

Fig. 68 Common oxygen sensor used on the 1989–90 MPI system

TESTING

1. Start the engine and bring it to normal operating temperature, then run the engine above 1200 rpm for two minutes.
2. Backprobe with a high impedance averaging voltmeter (set to the DC voltage scale) between the HO2S sensor signal wire and battery ground.
3. Verify that the sensor voltage fluctuates rapidly between 0.40–0.60 volts.
4. If the sensor voltage is stabilized at the middle of the specified range (approximately 0.45–0.55 volts) or if the voltage fluctuates very slowly between the specified range (HO2S signal crosses 0.5 volts less than 5 times in ten seconds), the sensor may be faulty.
5. If the sensor voltage stabilizes at either end of the specified range, the ECU is probably not able to compensate for a mechanical problem such as a vacuum leak. These types of mechanical problems will cause the sensor to report a constant lean or constant rich mixture. The mechanical problem will first have to be repaired and then the HO2S sensor test repeated.
6. Pull a vacuum hose located after the throttle plate. Voltage should drop to approximately 0.12 volts (while still fluctuating rapidly). This tests the ability of the sensor to detect a lean mixture condition. Reattach the vacuum hose.
7. Richen the mixture using a propane enrichment tool. Sensor voltage should rise to approximately 0.90 volts (while still fluctuating rapidly). This tests the ability of the sensor to detect a rich mixture condition.
8. If the sensor voltage is above or below the specified range, the sensor and/or the sensor wiring may be faulty. Check the wiring for any breaks, repair as necessary and repeat the test.
9. Further sensor operational testing requires the use of a special tester M.S.1700, or equivalent.

REMOVAL & INSTALLATION

1. Raise the vehicle and support it with jackstands.
2. Disengage the HO2S sensor wiring connector and remove it using tool YA 8875, or its equivalent.

To install:
3. Inspect the threads of the HO2S sensor. Apply an anti-seize compound only if there is none visible on the threads. Be careful not to contaminate the sensor tip with any foreign compounds.

4. Install the sensor using tool YA 8875, or its equivalent and engage the wiring connector.
5. Carefully lower the vehicle.

Throttle Position Sensor (TPS)

OPERATION

▶ **See Figure 69**

The throttle position sensor is mounted on the throttle plate assembly and provides the ECU with an input signal of up to 5 volts to indicate throttle position. At minimum throttle opening (idle speed), a signal input of approximately 1 volt is transmitted to the ECU. As the throttle opening increases, voltage increases to a maximum of approximately 5 volts at the wide open throttle position.

A dual TPS is used on models equipped with automatic transmission. This dual TPS not only provides the ECU with input voltages, but also supplies the Transmission Control Unit (TCU) with an input of throttle position.

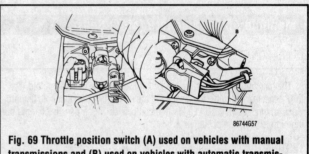

Fig. 69 Throttle position switch (A) used on vehicles with manual transmissions and (B) used on vehicles with automatic transmissions

TESTING

1. Unplug the connector at the TPS.
2. Check the voltage between the black and grey wires with the key **ON**. Voltage should be approximately 5 volts. If the proper voltage is not present, check the harness for shorts or opens.
3. Engage the wire connector to the TPS. With the key **ON**, and the throttle plate closed, check the voltage between the blue and the black wires. Voltage should be approximately 0.8 volts.
4. If voltage is not correct, loosen the screws securing the TPS and adjust until 0.8 volts is present.
5. If adjusting does not bring sensor voltage to specification, replace the TPS.

Coolant Temperature Sensor (CTS)

OPERATION

The coolant temperature sensor is located on the left side of the cylinder block, just below the exhaust manifold. The CTS provides an engine coolant temperature input to the ECU, which will then enrich the air/fuel mixture delivered by the injectors when the engine coolant is cold. Based on the CTS signal, the ECU will also control engine warmup idle speed, increase ignition advance and inhibit EGR operation when the coolant is cold.

TESTING

▶ **See Figure 70**

Disconnect the wire harness connector from the CTS and measure the resistance of the sensor with a high input impedance (digital) volt-ohmmeter. The resistance should be less than 1000 ohms with the engine warm. Refer to the resistance chart and replace the sensor if it is not within the range of resistance specified in the chart. Measure the resistance of the wire harness between ECU wire harness connector terminal D-3 and the sensor connector terminal, and

Temperature-to-Resistance Values (Approximate)		
°F	°C	Ohms
212	100	185
160	70	450
100	38	1,600
70	20	3,400
40	4	7,500
20	-7	13,500
0	-18	25,000
-40	-40	100,700

86744G58.

Fig. 70 CTS sensor resistance test chart—1989–90 vehicles

terminal C-10 to the sensor connector terminal and repair the wire harness if an open circuit is indicated.

Manifold Air Temperature (MAT) Sensor

OPERATION

The manifold air temperature sensor is located in the intake manifold. The MAT sensor reacts to the temperature of the air in the intake manifold and provides an input to the ECU to allow it to compensate for air density changes during high temperature operation.

TESTING

▶ **See Figure 64**

Disconnect the wire harness connector from the MAT and measure the resistance of the sensor with a high input impedance (digital) volt-ohmmeter. The resistance should be less than 1000 ohms with the engine warm. Refer to the resistance chart and replace the sensor if it is not within the range of resistance specified in the chart. Measure the resistance of the wire harness between ECU wire harness connector terminal D-3 and the sensor connector terminal, and terminal C-8 to the sensor connector terminal. Repair the wire harness if the resistance is greater than 1 ohm.

Manifold Absolute Pressure (MAP) Sensor

OPERATION

▶ **See Figure 63**

The manifold absolute pressure sensor is mounted on the dash panel behind the engine. The MAP sensor reacts to absolute pressure in the intake manifold and provides an input voltage to the ECU. Manifold pressure is used to supply mixture density information and ambient barometric pressure information to the ECU. A hose from the intake manifold provides the input pressure.

TESTING

▶ **See Figure 63**

1. Inspect the MAP sensor vacuum hose connection at the throttle body and sensor and repair as necessary.
2. Test the MAP sensor output voltage at the MAP sensor connector terminal B (as marked on the sensor body) with the ignition switch and the engine **OFF**. The output voltage should be 4–5 volts.

➡ **The voltage should drop to 0.5–1.5 volts with a hot, neutral idle speed condition.**

3. Test ECU terminal C-6 for the same voltage as in Step 2 to verify the wire harness condition and repair as necessary.
4. Test the MAP sensor supply voltage at the sensor connector terminal C with

the ignition **ON**. The voltage should be 4.5–5.5 volts. The same voltage should be present at terminal C-14 of the ECU wire harness connector. Repair or replace the wire harness as necessary. If the ECU is suspect, use Diagnostic Tester M.S.1700, or equivalent, to test ECU function. Follow the manufactures instructions.

5. Test the MAP sensor ground circuit at the sensor connector terminal A and ECU connector terminal D-3. Repair the wire harness as necessary.
6. Test the MAP sensor ground circuit at the ECU connector between terminal D-3 and terminal B-11 with an ohmmeter. If the ohmmeter indicates an open circuit, check for a defective sensor ground connection located on the right side of the cylinder block. If the ground connection is good, replace the ECU.

➡ **If terminal D-3 has a short circuit to 12 volts, correct this condition before replacing the ECU.**

Knock Sensor

OPERATION

The knock sensor is located on the lower left side of the cylinder block, just above the oil pan. The knock sensor provides and input to the ECU that indicates detonation (knock) during engine operation. When detonation occurs, the ECU retards the ignition timing advance to eliminate the detonation at the applicable cylinder.

TESTING

➡ **This procedure requires the use of a special tool M.S.1700, or an equivalent knock sensor tester.**

1. Connect diagnostic tester M.S.1700, or equivalent, to the vehicle according to the manufacturer's instructions.
2. Proceed to state display mode.
3. Start the engine.
4. Observe and note the knock unit value.
5. Using the tip of a screwdriver or a small hammer, gently tap on the cylinder block near the knock sensor and watch the knock value. The knock value should increase while tapping on the block.
6. If the knock value does not increase while tapping on the block, check the sensor connector. If the connection is good, replace the knock sensor.

Crankshaft Position Sensor (CKP)

OPERATION

▶ **See Figure 71**

The Crankshaft Position Sensor (CKP) is secured by special shouldered bolts to the flywheel/drive plate housing. It is preset in its mounting at the factory and is non-adjustable in the field. The sensor senses TDC and engine speed by detecting the flywheel teeth as they pass during engine operation.

The flywheel has a large trigger tooth and notch located 12 small teeth before each Top Dead Center (TDC) position. When a small tooth and notch pass the

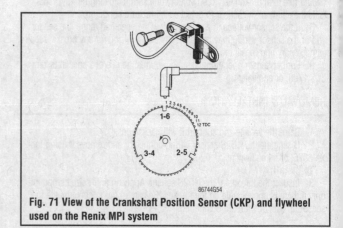

86744G54

Fig. 71 View of the Crankshaft Position Sensor (CKP) and flywheel used on the Renix MPI system

magnet core in the sensor, the concentration and then collapse of the magnetic flux induces a small voltage spike into the sensor pickup coil winding. These small voltage spikes enable the ECU to count the teeth as they pass the sensor.

When a large trigger tooth and notch pass the magnet core in the sensor, the increased concentration/collapse of the magnetic flux induces a higher voltage spike into the pickup coil winding. This higher voltage spike indicates to the ECU that a piston will soon be at the TDC position 12 teeth later. The ignition timing for the cylinder is either advanced or retarded as necessary by the ECU according to the sensor inputs.

TESTING

Unplug the sensor connector from the ignition control module and connect an ohmmeter between terminals **A** and **B** as marked on the connector. The ohm-meter should read 125–275 ohms on a hot engine. Replace the sensor if the readings are not as stated.

Latch Relay

OPERATION

▶ **See Figures 72 and 73**

The latch relay is located on the right inner fender panel. This relay is initially energized during engine startup and remains energized until 3–5 seconds after the engine is stopped. This enables the ECU to extend the idle speed stepper motor for the next startup, then cease operation.

TESTING

A relay in the de-energized position should have continuity between termi-nals 87A and 30. Resistance values between terminals 85 and 86 is 70–80 ohms for resistor relays and 81–91 ohms for diode relays. Not all relays have battery voltage connected to terminal 30. Some may have battery voltage con-nected to terminals 87 or 87A.

Camshaft Position Sensor (CMP)

OPERATION

The camshaft position sensor, or CMP sensor is located inside the distribu-tor. The ECU uses the CMP signal to determine the position of the No. 1 cylin-der piston during its power stroke. The ECU uses this information in conjunction with the crankshaft position sensor to determine spark timing among other things.

The CMP sensor contains a Hall effect device which sends either a 0.0 volt or a 5.0 volt signal to the ECU depending on the position of the distributor shaft.

If the cam signal is lost while the engine is running, the ECU will calculate spark timing based on the last CMP signal and the engine will continue to run. However, the engine will not run after it is shut off.

TESTING

1. Insert the positive (+) lead of a voltmeter into the blue wire at the distrib-utor connector and the negative (–) lead into the gray/white wire at the distribu-tor connector.

CHRYSLER MULTI-POINT FUEL INJECTION (MPI) SYSTEM

Powertrain Control Module (PCM)

OPERATION

▶ **See Figure 74**

All 1991 and later Jeep vehicles employ a sequential Multi-Point Fuel Injec-tion (MPI) System. The system, similar in construction to the Renix multi-point

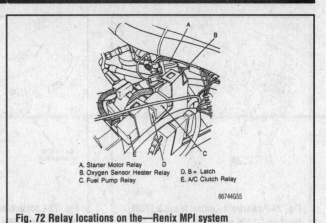

A. Starter Motor Relay
B. Oxygen Sensor Heater Relay
C. Fuel Pump Relay
D. B+ Latch
E. A/C Clutch Relay

86744G55

Fig. 72 Relay locations on the—Renix MPI system

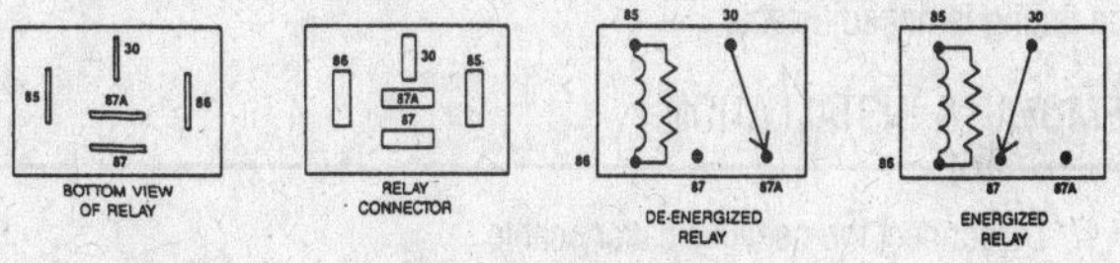

BOTTOM VIEW OF RELAY   RELAY CONNECTOR   DE-ENERGIZED RELAY   ENERGIZED RELAY

TERMINAL NUMBER

30 = usually connected to battery voltage — can be switched or B+ at all times.
87A = connected to 30 in the de-energized position.
87 = connected to 30 in the energized position which supplies battery voltage to the operated device.

86 = connected to the electromagnet and usually connected to a switched power source.
85 = also is connected to the electromagnet and is usually grounded by a switch or ECU.

86744G56

Fig. 73 Relay terminal identification—Renix MPI system

➡ **Do not unplug the distributor connector from the distributor. Insert the voltmeter leads into the back side of the connector to make contact with the terminals.**

2. Set the voltmeter on the 15 volt AC scale and turn the ignition switch **ON**. The voltmeter should read approximately 5 volts. If there is no voltage, check the voltmeter leads for a good connection.

3. If there is still no voltage, remove the ECU and check for voltage at pin C-16 and ground with the harness connected. If there is still no voltage present, perform a vehicle test using tester M.S.1700, or equivalent.

4. If voltage is present, check for continuity between the blue wire at the distributor connector and pin C-16 at the ECU. If there is no continuity, repair the wire harness as necessary.

5. Check for continuity between the gray/white wire at the distributor con-nector and pin C-5 at the ECU. If there is no continuity, repair the wire harness as necessary.

6. Check for continuity between the black wire at the distributor connector and ground. If there is no continuity, repair the wire harness as necessary.

7. Crank the engine while observing the voltmeter; the needle should fluctu-ate back and forth while the engine is cranking. This verifies that the stator in the distributor is operating properly. If there is no sync pulse, stator replacement is necessary.

fuel injection system, is controlled by a Powertrain Control Module, or PCM. The PCM is a pre-programmed, dual microprocessor digital computer. It regu-lates ignition timing, air-fuel ratio, emission control devices, charging system, speed control and idle speed.

Fuel is injected into the intake port directly above the intake valve in precise metered amounts through electrically operated injectors. The injectors are fired in a specific sequence by the PCM. The PCM maintains an air/fuel ratio of 14.7/1 by constantly adjusting injector pulse width. Injector pulse width is the length of time the injector is open.

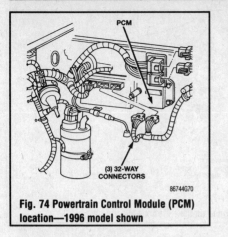

Fig. 74 Powertrain Control Module (PCM) location—1996 model shown

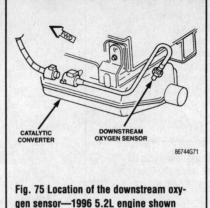

Fig. 75 Location of the downstream oxygen sensor—1996 5.2L engine shown

Fig. 76 Using a small flat bladed tool, separate the oxygen sensor wiring harness connector from the retaining bracket on the side of the lower part of the engine

The PCM adjusts ignition timing by controlling the ignition coil. Base ignition timing is not adjustable.

REMOVAL & INSTALLATION

1. Disconnect the negative battery cable.
2. Remove the coolant reserve tank and disengage the three electrical connectors from the PCM.
3. Remove the three PCM mounting bolts and carefully remove the PCM.
4. Installation is the reverse of removal.

Heated Oxygen (HO2S) Sensor

OPERATION

♦ **See Figure 75**

The heated oxygen sensor, or HO2S sensor is located at the exhaust system, usually near the catalytic converter. It produces a voltage signal of 0.1–1.0 volts based on the amount of oxygen in the exhaust gas. When a low amount of oxygen is present (caused by a rich air/fuel mixture), the sensor produces a low voltage. When a high amount of oxygen is present (caused by a lean air/fuel mixture), the sensor produces a high voltage. Because an accurate voltage signal is only produced if the sensor temperature is above approximately 600°F, a fast acting heating element is built into its body.

The PCM uses the HO2S sensor voltage signal to constantly adjust the amount of fuel injected which keeps the engine at its peek efficiency. 1996 and later vehicles are equipped with a second HO2S sensor which is used to monitor the efficiency of the catalytic converter.

TESTING

1. Start the engine and bring it to normal operating temperature, then run the engine above 1200 rpm for two minutes.

2. Backprobe with a high impedance averaging voltmeter (set to the DC voltage scale) between the HO2S sensor signal wire and battery ground.
3. Verify that the sensor voltage fluctuates rapidly between 0.40–0.60 volts.
4. If the sensor voltage is stabilized at the middle of the specified range (approximately 0.45–0.55 volts) or if the voltage fluctuates very slowly between the specified range (HO2S signal crosses 0.5 volts less than 5 times in ten seconds), the sensor may be faulty.
5. If the sensor voltage stabilizes at either end of the specified range, the PCM is probably not able to compensate for a mechanical problem such as a vacuum leak. These types of mechanical problems will cause the sensor to report a constant lean or constant rich mixture. The mechanical problem will first have to be repaired and then the HO2S sensor test repeated.
6. Pull a vacuum hose located after the throttle plate. Voltage should drop to approximately 0.12 volts (while still fluctuating rapidly). This tests the ability of the sensor to detect a lean mixture condition. Reattach the vacuum hose.
7. Richen the mixture using a propane enrichment tool. Sensor voltage should rise to approximately 0.90 volts (while still fluctuating rapidly). This tests the ability of the sensor to detect a rich mixture condition.
8. If the sensor voltage is above or below the specified range, the sensor and/or the sensor wiring may be faulty. Check the wiring for any breaks, repair as necessary and repeat the test.

REMOVAL & INSTALLATION

♦ **See Figures 76, 77, 78 and 79**

1. Raise the vehicle and support it with jackstands.
2. Disengage the HO2S sensor wiring connector and remove the sensor using an open end wrench, or an O2 sensor socket.

To install:

3. Inspect the threads of the HO2S sensor. Apply an anti-seize compound only if there is none visible on the threads. Be careful not to contaminate the sensor tip with any foreign compounds.
4. Install the sensor and engage the wiring connector.
5. Carefully lower the vehicle.

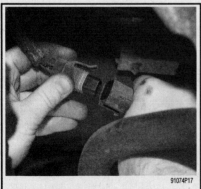

Fig. 77 Disengage the oxygen sensor wiring harness connector

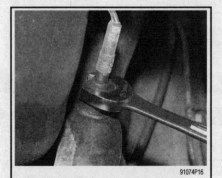

Fig. 78 Using a wrench, loosen the oxygen sensor from the exhaust pipe/manifold fitting . . .

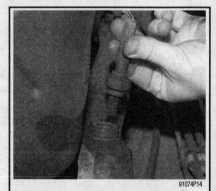

Fig. 79 . . . then remove the oxygen sensor from the engine

Idle Air Control (IAC) Valve

OPERATION

The Idle Air Control valve, or IAC valve is mounted on the back of the throttle body. The valve controls the idle speed of the engine by controlling the amount of air flowing through the air control passage. There is a factory pre-set throttle screw located by the valve which is not connected with the valve and should never be tampered with.

The IAC valve consists of electronic motors that move a pintle shaped plunger in and out of the air control passage. The valve receives an electronic signal from the PCM.

When the valve plunger is moved in, the air control passage flows more air. This raises the idle speed. When the valve plunger is moved out, the air control passage flows less air. This lowers the idle speed.

TESTING

1. Verify that there are no vacuum leaks or other mechanical problems that can affect the idle speed.
2. Start the engine, let it warm to a normal operating temperature and observe the idle speed.
3. Turn on various consumers such as the A/C system, high beams and/or the rear window defroster and observe the idle speed.
4. With the brake pedal firmly depressed, place the vehicle in gear (automatic transmission) or place the vehicle in fourth gear and slightly disengage the clutch (manual transmission). Observe the idle speed. Return the transmission to park or neutral.
5. If the idle speed does not immediately return to specification, the IAC valve may be faulty.

REMOVAL & INSTALLATION

▶ **See Figure 80**

1. Remove the air intake duct at the throttle body.
2. Disengage the IAC valve wiring connector, remove the two mounting screws and carefully pull the valve from the throttle body.
3. Installation is the reverse of removal.

Engine Coolant Temperature (ECT) Sensor

OPERATION

▶ **See Figures 81 and 82**

The engine coolant temperature sensor, or ECT sensor is mounted by the thermostat and provides the PCM with engine temperature information. The PCM supplies 5 volts to the ECT sensor circuit. The sensor is a thermistor which changes internal resistance as temperature changes. When the sensor is cold (internal resistance high), the PCM monitors a high signal voltage which it interprets as a cold engine. As the sensor warms (internal resistance low), the PCM monitors a low signal voltage which it interprets as warm engine.

TESTING

▶ **See Figures 83 and 84**

1. With the engine cold, remove the ECT sensor.
2. Immerse the tip of the sensor in container of water.
3. Connect a digital ohmmeter to the two terminals of the sensor.
4. Using a calibrated thermometer, compare the resistance of the sensor to the temperature of the water. Refer to the sensor resistance illustration.

Fig. 80 Removing the IAC valve from the throttle body

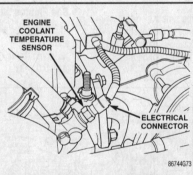

Fig. 81 View of the Engine Coolant Temperature (ECT) Sensor—1996 4.0L engine shown

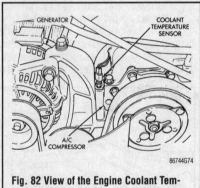

Fig. 82 View of the Engine Coolant Temperature (ECT) Sensor—1996 5.2L engine shown

Fig. 83 Submerge the end of the temperature sensor in cold or hot water and check resistance

TEMPERATURE		RESISTANCE (OHMS)	
C	F	MIN	MAX
−40	−40	291,490	381,710
−20	−4	85,850	108,390
−10	14	49,250	61,430
0	32	29,330	35,990
10	50	17,990	21,810
20	68	11,370	13,610
25	77	9,120	10,880
30	86	7,370	8,750
40	104	4,900	5,750
50	122	3,330	3,880
60	140	2,310	2,670
70	158	1,630	1,870
80	176	1,170	1,340
90	194	860	970
100	212	640	720
110	230	480	540
120	248	370	410

Fig. 84 Temperature-to-resistance relationship of the ECT and MAT sensors

5. Repeat the test at two other temperature points, heating or cooling the water as necessary.

6. If the sensor does not meet specification, it must be replaced.

REMOVAL & INSTALLATION

1. With the engine cold, partially drain the cooling system. Record the amount of coolant drained.

2. Carefully disengage the ECT sensor wiring connector.

3. Unscrew the sensor.

To install:

4. Coat the threads of the ECT sensor with sealant and install it into the block. Tighten the sensor to 8 ft. lbs. (11 Nm).

5. Engage the sensor wiring connector.

6. Fill the system with the same amount of coolant as was drained and check for leaks.

Intake Manifold Air Temperature (MAT) Sensor

OPERATION

▶ **See Figures 85 and 86**

The intake manifold air temperature sensor, or MAT sensor is mounted on the intake manifold and provides the PCM with intake air temperature information. The sensor is a temperature dependent resistor. As the temperature of the air rises, the sensor resistance drops and as the temperature of the air drops, the sensor resistance rises.

TESTING

▶ **See Figure 87**

1. Remove the MAT sensor from the intake manifold.

2. Connect a digital ohmmeter to the two terminals of the sensor.

3. Using a calibrated thermometer, compare the resistance of the sensor to the temperature of the ambient air. Refer to the Sensor Resistance Chart.

4. Repeat the test at two other temperature points, heating or cooling the air as necessary with a hair dryer or other suitable tool.

5. If the sensor does not meet specification, it must be replaced.

REMOVAL & INSTALLATION

1. Disengage the MAT sensor wiring harness and unscrew the sensor.

To install:

2. Screw in the sensor and tighten it to 20 ft. lbs. (28 Nm).

3. Engage the sensor wiring connector.

Manifold Air Pressure (MAP) Sensor

OPERATION

▶ **See Figures 88 and 89**

The Manifold Absolute Pressure sensor, or MAP sensor is mounted on the throttle body. It measures the changes in intake manifold pressure, which result from the engine load and speed changes, and converts this to a voltage output.

A closed throttle on engine coastdown will produce a low sensor output, while a wide-open throttle will produce a high output. This high output is produced because the pressure inside the manifold is the same as outside the manifold, so 100 percent of the outside air pressure is measured.

The MAP sensor reading is the opposite of what you would measure on a vacuum gauge. When manifold pressure is high, vacuum is low.

The PCM sends a 5 volt reference signal to the MAP sensor. As the manifold pressure changes, the electrical resistance of the sensor also changes. By monitoring the sensor output voltage, the PCM knows the the manifold pressure. A higher pressure, low vacuum (high voltage) requires more fuel, while a lower pressure, higher vacuum (low voltage) requires less fuel.

The PCM uses the MAP sensor to control fuel delivery and ignition timing.

TESTING

▶ **See Figures 90 and 91**

1. Backprobe with a high impedance voltmeter at MAP sensor terminal Nos. 1 and 3.

2. With the key **ON** and engine off, the voltmeter reading should be approximately 5.0 volts.

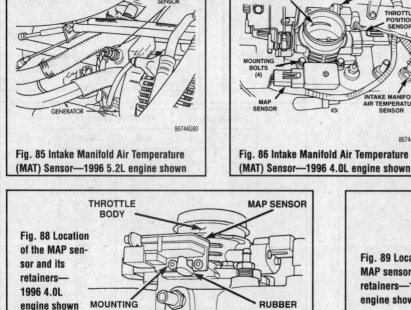

Fig. 85 Intake Manifold Air Temperature (MAT) Sensor—1996 5.2L engine shown

Fig. 86 Intake Manifold Air Temperature (MAT) Sensor—1996 4.0L engine shown

Fig. 87 Performing a resistance test on the MAT sensor

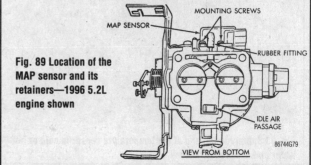

Fig. 88 Location of the MAP sensor and its retainers—1996 4.0L engine shown

Fig. 89 Location of the MAP sensor and its retainers—1996 5.2L engine shown

3. If the voltage is not as specified, either the wiring to the MAP sensor or the PCM may be faulty. Correct any wiring or PCM faults before continuing test.

4. Backprobe with the high impotence voltmeter at MAP sensor terminal Nos. 1 and 2.

5. Start the vehicle and verify that the sensor voltage is 0.5–1.8 volts with the engine at a normal idling speed.

6. Verify that the sensor voltage reaches 3.9–4.8. volts at Wide Open Throttle (WOT).

7. If the sensor voltage is not as specified, check the sensor and the sensor vacuum source for a leak or a restriction. If no leaks or restrictions are found, the sensor may be faulty.

REMOVAL & INSTALLATION

1. If the MAP sensor is mounted on the front of the throttle body, the throttle body must first be removed from the engine.

2. If the sensor is mounted on the side of the throttle body, the intake air tube must first be removed.

3. Remove the two sensor mounting screws and carefully pull the sensor away from the throttle body. Be careful not to lose the rubber L-shaped fitting that attaches the sensor to the throttle body.

To install:

4. Install rubber L-shaped fitting to the sensor.

5. Place the sensor into position being careful to guide the fitting onto the throttle body nipple.

6. Install the sensor mounting screws. Tighten the screws to 25 inch. lbs. (3 Nm).

7. Install the intake air tube or the throttle body as necessary.

Throttle Position (TPS) Sensor

OPERATION

▶ **See Figure 92**

The Throttle Position Sensor, or TPS is connected to the throttle shaft on the throttle body. It sends throttle valve angle information to the PCM. The PCM uses this information to determine fuel delivery volume.

The TPS is a potentiometer with one end connected to 5 volts from the PCM and the other to ground. A third wire is connected to the PCM to measure the voltage from the TPS.

As the throttle valve angle is changed (accelerator pedal moved), the output of the TPS also changes. At a closed throttle position, the output of the TPS is low (approximately .5 volts). As the throttle valve opens, the output increases so that, at wide-open throttle, the output voltage should be above 3.9 volts.

By monitoring the output voltage from the TPS, the PCM can determine fuel delivery based on throttle valve angle (driver demand).

TESTING

▶ **See Figures 93, 94 and 95**

1. With the key **ON** and engine **OFF**, backprobe with a high impedance voltmeter at the two end terminals of the TPS connector and battery ground. Verify that one terminal reads approximately 5.0 volts.

2. Backprobe with a high impedance ohmmeter between the end terminal that did not have the 5.0 volt signal and battery ground. Verify that the resistance is less than 5 ohms.

3. If the voltages are not as specified, either the wiring to the TPS or the PCM may be faulty. Correct any wiring or PCM faults before continuing test.

4. With the key **ON** and engine off and the throttle closed, the TPS voltage should be approximately 0.5–1.2 volts.

5. Verify that the TPS voltage increases or decreases smoothly as the throttle is opened or closed. Make sure to open and close the throttle very slowly in order to detect any abnormalities in the TPS voltage reading.

6. If the sensor voltage is not as specified, replace the sensor.

REMOVAL & INSTALLATION

▶ **See Figures 96 and 97**

1. Remove the air intake tube at the throttle body.

Fig. 90 Wiring harness connector terminal identifications for the MAP sensor harness side. Terminal 1 (left), terminal 3 (right)

Fig. 91 Performing a voltage test with a digital voltmeter on the harness side of the MAP sensor

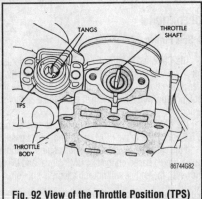

Fig. 92 View of the Throttle Position (TPS) Sensor—1996 4.0L engine

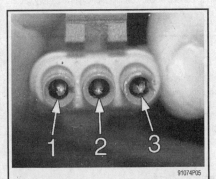

Fig. 93 Disengage the Throttle Position Sensor (TPS) wiring harness connector

Fig. 94 Connect a voltmeter to the middle terminal of the TPS (A) and battery ground (B). With the throttle closed, note the reading

Fig. 95 Check the voltage variation on the TPS while opening up the throttle to Wide Open Throttle (WOT)

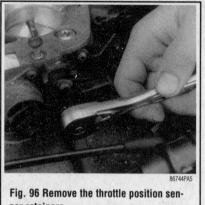

Fig. 96 Remove the throttle position sensor retainers . . .

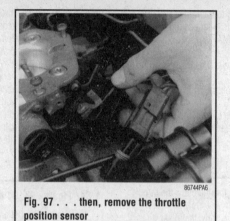

Fig. 97 . . . then, remove the throttle position sensor

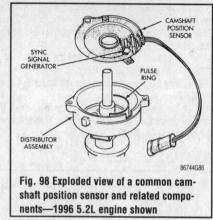

Fig. 98 Exploded view of a common camshaft position sensor and related components—1996 5.2L engine shown

2. Disengage the TPS wiring connector and remove the two mounting screws.

3. Carefully remove the TPS from the throttle body.

To install:

4. The throttle shaft end has a tang that can be fitted into the TPS two different ways. Only one of the installed positions is correct. When correctly positioned, the TPS can be rotated a few degrees. To determine correct positioning, place the TPS onto the throttle body with the throttle shaft tang on one side of the TPS socket. Verify that the TPS can be rotated. If the TPS cannot be rotated, place the TPS on the throttle body with the throttle shaft tang on the other side.

5. Tighten the two TPS mounting bolts to 60 inch lbs. (7 Nm) and engage the wiring connector.

6. Manually operate the throttle and check for any binding.

7. Install the air intake tube.

Camshaft Position (CMP) Sensor

Al Except 2000 and Later Inline Six-Cylinder Engines

OPERATION

▶ See Figure 98

The Camshaft Position Sensor, or CMP sensor is located inside the distributor. The PCM uses the CMP signal to determine the position of the No. 1 cylinder piston during its power stroke. The PCM uses this information in conjunction with the crankshaft position sensor to determine spark timing among other things.

The CMP sensor contains a Hall effect device which sends either a 0.0 volt or a 5.0 volt signal to the PCM depending on the position of the distributor shaft.

If the cam signal is lost while the engine is running, the PCM will calculate spark timing based on the last CMP signal and the engine will continue to run. However, the engine will not run after it is shut off.

TESTING

1. Make sure that the ignition is **OFF**, remove the distributor cap and turn the engine over by hand.

2. Verify that the distributor shaft turns. If the distributor shaft does not turn, the engine must be checked for proper mechanical operation.

3. Backprobe with a high impedance ohmmeter between the CMP sensor connector middle terminal and battery ground.

4. Verify that the resistance is less than 5 ohms. If the resistance is not as specified, repair or replace the wiring as necessary and continue the test.

5. With the ignition **ON** and the engine **OFF**, backprobe with a high impedance voltmeter between the sensor connector middle terminal and either of the end terminals.

6. Verify that a 5 volt or greater signal is present at one of the two terminals. If not as specified, repair or replace the wiring as necessary and continue the test.

7. With the ignition **ON** and the engine **OFF**, backprobe with a high impedance voltmeter between the sensor connector middle terminal and the end terminal that did not have the 5 volt or greater signal.

8. Crank the engine by hand and verify that the voltage reading alternates between 0.0 or 5.0 volts.

9. Install the distributor cap and crank the engine with starter. Verify that the voltage reading is 2.5 volts (averaging voltmeters only).

10. If the voltage readings are not as specified, the sensor may be faulty.

REMOVAL & INSTALLATION

1. Disconnect the negative battery cable and remove the intake air tube if necessary.

2. Remove the distributor cap and the rotor.

3. Disengage the CMP sensor wiring connector and carefully lift the sensor out of the distributor.

To install:

4. Carefully place the sensor into the distributor. Make sure that any alignment notches or tabs line up properly.

5. Install the distributor rotor and cap.

6. Engage the sensor wiring connector and connect the negative battery cable.

2000 and Later Inline Six-Cylinder Models

Operation

The camshaft position sensor provides information on camshaft position. The PCM uses this information, along with the crankshaft position sensor information, to control fuel injection synchronization. The camshaft position sensor on 2000 and later models is a separate unit installed where the distributor was located on earlier models.

Removal and Installation

▶ See Figures 99a and 99b

➡Note: The camshaft position sensor is located on top of the oil pump drive assembly. It is possible to replace the camshaft position sensor without removing the oil pump drive assembly, by removing the two screws securing the sensor to the drive assembly. If the oil pump drive assembly must be removed, the mounting flange must be precisely marked in relation to the engine block or it will be necessary to reset the camshaft position sensor with a scan tool.

1 Disconnect the electrical connector from the camshaft position sensor.

2 If removing the sensor only, remove the two mounting bolts and remove the sensor from the oil pump drive. Install the new sensor, tighten the bolts securely and connect the electrical connector.

3 If removing the oil pump drive assembly, position the number one cylinder at TDC on the compression stroke.

4 Remove the sensor. Insert an appropriate size alignment pin (such as a drill bit) through the holes in the sensor base and pulse ring. If the holes do not align, rotate the crankshaft until they do.

5 Mark the position of the oil pump drive mounting flange base to the engine block to ensure the oil pump drive can be re-installed in exactly the same position as originally installed.

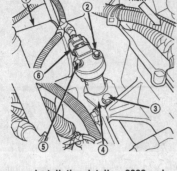

1 Oil filter
2 Camshaft position sensor
3 Clamp bolt
4 Oil pump drive clamp
5 Camshaft position sensor mounting bolts
6 Electrical connector

Fig. 99a Camshaft position sensor installation details – 2000 and later inline six-cylinder models

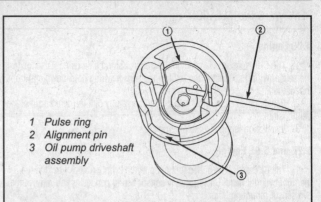

1 Pulse ring
2 Alignment pin
3 Oil pump driveshaft assembly

fig. 99b Before removing the camshaft position sensor on a 2000 and later inline six-cylinder model, position the engine with the number one cylinder at TDC and install an appropriate size alignment pin through the hole in the base of the pulse ring

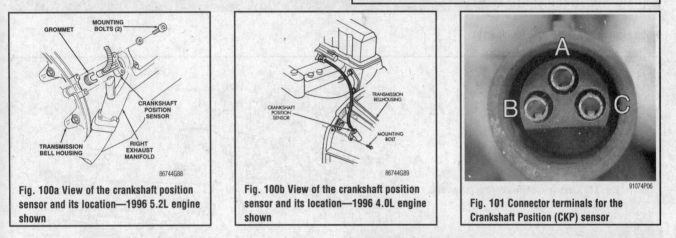

Fig. 100a View of the crankshaft position sensor and its location—1996 5.2L engine shown

Fig. 100b View of the crankshaft position sensor and its location—1996 4.0L engine shown

Fig. 101 Connector terminals for the Crankshaft Position (CKP) sensor

6 Remove the oil pump drive hold-down bolt and withdraw the oil pump drive assembly. Remove and discard the O-ring.

To install:

7 If the crankshaft has been moved while the oil pump drive is out, the number one piston must be repositioned at TDC. This can be done by feeling for compression pressure at the number one spark plug hole as the crankshaft is rotated. Once compression is felt, continue rotating the crankshaft until the mark on the crankshaft damper is aligned with the zero or TDC mark on the timing indicator.

8 Turn the pulse ring until the hole in the pulse ring aligns with the hole in the housing and install the alignment pin the holes. Install a new O-ring on the oil pump drive assembly.

9 Insert the oil pump drive into the engine block and align the marks made in Step 5.

10 Because of the helical-cut drive gear, the assembly will rotate clockwise as the gears engage. Be sure to compensate by starting the installation with the drive gear assembly positioned counterclockwise from the desired finished position. Installing the oil pump drive assembly is very similar to installing a distributor. The oil pump drive must be installed in the same position as originally installed before removal. When properly installed, a line drawn through the center of the camshaft position sensor and electrical connector should be parallel with the centerline of the engine.

Note: If the alignment marks are lost or poor driveability symptoms appear after installing the oil pump drive, take the vehicle to a dealer service department or other properly equipped repair facility and have the fuel system synchronization reset with a scan tool.

11 Install the oil pump drive hold-down clamp and tighten the bolt to 17 ft-lbs.

12 The remainder of installation is the reverse of removal.

Crankshaft Position (CKP) Sensor

OPERATION

▶ See Figures 100a and 100b

The Crankshaft Position Sensor, or CKP sensor provides the PCM with information about engine speed and crankshaft position. It is located near the bell-housing.

The CKP sensor contains a Hall effect device which sends either a 0.0 volt or a 5.0 volt signal to the PCM depending on the position of the distributor shaft.

The PCM uses the CKP sensor signal to determine fuel injection event time among other things. The engine will not run without the CKP sensor signal.

TESTING

▶ See Figures 101 and 102

1. Backprobe with a high impedance ohmmeter between the CKP sensor connector middle terminal and battery ground.

2. Verify that the resistance is less than 5 ohms. If the resistance is not as specified, repair or replace the wiring as necessary and continue the test.

3. With the ignition **ON** and the engine **OFF**, backprobe with a high impedance voltmeter between the sensor connector middle terminal and either of the end terminals.

4. Verify that a 5 volt or greater signal is present at one of the two terminals. If not as specified, repair or replace the wiring as necessary and continue the test.

5. With the ignition **ON** and the engine **OFF**, backprobe with a high impedance voltmeter between the sensor connector middle terminal and the end terminal that did not have the 5 volt or greater signal.

6. Crank the engine and verify that the voltage reading alternates between 0.0 and 5.0 volts or verify that the voltage reading is 2.5 volts (averaging voltmeters only).

7. If the voltage readings are not as specified, the sensor may be faulty.

REMOVAL & INSTALLATION

4.0L Engine

1. The CKP sensor is located on the transmission bellhousing. Disengage the sensor wiring connector and remove the sensor wiring hold-down clip from the fuel rail.
2. Remove the sensor mounting bolt and carefully pull the sensor out of the bellhousing.
3. Installation is the reverse of removal.

5.2L and 5.9L Engine

1. The CKP sensor is bolted to the top of the cylinder block near the rear of the right cylinder head. Disengage the sensor wiring connector and remove the two sensor mounting bolts.
2. Carefully pull the sensor out of the cylinder block.
3. Installation is the reverse of removal.

Fig. 102 Checking the CKP sensor voltage between the wiring harness side and battery ground

COMPONENT LOCATIONS

▶ See Figures 103, 104, 105, 106 and 107

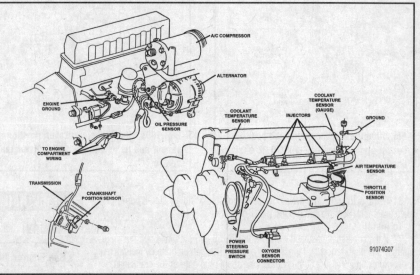

Fig. 103 Electronic engine control component locations—2.5L engine shown

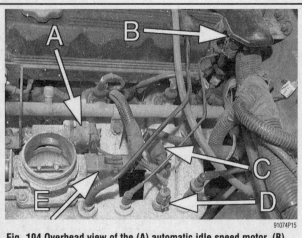

Fig. 104 Overhead view of the (A) automatic idle speed motor, (B) MAP sensor, (C) crankshaft position sensor wiring harness, (D) air temperature sensor, and (E) throttle position sensor—1992 Cherokee with the 4.0L engine shown

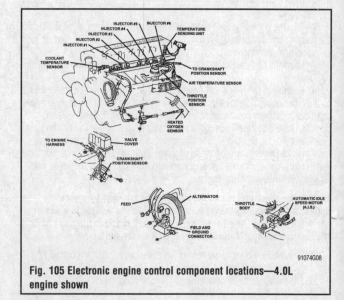

Fig. 105 Electronic engine control component locations—4.0L engine shown

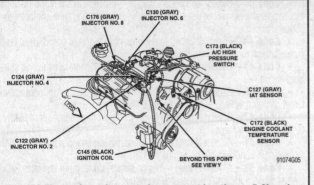

Fig. 106 Electronic engine control component locations—5.2L and 5.9L engines (Part 1 of 2)

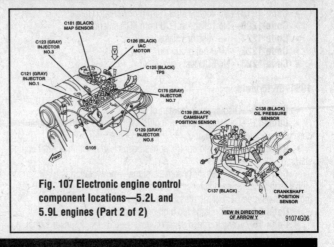

Fig. 107 Electronic engine control component locations—5.2L and 5.9L engines (Part 2 of 2)

TROUBLE CODES

Trouble Code Lists

CARBURETED ENGINES

- **CODE 12:** No distributor reference pulses to the ECM. This code is not stored in memory and will only flash while the trouble exists. This code is normal when the ignition is switched ON with the engine not running.
- **CODE 13:** Oxygen sensor circuit. The engine must operate for up to 5 minutes at part throttle, under road load, before this code will be set.
- **CODE 14:** Shorted coolant sensor circuit. The engine must operate for up to 5 minutes before this code will be set.
- **CODE 15:** Open coolant sensor circuit. The engine must operate for up to 5 minutes before this code will be set.
- **CODE 21:** Throttle position sensor circuit. The engine must operate for at least 25 seconds at curb idle speed before this code will be set.
- **CODE 23:** Mixture control solenoid circuit is shorted or open.

FUEL INJECTED ENGINES

Except 1991 and Later Models

- **Code 1000**—Ignition line low.
- **Code 1001**—Ignition line high.
- **Code 1002**—Oxygen heater line.
- **Code 1004**—Battery voltage low.
- **Code 1005**—Sensor ground line out of limits.
- **Code 1010**—Diagnostic enable line low.
- **Code 1011**—Diagnostic enable line high.
- **Code 1012**—MAP line low.
- **Code 1013**—MAP line high.
- **Code 1014**—Fuel pump line low.
- **Code 1015**—Fuel pump line high.
- **Code 1016**—Charge air temperature sensor low.
- **Code 1017**—Charge air temperature sensor high.
- **Code 1018**—No serial data from the ECU.
- **Code 1021**—Engine failed to start due to mechanical, fuel, or ignition problem.
- **Code 1022**—Start line low.
- **Code 1024**—ECU does not see start signal.
- **Code 1025**—Wide open throttle circuit low.
- **Code 1027**—ECU sees wide open throttle.
- **Code 1028**—ECU does not see wide open throttle.
- **Code 1031**—ECU sees closed throttle.
- **Code 1032**—ECU does not see closed throttle.
- **Code 1033**—Idle speed increase line low.
- **Code 1034**—Idle speed increase line high.
- **Code 1035**—Idle speed decrease line low.
- **Code 1036**—Idle speed decrease line high.
- **Code 1037**—Throttle position sensor reads low.

- **CODE 34:** Vacuum sensor circuit. The engine must operate for up to 5 minutes at curb idle speed before this code will be set.
- **CODE 41:** No distributor reference pulses to the ECM at the specified engine manifold vacuum. This code will be stored in memory.
- **CODE 42:** Electronic Spark Timing (EST) bypass circuit or EST circuit has short circuit to ground or an open circuit.
- **CODE 44:** Lean exhaust indication. The engine must operate for up to 5 minutes, be in closed loop operation and at part throttle before this code will be set.
- **CODE 44 & 45:** If these two codes appear at the same time, it indicates a problem in the oxygen sensor circuit.
- **CODE 45:** Rich exhaust indication. The engine must operate for up to 5 minutes, be in closed loop and at part throttle before this code will be set.
- **CODE 51:** Faulty calibration unit (PROM) or installation. It requires up to 30 seconds for this code to be set.
- **CODE 54:** Mixture Control (MC) solenoid circuit is shorted or the ECM is faulty.
- **CODE 55:** Voltage reference has short circuit to ground (terminal 21), faulty oxygen sensor or faulty ECM.

- **Code 1038**—Park/Neutral line high.
- **Code 1040**—Latched B+ line low.
- **Code 1041**—Latched B+ line high.
- **Code 1042**—No Latched B+ 1/2 volt drop.
- **Code 1047**—Wrong ECU.
- **Code 1048**—Manual vehicle equipped with automatic ECU.
- **Code 1049**—Automatic vehicle equipped with manual ECU.
- **Code 1050**—Idle RPM's less than 500.
- **Code 1051**—Idle RPM's greater than 2000.
- **Code 1052**—MAP sensor out of limits.
- **Code 1053**—Change in MAP reading out of limits.
- **Code 1054**—Coolant temperature sensor line low.
- **Code 1055**—Coolant temperature sensor line high.
- **Code 1056**—Inactive coolant temperature sensor.
- **Code 1057**—Knock circuit shorted.
- **Code 1058**—Knock value out of limits.
- **Code 1059**—A/C request line low.
- **Code 1060**—A/C request line high.
- **Code 1061**—A/C select line low.
- **Code 1062**—A/C select line high.
- **Code 1063**—A/C clutch line low.
- **Code 1064**—A/C clutch line high.
- **Code 1065**—Oxygen reads rich.
- **Code 1066**—Oxygen reads lean.
- **Code 1067**—Latch relay line low.
- **Code 1068**—Latch relay line high.
- **Code 1070**—A/C cutout line low.
- **Code 1071**—A/C cutout line high.
- **Code 1073**—ECU does not see speed sensor signal.
- **Code 1200**—ECU defective.
- **Code 1202**—Injector shorted to ground.
- **Code 1209**—Injector open.

- **Code 1218**—No voltage at ECU from power latch relay.
- **Code 1220**—No voltage at ECU from EGR solenoid.
- **Code 1221**—No injector voltage.
- **Code 1222**—MAP not grounded.
- **Code 1223**—No ECU tests run.

1991–95 Models

- **Code 88**—Display used for start of test.
- **Code 11**—Camshaft signal or Ignition signal—no reference signal detected during engine cranking.
- **Code 12**—Memory to controller has been cleared within 50–l00 engine starts.
- **Code 13**—MAP sensor pneumatic signal—no variation in MAP sensor signal is detected or no difference is recognized between the engine MAP reading and the stored barometric pressure reading..
- **Code 14**—MAP voltage too high or too low.
- **Code 15**—Vehicle speed sensor signal—no distance sensor signal detected during road load conditions.
- **Code 16**—Knock sensor circuit—Open or short has been detected in the knock sensor circuit.
- **Code 16**—Battery input sensor—battery voltage sensor input below 4 volts with engine running.
- **Code 17**—Low engine temperature—engine coolant temperature remains below normal operating temperature during vehicle travel; possible thermostat problem.
- **Code 21**—Oxygen sensor signal—neither rich or lean condition is detected from the oxygen sensor input.
- **Code 22**—Coolant voltage low—coolant temperature sensor input below the minimum acceptable voltage/Coolant voltage high—coolant temperature sensor input above the maximum acceptable voltage.
- **Code 23**—Air Charge or Throttle Body temperature voltage HIGH/LOW—charge air temperature sensor input is above or below the acceptable voltage limits.
- **Code 24**—Throttle Position sensor voltage high or low.
- **Code 25**—Automatic Idle Speed (AIS) motor driver circuit—short or open detected in 1 or more of the AIS control circuits.
- **Code 26**—Injectors No. 1, 2, or 3 peak current not reached, high resistance in circuit.
- **Code 27**—Injector control circuit—bank output driver stage does not respond properly to the control signal.
- **Code 27**—Injectors No. 1, 2, or 3 control circuit and peak current not reached.
- **Code 31**—Purge solenoid circuit—open or short detected in the purge solenoid circuit.
- **Code 32**—Exhaust Gas Recirculation (EGR) solenoid circuit—open or short detected in the EGR solenoid circuit/EGR system failure—required change in fuel/air ratio not detected during diagnostic test.
- **Code 33**—Air conditioner clutch relay circuit—open or short detected in the air conditioner clutch relay circuit. If vehicle doesn't have air conditioning ignore this code.
- **Code 34**—Speed control servo solenoids or MUX speed control circuit HIGH/LOW—open or short detected in the vacuum or vent solenoid circuits or speed control switch input above or below allowable voltage.
- **Code 35**—Radiator fan control relay circuit—open or short detected in the radiator fan relay circuit.
- **Code 35**—Idle switch shorted—switch input shorted to ground—some 1993 vehicles.
- **Code 37**—Part Throttle Unlock (PTU) circuit for torque converter clutch—open or short detected in the torque converter part throttle unlock solenoid circuit.
- **Code 37**—Baro Reed Solenoid—solenoid does not turn off when it should.
- **Code 37**—Shift indicator circuit (manual transaxle).
- **Code 41**—Charging system circuit—output driver stage for generator field does not respond properly to the voltage regulator control signal.
- **Code 42**—Fuel pump or no Autoshut-down (ASD) relay voltage sense at controller.
- **Code 43**—Ignition control circuit—peak primary circuit current not respond properly with maximum dwell time.
- **Code 43**—Ignition coil #1, 2, or 3 primary circuits—peak primary was not achieved within the maximum allowable dwell time.

- **Code 44**—Battery temperature voltage—problem exists in the PCM battery temperature circuit or there is an open or short in the engine coolant temperature circuit.
- **Code 44**—Fused J2 circuit in not present in the logic board; used on the single engine module controller system.
- **Code 44**—Overdrive solenoid circuit—open or short in overdrive solenoid circuit.
- **Code 46**—Battery voltage too high—battery voltage sense input above target charging voltage during engine operation.
- **Code 47**—Battery voltage too low—battery voltage sense input below target charging voltage.
- **Code 51**—Air/fuel at limit—oxygen sensor signal input indicates LEAN air/fuel ratio condition during engine operation.
- **Code 52**—Air/fuel at limit—oxygen sensor signal input indicates RICH air/fuel ratio condition during engine operation.
- **Code 53**—Internal controller failure—internal engine controller fault condition detected during self test.
- **Code 54**—Camshaft or (distributor sync.) reference circuit—No camshaft position sensor signal detected during engine rotation.
- **Code 55**—End of message.
- **Code 61**—Baro read solenoid—open or short detected in the baro read solenoid circuit.
- **Code 62**—EMR mileage not stored—unsuccessful attempt to update EMR mileage in the controller EEPROM.
- **Code 63**—EEPROM write denied—unsuccessful attempt to write to an EEPROM location by the controller.
- **Code 64**—Flex fuel sensor— Flex fuel sensor signal out of range—(new in 1993)—CNG Temperature voltage out of range—CN gas pressure out of range.
- **Code 66**—No CCD messages or no BODY CCD messages or no EATX CCD messages—messages from the CCD bus or the BODY CCD or the EATX CCD were not received by the PCM.
- **Code 76**—Ballast bypass relay—open or short in fuel pump relay circuit.
- **Code 77**—Speed control relay—an open or short has been detected in the speed control relay.
- **Code 88**—Display used for start of test.
- **Code Error**—Fault code error—Unrecognized fault ID received by DRBII.

1996 and Later Models

- **P0107** Manifold Absolute Pressure/Barometric Pressure Circuit Low Input
- **P0108** Manifold Absolute Pressure/Barometric Pressure Circuit High Input
- **P0112** Intake Air Temperature Circuit Low Input
- **P0113** Intake Air Temperature Circuit High Input
- **P0117** Engine Coolant Temperature Circuit Low Input
- **P0118** Engine Coolant Temperature Circuit High Input
- **P0121** Throttle/Pedal Position Sensor/Switch ìAî Circuit Range/Performance Problem
- **P0122** Throttle/Pedal Position Sensor/Switch ìAî Circuit Low Input
- **P0123** Throttle/Pedal Position Sensor/Switch ìAî Circuit High Input
- **P0125** Insufficient Coolant Temperature for Closed Loop Fuel Control
- **P0129** Catalyst Monitor Slow O2 Sensor (Bank no. 1 Sensor no. 2)
- **P0131** Left Bank and Upstream O2 Sensor Voltage Shorted to Ground
- **P0132** Left Upstream O2 Sensor Shorted to Voltage
- **P0133** Upstream O2 Sensor Circuit Slow Response (Bank no. 1 Sensor no. 1)
- **P0135** O2 Sensor Heater Circuit Malfunction (Bank no. 1 Sensor no. 1)
- **P0137** Left Bank Downstream or Downstream and Pre-Catalyst O2 Sensor Voltage Shorted to Ground
- **P0138** Left Bank Downstream or Downstream and Pre-Catalyst O2 Sensor Shorted to Voltage
- **P0141** Downstream, Left Bank Downstream or Pre-Catalyst O2 Sensor Heater Failure
- **P0152** Left Upstream O2 Sensor Slow Response
- **P0162** Charging System Voltage Too Low
- **P0171** Right Rear (or just) Fuel System Too Lean
- **P0172** Left Bank or Fuel System Too Rich
- **P0201** Injector no. 1 Control Circuit
- **P0202** Injector no. 2 Control Circuit

- **P0203** Injector no. 3 Control Circuit
- **P0204** Injector no. 4 Control Circuit
- **P0205** Injector no. 5 Control Circuit
- **P0206** Injector no. 6 Control Circuit
- **P0207** Injector no. 7 Control Circuit
- **P0208** Injector no. 8 Control Circuit
- **P0300** Random/Multiple Cylinder Misfire Detected
- **P0301** Cylinder no. 1—Misfire Detected
- **P0302** Cylinder no. 2—Misfire Detected
- **P0303** Cylinder no. 3—Misfire Detected
- **P0304** Cylinder no. 4—Misfire Detected
- **P0305** Cylinder no. 5—Misfire Detected
- **P0306** Cylinder no. 6—Misfire Detected
- **P0307** Cylinder no. 7—Misfire Detected
- **P0308** Cylinder no. 8—Misfire Detected
- **P0320** No Crank Reference Signal at PCM
- **P0340** No Cam Signal at PCM
- **P0351** Ignition Coil no. 1 Primary Circuit
- **P0420** Left Bank Catalytic Converter or just Catalytic Converter Efficiency Failure
- **P0441** Evaporative Purge Flow Monitor Failure
- **P0442** Evaporative Emission Control System Leak Detected (Small Leak)
- **P0443** Evap Purge Solenoid Circuit
- **P0455** Evaporative Emission Control System Leak Detected (Gross Leak)
- **P0460** Fuel Level Unit No Change Over Miles
- **P0462** Fuel Level Sending Unit Voltage Too Low
- **P0463** Fuel Level Sending Unit Voltage Too High
- **P0500** No Vehicle Speed Sensor Signal
- **P0505** Idle Air Control Motor Circuits
- **P0600** PCM/Serial Communication Link Malfunction
- **P0601** Internal Controller Failure
- **P0622** Generator Field Not Switching Properly
- **P0645** A/C Clutch Relay Circuit
- **P0711** Transmission Fluid Temperature Sensor, No Temperature Rise After Start
- **P0712** Transmission Fluid Temperature Sensor Voltage Too Low
- **P0713** Transmission Fluid Temperature Sensor Voltage Too High

- **P0720** Low Output Speed Sensor RPM Above 15 MPH
- **P0740** Torque Converter Clutch, No RPM Drop At Lockup
- **P0743** Torque Converter Clutch Solenoid/Trans Relay Circuits
- **P0748** Governor Pressure Solenoid Control/Trans Relay Circuits
- **P0751** Overdrive Switch Pressed (LO) More Than 5 Minutes
- **P0753** Trans 3–4 Shift Solenoid/Trans Relay Circuits
- **P0783** 3–4 Shift Solenoid, No RPM Drop @ 3–4 Shift
- **P1195** Catalyst Monitor Slow O2 Sensor (Bank no. 1 Sensor no. 1)
- **P1197** Catalyst Monitor Slow O2 Sensor (Bank no. 1 Sensor no. 2)
- **P1281** Engine is Cold Too Long
- **P1282** Fuel Pump Relay Control Circuit
- **P1294** Target Idle Not Reached
- **P1296** No 5 Volts To MAP Sensor
- **P1297** No Change In MAP From Start To Run
- **P1388** Auto Shutdown Relay Control Circuit
- **P1389** No ASD Relay Output Voltage at PCM
- **P1391** Intermittent Loss of CMP or CKP
- **P1398** Misfire Adaptive Numerator At Limit or No Crank Sensor Learn
- **P1486** EVAP Leak Monitor Pinched Hose Or Obstruction Found
- **P1492** Battery Temp Sensor Voltage Too High
- **P1493** Battery Temp Sensor Voltage Too Low
- **P1494** Leak Detection Pump Pressure Switch Or Mechanical Fault
- **P1495** Leak Detection Pump Solenoid Circuit
- **P1594** Charging System Voltage Too High
- **P1595** Speed Control Solenoid Circuits
- **P1596** Speed Control Switch Always High
- **P1597** Speed Control Switch Always Low
- **P1683** Speed Control Power Circuit
- **P1696** PCM Failure EEPROM Write Denied
- **P1698** PCM Failure EEPROM Write Denied
- **P1756** Governor Pressure Not Equal To Target @ 15–20 PSI
- **P1757** Governor Pressure Above 3 PSI In Gear with 0 MPH
- **P1762** Governor Pressure Sensor Offset Volts Too Low or High
- **P1763** Governor Pressure Sensor Volts Too High
- **P1764** Governor Pressure Sensor Volts Too Low
- **P1765** Trans 12 Volt Supply Relay Control Circuit
- **P1899** P/N Switch Stuck In Park Or In Gear

Diagnostic Connector

◆ See Figures 108, 109, 110 and 111

To read Diagnostic Trouble Codes (DTCí's), the test connector for the electronic engine control system must be used. The test connector is more commonly referred to as the Data Link Connector (DLC). On all Jeep models through 1990, the DLC is a 6-pin and a 15-pin connector located under the hood on the right side of the engine compartment. On 1991–93 models, the DLC is located under the hood on the left side of the engine compartment near the powertrain control module. On 1994–98 vehicles, the DLC is located in the passenger compartment, under the driver side dashboard.

Reading Codes

CARBURETED ENGINES

When a jumper wire is connected between the trouble code test terminals 6

and 7 of the 15-terminal diagnostic connector (D2), the CHECK ENGINE light will flash a trouble code or codes that indicate a problem area. For a bulb and system check, the CHECK ENGINE light will illuminate when the ignition switch is **ON** and the engine not started. If the test terminals are then grounded, the light will flash a code 12 that indicates the self-diagnostic system is operational. A code 12 consists of one flash, followed by a short pause, then two more flashes in quick succession. After a longer pause, the code will repeat two more times. If more than one trouble code is stored, each will be flashed three more times in numerical order, from the lowest to the highest numbered code.

➡Remember that the fault message identifies a circuit problem, not a component.

FUEL INJECTED ENGINES

Entering the self-diagnostic system on models prior to 1991 requires the use of a special adapter that connects with the Diagnostic Readout Box II (DRB-II). These systems require the adapter because all of the system diagnosis is done

Fig. 108 Data Link Connector (DLC) location—Jeep models through 1990

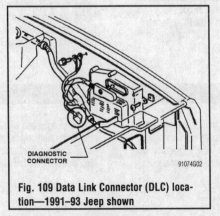

Fig. 109 Data Link Connector (DLC) location—1991–93 Jeep shown

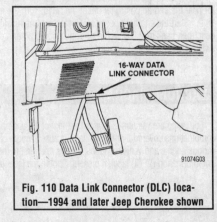

Fig. 110 Data Link Connector (DLC) location—1994 and later Jeep Cherokee shown

Fig. 111 Data Link Connector (DLC) location—1994–98 Jeep Grand Cherokee

Fig. 112 Plug the scan tool into the data link connector—location on the left side of the engine compartment of 1992 Jeep shown

Fig. 113 Using the scan tool to diagnose a problem—coolant temp sensor reading shown

Off-Board instead of On-Board like most vehicles. The adapter, which is a computer module itself, measures signals at the diagnostic connector and converts the signals into a form which the DRB-II can use to perform tests. The MIL or a scan tool can be used to read codes.

➠**Remember that the fault message identifies a circuit problem, not a component.**

MIL Method

➠**This procedure may be used on 1991–96 models.**

1. Start the engine, if possible, cycle the transmission selector and the A/C switch if applicable. Shut off the engine.
2. Turn the ignition switch **ON—OFF, ON—OFF, ON—OFF, ON** within 5 seconds.
3. Observe the MIL on the instrument panel.
4. Just after the last **ON** cycle, MIL will begin flashing the stored codes.
5. The codes are transmitted as two digit flashes. For example Code 21 will be displayed as a FLASH FLASH pause FLASH.
6. Be ready to write down the codes as they appear; the only way to repeat the codes is to start over at the beginning.

Scan Tool Method

▶ **See Figures 112 and 113**

The scan tool is the preferred choice for fault recovery and system diagnosis. Some hints on using the DRB include:
• To use the HELP screen, press and hold F3 at any time.
• To restart the DRB-II at any time, hold the MODE button and press ATM at the same time.
• Pressing the up or down arrows will move forward or backward one item within a menu.
• To select an item, either press the number of the item or move the cursor arrow to the selection, then press ENTER.
• To return to the previous display (screen), press ATM.
• Some test screens display multiple items. To view only one, move the cursor arrow to the desired item, then press ENTER.

To read stored faults with the DRB:
1. With the ignition switch **OFF**, connect the tool to the diagnostic connector near the engine controller under the hood. Turn the ignition **ON**.
2. Start the engine if possible. Cycle the transmission from **P** to a forward gear, then back to **P**, Cycle the air conditioning on and off. Turn the ignition switch **OFF**.

3. Turn the ignition switch **ON** but do not start the engine. The DRB-II will begin its power-up sequence; do not touch any keys on the scan tool during this sequence.
4. Reading faults must be selected from the FUEL/IGN MENU. To reach this menu on the DRB-II:
   a. When the initial menu is displayed after the power-up sequence, use the down arrow to display choice 4) SELECT SYSTEM and select this choice.
   b. Once on the —SELECT SYSTEM— screen, choose 1) ENGINE. This will enter the engine diagnostics section of the program.
   c. The screen will momentarily display the engine family and SBEC identification numbers. After a few seconds the screen displays the choices 1) With A/C and 2) Without A/C. Select and enter the correct choice for the vehicle.
   d. When the —ENGINE SYSTEM— screen appears, select 1) FUEL/IGNITION from the menu.
   e. On the next screen, select 2) READ FAULTS
5. If any faults are stored, the display will show how many are stored (1 of 4 faults, etc.) and issue a text description of the problem, such as COOLANT SENSOR VOLTAGE TOO LOW. The last line of the display shows the number of engine starts since the code was set. If the number displayed is 0 starts, this indicates a hard or current fault. Faults are displayed in reverse order of occurrence; the first fault shown is the most current and the last fault shown is the oldest.
6. Press the down arrow to read each fault after the first. Record the screen data carefully for easy reference.
7. If no faults are stored in the controller, the display will state NO FAULTS DETECTED and show the number of starts since the system memory was last erased.
8. After all faults have been read and recorded, press ATM.

Clearing Codes

Stored faults should only be cleared by use of the DRB-II or similar scan tool. Disconnecting the battery will clear codes but is not recommended as doing so will also clear all other memories on the vehicle and may affect driveability. Unplugging the PCM connector will also clear codes, but on newer models it may store a power loss code and will affect driveability until the vehicle is driven and the PCM can relearn its driveability memory.

The —ERASE— screen will appear when ATM is pressed at the end of the stored faults. Select the desired action from ERASE or DON'T ERASE. If ERASE is chosen, the display asks ARE YOU SURE? Pressing ENTER erases stored faults and displays the message FAULTS ERASED. After the faults are erased, press ATM to return the FUEL/IGN MENU.

VACUUM DIAGRAMS

Following are vacuum diagrams for most of the engine and emissions package combinations covered by this manual. Because vacuum circuits will vary based on various engine and vehicle options, always refer first to the Vehicle Emission Control Information (VECI) label, if present. Should the label be missing, or should

vehicle be equipped with a different engine from the vehicle's original equipment, refer to the diagrams below for the same or similar configuration.If you wish to obtain a replacement emissions label, most manufacturers make the labels available for purchase. The labels can usually be ordered from a local dealer.

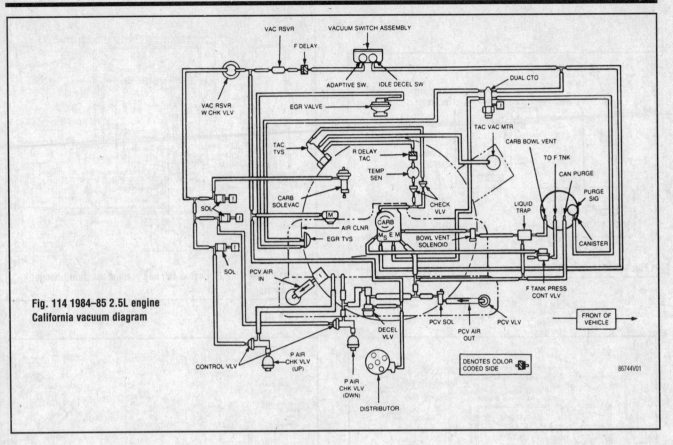

Fig. 114 1984–85 2.5L engine California vacuum diagram

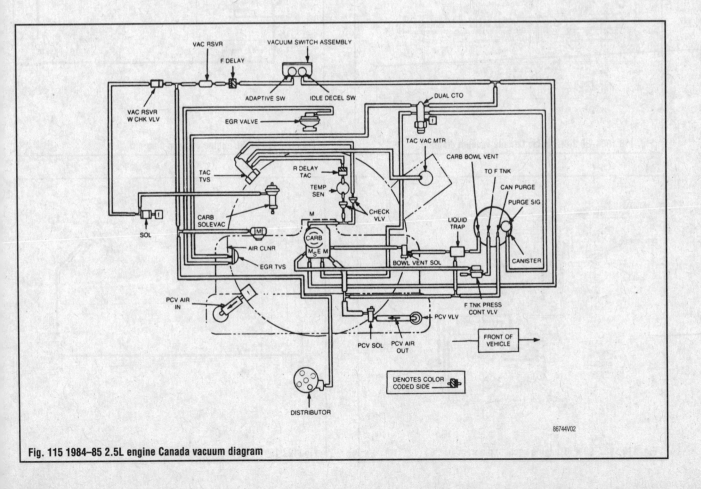

Fig. 115 1984–85 2.5L engine Canada vacuum diagram

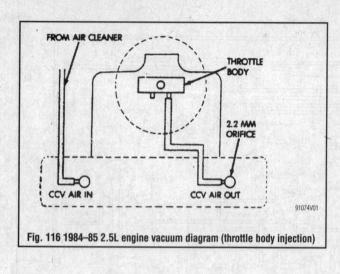

Fig. 116 1984–85 2.5L engine vacuum diagram (throttle body injection)

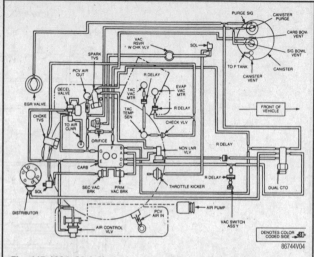

Fig. 117 1984–86 2.8L engine 49 state vacuum diagram (manual transmission)

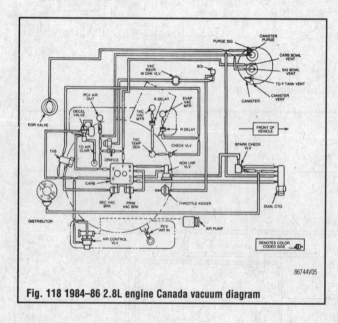

Fig. 118 1984–86 2.8L engine Canada vacuum diagram

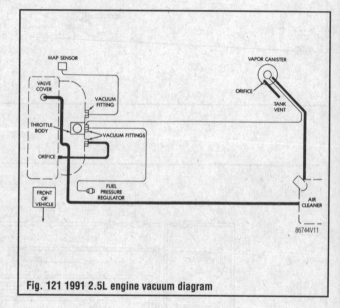

Fig. 121 1991 2.5L engine vacuum diagram

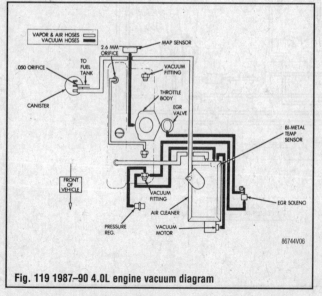

Fig. 119 1987–90 4.0L engine vacuum diagram

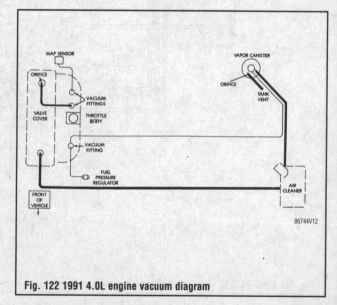

Fig. 122 1991 4.0L engine vacuum diagram

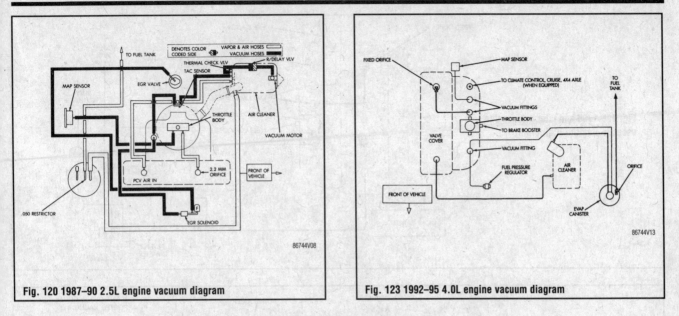

Fig. 120 1987–90 2.5L engine vacuum diagram

Fig. 123 1992–95 4.0L engine vacuum diagram

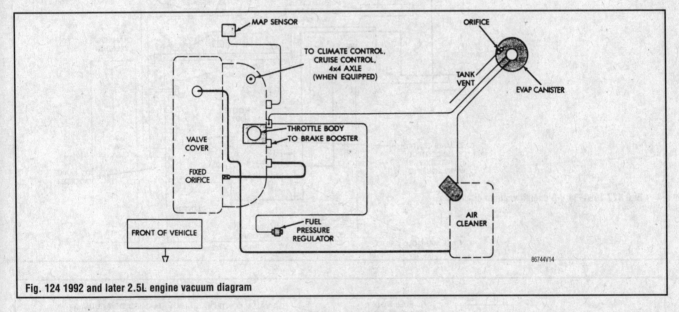

Fig. 124 1992 and later 2.5L engine vacuum diagram

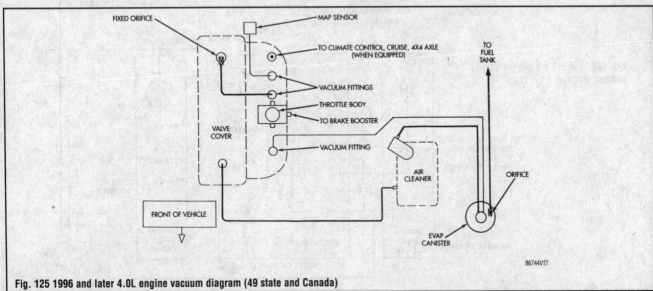

Fig. 125 1996 and later 4.0L engine vacuum diagram (49 state and Canada)

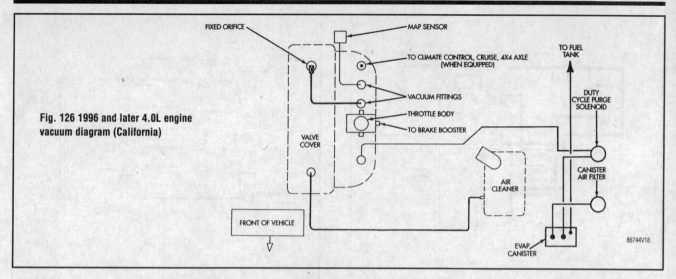

Fig. 126 1996 and later 4.0L engine vacuum diagram (California)

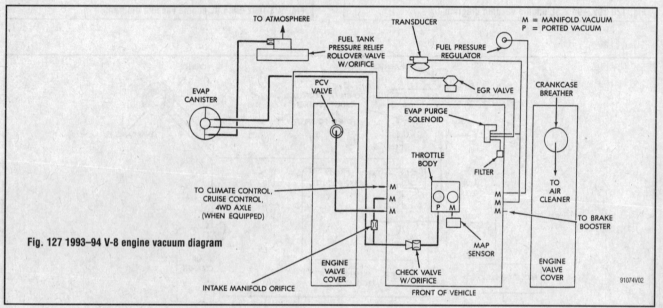

Fig. 127 1993–94 V-8 engine vacuum diagram

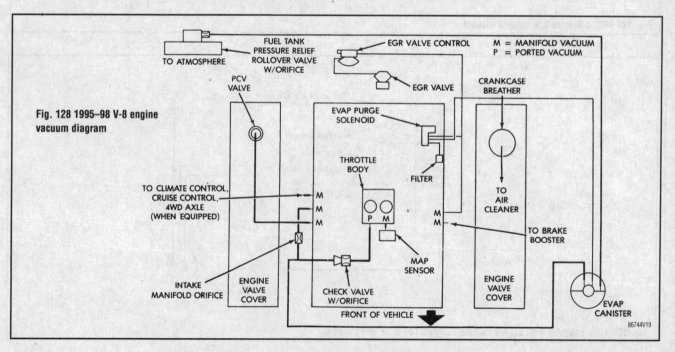

Fig. 128 1995–98 V-8 engine vacuum diagram

5

FUEL
SYSTEM

BASIC FUEL SYSTEM DIAGNOSIS

When there is a problem starting or driving a vehicle, two of the most important checks involve the ignition and the fuel systems. The questions most mechanics attempt to answer first, "is there spark?" and "is there fuel?" will often lead to solving most basic problems. For ignition system diagnosis and testing, please refer to the information on engine electrical components and ignition systems found earlier in this manual. If the ignition system checks out (there is spark), then you must determine if the fuel system is operating properly (is there fuel?).

FUEL LINES AND FITTINGS

Quick-Connect Fuel Line

REMOVAL & INSTALLATION

1988–93 Models

▶ See Figure 1

1. Release the fuel system pressure, then separate the quick-connect fuel line tubes at the inner fender panel by squeezing the two retaining tabs against the fuel line. Pull the tube and retainer from the fitting.
2. Remove the two O-rings and the spacer from the fitting. This can be accomplished by using a paper clip or piece of heavy wire bent into an L-shape.
3. Remove the retainer from the fuel tube and discard the O-rings, spacer and retainer.

To install:
4. Install the new retainer assembly by pushing it into the quick-connect fitting until it clicks.
5. Grasp the disposable plastic plug and remove it from the replacement fitting. By removing only the plastic plug, the O-rings, spacer and retainer will remain in the fitting.
6. Push the fuel line into the fitting until a click is heard and the connection is complete. Give the fuel line connection a firm tug to verify that it is seated and locked properly.

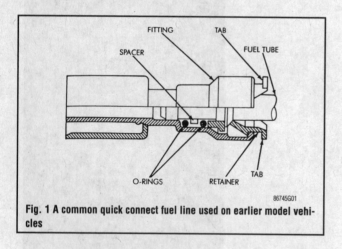

Fig. 1 A common quick connect fuel line used on earlier model vehicles

1994 and Later Models

SINGLE TAB TYPE

▶ See Figures 2 and 3

✳✳ CAUTION

The O-rings and spacers of this type of fitting are not serviced separately. Do not attempt to repair damaged fuel lines or fittings. If the lines, fittings and O-rings are defective the complete fuel line assembly must be replaced.

1. Disconnect the negative battery cable.
2. Relieve the fuel system pressure as outlined in this section.
3. Clean the fitting of any dirt and grime and press the release on the side of the fitting to release the tab.

4. While pressing the release tab, pry up the pull tab with a screwdriver.
5. Raise the tab until it separates from the fitting and discard the old tab. Disconnect the fitting from the component or line being serviced.

To install:
6. Inspect the line for damage and clean the fitting and lubricate with clean engine oil.
7. Engage the fitting to the line or component it was removed from.
8. Using a new pull tab, push the tab down until it locks into place in the fitting.
9. Verify the fitting is locked in place by pulling on the tube and fitting.
10. Connect the negative battery cable, start the vehicle and check for leaks.

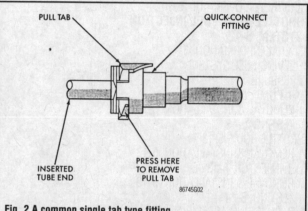

Fig. 2 A common single tab type fitting

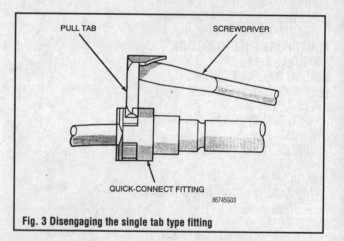

Fig. 3 Disengaging the single tab type fitting

TWO-TAB TYPE

▶ See Figures 4 and 5

✳✳ CAUTION

The O-rings and spacers of this type of fitting are not serviced separately. Do not attempt to repair damaged fuel lines or fittings. If the lines, fittings and O-rings are defective the complete fuel line assembly must be replaced.

1. Disconnect the negative battery cable.
2. Relieve the fuel system pressure as outlined in this section.
3. Clean the fitting of any dirt and grime.
4. Squeeze the release tabs against the sides of the fitting and pull the fitting from the component or line being serviced.

➡ **The plastic retainer will stay on the component being serviced after the fitting has been disconnected.**

To install:
5. Inspect the line for damage and clean the fitting and lubricate with clean engine oil.

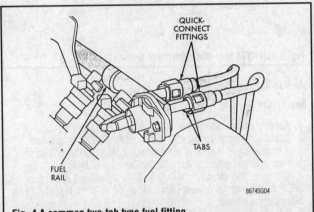

Fig. 4 A common two-tab type fuel fitting

Fig. 5 Disengaging the two-tab type quick connect fitting

6. Engage the fitting to the line or component it was removed from. The connection has been made when a click is heard.
7. Verify the fitting is locked in place by pulling on the tube and fitting.
8. Connect the negative battery cable, start the vehicle and check for leaks.

PLASTIC RETAINER TYPE

♦ **See Figure 6**

This type of fitting can be identified by the use of a full round plastic retainer ring usually black in color.
1. Disconnect the negative battery cable.
2. Relieve the fuel system pressure as outlined in this section.
3. Clean the fitting of any dirt and grime.
4. Release the fitting from the component or line being serviced by pushing the fitting towards the component while pushing the plastic retaining into the fitting. With the plastic ring fully depressed, pull the fitting from the component.

To install:

➡ **The plastic retainer will stay on the component being serviced after the fitting has been disconnected.**

5. Inspect the line for damage and clean the fitting and lubricate with clean engine oil.
6. Engage the fitting to the line or component it was removed from. The connection has been made when a click is felt.
7. Verify the fitting is locked in place by pulling on the tube and fitting.
8. Connect the negative battery cable, start the vehicle and check for leaks.

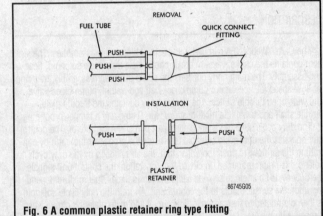

Fig. 6 A common plastic retainer ring type fitting

CARBURETED FUEL SYSTEM

Mechanical Fuel Pump

REMOVAL & INSTALLATION

♦ **See Figure 7**

1. Disconnect the inlet and outlet fuel lines and, on the 2.8L engine, the fuel return line.
2. Remove the fuel pump body attaching nuts and lock washers.
3. Pull the pump and gasket or O-ring free of the engine.

➡ **On the 2.8L engine, the actuating rod may fall from the engine.**

To install:
4. Make sure that the mating surfaces of the fuel pump and the engine are clean.
5. Cement a new gasket to the mounting flange of the fuel pump.
6. Position the fuel pump on the engine block so that the lever of the fuel pump rests on the fuel pump cam of the camshaft.

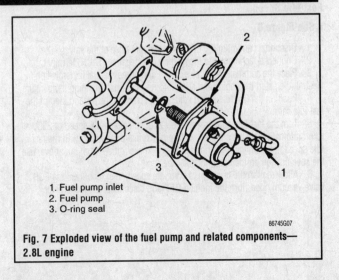

1. Fuel pump inlet
2. Fuel pump
3. O-ring seal

Fig. 7 Exploded view of the fuel pump and related components— 2.8L engine

7. Secure the fuel pump to the block with the capscrews and lock washers. tighten the capscrews to 16 ft. lbs. (21 Nm).

8. Connect the fuel lines to the fuel pump.

TESTING

Volume Check

1. Disconnect the fuel line from the carburetor and place the open end of the line into a graduated one quart container.

2. Start the engine and operate it at a normal idle speed. The pump should deliver at least one pint in 30 seconds.

3. Replace the pump if defective.

Pressure Check

1. Disconnect the fuel line at the carburetor.

2. Install a T-fitting on the open end of the fuel line and refit the line to the carburetor.

3. Plug a pressure gauge into the remaining opening of the T-fitting.

4. The hose leading to the pressure gauge should not be any longer than 6 in. (152mm). On pumps with a fuel return line, the line must be plugged. Start the engine.

5. Fuel pressures are as follows:
- 2.5L: 4.00–5.00 psi (27–34 kPa) at idle
- 2.8L: 6.00–7.50 psi (41–51 kPa) at idle

Carter YFA Feedback Carburetor

➡**The Carter model YFA feedback carburetor was used on the 2.5L engine.**

DESCRIPTION

The Carter/Weber YFA carburetor consists of three main assemblies. The air horn contains the choke, vacuum break, choke plate duty cycle solenoid, float and assembly. The main body contains the pump diaphragm assembly, metering jet, low-speed jet, accelerator pump check ball and weight, pump bleed valve and wide open throttle switch. The throttle body contains the throttle plate, throttle shaft and lever, idle mixture screw with O-ring and a tamper-proof plug.

The duty cycle solenoid is an integral part of the YFA carburetor. The control unit operates the duty cycle solenoid to provide the proper air/fuel ratio by controlling the air flow. In open loop operation, the air supplied by the duty cycle solenoid is preprogrammed. In closed loop operation, the control unit signals the duty cycle solenoid to provide additional air to the air/fuel mixture depending upon the sensor inputs to the control unit. Air from the duty cycle solenoid is then distributed to the carburetor idle circuit and main metering circuit where it mixes with the fuel.

ADJUSTMENTS

Fast Idle Speed

♦ **See Figure 8**

1. Disconnect and plug the EGR valve vacuum hose at the valve.

2. Connect a tachometer to the ignition coil negative (TACH) terminal.

3. Place the automatic transmission in Park, or the manual transmission in Neutral, then start the engine and allow it to reach normal operating temperature.

4. Position the fast idle speed adjustment screw on the second step of the fast idle cam.

5. Turn the fast idle adjustment screw to obtain a fast idle speed of 2300 rpm (automatic transmission) or 2000 rpm (manual transmission). If the fast idle speed listed on the underhood emission sticker differs from the above, use the specification on the underhood sticker.

6. Allow the throttle to return to curb idle speed, then reconnect the EGR valve vacuum hose. Turn the ignition **OFF** and disconnect the tachometer.

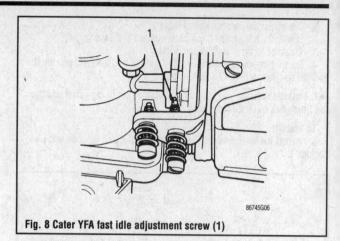

Fig. 8 Cater YFA fast idle adjustment screw (1)

Sole-Vac Vacuum Actuator

♦ **See Figure 9**

1. Connect a tachometer to the ignition coil TACH terminal.

2. Start the engine and allow it to reach normal operating temperature.

3. This adjustment is made with the automatic transmission in Drive or manual transmission in Neutral and all accessories turned **OFF**.

4. Disconnect the vacuum hose from the Sole-Vac vacuum actuator and plug. Connect an external vacuum source and apply 10–15 in. Hg (34–51 kPa) of vacuum to the actuator.

5. Adjust the idle speed to 850 rpm (auto. trans.), 950 rpm (manual trans.) using the vacuum actuator adjustment screw on the throttle lever. Use the specifications on the underhood sticker if they differ from the specifications.

6. Turn the ignition **OFF** and disconnect the tachometer and vacuum pump. The Sole-Vac curb idle speed should be adjusted following this procedure.

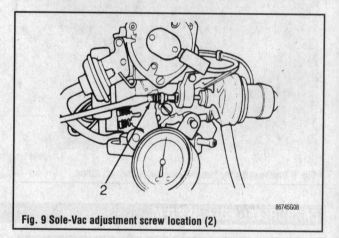

Fig. 9 Sole-Vac adjustment screw location (2)

Curb Idle Speed

♦ **See Figure 10**

1. Connect a tachometer to the ignition coil TACH terminal.

2. Place the automatic transmission in Drive, or the manual transmission in Neutral.

3. Start the engine and allow it to reach normal operating temperature.

4. Disconnect and plug the vacuum hose from the actuator.

5. Adjust the hex head curb idle speed adjustment screw to 700 rpm (auto. trans.) or 750 rpm (manual trans.). Use the specifications on the underhood sticker if they differ from the above specifications.

6. Turn the ignition switch **OFF**, then disengage the tachometer and reconnect the vacuum actuator hose.

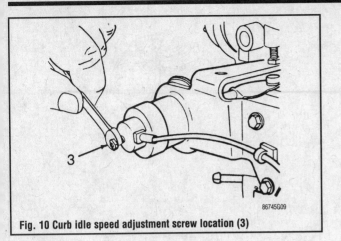

Fig. 10 Curb idle speed adjustment screw location (3)

Float Level

▶ See Figure 11

1. Remove and invert the air horn assembly and check the clearance from the top of the float to the surface of the air horn with a T-scale.

2. The air horn should be held at eye level when gauging and the float arm should be resting on the needle pin.

3. Do not exert pressure on the needle valve when measuring or adjusting the float. Bend the float arm as necessary to adjust the float level.

❈❈ CAUTION

Do not bend the tab at the end of the float arm as it prevent the float from striking the bottom of the fuel bowl when empty and keeps the needle in place.

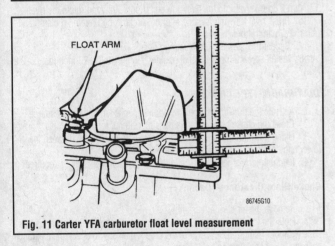

Fig. 11 Carter YFA carburetor float level measurement

Float Drop

1. Hold the air horn upright and let the float hang freely.

2. Measure the maximum clearance from the toe end of the float to the casting surface.

3. Hold the air horn at eye level when measuring To adjust, bend the tab at the end of the float arm.

Metering Rod

▶ See Figure 12

1. Remove the air horn. Back out the idle speed adjusting screw until the throttle plate is seated fully in its bore.

2. Press down on the upper end of the diaphragm shaft until the diaphragm bottoms in the vacuum chamber.

3. The metering rod should contact the bottom of the metering rod well. The lifter link at the outer end nearest the springs and at the supporting link should be bottomed.

4. Turn the rod adjusting screw until the metering rod just bottoms in the body casting. For final adjustment, turn the screw one additional turn clockwise.

5. Install the carburetor air horn and replacement gasket on the carburetor, then set the curb idle speed to specifications.

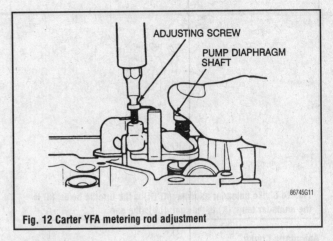

Fig. 12 Carter YFA metering rod adjustment

Fast Idle Cam Index

▶ See Figure 13

1. Put the fast idle screw on the second highest step of the fast idle cam, against the shoulder of the high step.

2. Measure the clearance between the lower edge of the choke valve and the air horn wall. It is not necessary to remove the air cleaner bracket when measuring clearance between the choke valve and air horn wall, position the gauge next to the bracket.

3. Adjust by bending the choke plate connecting rod to obtain the specified clearance between the lower edge of the choke plate and the air horn wall.

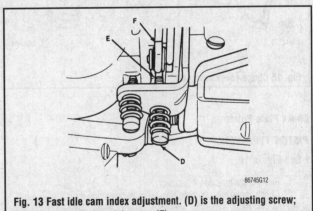

Fig. 13 Fast idle cam index adjustment. (D) is the adjusting screw; (E) is the second step of the cam (F)

Choke Unloader

▶ See Figure 14

1. Hold the throttle lever fully open and apply pressure on the choke valve toward the closed position.

2. Measure the clearance between the lower edge of the choke valve and the air horn wall. See the Specifications Chart.

➡ **DO NOT bend the unloader tang DOWN.**

3. Adjust by bending the unloader tang which contacts the fast idle cam. Bend toward the cam to increase clearance, away to decrease.

4. Ensure the unloader tang is at least 0.070 in. (1.8mm) from the main body flange when the throttle is open.

5. Check for full throttle opening when throttle is operated from inside vehicle.

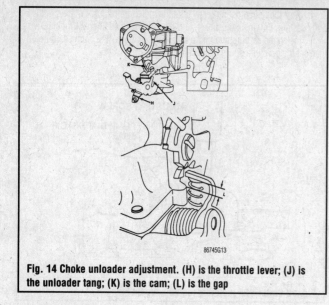

Fig. 14 Choke unloader adjustment. (H) is the throttle lever; (J) is the unloader tang; (K) is the cam; (L) is the gap

Automatic Choke

▶ See Figure 15

1. Loosen the choke cover retaining screws, then turn the choke cover so that the index mark on the cover lines up with the specified mark on the choke housing.

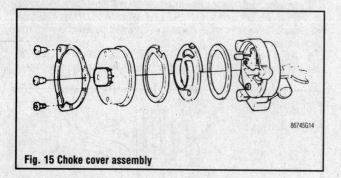

Fig. 15 Choke cover assembly

Choke Plate Pulldown

PISTON-TYPE CHOKE

▶ See Figure 16

1. Remove the air cleaner assembly.
2. Check choke cap retaining ring rivets to determine if mandrel is well below the rivet head. If mandrel appears to be at or within the rivet head thickness, drive it down or out with a 1/16 in. (1.5mm) diameter punch.
3. Use a 1/8 in. (3mm) diameter drill for drilling the rivet heads. Drill into the rivet head until the rivet head comes loose from the rivet body.
4. After the rivet head is removed, drive the remaining portion of the rivet out of the hole with a 1/8 in. (3mm) diameter punch.

➡This procedure must be followed to retain the hole size.

5. Repeat Steps 1–4 for the remaining rivet.
6. Remove screw in the conventional manner.
7. Bend a 0.026 in. (0.66mm) diameter wire gauge at a 90° angle approximately 1/8 in. (3mm) from one end. Insert the bent end of the gauge between the choke piston slot and the right hand slot in the choke housing. Rotate the choke piston lever counterclockwise until the gauge is shut in the piston slot.
8. Apply light pressure on the choke piston lever to hold the gauge in place, then measure the clearance between the lower edge of the choke plate and the carburetor bore using a drill with the diameter equal to the specified pulldown clearance.
9. Bend the choke piston lever to obtain the proper clearance.

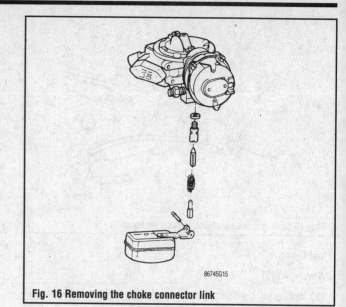

Fig. 16 Removing the choke connector link

10. Install choke cap gasket.
11. Install the locking and indexing plate.
12. Install the notched gasket.
13. Install choke cap, making certain that bi-metal loop is positioned around choke lever tang.
14. While holding cap in place, actuate choke plate to make certain bi-metal loop is properly engaged with lever tang. Set retaining clamp over choke cap and orient clamp to match holes in casting (holes are not equally spaced). Make sure retaining clamp is not upside down.
15. Place a 1/8 in. diameter x 1/2 in. long x 1/4 in. diameter head (3mm x 12.7mm x 6mm) rivet into the rivet gun and trigger lightly to retain the rivet.
16. Press rivet fully into casting after passing through retaining clamp and pop rivet (mandrel breaks off).
17. Repeat this step for the remaining rivet.
18. Install screw in conventional manner. Tighten to 17–20 inch lbs. (2–2.2 Nm).

DIAPHRAGM-TYPE CHOKE

1. Activate the pull-down motor by applying an external vacuum source.
2. Close the choke plate as far as possible without forcing it.
3. Using a drill of the specified size, measure the clearance between the lower edge of the choke plate and the air horn wall.
4. If adjustment is necessary, bend the choke diaphragm link as required.

Choke Plate Clearance (Dechoke)

1. Remove the air cleaner assembly.
2. Hold the throttle plate fully open and close the choke plate as far as possible without forcing it. Use a drill of the proper diameter to check the clearance between the choke plate and air horn.
3. If the clearance is not within specification, adjust by bending the arm on the choke lever of the throttle lever. Bending the arm downward will decrease the clearance, and bending it upward will increase the clearance. Always recheck the clearance after making any adjustment.

Mechanical Fuel Bowl Vent

1. Start the engine and wait until it has reached normal operating temperature before proceeding.
2. Check engine idle rpm and set to specifications.
3. Check DC motor operation by opening throttle off idle. The DC motor should extend.
4. Release the throttle, and the DC motor should retract when in contact with the throttle lever.
5. Disconnect the idle speed motor in the idle position.
6. Turn engine **OFF**.
7. Open the throttle lever so that the throttle lever actuating lever does not touch the fuel bowl vent rod.

8. Close the throttle lever to the idle set position and measure the travel of the fuel bowl vent rod at point A. The distance measured represents the travel of the vent rod from where there is no contact with the actuating lever to where the actuating lever moves the vent rod to the idle set position. The travel of the vent rod at point A should be 0.100–0.150 in. (2.5–3.8mm).

9. If adjustment is required, bend the throttle actuating lever at notch shown.

10. Reconnect the idle speed control motor.

Secondary Throttle Stop Screw

Back off the screw until it does not touch the lever. Turn the screw in until it touches the lever, then turn it an additional 1/4 turn.

REMOVAL & INSTALLATION

1. Remove the air cleaner.
2. Tag and disconnect all hoses leading to the carburetor.
3. Disconnect the control shaft from the throttle lever.
4. Disengage the inline fuel filter, pullback spring and all electrical connectors.
5. Remove the carburetor mounting nuts and lift off the carburetor.
6. Remove the carburetor mounting gasket from the spacer.

To install:

7. Clean all gasket mating surfaces on the spacer and carburetor.
8. Install a new gasket on the spacer, then install the carburetor and secure it with the mounting nuts.
9. Engage all vacuum hoses, fuel lines and electrical connectors.
10. Connect the control shaft and pullback spring.
11. Install the air cleaner and adjust the curb and fast idle speed, as previously described.

Rochester 2SE/E2SE Carburetor

➡The Rochester 2SE and E2SE carburetors were used on 2.8L engines. The carburetor part number is stamped vertically on the float bowl in the float. Refer to this part number when servicing the carburetor.

Make all adjustments with the engine at normal operating temperature, choke plate fully opened, air cleaner removed, thermac vacuum source plugged and A/C off (except if needed for a certain adjustment). Set the idle speeds only when the emission control system is in closed loop mode.

ADJUSTMENTS

Float Level

♦ **See Figures 17 and 18**

➡Special tools are needed for this procedure.

1. Run the engine to normal operating temperature.
2. Remove the vent stack screws and the vent stack.
3. Remove the air horn screw adjacent to the vent stack.
4. With the engine idling and the choke fully opened, carefully insert float gauge J-9789-136 or its equivalent for E2SE carburetors, or J-9789-138 or its equivalent for 2SE carburetors, into the air horn screw hole and vent hole.
5. Allow the gauge to rest freely on the float. Do not press down on the float!
6. With the gauge at eye level, observe the mark that aligns with the top of the casting at the vent hole. The float level should be within 0.06 in. (1.5mm) of the specification listed in the chart. If not, remove the air horn and adjust as follows:

a. Hold the retainer pin firmly in place and push the float down, lightly, against the inlet needle.

b. Using an adjustable T-scale, at a point 3/16 in. (4.8mm) from the end of the float, at the toe, measure the distance from the float bowl top surface (gasket removed) to the top of the float at the toe. If the distance isn't as specified in the Chart, remove the float and bend the float arm as necessary.

Fast Idle Speed

♦ **See Figure 19**

1. Place the fast idle screw on the high step of the fast idle cam.
2. Disconnect and plug the EGR valve hose and the canister purge line at the canister.

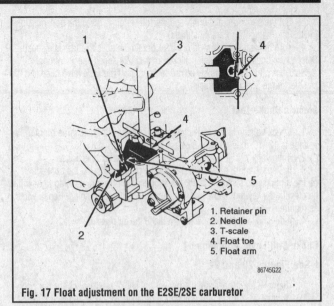

1. Retainer pin
2. Needle
3. T-scale
4. Float toe
5. Float arm

86745G22

Fig. 17 Float adjustment on the E2SE/2SE carburetor

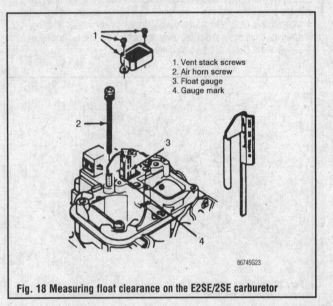

1. Vent stack screws
2. Air horn screw
3. Float gauge
4. Gauge mark

86745G23

Fig. 18 Measuring float clearance on the E2SE/2SE carburetor

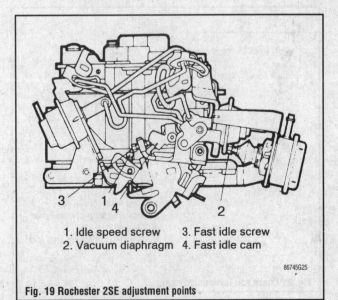

1. Idle speed screw   3. Fast idle screw
2. Vacuum diaphragm   4. Fast idle cam

86745G25

Fig. 19 Rochester 2SE adjustment points

3. Set the parking brake firmly and start the engine. Place the transmission in Neutral (manual) or Park (automatic).

4. Turn the fast idle screw in or out to obtain the specified fast idle speed. Refer to the underhood emission sticker for fast idle speed specifications.

5. Once all adjustments are complete, reconnect the EGR valve hose and the canister purge line at the canister.

Electric Choke Test

1. Check voltage at the choke heater connection with the engine running. If voltage is 12–15 volts, replace the electric choke unit.

2. If the voltage is low or zero, check all wires and connections.

3. If Steps 1 and 2 pass the test properly, check and see if the connection on the oil pressure switch is faulty, the temperature pressure warning light will be off with the key in the **ON** position and the engine not running. Repair wires as required.

4. If the choke is still inoperative, replace the oil pressure switch.

Choke Coil Lever Adjustment

▶ **See Figures 20 and 21**

1. Remove air cleaner and disconnect the choke electrical connector.

2. Align a 5/32 in. (4mm) drill on the retainer rivet head and drill only enough to remove rivet head. After removing rivet heads and retainers, use a drift and small hammer to drive the remainder of the rivet from the choke housing. Use care in drilling to prevent damage to the choke cover or housing. Remove the three rivets and choke cover assembly from choke housing.

3. Remove choke coil from housing.

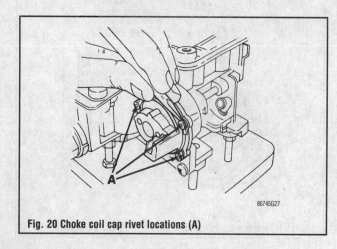

Fig. 20 Choke coil cap rivet locations (A)

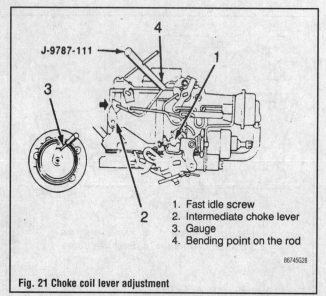

1. Fast idle screw
2. Intermediate choke lever
3. Gauge
4. Bending point on the rod

Fig. 21 Choke coil lever adjustment

➡**A choke stat cover retainer kit is required for reassembly.**

4. Place the fast idle screw on the high step of the dam.

5. Close the choke by pushing in on the intermediate choke lever. On front wheel drive models, the intermediate choke lever is behind the choke vacuum diaphragm.

6. Insert a drill or gauge of the specified size into the hole in the choke housing. The choke lever in the housing should be up against the side of the gauge.

7. If the lever does not just touch the gauge, bend the intermediate choke rod to adjust.

To install:

8. Install the choke cover and coil assembly in choke housing as follows:

a. Install the choke cover and coil assembly in the choke housing, aligning notch in cover with raised casting projection on housing cover flange. Make sure coil pickup tank engages the inside choke coil lever.

b. A choke cover retainer kit is required to attach the choke cover to the choke housing. Install a suitable blind rivet installing tool.

9. Engage choke electrical connector.

10. Start engine, check operation of choke and then install the air cleaner.

Electric Choke Setting

This procedure is only for those carburetors with choke covers retained by screws. Riveted choke covers are preset and non-adjustable.

1. Loosen the three retaining screws.

2. Place the fast idle screw on the high step of the cam.

3. Rotate the choke cover to align the cover mark with the specified housing mark.

➡**The specification "index" which appears in the specification table refers to the mark between "1 notch lean" and "1 notch rich".**

Secondary Lockout Adjustment

1. Pull the choke wide open by pushing out on the intermediate choke lever.

2. Open the throttle until the end of the secondary actuating lever is opposite the toe of the lockout lever.

3. Gauge clearance between the lockout lever and secondary lever should be as specified.

4. To adjust, bend the lockout lever where it contacts the fast idle cam.

Secondary Vacuum Break TVS Test

The secondary vacuum break Thermal Vacuum Switch (TVS), located in the air cleaner, improves cold starting and cold driveability by sensing carburetor air inlet temperature to control the carburetor secondary vacuum break.

1. With engine at normal operating temperature, the Thermal Vacuum Switch (TVS) must be open (air cleaner cover on).

2. Apply either engine or auxiliary vacuum to the TVS inlet port and check for vacuum at the outlet port (outlet port connects to secondary vacuum break).

3. If there is no vacuum, check air cleaner assembly for leaks, thermostatic air cleaner vacuum hoses and/or replace the TVS. Replace the TVS as follows:

a. Remove air cleaner cover and element.

b. Disconnect vacuum hoses.

c. Remove clip from TVS and remove TVS.

d. Install new TVS and replace clip.

e. Reconnect vacuum hoses (refer to Vehicle Emission Control Information Label).

f. Install air cleaner cover and element.

Idle Stop Solenoid Test

The solenoid should be checked to assure that the solenoid plunger extends when the solenoid is energized. an inoperative solenoid could cause stalling or a rough idle when hot, and should be replaced as necessary.

1. Turn the ignition **ON**, but do not start engine. Position transmission lever in Drive (A/T) or Neutral (M/T). On vehicles equipped with air conditioning, A/C switch must be on.

2. Open and close throttle. The solenoid plunger should retract from throttle lever. Disconnect the wire at the solenoid, the solenoid plunger should retract from the throttle lever.

3. Connect solenoid wire and the plunger should move out and contact the

throttle lever. the solenoid may not be strong enough to open the throttle, but the plunger should move.

4. If the plunger does not move in and out as the wire is disconnected and connected, check the voltage feed wire:

    a. If voltage is 12–15 volts, replace the solenoid.

    b. If voltage is low or zero, locate the cause of the open circuit in the solenoid feed wire and repair.

5. If necessary to replace the idle stop, proceed as follows.

    a. Remove carburetor air cleaner.

    b. Disengage electrical connector at the solenoid.

    c. Unfasten the large retaining nut, tabbed lock washer and remove the solenoid.

    d. Install the solenoid and retaining nut, bending the lock tabs against nut flats.

    e. Engage electrical connector.

    f. Install air cleaner and adjust idle speed as necessary.

Carburetor Pre-Set Procedure

▶ **See Figures 22 and 23**

1. Remove the carburetor from the engine following normal service procedures to gain access to the plug covering the idle mixture needle.

2. To remove the plug, make two parallel cuts in the throttle body, one on each side of the plug, with a hacksaw. There is a locator point marking the casting at the plug. The cuts should extend down to the steel plug, but should not extend more than 1/8 in. (3mm) beyond the locator point.

3. Place a flat punch at a point near the ends of the saw cuts the throttle body. Hold the punch at a 45° angle and drive it into the throttle body until the casting breaks away and exposes the steel plug. Hold a center punch in the vertical position and drive it into the plug, then hold the punch at a 45° angle and drive the plug out of the housing. The hardened steel plug will shatter rather than remain intact. It is not necessary to remove the plug completely; instead, remove the loose pieces, then turn the idle mixture needle in until lightly seated and back out 4 turns.

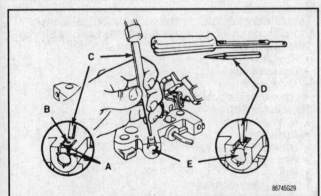

Fig. 22 Removing the idle mixture screw cover on the 2SE/E2SE carburetor

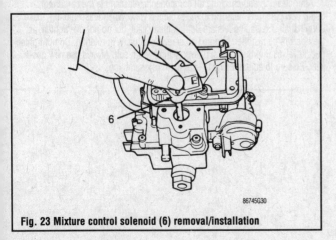

Fig. 23 Mixture control solenoid (6) removal/installation

4. If the plug in air horn covering the idle air has been removed replace air horn. If plug is still in place, do not remove plug.

5. Remove vent stack screen assembly to gain access to lean mixture screw. (Be sure to reinstall vent stack screen assembly after adjustment).

6. Using tool J-28696-10 BT 7928 or equivalent, turn lean mixture screw in until lightly bottomed and back out 2 1/2 turns.

7. Reinstall the carburetor on the engine and perform the following:

    a. Do not install air cleaner and gasket.

    b. Disconnect the bowl vent line at carburetor.

    c. Disconnect the EGR valve hose and canister purge hose at the carburetor and cap the carburetor ports.

    d. Refer to Vehicle Emission Control Information Label and observe hose from sensor and secondary vacuum break TVS. Disconnect hose at temperature sensor on air cleaner and plug open hose.

    e. Connect the positive lead of a dwell meter to the mixture control solenoid test lead (green connector). Connect the other meter lead to ground. Set dwell meter to 6 cylinder position. Connect a tachometer to distributor lead (brown connector). Tachometer should be connected to the distributor side of the tach filter if vehicle is equipped with a tachometer.

    f. Block the drive wheels.

    g. Place the transmission in Park (automatic transmission) or Neutral (manual transmission) and set the parking brake.

Mixture Adjustment

▶ **See Figure 24**

1. Perform carburetor pre-set procedure.

2. Run engine on high step of fast idle cam until engine cooling fan starts to cycle (at least three minutes and until in closed loop).

3. Run the engine at 3000 rpm and adjust the lean mixture screw slowly in small increments allowing time for the dwell to stabilize after turning the screw to obtain an average dwell of 35°.

4. If dwell is too low, back screw out, if too high, turn it in.

5. If unable to adjust to specifications, inspect main metering circuit for leaks, restrictions, etc.

6. The dwell reading of the M/C solenoid is used to determine calibration and is sensitive to changes in fuel mixture caused by heat, air leaks, etc. While idling, it is normal for the dwell to increase and decrease fairly constantly over a relatively narrow range, such as 5°. However, it may occasionally vary be as much as 10–15° momentarily due to temporary mixture changes.

7. The dwell reading specified is the average of the most consistent variation. The engine must be allowed a few moments to stabilize at idle or 3000 rpm as applicable before taking a dwell reading. Return to idle.

8. Adjust the idle mixture screw to obtain an average dwell of 25° with cooling fan in off cycle.

9. If reading is too low, back screw out. If too high, turn it in. Allow time for reading to stabilize after each adjustment. Adjustment is very sensitive. Make final check with adjusting tool removed.

10. If unable to adjust to specifications, inspect idle system for leaks, restrictions, etc.

11. Disconnect mixture control solenoid when cooling fan is in off cycle and check for an rpm change of at least 50 rpm. If rpm does not change enough, inspect idle air bleed circuit for restrictions, leaks, etc.

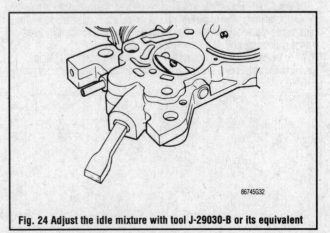

Fig. 24 Adjust the idle mixture with tool J-29030-B or its equivalent

12. Run engine at 3000 rpm for a few moments and note dwell reading. Dwell should be varying with an average reading of 35°. If not at 35° average dwell, reset the lean mixture screw as per Step 3. Then reset the idle mixture screw to obtain 25° dwell as per Step 5.

13. If at 35° average dwell, reconnect the systems disconnected earlier (purge and vent hoses, EGR valve, etc.), reinstall vent screen and set idle speed to specifications.

REMOVAL & INSTALLATION

Always replace all internal gaskets that are removed. Base gasket should be inspected and replaced only if damaged. Flooding, stumble on acceleration and other performance complaints are in many instances, caused by presence of dirt, water, or other foreign matter in carburetor. To aid in diagnosis, carburetor should be carefully removed from the engine without draining fuel from bowl. Contents of the fuel bowl may then be examined for contamination as the carburetor is disassembled. Be sure to check the fuel filter.

1. Remove the air cleaner and gasket.
2. Disconnect the fuel pipe and vacuum lines.
3. Disengage the electrical connectors.
4. Disconnect the accelerator linkage.
5. If equipped with automatic transmission, disconnect the downshift cable.
6. If equipped with cruise control, disconnect the linkage.
7. Remove the carburetor attaching bolts.
8. Remove the carburetor and EFE heater/insulator (if used).
9. Fill the carburetor bowl before installing carburetor. A small supply of fuel will enable the carburetor to be filled and the operation of the float and inlet needle and seat to be checked.
10. Operate throttle lever several times and check discharge from pump jets before installing carburetor.

To install:

11. Inspect EFE heater/insulator for damage. Be certain throttle body and EFE heater/insulator surfaces are clean.
12. Install EFE heater/insulator.
13. Install the carburetor and tighten the nuts alternately to the correct torque.
14. Connect the downshift cable as required.
15. Connect the cruise control cable as required.
16. Connect the accelerator linkage.
17. Engage the electrical connections.
18. Connect the fuel pipes and vacuum hoses.
19. Check the base (slow) and fast idle.
20. Install the air cleaner.

Carburetor Overhaul

➡**Specific directions and specifications for carburetor overhaul are usually contained in the rebuilding kit.**

Efficient carburetion depends greatly on careful cleaning and inspection during overhaul since dirt, gum, water, or varnish in or on the carburetor parts are often responsible for poor performance.

Overhaul your carburetor in a clean, dust-free area. Carefully disassemble the carburetor, referring often to the exploded views. Keep all similar and look-alike parts segregated during disassembly and cleaning to avoid accidentally interchange during assembly. Make a note of all jet sizes.

When the carburetor is disassembled, wash all parts (except diaphragms, electric choke units, pump plunger, and any other plastic, leather, fiber, or rubber parts) in clean carburetor solvent. Do not leave parts in the solvent any longer than is necessary to sufficiently loosen the deposits. Excessive cleaning may remove the special finish from the float bowl and choke valve bodies, leaving these parts unfit for service. Rinse all parts in clean solvent and blow them dry with compressed air or allow them to air dry. Wipe clean all cork, plastic, leather, and fiber parts with a clean, lint-free cloth.

Blow out all passages and jets with compressed air and be sure that there are no restrictions or blockages. Never use wire or similar tools to clean jets, fuel passages, or air bleeds. Clean all jets and valves separately to avoid accidental interchange.

Check all parts for wear or damage. If wear or damage is found, replace the defective parts. Especially check the following:

1. Check the float needle and seat for wear. If wear is found, replace the complete assembly.
2. Check the float hinge pin for wear and the float(s) for dents or distortion. Replace the float if fuel has leaked into it.
3. Check the throttle and choke shaft bores for wear or an out-of-round condition. Damage or wear to the throttle arm, shaft, or shaft bore will often require replacement of the throttle body. These parts require a close tolerance of fit. Wear may allow air leakage, which could adversely affect starting and idling.
4. Inspect the idle mixture adjusting needles for burrs or grooves. Any such condition requires replacement of the needle, since you will not be able to obtain a satisfactory idle.
5. Test the accelerator pump check valves. They should pass air one way but not the other. Test for proper seating by blowing and sucking on the valve. Replace the valve if necessary. If the valve is satisfactory, wash the valve again to remove breath moisture.
6. Check the bowl cover for warped surfaces with a straightedge.
7. Closely inspect the valves and seats for wear and damage, replacing as necessary.
8. After the carburetor is assembled, check the choke valve for freedom of operation.

Carburetor overhaul kits are recommended for each overhaul. These kits contain all gaskets and new parts to replace those that deteriorate most rapidly. Failure to replace all parts supplied with the kit (especially gaskets) can result in poor performance later.

Some carburetor manufacturers supply overhaul kits of three basic types: minor repair, major repair and gasket kits. Basically, they contain the following:

Minor Repair Kits
- All gaskets
- Float needle valve
- All diaphragms
- Spring for the pump diaphragm

Major Repair Kits
- All jets and gaskets
- All diaphragms
- Float needle valve
- Pump ball valve
- Float
- Complete intermediate rod
- Intermediate pump lever
- Some cover hold-down screws and washers

Gasket kits contain all gaskets.

After cleaning and checking all components, reassemble the carburetor, using new parts and referring to the exploded view. When reassembling, make sure that all screws and jets are tight in their seats, but do not overtighten, as the tips will be distorted. Tighten all screws gradually, in rotation. Do not tighten needle valves into their seats; uneven jetting will result. Always use new gaskets. Be sure to adjust the float level when reassembling.

CARTER YFA

Year	List Number	Application	Float Level mm (in) Set To	Float Level mm (in) OK Range	Initial Choke Valve Clearance mm (in) Set To	Initial Choke Valve Clearance mm (in) OK Range	Fast Idle Cam Setting Index mm (im) Set To	Fast Idle Cam Setting Index mm (im) OK Range	Automatic Choke Cover Setting Set To	Choke Unloader mm (in)	Fast Idle Speed Set To	Fast Idle Speed OK Range
1984	7701/ 7452	4-2.5L Auto 49-S	15.2 (0.600)	14.2–16.0 (0.570–0.630)	6.0 (0.240)	6.4–6.7 (0.255–0.265)	4.4 (0.175)	4.0–4.8 (0.160–0.190)	TR	7.6 (0.280)	2300*	±100
	7700/ 7453	4-2.5L Man 49-S	15.2 (0.600)	14.2–16.0 (0.570–0.630)	6.0 (0.240)	6.4–6.7 (0.255–0.265)	4.4 (0.175)	4.0–4.8 (0.160–0.190)	TR	7.6 (0.280)	2000*	±100
	7703/ 7454	4-2.5L Auto High Alt	15.2 (0.600)	14.2–16.0 (0.570–0.630)	6.0 (0.240)	6.4–6.7 (0.255–0.265)	4.4 (0.175)	4.0–4.8 (0.160–0.190)	TR	7.6 (0.280)	2300*	±100
	7702/ 7455	4-2.5L Man High Alt	15.2 (0.600)	14.2–16.0 (0.570–0.630)	6.0 (0.240)	6.4–6.7 (0.255–0.265)	4.4 (0.175)	4.0–4.8 (0.160–0.190)	TR	7.6 (0.280)	2000*	±100
1985	7705	4-2.5L Auto 49-S	15.2 (0.600)	14.2–16.0 (0.570–0.630)	7.1 (0.280)	6.7–7.5 (0.265–0.295)	4.4 (0.175)	4.0–4.8 (0.160–0.190)	TR	7.6 (0.280)	2300*	±100
	7704	4-2.5L Man 49-S	15.2 (0.600)	14.2–16.0 (0.570–0.630)	7.1 (0.280)	6.7–7.5 (0.265–0.295)	4.4 (0.175)	4.0–4.8 (0.160–0.190)	TR	7.6 (0.280)	2000*	±100
	7707	4-2.5L Auto High Alt	15.2 (0.600)	14.2–16.0 (0.570–0.630)	7.1 (0.280)	6.7–7.5 (0.265–0.295)	4.4 (0.175)	4.0–4.8 (0.160–0.190)	TR	7.6 (0.280)	2300*	±100
	7706	4-2.5L Man High Alt	15.2 (0.600)	14.2–16.0 (0.570–0.630)	7.1 (0.280)	6.7–7.5 (0.265–0.295)	4.4 (0.175)	4.0–4.8 (0.160–0.190)	TR	7.6 (0.280)	2000*	±100

*EGR Valve Disconnected and the engine fully warm.
TR—Tamper Resistant
(1) Measured at upper edge of choke valve and airhorn wall

86745C01

ROCHESTER 2SE/E2SE

Engine	Year	Carburetor Number	Float Level mm (in)	Air Valve Spring (Turns)	Choke Coil Lever mm (in)	Fast Idle Cam (Choke Rod) 2nd Step	Vacuum Break Primary	Air Valve Rod	Vacuum Break Secondary	Unloader
6-2.8L	1984	17084581	4.2 (5/32)	1	2.2 (0.085)	22°	26°	1°	32°	40°
		17084580	4.2 (5/32)	1	2.2 (0.085)	22°	26°	1°	32°	40°
		17084582	4.2 (5/32)	1	2.2 (0.085)	22°	26°	1°	32°	40°
		17084583	4.2 (5/32)	1	2.2 (0.085)	22°	26°	1°	32°	40°
		17084384	3.3 (1/8)	1	2.2 (0.085)	22°	25°	1°	30°	40°
	1985–86	17085380	4.2 (5/32)	1	2.2 (0.085)	22°	26°	1°	32°	40°
		17085381	4.2 (5/32)	1	2.2 (0.085)	22°	26°	1°	32°	40°
		17085382	4.2 (5/32)	1	2.2 (0.085)	22°	26°	1°	32°	40°
		17085383	4.2 (5/32)	1	2.2 (0.085)	22°	26°	1°	32°	40°
		17085384	3.3 (1/8)	1	2.2 (0.085)	22°	25°	1°	30°	40°

86745C02

Troubleshooting Basic Fuel System Problems

Problem	Cause	Solution
Engine cranks, but won't start (or is hard to start) when cold	• Empty fuel tank • Incorrect starting procedure • Defective fuel pump • No fuel in carburetor • Clogged fuel filter • Engine flooded • Defective choke	• Check for fuel in tank • Follow correct procedure • Check pump output • Check for fuel in the carburetor • Replace fuel filter • Wait 15 minutes; try again • Check choke plate
Engine cranks, but is hard to start (or does not start) when hot—(presence of fuel is assumed)	• Defective choke	• Check choke plate
Rough idle or engine runs rough	• Dirt or moisture in fuel • Clogged air filter • Faulty fuel pump	• Replace fuel filter • Replace air filter • Check fuel pump output
Engine stalls or hesitates on acceleration	• Dirt or moisture in the fuel • Dirty carburetor • Defective fuel pump • Incorrect float level, defective accelerator pump	• Replace fuel filter • Clean the carburetor • Check fuel pump output • Check carburetor
Poor gas mileage	• Clogged air filter • Dirty carburetor • Defective choke, faulty carburetor adjustment	• Replace air filter • Clean carburetor • Check carburetor
Engine is flooded (won't start accompanied by smell of raw fuel)	• Improperly adjusted choke or carburetor	• Wait 15 minutes and try again, without pumping gas pedal • If it won't start, check carburetor

86745C03

THROTTLE BODY FUEL INJECTION SYSTEM

General Information

The electronic fuel injection system is a fuel metering system with the amount of fuel delivered by the throttle body injectors (TBI) determined by an electronic signal supplied by the Electronic Control Module (ECM). The ECM monitors various engine and vehicle conditions to calculate the fuel delivery time (pulse width) of the injectors. The fuel pulse may be modified by the ECM to account for special operating conditions, such as cranking, cold starting, altitude, acceleration, and deceleration.

The ECM controls the exhaust emissions by modifying fuel delivery to achieve, as near as possible, and air/fuel ratio of 14.7:1. The injector "ON" time is determined by various inputs to the ECM. By increasing the injector pulse, more fuel is delivered, enriching the air/fuel ratio. Decreasing the injector pulse, leans the air/fuel ratio.

Relieving Fuel System Pressure

The fuel system on vehicles equipped with Throttle Body Fuel Injection (TBI) is only under pressure when the electric fuel pump is operating. As long as the fuel pump in not operating, TBI fuel system components can be removed without the need to release system pressure.

Fuel Pump

REMOVAL & INSTALLATION

▶ **See Figure 25**

1. Disconnect the negative battery cable.
2. Remove the fuel tank filler cap.
3. Using a siphon hose, drain the fuel tank below 1/4 full.
4. Block the front wheels and raise and support the rear of the vehicle with jackstands.

5. Remove the fuel inlet and outlet hoses from the sending unit Be ready to catch any spilled fuel.
6. Remove the sending unit wires.
7. Using a brass punch and hammer, remove the sending unit retaining lockring by tapping it counterclockwise.
8. Remove the sending unit, which incorporates the electric fuel pump, along with the O-ring seal from the fuel tank. Discard the O-ring.
9. Remove and discard the pump inlet filter.
10. Disconnect the fuel pump terminal wires.
11. Remove the pump outlet hose and clamp.
12. Remove the pump top mounting bracket nut and remove the pump.

To install:
13. Install a new inlet filter on the pump.
14. Assemble the pump and bracket. Connect the hose and wiring.
15. Install the unit and new O-ring in the tank. The rubber stopper on the end of the fuel return tube must be inserted into the cup in the fuel tank reservoir.

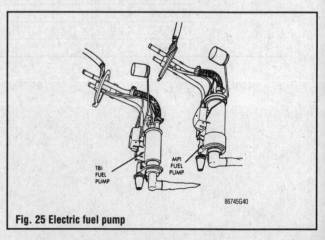

TBI FUEL PUMP

MPI FUEL PUMP

86745G40

Fig. 25 Electric fuel pump

16. Install the lockring. Carefully tap it into place until it seats against the stop on the tank.

17. Connect the hoses.

18. Connect the wiring.

19. Lower the truck, fill the tank, run the engine and check for leaks.

TESTING

1. Remove the plug from the test port and engage a test port fitting in its place.

2. Connect a fuel pressure gauge to the test port fitting.

3. Start the engine and let it idle.

4. The pressure gauge should read 14–15 psi (97–103 kPa).

5. If the pressure is correct the fuel pump is operating normally.

6. If the pressure is not correct, adjust the fuel pressure regulator to obtain the correct pressure by turning the screw at the bottom of the regulator inward to increase pressure or outward to decrease pressure.

7. If the fuel pressure is considerably above specification and adjusting fails to lower it within specification, inspect the return line for an obstruction.

8. If the fuel pressure is considerably below specification and adjusting fails to raise it within specification, momentarily pinch off the return line and recheck the pressure. If pressure has risen, replace the regulator. If it has not, check the filter and supply line for an obstruction.

✳✳ WARNING

Fuel pressure will rise to as much as 95 psi (655 kPa) when the return line is pinched shut. Shut the engine down immediately after pinching off the return line.

Throttle Body

REMOVAL & INSTALLATION

▶ **See Figure 26**

1. Disconnect the negative battery cable.

2. Remove the vacuum hoses from upper bonnet, unfasten the retaining clips and remove the upper bonnet assembly.

3. Remove the lower bonnet retaining bolts and lower bonnet.

4. Remove the throttle cable and the return spring.

5. Disengage the wire harness connector from the injector.

6. Disengage the wire harness connector from the WOT switch, ISA motor and TPS.

7. Disconnect the fuel supply and return lines from the throttle body.

8. Tag and disengage the vacuum hoses from the throttle body assembly.

9. Disengage the potentiometer wire connector.

10. Loosen throttle body retaining bolts and remove throttle body assembly from the intake manifold.

To install:

11. Clean the intake manifold and throttle body mating surfaces of old gasket material.

12. Install a new gasket and the throttle body assembly. Tighten the mounting bolts to 16 ft. lbs. (21 Nm).

13. Engage the potentiometer wire connector.

14. Engage the vacuum hoses to the throttle body.

15. Engage the fuel lines to the throttle body.

16. Engage the WOT switch, ISA motor, TPS, and injector electrical connections.

17. Install the return spring and throttle cable.

18. Install the lower bonnet and fasten the retainers.

19. Install the upper bonnet assembly, retaining clips and vacuum hoses.

20. Connect the negative battery cable.

21. Start the vehicle and check for fuel leaks.

Fuel Injector

REMOVAL & INSTALLATION

▶ **See Figure 27**

1. Disconnect the negative battery cable.

2. Remove the air cleaner and hose assembly.

3. Remove the throttle body upper and lower bonnets.

4. Remove the fuel injector wire by compressing the tabs and pulling it upwards.

5. Remove the fuel injector retainer clip screws. Remove the fuel injector retainer clip.

➡**The injector has a small locating tab that fits into a slot in the bottom of the injector bore of the throttle body. DO NOT twist the injector during removal!**

6. Using a small pair of pliers, gently grasp the center collar of the injector, between the electrical terminals, and carefully remove the injector using a lifting/rocking motion.

7. Discard the centering ring and the upper and lower O-rings.

To install:

8. Lubricate the upper and lower O-rings with transmission fluid and install them in the injector bore.

9. Install the centering ring on top of the upper O-ring and align locating ring on the injector with the slot in the housing.

10. Install the injector, retaining clip and retainer clip screws.

11. Engage the injector electrical connection.

12. Install the throttle body upper and lower bonnets and the air cleaner and hose assembly.

13. Connect the negative battery cable.

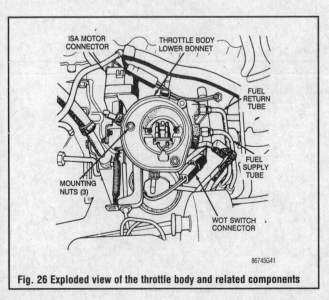

Fig. 26 Exploded view of the throttle body and related components

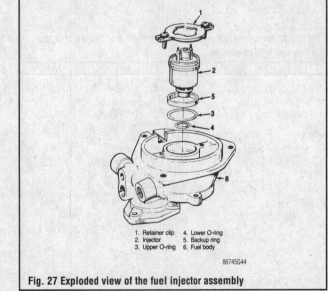

Fig. 27 Exploded view of the fuel injector assembly

TESTING

▶ **See Figures 28, 29 and 30**

1. With the ignition key/switch in the **OFF** position, unplug the fuel injector 2-way connector and use an ohmmeter to check the resistance between terminal B of the injector connector and terminal 6 of the diagnostic connector. If the resistance measures greater than 5 ohms, repair the open circuit between those terminals.

2. If the resistance measures below 5 ohms, check the resistance between terminal A of the injector connector and a good ground.

3. If the resistance measures below 5 ohms, turn the ignition key/switch to the **OFF** position and unplug the ECU connector, then check the resistance between terminal A of the injector connector and a good ground.

4. If the resistance measures greater than 5 ohms, replace the ECU.

5. Connect the ECU connector.

6. Check the resistance across the fuel injector terminals. If the resistance measures greater than 5 ohms, replace the fuel injector.

Fuel Charging Assembly

REMOVAL & INSTALLATION

▶ **See Figure 31**

1. Remove the throttle body assembly from the vehicle.
2. Remove the Torx® head screws that retain the fuel body to the throttle body. Remove and discard the gasket. Be sure to use a new gasket.
3. Installation is the reverse of removal. Be sure to use a new gasket.

Fuel Pressure Regulator

REMOVAL & INSTALLATION

▶ **See Figure 32**

1. Remove the throttle body assembly from the vehicle as outlined in this section.

✳✳ WARNING

To prevent spring pressure release, hold the regulator housing against the throttle body while removing the mounting screws.

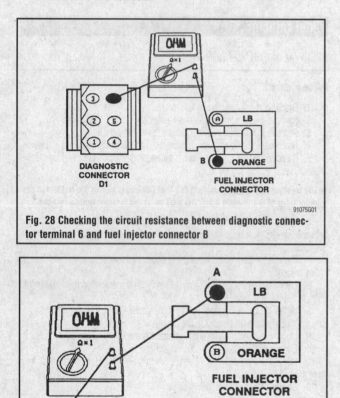

Fig. 28 Checking the circuit resistance between diagnostic connector terminal 6 and fuel injector connector B

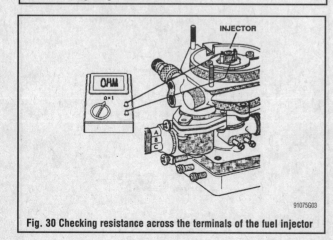

Fig. 29 Checking resistance between terminal A of the injector connector and a good ground

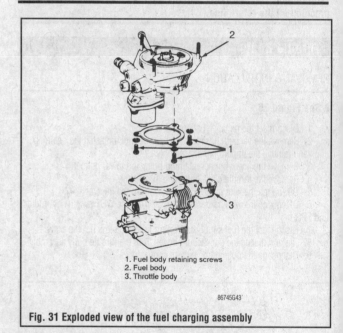

1. Fuel body retaining screws
2. Fuel body
3. Throttle body

Fig. 31 Exploded view of the fuel charging assembly

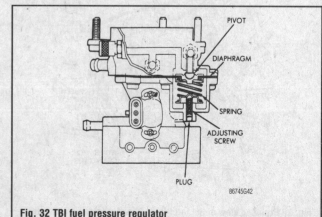

Fig. 30 Checking resistance across the terminals of the fuel injector

Fig. 32 TBI fuel pressure regulator

2. Remove the three retaining screws that hold the pressure regulator to the fuel body.

3. Disassemble the pressure regulator assembly. Note the location of the components for reassembly. Discard the gasket.

To install:

4. Install a new gasket and the regulator assembly. Tighten the three retaining screws.

MULTI-PORT FUEL INJECTION SYSTEM

General Information

All 4.0L engines from 1987 and all other engines from 1991 employ a Multi-Port Fuel Injection (MFI) system. The MFI system injects fuel into the intake manifold above the intake valve port of each cylinder through separate injectors.

The fuel system consists of the fuel tank, electric fuel pump, fuel filter, fuel tubes, fuel hoses, vacuum hoses, throttle body, and the fuel injectors.

A fuel return system is used on all vehicles. The system consists of the fuel tubes and hoses that route fuel back to the fuel tank, except on 1996 and later models. Jeep vehicles for 1996 and later do not utilize a separate fuel return line from the engine to the tank; instead, fuel is returned through the fuel pump module and back into the tank through the fuel pressure regulator (1996) or fuel filter/pressure regulator (1997 and later).

The fuel tank assembly consists of the tank, fuel gauge sending unit/fuel pump assembly, filler vent tube, rollover valve and a pressure filler cap (on some models).

Another part of the fuel system is the evaporation control system, which is designed to reduce the emission of fuel vapors into the atmosphere. The description and function of the evaporative control system is found in Section 4.

Relieving Fuel System Pressure

WITH FUEL PRESSURE TEST PORT

▶ **See Figures 33 and 34**

✳✳ CAUTION

Before opening any part of the fuel system, the pressure in the system must be relieved!

1. Disconnect the negative battery cable.
2. Remove the fuel filler cap.
3. Remove the cap from the pressure test port on the fuel rail in the engine compartment.

✳✳ CAUTION

Do not allow fuel to spray or spill on the engine exhaust manifold! Place heavy shop towels under the pressure port to absorb any escaped fuel!

Fig. 33 Removing the cap from test port on the fuel rail

5. Install the throttle body assembly as outlined in this section.

✳✳ WARNING

The pressure regulator diaphragm MUST be installed with the vent hole aligned with the vent holes in the throttle body and regulator housing!

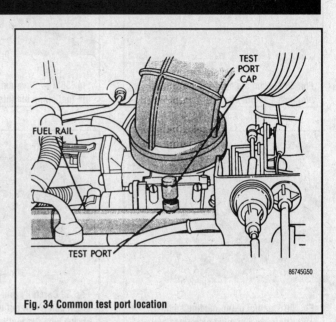

Fig. 34 Common test port location

4. Obtain the fuel pressure gauge/hose assembly from fuel pressure gauge tool 5069 or its equivalent and remove the gauge from the hose.

5. Place the gauge end of the hose into an approved gasoline container and place a shop towel under the test port.

6. To release fuel pressure, screw the other end of the hose onto the fuel pressure test port.

7. After the pressure has been relieved, remove the hose.

8. Install the test port cap.

WITHOUT FUEL PRESSURE TEST PORT

1. Remove the fuel pump relay from the Power Distribution Center (PDC). For location of the relay, refer to the label on the underside of the PDC cover.

2. Start the engine and allow it to run until it stalls out.

3. Attempt to start the engine until it will no longer run.

4. Turn the ignition key to the **OFF** position.

Fuel Pump

REMOVAL & INSTALLATION

1984–95 Models

▶ **See Figures 35 thru 41**

1. Disconnect the negative battery cable.
2. Remove the fuel tank filler cap.
3. Relieve the fuel system pressure as outlined in this section.
4. Drain the fuel from the fuel tank.
5. Raise and support the rear end on jackstands.
6. Remove the fuel inlet and outlet hoses from the sending unit. Be ready to catch any spilled fuel.
7. Disengage the sending unit wires.
8. Using a brass punch and hammer, remove the sending unit retaining lockring by tapping it counterclockwise.

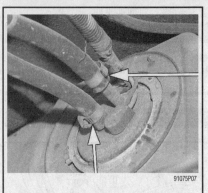

Fig. 35 Loosen the hose clamps and tag the fuel hoses before disconnecting them . . .

Fig. 36 . . . then detach the hoses from the fuel pump module/sending unit

Fig. 37 Disengage the fuel pump module/sending unit wiring harness connector

Fig. 38 The fuel pump module/sending unit retaining ring must be rotated counterclockwise for removal

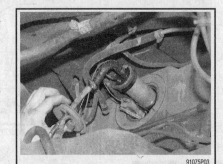

Fig. 39 Carefully pull the fuel pump module/sending unit out of the fuel tank—step shown with the fuel tank mounted on the vehicle

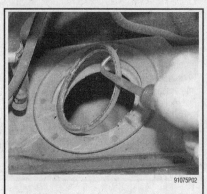

Fig. 40 Remove and discard the fuel pump module O-ring gasket

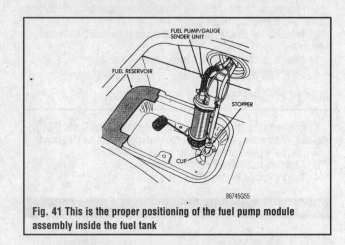

Fig. 41 This is the proper positioning of the fuel pump module assembly inside the fuel tank

9. Remove the sending unit, which incorporates the electric fuel pump, along with the O-ring seal from the fuel tank. Discard the O-ring.

10. Remove and discard the pump inlet filter.

11. Disengage the fuel pump terminal wires.

12. Remove the pump outlet hose and clamp.

13. Unfasten the pump top mounting bracket nut and remove the pump.

To install:

14. Install a new inlet filter on the pump.

15. Assemble the pump and bracket. Connect the hose and wiring.

16. Install the unit and new O-ring in the tank. The rubber stopper on the end of the fuel return tube must be inserted into the cup in the fuel tank reservoir.

17. Install the lockring. Carefully tap it into place until it seats against the stop on the tank.

18. Connect the hoses.

19. Engage the wiring.

20. Lower the vehicle, fill the tank, run the engine and check for leaks.

1996 and Later Models

▶ See Figures 42, 43 and 44

1. Drain and remove the fuel tank as outlined in this section.

2. Using tool 6856 or its equivalent, remove the module locknut which is threaded onto the fuel tank. The module will spring up when the nut is removed.

3. Remove the module.

To install:

4. Install a new gasket and place the module into the opening in the fuel tank.

5. Position a new locknut on top of the module and tighten the nut using tool 6856 or its equivalent to 40 ft. lbs. (54 Nm).

6. Install the fuel tank as outlined in this section.

TESTING

Fuel System Pressure

▶ See Figure 45

➟A DRB II scan tool is needed to perform this procedure.

1. Remove the cap from the fuel rail and connect a fuel gauge capable of reading up to 60 psi (0–414 kPa) to the test port fitting.

2. Start the vehicle and note the pressure reading at idle which should be 31 psi (214 kPa).

3. Disengage the vacuum line at the pressure regulator and note the reading. The reading should be 39 psi (269 kPa).

4. The fuel pressure should be 8–10 psi (55–69 kPa) higher with the vacuum line removed. If not check the pressure regulator vacuum line for leaks, kinks or blockage. If the line is not the problem, replace the pressure regulator.

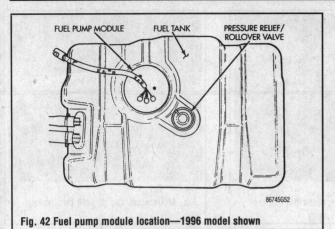

Fig. 42 Fuel pump module location—1996 model shown

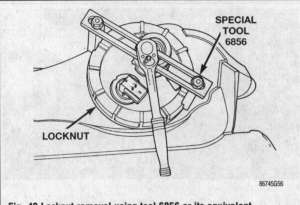

Fig. 43 Locknut removal using tool 6856 or its equivalent

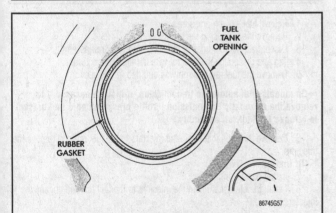

Fig. 44 Install a new gasket on the fuel tank opening

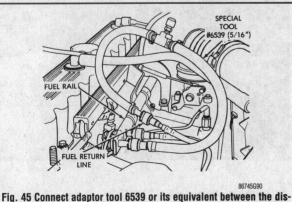

Fig. 45 Connect adaptor tool 6539 or its equivalent between the disconnected return line and fuel rail

5. If the pressure exceeds 45 psi (310 kPa) check the fuel return line for kinks or obstructions.

6. If the previous tests checked out properly and fuel pressure is correct. If not proceed as follows.

7. Disengage the fuel return line at the fuel rail and install fuel line pressure test adaptor tool 6539 or its equivalent between the disconnected return line and fuel rail.

8. Connect the fuel pressure gauge to the tool.

9. Using a DRB II scan tool activate the fuel pump and pressurize the system following the tool manufacturer's instructions.

10. Momentarily pinch the rubber hose portion of the adaptor tool. The pressure should rise 75 psi (517 (kPa) within two seconds. Do not pinch the hose for more than 3 seconds.

11. If the pressure does not rise relieve the fuel system pressure.

12. Raise the vehicle and support it safely with jackstands.

13. Disengage the fuel supply line at the inlet (fuel tank side) of the adaptor and connect fuel line pressure test adaptor tool 6631 between the fuel filter and supply line.

14. Using a DRB II scan tool activate the fuel pump and pressurize the system following the tool manufactures instructions.

15. Momentarily pinch the rubber hose portion of the adaptor tool. The pressure should rise 75 psi (517 (kPa) within two seconds. Do not pinch the hose for more than 3 seconds.

16. If the pressure does not rise, check for a restricted fuel filter and a restricted fuel supply line.

17. If the filter and line are not restricted perform the fuel pump capacity test.

Pump Capacity Test

➡**A DRB II scan tool is needed to perform this procedure.**

1. Perform the fuel system pressure test.
2. Relieve the fuel system pressure.
3. Disengage the fuel supply line at the fuel rail near the pressure regulator and connect fuel pressure test adaptor tool 6631 or its equivalent and insert the other end of the tool into an approved gasoline container.
4. Using a DRB II scan tool activate the fuel pump and pressurize the system following the tool manufactures instructions.
5. The fuel pump should deliver 0.2642 gal. (1 liter) per minute. If not the pump the pump is defective and must be replaced.

Throttle Body

REMOVAL & INSTALLATION

◆ **See Figures 46, 47, 48, 49 and 50**

1. Disconnect the battery ground cable.
2. Disconnect the air inlet tube from the throttle body.
3. Tag and disconnect the wiring and hoses from the throttle body.
4. Tag and disconnect all the control cables.
5. Remove the mounting bolts and remove the throttle body. Discard the gasket.

To install:

6. Install the new gasket, throttle body and mounting bolts. Tighten the bolts as follows;
   - On pre-1991 models; 23 ft. lbs. (31 Nm)
   - On 1991–1995 models; 9 ft. lbs. (12 Nm)
   - On the 1996–98 Grand Cherokee V-8 engines; 200 inch lbs. (23 Nm)
   - On the 1996–98 Grand Cherokee 4.0L engine; 100 inch lbs. (11 Nm)
   - On the 1996 and later Cherokee; 100 inch lbs. (11 Nm)
7. Engage the control cables.
8. Engage the wiring and hoses to the throttle body.
9. Engage the air inlet tube to the throttle body and connect the negative battery cable.
10. Installation is the reverse of removal. Tighten the mounting bolts to 23 ft. lbs. (31 Nm) pre-1991 models and 9 ft. lbs. (12 Nm) 1991 and later models.
11. If equipped with an automatic transmission, the throttle valve cable MUST be adjusted! See Section 7.

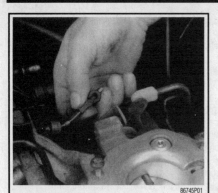

Fig. 46 Disconnect the throttle cable from the throttle body

Fig. 47 Disengage the electrical connections from the throttle body

Fig. 48 Unfasten the throttle body retaining bolts

Fig. 49 Remove the throttle body from the intake manifold

Fig. 50 Clean the old gasket from the intake manifold

Fuel Injectors

REMOVAL & INSTALLATION

▶ **See Figures 51, 52, 53, 54 and 55**

✳✳ CAUTION

Fuel system pressure must be relieved before disconnecting any fuel lines. Release fuel system pressure at the test connection using a suitable pressure gauge with a pressure bleed valve. Take precautions to avoid the risk of fire whenever working on or around any open fuel system.

1. Relieve fuel system pressure.
2. Remove the air duct at the throttle body.
3. Disconnect the fuel lines at the ends of the fuel rail assembly.
4. Tag and disengage the injector wire harness connectors.
5. Remove the fuel rail assembly as outlined in this section.

➡ **On models with automatic transmission, it may be necessary to remove the automatic transmission throttle pressure cable and bracket to remove the fuel rail assembly.**

6. Remove the clips that retain the injectors to the fuel rail and remove the injectors.
   To install:
7. Install new O-rings.
8. Install the clips that retain the injectors to the fuel rail and engage the injectors.

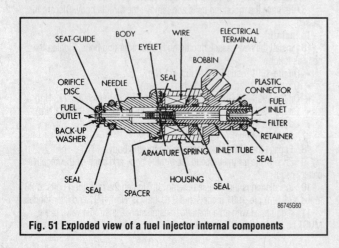

Fig. 51 Exploded view of a fuel injector internal components

Fig. 52 Remove the fuel rail . . .

Fig. 53 . . . then disengage the injector electrical connections

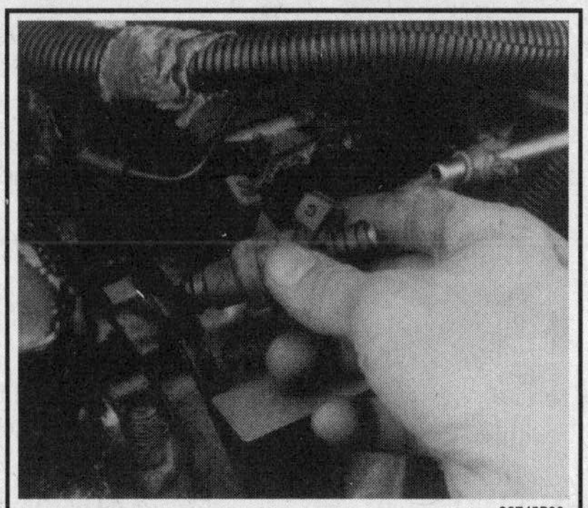

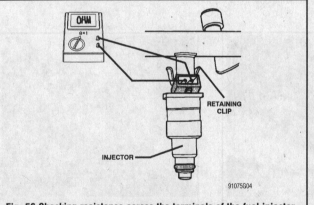

Fig. 54 Remove the fuel injector from the vehicle

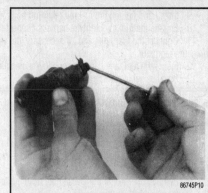

Fig. 55 Remove the old injector O-rings and replace them with new ones

9. Install the fuel rail as outlined in this section.
10. Engage the injector wire harness connectors.
11. Connect the fuel lines at the ends of the fuel rail assembly.
12. Connect the air duct at the throttle body.

TESTING

▶ See Figure 56

1. With the ignition key/switch in the **OFF** position, unplug the fuel injector connector.
2. Using an ohmmeter, check the resistance between the 2 fuel injector terminals.
3. If the resistance measures outside of 3–6 ohm range, replace the fuel injector.

Fig. 56 Checking resistance across the terminals of the fuel injector

Fuel Rail

REMOVAL & INSTALLATION

Except 5.2L and 5.9L Engines

▶ See Figures 57, 58 and 59

☀ CAUTION

Fuel system pressure must be relieved before disconnecting any fuel lines. Release fuel system pressure at the test connection using a suitable pressure gauge with a pressure bleed valve. Take precautions to avoid the risk of fire whenever working on or around any open fuel system.

1. Disconnect the negative battery cable and remove the fuel tank filler cap.
2. Relieve fuel system pressure.
3. Tag and disengage the injector wire harness connectors.

➡On models with automatic transmission, it may be necessary to remove the automatic transmission throttle pressure cable and bracket to remove the fuel rail assembly.

4. If located on the fuel rail, disengage the vacuum line from the fuel pressure regulator.
5. Disconnect the fuel supply line from the fuel rail and , if equipped, the fuel return line from the fuel pressure regulator.
6. Remove the fuel rail retaining bolts.
7. Remove the rail by gently rocking it until all the injectors are out of the intake manifold.
   To install:
8. Position the injector tips into the correct intake manifold bore and seat the injectors.

Fig. 57 Remove the fuel rail retaining bolts

Fig. 58 Disengage the vacuum line from the fuel pressure regulator, if equipped

Fig. 59 Remove the fuel rail by gently rocking it until all the injectors are out of the intake manifold

9. Install and tighten the fuel rail retaining bolts to 20 ft. lbs. (27 Nm).

10. Engage the fuel injector wire harness connectors.

11. Connect the fuel lines and , if necessary, the vacuum line to the fuel pressure regulator.

12. Install the fuel tank cap and connect the negative battery cable.

13. Start the vehicle and check for leaks.

5.2L and 5.9L Engines

▶ See Figure 60

1. Relieve the fuel system pressure as outlined in this section.

2. Disconnect the negative battery cable and remove the air duct from the throttle body.

3. Remove the throttle body assembly from the intake manifold. Refer to the proper procedure in this section.

4. If equipped with air conditioning, remove the A-shaped A/C compressor-to-intake manifold support bracket.

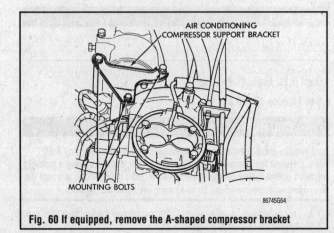

Fig. 60 If equipped, remove the A-shaped compressor bracket

5. Tag and disengage the fuel injector electrical connectors.

6. Disconnect the fuel line at the side of the fuel rail and remove the fuel rail retaining bolts.

7. Remove the rail by gently rocking the left and right fuel rail until all the injectors are out of the intake manifold.

To install:

8. Apply a small amount of engine oil to the injector O-rings.

9. Position the injector tips into the correct intake manifold bore and seat the injectors by pushing down on the left and right fuel rails until the injectors are firmly seated.

10. Install and tighten the fuel rail retaining bolts to 17 ft. lbs. (23 Nm).

11. Engage the fuel injector wire harness connectors.

12. Install the A/C compressor bracket, if equipped.

13. Install the throttle body assembly. Refer to the proper procedure as outlined in this section.

14. Engage the fuel line at the side of the fuel rail and install the air duct.

15. Connect the negative battery cable, start the vehicle and check for leaks.

Fuel Pressure Regulator

REMOVAL & INSTALLATION

Except 1996 and Later Models

▶ See Figures 61, 62, 63, 64 and 65

1. Relieve the fuel system pressure as outlined in this section.

2. Remove the vacuum line from the fuel pressure regulator.

3. Remove the regulator mounting clamp bolt and clamp from the fuel rail.

4. Remove the regulator and discard the O-ring seals.

To install:

5. Install the new O-ring seals.

6. Install the regulator and clamp onto the fuel rail and tighten the clamp mounting bolt.

Fig. 61 Disconnect the vacuum hose from the fuel pressure regulator

Fig. 62 Using a small box wrench, loosen the mounting clamp bolt . . .

Fig. 63 . . . then pull the mounting clamp off of the fuel rail assembly . . .

Fig. 64 . . . and pull the fuel pressure regulator out of the fuel rail assembly

Fig. 65 After removing the fuel pressure regulator, remove and discard the O-ring seals

7. Engage the vacuum line to the regulator, start the engine and check for leaks.

1996 Models

▶ **See Figure 66**

The fuel pressure regulator on 1996 models cannot be serviced separately. If it is found to be defective the entire fuel pump module must be replaced.

1997 and Later Models

The fuel pressure regulator is an integral component of the fuel filter, which is mounted on top of the fuel pump module, located in the fuel tank. When the fuel filter/regulator assembly requires service, the fuel tank must be removed from the vehicle, however, the fuel pump module does not need to be removed.

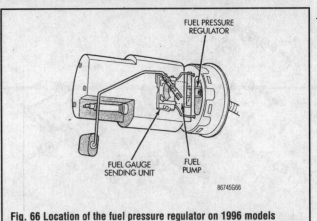

Fig. 66 Location of the fuel pressure regulator on 1996 models

DIESEL FUEL SYSTEM

The Renault-built diesel engine uses a Bosch VE4/9F injection pump, supplying Bosch KBE 48 57 injectors. A Stanadyne fuel filter cleans the system. Boost is developed by a Garret T-2 turbocharger.

Injectors

REMOVAL & INSTALLATION

▶ **See Figure 67**

➡ **A 13mm deep-well socket is necessary for this procedure.**

1. Disconnect the negative battery cable.
2. Remove the fuel return hoses and fittings from the injectors
3. Remove the high pressure lines from the injectors.
4. Remove both injector clamp nuts and washers from each injector.
5. Remove the injector clamp.
6. Pull the injector from the head.
7. Remove the copper seal and the heat shield.

To install:

8. Clean the injector bore with a brass brush.
9. Install a new heat shield and a new copper seal. Never reuse the old ones!
10. Install the injector, high pressure fuel lines (finger-tight at this time), clamps, washers and nuts.
11. Tighten the high pressure fuel lines.
12. Use new washers and install the fuel return lines. Tighten the fittings to 88 inch lbs. (10 Nm).

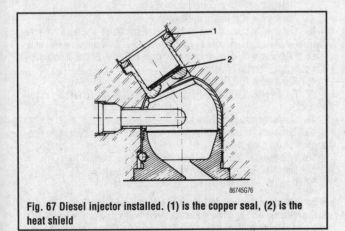

Fig. 67 Diesel injector installed. (1) is the copper seal, (2) is the heat shield

Injection Pump

REMOVAL & INSTALLATION

▶ **See Figures 68, 69, 70 and 71**

➡**Special tools are needed for this procedure.**

1. Disconnect the negative battery cable.
2. Using heavy clamps, clamp off the coolant inlet and outlet hoses at the cold start capsule. Then, disconnect them.
3. Disconnect the throttle cable and fuel shut-off solenoid wire.
4. If so equipped, disconnect the automatic transmission throttle cable, and cruise control cable.
5. Disconnect and plug the fuel delivery and return hoses.
6. Remove the alternator drive belt.
7. Remove the power steering drive belt.
8. Remove the timing belt cover.
9. Rotate the crankshaft clockwise, as viewed from the front, until No.1 piston is at TDC compression. Make sure that the camshaft sprocket timing mark is aligned with the center boss on the cylinder head cover. Make sure, also, that the injection pump sprocket timing mark is aligned with the center of the boss on the injection pump.
10. Rotate the crankshaft counterclockwise, moving the sprocket timing marks by 3 timing belt teeth.
11. Install sprocket holding tool MOT-854 or its equivalent. It may be necessary to turn the sprocket back and forth slightly to install the tool.
12. Loosen the sprocket retaining nut on the end of the injection pump shaft, and turn it out just to the end of the threads.
13. Assemble the sprocket removal tool jaws, B.Vi.48 and the short screw B.Vi.859, on the sprocket removal tool, B.Vi.2801 or there equivalents.
14. Attach the tool to the injection pump sprocket.
15. Disconnect all the fuel pipe fittings from the injectors. Plug the injectors to prevent dirt from entering the fuel system.
16. Disconnect the fuel pipe fittings from the fuel injection pump. Plug the fittings to prevent dirt from entering the system.
17. Remove the fuel line fittings from the vehicle. Remove all hoses and connectors from the injection pump assembly.
18. Remove the injection pump rear bracket retaining nuts.
19. Remove the plastic shield from under the injection pump.
20. Remove the three retaining nuts located at the front of the injection pump. The lower nut is hard to get at. It may be necessary to remove the alternator to get a wrench on it.
21. Using the sprocket removal tool, separate the injection pump from the sprocket.

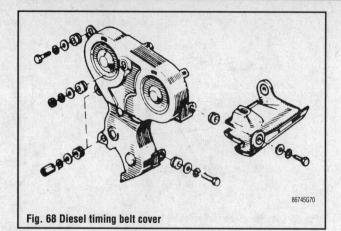

Fig. 68 Diesel timing belt cover

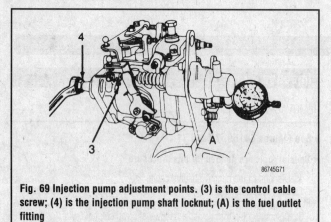

Fig. 69 Injection pump adjustment points. (3) is the control cable screw; (4) is the injection pump shaft locknut; (A) is the fuel outlet fitting

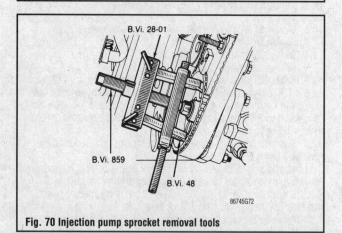

Fig. 70 Injection pump sprocket removal tools

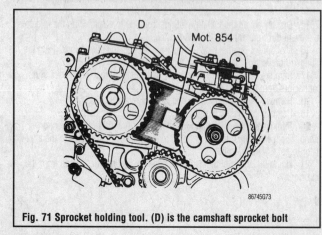

Fig. 71 Sprocket holding tool. (D) is the camshaft sprocket bolt

22. Remove the removal tool and the sprocket nut. The sprocket holding tool and the timing belt will hold the sprocket in plate. facilitating injection pump installation.

23. Remove the injection pump from the mounting brackets.

24. Remove the key from the shaft.

25. Remove the screw plug and copper washer located between the four high pressure fuel outlets, at the rear of the pump. Install dial indicator support tool Mot.856 or its equivalent in its place.

To install:

26. Install the stem of dial indicator Mot.LM in the support tool.

27. Position a locknut and nut on the end of the injection pump driveshaft.

28. Tighten the locknut against the nut.

29. Loosen the control cable set screw on the clevis, move the levers back slightly and turn the clevis pin 1/4 turn to disengage the cold start system.

30. Using the locknut, turn the pump driveshaft in the normal direction of rotation, to position the piston at bottom dead center. The dial indicator pointer will stop moving when the piston is at BDC. Zero the pointer.

31. The pump driveshaft keyway should be located just before the centerline of the number 1 fuel outlet fitting.

32. Remove the nut and locknut.

33. Insert the key in its keyway.

34. Mount the injection pump in the sprocket, aligning the key.

35. Loosely install the washers and retaining nuts on the mounting bracket studs.

36. Install the sprocket washer and retaining nut on the pump driveshaft. Tighten the nut to 37 ft. lbs. (50 Nm).

37. Remove the sprocket holding tool.

38. Rotate the crankshaft in a clockwise direction at least 2 full revolutions. Check the timing belt tension as follows:

   a. Loosen the timing belt tensioner bolts 1/2 turn each, maximum.

   b. The belt tensioner should, automatically, place the proper tension on the belt.

   c. Using belt tension gauge Ele.346-04 or its equivalent, at the straight, upper run, between the pump and camshaft sprockets, check belt deflection. Deflection should be 3–5mm when the gauge shoulder is flush with the plunger body.

39. Remove the threaded plug from the block, just behind the pump, and insert TDC Rod Mot.861 or its equivalent.

40. Slowly rotate the crankshaft clockwise until tool Mot.861 or its equivalent, can be inserted into the TDC slot in the crankshaft counterweight.

41. At this point, the dial indicator pointer should indicate a piston travel distance of 0.80–0.84mm.

42. If the indicated travel is not within specifications, adjust it as follows:

   a. Rotate the pump toward, then away from the engine to increase travel.

   b. Rotate the pump away from the engine to decrease travel

➡**Adjustment should always be made by rotation away from the engine. That's why rotation toward the engine is necessary in Step 42a.**

43. Tighten the injection pump mounting nuts.

44. Remove the TDC Rod from the counterweight slot.

45. Observe the dial indicator and rotate the crankshaft clockwise 2 full revolutions until the rod can, once again, be installed into the counterweight hole. The dial indicator should return to 0, then move to 0.80–0.84mm. If so, injection pump static timing is correct.

46. Remove the TDC Rod and install the plug.

47. Remove the dial indicator and install the washer and screw plug in the pump.

48. Connect the high pressure lines at the injectors.

49. Compress the timing control lever and install the clevis pin in the first position on the cable clamp.

50. With the lever against the clevis, tighten the setscrew.

51. Install and tighten the pump rear support bracket nuts.

52. Install all other parts in reverse order of removal.

➡**Don't confuse the fuel delivery and return hose banjo bolts. The delivery banjo bolt has two 4mm diameter holes; the return banjo bolt has a calibrated orifice. Never use the banjo bolts from one pump on another!**

STATIC TIMING ADJUSTMENT

▶ **See Figures 72 and 73**

➡**Special tools are needed for this job.**

1. Remove the injection pump as described above.
2. Remove the key from the shaft.
3. Remove the screw plug and copper washer located between the four high pressure fuel outlets, at the rear of the pump. Install dial indicator support tool Mot.856 or its equivalent in its place.
4. Install the stem of dial indicator Mot.LM or its equivalent in the support tool.
5. Position a locknut and nut on the end of the injection pump driveshaft.
6. Tighten the locknut against the nut.
7. Loosen the control cable setscrew on the clevis, move the levers back slightly and turn the clevis pin 1/4 turn to disengage the cold start system.
8. Using the locknut, turn the pump driveshaft in the normal direction of rotation, to position the piston at bottom dead center. The dial indicator pointer will stop moving when the piston is at BDC. Zero the pointer.
9. The pump driveshaft keyway should be located just before the centerline of the number 1 fuel outlet fitting.
10. Remove the nut and locknut.
11. Insert the key in its keyway.
12. Mount the injection pump in the sprocket, aligning the key.
13. Loosely install the washers and retaining nuts on the mounting bracket studs.
14. Install the sprocket washer and retaining nut on the pump driveshaft. Tighten the nut to 37 ft. lbs. (50 Nm).
15. Remove the sprocket holding tool.
16. Rotate the crankshaft in a clockwise direction at least 2 full revolutions. Check the timing belt tension as follows:
   a. Loosen the timing belt tensioner bolts 1/2 turn each, maximum.
   b. The belt tensioner should, automatically, place the proper tension on the belt.
   c. Using belt tension gauge Ele.346-04 or its equivalent, at the straight, upper run, between the pump and camshaft sprockets, check belt deflection. Deflection should be 3–5mm when the gauge shoulder is flush with the plunger body.
17. Remove the threaded plug from the block, just behind the pump, and insert TDC Rod Mot.861 or its equivalent.
18. Slowly rotate the crankshaft clockwise until tool Mot.861 or its equivalent can be inserted into the TDC slot in the crankshaft counterweight.
19. At this point, the dial indicator pointer should indicate a piston travel distance of 0.80–0.84mm.
20. If the indicated travel is not within specifications, adjust it as follows:
   a. Rotate the pump toward, then away from the engine to increase travel.
   b. Rotate the pump away from the engine to decrease lift.

➡**Adjustment should always be made by rotation away from the engine. That's why rotation toward the engine is necessary in Step 20a.**

21. Tighten the injection pump mounting nuts.
22. Remove the TDC Rod from the counterweight slot.
23. Observe the dial indicator and rotate the crankshaft clockwise 2 full revolutions until the rod can, once again, be installed into the counterweight hole. The dial indicator should return to 0, then move to 0.80–0.84mm. If so, injection pump static timing is correct.
24. Remove the TDC Rod and install the plug.
25. Remove the dial indicator and install the washer and screw plug in the pump.
26. Connect the high pressure lines at the injectors.
27. Compress the timing control lever and install the clevis pin in the first position on the cable clamp.
28. With the lever against the clevis, tighten the setscrew.
29. Install and tighten the pump rear support bracket nuts.
30. Install all other parts in reverse order of removal.

➡**Don't confuse the fuel delivery and return hose banjo bolts. The delivery banjo bolt has two 4mm diameter holes; the return banjo bolt has a calibrated orifice. Never use the banjo bolts from one pump on another!**

Cold Start Capsule

REMOVAL & INSTALLATION

▶ **See Figures 74 and 75**

➡**Two 6mm x 70mm threaded rods and nuts are necessary for this procedure.**

1. Using heavy clamps, clamp off the coolant lines at the cold start capsule.

✳✳ CAUTION

Follow this procedure exactly when removing the cold start capsule. There is a great deal of spring tension behind the housings.

2. Remove one of the capsule retaining bolts and replace it with a 6mm diameter x 70mm long threaded rod.
3. Thread a nut down the rod and tighten it.

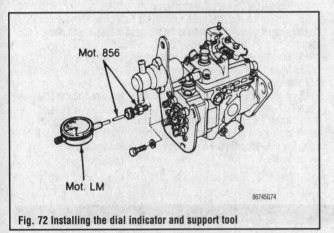
Fig. 72 Installing the dial indicator and support tool

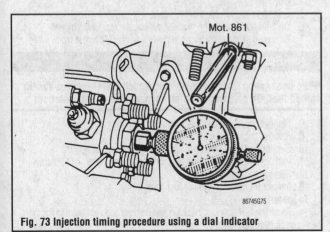
Fig. 73 Injection timing procedure using a dial indicator

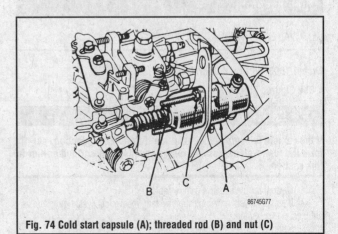
Fig. 74 Cold start capsule (A); threaded rod (B) and nut (C)

4. Remove the other bolt and replace it with a similar rod and nut.

5. Back off the two nuts, alternately and evenly, to release spring tension. Separate the capsule housing from the bracket and cable housing.

6. Remove the threaded rods.

7. Insert a 26mm OD section of tubing into the end of the capsule housing and hit the end sharply with a mallet to loosen the slotted retaining nut. Remove the nut, capsule and O-ring.

8. Assembly is the reverse of disassembly. Use the threaded rods to position the capsule housing, tightening them, alternately and evenly, then, replacing them, one at a time, with the bolts. Tighten the bolts securely.

Glow Plugs

REMOVAL & INSTALLATION

1. Disconnect the battery ground.
2. Disconnect the wire from the glow plug.
3. Unscrew the glow plug from the head.
4. Installation is the reverse of removal. Use a small amount of anti-seize compound on the glow plug threads. Tighten the glow plug to 20 ft. lbs. (27 Nm).

Cold Start System

ADJUSTMENT

➡**The engine must be cold, shut off for at least 2 1/2 hours, before starting this procedure. Special tools and shims are necessary for this procedure.**

1. Make sure that the timing control lever is contacting the stop. If not, loosen the setscrew and turn the clevis 1/4 turn.

2. Remove the TDC slot access hole plug from the block, just behind the pump.

3. Rotate the crankshaft clockwise 2 full revolutions and insert the TDC Rod Mot.861 or its equivalent, into the crankshaft counterweight TDC slot.

4. Move the timing control lever to the detent position.

5. Make sure that the clearance between the stop and the timing control lever is now 0.5mm. If not, turn the throttle stop
   adjustment screw, at the control lever, until it is.

6. Insert a 5.5mm shim between the timing control lever and the stop.

7. Insert a 3.0mm shim between the throttle lever and the idle stop screw.

8. Loosen the pivot ball nut and slide the pivot ball until it contacts the throttle lever. Tighten the nut.

9. Remove the shims.

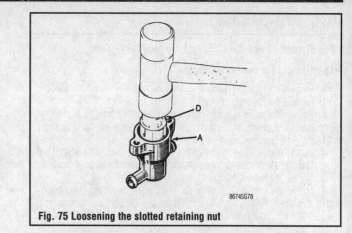

Fig. 75 Loosening the slotted retaining nut

10. The temperature of the capsule is now important. If the engine has been shut down for at least 2 1/2 hours, the capsule temperature should be the same as the ambient air temperature. Select a shim as follows:
   - below 66°F (19°C): 6.5mm
   - 66–71°F (19–22°C): 5.9mm
   - 72–76°F (22–24°C): 5.5mm
   - 77–85°F (25–29°C): 4.75mm
   - 86–94°F (30–34°C): 4.0mm
   - 95–104°F (35–40°C): 3.25mm

11. When the shim thickness has been determined, place the shim between the timing control lever and the stop.

12. Align the clevis and the throttle cable stop so that both screw heads are in the same plane.

13. Tighten the throttle cable and position the clevis and the throttle stop so that they contact the timing control lever.

14. Tighten the throttle cable stop screw.

15. Remove the shim and make sure that the distance between the stop and the timing control lever is the same as the thickness of the shim. Correct it if necessary.

16. Start the engine and run it to normal operating temperature.

17. Make sure that the throttle lever and timing control lever are against their stops and move freely.

18. If necessary, adjust the idle with the idle adjustment screw to obtain an idle of 800 rpm.

19. Insert a 6.5mm shim between the timing control lever and its stop and measure the clearance between the throttle control lever and its stop. The clearance should be 3.0mm. If not, repeat the above adjustments.

FUEL TANK

Tank Assembly

REMOVAL & INSTALLATION

Except 1996–98 Grand Cherokee

♦ See Figures 76 and 77

※※ CAUTION

If the vehicle is equipped with the Multi-Point Fuel Injection, perform the fuel system pressure release sequence described earlier in this section.

1. Disconnect the negative battery cable.
2. If equipped with a fuel injection system, relieve fuel system pressure as outlined in this section.
3. Remove the fuel filler cap.
4. Drain the fuel tank.
5. Raise and support the vehicle safely.
6. On 1986–91 Comanche models, remove the rear driveshaft.
7. Tag and disengage all hoses and wires connected to the tank.

※※ CAUTION

Wrap heavy shop towels around disconnected fuel lines to absorb spilled fuel. Be prepared to catch any fuel that is not absorbed!

8. Remove the skid plate, if equipped.
9. Remove the fuel tank shield.
10. Support the tank with a floor jack and remove the strap nuts.
11. Partially lower the tank and disconnect the tank vapor vent hoses.
12. Remove the tank.
13. Inspect for rotted or leaking fuel lines.

To install:

14. Raise the fuel tank into position and connect the vent hose to the filler neck and tighten the clamp.

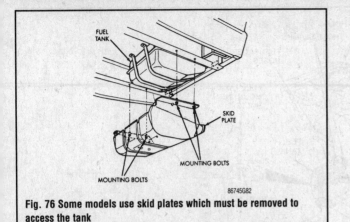

Fig. 76 Some models use skid plates which must be removed to access the tank

15. Wrap the support straps around the fuel tank, tighten them to 100 inch lbs. (11 Nm). If 3 straps are used, tighten the center strap to 43 inch lbs. (4 Nm) and the outer straps to 65 inch lbs. (7 Nm).

16. Install the tank shield and skid plate.

17. Engage all wires and hoses and lower the vehicle.

18. Fill the tank and install the filler cap.

19. Connect the negative battery cable.

20. Start the vehicle and check for leaks.

1996–98 Grand Cherokee

♦ See Figure 78

1. Disconnect the negative battery cable and relieve the fuel system pressure.

2. Raise and support the vehicle with jackstands.

3. Remove the fuel tank filler hose and vent hose clamps.

4. Remove both tubes at the filler tube.

5. If equipped remove the tow hooks and trailer hitch.

6. Remove the fuel tank skid plate retaining nuts/bolts, if equipped.

7. Unfasten the exhaust tailpipe heat shield retaining bolts and remove the shield.

8. Place a hydraulic jack under the tank.

❋❋ CAUTION

Place a shop towel around fuel lines to catch any fuel spillage.

9. Tag and disengage the fuel supply line, fuel vent line and fuel pump module electrical connection.

10. Remove the tank strap nuts and position the straps away from the tank.

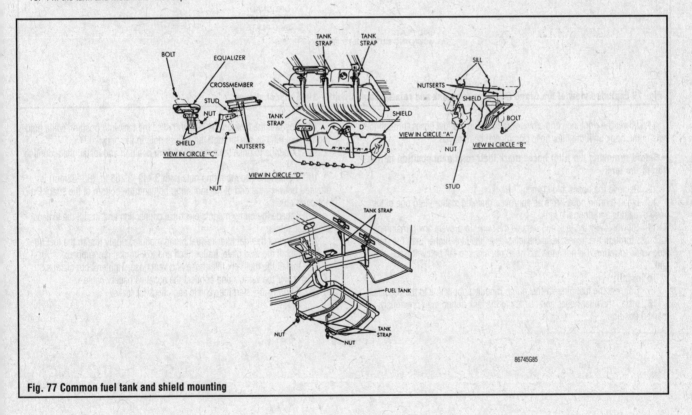

Fig. 77 Common fuel tank and shield mounting

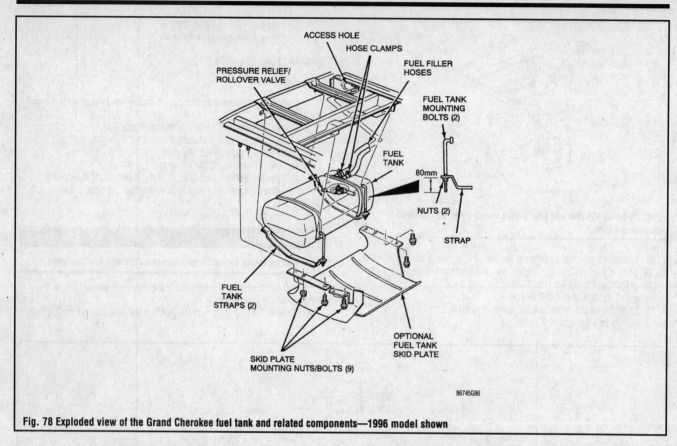

Fig. 78 Exploded view of the Grand Cherokee fuel tank and related components—1996 model shown

11. Lower the right side of the tank while feeding the fuel hoses through the hole in the body until the filler hose clamps can be removed.

➡**Before removing the filler hoses mark their rotational position in relation to the tank**

12. Remove the hoses and clamps.

13. Insert a drain hose (from an approved draining station) into one of the hose openings and drain the tank.

14. Slowly lower the jack and remove the tank. To prevent any remaining fuel loss through the hoses, keep the left side of the tank higher than the right side while lowering. Do not allow the hose openings to fall below the top of the tank.

To install:

15. Connect the fuel filter-to-fuel pump module supply line to the module.

16. Install the filler hoses and clamps to the tank noting their previously marked position.

17. Position the tank on the jack and raise the tank into position while guiding the fuel filler hoses through the access hole in the body.

18. Continue to raise the tank until it is in position and install the mounting straps.

19. Tighten the two mounting nuts until 3.149–3.268 in. (80–83mm) is attained between the end of the mounting bolt and the bottom of the strap. Do not overtighten.

20. Engage the pump module electrical connection and install the exhaust pipe heat shield.

21. Connect the fuel filter-to-fuel pump module supply line to the fuel filter.

22. Install the skid plate, trailer hitch and tow hooks, if equipped.

23. Install the fuel tank filler hose and vent hose. Tighten both clamps.

24. Lower the vehicle and connect the negative battery cable.

25. Fill the tank, start the vehicle and check for leaks.

6

CHASSIS ELECTRICAL

UNDERSTANDING AND TROUBLESHOOTING ELECTRICAL SYSTEMS

Basic Electrical Theory

♦ See Figure 1

For any 12 volt, negative ground, electrical system to operate, the electricity must travel in a complete circuit. This simply means that current (power) from the positive (+) terminal of the battery must eventually return to the negative (–) terminal of the battery. Along the way, this current will travel through wires, fuses, switches and components. If, for any reason, the flow of current through the circuit is interrupted, the component fed by that circuit will cease to function properly.

Perhaps the easiest way to visualize a circuit is to think of connecting a light bulb (with two wires attached to it) to the battery—one wire attached to the negative (–) terminal of the battery and the other wire to the positive (+) terminal. With the two wires touching the battery terminals, the circuit would be complete and the light bulb would illuminate. Electricity would follow a path from the battery to the bulb and back to the battery. It's easy to see that with longer wires on our light bulb, it could be mounted anywhere. Further, one wire could be fitted with a switch so that the light could be turned on and off.

The normal automotive circuit differs from this simple example in two ways. First, instead of having a return wire from the bulb to the battery, the current travels through the frame of the vehicle. Since the negative (–) battery cable is attached to the frame (made of electrically conductive metal), the frame of the vehicle can serve as a ground wire to complete the circuit. Secondly, most automotive circuits contain multiple components which receive power from a single circuit. This lessens the amount of wire needed to power components on the vehicle.

HOW DOES ELECTRICITY WORK: THE WATER ANALOGY

Electricity is the flow of electrons—the subatomic particles that constitute the outer shell of an atom. Electrons spin in an orbit around the center core of an atom. The center core is comprised of protons (positive charge) and neutrons (neutral charge). Electrons have a negative charge and balance out the positive charge of the protons. When an outside force causes the number of electrons to unbalance the charge of the protons, the electrons will split off the atom and look for another atom to balance out. If this imbalance is kept up, electrons will continue to move and an electrical flow will exist.

Many people have been taught electrical theory using an analogy with water. In a comparison with water flowing through a pipe, the electrons would be the water and the wire is the pipe.

The flow of electricity can be measured much like the flow of water through a pipe. The unit of measurement used is amperes, frequently abbreviated as amps

(a). You can compare amperage to the volume of water flowing through a pipe. When connected to a circuit, an ammeter will measure the actual amount of current flowing through the circuit. When relatively few electrons flow through a circuit, the amperage is low. When many electrons flow, the amperage is high.

Water pressure is measured in units such as pounds per square inch (psi); The electrical pressure is measured in units called volts (v). When a voltmeter is connected to a circuit, it is measuring the electrical pressure.

The actual flow of electricity depends not only on voltage and amperage, but also on the resistance of the circuit. The higher the resistance, the higher the force necessary to push the current through the circuit. The standard unit for measuring resistance is an ohm. Resistance in a circuit varies depending on the amount and type of components used in the circuit. The main factors which determine resistance are:

• Material—some materials have more resistance than others. Those with high resistance are said to be insulators. Rubber materials (or rubber-like plastics) are some of the most common insulators used in vehicles as they have a very high resistance to electricity. Very low resistance materials are said to be conductors. Copper wire is among the best conductors. Silver is actually a superior conductor to copper and is used in some relay contacts, but its high cost prohibits its use as common wiring. Most automotive wiring is made of copper.

• Size—the larger the wire size being used, the less resistance the wire will have. This is why components which use large amounts of electricity usually have large wires supplying current to them.

• Length—for a given thickness of wire, the longer the wire, the greater the resistance. The shorter the wire, the less the resistance. When determining the proper wire for a circuit, both size and length must be considered to design a circuit that can handle the current needs of the component.

• Temperature—with many materials, the higher the temperature, the greater the resistance (positive temperature coefficient). Some materials exhibit the opposite trait of lower resistance with higher temperatures (negative temperature coefficient). These principles are used in many of the sensors on the engine.

OHM'S LAW

There is a direct relationship between current, voltage and resistance. The relationship between current, voltage and resistance can be summed up by a statement known as Ohm's law.

Voltage (E) is equal to amperage (I) times resistance (R): $E = I \times R$
Other forms of the formula are $R = E/I$ and $I = E/R$

In each of these formulas, E is the voltage in volts, I is the current in amps and R is the resistance in ohms. The basic point to remember is that as the resistance of a circuit goes up, the amount of current that flows in the circuit will go down, if voltage remains the same.

The amount of work that the electricity can perform is expressed as power. The unit of power is the watt (w). The relationship between power, voltage and current is expressed as:

Power (w) is equal to amperage (I) times voltage (E): $W = I \times E$

This is only true for direct current (DC) circuits; The alternating current formula is a tad different, but since the electrical circuits in most vehicles are DC type, we need not get into AC circuit theory.

Electrical Components

POWER SOURCE

Power is supplied to the vehicle by two devices: The battery and the alternator. The battery supplies electrical power during starting or during periods when the current demand of the vehicle's electrical system exceeds the output capacity of the alternator. The alternator supplies electrical current when the engine is running. Just not does the alternator supply the current needs of the vehicle, but it recharges the battery.

The Battery

In most modern vehicles, the battery is a lead/acid electrochemical device consisting of six 2 volt subsections (cells) connected in series, so that the unit

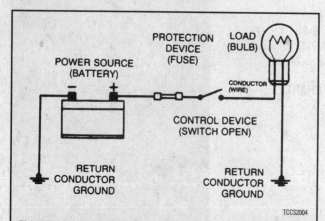

TCCS2004

Fig. 1 This example illustrates a simple circuit. When the switch is closed, power from the positive (+) battery terminal flows through the fuse and the switch, and then to the light bulb. The light illuminates and the circuit is completed through the ground wire back to the negative (–) battery terminal. In reality, the two ground points shown in the illustration are attached to the metal frame of the vehicle, which completes the circuit back to the battery

is capable of producing approximately 12 volts of electrical pressure. Each sub-section consists of a series of positive and negative plates held a short distance apart in a solution of sulfuric acid and water.

The two types of plates are of dissimilar metals. This sets up a chemical reaction, and it is this reaction which produces current flow from the battery when its positive and negative terminals are connected to an electrical load . The power removed from the battery is replaced by the alternator, restoring the battery to its original chemical state.

The Alternator

On some vehicles there isn't an alternator, but a generator. The difference is that an alternator supplies alternating current which is then changed to direct current for use on the vehicle, while a generator produces direct current. Alternators tend to be more efficient and that is why they are used.

Alternators and generators are devices that consist of coils of wires wound together making big electromagnets. One group of coils spins within another set and the interaction of the magnetic fields causes a current to flow. This current is then drawn off the coils and fed into the vehicles electrical system.

GROUND

Two types of grounds are used in automotive electric circuits. Direct ground components are grounded to the frame through their mounting points. All other components use some sort of ground wire which is attached to the frame or chassis of the vehicle. The electrical current runs through the chassis of the vehicle and returns to the battery through the ground (–) cable; if you look, you'll see that the battery ground cable connects between the battery and the frame or chassis of the vehicle.

➡️ **It should be noted that a good percentage of electrical problems can be traced to bad grounds.**

PROTECTIVE DEVICES

▶ **See Figure 2**

It is possible for large surges of current to pass through the electrical system of your vehicle. If this surge of current were to reach the load in the circuit, the surge could burn it out or severely damage it. It can also overload the wiring, causing the harness to get hot and melt the insulation. To prevent this, fuses, circuit breakers and/or fusible links are connected into the supply wires of the electrical system. These items are nothing more than a built-in weak spot in the system. When an abnormal amount of current flows through the system, these protective devices work as follows to protect the circuit:

• Fuse—when an excessive electrical current passes through a fuse, the fuse ``blows'' (the conductor melts) and opens the circuit, preventing the passage of current.
• Circuit Breaker—a circuit breaker is basically a self-repairing fuse. It will open the circuit in the same fashion as a fuse, but when the surge subsides, the circuit breaker can be reset and does not need replacement.
• Fusible Link—a fusible link (fuse link or main link) is a short length of special, high temperature insulated wire that acts as a fuse. When an excessive electrical current passes through a fusible link, the thin gauge wire inside the link melts, creating an intentional open to protect the circuit. To repair the circuit, the link must be replaced. Some newer type fusible links are housed in plug-in modules, which are simply replaced like a fuse, while older type fusible links must be cut and spliced if they melt. Since this link is very early in the electrical path, it's the first place to look if nothing on the vehicle works, yet the battery seems to be charged and is properly connected.

✳✳ CAUTION

Always replace fuses, circuit breakers and fusible links with identically rated components. Under no circumstances should a component of higher or lower amperage rating be substituted.

SWITCHES & RELAYS

▶ **See Figures 3 and 4**

Switches are used in electrical circuits to control the passage of current. The most common use is to open and close circuits between the battery and the various electric devices in the system. Switches are rated according to the amount of amperage they can handle. If a sufficient amperage rated switch is not used in a circuit, the switch could overload and cause damage.

Some electrical components which require a large amount of current to operate use a special switch called a relay. Since these circuits carry a large amount of current, the thickness of the wire in the circuit is also greater. If this large wire were connected from the load to the control switch, the switch would have to carry the high amperage load and the fairing or dash would be twice as large to accommodate the increased size of the wiring harness. To prevent these problems, a relay is used.

Relays are composed of a coil and a set of contacts. When the coil has a current passed though it, a magnetic field is formed and this field causes the contacts to move together, completing the circuit. Most relays are normally open, preventing current from passing through the circuit, but they can take any electrical form depending on the job they are intended to do. Relays can be considered ``remote control switches.'' They allow a smaller current to operate devices that require higher amperages. When a small current operates the coil, a larger

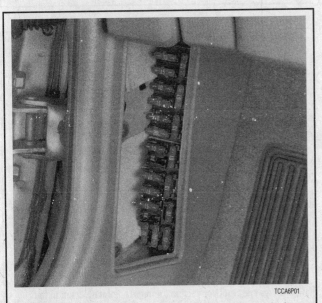

TCCA6P01

Fig. 2 Most vehicles use one or more fuse panels. This one is located on the driver's side kick panel

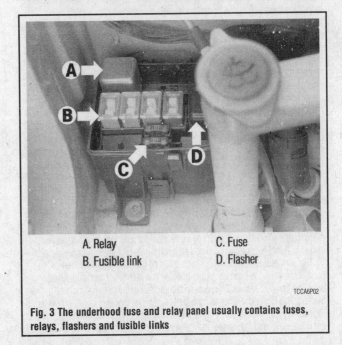

A. Relay   C. Fuse
B. Fusible link   D. Flasher

TCCA6P02

Fig. 3 The underhood fuse and relay panel usually contains fuses, relays, flashers and fusible links

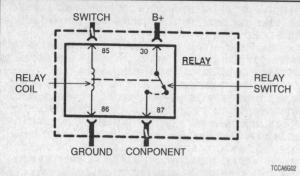

Fig. 4 Relays are composed of a coil and a switch. These two components are linked together so that when one operates, the other operates at the same time. The large wires in the circuit are connected from the battery to one side of the relay switch (B+) and from the opposite side of the relay switch to the load (component). Smaller wires are connected from the relay coil to the control switch for the circuit and from the opposite side of the relay coil to ground

current is allowed to pass by the contacts. Some common circuits which may use relays are the horn, headlights, starter, electric fuel pump and other high draw ciruits.

LOAD

Every electrical circuit must include a ``load" (something to use the electricity coming from the source). Without this load, the battery would attempt to deliver its entire power supply from one pole to another. This is called a ``short circuit." All this electricity would take a short cut to ground and cause a great amount of damage to other components in the circuit by developing a tremendous amount of heat. This condition could develop sufficient heat to melt the insulation on all the surrounding wires and reduce a multiple wire cable to a lump of plastic and copper.

WIRING & HARNESSES

The average vehicle contains meters and meters of wiring, with hundreds of individual connections. To protect the many wires from damage and to keep them from becoming a confusing tangle, they are organized into bundles, enclosed in plastic or taped together and called wiring harnesses. Different harnesses serve different parts of the vehicle. Individual wires are color coded to help trace them through a harness where sections are hidden from view.

Automotive wiring or circuit conductors can be either single strand wire, multi-strand wire or printed circuitry. Single strand wire has a solid metal core and is usually used inside such components as alternators, motors, relays and other devices. Multi-strand wire has a core made of many small strands of wire twisted together into a single conductor. Most of the wiring in an automotive electrical system is made up of multi-strand wire, either as a single conductor or grouped together in a harness. All wiring is color coded on the insulator, either as a solid color or as a colored wire with an identification stripe. A printed circuit is a thin film of copper or other conductor that is printed on an insulator backing. Occasionally, a printed circuit is sandwiched between two sheets of plastic for more protection and flexibility. A complete printed circuit, consisting of conductors, insulating material and connectors for lamps or other components is called a printed circuit board. Printed circuitry is used in place of individual wires or harnesses in places where space is limited, such as behind instrument panels.

Since automotive electrical systems are very sensitive to changes in resistance, the selection of properly sized wires is critical when systems are repaired. A loose or corroded connection or a replacement wire that is too small for the circuit will add extra resistance and an additional voltage drop to the circuit.

The wire gauge number is an expression of the cross-section area of the conductor. Vehicles from countries that use the metric system will typically describe the wire size as its cross-sectional area in square millimeters. In this method, the larger the wire, the greater the number. Another common system for expressing wire size is the American Wire Gauge (AWG) system. As gauge number increases, area decreases and the wire becomes smaller. An 18 gauge wire

is smaller than a 4 gauge wire. A wire with a higher gauge number will carry less current than a wire with a lower gauge number. Gauge wire size refers to the size of the strands of the conductor, not the size of the complete wire with insulator. It is possible, therefore, to have two wires of the same gauge with different diameters because one may have thicker insulation than the other.

It is essential to understand how a circuit works before trying to figure out why it doesn't. An electrical schematic shows the electrical current paths when a circuit is operating properly. Schematics break the entire electrical system down into individual circuits. In a schematic, usually no attempt is made to represent wiring and components as they physically appear on the vehicle; switches and other components are shown as simply as possible. Face views of harness connectors show the cavity or terminal locations in all multi-pin connectors to help locate test points.

CONNECTORS

▶ See Figures 5 and 6

Three types of connectors are commonly used in automotive applications—weatherproof, molded and hard shell.

• Weatherproof—these connectors are most commonly used where the connector is exposed to the elements. Terminals are protected against moisture

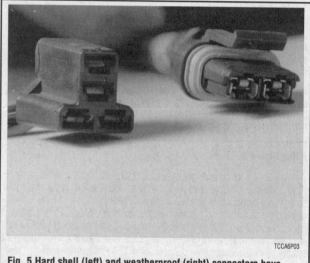

Fig. 5 Hard shell (left) and weatherproof (right) connectors have replaceable terminals

Fig. 6 Weatherproof connectors are most commonly used in the engine compartment or where the connector is exposed to the elements

and dirt by sealing rings which provide a weathertight seal. All repairs require the use of a special terminal and the tool required to service it. Unlike standard blade type terminals, these weatherproof terminals cannot be straightened once they are bent. Make certain that the connectors are properly seated and all of the sealing rings are in place when connecting leads.

- Molded—these connectors require complete replacement of the connector if found to be defective. This means splicing a new connector assembly into the harness. All splices should be soldered to insure proper contact. Use care when probing the connections or replacing terminals in them, as it is possible to create a short circuit between opposite terminals. If this happens to the wrong terminal pair, it is possible to damage certain components. Always use jumper wires between connectors for circuit checking and NEVER probe through weatherproof seals.
- Hard Shell—unlike molded connectors, the terminal contacts in hard-shell connectors can be replaced. Replacement usually involves the use of a special terminal removal tool that depresses the locking tangs (barbs) on the connector terminal and allows the connector to be removed from the rear of the shell. The connector shell should be replaced if it shows any evidence of burning, melting, cracks, or breaks. Replace individual terminals that are burnt, corroded, distorted or loose.

Test Equipment

Pinpointing the exact cause of trouble in an electrical circuit is most times accomplished by the use of special test equipment. The following describes different types of commonly used test equipment and briefly explains how to use them in diagnosis. In addition to the information covered below, the tool manufacturer's instructions booklet (provided with the tester) should be read and clearly understood before attempting any test procedures.

JUMPER WIRES

✷✷ CAUTION

Never use jumper wires made from a thinner gauge wire than the circuit being tested. If the jumper wire is of too small a gauge, it may overheat and possibly melt. Never use jumpers to bypass high resistance loads in a circuit. Bypassing resistances, in effect, creates a short circuit. This may, in turn, cause damage and fire. Jumper wires should only be used to bypass lengths of wire or to simulate switches.

Jumper wires are simple, yet extremely valuable, pieces of test equipment. They are basically test wires which are used to bypass sections of a circuit. Although jumper wires can be purchased, they are usually fabricated from lengths of standard automotive wire and whatever type of connector (alligator clip, spade connector or pin connector) that is required for the particular application being tested. In cramped, hard-to-reach areas, it is advisable to have insulated boots over the jumper wire terminals in order to prevent accidental grounding. It is also advisable to include a standard automotive fuse in any jumper wire. This is commonly referred to as a ``fused jumper''. By inserting an in-line fuse holder between a set of test leads, a fused jumper wire can be used for bypassing open circuits. Use a 5 amp fuse to provide protection against voltage spikes.

Jumper wires are used primarily to locate open electrical circuits, on either the ground (–) side of the circuit or on the power (+) side. If an electrical component fails to operate, connect the jumper wire between the component and a good ground. If the component operates only with the jumper installed, the ground circuit is open. If the ground circuit is good, but the component does not operate, the circuit between the power feed and component may be open. By moving the jumper wire successively back from the component toward the power source, you can isolate the area of the circuit where the open is located. When the component stops functioning, or the power is cut off, the open is in the segment of wire between the jumper and the point previously tested.

You can sometimes connect the jumper wire directly from the battery to the ``hot'' terminal of the component, but first make sure the component uses 12 volts in operation. Some electrical components, such as fuel injectors or sensors, are designed to operate on about 4 to 5 volts, and running 12 volts directly to these components will cause damage.

TEST LIGHTS

▶ **See Figure 7**

The test light is used to check circuits and components while electrical current is flowing through them. It is used for voltage and ground tests. To use a 12 volt test light, connect the ground clip to a good ground and probe wherever necessary with the pick. The test light will illuminate when voltage is detected. This does not necessarily mean that 12 volts (or any particular amount of voltage) is present; it only means that some voltage is present. It is advisable before using the test light to touch its ground clip and probe across the battery posts or terminals to make sure the light is operating properly.

✷✷ WARNING

Do not use a test light to probe electronic ignition, spark plug or coil wires. Never use a pick-type test light to probe wiring on computer controlled systems unless specifically instructed to do so. Any wire insulation that is pierced by the test light probe should be taped and sealed with silicone after testing.

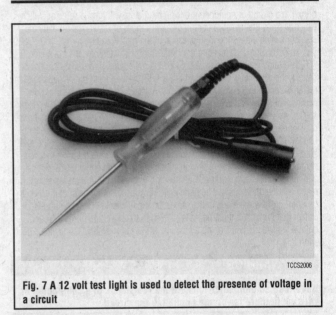

TCCS2006

Fig. 7 A 12 volt test light is used to detect the presence of voltage in a circuit

Like the jumper wire, the 12 volt test light is used to isolate opens in circuits. But, whereas the jumper wire is used to bypass the open to operate the load, the 12 volt test light is used to locate the presence of voltage in a circuit. If the test light illuminates, there is power up to that point in the circuit; if the test light does not illuminate, there is an open circuit (no power). Move the test light in successive steps back toward the power source until the light in the handle illuminates. The open is between the probe and a point which was previously probed.

The self-powered test light is similar in design to the 12 volt test light, but contains a 1.5 volt penlight battery in the handle. It is most often used in place of a multimeter to check for open or short circuits when power is isolated from the circuit (continuity test).

The battery in a self-powered test light does not provide much current. A weak battery may not provide enough power to illuminate the test light even when a complete circuit is made (especially if there is high resistance in the circuit). Always make sure that the test battery is strong. To check the battery, briefly touch the ground clip to the probe; if the light glows brightly, the battery is strong enough for testing.

➡ **A self-powered test light should not be used on any computer controlled system or component. The small amount of electricity transmitted by the test light is enough to damage many electronic automotive components.**

MULTIMETERS

Multimeters are an extremely useful tool for troubleshooting electrical problems. They can be purchased in either analog or digital form and have a price range to suit any budget. A multimeter is a voltmeter, ammeter and ohmmeter (along with other features) combined into one instrument. It is often used when testing solid state circuits because of its high input impedance (usually 10 megaohms or more). A brief description of the multimeter main test functions follows:

• Voltmeter—the voltmeter is used to measure voltage at any point in a circuit, or to measure the voltage drop across any part of a circuit. Voltmeters usually have various scales and a selector switch to allow the reading of different voltage ranges. The voltmeter has a positive and a negative lead. To avoid damage to the meter, always connect the negative lead to the negative (–) side of the circuit (to ground or nearest the ground side of the circuit) and connect the positive lead to the positive (+) side of the circuit (to the power source or the nearest power source). Note that the negative voltmeter lead will always be black and that the positive voltmeter will always be some color other than black (usually red).

• Ohmmeter—the ohmmeter is designed to read resistance (measured in ohms) in a circuit or component. Most ohmmeters will have a selector switch which permits the measurement of different ranges of resistance (usually the selector switch allows the multiplication of the meter reading by 10, 100, 1,000 and 10,000). Some ohmmeters are ``auto-ranging'' which means the meter itself will determine which scale to use. Since the meters are powered by an internal battery, the ohmmeter can be used like a self-powered test light. When the ohmmeter is connected, current from the ohmmeter flows through the circuit or component being tested. Since the ohmmeter's internal resistance and voltage are known values, the amount of current flow through the meter depends on the resistance of the circuit or component being tested. The ohmmeter can also be used to perform a continuity test for suspected open circuits. In using the meter for making continuity checks, do not be concerned with the actual resistance readings. Zero resistance, or any ohm reading, indicates continuity in the circuit. Infinite resistance indicates an opening in the circuit. A high resistance reading where there should be none indicates a problem in the circuit. Checks for short circuits are made in the same manner as checks for open circuits, except that the circuit must be isolated from both power and normal ground. Infinite resistance indicates no continuity, while zero resistance indicates a dead short.

✳✳ WARNING

Never use an ohmmeter to check the resistance of a component or wire while there is voltage applied to the circuit.

• Ammeter—an ammeter measures the amount of current flowing through a circuit in units called amperes or amps. At normal operating voltage, most circuits have a characteristic amount of amperes, called ``current draw'' which can be measured using an ammeter. By referring to a specified current draw rating, then measuring the amperes and comparing the two values, one can determine what is happening within the circuit to aid in diagnosis. An open circuit, for example, will not allow any current to flow, so the ammeter reading will be zero. A damaged component or circuit will have an increased current draw, so the reading will be high. The ammeter is always connected in series with the circuit being tested. All of the current that normally flows through the circuit must also flow through the ammeter; if there is any other path for the current to follow, the ammeter reading will not be accurate. The ammeter itself has very little resistance to current flow and, therefore, will not affect the circuit, but it will measure current draw only when the circuit is closed and electricity is flowing. Excessive current draw can blow fuses and drain the battery, while a reduced current draw can cause motors to run slowly, lights to dim and other components to not operate properly.

Troubleshooting Electrical Systems

When diagnosing a specific problem, organized troubleshooting is a must. The complexity of a modern automotive vehicle demands that you approach any problem in a logical, organized manner. There are certain troubleshooting techniques, however, which are standard:

• Establish when the problem occurs. Does the problem appear only under certain conditions? Were there any noises, odors or other unusual symptoms?

Isolate the problem area. To do this, make some simple tests and observations, then eliminate the systems that are working properly. Check for obvious problems, such as broken wires and loose or dirty connections. Always check the obvious before assuming something complicated is the cause.

• Test for problems systematically to determine the cause once the problem area is isolated. Are all the components functioning properly? Is there power going to electrical switches and motors? Performing careful, systematic checks will often turn up most causes on the first inspection, without wasting time checking components that have little or no relationship to the problem.

• Test all repairs after the work is done to make sure that the problem is fixed. Some causes can be traced to more than one component, so a careful verification of repair work is important in order to pick up additional malfunctions that may cause a problem to reappear or a different problem to arise. A blown fuse, for example, is a simple problem that may require more than another fuse to repair. If you don't look for a problem that caused a fuse to blow, a shorted wire (for example) may go undetected.

Experience has shown that most problems tend to be the result of a fairly simple and obvious cause, such as loose or corroded connectors, bad grounds or damaged wire insulation which causes a short. This makes careful visual inspection of components during testing essential to quick and accurate troubleshooting.

Testing

OPEN CIRCUITS

▶ See Figure 8

This test already assumes the existence of an open in the circuit and it is used to help locate the open portion.

1. Isolate the circuit from power and ground.
2. Connect the self-powered test light or ohmmeter ground clip to the ground side of the circuit and probe sections of the circuit sequentially.
3. If the light is out or there is infinite resistance, the open is between the probe and the circuit ground.
4. If the light is on or the meter shows continuity, the open is between the probe and the end of the circuit toward the power source.

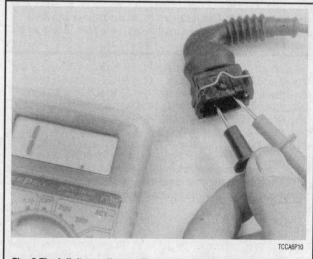

TCCA6P10

Fig. 8 The infinite reading on this multimeter indicates that the circuit is open

SHORT CIRCUITS

➡**Never use a self-powered test light to perform checks for opens or shorts when power is applied to the circuit under test. The test light can be damaged by outside power.**

1. Isolate the circuit from power and ground.
2. Connect the self-powered test light or ohmmeter ground clip to a good ground and probe any easy-to-reach point in the circuit.

3. If the light comes on or there is continuity, there is a short somewhere in the circuit.

4. To isolate the short, probe a test point at either end of the isolated circuit (the light should be on or the meter should indicate continuity).

5. Leave the test light probe engaged and sequentially open connectors or switches, remove parts, etc. until the light goes out or continuity is broken.

6. When the light goes out, the short is between the last two circuit components which were opened.

VOLTAGE

This test determines voltage available from the battery and should be the first step in any electrical troubleshooting procedure after visual inspection. Many electrical problems, especially on computer controlled systems, can be caused by a low state of charge in the battery. Excessive corrosion at the battery cable terminals can cause poor contact that will prevent proper charging and full battery current flow.

1. Set the voltmeter selector switch to the 20V position.

2. Connect the multimeter negative lead to the battery's negative (–) post or terminal and the positive lead to the battery's positive (+) post or terminal.

3. Turn the ignition switch **ON** to provide a load.

4. A well charged battery should register over 12 volts. If the meter reads below 11.5 volts, the battery power may be insufficient to operate the electrical system properly.

VOLTAGE DROP

▶ **See Figure 9**

When current flows through a load, the voltage beyond the load drops. This voltage drop is due to the resistance created by the load and also by small resistances created by corrosion at the connectors and damaged insulation on the wires. The maximum allowable voltage drop under load is critical, especially if there is more than one load in the circuit, since all voltage drops are cumulative.

1. Set the voltmeter selector switch to the 20 volt position.

2. Connect the multimeter negative lead to a good ground.

3. Operate the circuit and check the voltage prior to the first component (load).

4. There should be little or no voltage drop in the circuit prior to the first component. If a voltage drop exists, the wire or connectors in the circuit are suspect.

5. While operating the first component in the circuit, probe the ground side of the component with the positive meter lead and observe the voltage readings.

A small voltage drop should be noticed. This voltage drop is caused by the resistance of the component.

6. Repeat the test for each component (load) down the circuit.

7. If a large voltage drop is noticed, the preceding component, wire or connector is suspect.

RESISTANCE

▶ **See Figures 10 and 11**

※※ WARNING

Never use an ohmmeter with power applied to the circuit. The ohmmeter is designed to operate on its own power supply. The normal 12 volt electrical system voltage could damage the meter!

1. Isolate the circuit from the vehicle's power source.

2. Ensure that the ignition key is **OFF** when disconnecting any components or the battery.

3. Where necessary, also isolate at least one side of the circuit to be checked, in order to avoid reading parallel resistances. Parallel circuit resistances will always give a lower reading than the actual resistance of either of the branches.

4. Connect the meter leads to both sides of the circuit (wire or component) and read the actual measured ohms on the meter scale. Make sure the selector switch is set to the proper ohm scale for the circuit being tested, to avoid misreading the ohmmeter test value.

Wire and Connector Repair

Almost anyone can replace damaged wires, as long as the proper tools and parts are available. Wire and terminals are available to fit almost any need. Even the specialized weatherproof, molded and hard shell connectors are now available from aftermarket suppliers.

Be sure the ends of all the wires are fitted with the proper terminal hardware and connectors. Wrapping a wire around a stud is never a permanent solution and will only cause trouble later. Replace wires one at a time to avoid confusion. Always route wires exactly the same as the factory.

➡ **If connector repair is necessary, only attempt it if you have the proper tools. Weatherproof and hard shell connectors require special tools to release the pins inside the connector. Attempting to repair these connectors with conventional hand tools will damage them.**

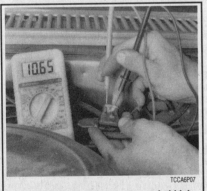

TCCA6P07

Fig. 9 This voltage drop test revealed high resistance (low voltage) in the circuit

TCCA6P08

Fig. 10 Checking the resistance of a coolant temperature sensor with an ohmmeter. Reading is 1.04 kilohms

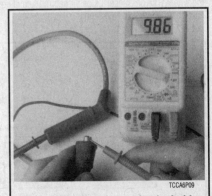

TCCA6P09

Fig. 11 Spark plug wires can be checked for excessive resistance using an ohmmeter

BATTERY CABLES

Disconnecting the Cables

When working on any electrical component on the vehicle, it is always a good idea to disconnect the negative (–) battery cable. This will prevent potential damage to many sensitive electrical components such as the Engine Control Module (ECM), radio, alternator, etc.

➡ **Any time you disengage the battery cables, it is recommended that you disconnect the negative (–) battery cable first. This will prevent your accidentally grounding the positive (+) terminal to the body of the vehicle when disconnecting it, thereby preventing damage to the above mentioned components.**

Before you disconnect the cable(s), first turn the ignition to the **OFF** position. This will prevent a draw on the battery which could cause arcing (electricity trying to ground itself to the body of a vehicle, just like a spark plug jumping the gap) and, of course, damaging some components such as the alternator diodes.

When the battery cable(s) are reconnected (negative cable last), be sure to check that your lights, windshield wipers and other electrically operated safety components are all working correctly. If your vehicle contains an Electronically Tuned Radio (ETR), don't forget to also reset your radio stations. Ditto for the clock.

AIR BAG (SUPPLEMENTAL RESTRAINT SYSTEM)

General Information

SYSTEM OPERATION

The supplemental restraint system is designed to work in concert with the seat belts to further prevent personal injury during a head-on collision with another object. The air bag system utilizes an air bag module, front impact sensors, a clockspring, and a diagnostic module.

With the battery cables connected, the air bag system system is energized and monitoring the front impact sensors and the safing sensor for collision confirmation messages. When the vehicle strikes, or is struck by, another object (such as a tree, wall, another vehicle, etc.), the front impact sensors and safing sensor send impulses to the diagnostic module, which determines the force and direction of the impact. Based on this information the diagnostic module either deploys or does not deploy the air bag.

The only time that the air bag system is completely disarmed with no chance of accidental deployment is when the battery cables have been disconnected from the battery and set aside, and at least 2 minutes have gone by to allow the system capacitor to discharge any residual energy.

SYSTEM COMPONENTS

▶ **See Figure 12**

Air Bag Module

The air bag module is the most visible part of the system. It contains the air bag cushion and its supporting components. The air bag module contains a housing to which the cushion and inflator are attached and sealed.

The inflator assembly is mounted to the back of the module housing. When supplied with the proper electrical signal, the inflator assembly produces a gas which discharges directly into the cushion. A protective cover is fitted to the front of the air bag module and forms a decorative cover in the center of the steering wheel. The driver's side air bag module is mounted directly to the steering wheel. The passenger's side air bag module, if equipped, is mounted on the dashboard ahed of the passenger.

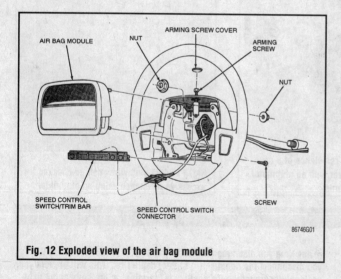

Fig. 12 Exploded view of the air bag module

Front Impact Sensors

The impact sensors provide verification of the direction and severity of the impact. Three impact sensors are used. One is called a safing sensor. It is located

inside the diagnostic module which is mounted on the floor pan, just forward of the center console. The other two sensors are mounted on the upper crossmember of the radiator closure panel on the left and right side of the vehicle under the hood.

The impact sensors are threshold sensitive switches that complete an electrical circuit when an impact provides a sufficient ``g force'' to close the switch. The sensors are calibrated for the specific vehicle and react to the severity and direction of the impact.

Clockspring

The clockspring is mounted on the steering column behind the steering wheel and is used to maintain a continuous electrical circuit between the wiring harness and the driver's air bag module. This assembly consists of a flat ribbon-like electrically conductive tape which winds and unwinds with the steering wheel rotation.

Diagnostic Module

The Air Bag System Diagnostic Module (ASDM) contains the safing sensor and energy reserve capacitor. The ASDM monitors the system to determine the system readiness. The ASDM will store sufficient energy to deploy the air bag for only two minutes after the battery is disconnected. The ASDM contains on-board diagnostics and will illuminate the AIR BAG warning lamp in the cluster when a fault occurs.

SERVICE PRECAUTIONS

When working on the air bag system or any components which require the removal of the air bag, adhere to all of these precautions to minimize the risks of personal injury or component damage:

• Before attempting to diagnose, remove or install air bag system components, you must first disconnect and isolate the negative (−) battery cable. Failure to do so could result in accidental deployment and possible personal injury.

• When an undeployed air bag assembly is to be removed from the steering wheel, after disconnecting the negative battery cable, allow the system capacitor to discharge for two minutes before commencing with the air bag system component removal.

• Replace the air bag system components only with Chrysler Mopar® specified replacement parts, or equivalent. Substitute parts may visually appear interchangeable, but internal differences may result in inferior occupant protection.

• The fasteners, screws, and bolts originally used for the air bag system have special coatings and are specifically designed for the system. They must never be replaced with any substitutes. Anytime a new fastener is needed, replace with the correct fasteners provided in the service package or fasteners listed in the parts books.

Handling A Live Air Bag Module

At no time should any source of electricity be permitted near the inflator on the back of the module. When carrying a live module, the trim cover should be pointed away from the body to minimize injury in the event of accidental deployment. In addition, if the module is placed on a bench or other surface, the plastic trim cover should be face up to minimize movement in case of accidental deployment.

When handling a steering column with an air bag module attached, never place the column on the floor or other surface with the steering wheel or module face down.

Handling A Deployed Air Bag Module

The vehicle interior may contain a very small amount of sodium hydroxide powder, a by-product of air bag deployment. Since this powder can irritate the skin, eyes, nose or throat, be sure to wear safety glasses, rubber gloves and long sleeves during clean up.

If you find that the clean up is irritating your skin, run cool water over the affected area. Also, if you experience nasal or throat irritation, exit the vehicle for fresh air until the irritation ceases. If irritation continues, see a physician.

Begin the clean up by putting tape over the two air bag exhaust vents so that no additional powder will find its way into the vehicle interior. Then remove the air bag and air bag module from the vehicle.

Use a vacuum cleaner to remove any residual powder from the vehicle interior. Work from the outside in so that you avoid kneeling or sitting in an uncleaned area.

Be sure to vacuum the heater and A/C outlets as well. In fact it's a good idea to run the blower on low and to vacuum up any powder expelled from the plenum. You may need to vacuum the interior of the car a second time to recover all of the powder.

Check with the local authorities before disposing of the deployed bag and module in your trash.

After an air bag has been deployed, the air bag module and clockspring must be replaced, because they cannot be reused. Other air bag system components should be replaced with new ones, if damaged.

DISARMING THE SYSTEM

To disarm the air bag system, simply disconnect the negative battery cable from the battery. Isolate the battery cable by taping up any exposed metal areas of the cable. This will keep the cable from accidentally contacting the battery and causing deployment of the air bag. Allow the system capacitor to discharge for at least 2 minutes, although 10 minutes is recommended, to allow for the dissipation of any residual energy.

ARMING THE SYSTEM

To arm the system, reconnect the negative battery cable. This will automatically enable the system.

HEATING AND AIR CONDTIONING

Blower Motor

REMOVAL & INSTALLATION

Except 4.0L Engines

▶ See Figure 13

1. Disengage the electrical connection.
2. Remove the blower motor attaching screws.
3. Remove the blower motor.
4. Remove the blower motor fan from the motor shaft for access to the motor attaching nuts.

To install:

5. Install the blower motor fan on the motor shaft.
6. Install the blower motor and fasten the attaching screws.
7. Engage the electrical connection.

4.0L Engine

▶ See Figures 14 and 15

1. Remove the coolant overflow bottle retaining strap. Remove the coolant overflow bottle and bracket.
2. Disengage the blower motor wiring.
3. Remove the blower motor mounting fasteners.
4. Remove the blower motor.
5. Remove the blower motor fan from the motor shaft for access to the motor attaching nuts.

To install:

6. Install the blower motor fan on the motor shaft.
7. Install the blower motor and tighten the mounting fasteners.
8. Engage the electrical connection.
9. Install the coolant overflow bracket, bottle and retaining strap.

Heater Core

REMOVAL & INSTALLATION

▶ See Figures 16, 17, 18, 19 and 20

1. Disconnect the negative battery cable.
2. If equipped with air conditioning, have the system discharged by a qualified professional mechanic using an approved recovery/recycling machine.
3. Drain the coolant.

❊❊ CAUTION

When draining coolant, keep in mind that cats and dogs are attracted by ethylene glycol antifreeze, and are quite likely to drink any that is left in an uncovered container or in puddles on the ground. This will prove fatal in sufficient quantity. Always drain the coolant into a sealable container. Coolant should be reused unless it is contaminated or several years old.

4. Disconnect the heater hoses at the core tubes.
5. Disconnect the blower motor wires and vent tube.

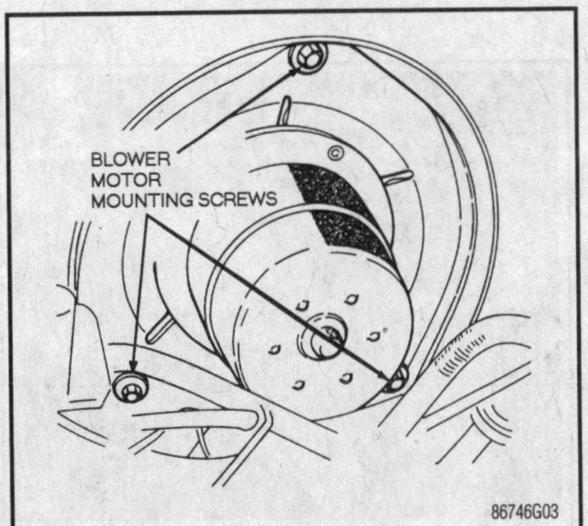

Fig. 14 Loosen and remove the blower motor retaining bolts

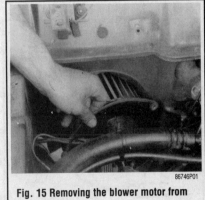

Fig. 15 Removing the blower motor from the vehicle

Fig. 13 Blower motor mounting screw locations

BLOWER MOTOR MOUNTING SCREWS

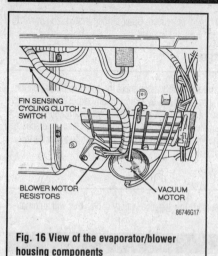

Fig. 16 View of the evaporator/blower housing components

FIN SENSING CYCLING CLUTCH SWITCH

BLOWER MOTOR RESISTORS

VACUUM MOTOR

86746G17

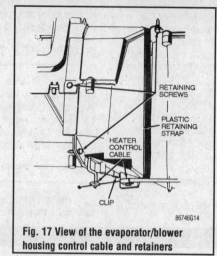

Fig. 17 View of the evaporator/blower housing control cable and retainers

RETAINING SCREWS

PLASTIC RETAINING STRAP

HEATER CONTROL CABLE

CLIP

86746G14

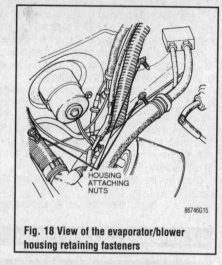

Fig. 18 View of the evaporator/blower housing retaining fasteners

HOUSING ATTACHING NUTS

86746G15

6. If equipped, remove the center console.

7. Remove the lower half of the instrument panel.

8. Disconnect the wiring at the A/C relay, blower motor resistors and A/C thermostat. Disconnect the vacuum hoses at the vacuum motor.

9. Cut the plastic retaining strap that retains the evaporator housing to the heater core housing.

10. Disconnect and remove the heater control cable.

11. Remove the clips at the rear blower housing flange and remove the retaining screws.

12. Remove the housing attaching nuts from the studs on the engine compartment side of the firewall.

13. Remove the evaporator drain tube.

14. Remove the right kick panel and the instrument panel support bolt.

15. Gently pull out on the right side of the dash and rotate the housing down and toward the rear to disengage the mounting studs from the firewall. Remove the housing.

16. Unbolt and remove the core from the housing.

To install:

17. Install the core in the housing. Ensure that the housing is positioned on the mounting studs on the firewall.

➡**When installing the housing, care must be taken not to trap wires between the housing fresh air inlet and the dash panel on the right side of the housing.**

18. Install the housing retaining screws and the rear housing clips.

19. Install the housing attaching nuts from the studs on the engine compartment side of the firewall.

20. Connect the blower motor wires and vent tube.

21. Connect the air conditioning hose at the expansion valve. Always use a back-up wrench!

22. Connect the wiring at the A/C relay, blower motor resistors and A/C thermostat.

23. Connect the heater control cable. Connect the vacuum hoses at the vacuum motor.

24. Install the right kick panel and the instrument panel support bolt.

25. Install the evaporator drain tube.

26. Install the lower half of the instrument panel.

27. Install the center console, if equipped.

28. Connect the heater hoses at the core tubes.

29. Fill the cooling system.

30. Connect the negative battery cable.

31. Have the system evacuated and recharged by a qualified professional mechanic, utilizing the proper equipment.

32. Start the vehicle and check for proper operation of system.

Heater Water Control Valve

▸ **See Figure 21**

The heater water control valve is spliced into the heater core hoses. It can be tested by attaching a hand vacuum pump to the valve to draw and release vacuum. If during this procedure the heating system functions properly, the valve is not defective. Check for vacuum leaks in the control panel or restrictions in the coolant system.

1. Allow the vehicle to cool before performing this procedure.

2. Label and disconnect all heater hoses attached to the valve.

3. Disconnect the vacuum hose which controls the valve.

4. Remove the valve.

5. Installation is the reverse of removal.

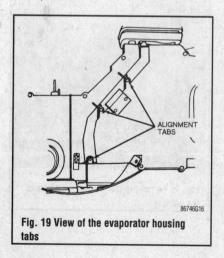

ALIGNMENT TABS

86746G16

Fig. 19 View of the evaporator housing tabs

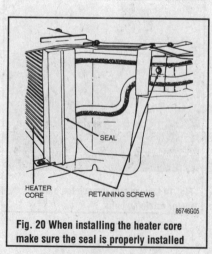

SEAL

HEATER CORE

RETAINING SCREWS

86746G05

Fig. 20 When installing the heater core make sure the seal is properly installed

91076P32

Fig. 21 The heater water control valve is spliced into the heater core hoses along with a vacuum hose to open and close the valve

Air Conditioning Components

REMOVAL & INSTALLATION

Repair or service of air conditioning components is not covered by this manual, because of the risk of personal injury or death, and because of the legal ramifications of servicing these components without the proper EPA certification and experience. Cost, personal injury or death, environmental damage, and legal considerations (such as the fact that it is a federal crime to vent refrigerant into the atmosphere), dictate that the A/C components on your vehicle should be serviced only by a Motor Vehicle Air Conditioning (MVAC) trained, and EPA certified automotive technician.

➡**If your vehicle's A/C system uses R-12 refrigerant and is in need of recharging, the A/C system can be converted over to R-134a refrigerant (less environmentally harmful and expensive). Refer to Section 1 for additional information on R-12 to R-134a conversions, and for additional considerations dealing with your vehicle's A/C system.**

Control Cables

REMOVAL & INSTALLATION

▶ **See Figures 22 and 23**

1. Remove the heater control panel as outlined in this section.
2. Remove the clip and the cable self-adjusting clip from the blend door lever at the bottom of the evaporator/blower housing.

3. Remove the cable by squeezing the tabs with needle nosed pliers, being careful not to break the housing.
   To install:
4. Install the cable and attach the clip and self adjusting clip to the blend door lever.
5. Install the heater control panel as outlined in this section.

Control Panel

REMOVAL & INSTALLATION

▶ **See Figures 24, 25, 26 and 27**

1. Disconnect the negative battery cable. Remove the ash tray.
2. Remove the instrument panel bezel fasteners and remove the bezel.
3. If necessary, remove the clock.
4. If necessary, unfasten the radio retaining screws and remove the radio. Refer to this section for the proper procedure.
5. Remove the control panel screws, pull the panel outward and disconnect and tag the hoses, wires and cable.
6. Remove the control cable locking tab by using a small prytool to release the tab.
   To install:
7. Engage the control cable and fasten the retaining tab.
8. Engage the hoses and wires, install the control panel and tighten the retaining screws.
9. Install the radio and clock. Refer to the proper procedure in this section.
10. Install the instrument panel bezel and fasteners then connect the negative battery cable. Check the control panel to verify proper operation.

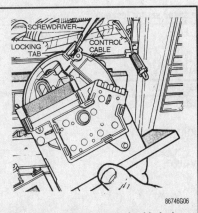

Fig. 22 Removing the control cable locking tab

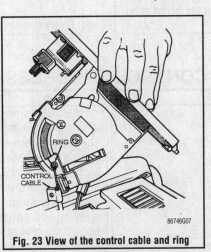

Fig. 23 View of the control cable and ring

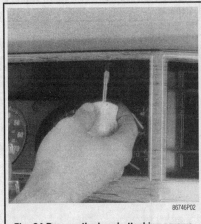

Fig. 24 Remove the bezel attaching screws

Fig. 25 Remove the control panel retaining screws . . .

Fig. 26 . . . then remove the control panel from the dash

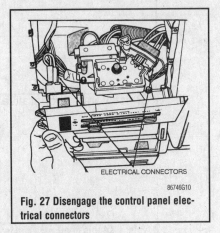

Fig. 27 Disengage the control panel electrical connectors

CRUISE CONTROL

General Information

▶ **See Figures 28 and 29**

The Cruise Command system is electrically actuated and vacuum operated. The turn signal lever on the steering column incorporates a slide switch which has three positions OFF, ON or RESUME. A SET button is located in the end of the lever. This device is designed to operate at speeds above approximately 35 mph (56 km/h).

The speed control module automatically controls throttle position to maintain a speed set by the operator. The vehicle will keep the set speed unless the driver presses the brake, clutch or accelerator pedal.

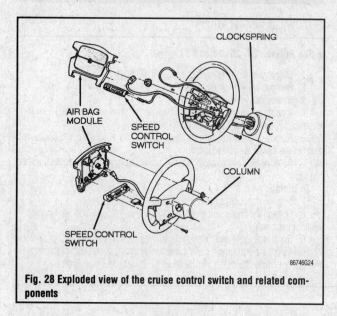

86746G24

Fig. 28 Exploded view of the cruise control switch and related components

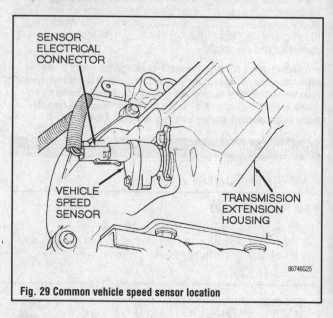

86746G25

Fig. 29 Common vehicle speed sensor location

CRUISE CONTROL TROUBLESHOOTING

Problem	Possible Cause
Will not hold proper speed	Incorrect cable adjustment
	Binding throttle linkage
	Leaking vacuum servo diaphragm
	Leaking vacuum tank
	Faulty vacuum or vent valve
	Faulty stepper motor
	Faulty transducer
	Faulty speed sensor
	Faulty cruise control module
Cruise intermittently cuts out	Clutch or brake switch adjustment too tight
	Short or open in the cruise control circuit
	Faulty transducer
	Faulty cruise control module
Vehicle surges	Kinked speedometer cable or casing
	Binding throttle linkage
	Faulty speed sensor
	Faulty cruise control module
Cruise control inoperative	Blown fuse
	Short or open in the cruise control circuit
	Faulty brake or clutch switch
	Leaking vacuum circuit
	Faulty cruise control switch
	Faulty stepper motor
	Faulty transducer
	Faulty speed sensor
	Faulty cruise control module

Note: Use this chart as a guide. Not all systems will use the components listed.

ENTERTAINMENT SYSTEMS

Radio Reciever/Amplifier/Tape Player/CD Player

REMOVAL & INSTALLATION

▶ See Figures 30, 31, 32 and 33

1. Disconnect the negative battery cable.
2. Remove the center cluster screws and bezel.
3. Remove the radio attaching screws.
4. Disconnect the radio from the instrument panel wiring harness and antenna.
5. Installation is the reverse of removal.

Speakers

REMOVAL & INSTALLATION

Instrument Panel

▶ See Figures 34, 35, 36, 37 and 38

This procedure applies to all vehicles covered by this manual. Some slight differences may arise; adjust the procedure accordingly.

Fig. 30 Remove the bezel retaining fasteners and the bezel . . .

Fig. 31 . . . then remove the radio retaining fasteners

Fig. 32 Slide the radio forward so that you may gain access to the electrical connections

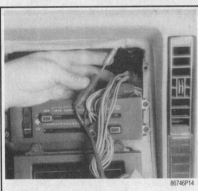
Fig. 33 Disengage the antenna and radio electrical connections

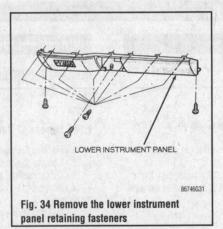
LOWER INSTRUMENT PANEL

Fig. 34 Remove the lower instrument panel retaining fasteners

Fig. 35 Pull the lower dash panel away from the dash board . . .

Fig. 36 . . . then disengage the speaker electrical connectors on each side

Fig. 37 Loosen the 2 lower speaker unit mounting screws . . .

Fig. 38 . . . then remove the speaker from the lower dash panel

1. Disconnect the negative battery cable.
2. On Cherokee/Wagoneer and Comanche models, remove the lower dashboard panel. On Grand Cherokee/Grand Wagoneer models, use a trim stick or other flat-bladed tool to pry the cowl top trim panel off the instrument panel top pad, then pull the cowl panel up far enough to disengage the solar sensor, if equipped.
3. Unplug the speaker wires.
4. Unfasten the speaker retaining screws and remove the speakers.

To install:
5. Install the speaker, fasten the retaining screws and engage the wires.
6. Install the lower dashboard panel, or cowl trim panel, making sure you engage the solar sensor electrical connection, if equipped.
7. Connect the negative battery cable.

Door Mounted

▶ **See Figures 39, 40 and 41**

This procedure applies to all vehicles covered by this manual, tailgate door as well as side doors. Some slight differences may arise; adjust the procedure accordingly.
1. Disconnect the negative battery cable.
2. Remove the door trim panel. Refer to Section 10 for this procedure.
3. Remove the speaker retaining screws.
4. Pull the speaker away from the door and unplug the electrical wires from the speaker.

To install:
5. Attach the electrical wires to the speaker.
6. Install the speaker to the door and secure in place with the retaining screws.
7. Install the door trim panel to the door. Refer to Section 10.
8. Connect the negative battery cable.

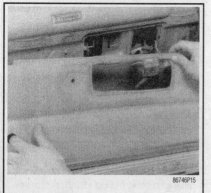

Fig. 39 Remove the door panel

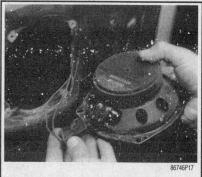

Fig. 40 Loosen the speaker retaining screws . . .

Fig. 41 . . . then remove the speaker and disengage the electrical connection

WINDSHIELD WIPERS AND WASHERS

Windshield Wiper Blade and Arm

REMOVAL & INSTALLATION

▶ **See Figures 42, 43, 44, 45 and 46**

1. Raise the blade end of the arm away from the windshield and move the spring tab away from the pivot shaft.
2. Disengage the auxiliary arm retainer clip from the pivot pin and pull the wiper arm from the pivot shaft.
3. Pivot the auxiliary over the pivot pin and engage the retainer clip. Push the wiper arm over the pivot shaft. Be sure that the shaft is in park and the wiper arm is positioned in the down mode.

Windshield Wiper Motor

REMOVAL & INSTALLATION

Front

▶ **See Figures 47 thru 54**

1. Remove the wiper arm and blade assemblies.
2. Remove the cowl trim panel.
3. Disconnect the washer hose.
4. Remove the cowl mounting bracket attaching nuts and pivot pin attaching screws.
5. Disconnect the wiring harness and unfasten the wiper motor retainers.

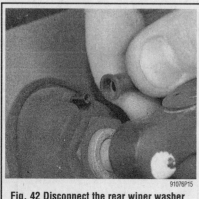

Fig. 42 Disconnect the rear wiper washer hose from the wiper motor shaft gromet (rear wiper arm)

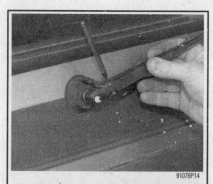

Fig. 43 To release wiper arm tension, lift the wiper arm away from the windshield and place a small diameter punch in the two holes of the arm and pivot lever

Fig. 44 This metal spring tab must be moved away from the pivot shaft using a small flat bladed tool

Fig. 45 After disengaging the spring tab, remove the wiper arm. If the wiper arm is to be reinstalled, leave the center punch in the arm to retain the spring tension

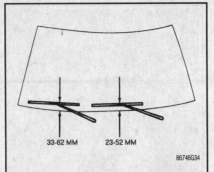

Fig. 46 After installing the wiper arms, check their distance above the windshield moulding

Fig. 47 Remove the wiper arms

Fig. 48 Remove the cowl panel retaining screws

Fig. 49 Remove the cowl panel

Fig. 50 Disengage the wiper motor electrical connection

Fig. 51 Unfasten the wiper motor retainers

6. Remove the wiper motor and the plastic motor cover, if equipped.
7. Remove the retainers holding the motor to the linkage assembly and bracket.

To install:

8. Install the retainers holding the motor to the linkage assembly and bracket.
9. Install the wiper motor and the plastic motor cover if equipped.
10. Engage the wiring harness and fasten the wiper motor retainers. Tighten the mounting nuts to 35 inch lbs. (4 Nm).
11. Install the cowl mounting bracket attaching nuts and pivot pin attaching screws.
12. Engage the washer hose, install the cowl trim panel and the wiper arm and blade assemblies.

Rear

◗ **See Figures 55 thru 62**

1. Remove the wiper arm assembly.
2. Disconnect the washer hose.

Fig. 52 Remove the wiper motor and linkage

Fig. 53 Unfasten the wiper motor-to-linkage retaining fasteners

Fig. 54 Separate the motor from the linkage

Fig. 55 Using a box wrench, loosen the pivot pin retaining nut . . .

Fig. 56 . . . then remove the nut from the pivot pin

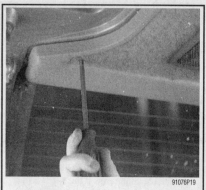

Fig. 57 Remove the tailgate interior panel retaining screws . . .

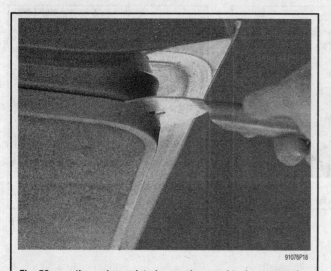

Fig. 58 . . . then using an interior panel removal tool, separate the panel from the tailgate door by disengaging the retaining clips

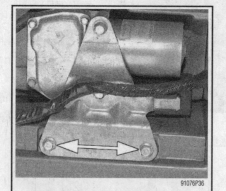

Fig. 59 After removing the screws and disengaging the retaining clips, remove the trim panel

Fig. 60 Unplug the electrical connector from the rear wiper motor

Fig. 61 Remove the rear wiper motor mounting bolts . . .

Fig. 62 . . . then remove the wiper motor from the tailgate door

3. Remove the pivot pin retaining nut.
4. Remove the liftgate interior trim panel.
5. Disconnect the wiper motor at the wiring harness.
6. Unbolt and remove the motor.

7. Installation is the reverse of removal. Torque the pivot pin attaching nut to 32 inch lbs. (4 Nm) and the motor mounting bracket to 40 inch lbs. (5 Nm).

Windshield Washer Motor

REMOVAL & INSTALLATION

▶ **See Figure 63**

1. Disconnect the negative battery cable.
2. Drain the washer fluid from the reservoir.
3. Disengage the wiring from the fluid level sensor, if equipped.
4. Remove the reservoir retaining fasteners and disengage the hoses from the reservoir.
5. Using a deep socket and an extension, remove the pump retaining fastener from inside the reservoir.
6. Remove the pump from the reservoir.
7. Installation is the reverse of removal.

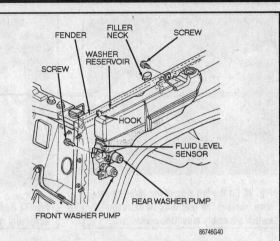

86746G40

Fig. 63 Windshield washer reservoir and washer pump (motor) assembly

---

INSTRUMENTS AND SWITCHES

Instrument Cluster

REMOVAL & INSTALLATION

▶ **See Figures 64 thru 75**

1. Disconnect the battery ground.
2. Remove the four instrument panel bezel screws and remove the instrument panel bezel. The bezel is a snap fit at several locations.
3. Remove the lighter housing screws.

4. Remove the rear window defroster switch housing screws.
5. Remove the instrument cluster screws.
6. Disconnect the speedometer cable.
7. Pull the cluster part way out and unplug the connectors.
8. Installation is the reverse of removal.

91076P43

Fig. 64 Remove the small plastic instrument panel trim piece from below the steering column by pulling away to disengage the retaining tabs (arrow)

91076P44

Fig. 65 Remove the 4 instrument cluster bezel retaining screws

91076P42

Fig. 66 Disengage the retaining clips from behind the istrument cluster bezel and pull the bezel away from the dashboard assembly

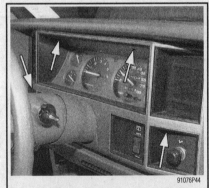

91076P61

Fig. 67 These are the metal clips located behind the instrument cluster bezel

91076P60

Fig. 68 Remove the 3 cigar lighter assembly mounting screws

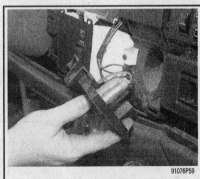

91076P59

Fig. 69 After removing the cigar lighter mounting screws, lower the cigar lighter out of the way

Fig. 70 On the left side of the steering column, remove the rear window defroster switch assembly mounting screw. . .

Fig. 71 Remove the instrument cluster assembly retaining screws

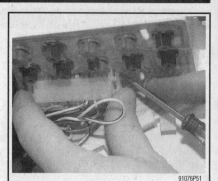
Fig. 72 Pull the instument cluster away from the dash board far enough to disengage the wiring connectors

Fig. 73 Remove the instrument cluster assembly from the dash board

Fig. 74 If bulbs in the instrument cluster assembly require replacement, simply turn over the housing to where the sockets are located . . .

Fig. 75 . . . then rotate the socket counterclockwise and pull it out

Speedometer/Tachometer Instrument Cluster Gauges

REMOVAL & INSTALLATION

▶ See Figure 76

1. Remove the instrument cluster.
2. Remove the cluster lens and gauge bezel. If equipped with a trip odometer remove the knob by gently pulling.
3. Remove attaching screws from the front and/or rear of the mounting bezel.
4. Remove the speedometer/tachometer assembly.
5. Installation is the reverse of removal.

Windshield Wiper Switch

REMOVAL & INSTALLATION

The wiper switch is part of the multi-function switch. See Section 8 for replacement.

Rear Window Wiper Switch

REMOVAL & INSTALLATION

▶ See Figures 77 thru 82

1. Remove the instrument cluster bezel.
2. If necessary, remove the cigar lighter housing panel.

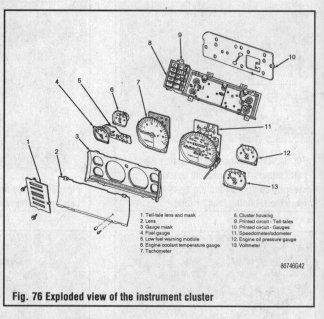

1. Tell-tale lens and mask
2. Lens
3. Gauge mask
4. Fuel gauge
5. Low fuel warning module
6. Engine coolant temperature gauge
7. Tachometer
8. Cluster housing
9. Printed circuit - Tell-tales
10. Printed circuit - Gauges
11. Speedometer/odometer
12. Engine oil pressure gauge
13. Voltmeter

Fig. 76 Exploded view of the instrument cluster

3. Remove the switch housing panel.
4. Unplug the switch connector.
5. Remove the bulb socket from the housing panel, if equipped.
6. The switch can be removed from the housing panel by unsnapping it from behind using a small, flat bladed tool.
7. Installation is the reverse of removal.

Fig. 77 After moving the cigar lighter housing out of the way, remove the rear wiper motor switch mounting screw . . .

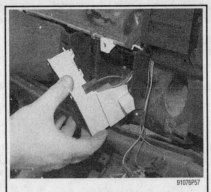

Fig. 78 . . . then pull the motor switch assembly out of the way

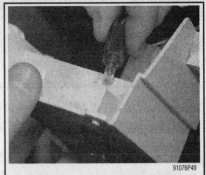

Fig. 79 After pulling the switch assembly away from the dashboard, rotate the bulb socket and pull out of the housing

Fig. 80 Disengage the electrical connector from behind the rear wiper motor switch

Fig. 81 Remove the rear wiper motor switch from the housing panel by pushing in the clip using a small flat bladed tool . . .

Fig. 82 . . . then pull the rear wiper motor switch out of the bezel

Headlight Switch

REMOVAL & INSTALLATION

▶ **See Figures 83 and 84**

This procedure applies only to models equipped with an instrument panel-mounted headlight switch.
1. Disconnect the battery ground cable.
2. Pull the switch to the full ON position.
3. Reach up under the panel and depress the switch shaft retainer button while pulling the switch control shaft straight out.

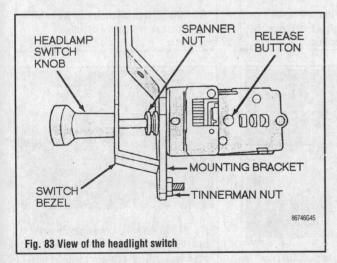

Fig. 83 View of the headlight switch

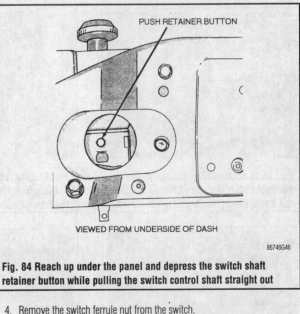

Fig. 84 Reach up under the panel and depress the switch shaft retainer button while pulling the switch control shaft straight out

4. Remove the switch ferrule nut from the switch.
5. Disconnect the switch from the harness.
6. Installation is the reverse of removal.

Back-up Light Switch

The back-up light switch is part of the neutral start switch if equipped with automatic transmission. See Section 7 for replacement.

LIGHTING

Headlights

REMOVAL & INSTALLATION

Cherokee, Wagoneer and Comanche Models

▶ **See Figures 85 thru 91**

1. Remove the headlamp bezel and retaining ring attaching screws. Remove the bezel and retaining ring.
2. Pull the headlight out, disconnect the wire harness and remove the headlight from the vehicle.
3. Install the headlight in the reverse order of removal.

Grand Cherokee and Grand Wagoneer Models

1. Open the hood, reach into the engine compartment and locate the lock ring supporting the bulb assembly.
2. Rotate the lock ring 1/8 turn counterclockwise and pull the bulb straight out from the housing.

To install:

3. Install a new bulb and position the bulb assembly in the lamp housing.
4. Rotate the lock ring 1/8 turn clockwise to secure.

HEADLIGHT AIMING

▶ **See Figures 92, 93 and 94**

The headlights must be properly aimed to provide the best, safest road illumination. The lights should be checked for proper aim, and adjusted if necessary, after installing a new sealed beam unit or if the front end sheet metal has been replaced. Certain state and local authorities have requirements for headlight aiming and you should check these before adjusting.

The truck's fuel tank should be about half full when adjusting the headlights. Tires should be properly inflated, and if a heavy load is carried in the pick-up bed, it should remain there.

Horizontal and vertical aiming of each sealed beam unit is provided by two adjusting screws, which move the mounting ring in the body against the tension of the coil spring. There is no adjustment for focus; this is done during headlight manufacturing.

1. If aiming is to be performed outdoors, it is advisable to wait until dusk in order to properly see the headlight beams on the wall. If done in a garage, darken the area around the wall as much as possible by closing shades or hanging cloth over the windows.

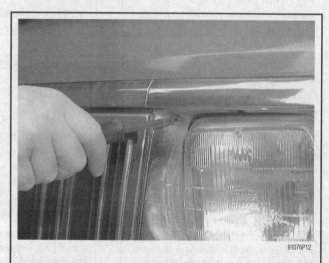

Fig. 85 Remove the top corner headlight bezel mounting screw

Fig. 86 To access the turn signal bulb or headlight bezel mounting screws, remove the 2 turn signal housing retaining screws

Fig. 87 After removing the turn signal housing from the headlight bezel, remove the 2 bezel mounting screws . . .

Fig. 88 . . . then carefully pull the headlight bezel away from the headlight assembly

Fig. 89 Remove the 4 headlight assembly retaining ring screws . . .

Fig. 90 . . . then pull the retaining ring off of the headlight assembly

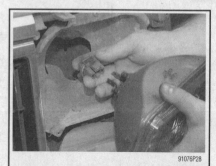

Fig. 91 Pull the headlight assembly away from the vehicle just far enough to disengage the electrical connector from behind the headlight

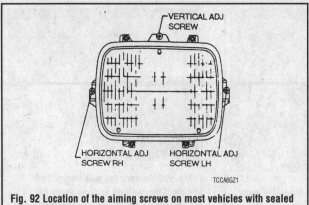

Fig. 92 Location of the aiming screws on most vehicles with sealed beam headlights

2. Turn the headlights **ON** and mark the wall at the center of each light's low beam, then switch on the brights and mark the center of each light's high beam. A short length of masking tape which is visible from the front of the vehicle may be used. Although marking all four positions is advisable, marking one position from each light should be sufficient.

Signal and Marker Lights

REMOVAL & INSTALLATION

Front Parking/Turn Signal Lights

▶ See Figures 95, 96 and 97

1. Remove the screws from the lens and separate the lens from the headlight bezel.
2. Remove the headlight bezel.
3. Remove the screws from the turn signal housing and pull it out.
4. Turn the bulb socket counterclockwise 1/3 turn and remove it.
5. Installation is the reverse of removal.

Side Marker Lights

▶ See Figure 86

1. Remove the screws from the marker lens and separate the lens from the headlight bezel.
2. Pull the bulb from its socket in the back of the lens.
3. Installation is the reverse of removal.

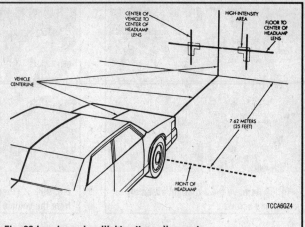

Fig. 93 Low-beam headlight pattern alignment

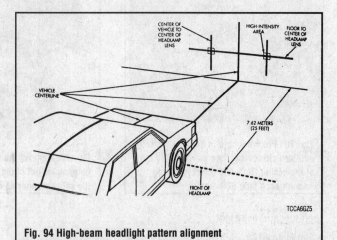

Fig. 94 High-beam headlight pattern alignment

Back-Up/Rear Turn Signal/Tail Lights

▶ See Figures 98 thru 103

1. Remove attaching screws and pull out the tail light assembly.
2. The bulbs can be removed by turning them 1/3 turn counterclockwise.

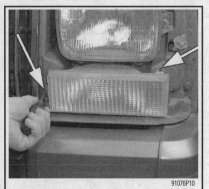

Fig. 95 Remove the 2 parking light housing retaining screws . . .

Fig. 96 . . . then pull the housing away from the vehicle far enough to remove the bulb socket from behind the housing. Turn the socket counterclockwise and pull

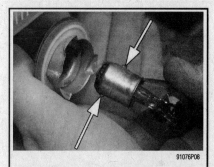

Fig. 97 Push the bulb in the socket gently and turn clockwise, then pull the bulb out of the socket. Note the offset retaining ears on each side of the bulb

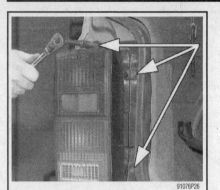

Fig. 98 Remove the 3 taillight assembly mounting screws . . .

Fig. 99 . . . then pull the assembly away from the vehicle

Fig. 100 Remove the bulb/socket from behind the taillight housing assembly by turning counterclockwise and pulling

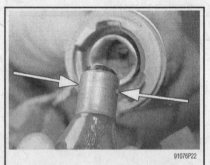

Fig. 101 Push the bulb in the socket gently and turn clockwise, then pull the bulb out of the socket. Note the offset retaining ears on each side of the bulb

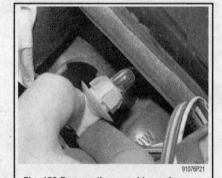

Fig. 102 Remove the rear side marker bulb/socket out of the taillight housing in the same manner as the taillight bulb . . .

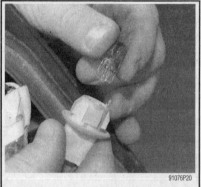

Fig. 103 . . . but just pull the rear side marker bulb straight out of the socket

High-mount Brake Light

♦ See Figure 104

1. Remove the brake light access door, if equipped.
2. Remove the brake light lamp mounting screws and then the socket and bulb assembly by turning it counterclockwise.
3. Remove the bulb from the socket.

To install:
4. Install the bulb in the socket.
5. Install the bulb and the socket by turning it clockwise.
6. Install the brake light and tighten the screws.
7. Install the brake light access door, if equipped.

Dome Light

♦ See Figure 105

1. Remove the dome lamp lens by squeezing it on both sides and pulling the lens down to gain access to the bulb.
2. Remove the bulb from the assembly.
3. Installation is the reverse of removal.

Cargo Lamp

♦ See Figure 106

1. Insert a flat blade tool into the slots on the lower portion of the lens.
2. Rotate the tool upwards until the lens snaps out of the housing.

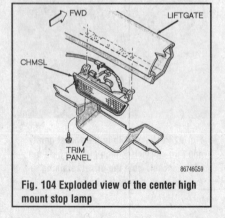

Fig. 104 Exploded view of the center high mount stop lamp

Fig. 105 Remove the dome light lens to access rhe bulb

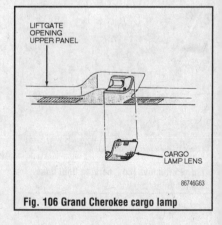

Fig. 106 Grand Cherokee cargo lamp

3. Remove the bulb from the socket.
To install:
4. Install the bulb in the socket.
5. Insert the upper tabs of the lens in the housing and snap the lens in place.

License Plate Light

COMANCHE

▶ **See Figure 107**

1. Remove the clip, located at the rear of the bumper, that retains the lamp and socket in the bumper.
2. Slide the bulb and socket out of bumper and replace the bulb.
3. Installation is the reverse of removal.

EXCEPT COMANCHE—WITHOUT SWING-OUT SPARE

▶ **See Figures 108, 109 and 110**

1. Unfasten the two lens screws and remove the bulb housing from liftgate.
2. Remove bulb from housing.
3. Installation is the reverse of removal

EXCEPT COMANCHE—WITH SWING-OUT SPARE

▶ **See Figure 111**

1. Remove screws holding lens assembly.
2. Pry housing cover from vehicle and remove bulb.
3. Installation is the reverse of removal.

Fog/Driving Lights

Fog lamps are installed on the front bumper. The switch is located to the left of the steering column on the dash panel. The fog lamps are turned off by the circuit relay when the high beam driving lamps are turned on. The circuit relay is located on the right front wheelhouse panel near the blower motor.

REMOVAL & INSTALLATION

Fog Lamp Element

▶ **See Figure 112**

1. Remove the lamp stone shields, the four bezel attaching screws, and the bezel.
2. Remove the reflector assembly from the lamp body.
3. Remove the bulb holder from the assembly. Remove the element from the bulb.

➡ **DO NOT handle elements with your bare hands, always handle with a clean cloth. Oil from your hands will cause the element to fail.**

4. Installation is the reverse of removal.

Fog Lamp Switch

The fog lamp switch is removed and installed by simply prying the switch from the instrument panel and unplugging the electrical connector.

FOGLAMP BEAM ADJUSTMENT

1. Position the vehicle on a level surface, facing a wall approximately 25 feet away. Remove the lamp stone shields and loosen the adjustment nuts.
2. Turn the fog lamps ON and adjust as follows:
   a. Distance between the light beam centers should be equal to the distance between the lamp assemblies on the bumper.
   b. Height of the light beams on the wall should be 4 inches less than the center of the lamp assemblies when mounted on the bumper.
3. Install all previously removed items after turning OFF the fog lamps.

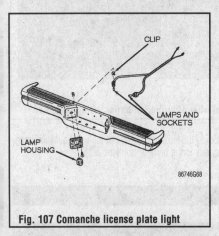

Fig. 107 Comanche license plate light

Fig. 108 Remove the license plate lamp cover retaining screws

Fig. 109 Remove the license plate lamp bulb housing

Fig. 110 Remove the license plate lamp bulb from the socket

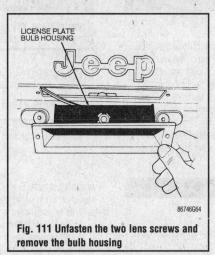

Fig. 111 Unfasten the two lens screws and remove the bulb housing

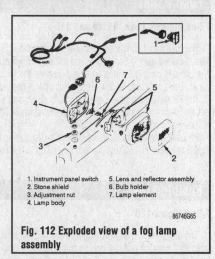

1. Instrument panel switch
2. Stone shield
3. Adjustment nut
4. Lamp body
5. Lens and reflector assembly
6. Bulb holder
7. Lamp element

Fig. 112 Exploded view of a fog lamp assembly

REPLACEMENT BULBS

Interior Lamps	Bulb Type
Ashtray Lamp	1891
Auto. Trans. Floor Shift Lamp	658
Cargo Lamp	561
Cigarette Lighter Lamp	53
Climate Control Lamp (2)	74
Dome Lamp	561
Dome/Reading Lamp	(1) 561 and (2) 906
Glove Box Lamp	194
Lighted Vanity Mirror (2)*	P/N 6501966
Map Reading Lamp in Overhead Console (4)	912
Rocker Switch Lamp	37
Transfer Case Lamp	658
Underpanel Courtesy Lamps (2)	168

*Available only at Chrysler Dealers.

Exterior Lamps	Bulb Type
Backup Lamps (2)	1156
Center High-Mounted Stoplamp (2)	922
Fog Lamps	H3
Front Park/Turn Lamps (2)	2057NA
Front Side Marker Lamps (2)	194
Headlights (2)	H 6054
Rear License Plate Lamp	168
(w/Outside Spare)	67
Rear Stop/Tail Lamps (2)	2057
Rear Turn Signal Lamps (2)	1156
Underhood Lamp	105

NOTE: Numbers refer to commercial bulb types that can be purchased from your local Jeep dealer.

91076C01

TRAILER WIRING

◆ See Figure 113

Wiring the vehicle for towing is fairly easy. There are a number of good wiring kits available and these should be used, rather than trying to design your own. All trailers will need brake lights and turn signals as well as tail lights and side marker lights. Most areas require extra marker lights for overwide trailers. Also, most areas have recently required back-up lights for trailers, and most trailer manufacturers have been building trailers with back-up lights for several years.

Additionally, some Class I, most Class II and just about all Class III and IV trailers will have electric brakes. Add to this number an accessories wire, to operate trailer internal equipment or to charge the trailer's battery, and you can have as many as seven wires in the harness.

Determine the equipment on your trailer and buy the wiring kit necessary. The kit will contain all the wires needed, plus a plug adapter set which includes the female plug, mounted on the bumper or hitch, and the male plug, wired into, or plugged into the trailer harness. When installing the kit, follow the manufacturer's instructions. The color coding of the wires is usually standard throughout the industry. One point to note: some domestic vehicles, and most imported vehicles, have separate turn signals. On most domestic vehicles, the brake lights and rear turn signals operate with the same bulb. For those vehicles without separate turn signals, you can purchase an isolation unit so that the brake lights won't blink whenever the turn signals are operated. One, final point, the best kits are those with a spring loaded cover on the vehicle mounted socket. This cover prevents

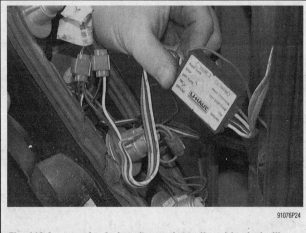

Fig. 113 An example of what after-market trailer wiring looks like

91076P24

dirt and moisture from corroding the terminals. Never let the vehicle socket hang loosely; always mount it securely to the bumper or hitch.

CIRCUIT PROTECTION

Fuse Panel

◆ See Figures 114a, 11.4b and 115

The fuse panel contains fuses which protect the various electrical systems. Also included are the turn signal and hazard flashers, and the chime module. The panel is usually located under the dash on the left hand side near the kick panel. There may also be an auxiliary fuse panel in the engine compartment.

The Power Distribution Center contains relays and fuses which further protect the electrical systems. It is usually located under the hood on the right side of the engine compartment.

Fuses and relays are replaced by simply unplugging the defective unit and inserting a new one. Ensure the ignition is **OFF** when replacing any fuse or relay.

✳✳ CAUTION

Never replace any fuse or relay with one of a different rating (amperage). Damage to the vehicle or personal injury could result.

REPLACEMENT

◆ See Figures 116, 117, 118 and 119

1. Using a fuse puller remove the defective fuse from the fuse panel.
2. Install a new fuse of the proper rating (amperage) in the fuse panel.

Fusible Link

◆ See Figure 120

The fusible link is a short length of special, Hypalon (high temperature) insulated wire, integral with the engine compartment wiring harness and should not be confused with standard wire. It is several wire gauges smaller than the circuit

which it protects. Under no circumstances should a fusible link replacement repair be made using a length of standard wire cut from bulk stock or from another wiring harness.

To repair any blown fusible link use the following procedure:
1. Determine which circuit is damaged, its location and the cause of the open fusible link. If the damaged fusible link is one of three fed by a common No. 10 or 12 gauge feed wire, determine the specific affected circuit.

Fig. 114a The main fuse panel on 1996 and earlier models is located in the vehicle, on the left side, under the steering column between the brake pedal and the left side kick panel

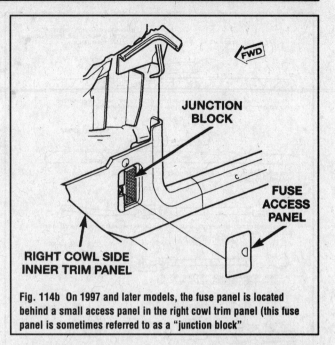

Fig. 114b On 1997 and later models, the fuse panel is located behind a small access panel in the right cowl trim panel (this fuse panel is sometimes referred to as a "junction block"

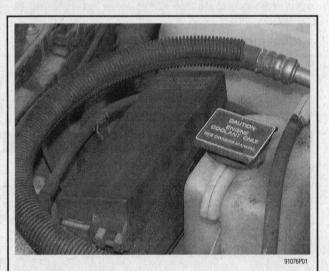

Fig. 115 The Power Distribution Center (PDC) box is located in the engine compartment

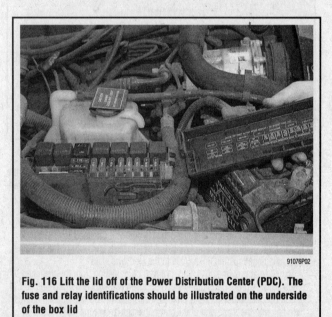

Fig. 116 Lift the lid off of the Power Distribution Center (PDC). The fuse and relay identifications should be illustrated on the underside of the box lid

Fig. 117 The large fuses can be lifted out by hand

Fig. 118 The smaller fuses may require the use of a special fuse puller tool

Fig. 119 The relays in the PDC box can be removed simply by pulling straight up

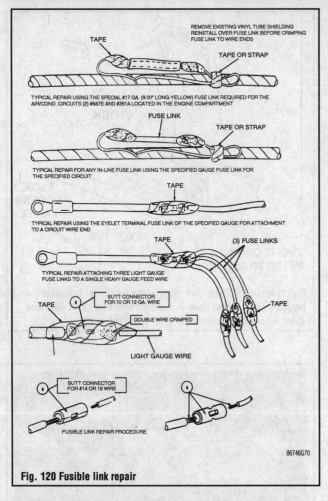

TAPE

REMOVE EXISTING VINYL TUBE SHIELDING
REINSTALL OVER FUSE LINK BEFORE CRIMPING
FUSE LINK TO WIRE ENDS

TAPE OR STRAP

TYPICAL REPAIR USING THE SPECIAL #17 GA. (9.00" LONG-YELLOW) FUSE LINK REQUIRED FOR THE
AIR/COND. CIRCUITS (2) #687E AND #261A LOCATED IN THE ENGINE COMPARTMENT

FUSE LINK

TAPE OR STRAP

TYPICAL REPAIR FOR ANY IN-LINE FUSE LINK USING THE SPECIFIED GAUGE FUSE LINK FOR
THE SPECIFIED CIRCUIT

TAPE

TYPICAL REPAIR USING THE EYELET TERMINAL FUSE LINK OF THE SPECIFIED GAUGE FOR ATTACHMENT
TO A CIRCUIT WIRE END

TAPE (3) FUSE LINKS

TYPICAL REPAIR ATTACHING THREE LIGHT GAUGE
FUSE LINKS TO A SINGLE HEAVY GAUGE FEED WIRE

TAPE

BUTT CONNECTOR
FOR 10 OR 12 GA. WIRE

DOUBLE WIRE CRIMPED

TAPE

LIGHT GAUGE WIRE

BUTT CONNECTOR
FOR #14 OR 16 WIRE

FUSIBLE LINK REPAIR PROCEDURE

86746G70

Fig. 120 Fusible link repair

2. Disconnect the negative battery cable.
3. Cut the damaged fusible link from the wiring harness and discard it. If the fusible link is one of three circuits fed by a single feed wire, cut it out of the harness at each splice end and discard it.
4. Identify and procure the proper fusible link and butt connectors for attaching the fusible link to the harness.
5. To repair any fusible link in a 3-link group with one feed:
   a. After cutting the open link out of the harness, cut each of the remaining undamaged fusible links close to the feed wire weld.
   b. Strip approximately 1/2 in. (13mm) of insulation from the detached ends of the two good fusible links. Then insert two wire ends into one end of a butt connector and carefully push one stripped end of the replacement fusible link into the same end of the butt connector and crimp all three firmly together.

➡**Care must be taken when fitting the three fusible links into the butt connector as the internal diameter is a snug fit for three wires. Make sure to use a proper crimping tool. Pliers, side cutters, etc. will not apply the proper crimp to retain the wires and withstand a pull test.**

   c. Using rosin core solder with a consistency of 60 percent tin and 40 percent lead, solder the connectors and the wires at the repairs and insulate with electrical tape.
6. To replace any fusible link on a single circuit in a harness, cut out the damaged portion, strip approximately 1/2 in. (13mm) of insulation from the two wire ends and attach the appropriate replacement fusible link to the stripped wire ends with two proper size butt connectors. Solder the connectors and wires and insulate with tape.
7. To repair any fusible link which has an eyelet terminal on one end such as the charging circuit, cut off the open fusible link behind the weld, strip approximately 1/2 in. (13mm) of insulation from the cut end and attach the appropriate new eyelet fusible link to the cut stripped wire with an appropriate size butt connector. Solder the connectors and wires at the repair and insulate with tape.
8. Connect the negative battery cable to the battery and test the system for proper operation.

➡**Do not mistake a resistor wire for a fusible link. The resistor wire is generally longer and has print stating, ``Resistor: don't cut or splice''.**

Circuit Breaker

Circuit breakers provide a similar protection to fuses. Unlike fuses most circuit breakers only have to be reset, and not replaced. Circuit breakers are used only in models equipped with power windows, and are located underneath the front seat.

REPLACEMENT

1. Remove the malfunctioning circuit breaker by pulling it out of its cavity.
2. Replace the circuit breaker with one of proper amp rating for the circuit, by pushing straight in until the fuse or circuit breaker seats itself fully into the cavity.

Flashers

REPLACEMENT

The turn signal flasher and hazard units are usually located located under the dash either to the left or right of the steering column on most models.
1. Remove the turn signal flasher unit or hazard unit by pulling them up from the electrical connection.
2. To install, push the unit(s) into the electrical connector.

FUSE BLOCK

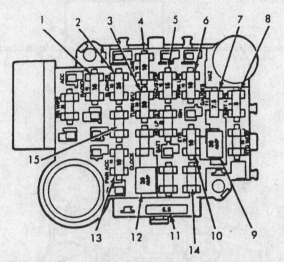

Located to left of steering column under instrument panel

Fuse	Amps	Protected Systems
1	15	Radio, cigarette lighter, clock illumination relay (1991-92), dome light (1992)
2	25	Blower motor (1986-91)
3	20	Turn signals, back-up lights (1986-91)
4	10	Illuminated entry (1992), interior dome lights, courtesy lights, glove box light, cargo box light, radio & clock memory (1989-92), telltale connector (1992)
5	15	Hazard warning system, stoplights (1986-90)
6	10 15	Parking lights, taillights, headlight warning chime/buzzer, instrument light dimmer (1986-90) Headlight switch, instrument panel lights, clock, radio/clock illumination, rear & front lights (1991-92)
7	7.5	Gauges, seat belt warning, instrument cluster (1992), headlight delay module (1992), chime module (1992)
8	5	Instrument panel illumination
9	30 (circuit breaker)	Power door locks, power seats (1989-90), trailer wiring (if equipped)
10	10	ETR radio, power antenna
11	5.5 (circuit breaker)	Front wiper/washer
12	30 (circuit breaker)	Power windows, trailer harness (1992)
13	10 25	Clock Blower motor (1992)
14	7.5	Transmission control unit (1989-90)
15	15	Flash-to-pass (1991), headlight dimmer switch (1992)

91076C02

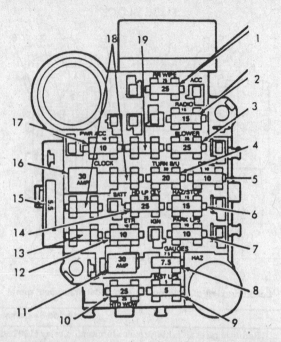

Fuse	Amps	Protected Systems
1	25	Rear washer/wiper
2	15	Radio and cigarette lighter (1985-95), dome light (1993-94)
3	25	Blower motor
4	20	Turn signal and back-up lights (1985-90), rear window defogger relay (1985-92), turn signal flasher (1993-95)
5	10	Dome light (1985-92), Radio and clock memory (1993-95), Telltale connectors (1994-95), Courtesy lights, glove box light, cargo light
6	15	Hazard warning system, stoplights
7	15 (1991-95)	Parking lights, taillights, headlights, warning chime/radio clock illumination (1993-95)
	10 (1985-90)	Parking lights, headlight warning chime/buzzer, instrument panel light dimmer/taillights (1989-90)
8	7.5	Seat belt warning (1985-92), headlight delay, chime module, and overhead console (1993-95), gauges
9	5	Instrument panel illumination, radio illumination (1994-95)
10	25	Rear window defogger
11	30 (Circuit breaker)	Power door locks (1985-89), power seats, trailer towing wiring harness
12	10 (1985-93)	ETR radio, power antenna
	20 (1994-95)	Power door locks
13	7.5 (1989-90)	Transmission control unit
	20 (1991-95)	Power door locks
14	25	Horn (1993-95), headlight delay
15	5.5 (Circuit breaker)	Front wiper (1985-88), front wiper/washer (1992-95)
	4.8 (Circuit breaker)	Front wiper (1989-91)
16	30 (Circuit breaker)	Power windows
17	10 (1985-92)	Clock
	- (1993-95)	Not used
18	2	Anti-lock brake system (1989-95)
19	15	Flash-to-pass (1989-95)

91076C03

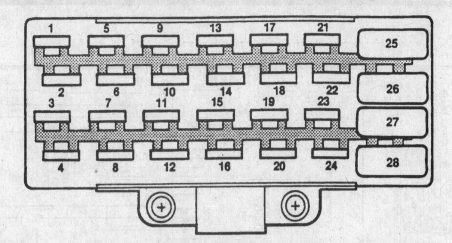

Fuse	Amps	Protected Systems
1	20	Power antenna relay (1993), trailer tow relay (1993-95)
2	15	Brake lamps
3	20	Hazard lamps
4	15	Security lamp
5	15	Interior lighting
6	15	Security alarm module
7	15	Security alarm relay, security alarm module, flash-to-pass
8	15	Overhead console, keyless entry, radio memory/clock/chime module, power locks, power mirrors, HEVAC and VIC
9	20	Rear wiper
10	15 (1993)	Radio accessory
	10 (1994-95)	Radio
11	15	Cigar lighter
12	15	Parking lamps, automatic headlamps
13	20	Horn relay
14	20	Power lock relay
15	3	ABS module and relay
16	20	Turn signals
17	7.5	Heater and A/C module
18	15	Air bag module
19	15	Interior mirror, auto headlamps, overhead console, VIC/GDM module, heated rear window relay, coil, illuminated entry relay, chime module
20	10	Heated rear window switch, overdrive switch, speed control
21	15	Cluster (1993), security alarm module, lamp outage module
22	15	Air bag module, speedometer, tachometer, telltales and gauges
23	15	Heated mirror feed, heated rear window switch
24	7.5	Instrument panel illumination
25	30 (Circuit breaker)	Power seats
26	30 (Circuit breaker)	Power windows (1993-95), power sunroof (1994-95)
27	10 (Circuit breaker)	Security alarm module, front wiper
28	30	Heated rear window relay

91076C04

WIRING DIAGRAMS

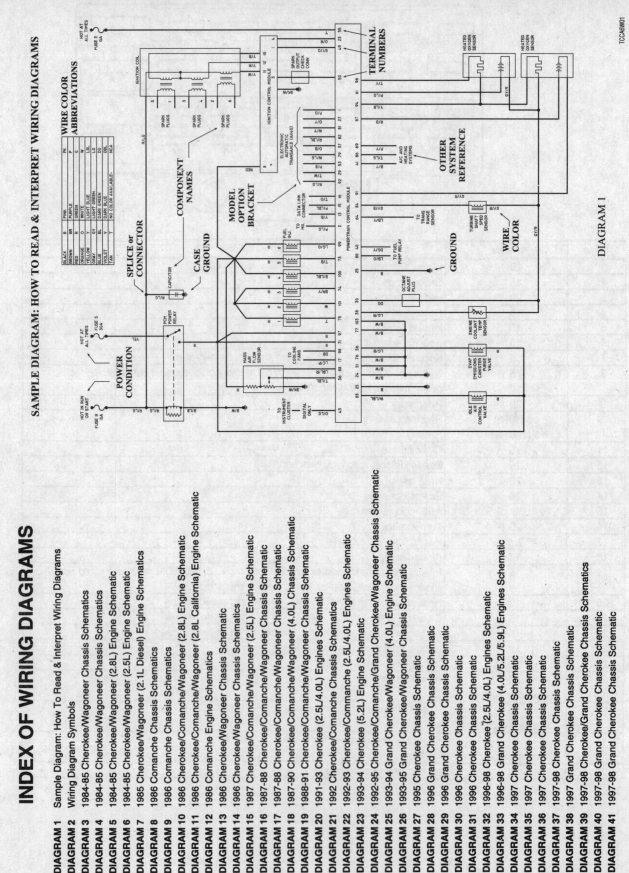

INDEX OF WIRING DIAGRAMS

WIRING DIAGRAM SYMBOLS

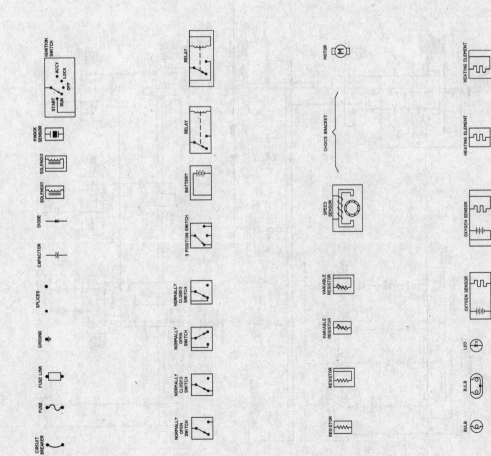

DIAGRAM 2

TCCA6W02

1984-85 CHEROKEE/WAGONEER CHASSIS SCHEMATICS

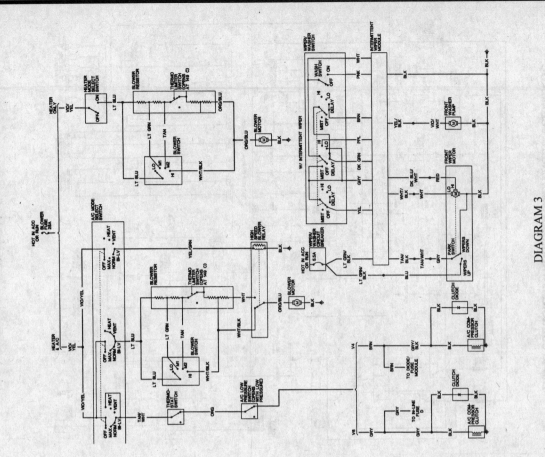

DIAGRAM 3

91076B05

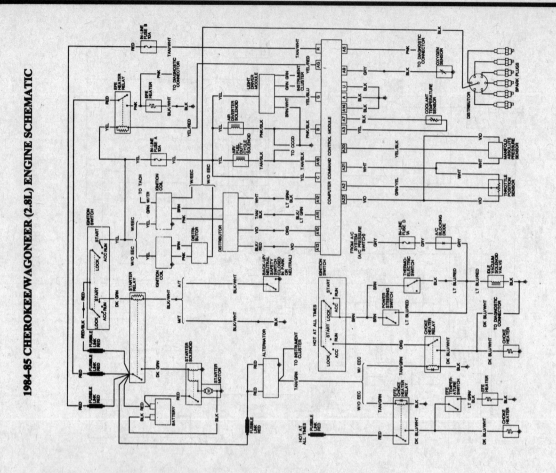

1984-85 CHEROKEE/WAGONEER (2.8L) ENGINE SCHEMATIC

DIAGRAM 5

1984-85 CHEROKEE/WAGONEER CHASSIS SCHEMATICS

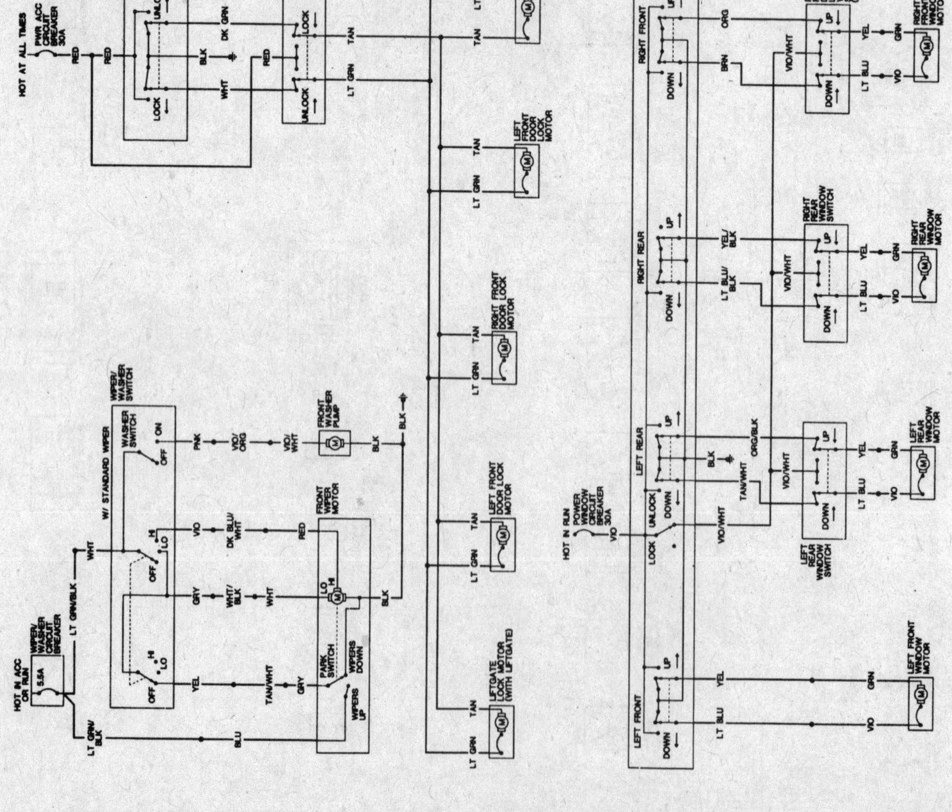

DIAGRAM 4

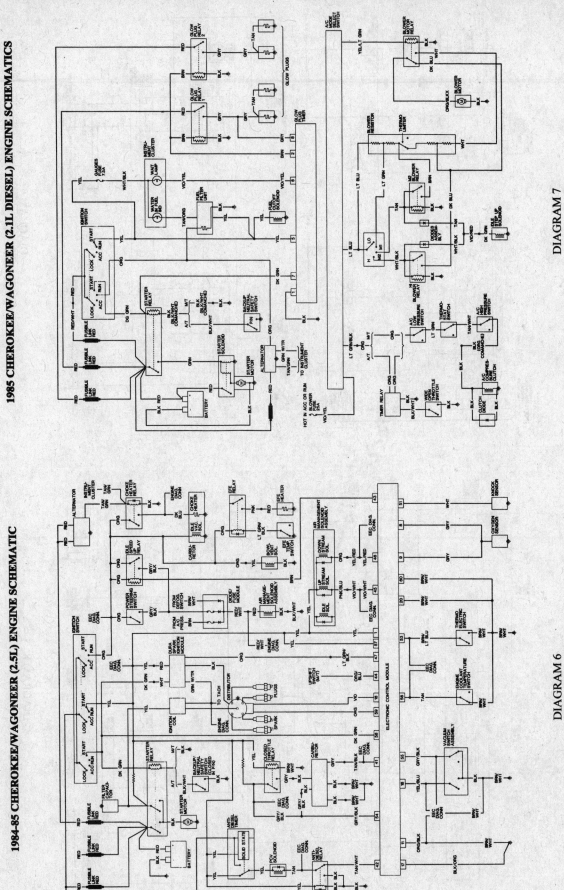

1985 CHEROKEE/WAGONEER (2.1L DIESEL) ENGINE SCHEMATICS

DIAGRAM 7

1984-85 CHEROKEE/WAGONEER (2.5L) ENGINE SCHEMATIC

DIAGRAM 6

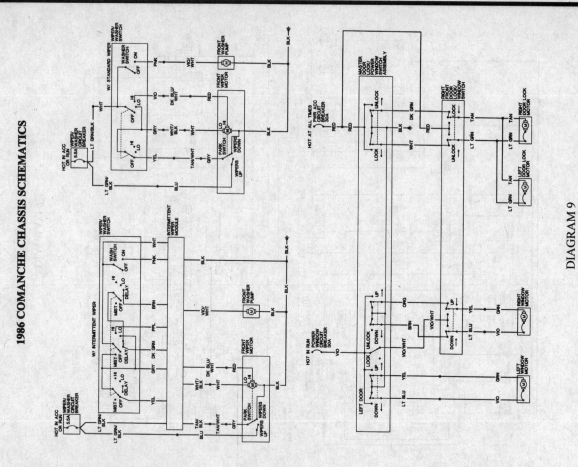

1986 COMANCHE CHASSIS SCHEMATICS

DIAGRAM 9

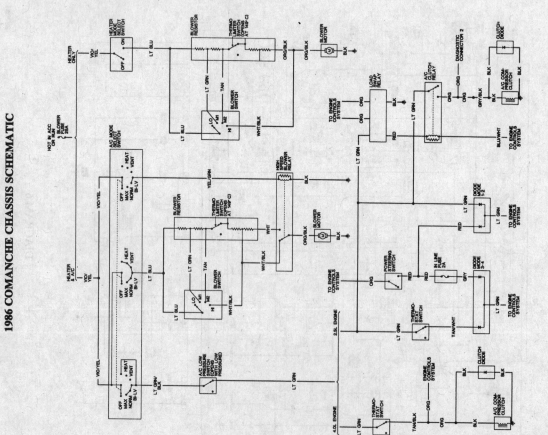

1986 COMANCHE CHASSIS SCHEMATIC

DIAGRAM 8

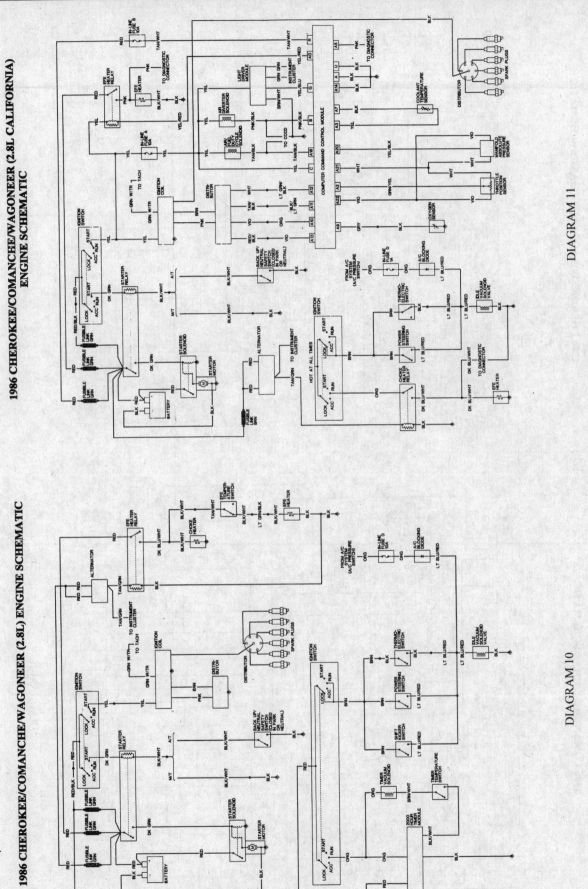

1986 CHEROKEE/COMANCHE/WAGONEER (2.8L CALIFORNIA) ENGINE SCHEMATIC

DIAGRAM 11

1986 CHEROKEE/COMANCHE/WAGONEER (2.8L) ENGINE SCHEMATIC

DIAGRAM 10

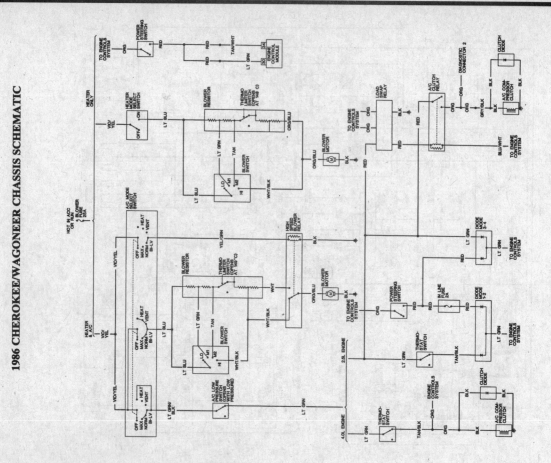

1986 CHEROKEE/WAGONEER CHASSIS SCHEMATIC

DIAGRAM 13

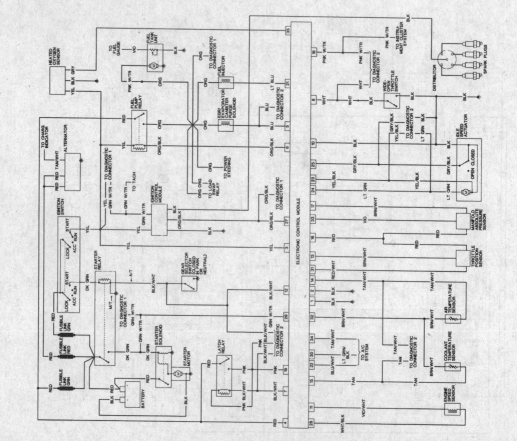

1986 COMANCHE ENGINE SCHEMATIC

DIAGRAM 12

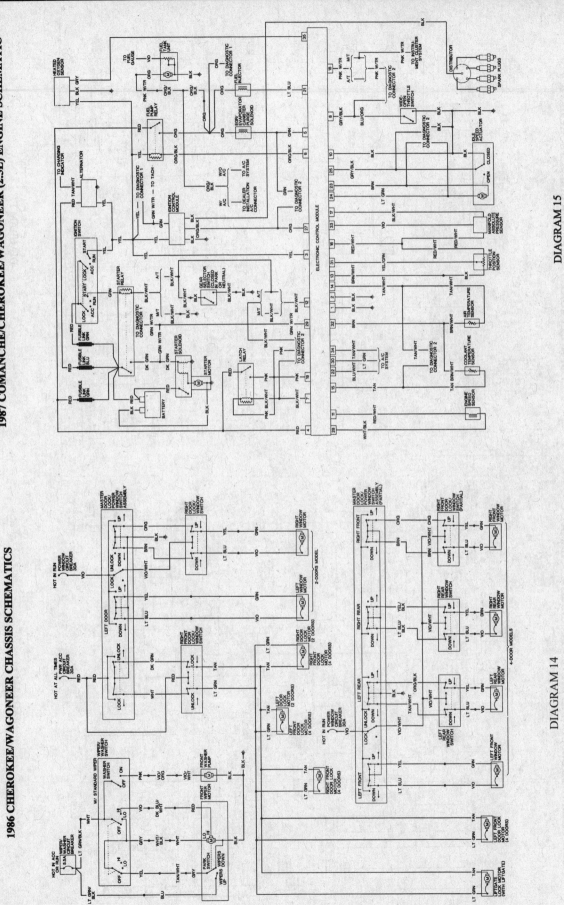

1987 COMANCHE/CHEROKEE/WAGONEER (2.5L) ENGINE SCHEMATIC

DIAGRAM 15

1986 CHEROKEE/WAGONEER CHASSIS SCHEMATICS

DIAGRAM 14

1987-88 CHEROKEE/WAGONEER CHASSIS SCHEMATICS

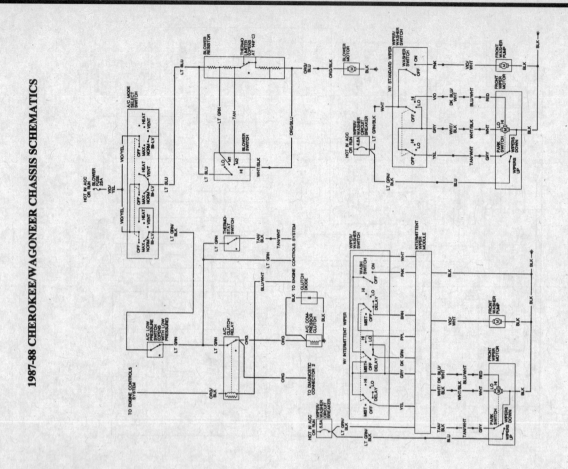

DIAGRAM 17

1987-88 CHEROKEE/COMANCHE/WAGONEER CHASSIS SCHEMATIC

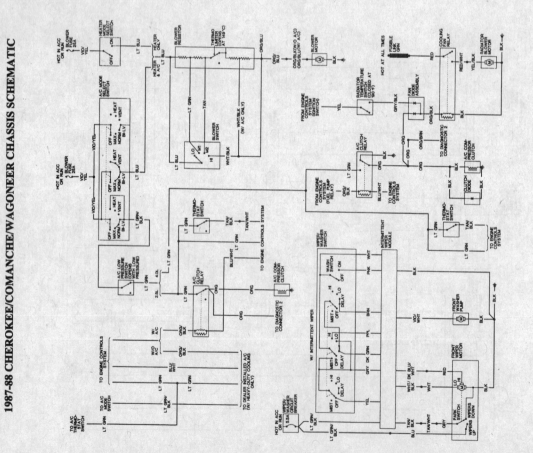

DIAGRAM 16

1988-91 CHEROKEE/COMANCHE/WAGONEER CHASSIS SCHEMATICS

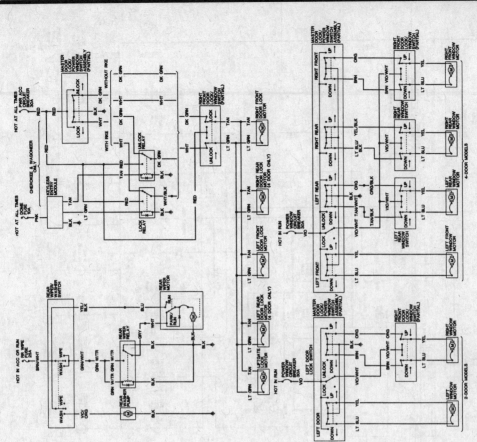

DIAGRAM 19

1987-90 CHEROKEE/COMANCHE/WAGONEER (4.0L) ENGINE SCHEMATIC

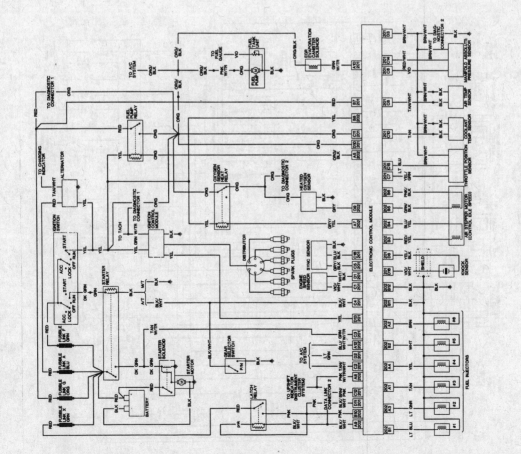

DIAGRAM 18

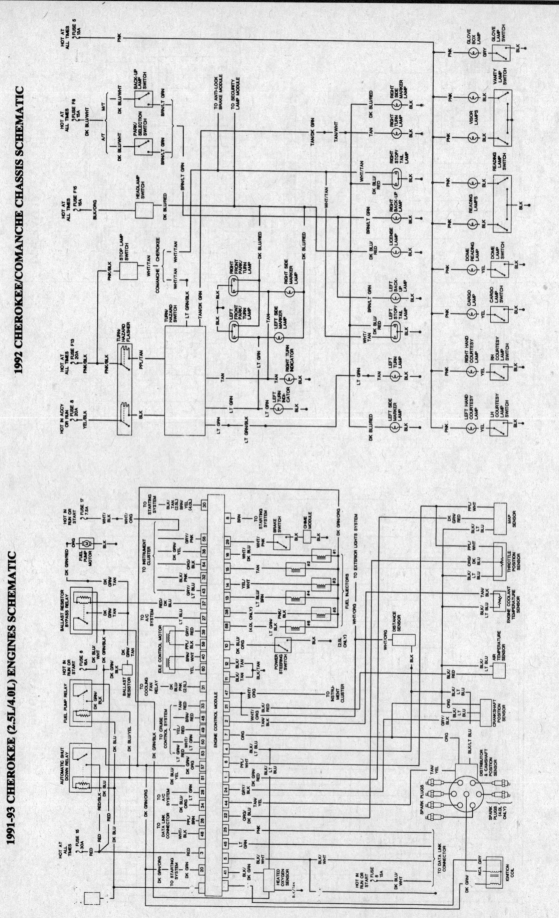

1992 CHEROKEE/COMANCHE CHASSIS SCHEMATIC

DIAGRAM 21

1991-93 CHEROKEE (2.5L/4.0L) ENGINES SCHEMATIC

DIAGRAM 20

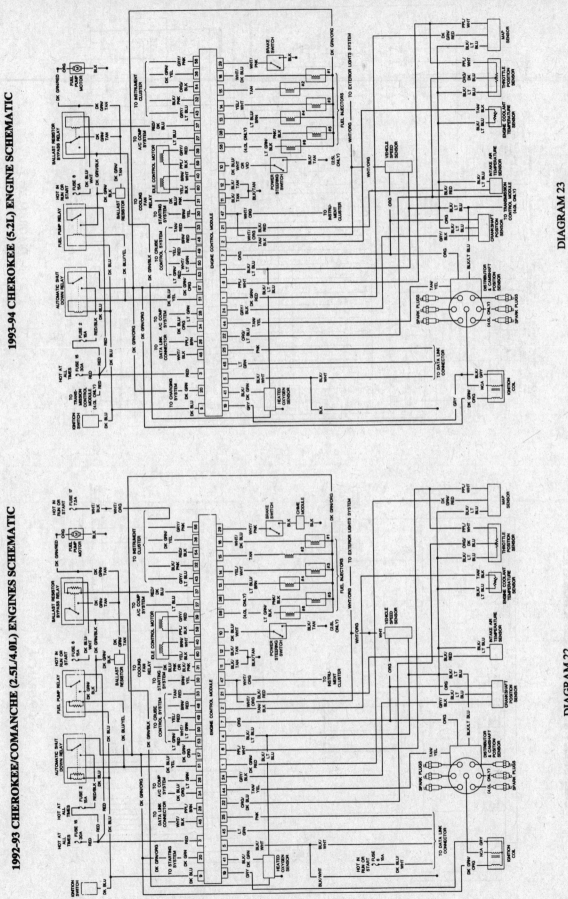

1993-94 CHEROKEE (5.2L) ENGINE SCHEMATIC

DIAGRAM 23

1992-93 CHEROKEE/COMANCHE (2.5L/4.0L) ENGINES SCHEMATIC

DIAGRAM 22

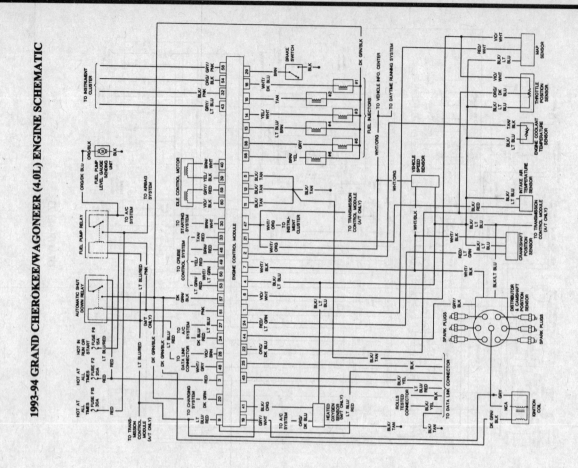

1993-94 GRAND CHEROKEE/WAGONEER (4.0L) ENGINE SCHEMATIC

DIAGRAM 25

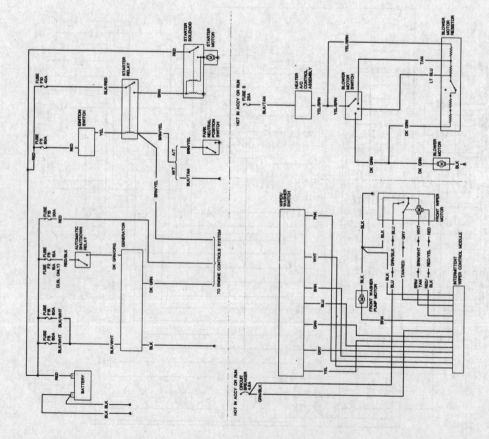

1992-95 CHEROKEE/COMANCHE/GRAND CHEROKEE/WAGONEER CHASSIS SCHEMATICS

DIAGRAM 24

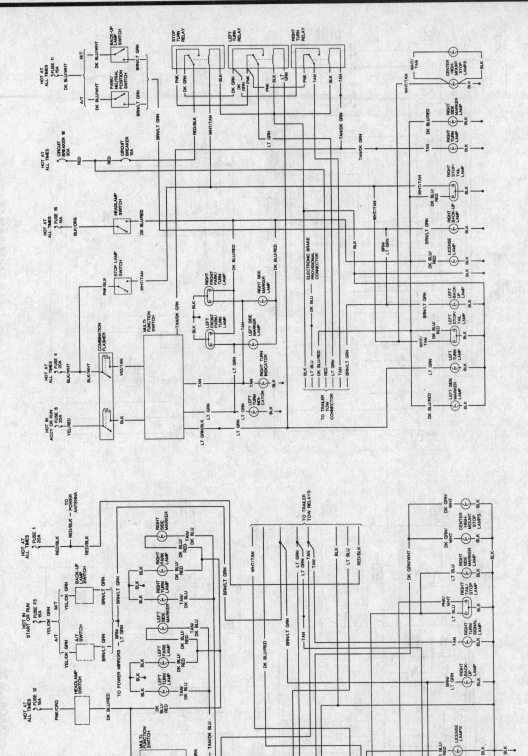

1995 CHEROKEE CHASSIS SCHEMATIC

DIAGRAM 27

1993-95 GRAND CHEROKEE/WAGONEER CHASSIS SCHEMATIC

DIAGRAM 26

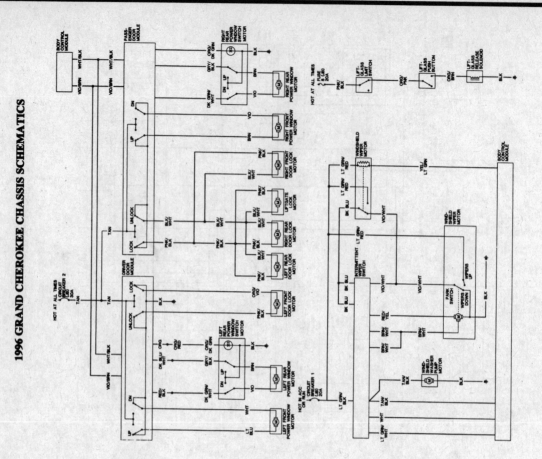

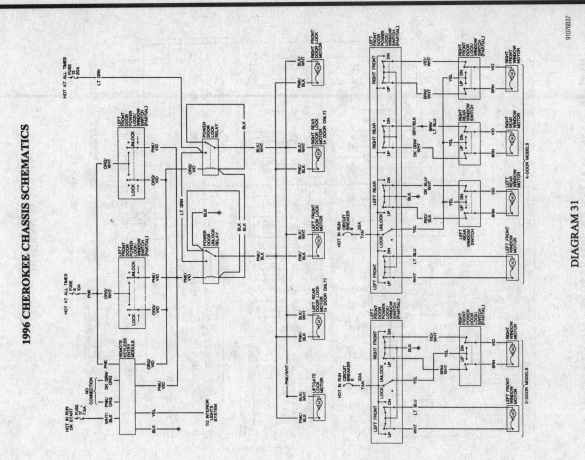

1996 CHEROKEE CHASSIS SCHEMATICS

DIAGRAM 31

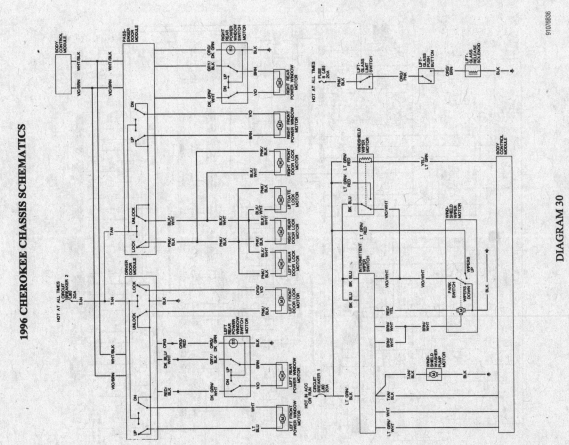

1996 CHEROKEE CHASSIS SCHEMATICS

DIAGRAM 30

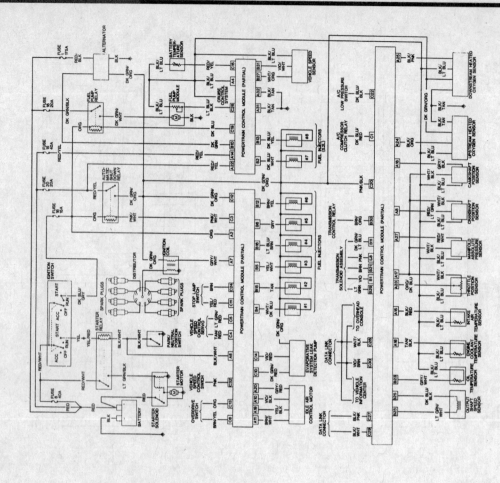

1996-98 GRAND CHEROKEE (4.0L/5.2L/5.9L) ENGINES SCHEMATIC

DIAGRAM 33

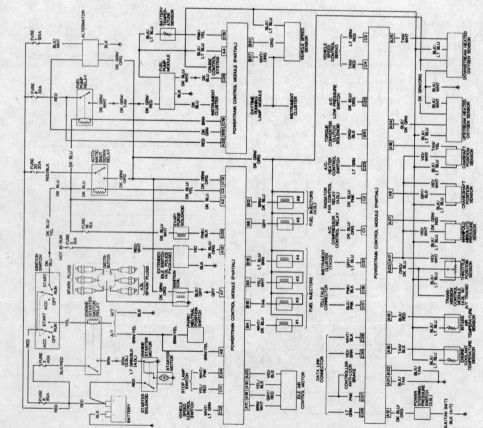

1996-98 CHEROKEE (2.5L/4.0L) ENGINES SCHEMATIC

DIAGRAM 32

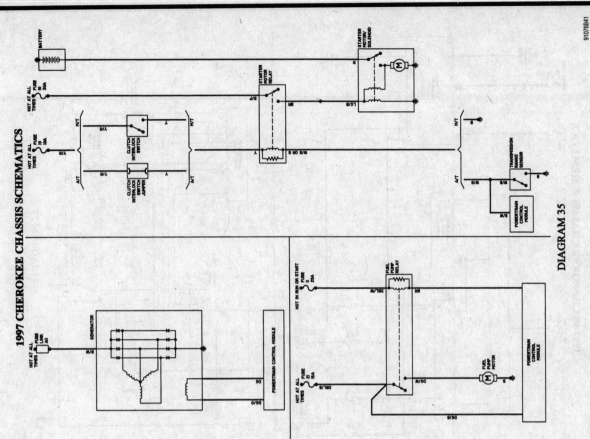

1997 CHEROKEE CHASSIS SCHEMATICS

DIAGRAM 35

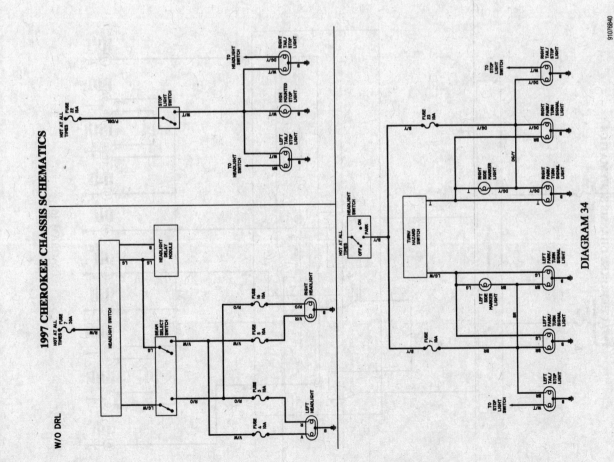

1997 CHEROKEE CHASSIS SCHEMATICS

W/O DRL

DIAGRAM 34

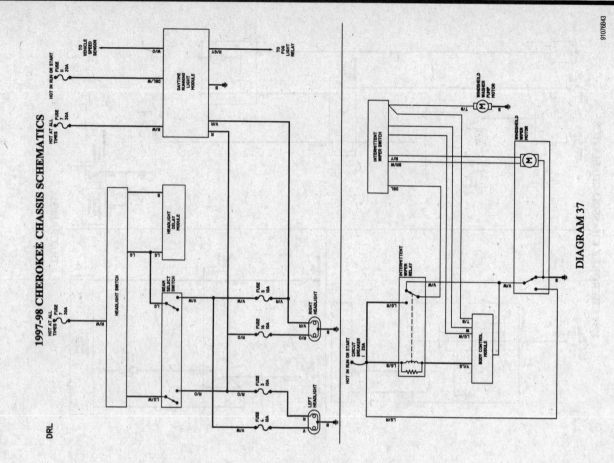

1997-98 CHEROKEE CHASSIS SCHEMATICS

DRL

DIAGRAM 37

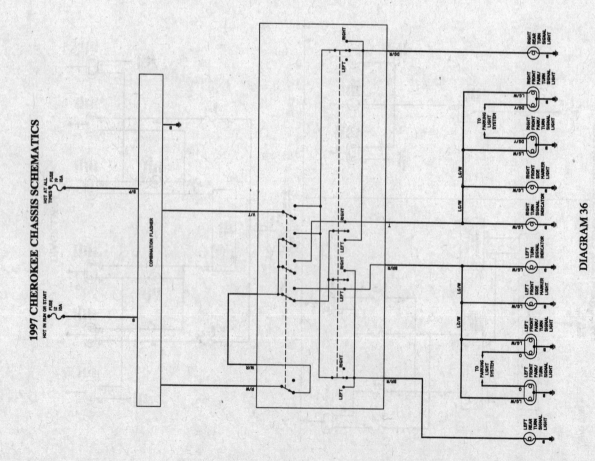

1997 CHEROKEE CHASSIS SCHEMATICS

DIAGRAM 36

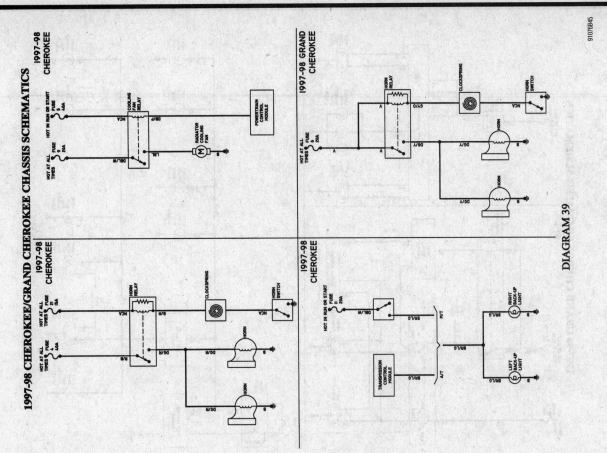

1997-98 CHEROKEE/GRAND CHEROKEE CHASSIS SCHEMATICS

DIAGRAM 39

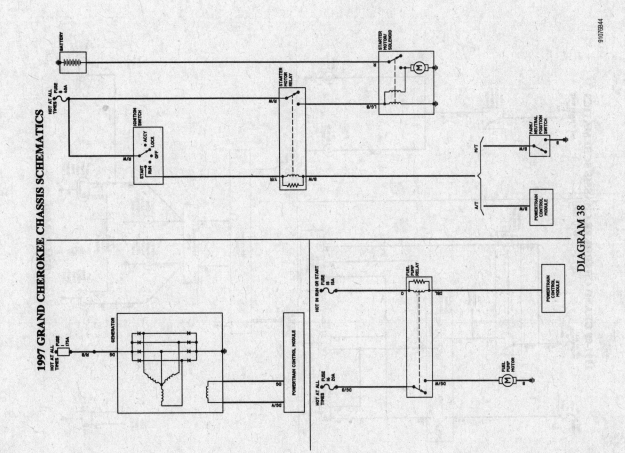

1997 GRAND CHEROKEE CHASSIS SCHEMATICS

DIAGRAM 38

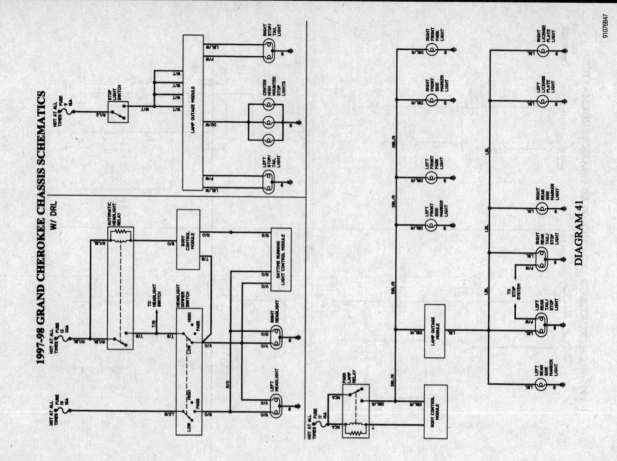

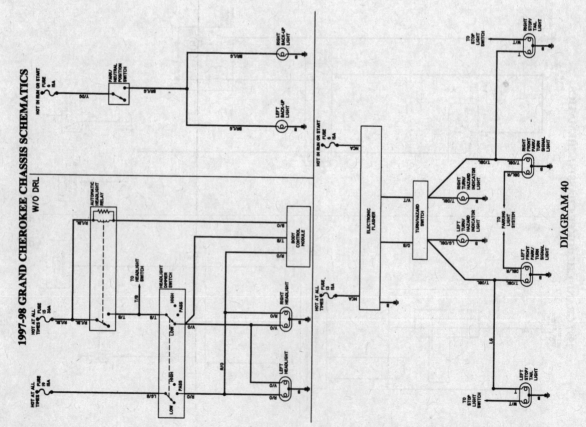

7

DRIVE TRAIN

MANUAL TRANSMISSION

Understanding the Manual Transmission

Because of the way an internal combustion engine breathes, it can produce torque (or twisting force) only within a narrow speed range. Most overhead valve pushrod engines must turn at about 2500 rpm to produce their peak torque. Often by 4500 rpm, they are producing so little torque that continued increases in engine speed produce no power increases.

The torque peak on overhead camshaft engines is, generally, much higher, but much narrower.

The manual transmission and clutch are employed to vary the relationship between engine RPM and the speed of the wheels so that adequate power can be produced under all circumstances. The clutch allows engine torque to be applied to the transmission input shaft gradually, due to mechanical slippage. The vehicle can, consequently, be started smoothly from a full stop.

The transmission changes the ratio between the rotating speeds of the engine and the wheels by the use of gears. 4-speed or 5-speed transmissions are most common. The lower gears allow full engine power to be applied to the rear wheels during acceleration at low speeds.

The clutch driveplate is a thin disc, the center of which is splined to the transmission input shaft. Both sides of the disc are covered with a layer of material which is similar to brake lining and which is capable of allowing slippage without roughness or excessive noise.

The clutch cover is bolted to the engine flywheel and incorporates a diaphragm spring which provides the pressure to engage the clutch. The cover also houses the pressure plate. When the clutch pedal is released, the driven disc is sandwiched between the pressure plate and the smooth surface of the flywheel, thus forcing the disc to turn at the same speed as the engine crankshaft.

The transmission contains a mainshaft which passes all the way through the transmission, from the clutch to the driveshaft. This shaft is separated at one point, so that front and rear portions can turn at different speeds.

Power is transmitted by a countershaft in the lower gears and reverse. The gears of the countershaft mesh with gears on the mainshaft, allowing power to be carried from one to the other. Countershaft gears are often integral with that shaft, while several of the mainshaft gears can either rotate independently of the shaft or be locked to it. Shifting from one gear to the next causes one of the gears to be freed from rotating with the shaft and locks another to it. Gears are locked and unlocked by internal dog clutches which slide between the center of the gear and the shaft. The forward gears usually employ synchronizers; friction members which smoothly bring gear and shaft to the same speed before the toothed dog clutches are engaged.

Shift Handle

REMOVAL & INSTALLATION

Warner T4/5 Models

▶ See Figure 1

1. Remove the screws attaching the the shift lever boot to the floor pan and slide the boot up.
2. Remove the bolts attaching the shift lever housing to the transmission and remove the lever and housing.
3. Installation is the reverse of removal. Make sure the lever is engaged with the shift rail before tightening the housing bolts to 18 ft. lbs. (24 Nm).

Aisin AX4/5/15 Models

▶ See Figures 2 and 3

1. Shift the transmission into first or third gear.
2. Raise and support the vehicle safely.
3. Support the transmission with a floor jack and remove the rear crossmember.
4. Lower the transmission assembly no more than 3 inches (8 cm) for access to the shift lever.
5. Reach up and around the transmission case to unseat the shifter lever dust boot from the transmission shift tower. Move the boot upward on the shift lever for access to the retainer that secures the lever in the tower.
6. Disengage the shift lever from the transmission by pressing the shift lever retainer downward and counterclockwise. Then lift the lever and retainer out of the shift tower. You can leave the shift lever in the floorpan boot for reassembly.
7. Installation is the reverse of removal. Tighten crossmember-to-frame bolts to 30 ft. lbs. (41 Nm); transmission-to-crossmember bolts to 33 ft. lbs. (45 Nm).

BA 10/5 Models

▶ See Figure 4

1. Remove the gearshift lever boot and remove the upper part of the console.
2. Remove the lower part of the console. Remove the inner gearshift lever boot.
3. Remove the gearshift lever.

➡On some BA 10/5 transmissions, the shift lever may be held in place with a snapring and spring washer.

4. Installation is the reverse of removal.

NV3550 Models

1. Shift the transmission into first or third gear.
2. Remove the center console and shift boot.
3. Install nuts on two M6 x 1.0 bolts and thread the bolts into the threaded holes at the base of the shift lever.
4. Tighten the nuts equally until the shift lever loosens on the shift tower stub shaft.
5. Remove the shift lever from the shift tower.
6. Installation is the reverse of removal.

Backup Light Switch

REMOVAL & INSTALLATION

The backup light switch on most transmissions is located on the right side of the case.

Fig. 1 Warner T4/5 shift lever

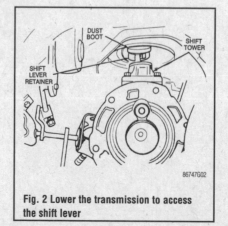

Fig. 2 Lower the transmission to access the shift lever

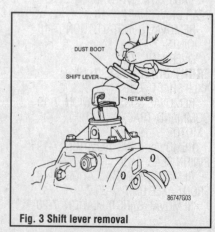

Fig. 3 Shift lever removal

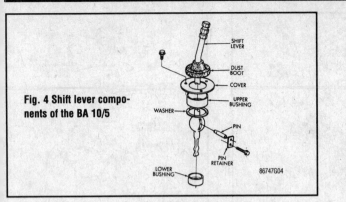

Fig. 4 Shift lever components of the BA 10/5

1. Unplug the electrical connector and unscrew the switch.
2. If the switch uses a gasket (washer), replace it when installing the new switch.
3. If a gasket (washer) is not used, coat the threads of the switch with sealer before installation.
4. Tighten the switch to 27 ft. lbs. (37 Nm) and engage the electrical connector.

Extension Housing Seal

REMOVAL & INSTALLATION

2WD Models

♦ **See Figures 5 and 6**

The extension seal on 2-wheel drive vehicles is located at the rear of the transmission case.
1. Raise and support the vehicle safely.
2. Drain the transmission of lubricant.
3. Matchmark the driveshaft to the yoke for reassembly and remove the driveshaft.
4. Remove the old seal using a seal puller or appropriate prytool.

To install:
5. Install a new seal, coated with sealing compound, using an appropriate seal installation tool.

➡**Tool J-35582 or equivalent is recommended for AX4/5/15 transmissions. Tool J-21426 or equivalent is recommended for Warner T4/5 transmissions.**

6. Install the driveshaft, making certain to align the matchmark. Tighten bolts to 20 ft. lbs. (27 Nm)
7. Fill the transmission to the level of the fill plug hole. Install the plug and lower the vehicle.

4WD Models

The extension seal on 4-wheel drive vehicles is located at the rear of the transfer case.
1. Raise and support the vehicle safely.

2. Drain the transfer case of lubricant.
3. Matchmark the driveshaft to the yoke for reassembly and remove the driveshaft.
4. Remove the old seal using a seal puller or appropriate prytool.

To install:
5. Install a new seal, coated with sealing compound, using an appropriate seal installation tool.
6. Install the driveshaft, making certain to align matchmark. Tighten bolts to 20 ft. lbs. (27 Nm)
7. Fill the transfer case with lubricant. Install the plug and lower the vehicle.

Transmission Assembly

REMOVAL & INSTALLATION

♦ **See Figures 7, 8, 9 and 10**

1. Shift the transmission into first or third gear.
2. Raise and support the vehicle safely.
3. Support the transmission with a floor jack and remove the rear crossmember.
4. Disconnect the transmission shift linkage, speedometer cable, transfer case vacuum lines (on 4WD) and clutch hydraulic lines.
5. Lower the transmission assembly no more than 3 inches (8 cm) for access to the shift lever.
6. Disengage the shift lever from the transmission. You can leave the shift lever in the floorpan boot for reassembly.
7. Matchmark the front and rear driveshafts for installation alignment and remove.
8. Disconnect the engine timing sensor, if equipped.
9. Disconnect the transmission (and transfer case on 4WD) vent hoses.
10. Disconnect the clutch master cylinder hydraulic line assembly. If equipped, disconnect it from the concentric bearing inlet line.
11. Secure the assembly to a floor jack with chains to prevent it from slipping during removal.

➡**It is a good idea to place a second support (floor jack or jackstand) under the oil pan of the engine to prevent the engine from falling rearward. This second support will also ease the installation of the transmission.**

12. Remove the clutch housing brace rod.
13. Remove the clutch housing to engine attaching bolts and remove the transmission assembly.
14. Separate the transmission from the clutch housing and transfer case (on 4WD).

➡**After separating the transmission from the clutch housing, resecure the bearing nylon straps to hold the bearing piston in place.**

To install:
15. Install the clutch housing on the transmission. Tighten the housing bolts to 27 ft. lbs. (37 Nm)
16. Install the concentric bearing. Secure the bearing to the mounting pin with a new retainer clip.
17. Mount the transmission on a floor jack, lightly lubricate the input shaft and install the transmission.

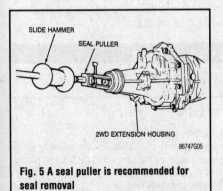

Fig. 5 A seal puller is recommended for seal removal

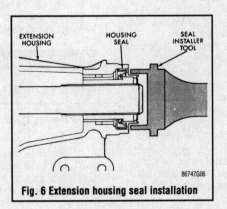

Fig. 6 Extension housing seal installation

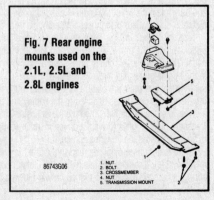

Fig. 7 Rear engine mounts used on the 2.1L, 2.5L and 2.8L engines

1. NUT
2. BOLT
3. CROSSMEMBER
4. NUT
5. TRANSMISSION MOUNT

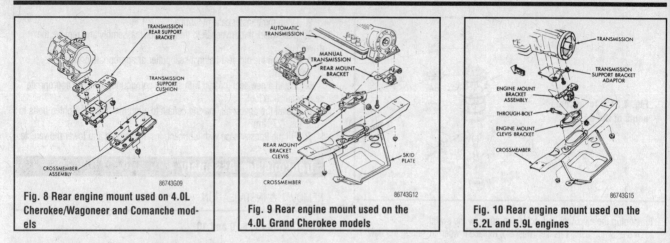

Fig. 8 Rear engine mount used on 4.0L Cherokee/Wagoneer and Comanche models

Fig. 9 Rear engine mount used on the 4.0L Grand Cherokee models

Fig. 10 Rear engine mount used on the 5.2L and 5.9L engines

18. Install and tighten the clutch housing-to-engine bolts to 28 ft. lbs. (38 Nm).

➡ **Be sure the housing is properly seated against the engine block before tightening the attaching bolts.**

19. Lower the transmission no more than 3 inches (8 cm) to allow installation of the shifter. Insert the shift lever in the shift tower. Press the lever retainer downward and turn clockwise to lock in place. Install the lever dust boot on the shift tower.

20. Connect the concentric bearing hydraulic line, if equipped, and the engine timing sensor wires.

21. Mount the transfer case (if equipped) on a jack and align with the transmission shafts. Install the transfer case and tighten the transfer case-to-transmission bolts to 26 ft. lbs. (35 Nm).

22. Connect the transmission (and transfer case on 4WD) vent hoses, backup light switch, and distance sensor wires.

23. Install the rear crossmember. Tighten the crossmember-to-frame bolts to 30 ft. lbs. (41 Nm); and the transmission-to-crossmember bolts to 33 ft. lbs. (45 Nm).

24. Align and install the front and rear propeller shafts. Tighten the U-joint clamp bolts to 170 inch lbs. (19 Nm).

25. Fill the transmission (and transfer case on 4WD) with lubricant and lower the vehicle.

CLUTCH

Understanding the Clutch

❊❊ CAUTION

The clutch driven disc may contain asbestos, which has been determined to be a cancer causing agent. Never clean clutch surfaces with compressed air! Avoid inhaling any dust from any clutch surface! When cleaning clutch surfaces, use a commercially available brake cleaning fluid.

The purpose of the clutch is to disconnect and connect engine power at the transmission. A vehicle at rest requires a lot of engine torque to get all that weight moving. An internal combustion engine does not develop a high starting torque (unlike steam engines) so it must be allowed to operate without any load until it builds up enough torque to move the vehicle. To a point, torque increases with engine rpm. The clutch allows the engine to build up torque by physically disconnecting the engine from the transmission, relieving the engine of any load or resistance.

The transfer of engine power to the transmission (the load) must be smooth and gradual; if it weren't, drive line components would wear out or break quickly. This gradual power transfer is made possible by gradually releasing the clutch pedal. The clutch disc and pressure plate are the connecting link between the engine and transmission. When the clutch pedal is released, the disc and plate contact each other (the clutch is engaged) physically joining the engine and transmission. When the pedal is pushed in, the disc and plate separate (the clutch is disengaged) disconnecting the engine from the transmission.

Most clutch assemblies consists of the flywheel, the clutch disc, the clutch pressure plate, the throw out bearing and fork, the actuating linkage and the pedal. The flywheel and clutch pressure plate (driving members) are connected to the engine crankshaft and rotate with it. The clutch disc is located between the flywheel and pressure plate, and is splined to the transmission shaft. A driving member is one that is attached to the engine and transfers engine power to a driven member (clutch disc) on the transmission shaft. A driving member (pressure plate) rotates (drives) a driven member (clutch disc) on contact and, in so doing, turns the transmission shaft.

There is a circular diaphragm spring within the pressure plate cover (transmission side). In a relaxed state (when the clutch pedal is fully released) this spring is convex; that is, it is dished outward toward the transmission. Push-

ing in the clutch pedal actuates the attached linkage. Connected to the other end of this is the throw out fork, which hold the throw out bearing. When the clutch pedal is depressed, the clutch linkage pushes the fork and bearing forward to contact the diaphragm spring of the pressure plate. The outer edges of the spring are secured to the pressure plate and are pivoted on rings so that when the center of the spring is compressed by the throw out bearing, the outer edges bow outward and, by so doing, pull the pressure plate in the same direction—away from the clutch disc. This action separates the disc from the plate, disengaging the clutch and allowing the transmission to be shifted into another gear. A coil type clutch return spring attached to the clutch pedal arm permits full release of the pedal. Releasing the pedal pulls the throw out bearing away from the diaphragm spring resulting in a reversal of spring position. As bearing pressure is gradually released from the spring center, the outer edges of the spring bow outward, pushing the pressure plate into closer contact with the clutch disc. As the disc and plate move closer together, friction between the two increases and slippage is reduced until, when full spring pressure is applied (by fully releasing the pedal) the speed of the disc and plate are the same. This stops all slipping, creating a direct connection between the plate and disc which results in the transfer of power from the engine to the transmission. The clutch disc is now rotating with the pressure plate at engine speed and, because it is splined to the transmission shaft, the shaft now turns at the same engine speed.

The clutch is operating properly if:
1. It will stall the engine when released with the vehicle held stationary.
2. The shift lever can be moved freely between 1st and reverse gears when the vehicle is stationary and the clutch disengaged.

Clutch Disc And Pressure Plate

REMOVAL & INSTALLATION

▶ **See Figures 11, 12, 13 and 14**

1. Raise and safely support the vehicle.
2. Remove the transmission or transmission/transfer case assembly.
3. Matchmark the pressure plate and flywheel. Loosen the pressure plate bolts, a little at a time, in rotation, to avoid warpage.
4. Remove the pressure plate and clutch disc.

5. Inspect the flywheel for scoring, cracks, warpage or other wear; resurface or replace as necessary.

6. Inspect the pilot bearing for excessive wear or damage and replace as necessary.

To install:

7. If removed, install the pilot bearing after lubricating lightly with grease. Seat the bearing in the crankshaft with a clutch alignment tool.

8. Check the clutch disc runout by installing the disc on the transmission input shaft. Runout should not exceed 0.020 in. (0.5mm) when measured 1/4 in. (5mm) from the outer edge of the facing.

9. Install the clutch alignment tool in the pilot bearing.

10. Install the clutch disc on the tool.

11. Install the pressure plate and tighten the bolts finger-tight. The pressure plate bolts must be tightened a little at a time, in rotation, to avoid warpage. Tighten the pressure plate bolts as follows:

- 2.1L diesel engines—16 ft. lbs. (22 Nm)
- 2.5L and 2.8L engines—23 ft. lbs. (31 Nm)
- 4.0L engine—40 ft. lbs. (54 Nm)
- 5.2L and 5.9L engines—5/16 nch bolts: 17 ft. lbs. (23 Nm) and 3/8 inch bolts 30 ft. lbs. (41 Nm)

12. Install the transmission or transmission/transfer case assembly and lower the vehicle.

Clutch Master Cylinder

REMOVAL & INSTALLATION

Comanche, Wagoneer and 1984–93 Cherokee

▶ See Figure 15

1. Disconnect the hydraulic line at the master cylinder. Cap the line.

2. Disconnect the pushrod at the clutch pedal. Remove the instrument panel lower trim cover for access, if necessary.

3. Unbolt the master cylinder from the firewall. One bolt is accessible from the engine compartment, the other is accessible from the passenger compartment.

4. Installation is the reverse of removal. Tighten the mounting nuts to 19 ft. lbs. (26 Nm); the hydraulic line fitting to 15 ft. lbs. (20 Nm). Refill and bleed the system.

Grand Cherokee and 1994 and Later Cherokee

▶ See Figure 16

The clutch master cylinder, reservoir, slave cylinder and connecting lines are sealed units and are serviced as an assembly only.

1. Raise and safely support the vehicle.

2. Remove the slave cylinder and clip from the clutch housing.

3. Disconnect the hydraulic fluid line from the body clips.

4. Lower the vehicle.

5. Remove the retaining ring, flat washer and wave washer attaching the clutch master cylinder pushrod to the clutch pedal.

6. Slide the master cylinder pushrod off the clutch pedal pin.

7. Inspect the clutch pedal bushing, replace as necessary.

8. Remove the clutch master cylinder reservoir from the dash panel.

9. Remove the clutch master cylinder stud nuts.

10. Remove the assembly from the vehicle.

To install:

11. Position the assembly into the vehicle.

12. Tighten the clutch master cylinder stud nuts to 200–300 inch lbs. (24–34 Nm).

13. Position the reservoir and tighten the screws.

14. Install the clutch master cylinder pushrod on the clutch pedal pin. Secure the rod with the wave washer, flat washer and retaining ring.

15. Raise and safely support the vehicle.

16. Insert the slave cylinder through the clutch housing into the release lever. Ensure the cap on the end of the rod is securely engaged in the lever. Tighten the bolts to 200–300 inch lbs. (24–34 Nm).

17. Insert the fluid line in the body clips.

Fig. 11 Be sure that the flywheel surface is clean, before installing the clutch

Fig. 12 Install a clutch alignment arbor, to align the clutch assembly during installation

Fig. 13 Use a locking agent on the clutch assembly bolts

Fig. 14 Install the clutch assembly bolts and tighten in steps, in an X pattern

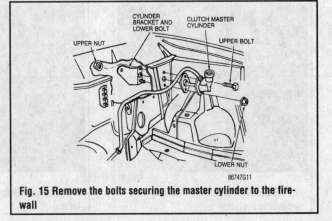

Fig. 15 Remove the bolts securing the master cylinder to the firewall

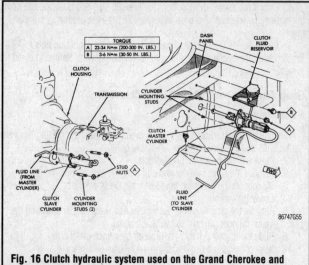

Fig. 16 Clutch hydraulic system used on the Grand Cherokee and 1994 and later Cherokee

Slave Cylinder

REMOVAL & INSTALLATION

Comanche, Wagoneer and 1984–93 Cherokee

▶ **See Figures 17 thru 23**

➥**The Comanche, Wagoneer and 1984–93 Cherokee models utilize what is referred to as a hydraulic concentric bearing, which performs the same function as a slave cylinder.**

The hydraulic concentric bearing incorporates the release bearing and the slave cylinder in a single assembly.

The hydraulic concentric bearing completely encircles the transmission input shaft. In operation, the piston movement causes the bearing to move in a straight line direction.

The hydraulic concentric bearing is serviced as an assembly only. The release bearing portion of the assembly is permanently attached to the piston. The hydraulic lines are also permanently attached.

1. Disconnect the negative battery cable.
2. Raise and support the vehicle safely.
3. Remove the transmission.
4. Disconnect the clutch master cylinder fluid line.
5. Remove the insulator plate bolts and slide the plate off the bleed line.
6. Remove the concentric bearing retaining nut.
7. Remove the concentric bearing from the transmission input shaft. If the bearing will be reused, secure the bearing and piston with rubber bands.

To install:

8. Inspect the bearing mounting pin and replace the front cover if the pin is damaged. Install the concentric bearing on the transmission input shaft.
9. Guide the bearing fluid and bleed lines through the openings in the clutch housing.
10. Position the bearing boss on the mounting pin and seat the bearing against the transmission. Install a new retaining nut and unhook the T-handle straps retaining the bearing.
11. Install the insulator and plate.
12. Install the transmission and transfer case and connect the clutch master cylinder fluid line.
13. Fill and bleed the clutch hydraulic system.

Grand Cherokee and 1994 and Later Cherokee

The clutch master cylinder, reservoir, slave cylinder and connecting lines are sealed units and are serviced as an assembly only. Refer to the Clutch Master Cylinder removal and installation procedure.

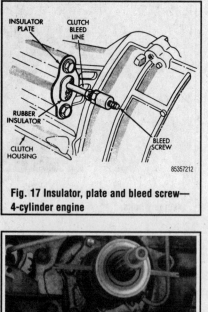

Fig. 17 Insulator, plate and bleed screw—4-cylinder engine

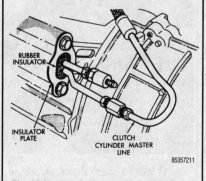

Fig. 18 Insulator, plate and bleed screw—6-cylinder engines

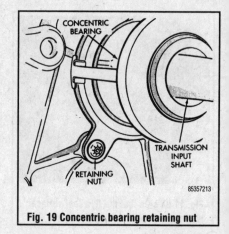

Fig. 19 Concentric bearing retaining nut

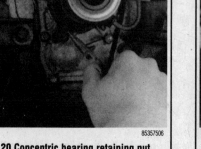

Fig. 20 Concentric bearing retaining nut removal/installation

Fig. 21 Concentric bearing removal/installation

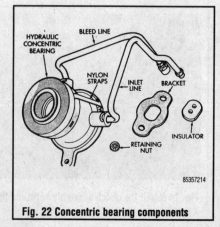

Fig. 22 Concentric bearing components

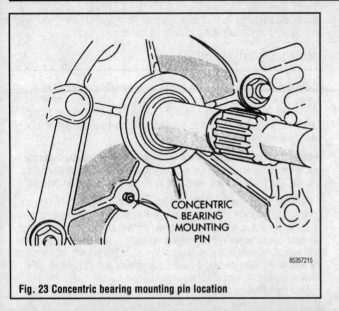

Fig. 23 Concentric bearing mounting pin location

SYSTEM BLEEDING

On the Grand Cherokee and 1994 and later Cherokee, the clutch master cylinder, reservoir, slave cylinder and connecting lines are sealed units and are serviced as an assembly only. System bleeding is not necessary or possible.

1. Fill the reservoir with clean brake fluid.
2. Raise and support the truck on jackstands.
3. Remove the slave cylinder from the clutch housing, but do not disconnect the hydraulic line. There is enough play in the line to do this.
4. Remove the slave cylinder pushrod.
5. Using a wood dowel, compress the slave cylinder plunger.
6. Attach one end of a rubber hose to the slave cylinder bleeder screw and place the other end in a glass jar, filled halfway with clean brake fluid. Make sure that the hose will stay submerged.
7. Loosen the bleeder screw.
8. Have an assistant press and hold the clutch pedal to the floor. Tighten the bleeder screw with the pedal at the floor. Bubbles will have appeared in the jar when the pedal was depressed.
9. Have your assistant release the pedal, then perform the sequence again, until bubbles no longer appear in the jar.
10. Install the slave cylinder and lower the truck. Test the clutch.

AUTOMATIC TRANSMISSION

Understanding Automatic Transmissions

The automatic transmission allows engine torque and power to be transmitted to the rear wheels within a narrow range of engine operating speeds. It will allow the engine to turn fast enough to produce plenty of power and torque at very low speeds, while keeping it at a sensible rpm at high vehicle speeds (and it does this job without driver assistance). The transmission uses a light fluid as the medium for the transmission of power. This fluid also works in the operation of various hydraulic control circuits and as a lubricant. Because the transmission fluid performs all of these functions, trouble within the unit can easily travel from one part to another. For this reason, and because of the complexity and unusual operating principles of the transmission, a very sound understanding of the basic principles of operation will simplify troubleshooting.

TORQUE CONVERTER

♦ **See Figure 24**

The torque converter replaces the conventional clutch. It has three functions:
1. It allows the engine to idle with the vehicle at a standstill, even with the transmission in gear.

2. It allows the transmission to shift from range-to-range smoothly, without requiring that the driver close the throttle during the shift.
3. It multiplies engine torque to an increasing extent as vehicle speed drops and throttle opening is increased. This has the effect of making the transmission more responsive and reduces the amount of shifting required.

The torque converter is a metal case which is shaped like a sphere that has been flattened on opposite sides. It is bolted to the rear end of the engine's crankshaft. Generally, the entire metal case rotates at engine speed and serves as the engine's flywheel.

The case contains three sets of blades. One set is attached directly to the case. This set forms the torus or pump. Another set is directly connected to the output shaft, and forms the turbine. The third set is mounted on a hub which, in turn, is mounted on a stationary shaft through a one-way clutch. This third set is known as the stator.

A pump, which is driven by the converter hub at engine speed, keeps the torque converter full of transmission fluid at all times. Fluid flows continuously through the unit to provide cooling.

Under low speed acceleration, the torque converter functions as follows:

The torus is turning faster than the turbine. It picks up fluid at the center of the converter and, through centrifugal force, slings it outward. Since the outer edge of the converter moves faster than the portions at the center, the fluid picks up speed.

The fluid then enters the outer edge of the turbine blades. It then travels back toward the center of the converter case along the turbine blades. In impinging upon the turbine blades, the fluid loses the energy picked up in the torus.

If the fluid was now returned directly into the torus, both halves of the converter would have to turn at approximately the same speed at all times, and torque input and output would both be the same.

In flowing through the torus and turbine, the fluid picks up two types of flow, or flow in two separate directions. It flows through the turbine blades, and it spins with the engine. The stator, whose blades are stationary when the vehicle is being accelerated at low speeds, converts one type of flow into another. Instead of allowing the fluid to flow straight back into the torus, the stator's curved blades turn the fluid almost 90° toward the direction of rotation of the engine. Thus the fluid does not flow as fast toward the torus, but is already spinning when the torus picks it up. This has the effect of allowing the torus to turn much faster than the turbine. This difference in speed may be compared to the difference in speed between the smaller and larger gears in any gear train. The result is that engine power output is higher, and engine torque is multiplied.

As the speed of the turbine increases, the fluid spins faster and faster in the direction of engine rotation. As a result, the ability of the stator to redirect the fluid flow is reduced. Under cruising conditions, the stator is eventually forced to rotate on its one-way clutch in the direction of engine rotation. Under these conditions, the torque converter begins to behave almost like a solid shaft, with the torus and turbine speeds being almost equal.

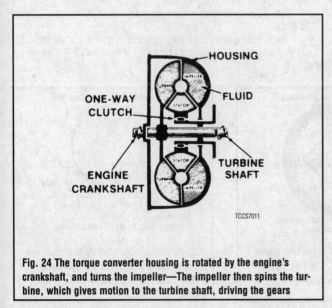

Fig. 24 The torque converter housing is rotated by the engine's crankshaft, and turns the impeller—The impeller then spins the turbine, which gives motion to the turbine shaft, driving the gears

PLANETARY GEARBOX

▶ **See Figures 25, 26 and 27**

The ability of the torque converter to multiply engine torque is limited. Also, the unit tends to be more efficient when the turbine is rotating at relatively high speeds. Therefore, a planetary gearbox is used to carry the power output of the turbine to the driveshaft.

Planetary gears function very similarly to conventional transmission gears. However, their construction is different in that three elements make up one gear system, and, in that all three elements are different from one another. The three elements are: an outer gear that is shaped like a hoop, with teeth cut into the inner surface; a sun gear, mounted on a shaft and located at the very center of the outer gear; and a set of three planet gears, held by pins in a ring-like planet carrier, meshing with both the sun gear and the outer gear. Either the outer gear or the sun gear may be held stationary, providing more than one possible torque multiplication factor for each set of gears. Also, if all three gears are forced to rotate at the same speed, the gearset forms, in effect, a solid shaft.

Most automatics use the planetary gears to provide various reductions ratios. Bands and clutches are used to hold various portions of the gearsets to the transmission case or to the shaft on which they are mounted. Shifting is accomplished, then, by changing the portion of each planetary gearset which is held to the transmission case or to the shaft.

SERVOS & ACCUMULATORS

▶ **See Figure 28**

The servos are hydraulic pistons and cylinders. They resemble the hydraulic actuators used on many other machines, such as bulldozers. Hydraulic fluid enters the cylinder, under pressure, and forces the piston to move to engage the band or clutches.

The accumulators are used to cushion the engagement of the servos. The transmission fluid must pass through the accumulator on the way to the servo. The accumulator housing contains a thin piston which is sprung away from the discharge passage of the accumulator. When fluid passes through the accumu-

lator on the way to the servo, it must move the piston against spring pressure, and this action smooths out the action of the servo.

HYDRAULIC CONTROL SYSTEM

The hydraulic pressure used to operate the servos comes from the main transmission oil pump. This fluid is channeled to the various servos through the shift valves. There is generally a manual shift valve which is operated by the transmission selector lever and an automatic shift valve for each automatic upshift the transmission provides.

➡**Many new transmissions are electronically controlled. On these models, electrical solenoids are used to better control the hydraulic fluid. Usually, the solenoids are regulated by an electronic control module.**

There are two pressures which affect the operation of these valves. One is the governor pressure which is effected by vehicle speed. The other is the modulator pressure which is effected by intake manifold vacuum or throttle position. Governor pressure rises with an increase in vehicle speed, and modulator pressure rises as the throttle is opened wider. By responding to these two pressures, the shift valves cause the upshift points to be delayed with increased throttle opening to make the best use of the engine's power output.

Most transmissions also make use of an auxiliary circuit for downshifting. This circuit may be actuated by the throttle linkage the vacuum line which actuates the modulator, by a cable or by a solenoid. It applies pressure to a special downshift surface on the shift valve or valves.

The transmission modulator also governs the line pressure, used to actuate the servos. In this way, the clutches and bands will be actuated with a force matching the torque output of the engine.

Neutral Start/Back-Up Light Switch

REMOVAL & INSTALLATION

Except AW-4 Models

▶ **See Figure 29**

To replace the switch, simply unbolt it from the transmission, disconnect the wires and install a new switch.

AW-4 Models

▶ **See Figure 30**

1. Raise and support the front end on jackstands.
2. Disconnect the wiring at the switch.
3. Pry open the locktabs and remove the switch retaining nut and washer.
4. Remove the switch adjusting bolt.
5. Slide the switch off the manual valve shaft.

To install:

6. Disconnect the shift linkage rod from the shift lever at the transmission.
7. Rotate the shift lever all the way rearward, then forward 2 detent positions to **N**.

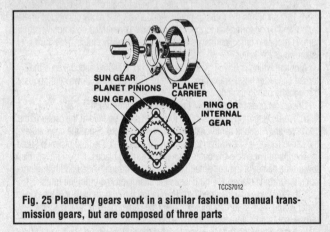

Fig. 25 Planetary gears work in a similar fashion to manual transmission gears, but are composed of three parts

Fig. 26 Planetary gears in the maximum reduction (low) range. The ring gear is held and a lower gear ratio is obtained

Fig. 27 Planetary gears in the minimum reduction (drive) range. The ring gear is allowed to revolve, providing a higher gear ratio

8.

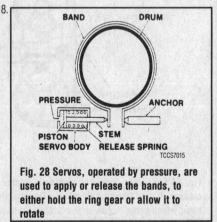

Fig. 28 Servos, operated by pressure, are used to apply or release the bands, to either hold the ring gear or allow it to rotate

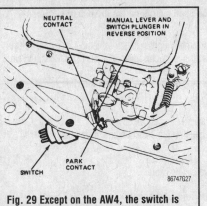

Fig. 29 Except on the AW4, the switch is screwed into the side of the transmission

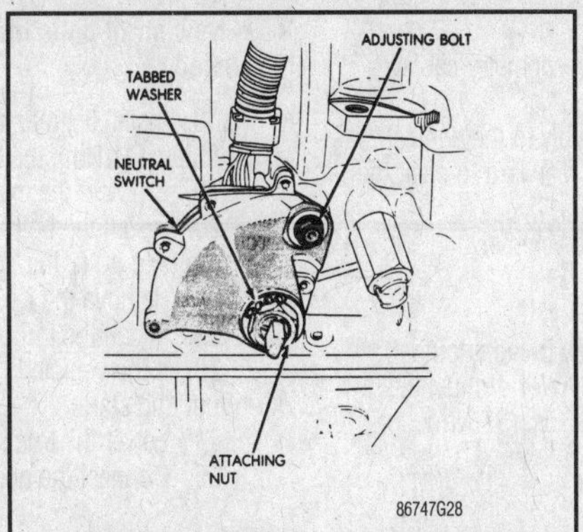

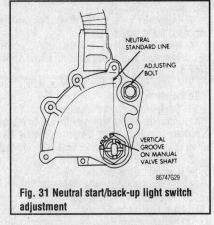

Fig. 30 Neutral start/back-up light switch removal on the AW4

Fig. 31 Neutral start/back-up light switch adjustment

Position the switch on the valve shaft and install the adjusting bolt finger-tight.

9. Install the washer and attaching nut and tighten the nut to 60 inch lbs. (7 Nm), but don't bend the tabbed washer yet.

10. Adjust the switch.

ADJUSTMENT

Except AW-4 Model

The switch is not adjustable on these transmissions.

AW-4 Models

♦ See Figure 31

1. Loosen the adjusting nut.
2. With the transmission in neutral, rotate the switch to align the neutral standard line with the groove on the valve shaft.
3. Hold the switch in this position and tighten the adjusting bolt to 108 inch lbs. (12 Nm).
4. Bend the tabbed washer over the retaining nut.
5. Connect the shift linkage rod.
6. Connect the switch wiring.
7. Check the switch operation. The engine should start in **P** and **N** only.

Extension Housing Seal

REMOVAL & INSTALLATION

2WD Models

The extension housing seal on 2-wheel drive vehicles is located at the rear of the transmission tail shaft.

1. Raise and support the vehicle safely.
2. Drain the transmission fluid, if necessary.

➡ In most cases it is not necessary to drain the transmission of fluid to change the seal. However, some fluid may leak out during the procedure.

3. Matchmark the driveshaft to the yoke for reassembly and remove driveshaft.
4. Remove the old seal using a seal puller or appropriate prytool.

To install:

5. Install a new seal, coated with sealing compound, using an appropriate seal installation tool.
6. Install the driveshaft, making certain to align the matchmark. Tighten bolts to 20 ft. lbs. (27 Nm).
7. Fill the transmission fluid to the proper level.

4WD Models

The extension seal on 4-wheel drive vehicles is located at the rear of the transfer case.

1. Raise and support the vehicle safely.
2. Drain transfer case of lubricant.

3. Matchmark driveshaft to yoke for reassembly and remove driveshaft.
4. Remove old seal using a seal puller or appropriate prytool.
5. Install a new seal, coated with sealing compound, using an appropriate seal installation tool.
6. Install the driveshaft, making certain to align matchmark. Tighten bolts to 20 ft. lbs. (27 Nm).
7. Fill transfer case with lubricant. Install plug and lower vehicle.

Transmission Assembly

REMOVAL & INSTALLATION

♦ See Figures 7, 9, 10 and 32

1984–91 Models

2WD MODELS

1. Disconnect the negative battery cable. Raise and support the vehicle on jackstands.
2. Matchmark the rear driveshaft and yoke for reassembly. Disconnect and remove the rear driveshaft.
3. Remove the torque converter inspection cover. Mark the converter driveplate and converter assembly for reassembly.
4. Remove the bolts attaching the torque converter to the flexplate. Support the transmission assembly on a floor jack.
5. Remove the bolts attaching the rear crossmember to the transmission side rail. Disconnect the exhaust pipe at the catalytic converter.
6. Lower the transmission slightly in order to disconnect the fluid cooler

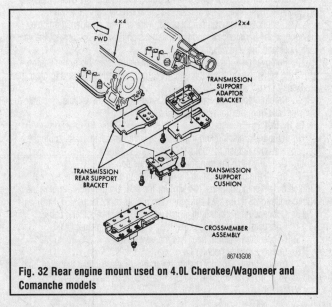

Fig. 32 Rear engine mount used on 4.0L Cherokee/Wagoneer and Comanche models

lines.

7. Disconnect the backup light switch wire and the speedometer cable. Disconnect the transmission linkage.

8. Remove the bolts attaching the transmission assembly to the engine. Move the transmission assembly and the torque converter rearward to clear the crankshaft.

9. Carefully lower the transmission assembly from the vehicle.

To install:

10. Carefully raise the transmission into position.

11. Install the bolts attaching the transmission assembly to the engine. Tighten the bolts to 25 ft. lbs. (34 Nm) for the 904. On the AW-4, tighten the 10mm bolts to 25 ft. lbs. (34 Nm); the 12mm bolts to 42 ft. lbs. (57 Nm).

12. Connect the backup light switch wire.

13. Connect the speedometer cable.

14. Connect the transmission linkage.

15. Connect the fluid cooler lines.

16. Install the rear crossmember. Tighten the crossmember bolts to 30 ft. lbs. (41 Nm); the transmission-to-crossmember bolts to 33 ft. lbs. (48 Nm).

17. Connect the exhaust pipe at the catalytic converter.

18. Install the bolts attaching the torque converter to the flexplate. Tighten the bolts to 40 ft. lbs. (54 Nm).

19. Remove the floor jack.

20. Install the torque converter inspection cover.

21. Install the driveshaft. Tighten the nuts to 14 ft. lbs. (19 Nm).

➡**New strap bolts must be used every time the driveshaft is disconnected.**

22. Lower the truck.

23. Connect the negative battery cable.

4WD MODELS

1. Disconnect the negative battery cable. Raise and support the vehicle safely.

2. Matchmark the rear driveshaft and yoke for reassembly. Disconnect and remove the rear driveshaft.

3. Remove the torque converter inspection cover. Mark the converter driveplate and converter assembly for reassembly.

4. Remove the bolts attaching the torque converter to the flexplate. Support the transmission assembly with a floor jack.

➡**If the vehicle is equipped with a diesel engine, support the engine with a jack under the crankshaft damper, and remove the left motor mount and starter in order to gain access to the torque converter driveplate bolts through the starter opening.**

5. Remove the rear crossmember-to-side rail attaching bolts. Disconnect the exhaust pipe at the catalytic converter.

6. Lower the transmission slightly in order to disconnect the fluid cooler lines. Matchmark the front driveshaft assembly for installation. Disconnect the driveshaft at the transfer case and secure the assembly out of the way.

7. Disconnect the backup light switch wire and the speedometer cable. Disconnect the transfer case and the transmission linkage. Disconnect the vacuum lines and the vent hose.

8. Remove the bolts attaching the transmission assembly to the engine. Move the transmission assembly and the torque converter rearward to clear the crankshaft.

9. Carefully lower the transmission assembly from the vehicle. Separate the transfer case from the transmission assembly.

To install:

10. If the transmission and transfer case were separated, reassemble the components and tighten the bolts to 26 ft. lbs. (35 Nm).

11. Carefully raise the transmission into position.

12. Install the bolts attaching the transmission assembly to the engine. Tighten the bolts to 25 ft. lbs. (34 Nm) for the 904. On the AW-4, tighten the 10mm bolts to 25 ft. lbs. (34 Nm); the 12mm bolts to 42 ft. lbs. (57 Nm).

13. Connect the backup light switch wire and the speedometer cable.

14. Connect the transfer case and the transmission linkage.

15. Connect the vacuum lines and the vent hose.

16. Connect the fluid cooler lines.

17. Connect the rear driveshaft to the transfer case. Tighten the strap bolt nuts to 14 ft. lbs. (19 Nm); the flange-to-case bolts to 35 ft. lbs. (47 Nm).

➡**New strap bolts must be used everytime the driveshaft is disconnected.**

18. Install the rear crossmember. Tighten the crossmember attaching bolts to 30 ft. lbs. (41 Nm); the transmission-to-crossmember bolts to 33 ft. lbs. (45 Nm).

19. Connect the exhaust pipe at the catalytic converter.

20. Install the bolts attaching the torque converter to the flexplate. Tighten the bolts to 40 ft. lbs. (54 Nm)

21. Remove the floor jack.

22. Install the torque converter inspection cover.

23. If the vehicle is equipped with a diesel engine, install the left motor mount and starter.

24. Lower the truck.

25. Connect the negative battery cable.

1992 and Later Cherokee and Comanche

2WD MODELS

1. Disconnect the negative battery cable.

2. Raise and support the vehicle safely.

3. Matchmark the rear driveshaft and yoke for reassembly.

4. Disconnect and remove the rear driveshaft.

5. Remove the torque converter inspection cover.

6. Matchmark the converter driveplate and converter assembly for reassembly.

7. Remove the bolts attaching the torque converter to the flexplate.

8. Remove the starter.

9. Support the transmission assembly using a jack.

10. Remove the bolts attaching the rear crossmember to the transmission side rail.

11. Disconnect the exhaust pipe at the catalytic converter.

12. Lower the transmission slightly in order to disconnect the fluid cooler lines.

13. Disconnect the backup light switch wire and speedometer cable.

14. Disconnect the transmission linkage.

15. Remove the bolts attaching the transmission assembly to the engine.

16. Move the transmission assembly and the torque converter rearward to clear the crankshaft.

17. Carefully lower the transmission assembly from the vehicle.

To install:

18. Carefully raise the transmission into position.

19. Install the bolts attaching the transmission assembly to the engine. Tighten the bolts to:
   - 10mm bolts: 25 ft. lbs. (34 Nm)
   - 12mm bolts: 42 ft. lbs. (57 Nm)

20. Connect the backup light switch wire.

21. Connect the speedometer cable.

22. Connect the transmission linkage.

23. Connect the fluid cooler lines.

24. Install the rear crossmember. Tighten the crossmember bolts to 30 ft. lbs. (41 Nm); the transmission-to-crossmember bolts to 33 ft. lbs. (45 Nm).

25. Connect the exhaust pipe at the catalytic converter.

26. Install the bolts attaching the torque converter to the flexplate. Tighten the bolts to 40 ft. lbs. (54 Nm).

27. Install the starter.

28. Remove the transmission jack.

29. Install the torque converter inspection cover.

30. Install the driveshaft. New strap bolts should be used every time the driveshaft is disconnected. Tighten the nuts to 14 ft. lbs. (19 Nm).

31. Lower the vehicle.

32. Connect the negative battery cable.

4WD MODELS

1. Disconnect the negative battery cable.

2. Raise and support the vehicle safely.

3. Matchmark the rear driveshaft and yoke for reassembly. Disconnect and remove the rear driveshaft.

4. Remove the torque converter inspection cover.

5. Matchmark the converter driveplate and converter assembly for reassembly.

6. Remove the bolts attaching the torque converter to the flexplate.

7. Support the transmission assembly with a jack.

8. Remove the bolts attaching the rear crossmember to the transmission side rail.

9. Disconnect the exhaust pipe at the catalytic converter.

10. Lower the transmission slightly in order to disconnect the fluid cooler lines.

11. Matchmark the front driveshaft assembly for installation.

12. Disconnect the driveshaft at the transfer case and secure the assembly aside.

13. Disconnect the backup light switch wire and speedometer cable.

14. Disconnect the transfer case and transmission linkage.

15. Disconnect the vacuum lines and vent hose.

16. Remove the bolts attaching the transmission assembly to the engine.

17. Move the transmission assembly and torque converter rearward to clear the crankshaft.

18. Carefully lower the transmission assembly from the vehicle.

19. Remove the transfer case retaining bolts from the transmission assembly.

To install:

20. If the transmission and transfer case were separated, re-attach them and tighten the bolts to 26 ft. lbs. (35 Nm).

21. Carefully raise the transmission into position.

22. Install the bolts attaching the transmission assembly to the engine. Tighten the bolts to:
- 10mm bolts: 25 ft. lbs. (34 Nm)
- 12mm bolts: 42 ft. lbs. (57 Nm)

23. Connect the backup light switch wire and speedometer cable.

24. Connect the transfer case and transmission linkage.

25. Connect the vacuum lines and the vent hose.

26. Connect the fluid cooler lines.

27. Connect the driveshaft at the transfer case. New strap bolts should be used whenever the driveshaft is disconnected. Tighten the strap bolt nuts to 14 ft. lbs (19 Nm); the flange-to-case bolts to 35 ft. lbs. (48 Nm).

28. Install the rear crossmember. Tighten the crossmember attaching bolts to 30 ft. lbs. (41 Nm); the transmission-to-crossmember bolts to 33 ft. lbs. (45 Nm).

29. Connect the exhaust pipe at the catalytic converter.

30. Install the bolts attaching the torque converter to the flexplate. Tighten the bolts to 40 ft. lbs. (61 Nm).

31. Remove the floor jack.

32. Install the torque converter inspection cover.

33. Install the rear driveshaft. Use new strap bolts. Tighten the strap bolt nuts to 14 ft. lbs. (19 Nm); the flange bolts to 35 ft. lbs. (48 Nm).

34. Lower the vehicle.

35. Connect the negative battery cable.

1993–98 Grand Cherokee/Wagoneer

2WD MODELS

1. Disconnect the negative battery cable.

2. Raise and support the vehicle safely.

3. If equipped, remove the skid plate.

4. If the transmission is being removed for repair, drain the fluid and reinstall the pan.

5. Matchmark the driveshaft yoke and remove the driveshaft.

6. Disconnect the vehicle speed wires, transmission solenoid wires and park-neutral position switch wires.

7. Disconnect the wires from the transmission speed sensor at the rear of the overdrive unit.

8. Remove the exhaust Y-pipe.

9. Unclip the wire harness from the transmission clips.

10. Disconnect the throttle valve and gearshift cables from the levers on the valve body manual shaft. Position the cables aside and secure them to the underbody.

11. Remove the dust cover from the transmission converter housing.

12. Remove the starter.

13. Remove the bolts attaching the converter to the driveplate.

14. Disconnect the cooler fluid lines from the transmission.

15. Support the transmission with a jack.

16. Remove the nuts and bolts securing the rear crossmember to the insulator and remove the crossmember.

17. Lower the jack to gain access to the upper portion of the transmission.

18. Remove the crankshaft position sensor.

19. Remove the transmission fill tube and discard the O-ring.

20. Remove the bolts attaching the transmission to the engine.

21. Slide the transmission back and secure a C-clamp to the converter.

22. Remove the transmission.

To install:

23. Ensure the torque converter hub and hub drive are free from sharp edges, scratches or nicks. Polish with 400 grit sandpaper if necessary.

24. Lubricate the converter hub and pump seal with high temperature grease.

25. Secure the C-clamp to the converter.

26. Ensure the dowel pins are seated in the engine block and protrude far enough to align the transmission.

27. Align the transmission with the engine dowels and converter with the driveplate. Install 2 transmission bolts to keep it in place.

28. Remove the C-clamp and install the torque converter bolts. Tighten the bolts to:
- 3 lug converter—40 ft. lbs. (54 Nm)
- 4 lug converter—270 inch lbs. (31 Nm)

29. Install and tighten the remaining transmission-to-engine bolts.

30. Install the crankshaft position sensor.

31. Install the dust cover on the converter housing.

32. Install the starter.

33. Connect the transmission shift and throttle valve cables to the transmission.

34. Fasten the wire harness to the transmission.

35. Engage the harness connectors unplugged during removal.

36. Install the transmission filler tube with a new O-ring.

37. Install the rear crossmember.

38. Connect the fluid cooler lines to the transmission.

39. Align and install the driveshaft.

40. Install the exhaust system components.

41. Lower the vehicle.

42. Connect the negative battery cable.

43. Check the transmission control cables; adjust if necessary.

44. If the transmission fluid was drained, fill the transmission with fluid to the proper level.

4WD MODELS

1. Disconnect the negative battery cable.

2. Raise and support the vehicle safely.

3. If equipped, remove the skid plate.

4. If the transmission is being removed for repair, drain the fluid and reinstall the pan.

5. Matchmark the driveshaft yokes and remove both driveshafts.

6. Disconnect the vehicle speed wires, transmission solenoid wires and park-neutral position switch wires.

7. Unclip the wire harness from the transmission clips.

8. Disconnect the transfer case shift linkage from the lever. Remove the linkage and bracket from the transfer case. Position the linkage aside.

9. Remove the nuts attaching the transfer case to the overdrive unit gear case.

10. Place a jack under the transfer case and remove the case.

11. Support the transmission with the jack.

12. Remove the rear transmission crossmember.

13. Remove the exhaust Y-pipe.

14. Remove the crankshaft position sensor.

15. Disconnect the gearshift linkage from the lever on the transmission.

16. Remove the transmission shift linkage torque shaft assembly from the transmission and frame rail. Position it aside.

17. Remove the transmission-to-engine brackets.

18. Remove the dust cover from the transmission converter housing.

19. Remove the starter.

20. Remove the bolts attaching the converter to the driveplate.

21. Disconnect the cooler fluid lines from the transmission.

22. Disconnect the solenoid and park/neutral position switch wires.

23. Remove the transmission fill tube and discard the O-ring.

24. Lower the jack to gain access to the upper portion of the transmission.

25. Remove the bolts attaching the transmission to the engine.

26. Slide the transmission back and secure a C-clamp to the converter.

27. Move the transmission rearward until it clears the engine block dowels.

➡On some models, part of the flange joining the vehicle cab and dash panel may interfere with transmission removal. If necessary peen this part of the flange over with a mallet.

28. Remove the transmission.

To install:

29. Ensure the torque converter hub and hub drive are free from sharp edges, scratches or nicks. Polish with 400 grit sandpaper if necessary.

30. Lubricate the converter hub and pump seal with high temperature grease.

31. Secure the C-clamp to the converter.

32. Ensure the dowel pins are seated in the engine block and protrude far enough to align the transmission.

33. Align the transmission with the engine dowels and converter with the driveplate. Install 2 transmission bolts to keep it in place.

34. Remove the C-clamp and install the torque converter bolts. Tighten the bolts as follows:
- 3 lug converter—40 ft. lbs. (54 Nm)
- 4 lug, except 10.75 inch converter—55 ft. lbs. (74 Nm)
- 4 lug, 10.75 inch converter—270 inch lbs. (31 Nm)

35. Install the starter.

36. Install the strut brackets securing the transmission to the engine and front axle.

37. Install and tighten the remaining transmission-to-engine bolts.

38. Install the crankshaft position sensor.

39. Install the transmission filler tube with a new O-ring.

40. Install the exhaust system components.

41. Install the shift linkage torque bracket.

42. Connect the shift linkage to the transmission.

43. Connect the harness connectors disconnected during removal.

44. Install the rear crossmember.

45. Install the transfer case. Tighten the nuts as follows:
- 3/8 stud nuts—35 ft. lbs. (47 Nm)
- 5/16 stud nuts—26 ft. lbs. (35 Nm)

46. Install the damper on the transfer case rear retainer if removed. Tighten the nuts to 40 ft. lbs. (54 Nm).

47. Connect the transfer case shift linkage.

48. Connect the fluid cooler lines to the transmission.

49. Align and install the driveshafts. Tighten the U-joint clamp bolts to 170 inch lbs. (19 Nm).

50. Fill the transfer case to the proper level with fluid.

51. Lower the vehicle.

52. Connect the negative battery cable.

53. Fill the transmission to the proper level with the appropriate fluid.

54. Check the transmission control cables, adjust if necessary.

55. Check and adjust the transmission and transfer case shift linkage.

ADJUSTMENTS

Shift Linkage/Cable

EXCEPT 30RH/32RH, 42RE/44RE AND AW4 MODELS

▶ See Figure 33

1. Raise and support the truck on jackstands.
2. Loosen the shift rod trunnion locknuts.
3. Remove the lockpin retaining the shift rod trunnion to the bellcrank and disengage the trunnion and shift rod from the bellcrank.
4. Place the shift lever in **P** and lock the steering column.

5. Move the lever on the transmission rearward to the **P** detent. Park is the last possible rearward position.

6. Check to make sure that **P** is engaged, by trying to rotate the driveshaft by hand.

7. Adjust the shift rod trunnion so that the pin fits freely in the bellcrank arm and tighten the trunnion locknuts. Prevent the shift rod from turning while tightening the locknuts.

➡All lash in the linkage must be eliminated to provide for proper adjustment. Lash can be eliminated by pulling downward on the shift rod and pressing upward on the bellcrank.

8. Check that the engine starts in only the **P** and **N** positions, and that all shift ranges work properly.

9. Lower the truck.

30RH/32RH, 42RE/44RE AND AW4 MODELS

▶ See Figures 34 and 35

1. Place gearshift lever in **P**.
2. Raise and support the vehicle safely.
3. Unlock the transmission shift control cable by prying upward on the T-shaped adjuster clamp to release.
4. Move the valve body manual lever rearward into P detent (last rearward detent). Ensure that vehicle is in **P** by attempting to rotate the driveshaft. The driveshaft should NOT rotate.
5. With the valve body manual lever in the **P** position, snap the cable into the lower reaction bracket.
6. Lock the cable by pressing the T-shaped adjuster clamp down until it snaps into place.
7. Check engine starting procedure to ensure engine will only start in **P** or **N**.
8. Lower vehicle.

Park Lock Cable

EXCEPT 42RE/44RE

▶ See Figure 36

1. Shift the transmission into **P**.
2. Turn the ignition switch to the **LOCK** position.
3. Remove the shifter lever bezel and console screws. Raise the console for access to the cable.
4. Pull the cable lock button up to the release cable.
5. Pull the cable forward. Then release the cable and press the lock button down until it snaps in place.
6. Check the movement of the release shift handle button (floor shift) or release lever (column shift). You should not be able to press the button inward or move the column lever.
7. Turn the ignition to the **ON** position. Move the shift or column lever into **N**. If the cable adjustment is correct, ignition should not return to **LOCK** position. Recheck with the shift or column lever in the **D** position.
8. Move the shift or column lever to the **P** position. Ignition should now return to the **LOCK** position. With the ignition in the **LOCK** position, the shift or column lever should not move.

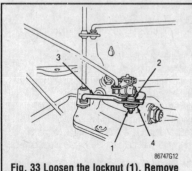

Fig. 33 Loosen the locknut (1). Remove the lockpin retaining the shift rod. Disengage the trunnion (2) and shift rod (3) at the bellcrank (4)

86747G12

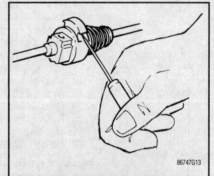

Fig. 34 Unlock transmission shift control cable by prying upward on the T-shaped adjuster clamp to release

86747G13

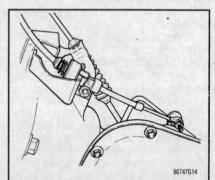

Fig. 35 With the valve body manual lever in the P position, snap the cable into the lower reaction bracket

86747G14

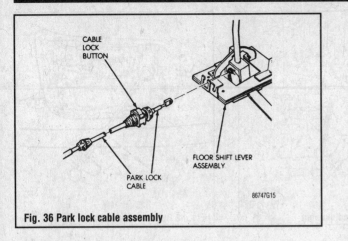

Fig. 36 Park lock cable assembly

42RE/44RE MODELS

1. Shift the transmission into **P**.
2. Turn ignition switch to the **ACC** position.
3. Remove the shifter lever bezel and console screws. Raise console for access to cable.
4. Pull the cable lock button up to release cable.
5. Pull the cable forward. Then release the cable and press the lock button down until it snaps in place.
6. With the shift lever in **P**, the ignition lock cylinder should move from **OFF** to **LOCK**. Cylinder should not rotate in any other position.
7. Turn the ignition to the **RUN** position. Press and hold the brake pedal. Check that the lever can be moved out of **P**.

Throttle Cable

AW-4 AND 30RH/32RH MODELS

▶ See Figure 37

1. Turn the ignition switch to **OFF**.
2. Press the throttle cable button all the way down, then, push the cable plunger inward.
3. Rotate the primary throttle lever to the wide open throttle position.
4. Hold the primary throttle lever in this position and let the cable plunger extend.
5. Release the lever when the plunger is fully extended.
6. The cable is now adjusted.

42RE/44RE MODELS

1. Turn the ignition switch to **OFF**.
2. Disconnect the cable from the stud.
3. Press the cable lock button inward to release the cable.
4. Center the end of the cable to the stud within 0.039 in. (1mm).
5. Install the cable onto the stud.

46RH MODELS

1. Turn the ignition switch to **OFF**.
2. Remove the air cleaner.
3. Position a 0.110–0.120 in. (2.8–3.0mm) feeler gauge between the idle stop and throttle lever.
4. Press the cable lock button to release the cable.
5. Raise the vehicle for access to the throttle valve lever.
6. Rotate the lever towards the front of the vehicle until the ratcheting sound stops.
7. Remove the feeler gauges and check the cable adjustment. The throttle lever should begin to move at the same time the lever on the throttle body moves off idle.
8. Lower the vehicle and install the air cleaner.

Throttle Valve Lever and Cable

2.1L DIESEL ENGINES

▶ See Figures 38, 39 and 40

➡ Special tool J-35514 and gauge J-35591 are necessary for this procedure.

1. Disconnect the throttle valve cable from the pin on the throttle valve lever.
2. Disconnect the cable from the transmission throttle lever. Remove and discard the cable.
3. Set the injection pump automatic advance lever at the curb idle position (seated against the stop).
4. Loosen the set screw and turn the cable clevis 1/4 turn counterclockwise. Tighten the set screw.
5. Install the special tool as shown.
6. Loosen the thumbscrew on the tool and move the sliding legs rearward.
7. Place the notched leg of the tool on the cable bracket. Then, rest the sliding legs on the lever.
8. Move the sliding legs forward until the rear leg lightly touches the cable attaching pin. Tighten the thumbscrew.
9. Move the lever to the wide open throttle position. The cable attaching pin should now lightly touch the forward leg of the sliding legs.
10. If the cable attaching pin does not touch the forward leg, or if the pin tends to move the special tool, hold the lever in the wide open throttle position, loosen the two lever adjusting screws and move the lever to adjust the travel. Tighten the screws to 66 inch lbs. Return the lever to the curb idle position and verify that the pin is, again, lightly touching the rear leg of the sliding legs. If the pin doesn't touch the rear leg at curb idle, loosen the thumbscrew and adjust the tool so that it does, and repeat the adjustment.
11. Install a new throttle valve cable, part number 8953 001 796.
12. The new cable should be supplied with a cable stop, or one can be obtained from a lawn mower shop, motorcycle repair shop or small engines outlet. The throttle stop should have an inside diameter of 1.07mm.
13. The new cable has a factory installed cable stop crimped onto the end of the cable. Cut this off and slide the inner cable stop off the cable. Slide the new cable stop into place and hand tighten the set screw.
14. Connect the new cable to the throttle valve lever pin.

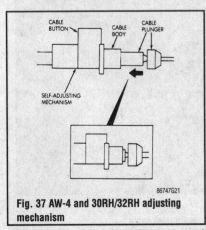

Fig. 37 AW-4 and 30RH/32RH adjusting mechanism

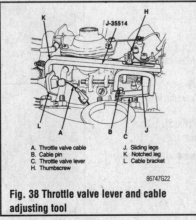

A. Throttle valve cable
B. Cable pin
C. Throttle valve lever
H. Thumbscrew
J. Sliding legs
K. Notched leg
L. Cable bracket

Fig. 38 Throttle valve lever and cable adjusting tool

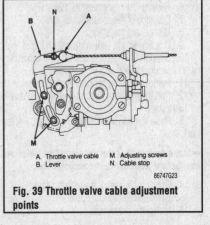

A. Throttle valve cable
B. Lever
M. Adjusting screws
N. Cable stop

Fig. 39 Throttle valve cable adjustment points

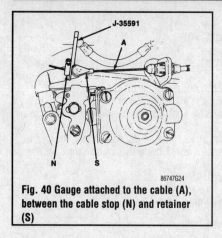

Fig. 40 Gauge attached to the cable (A), between the cable stop (N) and retainer (S)

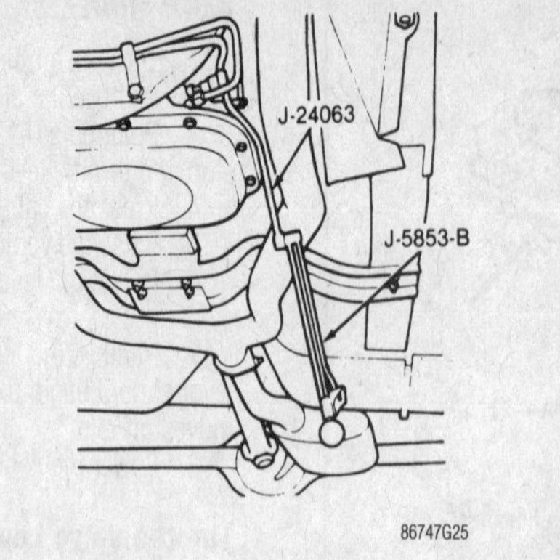

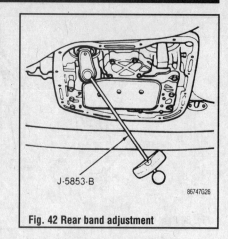

Fig. 41 Front band adjustment

Fig. 42 Rear band adjustment

15. Obtain a small coil spring and use it to hold the throttle valve lever against its stop.

16. Loosen the cable stop and install gauge J-35591 between the cable stop and the retainer.

17. Remove all slack from the cable.

18. Slide the cable stop rearward against the gauge and retainer. Securely tighten the set screw and remove the gauge. Remove the spring that you used on the throttle lever. Loosen the clevis set screw and turn the clevis screw back 1/4 turn.

Front Band

42RE/44RE, 46RH AND 30RH/32RH MODELS

▶ **See Figure 41**

1. Raise and support the truck on jackstands. The front band adjusting screw is located on the left side of the case, just above the control levers.

2. Loosen the locknut and back it off about five turns.

3. Make sure that the screw turns freely. Use penetrating oil if it binds.

4. Tighten the screw to 72 inch lbs. (8 Nm).

5. Back off the screw 2 1/2 turns on 42RE/44RE, 46RH and 30RH. On the

32RH, back it off 2 1/4 turns. On the 42RE/44RE back it off 2 7/8 turns.

6. Tighten the locknut to 30 ft. lbs. (41 Nm). Hold the screw still while tightening the locknut.

7. Lower the truck.

Rear Band

42RE/44RE, 46RH AND 30RH/32RH MODELS

▶ **See Figure 42**

1. Raise and support the truck on jackstands.

2. Drain the fluid and remove the pan.

3. Remove the adjusting screw locknut.

4. Tighten the adjusting screw to 41 inch lbs. (5 Nm) on 42RE/44RE and 30RH. On the 32RH and 46RH, tighten it to 72 inch lbs. (8 Nm).

5. Back off the adjusting screw 7 turns on 30RH. On the 32RH back it off 4 turns. On the 42RE/44RE and 46RH, back it off 2 turns.

6. Hold the adjusting screw still and tighten the locknut to 150 inch lbs. (17 Nm) on the 30RH/32RH. On the 42RE/44RE and 46RH, tighten it to 25 ft. lbs. (34 Nm).

7. Install the pan and fill the unit with the appropriate fluid.

TRANSFER CASE

Transfer Case Assembly

REMOVAL & INSTALLATION

▶ **See Figures 43 and 44**

1. Shift transfer case into **N**.

2. Raise and support the vehicle safely.

3. Drain the lubricant.

4. Matchmark and remove the front and rear driveshafts.

5. Raise and support the transmission with a floor jack.

6. Remove the rear crossmember.

7. Disconnect the speedometer cable.

8. Disconnect the linkage.

9. Disconnect the vent and vacuum hoses and the indicator wire.

10. Support the transfer case with a transmission jack. Make sure that the case is secured to the jack with chains.

11. Remove the transfer case-to-transmission bolts.

12. Pull the case rearward to disengage it and lower it from the truck.

To install:

13. Raise the transfer case into position. Tighten the bolts to 26 ft. lbs. (35 Nm).

➡ **Make certain that the case and transmission are mated without binding, before torquing the attaching bolts.**

14. Connect the shift linkage at the case.

15. Connect the vacuum hoses.

16. Install the driveshafts.

17. Install the rear crossmember. Tighten the crossmember-to-frame bolts to 30 ft. lbs. (41 Nm); the transmission-to-crossmember bolts to 33 ft. lbs. (45 Nm).

18. Remove the transmission floor jack.

19. Connect the speedometer cable and vent hose.

20. Connect the shift lever link at the operating lever.

21. Fill the case with lubricant. Lower the vehicle.

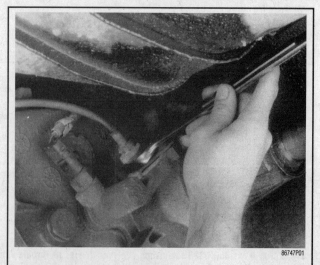

Fig. 43 Disconnect the speedometer cable . . .

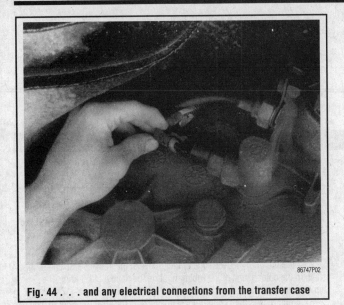

Fig. 44 . . . and any electrical connections from the transfer case

ADJUSTMENTS

Range Control Linkage

NP-207 MODELS

▶ See Figure 45

1. Place the range control lever in the **2WD** position.
2. Insert a 1/8 in. (3mm) spacer between the gate and the lever.
3. Hold the lever in this position.
4. Place the transfer case lever in the **2WD** position.

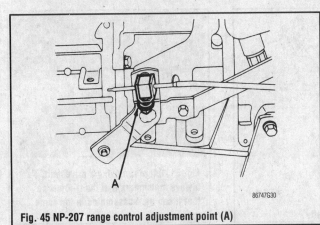

Fig. 45 NP-207 range control adjustment point (A)

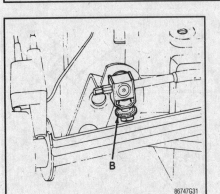

Fig. 46 NP-228/229 range control adjustment point (B)

5. Adjust the link, at the trunnion, to provide a free pin at the case outer lever.

NP-228 AND 229 MODELS

▶ See Figure 46

1. Place the range control lever in the **HIGH** position.
2. Insert a 1/8 in. (3mm) spacer between the shift gate and the lever.
3. Hold the lever in this position with tape.
4. Raise and support the vehicle safely.
5. Verify that the range lever is in the **HIGH** position.
6. Loosen the locknut and adjust the link, at the trunnion, to provide a free pin at the case outer lever. Tighten the locknut.
7. Lower the vehicle. Remove the spacer.

231 AND 242 MODELS

▶ See Figure 47

1. Remove the shifter lever bezel.
2. Place the range control lever in the **4 LOW** position.
3. Insert a 1/8 in. (4mm) spacer between the forward edge of the shift gate and the lever.
4. Hold the lever in this position with tape.
5. Raise and support the vehicle safely.
6. Loosen the trunnion lock bolt. The linkage rod should now slide freely in the trunnion.
7. Position the linkage rod so it is free in the range lever. Then tighten the locknut.
8. Lower the vehicle. Remove the spacer.

NV/NP-249 MODELS

1. Place the range control lever in the **N** position.
2. Raise and support the vehicle safely.
3. Loosen the trunnion lockbolt. The linkage rod should now slide freely in the trunnion.
4. Verify the shift lever on the transfer case is centered in the **N** position.
5. Tighten the lockbolt to 96–180 inch lbs. (11–20 Nm).
6. Lower the vehicle. Remove the spacer.

Mode Rod

NP-228 AND NP-229 MODELS

▶ See Figure 48

✳✳ WARNING

If this adjustment is not properly made, the transfer case may not fully engage 2WD/HIGH and internal damage will result.

1. Fully engage the **2WD/HIGH** position.
2. Refer to the accompanying illustration. The range lever and the mode lever must be aligned on the same centerline.

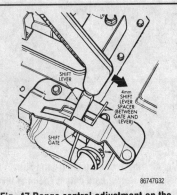

Fig. 47 Range control adjustment on the 231/242

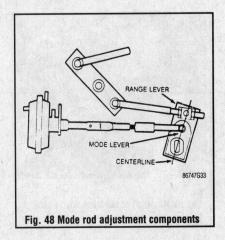

Fig. 48 Mode rod adjustment components

➡ To correctly position the mode lever, it is sometimes necessary to rotate the transfer case output shaft. To do this, raise and support the rear end on jackstands and rotate the rear driveshaft, while applying a load on the mode lever. Doing this will help align the spline for full engagement of 2WD/HIGH.

3. Adjust the length of the mode rod (4) to approximately 6 in. (152mm), to eliminate all free play.

4. Make sure all vacuum lines are secure.

5. Drive the vehicle a short distance, shifting between **4WD** and **2WD/HIGH**.

6. Check the mode lever position. The lever should be aligned as explained in Step 2. If not, repeat Steps 3 through 5, increasing the length of the mode rod one turn, until proper alignment is achieved.

7. With the transfer case vacuum motor shift rod fully extended and the transfer case in **2WD/HIGH**, adjust the mode rod so that the pin (6) moves freely in its hole.

DRIVELINE

Front Driveshaft

Jeep vehicles may come equipped with one of two different type front driveshafts. Type one has a conventional universal joint at the axle, but a double offset joint at the transfer case. Type two has a conventional universal joint at the axle and a double cardan joint at the transfer case.

Front driveshafts on 1984 vehicles use the type one universal joint only. Front driveshafts on 1985 and later vehicles use either type one or type two.

REMOVAL & INSTALLATION

▶ **See Figures 49, 50, 51, 52 and 53**

1. Matchmark the shaft ends, axle and transfer case.
2. Remove the U-joint strap bolts at the front axle yoke.
3. If equipped with a double offset U-joint, remove the double offset joint flange nuts at the transfer case.
4. If equipped with a double cardan U-joint, remove the double cardan joint flange nuts at the transfer case.
5. Installation is the reverse of removal. Install new strap bolts and tighten strap bolts to 14 ft. lbs. (19 Nm).

FRONT DRIVESHAFT LENGTH ADJUSTMENT

▶ **See Figure 54**

➡ **The length of the front driveshaft must be checked and adjusted if the shaft has been removed or replaced.**

1. Raise the vehicle on ramps.
2. Measure from the rear edge of the groove at the transfer case end of the shaft, to the outer flange of the rubber boot on the double offset joint. The dimension should be 1 1/2–1 3/4 in. (38.0–44.5mm).
3. If not, loosen the slip joint locknut and slide the shaft in or out of the double offset joint to correct the length.
4. Tighten the nut to 55 ft. lbs. (75 Nm).

Rear Driveshaft

REMOVAL & INSTALLATION

▶ **See Figures 55, 56, 57 and 58**

➡ **Two different driveshafts are used on these vehicles. With Command-Trac®, the driveshaft has welded yokes at each end. With Selec-Trac®,**

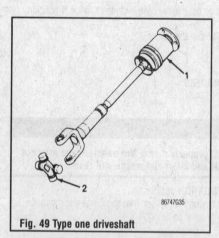

Fig. 49 Type one driveshaft

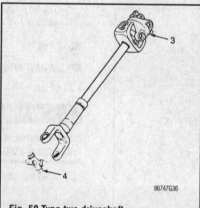

Fig. 50 Type two driveshaft

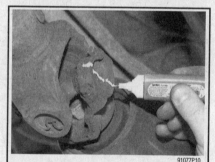

Fig. 51 Before removing a driveshaft, always matchmark it at the U-joints so that it can be reassembled in the same manner

Fig. 52 Removal of the front drive shaft U-joint strap bolts at the transfer case side

Fig. 53 After removing the U-joint strap bolts and straps, hold onto the joint at the needle bearing caps so that they cannot fall apart

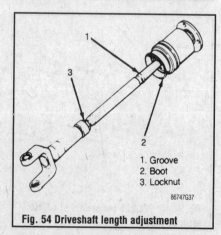

1. Groove
2. Boot
3. Locknut

Fig. 54 Driveshaft length adjustment

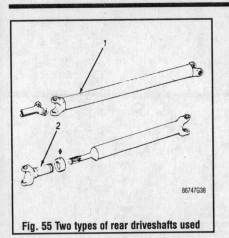

Fig. 55 Two types of rear driveshafts used

Fig. 56 Removal of the rear drive shaft U-joint strap bolts at the differential housing side

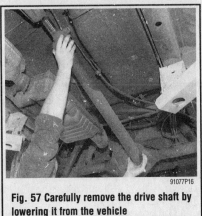

Fig. 57 Carefully remove the drive shaft by lowering it from the vehicle

Fig. 58 After removing the drive shaft, install a transmission plug into the tailshaft opening so that transmission fluid will not escape

a welded yoke is used at the rear and a splined slip yoke is used at the front.

1. Raise and support the vehicle on jackstands.
2. Place the transmission in **N**.
3. Matchmark the yokes and flanges.
4. On vehicles with Command-Trac®, the driveshaft may be removed by disconnecting it at the axle and sliding it from the front yoke, leaving the front yoke attached to the transfer case. If you do this, however, you MUST matchmark the driveshaft and front yoke BEFORE separation.
5. On vehicles with Selec-Trac®, disconnect the yokes from the axle and transfer case. Remove the driveshaft.
6. Installation is the reverse of removal. Install new strap bolts and tighten strap bolts to 170 inch lbs. (19 Nm).

U-Joints

There are five types of universal joints used: the Cardan cross-type with U-bolts and snaprings; a Cardan cross-type with just snaprings; a double Cardan cross-type; ball and trunnion-type universal joints which serve as a combination slip-joint and universal joint. Some models have a front driveshaft which, at the transfer case end, uses a double offset joint. This unit is not repairable and must be serviced by replacement only.

Universal joints fail for numerous reasons, the primary one being lack of lubrication. Others could be structural damage incurred from hitting something, an unbalanced driveshaft, the entrance of dirt or water due to a rotted rubber seal or just plain wear from excessive mileage.

Rebuilding kits are available for both types of universal joints. The kit for a Cardan cross-type universal joint includes the entire cross assembly, the cross bearing journal, roller bearings, bearing cap with new rubber seal and new snaprings.

The rebuilding kit for the ball and trunnion-type universal joint includes a new grease cover and gasket, universal joint body, two centering buttons and spring washers, two ball and roller bearing assemblies, two thrust washers, dust cover and two dust cover clamps.

Although U-joints can be rebuilt, most procedures today call for replacement rather than rebuilding.

OVERHAUL

Cardan Cross Type with Snaprings

▶ See Figure 59

1. Remove the driveshaft from the vehicle.
2. Remove the snaprings by pinching the ends together with a pair of pliers. If the rings do not readily snap out of the groove, tap the end of the bearing lightly to relieve pressure against the rings.
3. After removing the snaprings, press on the end of one bearing until the opposite bearing is pushed from the yoke arm. Turn the joint over and press the first bearing back out of that arm by pressing on the exposed end of the journal shaft. To drive it out, use a soft ground drift with a flat face, about 1/32 in. (0.8mm) smaller in diameter than the hole in the yoke; otherwise, there is danger of damaging the bearing.
4. Repeat the procedure for the other two bearings, then lift out the journal assembly by sliding it to one side.
5. Wash all parts in cleaning solvent and inspect the parts after cleaning. Replace the journal assembly if it is worn extensively. Make sure that the grease channel in each journal trunnion is open.
6. Pack all of the bearing caps 1/3 full of grease and install the rollers (bearings).
7. Press one of the cap/bearing assemblies into one of the yoke arms just far enough so that the cap will remain in position.
8. Place the journal in position in the installed cap, with a cap/bearing assembly placed on the opposite end.
9. Position the free cap so that when it is driven from the opposite end it will be inserted into the opening of the yoke. Repeat this operation for the other two bearings.
10. Install the retaining clips. If the U-joint binds when it is assembled, tap the arms of the yoke slightly to relieve any pressure on the bearings at the end of the journal.

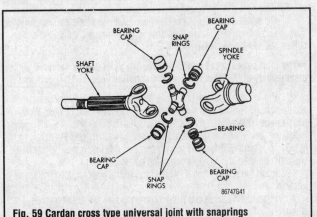

Fig. 59 Cardan cross type universal joint with snaprings

Cardan Cross Type with U-Bolts and Snaprings

▶ **See Figure 60**

1. Removal of the attaching U-bolt releases one set of bearing races. Slide the driveshaft into the yoke flange to remove that set of bearing races, being careful not to lose the rollers (bearings).

2. After removal of the first set of bearings, release the other set by pinching the ends of the snaprings with pliers and removing them from the sleeve yoke. Should the rings fail to snap readily from the groove, tap the end of the bearing lightly, to relieve the pressure against them.

3. Press on the end of one bearing, until the opposite bearing is pushed out of the yoke arm.

4. Turn the universal joint over and press the first bearing out by pressing on the exposed end of the journal assembly. Use a soft round drift with a flat face about 1/32 in. (0.8mm) smaller in diameter than the hole in the yoke arm. Then drive out the bearing.

5. Lift the journal out by sliding it to one side.

6. Install in the reverse order of removal, using the procedures for the snapring U-joints from Step 4 on as a guide.

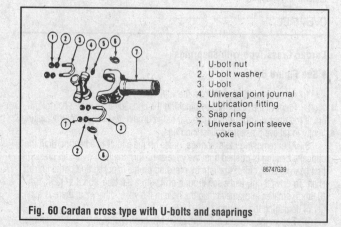

1. U-bolt nut
2. U-bolt washer
3. U-bolt
4. Universal joint journal
5. Lubrication fitting
6. Snap ring
7. Universal joint sleeve yoke

86747G39

Fig. 60 Cardan cross type with U-bolts and snaprings

Double Cardan Type

▶ **See Figure 61**

1. Use a punch to mark the coupling yoke and the adjoining yokes before disassembly, to ensure proper reassembly and driveline balance.

2. It is easiest to remove the bearings from the coupling yoke first.

3. Support the driveshaft horizontally on a press stand, or on the workbench if a vise is being used.

4. If snaprings are used to retain the bearing cups, remove them. Place the rear car of the coupling yoke over a socket large enough to receive the cup. Place a smaller socket, or a cross press made for the purpose, over the opposite cup. Press the bearing cup out of the coupling yoke ear. If the cup is not completely removed, insert a spacer and complete the operation, or grasp the cup with a pair of slip joint pliers and work it out. If the cups are retained by plastic, this will shear the retainers. Remove any bits of plastic.

5. Rotate the driveshaft and repeat the operation on the opposite cup.

6. Disengage the trunnions of the spider, still attached to the flanged yoke, from the coupling yoke, and pull the flanged yoke and spider from the center ball on the ball support tube yoke.

➡ **The joint between the shaft and coupling yoke can be serviced without disassembly of the joint between the coupling yoke and flanged yoke.**

7. Pry the seal from the ball cavity, remove the washers, spring and three seats. Examine the ball stud seat and the ball stud for scores or wear. Worn parts can be replaced with a kit. Clean the ball seat cavity and fill it with grease. Install the spring, washer, ball seats, and spacer (washer) over the ball.

8. To assembly, insert one bearing cup part way into one ear of the ball support tube yoke and turn this cup to the bottom.

9. Insert the spider (cross) into the tube so that the trunnion (arm) seats freely in the cup.

10. Install the opposite cup part way, making sure that both cups are straight.

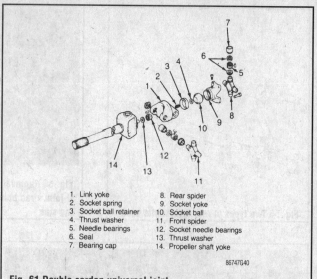

1. Link yoke
2. Socket spring
3. Socket ball retainer
4. Thrust washer
5. Needle bearings
6. Seal
7. Bearing cap
8. Rear spider
9. Socket yoke
10. Socket ball
11. Front spider
12. Socket needle bearings
13. Thrust washer
14. Propeller shaft yoke

86747G40

Fig. 61 Double cardan universal joint

11. Press the cups into position, making sure that both cups squarely engage the spider. Back off if there is a sudden increase in resistance, indicating that a cup is cocked or a needle bearing is out of place.

12. As soon as one bearing retainer groove clears the yoke, stop and install the retainer (plastic retainer models). On models with snaprings, press the cups into place, then install the snaprings over the cups.

13. If difficulty is encountered installing the plastic retainers or the snaprings, smack the yoke sharply with a hammer to spring the ears slightly.

14. Install one bearing cup part way into the ear of the coupling yoke, Make sure that the alignment marks are matched, then engaged the coupling yoke over the spider and press in the cups, installing the retainers or snaprings as before.

15. Install the cups and spider into the flanged yoke as with the previous yoke.

Ball and Trunnion Type

1. Remove the driveshaft from the vehicle.

2. Position the tube of the driveshaft near the ball-type universal joint, in a bench vise; clamp tightly.

3. Bend the lugs of the grease cover away from the universal joint body and remove the cover and the gasket.

4. Remove the two clamps from the dust cover. Push the joint body toward the driveshaft tube. Remove the two centering buttons and spring washers, the two ball and roller bearings and the two thrust washers from the trunnion pin.

5. Press the trunnion pin from the ball head with an arbor press.

➡ **It is strongly recommended that the trunnion pin be pressed out and in by an arbor press because of the possible damage that could result from other methods such as hammer and drift. This is a critical component in the assembly and any damage could result in premature failure or even necessitate replacement of the entire driveshaft.**

6. Clean the ball head of the driveshaft with a suitable solvent and dry thoroughly.

7. Secure the larger end of the dust cover to the universal joint body with the larger of the two clamps. Install the smaller clamp at the smaller end of the dust cover, then fit the cover over the ball head shaft.

8. Push the universal joint cover toward the driveshaft tube.

9. With an arbor press, press the trunnion pin into a centered position in the ball head.

➡ **The trunnion pin must project an equal distance from each side of the ball head. If it is not centered within 0.006 in. (0.15mm), driveshaft vibration may result.**

10. Hold the universal joint body toward the tube of the driveshaft to gain access to the trunnion pin. Install one thrust washer, one ball and roller bearing and one spring washer at one side of the ball head. Compress the centering buttons into the trunnion pin, then move the joint body away from the driveshaft tube, into position to surround the buttons and to hold them in place.

11. Insert the breather between the dust cover and ball head shaft, along the length of the shaft. The breather must extend no more than 1/2 in. (13mm) beyond the dust cover, along the shaft. Tighten the clamp screw to secure the cover to the shaft. Cut away any portion of the dust cover which protrudes from beneath either clamp.

12. Pack the raceways of the universal joint body (inner surfaces which surround the ball and roller bearings) with about 2 oz. of universal joint grease. Divide the grease equally between the raceways. Position the gasket and grease cover on the body of the universal joint and bend the lugs of the cover in place. Move the body inward and outward, toward and away from the driveshaft tube, to distribute the grease in the raceways.

13. Install the driveshaft on the vehicle.

FRONT DRIVE AXLE

Axle Shaft

REMOVAL & INSTALLATION

▶ **See Figure 62**

1. Raise and support the vehicle safely.

❋❋ CAUTION

Brake linings may contain asbestos. Asbestos is a known cancer-causing agent. When working on brakes, remember that the dust which accumulates on the brake parts and/or in the drum may contain asbestos. Always wear a protective face covering, such as a painter's mask, when working on the brakes. NEVER blow the dust from the brakes or drum! There are solvents made for the purpose of cleaning brake parts. Use them!

2. Remove the wheels and brake assemblies.

➡ **Refer to Section 9 for the proper procedures concerning brake removal.**

3. Remove the cotter pin, locknut and axle hub nut.
4. Remove the hub-to-knuckle attaching bolts.
5. Remove the hub and splash shield from the steering knuckle.
6. Remove the left axle shaft from the housing.
7. If equipped with Command-Trac, disconnect the vacuum harness from the shift motor and remove the shift motor from the housing.
8. Remove the right axle shaft from the housing.

To install:

9. Insert the left and right axle shafts into the axle tube.
10. To install the right axle shaft (with Command-Trac) first be sure that the shift collar is in position on the intermediate shaft and that the axle shaft is fully engaged in the intermediate shaft end.
11. If equipped with Command-Trac, install the shift motor, making sure that the fork engages with the collar. Tighten the bolts to 8 ft. lbs. (11 Nm).
12. On the left side, install the axle shaft in the housing.
13. Partially fill the hub cavity of the knuckle with chassis lube and install the hub and splash shield.

14. Tighten the hub bolts to 75 ft. lbs. (102 Nm).
15. Install the hub washer and nut. Tighten the nut to 175 ft. lbs. (237 Nm). Install the locknut. Install a new cotter pin.
16. Install the brake assemblies.
17. Lower the vehicle.

Command-Trac Axle Shift Motor

REMOVAL & INSTALLATION

▶ **See Figure 63**

1. Raise and support the vehicle safely. Position a drain pan under the shift motor.
2. Disconnect the vacuum harness. Remove the housing attaching bolts. Remove the housing, motor and shift fork as a unit. Mark the shift fork for installation reference.
3. Rotate the shift motor and remove the shift fork and motor retaining snaprings. Remove the shift motor from the housing.
4. Remove the O-ring seal and discard.

To install:

5. Add 5 oz. of gear lubricant to the axle through the shift motor housing opening.
6. Install a replacement O-ring seal on the shift motor. Install the motor in the housing with the retaining snaprings and slide the shift fork onto the shaft with the reference marks aligned.
7. Engage the shift fork with the shift collar and install the attaching bolts. Tighten to 101 inch lbs. (137 Nm).
8. Connect the vacuum harness, lower the vehicle and road test.

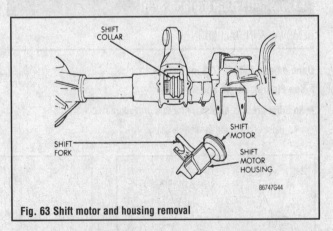

Fig. 63 Shift motor and housing removal

Pinion Seal

REMOVAL & INSTALLATION

1. Raise and support the vehicle safely.
2. Matchmark and remove the driveshaft.
3. Rotate the pinion gear three or four times with a torque wrench attached to the yoke nut. Measure the amount of torque necessary to rotate the pinion. Note for installation reference.

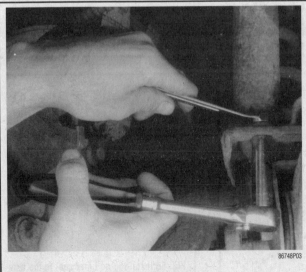

Fig. 62 Removing the axle shaft from the housing

4. Matchmark the pinion yoke and gear for installation reference.

5. Using a holding tool, remove the pinion yoke nut and washer. Discard the nut.

6. Punch the seal with a pin punch and pry it from the seal bore.

To install:

7. Apply gear lubricant to the lip of the replacement seal and install using a seal installation tool.

8. Install the yoke, noting the reference marks. Tighten just enough to remove the end-play.

9. On 1984–89 models, install the yoke, washer and a new nut. Tighten the nut to 210 ft. lbs. (285 Nm).

10. On 1990 and later models, set bearing preload as follows:

a. The required pinion gear bearing preload torque is 1/2 ft. lbs over the noted release torque as measured above.

b. Rotate the pinion gear three or four times with a torque wrench attached to the yoke nut. Measure the amount of torque necessary to rotate the pinion.

c. Using a holding tool and tighten the yoke nut in small increments and remeasure until the specified torque is obtained.

11. Install the driveshaft. Tighten the strap bolt nuts to 14 ft. lbs. (19 Nm).

➡️**New strap bolts be used whenever the driveshaft is disconnected.**

12. Add lubricant if necessary. Lower vehicle.

Front Axle Unit

REMOVAL & INSTALLATION

1. Raise and support the vehicle safely.

❋❋ CAUTION

Brake linings may contain asbestos. Asbestos is a known cancer-causing agent. When working on brakes, remember that the dust which accumulates on the brake parts and/or in the drum may contain asbestos. Always wear a protective face covering, such as a painter's mask, when working on the brakes. NEVER blow the dust

from the brakes or drum! There are solvents made for the purpose of cleaning brake parts. Use them!

2. Remove the wheels, and brake assemblies.

➡️**Refer to Section 9 for the proper procedures concerning brake removal.**

3. If equipped with Command-Trac, connect the axle shift motor vacuum harness.

4. Matchmark the front driveshaft and yoke.

5. Disconnect the stabilizer bar, rod and center link, front driveshaft, shock absorbers, steering damper, track bar and ABS sensor if equipped.

6. Place a floor jack under the axle to take up the weight.

7. Disconnect the upper and lower control arms at the axle and lower the axle from the truck.

To install:

8. Install the upper and lower suspension arms to the axle and the track bar. Finger-tighten the bolts and nuts.

9. Connect the following components to the axle:
- Steering damper
- Shock absorber
- Center link-to-knuckle
- Stabilizer bar
- U-joint strap nuts
- ABS brake sensor
- Axle vent hose
- U-joint straps

➡️**New replacement U-joint straps must be used whenever the driveshafts are removed.**

10. If equipped with Command-Trac, connect the axle shift motor vacuum harness.

11. Install the brake assemblies and wheels.

12. Lower the vehicle. Tighten the upper control arm bolts to 55 ft. lbs. (75 Nm). Tighten the lower nuts to 133 ft. lbs. (180 Nm) on Comanche, Wagoneer and Cherokee. On Grand Cherokee/Grand Wagoneer, tighten to 85 ft. lbs. (115 Nm). Tighten the track bar to 74 ft. lbs. (100 Nm). Have the front wheel alignment checked.

REAR AXLE

Axle Shaft, Bearing and Seal

REMOVAL & INSTALLATION

Dana 44 and AMC 7 7/16 in. Models

▶ **See Figures 64, 65 and 66**

➡️**An arbor press is necessary for this procedure.**

1. Raise and support the vehicle safely.

2. Remove the wheel and tire and brake drum/disc assembly.

❋❋ CAUTION

Brake linings may contain asbestos. Asbestos is a known cancer-causing agent. When working on brakes, remember that the dust which accumulates on the brake parts and/or in the drum may contain asbestos. Always wear a protective face covering, such as a painter's mask, when working on the brakes. NEVER blow the dust from the brakes or drum! There are solvents made for the purpose of cleaning brake parts. Use them!

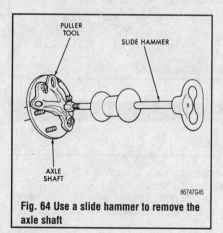

Fig. 64 Use a slide hammer to remove the axle shaft

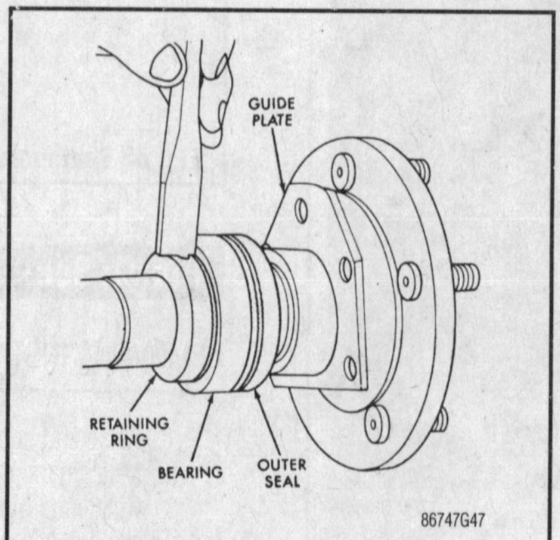

Fig. 65 Splitting the retaining ring

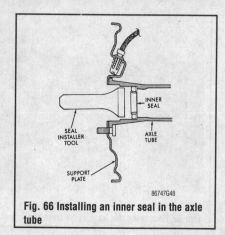

Fig. 66 Installing an inner seal in the axle tube

3. Remove the nuts that attach the outer seal retainer (and brake backing plate) to the axle shaft tube. Discard the nuts.

Remove the axle shaft from the housing with an axle puller attached to a slide hammer.

4. Discard the inner axle seal. Position the axle shaft in a vise.

5. Remove the retaining ring by drilling a 1/4 in. (6mm) hole about 3/4 of the way through the ring, then using a cold chisel over the hole, split the ring.

6. Remove the bearing with an arbor press, discard the seal and remove the retainer plate.

To install:

7. Clean and then apply a thin coating of wheel bearing lubricant to the bearing and seal contact surfaces. Apply wheel bearing lubricant to the lips of the replacement inner and outer seals.

8. Install the inner seal with the open end of the seal facing inward. Ensure it is completely seated.

➡ **It is helpful to cool the axle shaft before pressing on the bearing and retainer. Leave the bearing and retainer at room temperature.**

9. Install the retainer plate and the outer seal on the shaft. Ensure the open end of the seal faces toward the axle shaft bearing.

10. Pack the replacement bearing with wheel bearing lubricant and position on the axle shaft. Press into place.

11. Press a replacement bearing retainer on the axle shaft against the bearing.

12. Install the axle into the axle tube. Position and align the seal retainer and brake support plate and install replacement attaching nuts. Tighten nuts to 32 ft. lbs. (43 Nm).

13. Install brake assembly wheels and tires. Lower vehicle.

Except Dana 44 and AMC 7 7/16 in. Models

▶ See Figures 67 thru 76

1. Raise and support the vehicle safely.

2. Remove the wheels and brake assemblies.

➡ **Refer to Section 9 for the proper procedures concerning brake removal.**

3. Loosen the differential housing cover and drain the lubricant. Remove the housing cover.

4. Rotate the differential so the pinion gear mate shaft lock screw is accessible. Remove the lock screw and the pinion gear mate shaft.

5. Move the axle shafts inward and remove the C-clip lock from the recessed groove in the axle shaft.

6. Remove the axle shaft from the case.

7. Remove the axle shaft seal and bearing using removal tool set 6310.

To install:

8. Wipe the bearing bore and axle shaft tube clean.

9. Install the bearing using tools C-4171 and 6436. Seat the bearing against the shoulder in the axle tube.

10. Install the replacement axle shaft seal with tool 6437 and C-4171. When the installation tool face contacts the axle tube, the seal is at the correct depth.

11. Lubricate the bearing bore and the seal lip. Insert the axle shaft into the tube and engage its splines with the differential.

12. Install the C-clip locks and force the axles outward to seat them.

13. Insert the differential pinion gear mate shaft into the case and through the thrust washers and the pinion gears. Align the hole in the shaft with the lock screw hole. Install the lock screw and tighten to 14 ft. lbs.

Fig. 67 Using a small box wrench loosen the pinion gear mate shaft lock screw . . .

Fig. 68 . . . then remove the lock screw . . .

Fig. 69 . . . and carefully pull out the pinion gear mate shaft

Fig. 70 Notice how the axle shafts are retained in the housing with C-clips

Fig. 71 To remove the C-clip to free the axle shaft, simply move the shaft inward toward the center of the differential from the outside . . .

Fig. 72 . . . this will give enough room to remove the clip from out of the differential gear assembly

Fig. 73 Using a pair of long needle nose pliers, remove the C-clip from the axle shaft . . .

Fig. 74 . . . then carefully pull the axle shaft out of the housing

Fig. 75 After removing the shaft, examine the axle bearings and seal for damage or excessive wear and replace if necessary

Fig. 76 After removing the shaft, examine it for damage or excessive wear. If it is equipped with ABS, inspect the tone ring for damage

14. Apply an 1/8 in. (3mm) bead of RTV to the differential cover after cleaning the differential and cover with solvent.

15. Install the cover and tighten bolts to 35 ft. lbs. (47 Nm).

16. Install the brake assemblies and wheels.

➡ **For Trac-Lok differentials, a special limited slip additive is needed.**

17. Fill the differential with lubricant. Lower the vehicle and test for proper operation.

18. For vehicles equipped with Trac-Lok differentials, drive the vehicle and make 10 to 12 slow, figure-eight turns to pump lubricant through the clutch discs.

Pinion Seal

REMOVAL & INSTALLATION

▶ **See Figures 77 and 78**

1. Raise and support the vehicle.

2. Mark the driveshaft and yoke for reference during assembly and disconnect the driveshaft at the yoke.

3. Remove the pinion shaft nut and washer. Discard the nut.

4. Remove the yoke from the pinion shaft, using a puller.

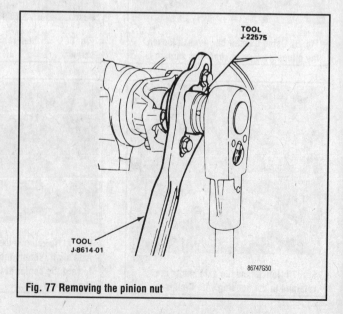

Fig. 77 Removing the pinion nut

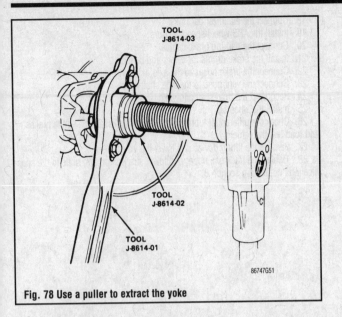

Fig. 78 Use a puller to extract the yoke

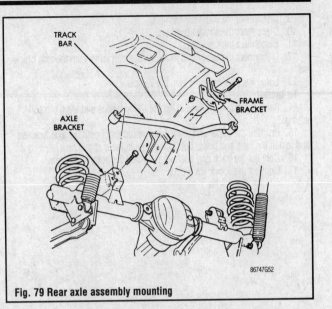

Fig. 79 Rear axle assembly mounting

5. Remove the pinion shaft oil seal with tool J-25180 on semi-floating axles, or tool J-25144 on full floating axles.

To install:

6. Install the new seal with a suitable driver.

7. On 1984–90 models, install the yoke, washer and a new nut. Tighten the nut to 210 ft. lbs. (285 Nm).

8. On 1990 and later models, set bearing preload as follows:

a. The required pinion gear bearing preload torque is 1/2 ft. lbs. over the noted release torque as measured above.

b. Rotate the pinion gear three or four times with a torque wrench attached to the yoke nut. Measure the amount of torque necessary to rotate the pinion.

c. Using a holding tool, tighten the yoke nut in small increments and remeasure until the specified torque is obtained.

9. Align the index marks on the driveshaft and yoke and install the driveshaft. Tighten the attaching bolts or nuts to 170 inch lbs. (19 Nm).

10. Add lubricant to the rear if necessary and lower the vehicle.

Rear Axle Unit

REMOVAL & INSTALLATION

Cherokee/Wagoneer and Comanche

▶ See Figure 79

1. Raise and support the vehicle safely.

❊❊ CAUTION

Brake linings may contain asbestos. Asbestos is a known cancer-causing agent. When working on brakes, remember that the dust which accumulates on the brake parts and/or in the drum may contain asbestos. Always wear a protective face covering, such as a painter's mask, when working on the brakes. NEVER blow the dust from the brakes or drum! There are solvents made for the purpose of cleaning brake parts. Use them!

2. Remove the wheels and brake drums.

➡**For vehicles equipped with Anti-Lock Brakes (ABS), refer to Section 9 for the proper procedures concerning brake removal.**

3. Disconnect the shock absorbers.

4. Disconnect the brake hose at the frame rail and cap to prevent the entry of dirt.

➡**On Comanche models a height sensing rear proportioning valve is mounted on the rear axle. This valve must be adjusted after the axle is reinstalled. If not adjusted unsatisfactory brake action could result.**

5. Disconnect the parking brake cables at the equalizer.

6. Matchmark the driveshaft and yoke, and disconnect the driveshaft.

7. Place a floor jack under the axle to take up the weight.

8. Remove the axle-to-spring U-bolts and lower the axle.

To install:

9. Raise the axle into place. Install the axle-to-spring U-bolts and tighten to 52 ft. lbs. (70 Nm).

10. Reconnect the driveshaft and tighten U-joint strap bolts.

11. Connect the parking brake cables at the equalizer.

12. Connect the brake hoses at the frame rail.

13. Connect the shock absorbers.

14. Install the wheels and brake drums.

15. Check the differential lubricant, bleed the brakes and road test the vehicle.

Grand Cherokee/Grand Wagoneer

1. Raise and support the vehicle safely.

❊❊ CAUTION

Brake linings may contain asbestos. Asbestos is a known cancer-causing agent. When working on brakes, remember that the dust which accumulates on the brake parts and/or in the drum may contain asbestos. Always wear a protective face covering, such as a painter's mask, when working on the brakes. NEVER blow the dust from the brakes or drum! There are solvents made for the purpose of cleaning brake parts. Use them!

2. Place a suitable lifting device under the axle. Secure the axle housing to the device.

3. Remove the wheels and brake drums/rotors.

4. Disconnect the parking brake cables.

➡**For vehicles equipped with Anti-Lock Brakes (ABS), refer to Section 9 for the proper procedures concerning brake removal.**

5. Remove the ABS wheel speed sensors.

6. Disconnect the brake hose at the axle junction block. DO NOT disconnect the brake hoses at the calipers. Cap the brake hose opening to prevent the entry of dirt into the system.

7. Disconnect the vent hose from the axle shaft tube.

8. Matchmark the driveshaft and yoke, and disconnect the driveshaft.

9. Disconnect the stabilizer bar links.
10. Disconnect the shock absorbers.
11. Disconnect the track bar.
12. Disconnect the upper and lower suspension arms from the axle brackets.
13. Lower the axle housing from the vehicle.

To install:

14. Raise the axle into place using the lifting device and align the coil springs.
15. Position the upper and lower suspension arms onto the axle brackets and install the nuts and bolts, but do not tighten them at this time.
16. Connect the track bar, but do not tighten the bolts at this time.
17. Connect the shock absorbers.

18. Connect the stabilizer bar links.
19. Install the ABS wheel speed sensors.
20. Connect the parking brake cables.
21. Install the brake drums, or rotors and calipers.
22. Connect the brake hoses to the axle junction block.
23. Connect the vent hose to the axle shaft tube.
24. Reconnect the driveshaft and yoke.
25. Install the wheels.
26. Check the differential lubricant and add if necessary, bleed the brakes and road test the vehicle.
27. Remove the lifting device and lower the vehicle.
28. Tighten the track bar, upper and lower suspension arm bolts to the specifications outlined in section 8.

8

SUSPENSION AND STEERING

WHEELS

Wheel Assembly

REMOVAL & INSTALLATION

♦ See Figure 1

1. Remove the wheel cover, if equipped, by prying it off with an appropriate tool.
2. With the vehicle still on the ground loosen the lug nuts just enough to ease removal with the wheel off the ground.
3. Raise and support the vehicle safely.
4. Remove the lug nuts and remove the wheel.
5. Installation is the reverse of removal. Tighten the lug nuts to 75 ft. lbs. (102 Nm) observing the tightening sequence in the illustration.

INSPECTION

The wheels should be inspected on a frequent basis. Replace any wheel that is cracked, bent, severely dented, has excessive runout or has a broken weld. The tire inflation valve should also be inspected frequently for wear, leaks, cuts and looseness. It should be replaced if defective or its condition is doubtful.

Clean all the wheels with a mild soap and water solution only and rinse thoroughly with water. Never use abrasive or caustic materials, especially on aluminum or chrome-plated wheels because the surface will be etched or the plating severely damaged. After cleaning aluminum or chrome-plated wheels, apply a coating of protective wax to preserve the finish and luster.

➡DO NOT wax open pore aluminum wheels. The wax will become embedded in the pores and will be very difficult to remove.

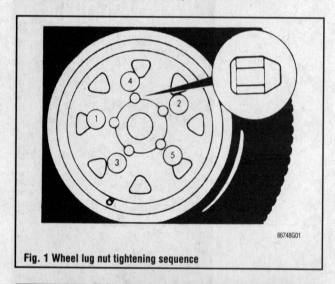

Fig. 1 Wheel lug nut tightening sequence

Wheel Lug Studs

REPLACEMENT

With Disc Brakes

♦ See Figure 2

1. Raise and support the appropriate end of the vehicle safely using jackstands, then remove the wheel.

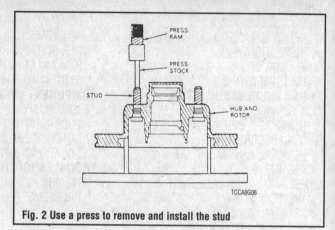

Fig. 2 Use a press to remove and install the stud

2. Remove the brake pads and caliper. Support the caliper aside using wire or a coat hanger. For details, please refer to Section 9 of this manual.
3. Remove the outer wheel bearing and lift off the hub/rotor. For details on wheel bearing removal, installation and adjustment, please refer to Section 1 of this manual.
4. Properly support the hub/rotor using press bars, then drive the stud out using an arbor press.

➡If a press is not available, CAREFULLY drive the old stud out using a blunt drift. MAKE SURE the hub/rotor is properly and evenly supported or it may be damaged.

To install:
5. Clean the stud hole with a wire brush and start the new stud with a hammer and drift pin. Do not use any lubricant or thread sealer.
6. Finish installing the stud with the press.

➡If a press is not available, start the lug stud through the bore in the hub/rotor, then position about 4 flat washers over the stud and thread the lug nut. Hold the hub/rotor while tightening the lug nut, and the stud should be drawn into position. MAKE SURE THE STUD IS FULLY SEATED, then remove the lug nut and washers.

7. Install the hub/rotor and adjust the wheel bearings.
8. Install the brake caliper and pads.
9. Install the wheel, then remove the jackstands and carefully lower the vehicle.
10. Tighten the lug nuts to 85 ft. lbs. (115 Nm).

With Drum Brakes

1. Raise the vehicle and safely support it with jackstands, then remove the wheel.
2. Remove the brake drum.
3. If necessary to provide clearance, remove the brake shoes, as outlined in Section 9 of this manual.
4. Using a large C-clamp and socket, press the stud from the axle flange.
To install:
5. Coat the serrated part of the stud with liquid soap and place it into the hole.
6. Position about 4 flat washers over the stud and thread the lug nut. Hold the flange while tightening the lug nut, and the stud should be drawn into position. MAKE SURE THE STUD IS FULLY SEATED, then remove the lug nut and washers.
7. If applicable, install the brake shoes.
8. Install the brake drum.
9. Install the wheel, then remove the jackstands and carefully lower the vehicle.
10. Tighten the lug nuts to 85 ft. lbs. (115 Nm).

FRONT SUSPENSION

FRONT SUSPENSION COMPONENT LOCATIONS

1. Coil springs
2. Lower ball joints
3. Stabilizer (sway) bar
4. Stabilizer (sway) bar links
5. Track bar
6. Upper control arms
7. Lower control arms
8. Steering knuckle
9. Pitman arm
10. Center link
11. Steering damper
12. Tie rod
13. Tie rod end
14. Drive axle

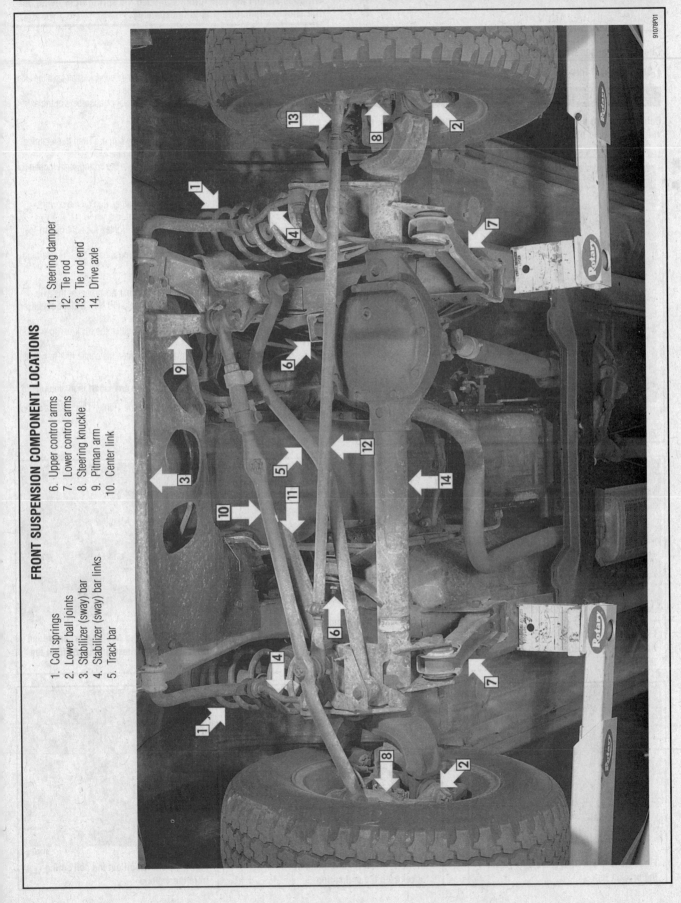

91078P01

Coil Springs

REMOVAL & INSTALLATION

Cherokee/Wagoneer and Comanche

▶ See Figures 3 thru 9

❊❊ CAUTION

Coil springs are under a great deal of tension when installed in the vehicle. Serious injury or death may result from being hit by an expanding spring. A piece of chain fastened to the frame and wrapped around the coil spring will keep the spring from flying out if it should slip before it is fully expanded.

1. Raise and support the vehicle safely.
2. Support the axle with a floor jack.
3. Remove the wheels.
4. On 4WD trucks, matchmark and disconnect the front driveshaft from the axle.
5. Disconnect the lower control arm at the axle.
6. Disconnect the stabilizer bar links and the shock absorbers at the axle.
7. Disconnect the track bar at the sill bracket.
8. Disconnect the tie rod at the pitman arm.
9. If equipped with ABS, disengage the wiring harness from the retaining brackets to prevent possible damage when lowering the axle.
10. Lower the axle until tension is removed from the spring, then loosen the spring retainer and remove the spring.

To install:

11. Position the replacement spring on the retainer, tighten the spring retainer bracket screw and lift the axle into position.
12. Connect the lower control arm to the axle. Tighten the control arm-to-axle bolt to 133 ft. lbs. (180 Nm).
13. If equipped with ABS, install the wiring harness back into the retaining brackets.
14. Remove the support jack.
15. Connect the stabilizer bar links and the shock absorbers at the axle. Tighten the shock absorber-to-axle bolt to 14 ft. lbs. (19 Nm) and the stabilizer bar-to-axle bolt to 70 ft. lbs. (95 Nm).
16. Connect the track bar at the sill bracket. Tighten the track bar-to-frame rail bolt to 35 ft. lbs. (47 Nm).
17. Connect the tie rod at the pitman arm. Tighten the center link-to-pitman arm bolt to 35 ft. lbs. (47 Nm).

➡ **New strap bolts must be used each time the driveshaft is disconnected.**

18. On 4WD trucks, connect the front driveshaft. Tighten U-joint-to-axle bolt to 14 ft. lbs. (19 Nm).
19. Install the wheels and lower the vehicle.

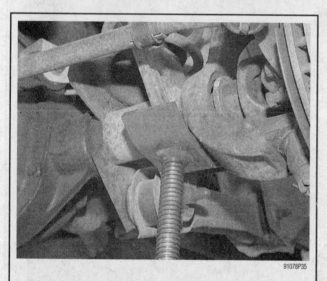

91078P35

Fig. 3 Be sure to support the front axle with a jack stand

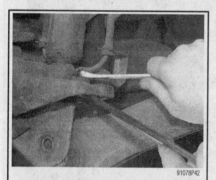

91078P42

Fig. 4 Using a backup wrench, loosen the front shock absorber mounting bracket fasteners

91078P31

Fig. 5 Loosen then **remove the ball stud nut,** then separate the front suspension track bar from the bracket on the left side frame rail

91078P43

Fig. 6 Separate the ABS front wheel speed sensor wiring harness grommets from the routing clips

91078P34

Fig. 7 Loosen the front coil spring retaining bracket bolt . . .

91078P33

Fig. 8 . . . then remove the bolt and bracket from the coil spring

91078P32

Fig. 9 Carefully pull out the coil spring from the vehicle

Grand Cherokee/Grand Wagoneer

▶ See Figure 10

1. Raise and safely support the vehicle, allowing the front axle to hang.
2. Support the axle with a jack.
3. Paint or scribe alignment marks on the cam adjusters and axle bracket for installation reference.
4. Matchmark and disconnect the front driveshaft from the axle.
5. Disconnect the lower suspension arm nut, cam and cam bolt from the axle.
6. Disconnect the stabilizer bar links and shock absorbers at the axle.
7. Disconnect the track bar at the frame rail bracket.
8. Disconnect the drag link at the pitman arm.
9. Lower the axle until spring is free from the upper mount, then remove the coil spring clip screw and remove the spring.
10. If necessary, remove the jounce bumper from the upper spring mount.

To install:

11. If removed, install the jounce bumper and tighten the bolts to 31 ft. lbs. (42 Nm).
12. Position the replacement spring on axle pad. Install the spring clip and tighten the screw to 16 ft. lbs. (21 Nm).
13. Raise the axle into position until the spring seats in the upper mount.
14. Connect the stabilizer bar links and shock absorbers to the axle bracket. Connect the track bar to the frame rail bracket.
15. Install the lower suspension arm to the axle.
16. Connect the driveshaft to the yoke.
17. Lower the vehicle.

Shock Absorbers

REMOVAL & INSTALLATION

Cherokee/Wagoneer and Comanche

▶ See Figures 11, 12, 13 and 14

1. Remove the locknuts and washers from the upper stud.
2. Raise and support the vehicle safely.
3. If necessary for access, remove the wheels.
4. Remove the lower attaching nuts and bolts.
5. Pull the shock absorber eyes and rubber bushings from the mounting pins.

To install:

➡ **Before installing new shocks, they should be purged of air. To do this, hold the shock upright and fully extend it, then invert and compress it. Do this several times.**

6. Position the shock on the vehicle and install the mounting hardware.
7. Tighten the upper end nut to 8 ft. lbs. (11 Nm) and the lower end bolts to 14 ft. lbs. (19 Nm).
8. Install the wheels and lower the vehicle.

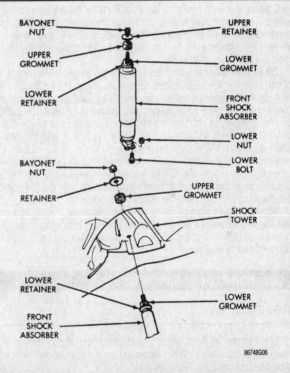

Fig. 11 Exploded view of the shock absorber mounting

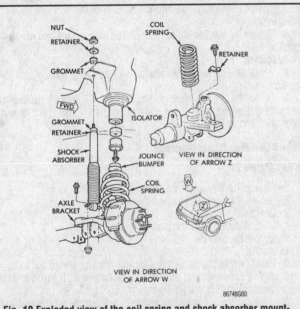

Fig. 10 Exploded view of the coil spring and shock absorber mounting

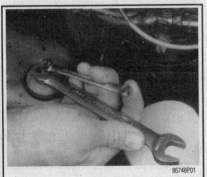

Fig. 12 Remove the locknut from the upper stud

Fig. 13 Keep all parts in the order removed

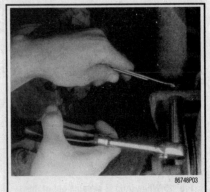

Fig. 14 Remove the lower nuts and bolts

Grand Cherokee/Grand Wagoneer

♦ **See Figure 10**

1. Remove the upper nut, retainer and grommet from the engine compartment,
2. Remove the lower bolt and nut from the mounting bracket.
3. Remove the shock absorber.

To install:

➡**Before installing new shocks, they should be purged of air. To do this, hold the shock upright and fully extend it, then invert and compress it. Do this several times.**

4. Position the shock on the vehicle and install the mounting hardware.
5. Tighten the upper retaining nut to 14 ft. lbs. (19 Nm) and lower bolt and nut to 17 ft. lbs. (23 Nm).
6. Install the wheels and lower the vehicle.

TESTING

♦ **See Figure 15**

The purpose of the shock absorber is simply to limit the motion of the spring during compression and rebound cycles. If the vehicle is not equipped with these motion dampers, the up and down motion would multiply until the vehicle was alternately trying to leap off the ground and to pound itself into the pavement.

Contrary to popular rumor, the shocks do not affect the ride height of the vehicle. This is controlled by other suspension components such as springs and tires. Worn shock absorbers can affect handling; if the front of the vehicle is rising or falling excessively, the ``footprint'' of the tires changes on the pavement and steering is affected.

The simplest test of the shock absorber is simply push down on one corner of the unladen vehicle and release it. Observe the motion of the body as it is released. In most cases, it will come up beyond it original rest position, dip back below it and settle quickly to rest. This shows that the damper is controlling the spring action. Any tendency to excessive pitch (up-and-down) motion or failure to return to rest within 2-3 cycles is a sign of poor function within the shock absorber. Oil-filled shocks may have a light film of oil around the seal, resulting from normal breathing and air exchange. This should NOT be taken as a sign of failure, but any sign of thick or running oil definitely indicates failure. Gas filled shocks may also show some film at the shaft; if the gas has leaked out, the shock will have almost no resistance to motion.

While each shock absorber can be replaced individually, it is recommended that they be changed as a pair (both front or both rear) to maintain equal response on both sides of the vehicle. Chances are quite good that if one has failed, its mate is weak also.

Upper and Lower Ball Joint

INSPECTION

To inspect the ball joints, unload the suspension and support the vehicle safely. Upper ball joints on 2WD vehicles and any ball joint on 4WD vehicles should be replaced if any play exists at all.

REMOVAL & INSTALLATION

♦ **See Figure 16**

➡**This procedure requires the use of a special ball joint removal tool.**

1. Raise and support the vehicle safely.
2. Remove the wheel. Remove the steering knuckle.
3. Position a ball joint removal tool (J-34503-1 and 34503-3 or equivalent), as illustrated, to remove the ball joint.
4. Tighten the clamp screw to remove the joint.

To install:

5. Use a ball joint installation tool (J-34503-5 or J-34503-4 or equivalent), as illustrated, to install the ball joint.
6. Install the knuckle. Tighten steering knuckle-to-ball joint nuts to 100 ft. lbs. (135 Nm).

Front Stabilizer Bar

REMOVAL & INSTALLATION

Cherokee/Wagoneer and Comanche

♦ **See Figures 17, 18, 19 and 20**

1. Raise and support the vehicle safely.
2. Disconnect the stabilizer bar at the connecting links. If necessary, disengage the connecting links from the brackets on the front axle housing.
3. Remove the stabilizer bar-to-frame clamps and cushions, and remove the stabilizer bar.

To install:

4. Position the bar on the vehicle and install the clamps and cushions finger-tight.
5. Tighten the clamp-to-frame bolts to 55 ft. lbs. (75 Nm), the stabilizer bar-to-connecting link nuts to 27 ft. lbs. (37 Nm), and the connecting link-to-axle bolts to 70 ft. lbs. (95 Nm).

Grand Cherokee/Grand Wagoneer

♦ **See Figure 21**

1. Raise and safely support the vehicle.
2. Remove the sway bar links from the axle brackets.
3. Disconnect the sway bar from the links.
4. Disconnect the sway bar clamps from the frame rails.
5. Remove the sway bar.

To install:

6. Install the sway bar on the frame rail and install the clamps and bolts. Ensure the bar is centered with equal spacing on both sides. Tighten the retaining bracket bolts to 55 ft. lbs. (75 Nm).
7. Install the connecting rod link and grommets onto the stabilizer bar and brackets. Tighten the nuts to 70 ft. lbs. (96 Nm).

TCCA8P73

Fig. 15 When fluid is seeping out of the shock absorber, it's time to replace it

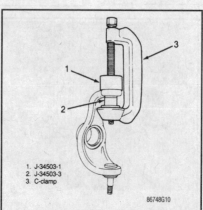

1. J-34503-1
2. J-34503-3
3. C-clamp

86748G10

Fig. 16 Press the ball joint out to remove it

91078P41

Fig. 17 Using a box wrench, loosen the stabilizer bar at the connecting links

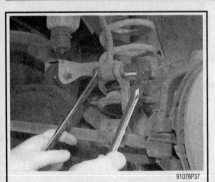

Fig. 18 If necessary, loosen the nut and bolt of the stabilizer bar link at the axle housing . . .

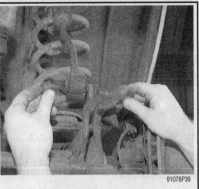

Fig. 19 . . . then separate the link fom the axle housing

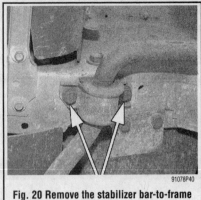

Fig. 20 Remove the stabilizer bar-to-frame clamp bolts

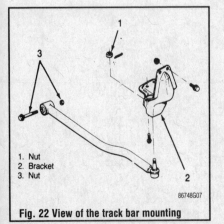

Fig. 21 Exploded view of the stabilizer bar mounting

8. Tighten the sway bar-to-connecting link nut to 27 ft. lbs. (36 Nm).
9. Lower the vehicle.

Track Bar

REMOVAL & INSTALLATION

▶ **See Figure 22**

1. Raise and support the vehicle safely.
2. Remove the cotter pin and nut securing the track bar to the frame bracket.
3. Remove the bolt and nut securing the track bar to the axle.

➡ A puller tool may be necessary to separate the ball stud from the frame rail bracket.

To install:
4. Position the track bar on the vehicle. Install both ends finger-tight.
5. Lower the vehicle.
6. Tighten the frame-end nut to 35 ft. lbs. (47 Nm) and the axle end bolt to 55 ft. lbs. (75 Nm).

Upper Control Arm

REMOVAL & INSTALLATION

Cherokee/Wagoneer and Comanche

▶ **See Figures 23 and 24**

1. Raise and support the vehicle safely.
2. On trucks with the 2.8L engine, disconnect the right engine mount and raise the engine so that the rear bolt will clear the exhaust pipe.
3. Remove the wheels.
4. Remove the control arm-to-axle bolt.
5. Remove the control arm-to-frame bolt and remove the arm.

To install:
6. Install the replacement control arm and all nuts and bolts finger-tight.
7. Install the wheels.
8. On 2.8L engines, connect the right engine mount.
9. Lower the vehicle.

➡ It is important to have the front springs at their normal ride height when the upper control arm attaching nuts are tightened. Vehicle ride comfort could be adversely affected.

10. Tighten the control arm bolts to 55 ft. lbs. (75 Nm) at the axle; 66 ft. lbs. (89 Nm) at the frame.

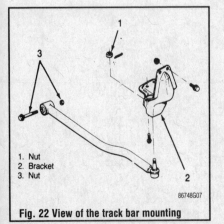

1. Nut
2. Bracket
3. Nut

Fig. 22 View of the track bar mounting

Fig. 23 Using a socket and box wrench, remove the upper control arm-to-axle housiung bolt

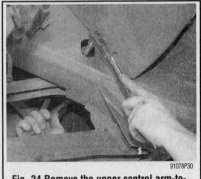

Fig. 24 Remove the upper control arm-to-frame bolt. Notice the access hole in the frame rail

Grand Cherokee/Grand Wagoneer

▶ **See Figure 25**

1. Raise and support the vehicle safely.
2. Remove the upper control arm-to-axle bracket nut and bolt.
3. Remove the upper control arm-to-frame nut and bolt.
4. Remove the arm.
To install:
5. Install the upper control arm and tighten the bolts and nuts finger-tight.
6. Lower the vehicle.
7. Tighten the upper control arm bolts to 55 ft. lbs. (75 Nm).

Lower Control Arm

REMOVAL & INSTALLATION

Cherokee/Wagoneer and Comanche

▶ **See Figures 26 and 27**

1. Raise and support the vehicle safely.
2. Remove the wheels.
3. Remove the bolts securing the lower control arm at the axle and rear bracket.
4. Remove the arm.
To install:
5. Install the replacement arm and tighten the attaching bolts finger-tight.
6. Install the wheels, then lower the vehicle.

➡It is important to have the front springs at their normal ride height when the lower control arm attaching nuts are tightened. Vehicle ride comfort could be adversely affected.

7. Tighten the lower control arm attaching bolts to 133 ft. lbs. (180 Nm).

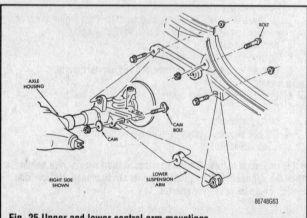

Fig. 25 Upper and lower control arm mountings

Grand Cherokee/Grand Wagoneer

▶ **See Figure 25**

1. Raise and safely support the vehicle, allowing the suspension to hang freely.
2. Paint or scribe alignment marks on the cam adjusters and suspension arm for installation reference.
3. Remove the lower control arm nut, cam and cam bolt from the axle.
4. Remove the nut and bolt from the frame rail bracket.
5. Remove the arm.
To install:
6. Install the lower control arm.
7. Tighten the rear bolts finger-tight.
8. Install the cam bolt, cam and nut in the axle while realigning the reference marks.
9. Lower the vehicle.
10. Tighten the nuts to 130 ft. lbs. (176 Nm).

Steering Knuckle

REMOVAL & INSTALLATION

▶ **See Figure 28**

1. Raise and support the vehicle.
2. Remove the wheels.
3. On 4WD models, remove the axle shaft.
4. Remove the disc brake caliper. See Section 9 for additional service information.

❊❊ CAUTION

Brake linings may contain asbestos. Asbestos is a known cancer-causing agent. When working on brakes, remember that the dust which accumulates on the brake parts may contain asbestos. Always wear a protective face covering, such as a painter's mask, when working on the brakes. NEVER blow the dust from the brakes or drum! There are solvents made for the purpose of cleaning brake parts. Use them!

5. Remove the knuckle-to-ball joint cotter pins and nuts.
6. Drive the knuckle out with a brass hammer.
To install:

➡A split ring seat is located in the bottom of the knuckle. During installation, this ring seat must be set to a depth of 0.20 in. (5.23mm). Measure the depth to the top of the ring seat.

7. Position the knuckle on the vehicle. Tighten the knuckle retaining nuts to 75 ft. lbs. (102 Nm). Use new cotter pins to secure the nuts.
8. Install the brake caliper. Tighten the disc brake caliper bolts to 77 ft. lbs. (104 Nm).
9. If applicable, install the axle shaft.
10. Install the wheels and lower the vehicle.

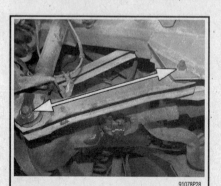

Fig. 26 The control arm assembly is secured in only two places (frame rail and axle housing)

Fig. 27 Remove the bolt securing the lower control arm to the front axle housing

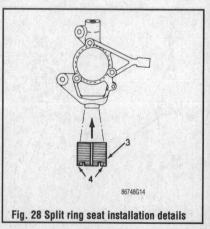

Fig. 28 Split ring seat installation details

Front Wheel Bearings

REPLACEMENT

➡Sodium-based grease is not compatible with lithium-based grease. Read the package labels and be careful not to mix the two types. If there is any doubt as to the type of grease used, completely clean the old grease from the bearing and hub before replacing.

Cherokee/Wagoneer and Comanche

2WD MODELS

▶ See Figure 29

1. Raise and support the vehicle safely.
2. Remove the wheels.
3. Remove the caliper without disconnecting the brake line. Suspend it out of the way using a piece of wire to prevent damage. See Section 9 for additional service information.

✳✳ CAUTION

Brake linings may contain asbestos. Asbestos is a known cancer-causing agent. When working on brakes, remember that the dust which accumulates on the brake parts may contain asbestos. Always wear a protective face covering, such as a painter's mask, when working on the brakes. NEVER blow the dust from the brakes or drum! There are solvents made for the purpose of cleaning brake parts. Use them!

4. Remove the grease cap, cotter pin, nut cap, nut, and washer from the spindle. Discard the cotter pin.
5. Slowly remove the hub and rotor. Catch the outer bearing as it falls.
6. Carefully drive out the inner bearing and seal from the hub, using a wood block.
7. Inspect the bearing races for excessive wear, pitting or grooves. If they are cracked or grooved, or if pitting and excess wear is present, drive them out with a drift or punch.
8. Check the bearing for excess wear, pitting or cracks, or excess looseness.

➡If it is necessary to replace either the bearing or the race, replace both. Never replace just a bearing or a race. These parts wear in a mating pattern. If just one is replaced, premature failure of the new part will result.

To install:

9. Thoroughly clean the spindle and the inside of the hub.
10. Pack the inside of the hub with high temperature wheel bearing grease. Add grease to the hub until it is flush with the inside diameter of the bearing cup.
11. Pack the bearings with the same grease. A needle-shaped wheel bearing packer is best for this operation. If one is not available, place a large amount of grease in the palm of your hand and slide the edge of the bearing cage through the grease to pick up as much as possible, then work the grease in until it squeezes through the bearing.

12. If a new race is being installed, very carefully drive it into position until it bottoms all around, using a brass drift. Be careful to avoid scratching the surface.
13. Place the inner bearing in the race and install a new grease seal.
14. Clean the rotor contact surface if necessary.
15. Position the hub and rotor on the spindle and install the outer bearing.
16. Install the washer and nut.
17. While turning the rotor, tighten the nut to 25 ft. lbs. (34 Nm) to seat the bearings.
18. Back the nut off 1/2 a turn. While turning the rotor, tighten the nut to 19 inch lbs. (2 Nm).
19. Install the nut cap and a new cotter pin. Install the grease cap.
20. Install the caliper.
21. Install the wheels.

4WD MODELS

▶ See Figures 30 thru 37

➡If the hub is equipped with ball bearings, the entire unit must be replaced if defective. If the hub is equipped with tapered roller bearings, its internal components can be serviced or replaced as necessary.

1. Raise and support the vehicle safely.
2. Remove the wheels.
3. Remove, but do not disconnect, the caliper. Suspend it out of the way. See Section 9 for additional service information.

✳✳ CAUTION

Brake linings may contain asbestos. Asbestos is a known cancer-causing agent. When working on brakes, remember that the dust which accumulates on the brake parts and/or in the drum may contain asbestos. Always wear a protective face covering, such as a painter's mask, when working on the brakes. NEVER blow the dust from the brakes or drum! There are solvents made for the purpose of cleaning brake parts. Use them!

4. Remove the rotor.
5. Remove the cotter pin, nut retainer, axle nut and washer.
6. Remove the 3 hub-to-steering knuckle attaching bolts.

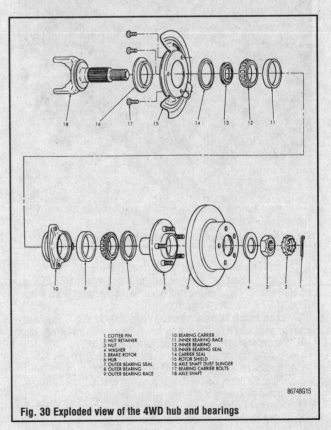

1. COTTER PIN
2. NUT RETAINER
3. NUT
4. WASHER
5. BRAKE ROTOR
6. HUB
7. OUTER BEARING SEAL
8. OUTER BEARING
9. OUTER BEARING RACE
10. BEARING CARRIER
11. INNER BEARING RACE
12. INNER BEARING
13. INNER BEARING SEAL
14. CARRIER SEAL
15. ROTOR SHIELD
16. AXLE SHAFT DUST SLINGER
17. BEARING CARRIER BOLTS
18. AXLE SHAFT

86748G15

Fig. 30 Exploded view of the 4WD hub and bearings

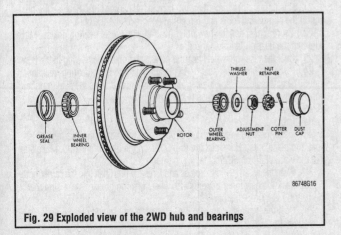

GREASE SEAL — INNER WHEEL BEARING — ROTOR — OUTER WHEEL BEARING — THRUST WASHER — ADJUSTMENT NUT — NUT RETAINER — COTTER PIN — DUST CAP

86748G16

Fig. 29 Exploded view of the 2WD hub and bearings

Fig. 31 Remove the cotter pin . . .

Fig. 32 . . . and the nut retainer

Fig. 33 Loosen . . .

Fig. 34 . . . then remove the nut . . .

Fig. 35 . . . and washer

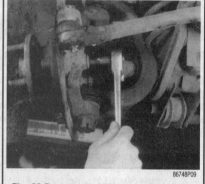

Fig. 36 Remove the hub-to-knuckle attaching bolts . . .

Fig. 37 . . . then remove the hub assembly and rotor shield

7. Remove the hub/bearing carrier and the rotor shield.

8. Using an arbor press, press the hub out of the bearing carrier. Special tools 5073 and 5074 are available for this job. Secure the carrier to the press plate with M12 x 1.75mm x 40mm bolts.

9. Cut and remove the plastic cage from the hub inner bearing. Using diagonal pliers or tin snips, cut the bearing cage. Discard the rollers after removing the cage.

10. Remove what remains of the inner bearing as follows:

a. Install a bearing separator tool on the inner bearing.

b. Position the separator tool and hub in an arbor press.

c. Force the hub out of the inner bearing with press pin tool 5074.

11. Remove the bearing carrier outer seal and discard it.

12. Drive the inner bearing seal out and discard it. If you're using tool 5078, make sure that the word JEEP faces downward.

13. Attach press plate tool 5073 to the rear of the carrier. Secure it in the press using M12 x 1.75mm x 40mm bolts.

14. Position bearing race remover 5076 in the carrier bore between the inner and outer bearing races.

15. Position the press pin tool 5074 on tool 5076.

16. Place the bearing carrier in the press and force the inner bearing race from the carrier bore. Reverse the position of the carrier and tools and force the outer bearing race from the bore.

To assemble and install:

17. Thoroughly clean all reusable parts with a safe solvent. Discard any parts that appear worn or damaged.

18. Attach press plate tool 5073 on the bearing carrier. Secure it in the press using M12 x 1.75mm x 40mm bolts.

19. Position the new outer bearing race in the bore.

20. Position bearing race installation tool 5077 on the race. Make sure that the word JEEP faces the downward. Press the race into the bore. The race should be flush with the machined shoulder of the carrier.

21. Position the new inner bearing race in the carrier bore. Reverse the position of the carrier and tools and force the inner race into the bore.

22. Thoroughly pack the new outer bearing with wheel bearing grease. Make sure that the bearing is fully packed.

23. Coat the race with wheel bearing grease and place the bearing in the bore.

24. Place the new outer seal on the bearing and position bearing installation tool 5079 on the seal. Place the carrier in the press and force the seal into the bore. Apply wheel bearing grease to the seal lip.

25. Insert the hub through the seal and outer bearing and into the bearing carrier bore.

26. Install bearing installation tool 5078 into the rear of the bearing carrier bore and place the race installation tool 5077 on the front of the hub. Make sure that the word JEEP on 5077 is facing the hub.

27. Place the assembly in the press and force the hub shaft into the carrier bore.

28. Pack the new inner bearing with wheel bearing grease. Make sure that the bearing is thoroughly packed.

29. Coat the inner seal lip with wheel bearing grease and place it on the inner bearing.

30. Coat the inner bearing race with wheel bearing grease.
31. Place the carrier in a press along with tool 5077. The word JEEP must face the hub. Position the bearing and seal in the carrier. Place seal installation tool 5080 on the seal.
32. Force the bearing and seal into the bore and onto the hub shaft.

✲✲ WARNING

Use extreme care when forcing the assembly into position! The carrier must rotate freely after installation of the bearing! Do not attempt to eliminate bearing lash with the press. Final bearing preload is attained by tightening the drive axle nut.

33. Install the new outer seal on the carrier.
34. Thoroughly clean the axle shaft and apply a thin coating of lithium-based grease to the splines and seal contact surfaces.
35. Install the slinger, rotor shield and hub/bearing assembly on the axle shaft.
36. Coat the carrier bolt threads with Loctite®. Install them and tighten to 75 ft. lbs. (102 Nm).
37. Install the rotor and caliper.
38. Install the washer and axle shaft nut. Tighten the nut to 175 ft. lbs. (237 Nm).
39. Install the nut retainer and cotter pin. NEVER back off the nut to install the cotter pin! ALWAYS advance it!
40. Install the wheel.

Grand Cherokee/Grand Wagoneer

1. Raise and support the vehicle safely.
2. Remove the wheel.
3. Remove the caliper and rotor.
4. Remove the cotter pin, nut retainer and axle hub nut.
5. Remove the hub-to-knuckle bolts. Remove the hub from the steering knuckle.

To install:

6. Install the hub to the steering knuckle. Tighten the bolts to 75 ft. lbs. (102 Nm).
7. Install the hub washer and nut. Tighten the nut to 175 ft. lbs. (237 Nm). Install the nut retainer and a new cotter pin.
8. Install the rotor and caliper.
9. Install the wheel and lower the vehicle.

Wheel Alignment

If the tires are worn unevenly, if the vehicle is not stable on the highway or if the handling seems poor, the wheel alignment should be checked. If an alignment problem is suspected, first check for improper tire inflation and other possible causes. These can be worn suspension or steering components, accident damage or even unmatched tires. If any worn or damaged components are found, they must be replaced before the wheels can be properly aligned. Wheel alignment requires very expensive equipment and involves minute adjustments which must be accurate; it should only be performed by a trained technician. Take your vehicle to a properly equipped shop.

Following is a description of the alignment angles which are adjustable on most vehicles and how they affect vehicle handling. Although these angles can apply to both the front and rear wheels, usually only the front suspension is adjustable.

CASTER

▶ **See Figure 38**

Looking at a vehicle from the side, caster angle describes the steering axis rather than a wheel angle. The steering knuckle is attached to the axle yoke through ball joints or king pins. The wheel pivots around the line between these points to steer the vehicle. When the upper point is tilted back, this is described as positive caster. Having a positive caster tends to make the wheels self-centering, increasing directional stability. Excessive positive caster makes the wheels hard to steer, while an uneven caster will cause a pull to one side. Overloading the vehicle or sagging rear springs will affect caster, as will raising the rear of the vehicle. If the rear of the vehicle is lower than normal, the caster becomes more positive.

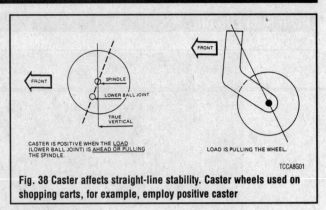

Fig. 38 Caster affects straight-line stability. Caster wheels used on shopping carts, for example, employ positive caster

CAMBER

▶ **See Figure 39**

Looking from the front of the vehicle, camber is the inward or outward tilt of the top of wheels. When the tops of the wheels are tilted in, this is negative camber; if they are tilted out, it is positive. In a turn, a slight amount of negative camber helps maximize contact of the tire with the road. However, too much negative camber compromises straight-line stability, increases bump steer and torque steer.

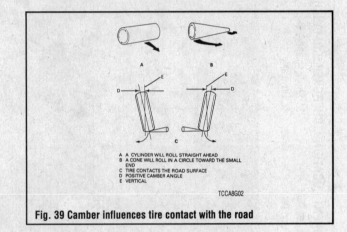

Fig. 39 Camber influences tire contact with the road

TOE

▶ **See Figure 40**

Looking down at the wheels from above the vehicle, toe angle is the distance between the front of the wheels relative to the distance between the back of the wheels. If the wheels are closer at the front, they are said to be toed-in or to have negative toe. A small amount of negative toe enhances directional stability and provides a smoother ride on the highway.

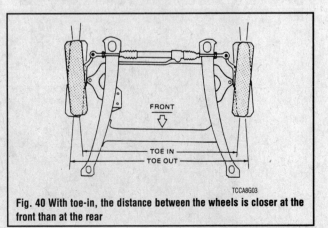

Fig. 40 With toe-in, the distance between the wheels is closer at the front than at the rear

REAR SUSPENSION

REAR SUSPENSION COMPONENT LOCATIONS (CHEROKEE, COMANCHE, WAGONEER)

1. Leaf springs
2. Stabilizer (sway) bar
3. Shock absorbers
4. Drive axle

91078P02

Coil Springs

REMOVAL & INSTALLATION

▶ See Figure 41

➡Coil springs are used only on the Grand Cherokee/Grand Wagoneer models.

1. Raise and safely support the vehicle.
2. Support the axle with a suitable jack.
3. Disconnect the sway bar links and shock absorbers from the axle bracket.
4. Disconnect the track bar from the frame rail bracket.
5. Lower the axle until the spring is free from the upper mount seat. Remove the coil spring clip screw and remove the spring.

To install:

6. Position the coil spring on the axle pad, then install the spring clip and screw. Tighten the screw to 16 ft. lbs. (22 Nm).
7. Raise the axle into position until the spring seats in the upper mount.
8. Connect the sway bar links and shock absorbers to the axle bracket. Connect the track bar to the frame rail bracket.
9. Remove the supports and lower the vehicle.

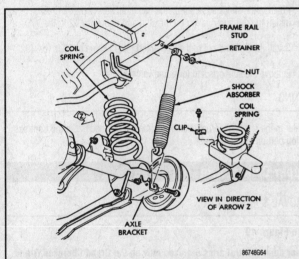

Fig. 41 Exploded view of the coil spring and shock absorber mounting

Leaf Springs

REMOVAL & INSTALLATION

▶ See Figures 42, 43, 44, 45 and 46

➡Leaf springs are used on Cherokee, Wagoneer and Comanche models.

1. Raise and support the vehicle safely.
2. Remove the wheels.
3. Take up the weight of the axle with a floor jack.
4. Disconnect the shock absorbers at the axle.
5. Disconnect the stabilizer bar links (if equipped) at the spring plate.
6. Remove the spring bracket U-bolts and spring plates.
7. Remove the rear spring-to-shackle bolt, then the front spring-to-shackle bolt.
8. Lower the axle and remove the spring.

To install:

9. Position the spring on the axle, then align the ends of the spring with the shackles.

10. Install the shackle bolts, then the spring bracket U-bolts. Tighten the shackle bolts to 111 ft. lbs. (151 Nm) on 1984–88 models, 105 ft. lbs. (142 Nm) on 1989 models and 65 ft. lbs. (88 Nm) on 1990–98 models. Tighten the U-bolt nuts to 52 ft. lbs. (71 Nm) for Cherokee and Wagoneer or 100 ft. lbs. (135 Nm) on Comanche.
11. Connect the stabilizer bar to the spring plate.
12. Connect the shock absorbers to the axle.
13. Install the wheels, then lower the vehicle to the ground. Double check the tightness of the fasteners.

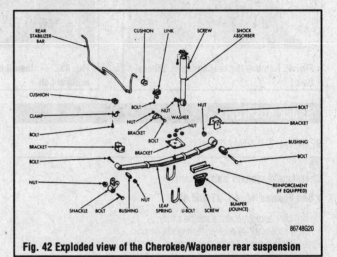

Fig. 42 Exploded view of the Cherokee/Wagoneer rear suspension

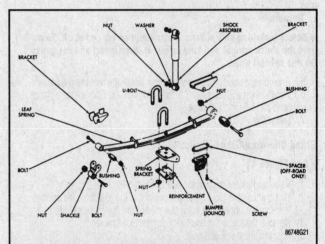

Fig. 43 Exploded view of the Comanche rear suspension

Fig. 44 Be sure to support the rear axle with a jackstand

Fig. 45 Remove the rear spring-to-shackel bolt . . .

Fig. 46 . . . then the front spring-to-shackel bolt

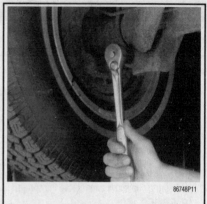

Fig. 47 Remove the lower attaching bolt

Shock Absorbers

REMOVAL & INSTALLATION

Cherokee/Wagoneer and Comanche

♦ See Figures 44, 45, 47 and 48

1. Raise and support the vehicle safely.
2. If necessary for access, remove the wheels.
3. Remove the locknuts and washers.
4. Pull the shock absorber eyes and rubber bushings from the mounting pins.

To install:

➡ Before installing new shocks, they should be purged of air. To do this, hold the shock upright and fully extend it, then invert and compress it. Do this several times.

5. Position the shock on the vehicle and install the mounting hardware.
6. Tighten the nuts/bolts to 44 ft. lbs. (60 Nm). On Comanche, tighten upper bolts to 15 ft. lbs. (20 Nm).
7. Lower the vehicle.

Grand Cherokee/Grand Wagoneer

♦ See Figure 41

1. Raise and safely support the rear of the vehicle.
2. Using a suitable jack, relieve the weight of the axle from the springs.
3. Remove the upper stud nut and washer from the frame rail stud.
4. Remove the lower nut and bolt from the axle bracket.
5. Remove the shock absorber.

To install:

➡ Before installing new shocks, they should be purged of air. To do this, hold the shock upright and fully extend it, then invert and compress it. Do this several times.

6. Position the shock absorber on the frame rail stud and axle bracket.
7. Install the nut and retainer on the stud and tighten to 52 ft. lbs. (70 Nm).
8. Install the bolt and nut to the axle bracket and tighten to 68 ft. lbs. (92 Nm).
9. Remove the supports and lower the vehicle.

TESTING

Refer to the shock absorber testing information outlined under the front suspension portion of this section.

Upper Control Arm

REMOVAL & INSTALLATION

♦ See Figure 49

➡ Rear upper control arms are used only on the Grand Cherokee/Grand Wagoneer models.

1. Raise and support the vehicle safely.
2. Remove the wheels.
3. Remove the control arm-to-axle bolt.
4. Remove the control arm-to-frame bolt and remove the arm.

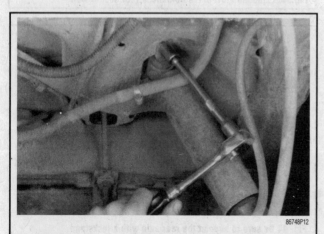

Fig. 48 Use an extension to access the upper mounting bolts

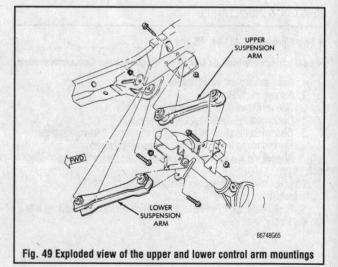

Fig. 49 Exploded view of the upper and lower control arm mountings

To install:

5. Position the control arm on the vehicle. Install the nuts and bolts finger-tight.
6. Install the wheels.
7. Lower the vehicle.

➡ **It is important to have the front springs at their normal ride height when the upper control arm attaching nuts are tightened. Vehicle ride comfort could be adversely affected.**

8. Tighten the control arm bolts to 55 ft. lbs. (75 Nm) at the axle; 66 ft. lbs. (90 Nm) at the frame.

Lower Control Arm

REMOVAL & INSTALLATION

▶ **See Figure 49**

➡ **Rear lower control arms are used only on the Grand Cherokee/Grand Wagoneer models.**

1. Raise and support the vehicle safely.
2. Remove the wheels.
3. Remove the fasteners securing the lower control arm at the axle and rear bracket.
4. Remove the arm.

To install:

5. Position the arm on the vehicle. Install the attaching bolts finger-tight.
6. Install the wheels.
7. Lower the vehicle.

➡ **It is important to have the front springs at their normal ride height when the lower control arm attaching nuts are tightened. Vehicle ride comfort could be adversely affected.**

8. Tighten the lower control arm attaching bolts to 133 ft. lbs. (180 Nm).

Rear Stabilizer Bar

REMOVAL & INSTALLATION

Cherokee, Wagoneer and Comanche

▶ **See Figures 44, 50 and 51**

1. Raise and support the vehicle safely.
2. Disconnect the sway bar links from the springs.
3. Disconnect the sway bar from the frame rails.
4. Remove the sway bar.

To install:

5. Install the sway bar and tighten the bar link bolts to 55 ft. lbs. (74 Nm).
6. Connect the sway bar to the frame rail and tighten the bolts to 40 ft. lbs. (54 Nm).
7. Lower the vehicle.

Grand Cherokee/Grand Wagoneer

▶ **See Figure 52**

1. Raise and support the vehicle safely.
2. Remove the wheels.
3. Disconnect the stabilizer bar links from the axle brackets.
4. Lower the exhaust by disconnecting the muffler and tail pipe hangers.
5. Disconnect the stabilizer bar from the links.
6. Disconnect the stabilizer bar clamps from the frame rails. Remove the stabilizer bar.

To install:

7. Position the stabilizer bar on the frame rail and install the clamps and bolts.
8. Ensure the bar is centered with equal spacing on both sides. Tighten the bolts to 40 ft. lbs. (54 Nm).
9. Install the links and grommets onto the stabilizer bar and axle brackets. Install the nuts and tighten them to 27 ft. lbs. (36 Nm).
10. Connect the muffler and tail pipe to their hangers.
11. Install the wheel and lower the vehicle.

Fig. 50 Disconnect the rear sway bar links from the springs

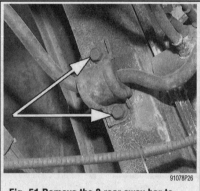

Fig. 51 Remove the 2 rear sway bar-to-frame rail clamp bolts

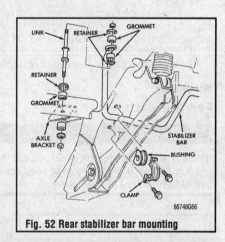

Fig. 52 Rear stabilizer bar mounting

STEERING

Steering Wheel

REMOVAL & INSTALLATION

Without Air Bag

▶ **See Figures 53 thru 58**

1. Disconnect the negative battery cable.
2. Set the front tires in the straight ahead position.
3. If equipped with the standard steering wheel:

    a. Remove the trim cover attaching screws from the underside of the wheel and remove the cover.

    b. Unplug the horn wire connectors from the contact switch.

4. If equipped with the sport steering wheel:

    a. Remove the horn button by prying outward.

    b. Remove the horn contact assembly, bushing, receiver and flex plate from the steering wheel.

5. Remove the steering wheel nut and vibration damper.
6. Scribe a line mark on the steering wheel and steering shaft if there is not one already. Release the turn signal assembly from the steering post and install a puller.
7. Remove the steering wheel and spring.

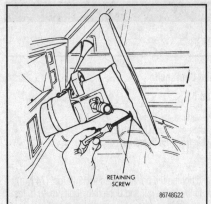

Fig. 53 Standard wheel trim pad removal

Fig. 54 Remove the horn button

Fig. 55 Remove the screws securing the horn contact assembly

Fig. 56 Loosen and remove the steering wheel nut

Fig. 57 A puller must be used to remove the steering wheel

Fig. 58 Align the scribe marks and install the wheel

To install:

8. Align the scribe marks on the steering shaft with the steering wheel and secure the steering wheel spring, steering wheel, and horn button contact cup with the steering wheel nut. Tighten to 25 ft. lbs. (34 Nm).

9. Install the horn assembly in the reverse order of removal.

10. Connect the battery cable and test for horn operation.

With Air Bag

♦ **See Figures 59, 60 and 61**

❋ CAUTION

Before removing the steering wheel, disable the air bag system (refer to Section 6). Failure to do so could result in accidental air bag deployment and possible injury.

1. Disconnect the negative battery cable and disable the air bag system.

2. Set the front tires in a straight-ahead position.

3. Remove the air bag module retaining nuts from behind the steering wheel.

4. Remove the air bag module.

5. If equipped, remove the cruise control switch.

6. Disconnect the horn wiring.

7. Remove the steering wheel retaining nut.

8. Scribe a line mark on the steering wheel and steering shaft if there is not one already.

9. Remove the steering wheel using a suitable puller.

To install:

10. To install, align the scribe marks on the steering shaft with the steering wheel.

11. Ensure the wheel compresses the 2 locktabs on the clockspring.

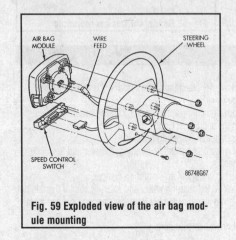

Fig. 59 Exploded view of the air bag module mounting

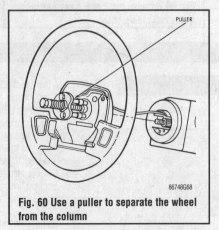

Fig. 60 Use a puller to separate the wheel from the column

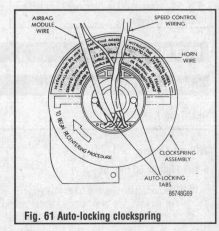

Fig. 61 Auto-locking clockspring

12. Pull the air bag and if equipped, cruise control wires through the larger hole and horn wire through the smaller hole. Ensure they are not pinched.

13. Install the steering wheel nut and tighten it to 45 ft. lbs. (61 Nm) while forcing the steering wheel down the shaft with the nut.

14. Connect the wire feed to the horn buttons.

15. Connect the feed wires and tighten the air bag retaining nuts to 90 inch lbs. (10 Nm). Ensure the air bag is completely seated. The latching clip arms must be visible on top of the connector housing on the module.

16. Enable the air bag system and connect the battery cable.

17. From the right side of the vehicle (in case of accidental deployment), turn the ignition switch to the **ON** position.

18. Check for proper air bag warning light operation.

Turn Signal (Combination) Switch

REMOVAL & INSTALLATION

Without Air Bag

▶ **See Figures 62 thru 78**

1. Disconnect the negative battery cable.
2. Remove the steering wheel.
3. Remove the lockplate cover with tool C-4156 or an equivalent lockplate compressing tool. Release the steering shaft retaining snapring.

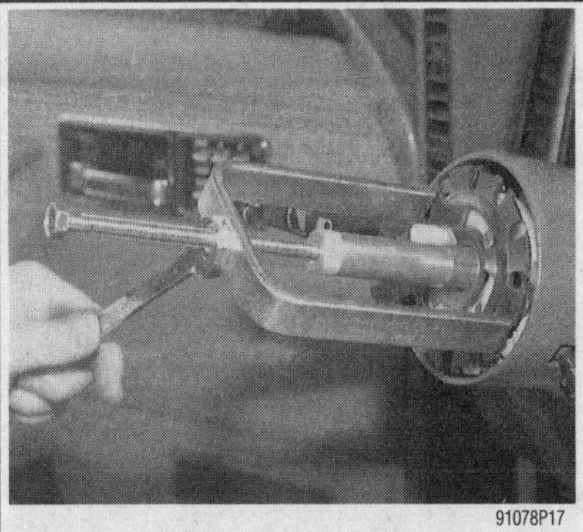

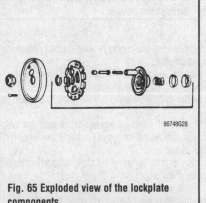

Fig. 62 Compress the lock plate spring . . .

Fig. 63 . . . enough to expose the steering wheel lock plate retaining snapring

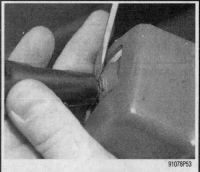

Fig. 64 If snapring pliers are not available, use a flat bladed tool to move the snapring off of the steering column shaft

Fig. 65 Exploded view of the lockplate components

Fig. 66 Remove the hazard warning switch knob

Fig. 67 Using a small flat bladed tool, gently pry out the combination switch stalk handle

Fig. 68 Unplug the combination switch wiring harness connector located underneath the steering column

Fig. 69 Wrap the harness connector flat against the wires so that it can be removed from the steering column

Fig. 70 Remove the (1) steering column bracket-to-dashboard nuts, and (2) steering column-to-bracket bolts

Fig. 71 . . . then remove the support bracket from the vehicle

Fig. 72 Remove the wiring harness plastic protector

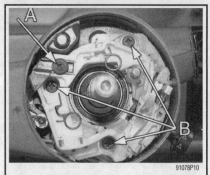

Fig. 73 Remove the mounting screw and turn signal actuater arm (A), then remove the turn signal switch attaching screws (B)

Fig. 74 Remove the 3 Torx® head screws from the steering column barrell . . .

Fig. 75 . . . then pull the turn signal switch, steering column barrel and combination switch assembly from the steering column

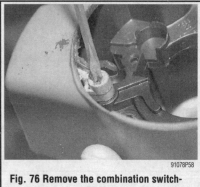

Fig. 76 Remove the combination switch-to-steering column pivot peg by pushing it through the bottom . . .

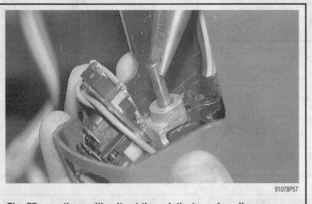

Fig. 77 . . . then pulling it out through the top using pliers . . .

Fig. 78 . . . then pull the combination switch out of the steering column barrel

4. Remove the lockplate, canceling cam, upper bearing preload spring and thrust washer from the steering column.

5. Remove the hazard warning switch knob. Press the knob inward and remove it from the column by turning counterclockwise.

6. If equipped with a column shift, remove the two retaining screws and the gear selector indicator cover.

7. If equipped with a column shift, remove the gear selector indicator lamp bracket retaining screw. DO NOT remove the lamp and bracket at this time.

8. Unscrew the tilt-release lever.

9. Remove the combination lever by pulling it out straight from the column. The wiper switch must be in the off position.

10. Disconnect the turn signal wiring harness located at the lower end of the steering column. Wrap it with tape to prevent it from becoming entangled.

11. Remove the plastic protector from the wire harness.

12. Remove the turn signal switch retaining screws and the dimmer switch actuator arm, then remove the switch. Guide the switch straight up out of the steering column.

To install:

13. Install the turn signal switch and wiring harness. Install the dimmer switch actuator arm and turn signal switch retaining screws. Tighten turn signal and dimmer switch attaching screws to 35 inch lbs. (4 Nm).

14. Install the combination lever and tilt release lever.

15. If equipped with a column shift, install the two retaining screws and the gear selector indicator cover.

16. If equipped with a column shift, install the gear selector indicator lamp bracket retaining screw.

17. Install the hazard warning switch knob. Press the knob inward and install it from the column by turning clockwise.

18. Install the lockplate, canceling cam, upper bearing preload spring and thrust washer from the steering column.

19. Install the lockplate cover and install the steering shaft retaining snapring.

20. Install the steering wheel. Tighten the nut to 25 ft. lbs. (34 Nm).

21. Connect the negative battery cable.

With Air Bag

▶ **See Figures 79 and 80**

✳✳ CAUTION

Before performing this procedure, disable the air bag system (refer to Section 6). Failure to do so could result in accidental air bag deployment and possible injury.

1. Disconnect the negative battery cable and disable the air bag system.
2. If equipped, remove the tilt lever.
3. Remove the upper and lower steering column covers with a suitable Torx® driver.
4. Remove the steering column trim panel.
5. Remove the knee blocker.
6. Remove the steering column retaining nut and lower the column.
7. Using Snap-On® tamper-proof bit TTXR20B2 or equivalent, remove the multi-function switch screws.
8. Pull the switch away from the column, loosen the connector screw (which will remain in the connector) and unplug the electrical connector.

To install:

9. Engage the electrical connector to the multi-function switch and tighten the retaining screw.
10. Mount the multi-function switch to the steering column and tighten the screws.
11. Position the steering column and tighten the retaining nuts.
12. Install the knee blocker, lower trim panel and steering column covers.
13. If equipped, install the tilt steering lever.
14. Enable the air bag system and connect the negative battery cable.
15. From the right side of the vehicle (in case of accidental deployment), turn the ignition switch to the **ON** position.
16. Check for proper air bag warning light operation.

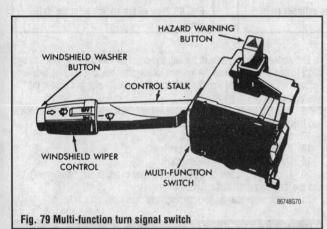

Fig. 79 Multi-function turn signal switch

Ignition Switch

REMOVAL & INSTALLATION

Without Air Bag

▶ **See Figures 81 and 82**

The ignition switch is located on the lower part of the steering column.
1. Place the ignition in the **LOCK** position.
2. Remove any components necessary to access the switch.
3. Remove the two switch mounting screws.
4. Disconnect the switch from the rod.
5. Disconnect the wiring and remove the switch.

To install:

6. On non-tilt columns:
   a. Move the ignition switch slider to the **OFF** unlocked position (move the slider all the way down, then back two clicks). The remote rod hole in the ignition switch slider should now be centered.
   b. Insert the remote rod in the ignition switch slider hole and install the ignition switch on the steering column. Tighten the attaching screws to 35 inch lbs. (4 Nm).
7. On tilt columns:
   a. Insert the ignition key in the lock cylinder and turn the cylinder to the **OFF** unlocked position.
   b. Move the ignition switch downward to eliminate any slack and tighten the attaching screws to 35 inch lbs. (4 Nm).
8. Install any components removed for switch access.

With Air Bag

▶ **See Figures 83 thru 89**

✳✳ CAUTION

Before performing this procedure, disable the air bag system (refer to Section 6). Failure to do so could result in accidental air bag deployment and possible injury.

1. Disconnect the negative battery cable and disable the air bag system.
2. If equipped, remove the tilt lever.
3. Remove the upper and lower steering column covers with a suitable Torx® driver.
4. Using Snap-On® tamper-proof bit TTXR20BO or equivalent, remove the ignition switch screws.
5. Pull the ignition switch away from the column.
6. Release the 2 connector locks on the 7-terminal wiring connector and remove the connector from the ignition switch.
7. Release the connector lock on the key-in-switch and halo light 4-terminal connector and remove the connector from the ignition switch.

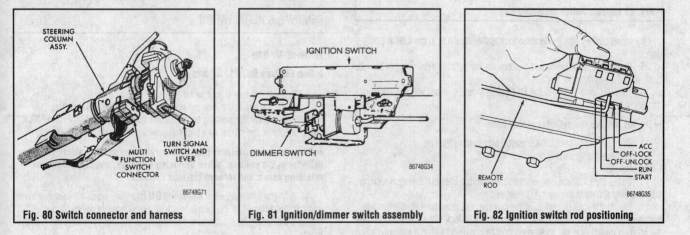

Fig. 80 Switch connector and harness

Fig. 81 Ignition/dimmer switch assembly

Fig. 82 Ignition switch rod positioning

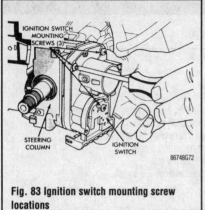

Fig. 83 Ignition switch mounting screw locations

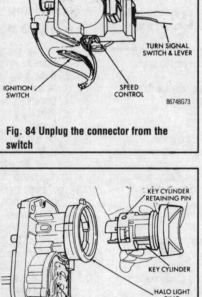

Fig. 84 Unplug the connector from the switch

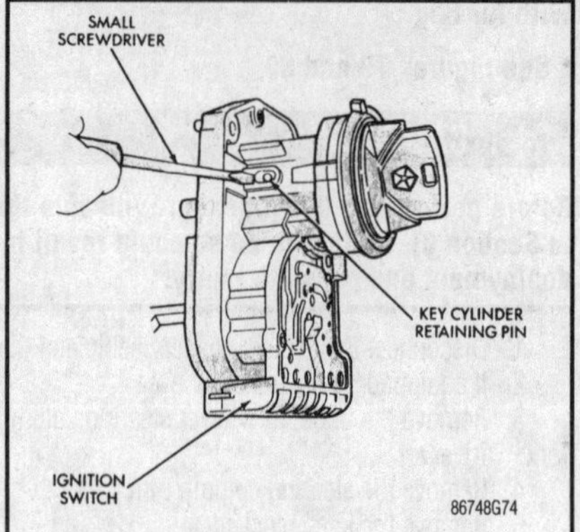

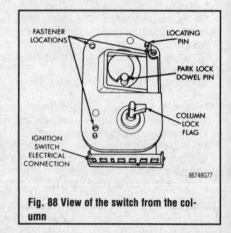

Fig. 85 Key cylinder retaining pin

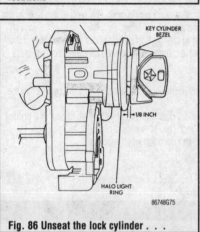

Fig. 86 Unseat the lock cylinder . . .

Fig. 87 . . . then pull the cylinder from the switch

Fig. 88 View of the switch from the column

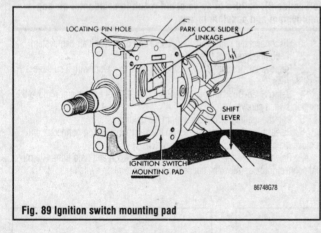

Fig. 89 Ignition switch mounting pad

8. Insert the key into the ignition lock and ensure it is in the **LOCK** position.

9. Using a small screwdriver, depress the key cylinder retaining pin so it is flush with the key cylinder surface.

10. Turn the ignition key to the **OFF** position and the lock will release from its seated position.

➡**Do not remove the cylinder at this time.**

11. Turn the key to the **LOCK** position and remove the key.

12. Remove the ignition lock.

To install:

13. Install the electrical connectors to the switch. Ensure the switch locking tabs are fully seated in the wiring connectors.

14. Mount the ignition switch to the column. The dowel pin on the ignition switch assembly must engage with the column park-lock slider linkage. Ensure the ignition switch is in the lock position (flag is parallel with the ignition switch terminals).

15. Apply a dab of grease to the flag and pin. Position the park-lock link and slider to mid-travel. Position the ignition lock against the lock housing face. Ensure the pin is inserted into the park-lock link contour slot and tighten the retaining screw.

16. With the ignition lock and switch in the **LOCK** position, insert the lock into the switch assembly until it bottoms.

17. Assemble the column covers.

18. If equipped, install the tilt wheel lever.

19. Connect the negative battery cable.

20. From the right side of the vehicle (in case of accidental deployment), turn the ignition switch to the **ON** position.

21. Check for proper air bag warning light operation.

Ignition Lock Cylinder

REMOVAL & INSTALLATION

Without Air Bag

▶ **See Figures 90, 91, 92 and 93**

1. Remove the turn signal switch.

2. Insert the key in the lock cylinder and turn it to the **ON** position.

3. Remove the key warning buzzer switch and contacts AS AN ASSEMBLY using needle-nosed pliers, or a paper clip with a 90° bend.

➡**Some steering columns may have a retaining screw holding the lock cylinder in the column. When servicing this type, simply remove the retaining screw and remove the lock cylinder.**

4. With the ignition switch still in the **ON** position, insert a thin screwdriver into the slot adjacent to the switch attaching screw boss (right-hand slot). Depress the spring latch located at the bottom of the slot to release the lock cylinder.

5. Remove the lock cylinder.

Fig. 90 Using a pair of needle nose pliers, remove the key warning buzzer switch and contacts from the steering column

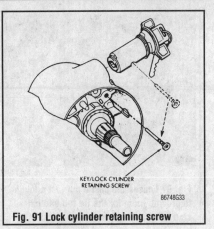

KEY/LOCK CYLINDER RETAINING SCREW

86748G33

Fig. 91 Lock cylinder retaining screw

Fig. 92 Using a small thin bladed tool, press in the ignition lock clinder retaining tab . . .

91078P03

Fig. 93 . . . then pull out the lock cylinder from the steering column

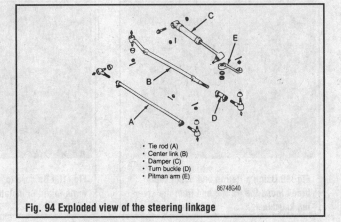

- Tie rod (A)
- Center link (B)
- Damper (C)
- Turn buckle (D)
- Pitman arm (E)

86748G40

Fig. 94 Exploded view of the steering linkage

To install:

6. To install the lock cylinder, turn the key to the **LOCK** position. Insert the lock cylinder in to the housing far enough to contact the drive tang. Force it inward and move the ignition switch actuator rod up and down to align the components. When the components align, the cylinder will move inward and the spring-loaded retainer will snap into place locking the lock cylinder in the housing.

➡️**If the lock cylinder is retained by a screw, tighten the screw to 40 inch lbs. (5 Nm).**

7. Install the key warning buzzer switch.
8. Follow the ignition switch installation procedures to adjust the ignition switch.
9. Install the turn signal switch.

With Air Bag

Please refer to the ignition switch removal and installation procedure.

Steering Linkage

REMOVAL & INSTALLATION

Pitman Arm (Steering Arm)

▸ **See Figure 94**

➡️**It is recommended that that front end alignment be checked after performing this procedure.**

1. Raise and support the vehicle safely.
2. Place the wheels in a straight ahead position.
3. Remove the cotter pin and nut, then disconnect the connecting rod from the pitman arm.
4. Matchmark the pitman arm and steering gear housing for installation alignment.

5. Remove the pitman arm nut. Some steering gears have a staked washer securing the nut. The arms of this washer must be bent out of the way to remove the nut.
6. Installation is the reverse of removal. Tighten the pitman arm nut to 185 ft. lbs. (250 Nm).

Tie Rod End

➡️**It is recommended that that front end alignment be checked after performing this procedure.**

CHEROKEE/WAGONEER AND COMANCHE

▸ **See Figures 95 thru 100**

1. Raise and support the vehicle safely.
2. Remove the cotter pins and retaining nuts at both ends of the tie rod.

91078P05

Fig. 95 Using a pair of wire cutters, unbend the tie rod end cotter pin so that it is straight . . .

Fig. 96 . . . then pull it out from the tie rod end ball stud

Fig. 97 Loosen the castle nut just enough to provide room for the tie rod end ball stud to break loose from the knuckle

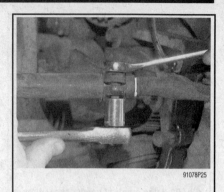

Fig. 98 Using a socket and backup wrench, loosen the tie rod end clamp nut and bolt

Fig. 99 Using a tie rod end puller tool, break loose the tie rod end from the steering knuckle

Fig. 100 Be sure to count the number of turns to aid in installation of the new tie rod

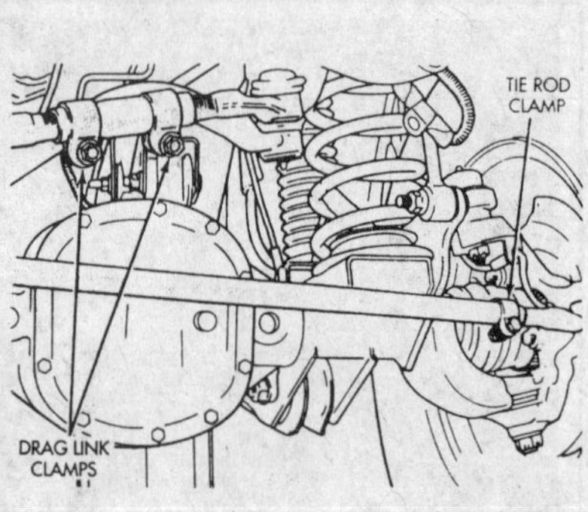

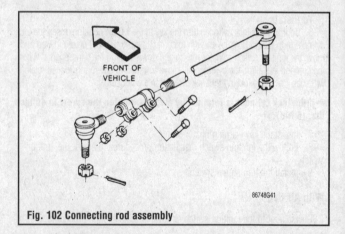

Fig. 101 Tie rod/drag link clamp bolts

3. Remove the tie rod ends from the steering arm and center link.

4. Count the number of visible threads on the tie rod and unscrew the tie rod ends.

5. Installation is the reverse of removal. Install the tie rod ends, leaving the same number of threads exposed. Tighten the retaining nuts to 35 ft. lbs. (47 Nm).

GRAND CHEROKEE/GRAND WAGONEER

▶ See Figure 101

1. Remove the cotter pins at the steering knuckle and drag link.
2. Loosen the ball studs using a suitable puller.
3. If necessary, loosen the end clamp bolts and remove the tie rod ends from the tube. Count the number of turns required to remove the tie rod ends so the replacement tie rod ends can be reinstalled in the same approximate position.

To install:

4. If removed, install the tie rod ends in the tube. Thread the tie rod ends into the tube the same number of turns required to remove the old ones.
5. Position the tie rod clamps and tighten to 20 ft. lbs. (27 Nm).
6. Install the tie rod on the drag link and steering knuckle and install the retaining nuts.
7. Tighten the ball stud nuts to 55 ft. lbs. (75 Nm) and install new cotter pins. If the ball stud hole does not align with the nut castellation, further tighten the nut in order to install the cotter pin.
8. Have the wheel alignment checked.

Steering Connecting Rod (Drag Link)

➡It is recommended that that front end alignment be checked after performing this procedure.

CHEROKEE/WAGONEER AND COMANCHE

▶ See Figures 94 and 102

1. Raise and support the vehicle safely.
2. Place the wheels in a straight ahead position.

Fig. 102 Connecting rod assembly

3. Remove the cotter pin and nut and disconnect the steering damper from the connecting rod.
4. Remove the cotter pins and nuts at each end of the rod, then disconnect the connecting rod from the knuckle and the pitman arm.
5. Install the connecting rod, with the wheels straight ahead and the pitman arm parallel with the vehicle centerline. Install the nuts and tighten all three to 35 ft. lbs. (47 Nm).

GRAND CHEROKEE/GRAND WAGONEER

1. Remove the cotter pins and nuts at the steering knuckle and drag link.
2. Remove the steering dampener ball stud from the drag link using a suitable puller tool.
3. Remove the tie rod from the drag link and remove the drag link from the steering knuckle and pitman arm using a suitable puller tool.
4. If necessary, loosen the end clamp bolts and remove the tie rod end from the link. Count the number of turns required to remove the tie rod end so the replacement tie rod end can be reinstalled in the same approximate position.

To install:

5. Install the drag link adjustment sleeve and tie rod end. Thread the tie rod end and sleeve onto the drag link the same number of turns required to remove the old ones.

6. Position the clamp bolts and tighten to 36 ft. lbs. (49 Nm).

7. Install the drag link to the steering knuckle, tie rod and pitman arm. Install the nuts and tighten to 55 ft. lbs. (75 Nm). Install new cotter pins. If the ball stud hole does not align with the nut castellation, further tighten the nut in order to install the cotter pin.

8. Install the steering dampener onto the drag link and tighten the nut to 55 ft. lbs. (75 Nm). Install a new cotter pin. If the ball stud hole does not align with the nut castellation, further tighten the nut in order to install the cotter pin.

9. Have the wheel alignment checked.

Steering Dampener

▶ **See Figures 94, 103, 104 and 105**

➡ It is recommended that that front end alignment be checked after performing this procedure.

1. Raise and support the vehicle safely.
2. Place the wheels in a straight ahead position.

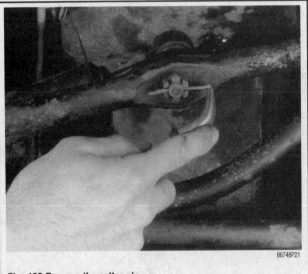

Fig. 103 Remove the cotter pin . . .

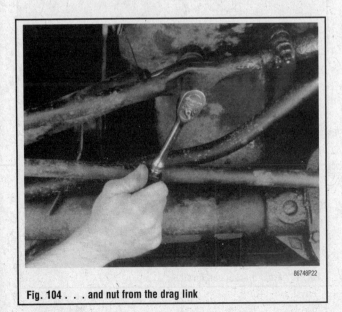

Fig. 104 . . . and nut from the drag link

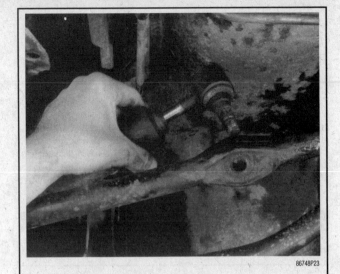

Fig. 105 Separate the stud from the drag link

3. Remove the steering dampener retaining nut and bolt from the axle bracket.

4. Remove the cotter pin and nut from the piston rod ball stud at the drag link.

5. Remove the steering dampener ball stud from the drag link.

6. Installation is the reverse of removal. Tighten retaining bolts to 55 ft. lbs. (75 Nm).

Manual Steering Gear

REMOVAL & INSTALLATION

1. Disconnect the steering shaft from the gear.
2. Raise and support the truck on jackstands.
3. Disconnect the center link from the pitman arm.
4. Remove the front stabilizer bar.
5. Remove the pitman arm nut. Matchmark the arm and shaft, and remove the arm with a puller.
6. Unbolt and remove the gear.
7. Installation is the reverse of removal. The pitman arm nut MUST be securely staked. Observe the following torque specifications:
- Steering gear-to-frame: 65 ft. lbs. (88 Nm).
- Pitman arm-to-shaft: 185 ft. lbs. (250 Nm).
- Stabilizer bar-to-frame: 55 ft. lbs. (75 Nm).
- Stabilizer bar-to-link: 27 ft. lbs. (37 Nm).
- Center link-to-pitman arm: 55 ft. lbs. (75 Nm).

ADJUSTMENT

✳✳ WARNING

Adjust the wormshaft bearing preload and pitman shaft overcenter drag torque in the order listed below. Failure to follow the procedures exactly may result in gear failure.

1. Raise and support the vehicle safely.
2. Check the steering gear mounting bolt torque. It should be 65 ft. lbs. (88 Nm).
3. Matchmark the pitman arm and shaft, and remove the pitman arm nut. Remove the arm with a puller.
4. Loosen the pitman adjusting screw locknut, then back off the adjusting screw 2–3 turns.
5. Remove the horn button and cover. Slowly turn the steering wheel in one direction as far as it will go, then back 1/2 turn.
6. Install a socket and inch-pound torque wrench on the steering wheel nut. Measure the worm bearing preload by turning the wheel through a 90° arc (1/4 turn) with the wrench. Preload should be 5–8 inch lbs.

7. If preload is not within specifications, turn the adjuster screw clockwise to increase, or counterclockwise to decrease, the preload.

8. When the desired preload is attained, tighten the adjuster locknut to 50 ft. lbs. (68 Nm) and recheck the adjustment.

9. Rotate the steering wheel slowly from lock-to-lock, counting the number of turns. Turn the wheel back, 1/2 the number of turns to center the gear, then turn the wheel 1/2 turn off center.

10. Install the inch-pound torque wrench and socket on the steering wheel nut. Measure the torque required to tun the gear through the center point of travel. The drag should equal the worm bearing preload torque plus 4–10 inch lbs., but not exceed a total of 18 inch lbs.

11. If adjustment is required, loosen the pitman shaft screw locknut and turn the adjusting screw to obtain the desired torque. Tighten the locknut to 25 ft. lbs. (34 Nm) and recheck the overcenter drag.

12. Install all parts and check steering wheel alignment.

Power Steering Gear

REMOVAL & INSTALLATION

1. Place the front wheels in a straight-ahead position. Place a drain pan under the steering gear.

2. Disconnect the fluid hoses from the steering gear. Raise and secure the hoses above the level of the pump to prevent excess steering fluid loss. Plug the hoses to prevent the entry of dirt.

3. Disconnect the steering shaft from the gear.

4. Raise and support the truck on jackstands.

5. Disconnect the center link from the pitman arm.

6. Remove the front stabilizer bar.

7. Remove the pitman arm nut. Matchmark the arm and shaft, and remove the arm with a puller.

8. Unbolt and remove the gear.

9. Installation is the reverse of removal. The pitman arm nut MUST be securely staked. Observe the following torque specifications:
- Steering gear-to-frame: 65 ft. lbs. (88 Nm)
- Pitman arm-to-shaft: 185 ft. lbs. (250 Nm)
- Stabilizer bar-to-frame: 55 ft. lbs. (75 Nm)
- Stabilizer bar-to-link: 27 ft. lbs. (37 Nm)
- Center link-to-pitman arm: 55 ft. lbs. (75 Nm)

ADJUSTMENT

❋❋ WARNING

Adjust the wormshaft bearing preload and pitman shaft overcenter drag torque in the order listed below. Failure to follow the procedures exactly may result in gear failure.

1. Ensure the wormshaft bearing adjustment cap is seated. Score an index mark on the steering gear housing adjacent to one of the spanner wrench tightening holes.

2. Measure counterclockwise 0.19–0.23 in. (5–6mm) from the index mark and score an adjustment reference mark on the housing. Rotate the adjustment cap counterclockwise until the spanner wrench tightening hole in the cap is aligned with the adjustment reference mark on the housing.

3. Install the adjustment cap locknut and tighten to 85 ft. lbs. (115 Nm). Ensure that the adjustment cap does not rotate. Rotate the stub shaft clockwise to the stop, then rotate it counterclockwise 1/4 of a turn.

4. Measure the preload torque by rotating at a constant speed with a inch pound torque wrench installed. It should be between 4–10 inch lbs.

5. Rotate the pitman shaft adjustment screw counterclockwise until it is fully extended, then rotate it 180° clockwise. Rotate the stub shaft from stop-to-stop counting the number of turns. Turn the wheel back, 1/2 the number of turns. Make sure the steering gear is centered. The flat area on the stub shaft should face upward and be parallel with the adjustment screw cover.

6. Measure the drag by rotating the stub shaft 45° on each side of vertical and record the highest drag torque measured at or near the steering gear center position.

7. Specifications are as follows:
- New Gears: 4–8 inch lbs. greater than wormshaft bearing preload, to a maximum of 18 inch lbs.
- Used Gears: 4–5 inch lbs. greater than wormshaft bearing preload, to a maximum of 18 inch lbs.

8. If necessary, rotate the pitman shaft adjustment screw until the correct torque is obtained. Tighten the locknut to 20 ft. lbs. (27 Nm). DO NOT allow the adjustment screw locknut to rotate.

Power Steering Pump

REMOVAL & INSTALLATION

Cherokee, Wagoneer and Comanche

▶ **See Figures 106 and 107**

1. Loosen the alternator adjustment and pivot bolts.

2. Insert the drive lug of a 1/2 in. drive ratchet into the adjustment hole in the alternator bracket and move the alternator to relieve tension on the belt.

3. Remove the drive belt.

4. Remove the air cleaner.

5. Disconnect the hoses at the pump and cap the hose ends.

6. Remove the front bracket-to-engine bolts.

7. Support the pump with your hand. Remove the pump-to-rear bracket nuts.

8. Lift out the pump.

To install:

9. Position the pump on the engine.

10. Install and tighten the pump-to-bracket nuts to 28 ft. lbs. (38 Nm) and the bracket-to-engine bolts to 33 ft. lbs. (45 Nm).

11. Install the air cleaner.

12. Install and tension the drive belt.

13. Fill the reservoir with power steering fluid. Bleed the system.

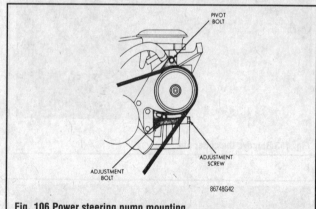

Fig. 106 Power steering pump mounting

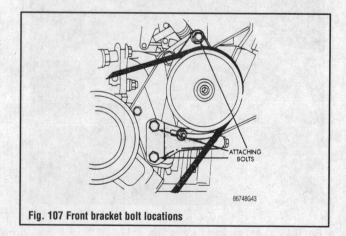

Fig. 107 Front bracket bolt locations

Grand Cherokee/Wagoneer

4.0L ENGINE

▶ **See Figure 108**

1. Disconnect the negative battery cable.
2. Loosen and remove the serpentine drive belt.
3. Place a drain pan under the power steering pump.
4. Clamp the power steering pump pressure and return fluid lines and disconnect the lines from the hose from the pump.
5. Remove the rear bracket-to-pump bolts.
6. Remove the lower nut and adjustment bracket.
7. Remove the adjuster and pivot bolts.
8. Tilt the pump forward and remove the pump and front bracket assembly from the engine bracket.
9. Remove the bracket from the pump.

To install:

10. Install the bracket to the pump and tighten the bolts to 21 ft. lbs. (28 Nm).
11. Position the pump and bracket on the engine bracket.
12. Install the pivot bolt.
13. Install the adjuster bolt.
14. Install the adjuster stud nut.
15. Install the rear bracket-to-pump bolts and tighten them to 21 ft. lbs. (28 Nm).
16. Install the serpentine belt.
17. Connect the power steering lines and remove the clamps.
18. Fill the pump reservoir to the proper level with fluid.
19. Connect the negative battery cable.
20. Bleed the system.

5.2L AND 5.9L ENGINES

1. Disconnect the negative battery cable.
2. Loosen and remove the serpentine drive belt.
3. Place a drain pan under the power steering pump.
4. Disconnect the return and pressure lines from the pump.
5. Remove the bolts attaching the pump to the bracket on the engine block.
6. If necessary, remove the bracket-to-engine block bolts.

To install:

7. Install the bracket to the engine block and tighten the bolts to 30 ft. lbs. (41 Nm).

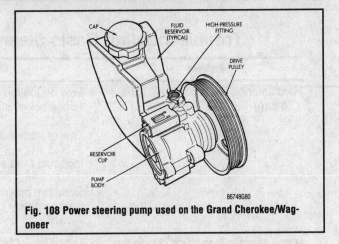

Fig. 108 Power steering pump used on the Grand Cherokee/Wagoneer

86748G80

8. Mount the pump on the bracket and tighten the bolts 20 ft. lbs. (27 Nm).
9. Install the serpentine belt.
10. Connect the fluid lines to the pump and remove the clamps.
11. Fill the power steering reservoir to the proper level with fluid.
12. Connect the negative battery cable.
13. Bleed the system.

SYSTEM BLEEDING

1. Fill the steering pump with fluid. Operate the engine until it reaches normal operating temperature, then stop the engine.
2. Turn the wheels to the full left and full right position to circulate the fluid. Add fluid to reservoir to maintain full level. Start the engine. Check the fluid level and add if necessary.
3. Purge the system of air by turning the wheels from side-to-side without going to the full left or right position.
4. Return the wheels to straight ahead position and operate the engine for 2–3 minutes, then stop the engine. Add fluid if necessary. Road test the vehicle.

Troubleshooting Basic Steering and Suspension Problems

Problem	Cause	Solution
Hard steering (steering wheel is hard to turn)	• Low or uneven tire pressure • Loose power steering pump drive belt • Low or incorrect power steering fluid • Incorrect front end alignment • Defective power steering pump • Bent or poorly lubricated front end parts	• Inflate tires to correct pressure • Adjust belt • Add fluid as necessary • Have front end alignment checked/adjusted • Check pump • Lubricate and/or replace defective parts
Loose steering (too much play in the steering wheel)	• Loose wheel bearings • Loose or worn steering linkage • Faulty shocks • Worn ball joints	• Adjust wheel bearings • Replace worn parts • Replace shocks • Replace ball joints
Car veers or wanders (car pulls to one side with hands off the steering wheel)	• Incorrect tire pressure • Improper front end alignment • Loose wheel bearings • Loose or bent front end components • Faulty shocks	• Inflate tires to correct pressure • Have front end alignment checked/adjusted • Adjust wheel bearings • Replace worn components • Replace shocks
Wheel oscillation or vibration transmitted through steering wheel	• Improper tire pressures • Tires out of balance • Loose wheel bearings • Improper front end alignment • Worn or bent front end components	• Inflate tires to correct pressure • Have tires balanced • Adjust wheel bearings • Have front end alignment checked/adjusted • Replace worn parts
Uneven tire wear	• Incorrect tire pressure • Front end out of alignment • Tires out of balance	• Inflate tires to correct pressure • Have front end alignment checked/adjusted • Have tires balanced

TCCA8C01

9

BRAKES

BRAKE OPERATING SYSTEMS

Basic Operating Principles

Hydraulic systems are used to actuate the brakes of all modern automobiles. The system transports the power required to force the frictional surfaces of the braking system together from the pedal to the individual brake units at each wheel. A hydraulic system is used for two reasons.

First, fluid under pressure can be carried to all parts of an automobile by small pipes and flexible hoses without taking up a significant amount of room or posing routing problems.

Second, a great mechanical advantage can be given to the brake pedal end of the system, and the foot pressure required to actuate the brakes can be reduced by making the surface area of the master cylinder pistons smaller than that of any of the pistons in the wheel cylinders or calipers.

The master cylinder consists of a fluid reservoir along with a double cylinder and piston assembly. Double type master cylinders are designed to separate the front and rear braking systems hydraulically in case of a leak. The master cylinder coverts mechanical motion from the pedal into hydraulic pressure within the lines. This pressure is translated back into mechanical motion at the wheels by either the wheel cylinder (drum brakes) or the caliper (disc brakes).

Steel lines carry the brake fluid to a point on the vehicle's frame near each of the vehicle's wheels. The fluid is then carried to the calipers and wheel cylinders by flexible tubes in order to allow for suspension and steering movements.

In drum brake systems, each wheel cylinder contains two pistons, one at either end, which push outward in opposite directions and force the brake shoe into contact with the drum.

In disc brake systems, the cylinders are part of the calipers. At least one cylinder in each caliper is used to force the brake pads against the disc.

All pistons employ some type of seal, usually made of rubber, to minimize fluid leakage. A rubber dust boot seals the outer end of the cylinder against dust and dirt. The boot fits around the outer end of the piston on disc brake calipers, and around the brake actuating rod on wheel cylinders.

The hydraulic system operates as follows: When at rest, the entire system, from the piston(s) in the master cylinder to those in the wheel cylinders or calipers, is full of brake fluid. Upon application of the brake pedal, fluid trapped in front of the master cylinder piston(s) is forced through the lines to the wheel cylinders. Here, it forces the pistons outward, in the case of drum brakes, and inward toward the disc, in the case of disc brakes. The motion of the pistons is opposed by return springs mounted outside the cylinders in drum brakes, and by spring seals, in disc brakes.

Upon release of the brake pedal, a spring located inside the master cylinder immediately returns the master cylinder pistons to the normal position. The pistons contain check valves and the master cylinder has compensating ports drilled in it. These are uncovered as the pistons reach their normal position. The piston check valves allow fluid to flow toward the wheel cylinders or calipers as the pistons withdraw. Then, as the return springs force the brake pads or shoes into the released position, the excess fluid reservoir through the compensating ports. It is during the time the pedal is in the released position that any fluid that has leaked out of the system will be replaced through the compensating ports.

Dual circuit master cylinders employ two pistons, located one behind the other, in the same cylinder. The primary piston is actuated directly by mechanical linkage from the brake pedal through the power booster. The secondary piston is actuated by fluid trapped between the two pistons. If a leak develops in front of the secondary piston, it moves forward until it bottoms against the front of the master cylinder, and the fluid trapped between the pistons will operate the rear brakes. If the rear brakes develop a leak, the primary piston will move forward until direct contact with the secondary piston takes place, and it will force the secondary piston to actuate the front brakes. In either case, the brake pedal moves farther when the brakes are applied, and less braking power is available.

All dual circuit systems use a switch to warn the driver when only half of the brake system is operational. This switch is usually located in a valve body which is mounted on the firewall or the frame below the master cylinder. A hydraulic piston receives pressure from both circuits, each circuit's pressure being applied to one end of the piston. When the pressures are in balance, the piston remains stationary. When one circuit has a leak, however, the greater pressure in that circuit during application of the brakes will push the piston to one side, closing the switch and activating the brake warning light.

In disc brake systems, this valve body also contains a metering valve and, in some cases, a proportioning valve. The metering valve keeps pressure from traveling to the disc brakes on the front wheels until the brake shoes on the rear wheels have contacted the drums, ensuring that the front brakes will never be used alone. The proportioning valve controls the pressure to the rear brakes to lessen the chance of rear wheel lock-up during very hard braking.

Warning lights may be tested by depressing the brake pedal and holding it while opening one of the wheel cylinder bleeder screws. If this does not cause the light to go on, substitute a new lamp, make continuity checks, and, finally, replace the switch as necessary.

The hydraulic system may be checked for leaks by applying pressure to the pedal gradually and steadily. If the pedal sinks very slowly to the floor, the system has a leak. This is not to be confused with a springy or spongy feel due to the compression of air within the lines. If the system leaks, there will be a gradual change in the position of the pedal with a constant pressure.

Check for leaks along all lines and at wheel cylinders. If no external leaks are apparent, the problem is inside the master cylinder.

DISC BRAKES

Instead of the traditional expanding brakes that press outward against a circular drum, disc brake systems utilize a disc (rotor) with brake pads positioned on either side of it. An easily-seen analogy is the hand brake arrangement on a bicycle. The pads squeeze onto the rim of the bike wheel, slowing its motion. Automobile disc brakes use the identical principle but apply the braking effort to a separate disc instead of the wheel.

The disc (rotor) is a casting, usually equipped with cooling fins between the two braking surfaces. This enables air to circulate between the braking surfaces making them less sensitive to heat buildup and more resistant to fade. Dirt and water do not drastically affect braking action since contaminants are thrown off by the centrifugal action of the rotor or scraped off the by the pads. Also, the equal clamping action of the two brake pads tends to ensure uniform, straight line stops. Disc brakes are inherently self-adjusting. There are three general types of disc brake:
1. A fixed caliper.
2. A floating caliper.
3. A sliding caliper.

The fixed caliper design uses two pistons mounted on either side of the rotor (in each side of the caliper). The caliper is mounted rigidly and does not move.

The sliding and floating designs are quite similar. In fact, these two types are often lumped together. In both designs, the pad on the inside of the rotor is moved into contact with the rotor by hydraulic force. The caliper, which is not held in a fixed position, moves slightly, bringing the outside pad into contact with the rotor. There are various methods of attaching floating calipers. Some pivot at the bottom or top, and some slide on mounting bolts. In any event, the end result is the same.

DRUM BRAKES

Drum brakes employ two brake shoes mounted on a stationary backing plate. These shoes are positioned inside a circular drum which rotates with the wheel assembly. The shoes are held in place by springs. This allows them to slide toward the drums (when they are applied) while keeping the linings and drums in alignment. The shoes are actuated by a wheel cylinder which is mounted at the top of the backing plate. When the brakes are applied, hydraulic pressure forces the wheel cylinder's actuating links outward. Since these links bear directly against the top of the brake shoes, the tops of the shoes are then forced against the inner side of the drum. This action forces the bottoms of the two shoes to contact the brake drum by rotating the entire assembly slightly (known as servo action). When pressure within the wheel cylinder is relaxed, return springs pull the shoes back away from the drum.

Most modern drum brakes are designed to self-adjust themselves during application when the vehicle is moving in reverse. This motion causes both shoes to rotate very slightly with the drum, rocking an adjusting lever, thereby causing rotation of the adjusting screw. Some drum brake systems are designed to self-adjust during application whenever the brakes are applied. This on-board adjustment system reduces the need for maintenance adjustments and keeps both the brake function and pedal feel satisfactory.

Brake Light Switch

REMOVAL & INSTALLATION

▶ **See Figure 1**

The brake light switch is mounted in the pedal support bracket and is operated by the pedal.

1. Remove the steering column cover and lower the trim panel, if necessary.
2. Disengage the switch electrical connection.
3. Screw the switch out of the retainer, or rock the switch up and down, then pull it rearward out of the retainer.
4. Installation is the reverse of removal.

Fig. 1 Brake light switch is located on top of brake pedal lever under the dashboard

Master Cylinder

REMOVAL & INSTALLATION

Non-ABS Equipped Models

▶ **See Figures 2, 3 and 4**

1. Disconnect and plug the brake lines.
2. Remove the combination valve (if necessary).
3. Remove all attaching bolts and nuts, and lift the assembly from the vehicle.

To install:

4. Remove the protective cover from the end of the primary piston (if necessary).
5. Clean the cylinder mounting surface on the booster.
6. Install the master cylinder onto the brake booster studs.
7. Install the nuts and tighten to 18 ft. lbs. (25 Nm).
8. Connect the brake lines, fill the reservoir and bleed the brake system.

ABS Equipped Models

▶ **See Figures 5 thru 12**

➡ **This procedure applies to all models equipped with ABS except for 1989–91 Jeep models which are equipped with a Bendix anti-lock brake system. Refer to that removal procedure later in this section.**

1. Disengage the pedal travel sensor wires and remove the air cleaner.
2. Before disconnecting any brake lines, suck out as much of the brake fluid as possible from the reservoir.
3. Remove the clamps that secure the reservoir hoses to the Hydraulic Control Unit (HCU) pipes.
4. Drain the fluid into a container and discard the fluid.
5. Pump the brake pedal to exhaust all vacuum from the booster.

Fig. 2 Loosening the brake lines using a backup wrench

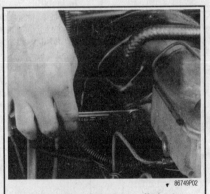

Fig. 3 Removing the master cylinder-to-booster retaining nuts

Fig. 4 Removing the master cylinder from the vehicle

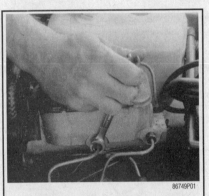

Fig. 5 Disengage the wiring harness connector from the pedal travel sensor, located on the power booster

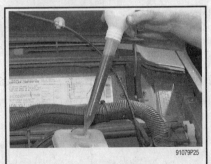

Fig. 6 Before disconnecting any brake lines to the master cylinder, suck out as much of the brake fluid as possible from the reservoir

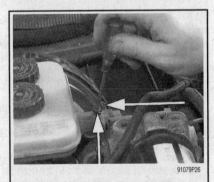

Fig. 7 Loosen the hose clamps and disconnect the brake fluid reservoir-to-HCU hoses

Fig. 8 Using a flare nut wrench, loosen the brake line fittings at the master cylinder . . .

Fig. 9 . . . then remove the fitting and disconnect the brake line

Fig. 10 Remove the mounting bolt securing the combination valve bracket to the master cylinder

Fig. 11 Using a box wrench, remove the master cylinder mounting nuts

Fig. 12 Carefully pull the brake master cylinder assembly off of the power booster and out of the vehicle

6. Disengage the brake lines and the combination valve bracket bolt at the master cylinder.

7. Unfasten the master cylinder attaching bolts and remove the master cylinder from the vehicle.

To install:

8. If installing a new master cylinder, bleed the cylinder on a bench before installation.

9. Install the master cylinder in position and engage the reservoir hoses to the HCU pipes.

10. Tighten the master cylinder retaining bolts to 25 ft. lbs. (34 Nm) and connect the brake lines.

11. Install the combination valve and bracket bolt (if removed).

12. Connect the sensor wires and fill the reservoir.

13. Bleed the brakes. Refer to the procedure outlined later in this section.

14. Install the air cleaner and test drive the vehicle to verify proper brake operation.

Power Brake Boosters

REMOVAL & INSTALLATION

Non-ABS Equipped Models

▶ See Figure 13

1. Loosen, but do not remove the master cylinder retaining nuts.

2. Remove the instrument panel lower trim cover.

3. Remove the retaining clip attaching the booster pushrod to the brake pedal.

4. Loosen the vacuum hose clip and disconnect the hose from the check valve.

5. Remove the master cylinder retaining nuts and carefully move the master cylinder aside with the brake lines still attached.

6. Unfasten the booster retaining nuts/bolts and remove the booster.

To install:

7. Install the check valve and grommet in the booster.

8. Install the spacer on the booster (if equipped).

9. Position the booster on the firewall and fasten the booster mounting bolts/nuts.

10. Working inside the vehicle, install the nuts on the booster mounting studs. Tighten the bolts to 30 ft. lbs. (41 Nm).

11. Tighten the pedal pushrod bolt inner nut to 25 ft. lbs. (34 Nm) and then tighten the outer locknut to 75 inch lbs. (8 Nm).

12. Install the master cylinder and check for proper operation.

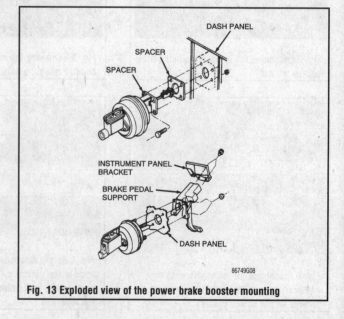

Fig. 13 Exploded view of the power brake booster mounting

ABS Equipped Models

BENDIX ANTI-LOCK BRAKE SYSTEM

The power booster unit on the Bendix anti-lock brake system is an integral component of the master cylinder/pressure modulator/accumulator assembly. Refer to that removal procedure under the Bendix ABS portion later in this section.

TEVES MK-IV ANTI-LOCK BRAKE SYSTEM

➡A Diagnostic Readout Box (DRB II), or the equivalent type of scan tool, is essential to perform the bleeding of the ABS system.

1. Pump the brake pedal until all vacuum is expelled from the booster.
2. Disengage the pedal travel sensor and remove the air cleaner.
3. Unfasten the clamps securing the reservoir hoses to the HCU pipes. Remove the hoses from the pipes.
4. Disengage the brake lines at the master cylinder.
5. Remove the combination valve bracket bolt (if necessary).
6. Remove the nuts attaching the master cylinder to the booster mounting. Remove the master cylinder from the vehicle.
7. Tag and disconnect vacuum hose at the booster check valve.
8. Disconnect the booster pushrod from the brake pedal.
9. Remove the nuts attaching the booster to the passenger compartment side of the dash panel.
10. Slide the booster forward and remove it from the vehicle.

To install:

11. Install the booster on the dash panel. Align the booster mounting studs with the holes in the panel and seat the booster.
12. In the passenger compartment, install the booster attaching nuts on the mounting studs. Tighten the attaching nuts to 30 ft. lbs. (41 Nm).
13. Install the seal on the master cylinder.
14. Install the pedal travel sensor and the booster pushrod.
15. Attach the vacuum hose to the booster check valve and install the master cylinder on the booster. Tighten the bolts to 18–22 ft. lbs. (25–30 Nm).
16. Engage the brake lines to the master cylinder and install the combination valve bracket bolt.
17. Engage the reservoir hoses to the HCU pipes.
18. Engage the sensor wires, bleed the brake system, install the air cleaner assembly and test drive the vehicle to verify proper brake operation.

TEVES MK-IVG ANTI-LOCK BRAKE SYSTEM

➡A Diagnostic Readout Box (DRB II), or the equivalent type of scan tool, is essential to perform the bleeding of the ABS system.

1. Disconnect the negative battery cable and remove the air cleaner assembly.
2. Remove the windshield washer fluid reservoir retainers and move the reservoir to one side.
3. Remove the master cylinder, combination valve and HCU. Refer to the proper procedures in this section and disengage the vacuum hose at the booster check valve.
4. In the passenger compartment, remove the booster pushrod to pedal pin retaining clip. Then slide the pushrod off the pin.
5. Remove the locknuts that retain the booster to the dash panel.
6. In the engine compartment, remove the booster by pulling it forward and tilted slightly upward.

To install:

7. Check the condition of the grommet that secures the check valve in the booster. If the grommet is defective it must be replaced.
8. Install the booster on the firewall.
9. In the passenger compartment, lubricate the pedal pin and bushing, then fasten the booster attaching nuts to 30 ft. lbs. (41 Nm).
10. Slide the booster pushrod onto the pedal pin and secure the rod to pin with the retaining clip.
11. In the engine compartment, engage the vacuum hose to the booster check valve.
12. Install the master cylinder, combination valve and HCU. Refer to the proper procedures in this section.
13. Bleed the brake system. Refer to the proper procedure in this section.

14. Install the air cleaner assembly and hoses. Test drive the vehicle and verify proper brake operation.

Pressure Differential Valve

▶ **See Figure 14**

Jeep vehicles use a pressure differential valve, mounted immediately below the master cylinder. The valve is not a serviceable part, and must be replaced if defective.

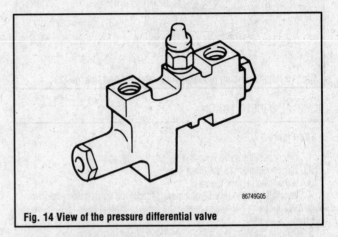

Fig. 14 View of the pressure differential valve

REMOVAL & INSTALLATION

1. Disconnect the brake lines at the valve and plug them.
2. Unbolt and remove the valve.
3. Installation is the reverse of removal. Bleed the system.

Height Sensing Proportioning Valve

▶ **See Figures 15 and 16**

In addition to the pressure differential valve, a mechanically activated height sensing proportioning valve is used on Comanche models. This valve, located above the rear axle, must be adjusted any time rear springs are replaced, or the valve is removed during service operations.

➡Any time the valve is adjusted, the lever bushing must be replaced. The adjustment must be made with the vehicle level and at curb weight. Special tools are needed for this job.

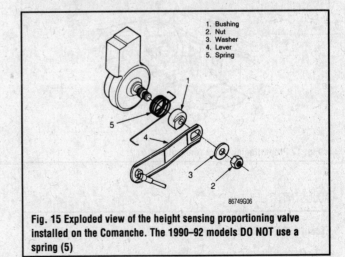

Fig. 15 Exploded view of the height sensing proportioning valve installed on the Comanche. The 1990–92 models DO NOT use a spring (5)

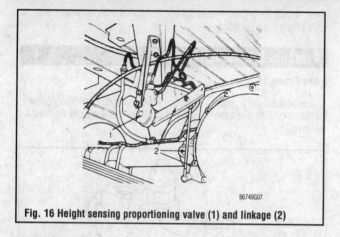

Fig. 16 Height sensing proportioning valve (1) and linkage (2)

REMOVAL & INSTALLATION

▶ **See Figure 17**

1. Disconnect the valve lever and spring, if equipped.
2. Disconnect and cap the brake lines.
3. Unbolt and remove the valve.
4. Installation is the reverse of removal. Torque the Valve bracket-to-frame bolts to 13 ft. lbs. (17 Nm) and tighten the valve-to-bracket bolts to 10 ft. lbs. (13 Nm).
5. Perform the valve adjusting procedure outlined in this section.

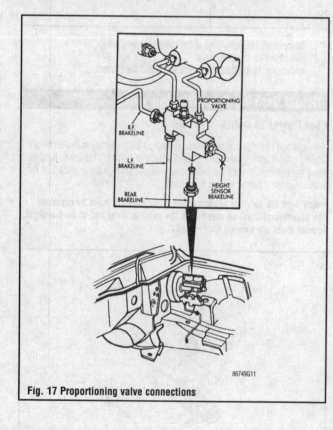

Fig. 17 Proportioning valve connections

ADJUSTMENT

Except 1990–92 Comanche Models

1. Remove the valve shaft nut and washer.
2. Disconnect the valve lever and remove the spring.

3. Remove and discard the bushing.
4. Rotate the valve shaft and install adjusting gauge tool J-35853-2 or its equivalent.

➡ **The gauge must be properly seated on the D shape of the shaft and the valve lower mounting bolt. All 1inkage components, except the spring, must be connected before installing the new bushing.**

5. Place the bushing in the lever, and, using bushing aligning tool J-35853-1 or its equivalent, press the bushing and lever onto the shaft.
6. Remove the lever and adjusting tool J-35853-2 or its equivalent and install the spring.
7. Install the lever, washer and nut. Tighten the nut to 100 inch. lbs. (11 Nm).
8. Connect the spring.

1990–92 Comanche Models

➡ **Valve adjustment requires Calibration Kit 6229 or its equivalent.**

1. Raise the vehicle and support it safely with jackstands.
2. Unload the vehicle and place on a level surface for accurate valve adjustment.
3. Remove the nut attaching lever to the valve shaft.
4. Pull the lever and retainer off the valve shaft and remove old the bushing. Discard the bushing.
5. Clean the threads and splines on the valve shaft. If valve the link was disconnected from axle the bracket or lever, reconnect the link before continuing.
6. Loosen the valve mounting bolts two full turns. Then turn valve shaft until the shaft flat is approximately between the 5 and 6 o'clock position.
7. Install the valve adjusting gauge and it position on the mounting bolts and shaft. There should be no clearance between the gauge, shaft and bolts. The gauge should be seated on the shaft flat.
8. Install the retainer on the lever, and the bushing on the retainer. Start the bushing and the lever on the valve shaft and press into place with the tools provided in kit 6229 or its equivalent.
9. Remove the adjustment gauge and the bushing installer tool. Tighten the valve mounting bolts to 10 ft. lbs. (13 Nm) and tighten the lever nut to 100 inch lbs. (11 Nm).

Combination Valve

REMOVAL & INSTALLATION

▶ **See Figures 18, 19 and 20**

➡ **A Diagnostic Readout Box (DRB II), or the equivalent type of scan tool, is essential to perform the bleeding of the ABS system.**

The combination valve is not repairable and must be replaced if defective.
1. Disengage the brake lines that connect the master cylinder to the combination valve.
2. On ABS equipped vehicles, disengage the brake lines that connect the combination valve to the Hydraulic Control Unit (HCU).
3. Disengage the electrical connection from the combination valve.
4. On ABS equipped vehicles, slide the HCU solenoid harness connectors off the combination valve bracket and move the harness out of the way.
5. Unfasten the combination valve bracket retaining nuts and remove combination valve from the vehicle.

To install:
6. Install the valve bracket on the mounting studs and tighten the nuts to 10–18 ft. lbs. (13–25 Nm).
7. Align and start the brake lines fittings in the combination valve by hand to prevent cross threading.
8. Tighten the fittings just enough to prevent leakage.
9. Install and tighten the brake lines to the master cylinder and engage all electrical connections.
10. Bleed the brake system. Refer to the proper procedure in this section.
11. Test drive the vehicle and verify proper brake operation.

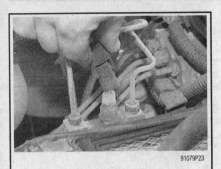

Fig. 18 Unplugging the pressure differential switch wiring harness coinnector from the top of the combination valve—1992 model shown

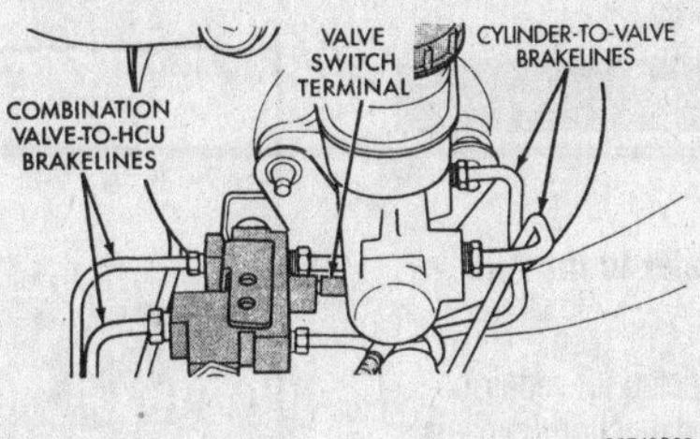

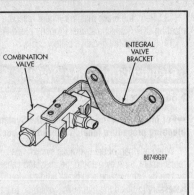

Fig. 19 Combination valve hydraulic connections—1995 model shown

Fig. 20 Combination valve and bracket—1995 model shown

Brake Hoses and Lines

Metal lines and rubber brake hoses should be checked frequently for leaks and external damage. Metal lines are particularly prone to crushing and kinking under the vehicle. Any such deformation can restrict the proper flow of fluid and therefore impair braking at the wheels. Rubber hoses should be checked for cracking or scraping; such damage can create a weak spot in the hose and it could fail under pressure.

Any time the lines are removed or disconnected, extreme cleanliness must be observed. Clean all joints and connections before disassembly (use a stiff bristle brush and clean brake fluid); be sure to plug the lines and ports as soon as they are opened. New lines and hoses should be flushed clean with brake fluid before installation to remove any contamination.

REMOVAL & INSTALLATION

▶ See Figures 21, 22, 23 and 24

1. Disconnect the negative battery cable.
2. Raise and safely support the vehicle on jackstands.
3. Remove any wheel and tire assemblies necessary for access to the particular line you are removing.
4. Thoroughly clean the surrounding area at the joints to be disconnected.
5. Place a suitable catch pan under the joint to be disconnected.
6. Using two wrenches (one to hold the joint and one to turn the fitting), disconnect the hose or line to be replaced.
7. Disconnect the other end of the line or hose, moving the drain pan if necessary. Always use a back-up wrench to avoid damaging the fitting.
8. Disconnect any retaining clips or brackets holding the line and remove the line from the vehicle.

➡If the brake system is to remain open for more time than it takes to swap lines, tape or plug each remaining clip and port to keep contaminants out and fluid in.

To install:

9. Install the new line or hose, starting with the end farthest from the master cylinder. Connect the other end, then confirm that both fittings are correctly threaded and turn smoothly using finger pressure. Make sure the new line will not rub against any other part. Brake lines must be at least 1/2 in. (13mm) from the steering column and other moving parts. Any protective shielding or insulators must be reinstalled in the original location.

✳✳ WARNING

Make sure the hose is NOT kinked or touching any part of the frame or suspension after installation. These conditions may cause the hose to fail prematurely.

10. Using two wrenches as before, tighten each fitting.
11. Install any retaining clips or brackets on the lines.
12. If removed, install the wheel and tire assemblies, then carefully lower the vehicle to the ground.

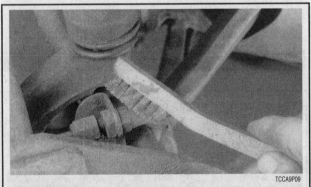

Fig. 21 Use a brush to clean the fittings of any debris

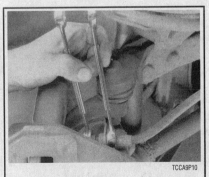

Fig. 22 Use two wrenches to loosen the fitting. If available, use flare nut type wrenches

Fig. 23 Any gaskets/crush washers should be replaced with new ones during installation

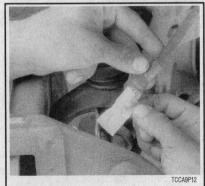

Fig. 24 Tape or plug the line to prevent contamination

13. Refill the brake master cylinder reservoir with clean, fresh brake fluid, meeting DOT 3 specifications. Properly bleed the brake system.

14. Connect the negative battery cable.

Bleeding The Brake System

▶ **See Figures 25 and 26**

➡**For bleeding of the Anti-lock Brake System (ABS), refer to the ABS bleeding procedure located later in this section.**

When any part of the hydraulic system has been disconnected for repair or replacement, air may get into the lines and cause spongy pedal action (because air can be compressed and brake fluid cannot). To correct this condition, it is necessary to bleed the hydraulic system so to be sure all air is purged.

When bleeding the brake system, bleed one brake cylinder at a time, beginning at the cylinder with the longest hydraulic line (farthest from the master cylinder) first. ALWAYS Keep the master cylinder reservoir filled with brake fluid during the bleeding operation. Never use brake fluid that has been drained from the hydraulic system, no matter how clean it is.

The primary and secondary hydraulic brake systems are separate and are bled independently. During the bleeding operation, do not allow the reservoir to run dry. Keep the master cylinder reservoir filled with brake fluid.

1. Clean all dirt from around the master cylinder fill cap, remove the cap and fill the master cylinder with brake fluid until the level is within 1/4 in. (6mm) of the top edge of the reservoir.

2. Clean the bleeder screws at all 4 wheels. The bleeder screws are located on the back of the brake backing plate (drum brakes) and on the top of the brake calipers (disc brakes).

3. Attach a length of rubber hose over the bleeder screw and place the other end of the hose in a glass jar, submerged in brake fluid.

4. Open the bleeder screw 1/2 - 3/4 turn. Have an assistant slowly depress the brake pedal.

5. Close the bleeder screw and tell your assistant to allow the brake pedal to return slowly. Continue this process to purge all air from the system.

6. When bubbles cease to appear at the end of the bleeder hose, close the bleeder screw and remove the hose. Tighten the bleeder screw.

7. Check the master cylinder fluid level and add fluid accordingly. Do this after bleeding each wheel.

8. Repeat the bleeding operation at the remaining 3 wheels, ending with the one closet to the master cylinder.

9. Fill the master cylinder reservoir to the proper level.

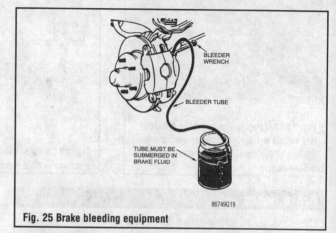

Fig. 25 Brake bleeding equipment

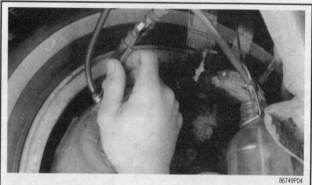

Fig. 26 Open the bleeder screw until brake fluid starts to flow through the tube

DISC BRAKES

NON-ABS DISC BRAKE COMPONENTS (ABS SIMILAR)

1. Brake line hose
2. Inboard brake pad
3. Caliper
4. Outboard brake pad
5. Brake rotor

Brake Pads

REMOVAL & INSTALLATION - MODELS WITH CALIPER BRACKET-MOUNTED PADS

▶ **See Figures 27 thru 41**

➡**Even though the accompanying photos show the replacement of the front brake pads, this procedure also applies to the replacement of rear disc brake pads.**

Fig. 27 Raise the vehicle using a hydraulic jack

❊❊ CAUTION

Brake pads may contain asbestos, which has been determined to be a cancer causing agent. Never clean the brake surfaces with compressed air! Avoid inhaling any dust from any brake surface! When cleaning brake surfaces, use a commercially available brake cleaning fluid.

1. Raise and support the vehicle safely using jackstands. Remove the wheel(s) on the side to be worked on.

➡**For vehicles equipped with Anti-Lock Brakes (ABS), refer to the proper procedures concerning brake system servicing.**

2. Drain a small amount of the brake fluid from the front reservoir using a suction gun or a turkey baster.

3. Place a C-clamp on the caliper so that the solid end contacts the back of the caliper and the screw end contacts the metal part of the outboard brake pad.

4. Tighten the clamp until the caliper moves far enough to force the piston to the bottom of the piston bore. This will back the brake pads off of the rotor surface to facilitate the removal and installation of the caliper assembly.

5. Remove the C-clamp.

➡**Do not push down on the brake pedal or the piston and brake pads will return to their original positions up against the rotor.**

6. Remove the caliper mounting bolts. Tilt the top of the caliper outward and lift it off the rotor.

7. Hold the anti-rattle clip against the caliper anchor plate and remove the outboard brake pad.

8. Remove the inboard pad and the anti-rattle clip. Be sure that the support spring is removed with the inboard pad.

9. Use a piece of wire to support the caliper so that no tension is placed on the brake hose. Do not allow the caliper to hang by the brake hose.

To install:

10. Clean all the mounting holes and bushing grooves in the caliper ears. Clean the mounting bolts. Replace the bolts if they are corroded or if the threads

are damaged. If you're working on a 1995 or later Grand Cherokee, measure the length of the caliper mounting bolts (see Fig. 42g), replacing them if they aren't within specifications. Wipe the inside of the caliper clean, including the exterior of the dust boot. Inspect the dust boot for cuts or cracks and for proper seating in the piston bore. If evidence of fluid leakage is noted, the caliper should be rebuilt.

➡**Do not use abrasives on the bolts in order not to destroy their protective plating. You should not use compressed air to clean the inside of the caliper, as it may unseat the dust boot seal.**

11. If not already in place, attach the support spring to the inboard brake pad.

12. Install the anti-rattle clip on the trailing end of the inboard pad's anchor plate. The split end of the clip must face away from the rotor.

13. Install the inboard pad in the caliper. The pad must lay flat against the piston.

14. Install the outboard pad in the caliper while holding the anti-rattle clip.

15. With the pads installed, position the caliper over the rotor.

➡**Before securing the caliper, ensure the brake hose is not twisted, kinked or touching any chassis parts.**

16. Lubricate the caliper pins and bushings with silicone grease. Line up the mounting holes in the caliper and the support bracket and insert the mounting bolts. Make sure that the bolts pass under the retaining ears on the inboard shoes. Push the bolts through until they engage the holes of the outboard pad and caliper ears. Thread the bolts into the support bracket and tighten them to:

Grand Cherokee	132 in-lbs (15 Nm)
Grand Wagoneer	132 in-lbs (15 Nm)
Cherokee, Wagoneer, Comanche	
1989 and earlier models	25 to 35 ft-lbs (34 to 47 Nm)
1990 through 1996 models	
2WD	25 to 35 ft-lbs (34 to 47 Nm)
4WD	15 ft-lbs (20 Nm)
1997 and later models	132 in-lbs (15 Nm)

Fig. 28 Support the vehicle using safety stands

Fig. 29 Removing a small amount of brake fluid from the master cylinder using a turkey baster

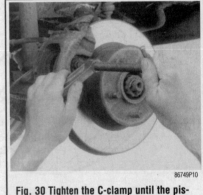

Fig. 30 Tighten the C-clamp until the piston reaches the bottom of its bore

Fig. 31 Remove the caliper mounting bolts

Fig. 32 Slide the caliper off the brake rotor

Fig. 33 Support the caliper so that no tension is placed on the brake hose

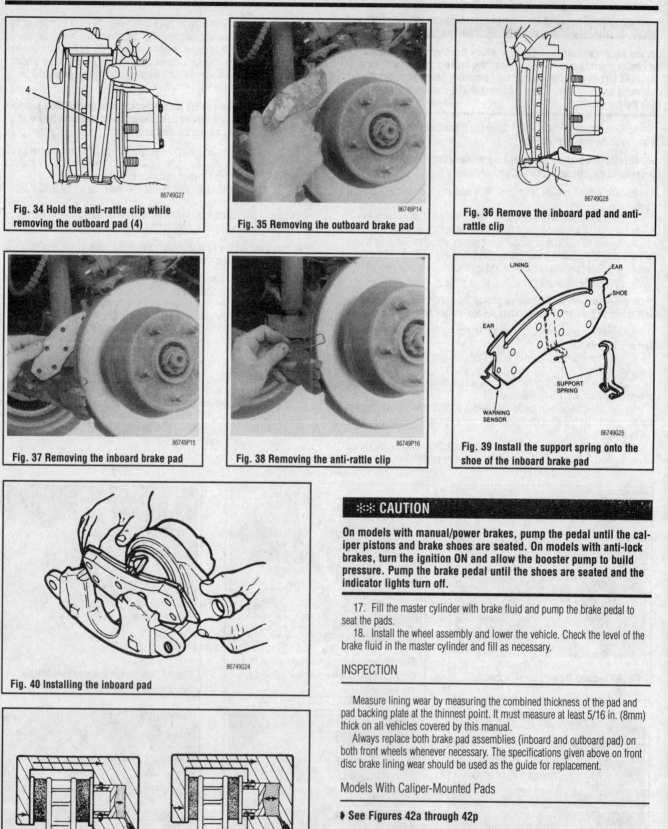

Fig. 34 Hold the anti-rattle clip while removing the outboard pad (4)

Fig. 35 Removing the outboard brake pad

Fig. 36 Remove the inboard pad and anti-rattle clip

Fig. 37 Removing the inboard brake pad

Fig. 38 Removing the anti-rattle clip

Fig. 39 Install the support spring onto the shoe of the inboard brake pad

Fig. 40 Installing the inboard pad

Fig. 41 Piston extension on new and worn brake pads

✳✳ CAUTION

On models with manual/power brakes, pump the pedal until the caliper pistons and brake shoes are seated. On models with anti-lock brakes, turn the ignition ON and allow the booster pump to build pressure. Pump the brake pedal until the shoes are seated and the indicator lights turn off.

17. Fill the master cylinder with brake fluid and pump the brake pedal to seat the pads.

18. Install the wheel assembly and lower the vehicle. Check the level of the brake fluid in the master cylinder and fill as necessary.

INSPECTION

Measure lining wear by measuring the combined thickness of the pad and pad backing plate at the thinnest point. It must measure at least 5/16 in. (8mm) thick on all vehicles covered by this manual.

Always replace both brake pad assemblies (inboard and outboard pad) on both front wheels whenever necessary. The specifications given above on front disc brake lining wear should be used as the guide for replacement.

Models With Caliper-Mounted Pads

♦ See Figures 42a through 42p

1 Remove the cover from the brake fluid reservoir.

2 Loosen the wheel lug nuts, raise the front of the vehicle and support it securely on jackstands.

3 Remove the front wheels. Work on one brake assembly at a time, using the assembled brake for reference if necessary.

4 Push the piston back into the bore to provide room for the new brake

42a Before removing the caliper, wash off all traces of brake dust with brake system cleaner

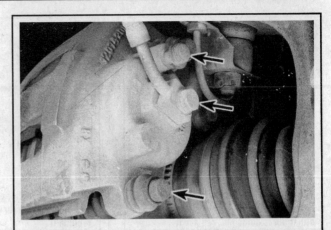

42b To remove the caliper, remove these two mounting bolts (upper and lower arrows); don't remove the brake hose-to-caliper banjo bolt (center arrow) unless you intend to replace the caliper or hose

42c Remove the caliper; this is a good time to check for fluid leakage around the caliper piston boot, which would indicate the need for replacement

42d Whenever you have to let go of the caliper, hang it from the coil spring with a piece of wire - DON'T let it hang by the brake hose!

42e To remove the outer brake pad from the caliper, push up on the ears at either end of the pad, disengage the pad retaining clips from the caliper and remove the pad

pads. A C-clamp can be used to accomplish this (see illustration). As the piston is depressed to the bottom of the caliper bore, the fluid in the master cylinder will rise. Make sure it doesn't overflow. If necessary, siphon off some of the fluid.

5   Inspect the brake disc carefully. If machining is necessary, remove the disc, at which time the pads can be removed from the calipers as well.

6   Follow the accompanying illustrations, beginning with Figure 42a, for the actual pad replacement procedure. Be sure to stay in order and read the caption under each illustration.

7   When reinstalling the caliper, be sure to tighten the mounting pins to 21 to 30 ft-lbs (31 to 40.5 Nm). After the job has been completed, firmly depress the brake pedal a few times to bring the pads into contact with the disc.

8   Check for fluid leakage and make sure the brakes operate normally before driving in traffic.

42f To remove the inner brake pad, pull on the pad to disengage the retaining clips from the bore of the piston

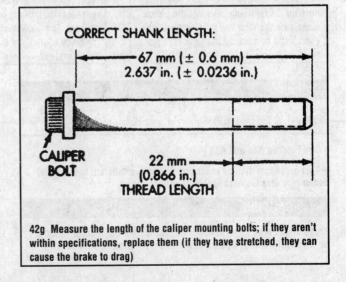

CORRECT SHANK LENGTH:

67 mm (± 0.6 mm)
2.637 in. (± 0.0236 in.)

CALIPER BOLT

22 mm (0.866 in.) THREAD LENGTH

42g Measure the length of the caliper mounting bolts; if they aren't within specifications, replace them (if they have stretched, they can cause the brake to drag)

42h Pull out both pin bushings and inspect them for corrosion and wear; if either pin is damaged, replace it

42i If either rubber dust boot for the pins and bushings is cracked, torn or dried out, replace it

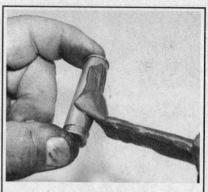

42j Coat the bushings with high temperature grease

42k Install the bushings

42l Before installing the new brake pads, depress the piston all the way into the caliper to facilitate installation of the new pads over the disc

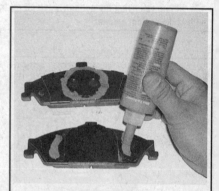

42m Apply anti-squeal compound to the backs of the new pads (follow the instructions on the container)

42n Install the new inner brake pad by pushing the retaining clips into the piston; make sure the clips are fully engaged (the pad should be seated flat against the piston)

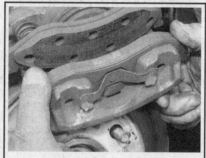

42o Install the new outer brake pad by pushing down firmly on the pad with your thumbs as shown; make sure the pad is properly seated and the retaining clips fully engaged

42p Install the caliper and pads over the disc, install the caliper bolts and tighten them to the torque listed in this Chapter's Specifications

Calipers

REMOVAL & INSTALLATION

▶ See Figures 43a and 43b

➡This procedure applies to the removal and installation of the front and/or rear disc brake caliper assemblies.

✳✳ CAUTION

Brake shoes may contain asbestos, which has been determined to be a cancer causing agent. Never clean the brake surfaces with compressed air! Avoid inhaling any dust from any brake surface! When cleaning brake surfaces, use a commercially available brake cleaning fluid.

1. Raise and support the vehicle safely using jackstands. Remove the wheel(s) on the side to be worked on.

➡For vehicles equipped with Anti-Lock Brakes (ABS), refer to the proper procedures concerning brake system servicing.

2. Drain a small amount of the brake fluid from the front reservoir using a suction gun or a turkey baster.
3. Place a C-clamp on the caliper so that the solid end contacts the back of the caliper and the screw end contacts the metal part of the outboard brake pad.

4. Tighten the clamp until the caliper moves far enough to force the piston to the bottom of the piston bore. This will back the brake pads off of the rotor surface to facilitate the removal and installation of the caliper assembly.

5. Remove the C-clamp.

➥Do not push down on the brake pedal or the piston and brake pads will return to their original positions up against the rotor.

6. Remove the caliper mounting bolts. Tilt the top of the caliper outward and lift off the rotor.

7. Remove the brake pads from the caliper.

➥If the caliper is not being removed for overhaul, it is not necessary to remove the caliper assembly entirely from the vehicle. DO NOT remove the brake line. Suspend the caliper with a piece of wire. DO NOT allow the brake hose to support the weight of the caliper.

8. Remove the caliper fitting bolt and disconnect the brake line at the caliper. Discard the fitting bolt washers, they are not reusable. Cap or tape the open ends of the hose to keep dirt out.

To install:

9. Clean all the mounting holes and bushing grooves in the caliper ears. Clean the mounting bolts. Do not use abrasives on the bolts it will destroy their protective plating. Replace the bolts if they are corroded or if the threads are damaged.

10. Reconnect the brake hose to the caliper. Tighten the bolt to 23 ft. lbs. (31 Nm).

11. Install the brake pads and position the caliper over the rotor.

➥Before securing the caliper, ensure the brake hose is not twisted, kinked or touching any chassis parts.

12. Lubricate the caliper pins and bushings with silicone grease. Line up the mounting holes in the caliper and the support bracket and insert the mounting bolts. Make sure that the bolts pass under the retaining ears on the inboard shoes. Push the bolts through until they engage the holes of the outboard pad and caliper ears. Thread the bolts into the support bracket and tighten them.

✳✳ CAUTION

On models with manual/power brakes, pump the pedal until the caliper pistons and brake shoes are seated. On models with anti-lock brakes, turn the ignition ON and allow the booster pump to build pressure. Pump the brake pedal until the shoes are seated and the indicator lights turn off.

13. Fill the master cylinder with brake fluid and pump the brake pedal to seat the pads.

14. Install the wheel assembly and lower the vehicle. Check the level of the brake fluid in the master cylinder and fill as necessary.

OVERHAUL

◆ **See Figures 44 thru 50**

➥Some vehicles may be equipped dual piston calipers. The procedure to overhaul the caliper is essentially the same with the exception of multiple pistons, O-rings and dust boots.

1. Remove the caliper from the vehicle and place on a clean workbench.

✳✳ CAUTION

NEVER place your fingers in front of the pistons in an attempt to catch or protect the pistons when applying compressed air. This could result in personal injury!

➥Depending upon the vehicle, there are two different ways to remove the piston from the caliper. Refer to the brake pad replacement procedure to make sure you have the correct procedure for your vehicle.

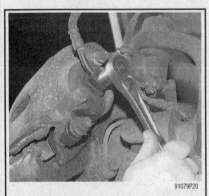

Fig. 43a Loosen the banjo bolt at the brake caliper . . .

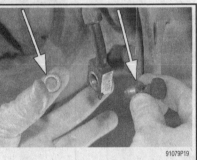
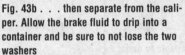

Fig. 43b . . . then separate from the caliper. Allow the brake fluid to drip into a container and be sure to not lose the two washers

Fig. 44 For some types of calipers, use compressed air to drive the piston out of the caliper, but make sure to keep your fingers clear

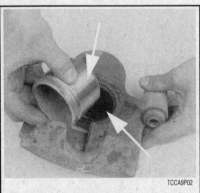

Fig. 45 Withdraw the piston from the caliper bore

Fig. 46 On some vehicles, you must remove the anti-rattle clip

Fig. 47 Use a prytool to carefully pry around the edge of the boot . . .

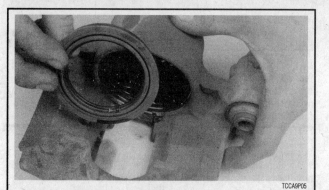

Fig. 48 . . . then remove the boot from the caliper housing, taking care not to score or damage the bore

Fig. 49 Use the proper size driving tool and a mallet to properly seal the boots in the caliper housing

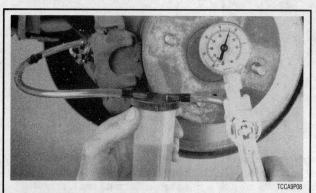

Fig. 50 There are tools, such as this Mighty-Vac, available to assist in proper brake system bleeding

2. The first method is as follows:

a. Stuff a shop towel or a block of wood into the caliper to catch the piston.

b. Remove the caliper piston using compressed air applied into the caliper inlet hole. Inspect the piston for scoring, nicks, corrosion and/or worn or damaged chrome plating. The piston must be replaced if any of these conditions are found.

3. For the second method, you must rotate the piston to retract it from the caliper.

4. If equipped, remove the anti-rattle clip.

5. Use a prytool to remove the caliper boot, being careful not to scratch the housing bore.

6. Remove the piston seals from the groove in the caliper bore.

7. Carefully loosen the brake bleeder valve cap and valve from the caliper housing.

8. Inspect the caliper bores, pistons and mounting threads for scoring or excessive wear.

9. Use crocus cloth to polish out light corrosion from the piston and bore.

10. Clean all parts with denatured alcohol and dry with compressed air.

To assemble:

11. Lubricate and install the bleeder valve and cap.

12. Install the new seals into the caliper bore grooves, making sure they are not twisted.

13. Lubricate the piston bore.

14. Install the pistons and boots into the bores of the calipers and push to the bottom of the bores.

15. Use a suitable driving tool to seat the boots in the housing.

16. Install the caliper in the vehicle.

17. Install the wheel and tire assembly, then carefully lower the vehicle.

18. Properly bleed the brake system.

Brake Rotor

REMOVAL & INSTALLATION

Front

4-WHEEL DRIVE

▶ **See Figures 51 and 52**

1. Loosen the lug nuts on the front wheels.
2. Raise and support the vehicle safely.
3. Remove the front wheels.
4. Remove the calipers, but don't disconnect the brake lines. Suspend the calipers out of the way.

Fig. 51 Removing the brake rotor

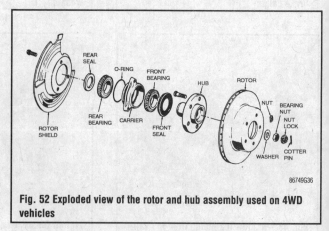

Fig. 52 Exploded view of the rotor and hub assembly used on 4WD vehicles

5. Remove the rotor.

6. Installation is the reverse of removal. Tighten wheel lug nuts to 75 ft. lbs. (101 Nm).

2-WHEEL DRIVE

♦ **See Figure 53**

1. Raise and safely support the front end on jackstands.
2. Remove the wheels.
3. Remove the caliper without disconnecting the brake line. Suspend it out of the way. Refer to the caliper removal procedure in this section.
4. Remove the grease cap, cotter pin, nut cap, nut, and washer from the spindle.
5. Pull slowly on the hub and catch the outer bearing as it falls.
6. Remove the hub and rotor. The inner bearing and seal can be removed by prying out and discarding the inner seal.

To install:

7. Clean and repack the hub and bearings, install the inner bearing and a new seal.
8. Position the hub and rotor on the spindle and install the outer bearing.
9. Install the washer and nut.
10. While turning the rotor, tighten the nut to 25 ft. lbs. (33 Nm) to seat the bearings.
11. Back off the nut 1/2 turn, and, while turning the rotor, tighten the nut to 19 inch lbs. (2 Nm).
12. Install the nut cap and a new cotter pin. Install the grease cap.
13. Install the caliper.
14. Install the wheels.

Rear

> **** CAUTION**
>
> Brake shoes may contain asbestos, which has been determined to be a cancer causing agent. Never clean the brake surfaces with compressed air! Avoid inhaling any dust from any brake surface! When cleaning brake surfaces, use a commercially available brake cleaning fluid.

1. Loosen the lug nuts on the rear wheels.
2. Raise and support the vehicle safely.
3. Remove the rear wheels.
4. Remove the calipers, but don't disconnect the brake lines. Suspend the calipers out of the way.
5. If equipped, remove and discard the push nuts securing the rotor to the wheel studs.
6. If the rotor and/or axle hub contact surfaces appear to have heavy rust, apply a rust penetrating oil to those surfaces as well as through the spaces around the wheel studs. If necessary, use a plastic or rawhide mallet to loosen the rotor.

7. Remove the rotor. If necessary, remove the access plug from the splash shield and back off the parking brake shoes enough to allow removal of the rotor.

8. Installation is the reverse of removal. Tighten wheel lug nuts to 75 ft. lbs. (101 Nm).

INSPECTION

♦ **See Figures 54 and 55**

➡**This inspection procedure also applies to the rear brake rotors.**

Check the rotor for surface cracks, nicks, broken cooling fins and scoring of both contact surfaces. Some scoring of the surfaces may occur during normal use. Scoring that is 0.015 in. (0.38mm) deep or less is not detrimental to the operation of the brakes.

If the rotor surface is heavily rusted or scaled, clean both surfaces on a disc brake lathe using flat sanding discs before attempting any measurements.

With the rotor assembly mounted on the vehicle or a disc brake lathe and all play removed from the wheel bearings (front), assemble a dial indicator so that the stem contacts the center of the rotor braking surface. Zero the dial indicator before taking any measurements. Lateral run-out must not exceed 0.005 in. (0.13mm) with a maximum rate of change not to exceed 0.001 in. (0.025mm) in 30° of rotation.

Excessive run-out will cause the rotor to wobble and knock the piston back into the caliper, causing increased pedal travel, noise and vibration.

Check the Brake Specifications Chart for rotor thickness. Discard the rotor if it is not within the specification.

➡**Remember to adjust the preload on the wheel bearings after the run-out measurement has been taken.**

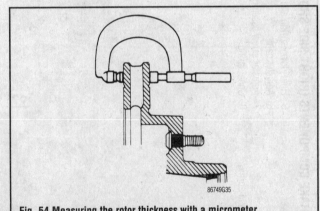

Fig. 54 Measuring the rotor thickness with a micrometer

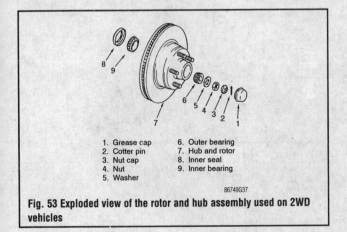

1. Grease cap	6. Outer bearing
2. Cotter pin	7. Hub and rotor
3. Nut cap	8. Inner seal
4. Nut	9. Inner bearing
5. Washer	

Fig. 53 Exploded view of the rotor and hub assembly used on 2WD vehicles

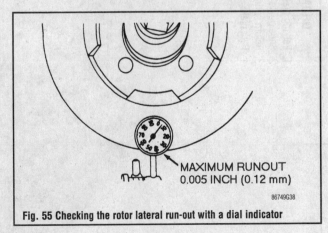

MAXIMUM RUNOUT
0.005 INCH (0.12 mm)

Fig. 55 Checking the rotor lateral run-out with a dial indicator

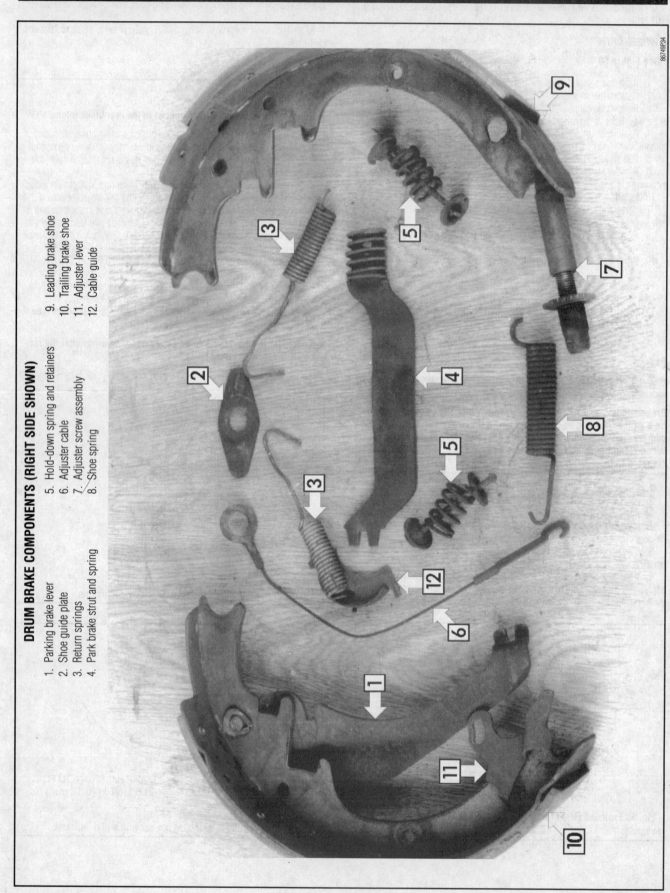

DRUM BRAKE COMPONENTS (RIGHT SIDE SHOWN)

1. Parking brake lever
2. Shoe guide plate
3. Return springs
4. Park brake strut and spring
5. Hold-down spring and retainers
6. Adjuster cable
7. Adjuster screw assembly
8. Shoe spring
9. Leading brake shoe
10. Trailing brake shoe
11. Adjuster lever
12. Cable guide

Brake Drums

REMOVAL & INSTALLATION

▶ See Figures 56 and 57

✳ CAUTION

Brake shoes may contain asbestos, which has been determined to be a cancer causing agent. Never clean the brake surfaces with compressed air! Avoid inhaling any dust from any brake surface! When cleaning brake surfaces, use a commercially available brake cleaning fluid.

1. Raise and support the rear end on jackstands. Block the front wheels
2. Remove the wheel, then the drum from the vehicle. On some models you may have to remove spring nuts securing the drums to the wheel studs before removing the drum.

➡ It may be necessary to back off the brake adjusters to remove the drum.

3. When placing the drum on the hub, make sure that the contacting surfaces are clean and flat.

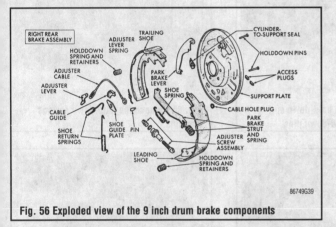

Fig. 56 Exploded view of the 9 inch drum brake components

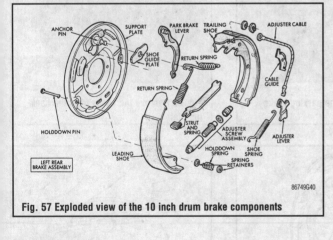

Fig. 57 Exploded view of the 10 inch drum brake components

INSPECTION

▶ See Figure 58

Using an inside micrometer, check all drums. Should a brake drum be scored or rough, it may be reconditioned by grinding or turning on a lathe. Do not remove more than 0.030 in. (0.76mm) thickness of metal. If a drum is reconditioned in this manner, it is recommended that either the correct factory supplied 0.030 in. (0.76mm) oversize lining be installed, or a shim equal in thickness to

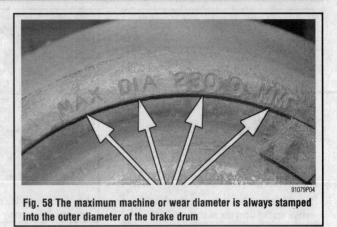

Fig. 58 The maximum machine or wear diameter is always stamped into the outer diameter of the brake drum

the metal removed be placed between the lining and the brake shoe so that the arc of the lining will be the same as that of the drum.

Brake Shoes

REMOVAL & INSTALLATION

▶ See Figures 59 thru 73

✳ CAUTION

Brake shoes may contain asbestos, which has been determined to be a cancer causing agent. Never clean the brake surfaces with compressed air! Avoid inhaling any dust from any brake surface! When cleaning brake surfaces, use a commercially available brake cleaning fluid.

➡ A brake spring removal tool and a brake adjusting gauge are required for this procedure.

1. Raise and support the vehicle safely with jackstands.
2. If the brakes have never been serviced before, the drums will be held on the wheel studs with spring nuts. Remove the spring nuts and discard.
3. Turn the adjustment starwheel so that the brake shoes are retracted from the brake drum and remove the brake drum.
4. Install wheel cylinder clamps to retain the wheel cylinder pistons in place and prevent leakage of brake fluid while replacing the shoes.
5. Remove the U-clip and washer securing the adjuster cable to the parking brake lever.
6. Remove the adjuster cable, cable guide, adjuster lever and adjuster springs. Remove the return springs with a brake spring remover tool.
7. Remove the hold-down retainers and springs, then remove the brake shoes.

Fig. 59 Use a brake cleaner to clean the brake surfaces

Fig. 60 Using a brake tool, remove the return spring from the anchor pin

Fig. 61 Remove the return spring and the adjuster cable guide

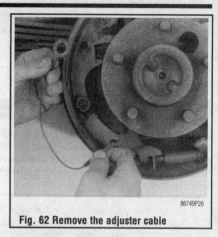

Fig. 62 Remove the adjuster cable

Fig. 63 Remove the shoe guide plate

Fig. 64 Disengage the hold-down spring retainers from the hold-down pins

Fig. 65 Remove the hold-down springs and pins

Fig. 66 Pull the shoes apart and then . . .

Fig. 67 . . . remove the parking brake strut and spring

Fig. 68 Remove the shoes from the backing plate

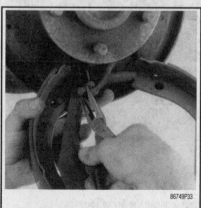

Fig. 69 Disengage the parking brake cable

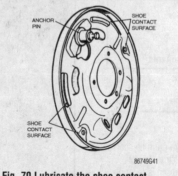

Fig. 70 Lubricate the shoe contact points—10 inch drum brake backing plate shown

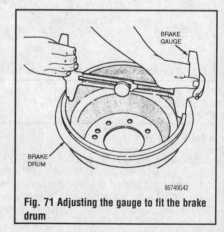

Fig. 71 Adjusting the gauge to fit the brake drum

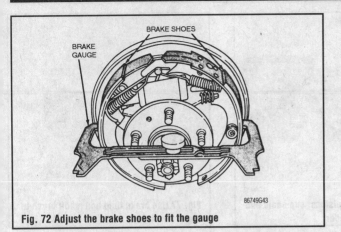

Fig. 72 Adjust the brake shoes to fit the gauge

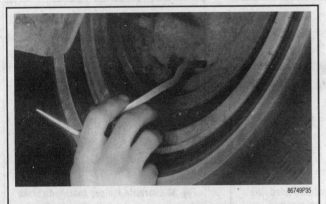

Fig. 73 Adjusting the drum brakes using a brake spoon

To install:

8. Clean the backing plate with a brush or cloth. Place a dab of Lubriplate® on each spot where the brake shoes rub on the backing plate.

➡**Always replace brake linings in axle sets. Never replace linings on one side or just on one wheel.**

9. Thoroughly clean and lubricate the adjuster cable guides, adjuster screw and pivot, parking brake lever and lever pivot pin with multi-purpose grease.

10. Apply a thin coat of multi-purpose chassis lube to the mounting pads on the backing plate.

11. Transfer the parking brake actuating lever to the new secondary shoe.

12. Position the brake shoes on the backing plate, then install the hold-down springs and retainers. Don't forget to engage the parking brake lever with the cable.

13. Install the parking brake actuating bar and spring between the parking brake lever and primary shoe.

14. Install the self-adjusting cable, cable guide and upper return springs.

15. Thoroughly clean the starwheel and lightly lubricate the threads with lithium based grease.

16. Install the starwheel.

17. Install the self-adjusting cam and lower spring. A big pair of locking pliers is good for this job.

18. Check the surface of the brake shoes for any grease that may have gotten on them. If dirty, lightly clean with a piece of sandpaper.

19. Adjust the brakes, install the brake drum and wheel. Lower the vehicle and test drive.

ADJUSTMENT

These brakes are equipped with self-adjusters and no manual adjustment is necessary, except when brake linings are replaced. After replacing the brake shoes, perform the following adjustment procedure:

1. Insert the brake gauge in the drum and fully expand until the gauge inner legs contact the drum braking surface. Then lock the gauge in position.

2. Reverse the gauge and install it on the brake shoes. Position the gauge legs at the shoe centers. If the gauge does not have a light drag fit, adjust the shoes.

3. Pull the starwheel away from the automatic adjuster lever. Turn the starwheel by hand to expand or retract the shoes and recheck with the brake gauge.

4. Install the brake drums, lower vehicle and make final adjustment.

5. Final adjustments on drum brakes take advantage of the systems self-adjustment mechanism. Drive the vehicle and make one forward stop followed by on reverse stop. Repeat the procedure 8–10 times to equalize adjustment between the two sides. Bring the vehicle to a complete stop each time. Rolling stops will not activate the self-adjuster mechanism

Wheel Cylinders

REMOVAL & INSTALLATION

✵✵ CAUTION

Brake shoes may contain asbestos, which has been determined to be a cancer causing agent. Never clean the brake surfaces with compressed air! Avoid inhaling any dust from any brake surface! When cleaning brake surfaces, use a commercially available brake cleaning fluid.

➡**For vehicles equipped with Anti-Lock Brakes (ABS), refer to the proper procedures concerning brake system servicing.**

1. Raise and support the vehicle safely using jackstands. Remove the wheel.

2. Disconnect the brake line at the fitting on the brake backing plate.

➡**In most cases the flare fittings that attach the brake lines to the wheel cylinders will be frozen. Clean the fittings with solvent and use penetrating oil to loosen the rust. Use the proper size flare nut wrench to avoid stripping the fitting.**

3. Remove the brake assemblies. Disconnect the brake line from the rear of the wheel cylinder.

4. Remove the screws or nuts that hold the wheel cylinder to the backing plate and remove the wheel cylinder from the vehicle.

To install:

5. Position the wheel cylinder on the backing plate and start the brake line in the cylinder fitting.

6. Install the cylinder mounting bolts and tighten to 90 inch lbs. (10 Nm).

7. To avoid stripping the fitting, tighten the brake line fitting to 11 ft. lbs. (15 Nm) using a flare nut wrench.

OVERHAUL

▶ **See Figures 74 thru 83**

Wheel cylinder overhaul kits may be available, but often at little or no savings over a reconditioned wheel cylinder. It often makes sense with these components to substitute a new or reconditioned part instead of attempting an overhaul.

Fig. 74 Remove the outer boots from the wheel cylinder

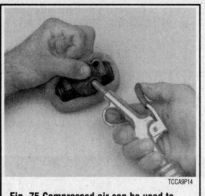

Fig. 75 Compressed air can be used to remove the pistons and seals

Fig. 76 Remove the pistons, cup seals and spring from the cylinder

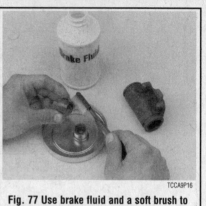

Fig. 77 Use brake fluid and a soft brush to clean the pistons . . .

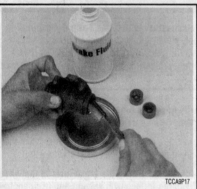

Fig. 78 . . . and the bore of the wheel cylinder

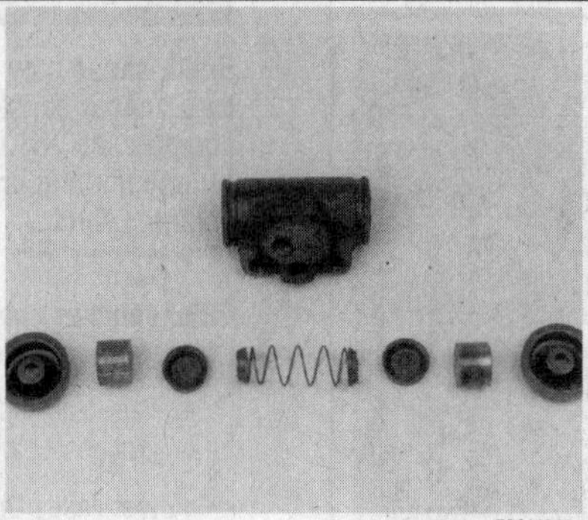

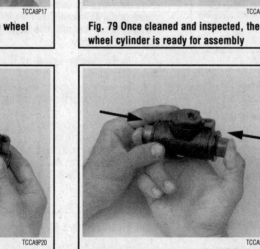

Fig. 79 Once cleaned and inspected, the wheel cylinder is ready for assembly

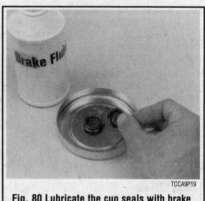

Fig. 80 Lubricate the cup seals with brake fluid

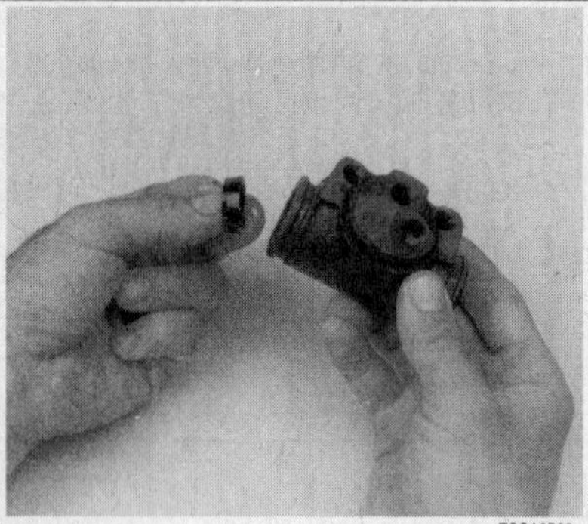

Fig. 81 Install the spring, then the cup seals in the bore

Fig. 82 Lightly lubricate the pistons, then install them

Fig. 83 The boots can now be installed over the wheel cylinder ends

If no replacement is available, or you would prefer to overhaul your wheel cylinders, the following procedure may be used. When rebuilding and installing wheel cylinders, avoid getting any contaminants into the system. Always use clean, new, high quality brake fluid. If dirty or improper fluid has been used, it will be necessary to drain the entire system, flush the system with proper brake fluid, replace all rubber components, then refill and bleed the system.

1. Remove the wheel cylinder from the vehicle and place on a clean workbench.

2. First remove and discard the old rubber boots, then withdraw the pistons. Piston cylinders are equipped with seals and a spring assembly, all located behind the pistons in the cylinder bore.

3. Remove the remaining inner components, seals and spring assembly. Compressed air may be useful in removing these components. If no compressed air is available, be VERY careful not to score the wheel cylinder bore when removing parts from it. Discard all components for which replacements were supplied in the rebuild kit.

4. Wash the cylinder and metal parts in denatured alcohol or clean brake fluid.

⁕⁕ WARNING

Never use a mineral-based solvent such as gasoline, kerosene or paint thinner for cleaning purposes. These solvents will swell rubber components and quickly deteriorate them.

5. Allow the parts to air dry or use compressed air. Do not use rags for cleaning, since lint will remain in the cylinder bore.

6. Inspect the piston and replace it if it shows scratches.

7. Lubricate the cylinder bore and seals using clean brake fluid.

8. Position the spring assembly.

9. Install the inner seals, then the pistons.

10. Insert the new boots into the counterbores by hand. Do not lubricate the boots.

11. Install the wheel cylinder.

PARKING BRAKE

Cables

REPLACEMENT

Cherokee, Comanche and Wagoneer Models

REAR CABLE

▶ See Figures 84 and 85

1. Raise and support the vehicle safely with jackstands. Fully release the parking brake.

※※ **CAUTION**

Take care to support the vehicle safely. Place wheel chocks behind the wheels and use jackstands under the frame for support. Remember, the parking brake is released!

2. Remove the rear wheel and brake drum.
3. Remove the secondary (rear) brake shoe and disengage the cable from the lever on the brake shoe.
4. Compress the cable retainer with a worm drive hose clamp as illustrated.
5. Remove the cable from the backing plate, then remove the cable mounting clips.
6. Disengage the cable from the equalizer and remove the cable.
7. Installation is the reverse of removal. Adjust the drum brakes and parking brakes as described in this section.

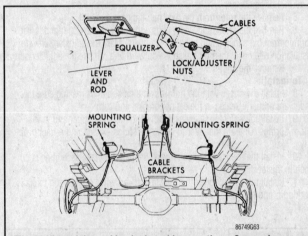

Fig. 84 View of the parking brake cable mounting—Comanche shown

FRONT CABLE (COMANCHE ONLY)

▶ See Figures 86 and 87

1. Raise and support the vehicle safely. Fully release the parking brake.

※※ **CAUTION**

Take care to support the vehicle safely. Place wheel chocks behind the wheels and use jackstands under the frame for support. Remember, the parking brake is released!

2. Remove the equalizer nuts and remove the front cable from the equalizer and cable bracket.
3. Lower the vehicle.
4. Move the carpet away from the pedal assembly. Then remove the pedal mounting bolts and move the pedal assembly away from the kick panel. Disconnect the front cable from the pedal.
5. Move the carpet at the driver's side and rear of the cab to gain access to the cable floorpan clamps. Remove the clamps, unseat the cable grommet and remove the cable through the floorpan.
6. Installation is the reverse of removal. Adjust the parking brake cable.

Grand Cherokee/Grand Wagoneer Models

REAR CABLE

1. Raise the vehicle and safely support it with jackstands. Release the parking brake.
2. Loosen the adjusting nut at the equalizer to provide slack in the cable.
3. Disengage the cable(s) from the equalizer, chassis/body clips and retainers.
4. If equipped with rear drums, perform the following:
   a. Remove the rear wheel and brake drum.
   b. Remove the secondary brake shoe.
   c. Disengage the cable from the lever on the secondary brake shoe.
   d. Using a worm drive hose clamp, compress the cable retainer then remove from the brake support plate.
5. If equipped with rear disc brakes, perform the following:
   a. Slide the cable eyelet off the actuating lever.
   b. Compress the retainer holding the cable in the bracket attached to the caliper bracket, then remove the cable.
6. Installation is the reverse of removal. Adjust the drum brakes (if equipped) and parking brakes as described in this section.

FRONT CABLE

1. Disconnect the negative battery cable and raise the vehicle. Safely support the vehicle using jackstands and release the parking brake.
2. Remove the front cable adjusting nut and disengage the tensioner from the equalizer.
3. Remove the cable from the tensioner. Disengage the cable from the floorpan insert, and insert from the floorpan.

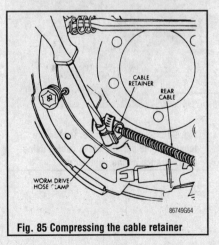

Fig. 85 Compressing the cable retainer

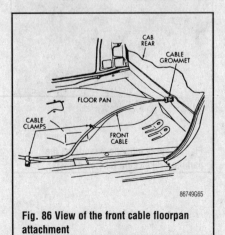

Fig. 86 View of the front cable floorpan attachment

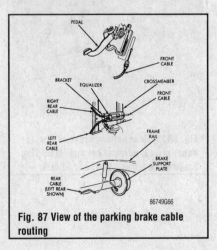

Fig. 87 View of the parking brake cable routing

4. Lower the vehicle and remove the console. Refer to Section 10, if this procedure is applicable to your vehicle.

5. Disengage the wiring harness connector at the parking brake switch and air bag module, if located there.

6. If necessary, remove the screws that the mount the air bag module to the floorpan and parking brake lever. Then move the module off to the side for access to the lever.

7. Remove the parking brake lever. Disconnect the cable from the parking lever and remove the cable.

8. Installation is the reverse of removal. Adjust the parking cable as outlined in this section.

ADJUSTMENT

1984–93 Models

CHEROKEE, COMANCHE AND WAGONEER MODELS

▶ **See Figures 88, 89 and 90**

➡This procedure requires the use of a special tool.

1. Ensure the rear brakes are properly adjusted.

2. Fully apply and release the parking brake lever four or five times. Then place the lever on the fifth notch.

3. Raise and support the vehicle safely.

4. Loosen the equalizer locknut.

5. Install cable gauge tool J-34651 on an inch pound torque wrench, then position the gauge on one rear cable (Cherokee/Wagoneer) or on the front cable (Comanche).

6. Apply and hold torque of 45–50 inch lbs. (5–6 Nm) on the adjustment gauge and note the position of the gauge pointer.

7. Hold the equalizer rod and turn the equalizer nut until the cables are tight.

8. Apply and release the brake lever fully, five times, and recheck the adjustment.

9. If the brake lever does not reach the fifth notch, loosen the adjusting nut and if the lever goes past the fifth notch, tighten the adjusting nut.

10. When adjustment is correct, stake the adjusting nut.

1993 GRAND CHEROKEE MODELS

1. Ensure the rear brakes are properly adjusted.

2. Fully apply the parking brakes.

3. Raise and support the vehicle safely.

4. Using chalk or grease pencil, matchmark the position of the adjusting nut on the threaded end of the cable tensioner.

5. Tighten the adjusting nut approximately 1/2 in. (13mm) farther down the threaded end of the cable tensioner.

6. Release the parking brake and verify that there is no drag on the wheels.

7. Lower the vehicle.

1994 and Later Models

1. Raise the vehicle and safely support it with jackstands.

2. Back off the adjusting nut to create slack in the cables and remove the wheels and drums.

3. Ensure the rear brakes are properly adjusted and that the parking brake cables are in good condition.

4. Reinstall the wheels and drums if the brake shoe adjustment is correct.

5. Fully apply the parking brakes and leave them applied.

6. Mark the tensioner rod 1/4 in. (6.5mm) from the tensioner bracket.

7. Tighten the adjusting nut until the mark at the tensioner rod moves into alignment with the tensioner bracket.

8. Release the parking brake and verify that there is no drag on the wheels.

9. Lower the vehicle.

Brake Shoes

➡These procedures apply only to 1994 and Later Grand Cherokee models equipped with rear disc brakes.

REMOVAL & INSTALLATION

1. Raise the vehicle and safely support it with jackstands. Remove the wheel.

2. Remove the caliper from the rotor and support the caliper with a piece of wire to a suspension component.

3. Remove the rubber access plug from the rear of the disc brake splash shield.

4. Retract the parking brake shoes by rotating the star wheel downwards in a clockwise direction (while facing the front of the vehicle) using a brake adjustment tool or equivalent.

5. Remove the rotor from the axle hub flange.

6. Remove the shoe hold-down clips and pins and the upper and lower springs from the shoes using needle nose pliers. Mark the adjuster screw for installation reference, then tilt the shoes outward and remove the adjuster screw.

7. Remove the shoes.

To install:

8. Install the shoes with the hold-down pins and clips making sure the shoes are properly seated in the caliper bracket and cam.

9. Install the adjuster screw assembly and the shoe upper and lower return springs. Operate the lever to verify the shoes expand and retract properly.

10. Install the rotor and caliper. Adjust the parking brake assembly as outlined in this section.

11. Install the wheel, lower the vehicle and verify that the parking brake is working properly.

Fig. 88 (1) Rear parking brake cables, (2) equalizer, (3) adjuster nut and (4) parking brake cable tension threaded adjuster

Fig. 89 Spray lube the threads on the parking brake cable tension adjuster . . .

Fig. 90 . . . then tighten or loosen the tension of the parking brake cables using a box wrench on the adjuster nut

ADJUSTMENT

1. Raise the vehicle and safely support it with jackstands.
2. Remove the wheel and secure the rotor with two wheel nuts.
3. Remove the rubber access plug from the rear of the splash shield and insert a brake tool.

4. Position the brake tool at the bottom of the star wheel and rotate the star wheel upward (counterclockwise) to expand the shoes.
5. Expand the shoes until a slight drag is experienced, then back off the adjuster so that the drag is barely eliminated.
6. Replace the access plug, install the wheel and lower the vehicle.

BENDIX ANTI-LOCK BRAKE SYSTEM

General Information

▶ **See Figures 91 and 92**

The Bendix anti-lock braking system is available on 1989–91 Jeep Cherokee and Wagoneer vehicles (model designation XJ) with SelecTrac 4-wheel drive. Anti-lock Brake Systems (ABS) are designed to prevent wheel lockup under heavy braking conditions on virtually any type of road surface. The Jeep ABS limits wheel lockup by modulating the brake fluid pressure to the brakes at each wheel. A vehicle which is stopped without locking the wheels will normally stop in a shorter distance than a vehicle with locked wheels. Additionally, vehicle control can be maintained during hard braking because the front wheels do not lock. The Jeep system is an electronically operated, power assisted brake system controlled by an isolated Electronic Control Unit (ECU).

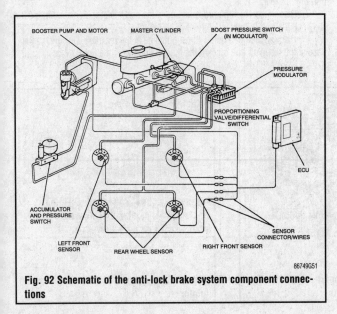

Fig. 91 Anti-lock brake system component locations

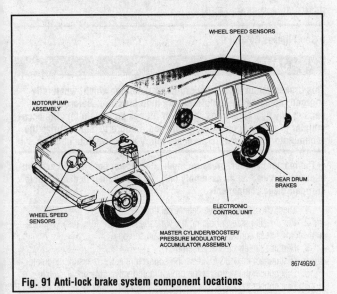

Fig. 92 Schematic of the anti-lock brake system component connections

SERVICE PRECAUTIONS

> ✳✳ **CAUTION**
>
> **This brake system uses a hydraulic accumulator which, when fully charged, contains brake fluid at very high pressure. Before disconnecting any hydraulic lines, hoses or fittings be certain that the accumulator pressure is completely relieved. Failure to depressurize the accumulator may result in personal injury and/or vehicle damage.**

• Certain components within the ABS system are not intended to be serviced or repaired individually. Only those components with removal and installation procedures should be serviced.
• Both the external accumulator and the smaller accumulator within the pump contain high pressure nitrogen charges to assistance in pressurizing the system. The gas pressure is maintained even after fluid pressure in the system is reduced. Never puncture or attempt to disassemble either of these components.
• Do not use rubber hoses or other parts not specifically specified for the ABS system. When using repair kits, replace all parts included in the kit. Partial or incorrect repair may lead to functional problems and require the replacement of components.
• Lubricate rubber parts with clean, fresh brake fluid to ease assembly. Do not use lubricated shop air to clean parts; damage to rubber components may result.
• Use only DOT 3 or its superceding brake fluid from an unopened container.
• If any hydraulic component or line is removed or replaced, it may be necessary to bleed the entire system.
• A clean repair area is essential. Always clean the reservoir and cap thoroughly before removing the cap. The slightest amount of dirt in the fluid may plug an orifice and impair the system function. Perform repairs after components have been thoroughly cleaned; use only denatured alcohol to clean components. Do not allow ABS components to come into contact with any substance containing mineral oil; this includes used shop rags.
• The anti-lock ECM is a microprocessor similar to other computer units in the vehicle. Insure that the ignition switch is **OFF** before removing or installing controller harnesses. Avoid static electricity discharge at or near the controller.

DEPRESSURIZING THE SYSTEM

> ✳✳ **CAUTION**
>
> **Depressurize the ABS accumulator and master cylinder assembly before performing any service operations. Failure to completely relieve the system could result in brake fluid under high pressure being sprayed on the technician and the vehicle. This can result in serious personal injury and vehicle damage.**

1. Turn the ignition switch **OFF** and leave it **OFF** during repairs, unless specifically directed otherwise.
2. Firmly apply and release the brake pedal a minimum of 45–50 times.
3. The pedal feel will become noticeably harder when the accumulator is completely discharged.
4. Do not turn the ignition switch **ON** after depressurizing the system, unless service procedures specifically require it or all service operations have been performed.

➡️After the reserve pressure is depleted, the fluid level in the reservoir will rise above the MAX fill mark. This is normal; the reservoir will not overflow unless the system was originally overfilled.

5. Always wear safety goggles when disconnecting lines and fittings.

PRE—DIAGNOSIS INSPECTION

Before diagnosing an apparent ABS problem, make absolutely certain that the normal braking system is in correct working order. Many common brake problems (dragging shoe, seepage, etc.) will affect the ABS system. A visual check of specific system components may reveal problems creating an apparent ABS malfunction. Performing this inspection may reveal a simple failure, thus eliminating extended diagnostic time. The steps should be performed in order.

1. Depressurize the system.
2. Inspect the brake fluid level in the reservoir.
3. Inspect brake lines, hoses, master cylinder assembly, brake calipers and cylinders for leakage.
4. Visually check brake lines and hoses for excessive wear, heat damage, punctures, contact with other parts, missing clips or holders, blockage or crimping.
5. Check the calipers and wheel cylinders for rust or corrosion. Check for proper sliding action, if applicable.
6. Check the caliper and wheel cylinder pistons for freedom of motion during application and release.
7. Inspect the wheel speed sensors for proper mounting and connections.
8. Inspect the tone wheels for broken teeth or poor mounting.
9. Inspect the wheels and tires on the vehicle. They must be of the same size and type to generate accurate speed signals.
10. Confirm the fault occurrence with the operator. Certain driver induced faults, such as not releasing the parking brake fully, will set a fault code and trigger the dash warning light(s). Excessive wheel spin on low-traction surfaces, high speed acceleration or riding the brake pedal may also set fault codes and trigger a warning lamp. These induced faults are not system failures but examples of vehicle performance outside the parameters of the ECM.
11. Many system shutdowns are due to loss of sensor signals to or from the ECM. The most common cause is not a failed sensor but a loose, corroded or dirty connector. Incorrect adjustment of the wheel speed sensor will cause a loss of wheel speed signal. Check harness and component connectors carefully.

Diagnosis and Testing

▶ See Figure 93

After performing the preliminary visual checks, observe the behavior and timing of the dashboard warning lamps. Their function, when used in diagnostics, can point to possible causes and eliminate others.

Use the DRB scan tool with the correct cartridge to determine the specific circuit at fault. The tester with the correct adapter should be engaged to the diagnostic connector on the right side of the engine compartment. Any fault read by the tester on initial hook-up should be considered as a guide only. After initial repairs, clear the fault code, drive the vehicle and recheck for any stored code. Once the fault is identified, the DRB may be used to test or energize system components.

Trouble Codes

The following is a list of the ABS system trouble codes for 1989–91 Jeep Cherokee and Wagoneer models:

- Code 801: Solenoid undervoltage
- Code 802: Parking brake not seen
- Code 803: Anti-lock/brake warning lamp inoperable
- Code 805: Differential pressure fault
- Code 806: Boost pressure fault
- Code 807: Low accumulator
- Code 808: Modulator fault
- Code 809: Self test failure
- Code 811: Relay fault
- Code 812: Pump/motor fault
- Code 813: Brake switch fault
- Code 814: Low fluid
- Code 815: Right rear speed sensor fault
- Code 816: Left rear speed sensor fault
- Code 817: Right front speed sensor fault
- Code 818: Left front speed sensor fault

Master Cylinder/Pressure Modulator/Power Booster/Accumulator Assembly

REMOVAL & INSTALLATION

▶ See Figures 94 and 95

❊❊ CAUTION

This brake system uses a hydraulic accumulator which, when fully charged, contains brake fluid at very high pressure. Before disconnecting any hydraulic lines, hoses or fittings be certain that the accumulator pressure is completely relieved. Failure to depressurize the accumulator may result in personal injury and/or vehicle damage.

➡️The master cylinder, pressure modulator, power booster and accumulator are serviced as an assembly only. Do not attempt to disassemble or repair these components.

1. Disconnect the negative battery cable.
2. Remove the screws holding the windshield washer fluid reservoir. Disconnect the hoses and wires and remove the reservoir.
3. Remove the air cleaner assembly.
4. Disconnect the ABS ECM wiring connectors at the pressure modulator.
5. Disconnect the wiring at the proportioning valve/differential switch.
6. Disconnect the brake line at the coupling on the underside of the proportioning valve.
7. Disconnect the high pressure line at the accumulator block and immediately cap the port to prevent entry of dirt.
8. Place a catch pan below the supply line at the reservoir. Disconnect the hose at the reservoir and discard the fluid drained from the line.

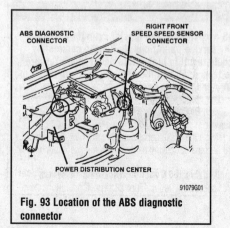

Fig. 93 Location of the ABS diagnostic connector

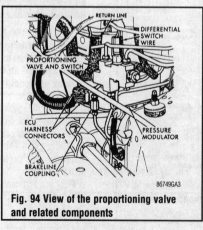

Fig. 94 View of the proportioning valve and related components

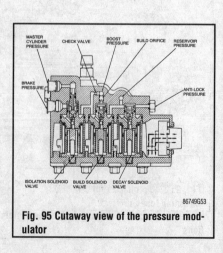

Fig. 95 Cutaway view of the pressure modulator

9. Remove the wires from the low pressure switch on the accumulator block, the modulator boost pressure switch and the fluid level switch.

10. Disconnect the front brake lines at the outboard side of the pressure modulator.

11. Inside the car, disconnect the wiring to the brake pedal switch. It may be necessary to remove the instrument panel lower trim for access.

12. Remove the master cylinder pushrod bolt; disconnect the pushrod from the pedal. Immediately discard the nuts from the pushrod bolt; they are not reusable.

13. Remove the nuts from the brake mounting bracket studs.

14. Under the hood, carefully pull the hydraulic components and bracket forward until the studs clear the firewall. Lift the assembly up and out of the engine compartment.

To install:

15. Install the pad onto the new bracket and place the bracket with the brake components in place against the firewall. Make certain the studs are correctly seated in the holes.

16. Position the master cylinder/modulator/accumulator on the firewall and tighten the mounting nuts to 27 ft. lbs. (31 Nm).

17. Connect the wiring harness to the low pressure switch, the differential switch, the pressure modulator, the low fluid and boost pressure switches.

18. Inside the vehicle, install the nuts on the mounting studs and tighten them to 31 ft. lbs (42 Nm).

19. Align the brake pedal, the brake lamp switch and the master cylinder pushrod. Install the pushrod bolt. The pushrod bolt must be correctly installed to avoid interference with the bracket. The bolt head must be on the left side of the brake pedal.

20. Use new nuts on the pushrod bolt. The inner locknut should be tightened to 25 ft. lbs. (34 Nm); the outer jam nut should be tightened to 75 inch lbs. (8.5 Nm).

21. Connect the wiring to the brake switch and install the lower dashboard trim, if it was removed.

22. In the engine compartment, connect the brake lines to the proportioning valve.

23. Connect the pressure and return lines to the accumulator.

24. Install the air cleaner assembly.

25. Connect hoses and wires to the windshield washer fluid reservoir and install it in position.

26. Inspect the high-pressure and return lines; make certain they are not kinked or touching the engine.

27. Fill the master cylinder to the MAX level.

28. Connect the negative battery cable.

29. Turn the ignition switch **ON**; the pump should start running. Listen for a drop in pump rpm; this shows the pump is pressurizing the system. If there is no drop in pump rpm within 20 seconds, immediately shut the ignition **OFF** and check for hydraulic leaks.

➡**Severe pump damage will result if the pump runs without pressurizing the system for any length of time.**

30. Add fluid to the reservoir as necessary. Do not overfill.

31. Bleed the brake system.

Electronic Control Unit (ECU)

REMOVAL & INSTALLATION

▶ **See Figure 96**

1. Confirm that the ignition switch is **OFF**.
2. Fold the rear seat cushion forward for access to the ECU.
3. Remove the bracket holding the ECU from the floorpan, then remove the control unit from the bracket.
4. Carefully disengage the wiring connectors from the ECU.

To install:

5. Connect the wiring harnesses to the replacement unit.
6. Mount the control unit on the bracket, then install the bracket to the floorpan. Make certain the bracket is in the correct position.
7. Reposition the rear seat cushion.

Speed Sensors

TESTING

▶ **See Figure 97**

1. Check the wheel speed sensor air gap using a brass feeler gauge. If the air gap measures out of specifications, adjust to the correct specifications.
2. Disengage the speed sensor wiring harness connector. Inspect the condition of the connector and repair if necessary.
3. Using an ohmmeter, measure the resistance between the wheel speed sensor connector terminals.
4. The resistance should measure between 5000–8000 ohms. If the resistance measures outside this value, replace the wheel speed sensor.

REMOVAL & INSTALLATION

Front

▶ **See Figures 98, 99 and 100**

1. Elevate and safely support the vehicle. Turn the front wheel outward for easier access to the sensor.
2. Before disassembly, note sensor wire routing including location of all clips and retainers. The sensor wire must be routed correctly during reassembly to avoid damage from moving parts.
3. Carefully remove the wire ties holding the sensor wire to the brake lines and the steering knuckle.
4. If the sensor is coated with mud, slush, etc., clean the sensor and surrounding area. This will prevent damage to the sensor and tone wheel during removal.

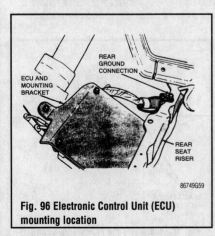

86749G59

Fig. 96 Electronic Control Unit (ECU) mounting location

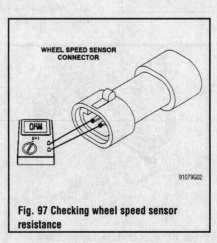

91079G02

Fig. 97 Checking wheel speed sensor resistance

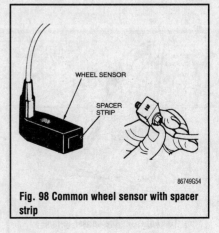

86749G54

Fig. 98 Common wheel sensor with spacer strip

5. Remove the sensor attaching screw and remove the sensor from the steering knuckle.

6. Loosen the grommet holding the sensor wire from the wheel arch panel.

7. In the engine compartment, disconnect the sensor wire connector from the ABS harness. Carefully remove the sensor and harness from the car.

To install:

8. The wheel sensors have a plastic spacing strip attached to the contact face. Inspect this spacer and note the condition. If the strip is securely attached and in good condition, no adjustment will be needed after installation. If the strip is damaged or not present, an air gap adjustment will be required.

9. Feed the sensor wire through the grommet hole in the wheelwell panel. Connect the sensor connector to the ABS harness and seat the rubber grommet in the panel.

10. Position the sensor on the steering knuckle and install the attaching bolt finger-tight.

11. If the spacer strip was intact and in good condition, lightly press the sensor against the tone wheel. Hold the sensor in this position and tighten the retaining bolt to 11 ft. lbs (14 Nm).

12. If the spacer was missing or damaged, clean the contacts on the sensor with a clean shop towel. Remove the spacer strip completely if loose or torn. After the sensor is loosely held in position by the retaining bolt, use a brass feeler gauge to set the air gap from the sensor to the tone wheel. Correct air gap is 0.013–0.019 in. (0.33–0.48mm). Tighten the retaining bolt to 11 ft. lbs. (14 Nm) and recheck the air gap with the feeler gauge.

➡Use of a brass or non-magnetic gauge is required. Do not use common steel feelers; the small magnets within the sensor may be damaged. Correct air gap is critical to the proper operation of the sensor.

13. Use new wire ties to secure the sensor wire to the brake lines and steering knuckle.

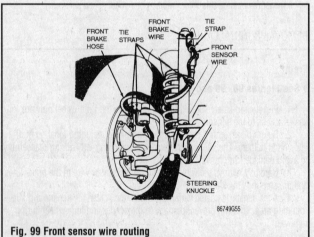

Fig. 99 Front sensor wire routing

Rear

▶ **See Figures 101 and 102**

1. Raise and fold forward the rear seat to gain access to the rear sensor connectors.

2. Disengage the sensor connector from the ABS harness; push the sensor grommet and wiring through the floor pan.

3. Elevate and safely support the vehicle.

4. Remove the wheel and brake drum.

5. Carefully remove the wire ties holding the sensor wires to the brake lines and rear axle.

6. Loosen or unseat the backing plate grommet holding the sensor wire.

7. Remove the bolt holding the sensor to the bracket. Remove the sensor by pulling the wire through the grommet hole in the backing plate.

To install:

8. The wheel sensors have a plastic spacing strip attached to the contact face. Inspect this spacer and note the condition. If the strip is securely attached and in good condition, no adjustment will be needed after installation. If the strip is damaged or not present, an air gap adjustment will be required.

9. Feed the sensor wire through the grommet hole in the backing plate and seat the grommet in the plate.

10. If the spacer strip was intact and in good condition, lightly press the sensor against the tone wheel. Hold the sensor in this position and tighten the retaining bolt to 11 ft. lbs (14 Nm).

11. If the spacer was missing or damaged, clean the contacts on the sensor with a clean shop towel. Remove the spacer strip completely if loose or torn. After the sensor is loosely held in position by the retaining bolt, use a brass feeler gauge to set the air gap from the sensor to the tone wheel. Correct air gap is 0.030–0.036 in. (0.76–0.91mm). Tighten the retaining bolt to 11 ft. lbs. (14 Nm) and recheck the air gap with the feeler gauge.

➡Use of a brass or non-magnetic gauge is required. Do not use common steel feelers; the small magnets within the sensor may be damaged. Correct air gap is critical to the proper operation of the sensor.

12. Route the sensor wire to the rear seat area and feed through the access hole. Seat the sensor wire grommets in the floorpan.

13. Use new wire ties to secure the sensor wiring to the brake lines and rear axle. Make certain that the wiring is clear of all moving and/or hot components.

14. Install the brake drum and wheel. Lower the vehicle to the ground.

15. Within the car, connect the sensor to the ABS harness. Reposition the seat and carpet.

Booster Pump and Motor

TESTING

▶ **See Figures 103 and 104**

1. Turn the ignition key to the **ON** position.

2. If the booster pump and motor does not run continuously, check the relay. If the pump and motor does run continuously, inspect the brake lines and fluid level carefully. If any fluid leaks are found, repair then add fluid as necessary.

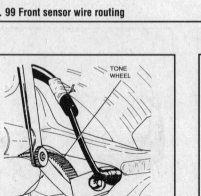

Fig. 100 Adjusting the sensor-to-tone wheel air gap

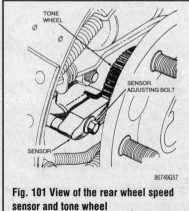

Fig. 101 View of the rear wheel speed sensor and tone wheel

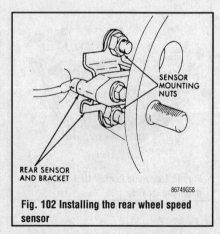

Fig. 102 Installing the rear wheel speed sensor

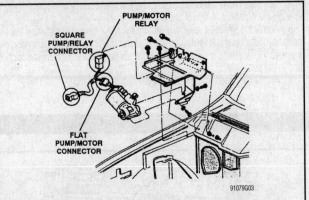

Fig. 103 Location of the booster pump/motor, connectors and relay

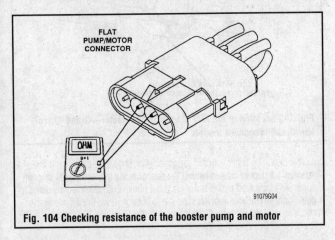

Fig. 104 Checking resistance of the booster pump and motor

3. Disengage the flat booster pump/motor wiring harness connector. Inspect the condition of the connector and repair as necessary.

4. Using an ohmmeter, check the resistance between cavities B and C of the connector on the component side.

5. If the resistance measures below 10 ohms, replace the booster pump and motor assembly.

REMOVAL & INSTALLATION

♦ **See Figures 105, 106 and 107**

❋❋ CAUTION

This brake system uses hydraulic accumulators, which, when fully charged, contain brake fluid at very high pressure. Before disconnecting any components, hydraulic lines, hoses or fittings, be certain that the accumulator pressure is completely relieved. Failure to

depressurize the system may result in personal injury and/or vehicle damage.

1. Depressurize the brake system
2. Disconnect the negative battery cable.
3. Remove the strap holding the coolant reservoir bottle and move the bottle aside. The hoses may be left attached; moving the bottle allows better access.
4. Remove the bolts holding the 2-piece mounting bracket to the firewall and inner fender panels.
5. Move or rotate the bracket with the pump assembly to one side for access to the wiring and hoses. Disconnect the pump motor wiring harness from the engine harness.
6. Slowly loosen the high pressure line at the pump and allow any residual high pressure to bleed off. Wear eye protection and wrap the joint in a clean shop towel to suppress any spray. Disconnect the line from the pump.
7. Place a container or catch pan under the return line to the pump. Loosen the hose clamp and remove the line. Do not reuse the brake fluid which drains from the line.
8. Remove the pump/motor and bracket as a complete assembly.
9. Remove the screw holding the relay to the bracket. Remove the screws holding the pump and motor to the bracket and remove the bracket.

To install:

10. Position the pump assembly onto the bracket and install the assembly attaching screws. Attach the pump/motor to the mounting bracket and attach the pump relay to the mounting bracket.
11. Connect the high-pressure and return lines to the pump.
12. Connect the electrical harness from the pump to the engine harness.
13. Place the bracket with the pump/motor and relay in place and install the retaining bolts.
14. Inspect the high-pressure and return lines; make certain they are not kinked or touching the engine.
15. Fill the master cylinder to the MAX level.
16. Connect the negative battery cable.
17. Turn the ignition switch **ON**; the pump should start running. Listen for a drop in pump rpm; this shows the pump is pressurizing the system. If there is no drop in pump rpm within 20 seconds, immediately shut the ignition **OFF** and check for hydraulic leaks.

➥**Severe pump damage will result if the pump runs without pressurizing the system for any length of time.**

18. Add fluid to the reservoir as necessary. Do not overfill.
19. Reposition and secure the coolant reservoir.

Bleeding The ABS System

1. Fill the reservoir to the MAX mark with clean, fresh brake fluid.
2. The brake system must be bled in the correct order. For all vehicles, the wheel order is: right rear, left rear, right front, left front. For 1991 vehicles, the master cylinder/power booster must be bled before the wheels are bled.
3. For 1991 vehicles, bleed the master cylinder/booster assembly. Loosen and bleed the brake lines at the side of the modulator one at a time. Have a helper turn the ignition **ON** and operate the brake pedal in the usual manner

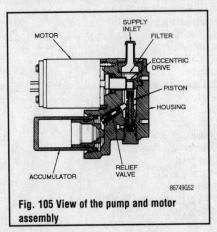

Fig. 105 View of the pump and motor assembly

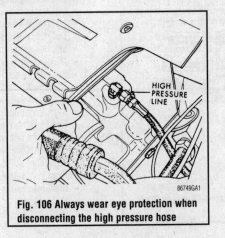

Fig. 106 Always wear eye protection when disconnecting the high pressure hose

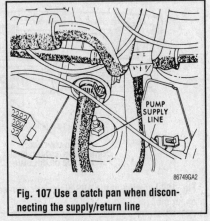

Fig. 107 Use a catch pan when disconnecting the supply/return line

while each line is loosened, bled and re-tightened. Bleed each circuit until the fluid is clear and free of air bubbles.

4. Attach a clear plastic bleed hose to the caliper or wheel cylinder fitting. Place the other end of the hose in a clear container of fresh brake fluid. Make certain the hose end is submerged in the fluid.

5. Turn the ignition switch **ON** to cycle the pump.

6. Have an assistant apply and hold brake pedal pressure to pressurize the system.

7. Open the bleed screw 1/2 turn. Close the bleed screw when the fluid entering the container is free of bubbles.

8. Check the reservoir level and refill to the MAX mark. Do not allow the master cylinder reservoir to run dry while bleeding. If the reservoir runs dry, air re-enters the system; the pump may be severely damaged if a constant supply of fluid is not available.

9. Repeat the bleeding procedure at the remaining wheels.

TEVES MK-IV ANTI-LOCK BRAKE SYSTEM (ABS)

General Information

▶ **See Figure 108**

The Jeep Anti-lock Brake System (ABS) used on 1992–94 models is an electronically operated, all wheel brake control system. Major components include the master cylinder, vacuum power brake booster, Electronic Control Unit (ECU), Hydraulic Control Unit (HCU) and various control sensors.

The brake system is a three channel design. The front brakes are controlled individually and the rear brakes in tandem.

The system is designed to retard wheel lockup during periods of high wheel slip when braking. Retarding wheel lockup is accomplished by modulating fluid pressure to the wheel brake units.

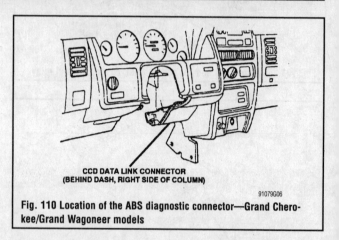

**CCD DATA LINK CONNECTOR
(BEHIND DASH, RIGHT SIDE OF COLUMN)**

91079G06

Fig. 110 Location of the ABS diagnostic connector—Grand Cherokee/Grand Wagoneer models

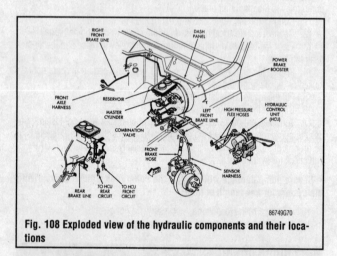

Fig. 108 Exploded view of the hydraulic components and their locations

Diagnosis and Testing

▶ **See Figures 109 and 110**

After performing the preliminary visual checks, observe the behavior and timing of the dashboard warning lamps. Their function, when used in diagnostics, can point to possible causes and eliminate others.

Use the DRB scan tool with the correct cartridge to determine the specific

circuit at fault. The tester with the correct adapter should be engaged to the diagnostic connector, located behind the dashboard to the right of the steering column. Any fault read by the tester on initial hook-up should be considered as a guide only. After initial repairs, clear the fault code, drive the vehicle and recheck for any stored code. Once the fault is identified, the DRB may be used to test or energize system components.

Trouble Code Displays

The following is a list of the ABS system trouble code the DRB may display for 1992–94 Jeep models:

- Controller failure
- G switch not processable
- Hydraulic failure
- Left front inlet valve
- Left front outlet valve
- Left front sensor circuit failure
- Left front sensor continuity (greater than) 25 MPH
- Left front sensor continuity (less than) 25 MPH
- Left front sensor signal missing
- Left front wheel speed comparison
- Rear inlet valve
- Rear outlet valve
- Left rear sensor circuit failure
- Left rear sensor continuity (greater than) 25 MPH
- Left rear sensor continuity (less than) 25 MPH
- Left rear sensor signal missing
- Left rear wheel speed comparison
- Main relay/power circuit failure
- Pedal travel sensor circuit
- Pump motor circuit not working properly
- Right front inlet valve
- Right front outlet valve
- Right front sensor circuit failure
- Right front sensor continuity (greater than) 25 MPH
- Right front sensor continuity (less than) 25 MPH
- Right front sensor signal missing
- Right front wheel speed comparison
- Right rear sensor circuit failure
- Right rear sensor continuity (greater than) 25 MPH
- Right rear sensor continuity (less than)25 MPH

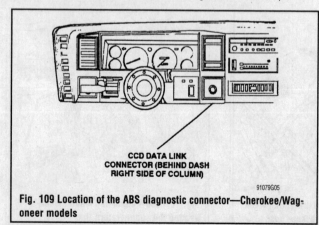

**CCD DATA LINK
CONNECTOR (BEHIND DASH
RIGHT SIDE OF COLUMN)**

91079G05

Fig. 109 Location of the ABS diagnostic connector—Cherokee/Wagoneer models

- Right rear sensor signal missing
- Right rear wheel speed comparison
- DRB II "No Response" message
- System verification test

Accelerator Sensor

REMOVAL & INSTALLATION

▶ See Figure 111

1. Tilt the rear seat forward to gain access to the sensor.
2. Disengage the sensor harness and unfasten the screws attaching the sensor to the bracket. Remove the sensor from the vehicle.

To install:

➡**Note the position of the locating arrow on the sensor. The sensor must be positioned so that the arrow faces forward.**

3. Install the sensor in the bracket and tighten the screws to 17–32 inch lbs. (2–4 Nm).
4. Engage the harness sensor and move the seat back to its normal position.

Pedal Travel Sensor

REMOVAL & INSTALLATION

▶ See Figure 112

➡**The pedal travel sensor and booster must form a matched set. The cap on the sensor and on the booster shell are color coded for identification, and to ensure that they are used as matched sets. Be sure the color of the sensor cap and the color dot on the booster shell are the**

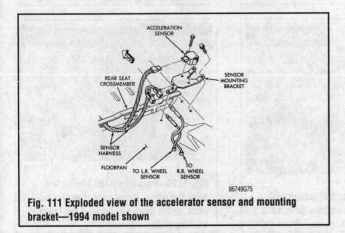

Fig. 111 Exploded view of the accelerator sensor and mounting bracket—1994 model shown

same before installation.

1. Disengage the wires at the sensor and pump the brake pedal until all vacuum is depleted from the booster.
2. Unseat the sensor retaining ring and remove the sensor from the booster.

To install:

3. Check the color dot on the face of the brake booster. Then check the color cap on the sensor plunger. If the colors match, proceed with the installation. If the colors do not match, install the correct color cap on the end of the plunger.
4. Install the O-ring on the sensor.
5. Install the sensor retaining ring on the booster flange and insert the sensor in the retaining ring and booster.
6. Verify that the sensor is properly engaged, then connect the sensor wires.

Electronic Control Unit (ECU)

REMOVAL & INSTALLATION

▶ See Figure 113

1. Turn the ignition **OFF** and remove the screws securing the ECU to the mounting bracket.
2. Disengage the ECU wiring harness and remove the ECU.

To install:

➡**IF a new ECU is to be installed, transfer the mounting bracket to the new ECU. Tighten the ECU-to-mounting bracket screws to 75–115 inch lbs. (8–13 Nm).**

3. Engage the wire harness to the ECU. Install the the ECU. Tighten the fasteners to 85–125 inch lbs. (10–14 Nm).
4. Test drive the vehicle and verify proper brake operation.

Speed Sensors

TESTING

▶ See Figure 114

1. Check the wheel speed sensor air gap using a brass feeler gauge. On the rear sensors, if the air gap measures out of specifications, adjust to the correct specifications. On the front sensors, if the air gap measures out of specifications, the sensor is broken or loose.
2. Disengage the speed sensor wiring harness connector. Inspect the condition of the connector and repair if necessary.
3. Using an ohmmeter, measure the resistance between the wheel speed sensor connector terminals.
4. The resistance should measure between 900–1300 ohms. If the resistance measures outside this value, replace the wheel speed sensor.

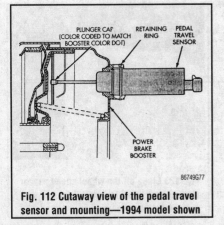

Fig. 112 Cutaway view of the pedal travel sensor and mounting—1994 model shown

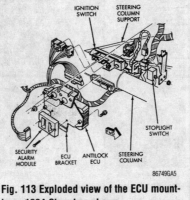

Fig. 113 Exploded view of the ECU mounting—1994 Cherokee shown

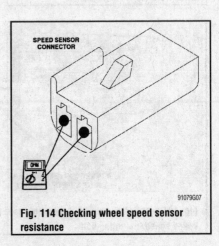

Fig. 114 Checking wheel speed sensor resistance

REMOVAL & INSTALLATION

Front

▶ See Figures 115, 116, 117 and 118

1. Raise the vehicle and safely support it with jackstands.
2. Turn the wheel outward.
3. Disengage the sensor wire and clean the sensor and surrounding area.
4. Unfasten the sensor attaching bolt
5. Remove the grommet retaining the sensor wire in the wheel house panel.
6. Disengage the sensor wire from the harness plug in the engine compartment and remove the sensor.

To install:

➡There is no front sensor air gap adjustment. The air gap should be 0.057–0.051 in. (0.04–1.30mm). If the air gap is incorrect, the sensor is broken or loose.

7. Install the sensor on the steering knuckle, apply Loctite® to the sensor bolt and tighten the bolt finger-tight only.
8. Tighten the bolt to 11 ft. lbs. (14 Nm) and attach the sensor wire to the steering knuckle with grommets.
9. Route the sensor wire to its original locations.
10. Seat the sensor wire grommet in the body panel and clip the wire to the brake line at the grommet location.
11. Engage the sensor wire to the harness in the engine compartment.
12. Lower the vehicle.

Rear

▶ See Figures 119 thru 124

1. Raise and fold the rear seat to gain access to the rear sensor connectors.
2. Disengage the sensors at the rear harness connectors and push the sensor grommets and wires through the floorpan.
3. Raise the vehicle and support it with jackstands.

Fig. 115 Location of the front ABS wheel speed sensor (1) in the steering knuckle and sensor tone ring (2)

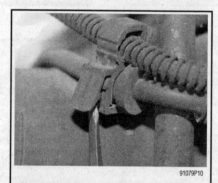

Fig. 116 Remove the speed sensor mounting bolt . . .

Fig. 117 . . . then remove the sensor from the steering knuckle

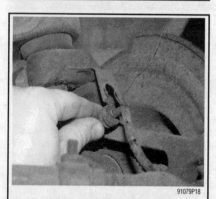

Fig. 118 Disengage the speed sensor wires from the routing brackets

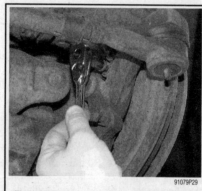

Fig. 119 Using a small flat bladed tool, pry open the plastic retainers to free the speed sensor wiring harness

Fig. 120 Using a small flat bladed tool, push the wheel speed sensor wiring harness rubber grommet through the brake backing plate

Fig. 121 Using a box wrench, loosen the speed sensor mounting bolt

Fig. 122 Remove the speed sensor by passing it throiugh the backing plate hole

Fig. 123 Clean off the wheel speed sensor with a shop rag and inspect it for damage, corrosion or excessive wear

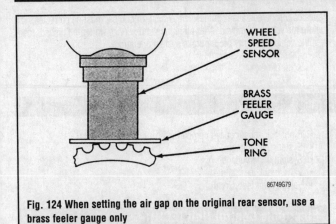

Fig. 124 When setting the air gap on the original rear sensor, use a brass feeler gauge only

4. Disengage the sensor wires at the rear axle connectors. Remove the wheels.

5. Remove the brake drum and the clips securing the sensor wires to the brake lines, hoses and rear axle.

6. Unseat the sensor support plate grommet and unfasten the bolt securing the sensor to the bracket. Remove the sensor from the vehicle.

To install:

7. Insert the sensor wire through the support plate hole and seat the sensor grommet in the support plate.

8. Apply Loctite® to the bolt and install the sensor. Fasten the bolt finger-tight only at this time.

9. Set the sensor air gap as follows:

a. If installing the original sensor, remove any remaining pieces of cardboard from the pickup face. Then, using a brass feeler gauge, adjust the gap to 0.043 in. (1.1mm).

b. Tighten the sensor retaining bolt to 11 ft. lbs. (14 Nm).

c. If installing a new sensor, push the cardboard spacer on the sensor face against the tone face.

d. Tighten the sensor retaining bolt to 6 ft. lbs. (8 Nm). The correct air gap will be established as the tone ring rotates and peels the spacer off the sensor face.

10. Route the sensor wires to the rear seat area. Feed the wires through the floorpan and install the sensor grommets.

11. Secure the sensor wires with the retaining clips located on the brake hoses, lines and rear axle.

12. Install the brake drum and wheel and lower the vehicle.

13. Engage the sensor wire to harness connector and return the carpet and seat to their proper position.

Hydraulic Control Unit (HCU)

REMOVAL & INSTALLATION

♦ See Figure 125

➡A Diagnostic Readout Box (DRB II), or the equivalent type of scan tool, is essential to perform the bleeding of the ABS system.

1. Remove the air cleaner and the clamp that secures the air cleaner hose and pipe to the fender apron.

2. Place a suitable size drain container under the master cylinder reservoir hoses and disengage the reservoir hoses from the HCU.

3. Remove the reservoir and disengage the pump motor and solenoid harness wires at the HCU.

4. Tag and disconnect the HCU hydraulic lines at the HCU.

5. Move the HCU harness and air cleaner hose pipe aside for access to the HCU bracket fasteners and remove the fasteners.

6. Remove the HCU, being careful not to damage the brake lines or master cylinder.

To install:

7. Engage the reservoir hoses to the HCU pipes and position the HCU assembly on the bracket. Tighten the fasteners to 92–112 inch lbs. (10–13 Nm).

8. Install and tighten the HCU hydraulic lines. Check the lines and hose routing so that they are clear of engine components and have no kinks.

Fig. 125 HCU is located on the left side of the engine compartment next to the brake master cylinder. (1) HCU pump motor harness and (2) HCU solenoid harness connector locations are shown

9. Fill the master cylinder with DOT 3 brake fluid and bleed the brake system. Refer to the bleeding procedure for this system in this section.

10. Install the air cleaner and hoses. Fasten the air cleaner hose to the fender apron with the clamp.

11. Test drive the vehicle and test for proper brake operation.

Bleeding The ABS System

➡A Diagnostic Readout Box (DRB II), or the equivalent type of scan tool, is essential to perform the bleeding of the ABS system.

The brake system must be bled any time air is permitted to enter the system through loosened or disconnected lines or hoses, or anytime the modulator is removed. Excessive air within the system will cause a soft or spongy feel in the brake pedal.

When bleeding any part of the system, the reservoir must remain as close to full as possible at all times. Check the level frequently and top off fluid as needed.

This is basically a three step process consisting of: a conventional manual bleeding procedure, a second bleeding procedure using a DRB II, followed by a repeat of the first bleeding procedure.

1. Clean around the reservoir cap and remove the cap. Fill the master cylinder with the recommended fluid.

2. The recommended bleeding sequence is: master cylinder, HCU valve body (at the fluid lines), right rear wheel, left rear wheel, right front wheel and left front wheel.

3. Clean all the bleeder screws. You may want to give each one a shot of penetrating solvent to loosen it; seizure is a common problem with bleeder screws, which then break off, sometimes requiring replacement of the part to which they are attached.

➡Brake fluid absorbs moisture from the air. Don't leave the master cylinder or the fluid container uncovered any longer than necessary. Be careful handling the fluid; spilled fluid will damage the vehicle's paint.

Check the level of the fluid often when bleeding, and refill the reservoirs as necessary. Don't let them run dry, or you will have to repeat the process.

4. Attach a length of clear vinyl tubing to the bleeder screw on the wheel cylinder. Insert the other end of the tube into a clear, clean jar half filled with brake fluid.

5. Have your assistant slowly depress the brake pedal. As this is done, open the bleeder screw until the brake fluid starts to flow through the tube. Then, close the bleeder screw when the brake pedal reaches the end of its travel. After the bleeder valve is fully closed, have your assistant slowly release the pedal. Repeat this process until no air bubbles appear in the expelled fluid.

6. Repeat the procedure on the other three brake cylinders/calipers, checking the level of brake fluid in the master cylinder reservoir often.

7. Perform the "Bleed Brake" procedure with the DRB II scan tool:

a. Engage the DRB II scan tool to the diagnostic connector.

b. Run the test as described in the manufacturers tester manual.

8. Repeat the manual bleeding procedure as outlined in Steps 1 through 6. Check and replenish the master cylinder fluid level if necessary.

After finishing, there should be no feeling of sponginess in the brake pedal. If there is, either there is still air in the line, in which case the process must be repeated, or there is a leak somewhere, which, of course, must be corrected before the vehicle is moved. After all repairs and service work are finished, road test the vehicle to verify proper brake system operation.

TEVES MK-IVG ANTI-LOCK BRAKE SYSTEM (ABS)

General Information

The Jeep Anti-lock Brake System (ABS) used on 1995 and later models is an electronically operated, all wheel brake control system. Major components include the master cylinder, vacuum power brake booster, Electronic Control Unit (ECU), Hydraulic Control Unit (HCU) and various control sensors.

The brake system is a three channel design. The front brakes are controlled individually and the rear brakes in tandem.

The system is designed to retard wheel lockup during periods of high wheel slip when braking. Retarding wheel lockup is accomplished by modulating fluid pressure to the wheel brake units.

Diagnosis and Testing

▶ **See Figures 109 and 110**

After performing the preliminary visual checks, observe the behavior and timing of the dashboard warning lamps. Their function, when used in diagnostics, can point to possible causes and eliminate others.

Use the DRB scan tool with the correct cartridge to determine the specific circuit at fault. The tester with the correct adapter should be engaged to the diagnostic connector, located behind the dashboard to the right of the steering column. Any fault read by the tester on initial hook-up should be considered as a guide only. After initial repairs, clear the fault code, drive the vehicle and recheck for any stored code. Once the fault is identified, the DRB may be used to test or energize system components.

Trouble Code Displays

The following is a list of the ABS system trouble codes the DRB may display for 1995 and later Jeep models:
- Diagnostic compare
- G switch not processable
- Left front inlet valve
- Left front outlet valve
- Left front sensor circuit failure
- Left front sensor continuity (less than) 25 MPH
- Left front sensor continuity (greater than) 25 MPH
- Left front sensor signal missing
- Left front sensor speed comparison
- Left rear sensor circuit failure
- Left rear sensor continuity (less than) 25 MPH
- Left rear sensor continuity (greater than) 25 MPH
- Left rear sensor signal missing
- Left rear sensor speed comparison
- Pump motor circuit not working properly
- Pump motor not running
- Rear inlet valve
- Rear outlet valve
- Right front inlet valve
- Right front outlet valve
- Right front sensor circuit failure
- Right front sensor continuity (less than) 25 MPH
- Right front sensor continuity (greater than) 25 MPH
- Right front sensor signal missing
- Right front sensor speed comparison
- Right rear sensor circuit failure
- Right rear sensor continuity (less than) 25 MPH
- Right rear sensor continuity (greater than) 25 MPH
- Right rear sensor signal missing
- Right rear sensor speed comparison
- System overvoltage
- System undervoltage
- Valve block feed failure
- Valve power feed circuit

Electronic Control Unit (ECU)

➡**The Electronic Control Unit (ECU) was utilized on the 1995–96 models. The Hydraulic Control Unit (HCU) on 1997 and later Jeep models has a Controller Antilock Brakes (CAB) unit mounted to it, which serves the same function as the ABS-ECU.**

REMOVAL & INSTALLATION

▶ **See Figure 126**

The Electronic Control Unit (ECU) is usually located in the engine compartment, mounted on the driver's side inner fender panel.
1. Turn the ignition to the **OFF** position.
2. Remove the lower finish panel from the instrument panel.
3. Remove the ECU retaining bolts/nuts and release the metal strap that secures the ECU harness connector to the pin terminals.
4. Disengage the harness connector from the ECU. This is achieved by tilting the connector upward to disengage it from the pins and then sliding it out of the retaining tangs.
5. Remove the ECU and mounting bracket as an assembly.
To install:
6. If a new ECU is to be installed, first install the mounting bracket on the ECU and tighten the fasteners to 85–125 inch. lbs (10–14 Nm).

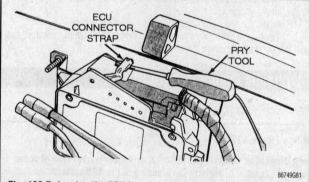

Fig. 126 Releasing the ECU harness connector strap—1995 model shown

❊❊ WARNING

Use care when connecting the harness connector to the ECU, the pins may be easily damaged.

7. Engage the harness connector to the ECU making sure it is fully seated and engages the tangs on the ECU.
8. Position the ECU bracket under the dash and install the retainers. Tighten the retainers to 75–125 inch lbs. (8–14 Nm).
9. Install the finish panel on the instrument panel.

Accelerator Sensor

REMOVAL & INSTALLATION

▶ **See Figure 127**

1. Tilt the rear seat forward to gain access to the sensor.
2. Disengage the sensor harness and unfasten the screws attaching the sensor to the bracket. Remove the sensor from the vehicle.

To install:

➡**Note the position of the locating arrow on the sensor. The sensor must be positioned so that the arrow faces forward.**

3. Install the sensor in the bracket and tighten the screws to 17–32 inch lbs. (2–4 Nm).
4. Engage the harness sensor and move the seat back to its normal position.

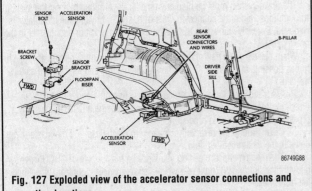

Fig. 127 Exploded view of the accelerator sensor connections and mounting locations

Speed Sensors

TESTING

▶ **See Figure 114**

1. Check the wheel speed sensor air gap using a brass feeler gauge. On the rear sensors, if the air gap measures out of specifications, adjust to the correct specifications. On the front sensors, if the air gap measures out of specifications, the sensor is broken or loose.
2. Disengage the speed sensor wiring harness connector. Inspect the condition of the connector and repair if necessary.
3. Using an ohmmeter, measure the resistance between the wheel speed sensor connector terminals.

4. The resistance should measure between 900–1300 ohms. If the resistance measures outside this value, replace the wheel speed sensor.

REMOVAL & INSTALLATION

Front

▶ **See Figures 128 and 129**

1. Raise the vehicle and support it with jackstands.
2. Turn the wheel outward.
3. Disengage the sensor wire and clean the sensor and surrounding area.
4. Unfasten the sensor attaching bolt
5. Remove the grommet retaining the sensor wire in the wheel house panel.
6. Disengage the sensor wire from the harness plug in the engine compartment and remove the sensor.

To install:

➡**There is no front sensor air gap adjustment. The air gap should be 0.057–0.051 in. (0.04–1.30mm). If the air gap is incorrect, the sensor is broken or loose.**

7. Install the sensor on the steering knuckle, apply Loctite® to the sensor bolt and tighten the bolt finger-tight only.
8. Tighten the bolt to 11 ft. lbs. (14 Nm) and attach the sensor wire to the steering knuckle with grommets.
9. Route the sensor wire to its original locations.
10. Seat the sensor wire grommet in the body panel and clip the wire to the brake line at the grommet location.
11. Engage the sensor wire to the harness in the engine compartment.
12. Lower the vehicle.

Rear

▶ **See Figure 130**

1. Raise and fold the rear seat to gain access to the rear sensor connectors.
2. Disengage the sensors at the rear harness connectors and push the sensor grommets and wires through the floorpan.
3. Raise the vehicle and support it with jackstands.
4. Disengage the sensor wires at the rear axle connectors. Remove the wheels.
5. Remove the brake drum and the clips securing the sensor wires to the brake lines, hoses and rear axle.
6. Unseat the sensor support plate grommet and unfasten the bolt securing the sensor to the bracket. Remove the sensor from the vehicle.

To install:

7. Insert the sensor wire through the support plate hole and seat the sensor grommet in the support plate.
8. Apply Loctite® to the bolt and install the sensor. Fasten the bolt finger-tight only at this time.
9. Set the sensor air gap as follows:
   a. If installing the original sensor, remove any remaining pieces of cardboard from the pickup face. Then using a brass feeler gauge adjust the gap to 0.043 in. (1.1mm).

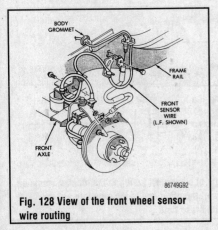

Fig. 128 View of the front wheel sensor wire routing

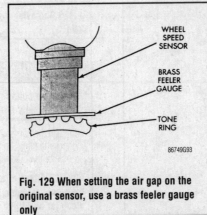

Fig. 129 When setting the air gap on the original sensor, use a brass feeler gauge only

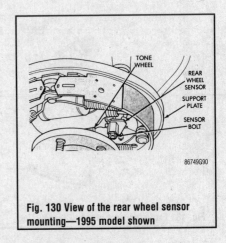

Fig. 130 View of the rear wheel sensor mounting—1995 model shown

b. Tighten the sensor retaining bolt to 11 ft. lbs. (14 Nm).

c. If installing a new sensor, push the cardboard spacer on the sensor face against the tone face.

d. Tighten the sensor retaining bolt to 6 ft. lbs. (8 Nm). The correct air gap will be established as the tone ring rotates and peels the spacer off the sensor face.

10. Route the sensor wires to the rear seat area. Feed the wires through the floorpan and install the sensor grommets.

11. Secure the sensor wires with the retaining clips located on the brake hoses, lines and rear axle.

12. Install the brake drum and wheel and lower the vehicle.

13. Engage the sensor wire to harness connector and return the carpet and seat to their proper position.

Hydraulic Control Unit (HCU)

→The Hydraulic Control Unit (HCU) on 1997 and later Jeep models also has the Controller Antilock Brakes (CAB) unit mounted to it. It serves the same function as the ABS-ECU does on 1995–96 models. The HCU/CAB is removed as an assembly.

REMOVAL & INSTALLATION

▶ See Figure 131

→A Diagnostic Readout Box (DRB), or the equivalent type of scan tool, is essential to perform the bleeding of the ABS system.

1. Disengage the vent hoses and air cleaner cover.
2. Loosen the clamp securing the air cleaner hose to the intake manifold and slide the clamp out of the way.
3. Remove the air cleaner cover, hose and filter.
4. Unfasten the air cleaner housing to panel bolts and nut, then remove the air cleaner housing.
5. Disengage the flex lines at the HCU.
6. Disengage the HCU solenoid harness from the main harness and the HCU pump motor harness.
7. Disengage the brake lines at the lower left side of the HCU.
8. If removing the HCU only:

a. Remove the HCU solenoid by squeezing the connector fasteners with needle nose pliers then pulling them out of the bracket.

b. Unfasten the shoulder bolts attaching HCU to the bracket and remove the HCU.

9. If removing the HCU and bracket:

a. Unfasten the fasteners retaining the HCU to the bracket and remove the HCU.

To install:

10. If only the HCU was removed:

a. Install the HCU in the bracket and tighten the shoulder bolts.

b. Install the HCU solenoid by pressing the connector fasteners into the bracket.

11. If installing the HCU and bracket as an assembly:

a. Install the bracket on the studs and tighten the fasteners to 92–112 inch lbs. (10–13 Nm).

12. Engage the HCU pump motor and solenoid harnesses.

13. Start the brake line fittings into the HCU by hand to avoid cross-threading and then tighten the fittings until they are snug.

14. Start the flex line fittings into the HCU by hand to avoid cross-threading and then tighten the fittings until they are snug.

15. Bleed the brake system. Refer to the proper procedure in this section.

16. Tighten the brake line fittings to 130–160 inch lbs. (15–18 Nm) at the HCU and master cylinder, and 160–210 inch lbs. (18–24 Nm) at the combination valve.

17. Install the air cleaner assembly, hoses and vacuum lines to the manifold.

18. Check the brake pedal action before moving the vehicle and bleed the brakes again if the pedal is not firm, (soft or spongy).

19. Test drive the vehicle and verify proper brake operation.

Bleeding The ABS System

▶ See Figure 132

→A Diagnostic Readout Box (DRB), or the equivalent type of scan tool, is essential to perform the bleeding of the ABS system.

The brake system must be bled any time air is permitted to enter the system through loosened or disconnected lines or hoses, or anytime the modulator is removed. Excessive air within the system will cause a soft or spongy feel in the brake pedal.

When bleeding any part of the system, the reservoir must remain as close to full as possible at all times. Check the level frequently and top off fluid as needed.

This is basically a three step process consisting of: a conventional manual bleeding procedure, a second bleeding procedure using a DRB, followed by a repeat of the first bleeding procedure.

1. Clean around the reservoir cap and remove the cap. Fill the master cylinder with the recommended fluid.

2. The recommended bleeding sequence is: master cylinder, HCU valve body (at the fluid lines), right rear wheel, left rear wheel, right front wheel and left front wheel.

3. Clean all the bleeder screws. You may want to give each one a shot of penetrating solvent to loosen it; seizure is a common problem with bleeder screws, which then break off, sometimes requiring replacement of the part to which they are attached.

→Brake fluid absorbs moisture from the air. Don't leave the master cylinder or the fluid container uncovered any longer than necessary. Be careful handling the fluid—it will damage the vehicle's paint.

Check the level of the fluid often when bleeding, and refill the reservoirs as necessary. Don't let them run dry, or you will have to repeat the process.

4. Attach a length of clear vinyl tubing to the bleeder screw on the wheel cylinder. Insert the other end of the tube into a clear, clean jar half filled with brake fluid.

5. Have your assistant slowly depress the brake pedal. As this is done, open the bleeder screw until the brake fluid starts to flow through the tube. Then, close the bleeder screw when the brake pedal reaches the end of its travel. After the bleeder valve is fully closed, have your assistant slowly release the pedal. Repeat this process until no air bubbles appear in the expelled fluid.

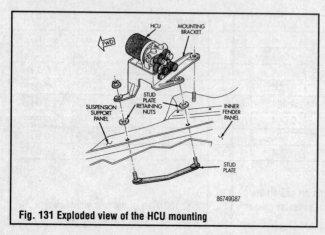

86749G87

Fig. 131 Exploded view of the HCU mounting

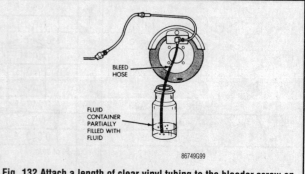

86749G99

Fig. 132 Attach a length of clear vinyl tubing to the bleeder screw on the wheel cylinder. Insert the other end of the tube into a clear, clean jar half filled with brake fluid

6. Repeat the procedure on the other three brake cylinders/calipers, check-ing the lever of brake fluid in the master cylinder reservoir often.

7. Perform the "Bleed Brake" procedure with the DRB scan tool:
   a. Engage the DRB scan tool to the diagnostic connector.
   b. Run the test as described in the tester manual.

8. Repeat the manual bleeding procedure as outlined in Steps 1 through 6. Check and replenish the master cylinder fluid level if necessary.

After finishing, there should be no feeling of sponginess in the brake pedal. If there is, either there is still air in the line, in which case the process must be repeated, or there is a leak somewhere, which, of course, must be corrected before the vehicle is moved. After all repairs and service work are finished, road test the vehicle to verify proper brake system operation.

BRAKE SPECIFICATIONS
All measurements in inches unless noted

| Year | Model | Master Cylinder Bore | Brake Disc | | | Brake Drum Diameter | | | Minimum Lining Thickness | |
			Original Thicknes	Minimum Thickness	Maximum Runout	Original Inside Diameter	Max. Wear Limit	Maximum Machine Diameter	Front	Rear
1984	Cherokee	0.937	NA	0.815	0.004	NA	1	NA	0.031	0.031
	Comanche	0.937	NA	0.815	0.004	NA	1	NA	0.031	0.031
	Wagoneer	0.937	NA	0.815	0.004	NA	1	NA	0.031	0.031
1985	Cherokee	0.937	NA	0.815	0.004	NA	1	NA	0.031	0.031
	Comanche	0.937	NA	0.815	0.004	NA	1	NA	0.031	0.031
	Wagoneer	0.937	NA	0.815	0.004	NA	1	NA	0.031	0.031
1986	Cherokee	0.937	NA	0.815	0.004	NA	1	NA	0.031	0.031
	Comanche	0.937	NA	0.815	0.004	NA	1	NA	0.031	0.031
	Wagoneer	0.937	NA	0.815	0.004	NA	1	NA	0.031	0.031
1987	Cherokee	0.937	NA	0.815	0.004	NA	1	NA	0.031	0.031
	Comanche	0.937	NA	0.815	0.004	NA	1	NA	0.031	0.031
	Wagoneer	0.937	NA	0.815	0.004	NA	1	NA	0.031	0.031
1988	Cherokee	0.937	NA	0.815	0.004	NA	1	NA	0.031	0.031
	Comanche	0.937	NA	0.815	0.004	NA	1	NA	0.031	0.031
	Wagoneer	0.937	NA	0.815	0.004	NA	1	NA	0.031	0.031
1989	Cherokee	0.937	NA	0.815	0.004	NA	1	NA	0.031	0.031
	Comanche	0.937	NA	0.815	0.004	NA	1	NA	0.031	0.031
	Wagoneer	0.937	NA	0.815	0.004	NA	1	NA	0.031	0.031
1990	Cherokee	0.937	NA	0.860 [2]	0.004	NA	1	NA	0.031	0.031
	Comanche	0.937	NA	0.860 [2]	0.004	NA	1	NA	0.031	0.031
	Wagoneer	0.937	NA	0.860 [2]	0.004	NA	1	NA	0.031	0.031
1991	Cherokee	0.937	NA	0.860 [3]	0.004	NA	1	NA	0.031	0.031
	Comanche	0.937	NA	0.860 [3]	0.004	NA	1	NA	0.031	0.031
1992	Cherokee	0.937	NA	0.860 [3]	0.004	NA	1	NA	0.031	0.031
	Comanche	0.937	NA	0.860 [3]	0.004	NA	1	NA	0.031	0.031
1993	Cherokee	0.937	NA	0.860 [3]	0.004	NA	1	NA	0.031	0.031
	Grand Cherokee	NA	0.940 [4]	0.890	0.004	-		-	0.031	0.031
	Grand Wagoneer	NA	0.940 [4]	0.890	0.004	-		-	0.031	0.031
1994	Cherokee	0.937	NA	0.860 [3]	0.004	9.00	1	9.06	0.031	0.031
	Grand Cherokee	NA	0.940 [4]	0.890	0.004	-		-	0.031	0.031
1995	Cherokee	0.937	NA	0.860 [3]	0.004	9.00	1	9.06	0.031	0.031
	Grand Cherokee	NA	0.940 [4]	0.890	0.004	-		-	0.031	0.031
1996	Cherokee	0.937	NA	0.860 [3]	0.004	9.00	1	9.06	0.031	0.031
	Grand Cherokee	NA	0.940 [4]	0.890	0.004	-		-	0.031	0.031
1997	Cherokee	0.937	NA	0.860 [3]	0.004	9.00	1	9.06	0.031	0.031
	Grand Cherokee	NA	0.940 [4]	0.890	0.004	-		-	0.031	0.031
1998 [5]	Cherokee	0.937	NA	0.860 [6]	0.004	9.00	1	9.06	0.031	0.031
	Grand Cherokee	NA	0.940 [4]	0.890	0.004	-		-	0.031	0.031

1: Maximum wear limit is listed on outside of drum
2: 0.940 with 4WD
3: 0.890 with 4WD
4: Rear rotor original thickness is 0.370
5: And 1999 and later Cherokee
6: Refer to the minimum thickness dimension stamped into the disc

91079C01

Troubleshooting the Brake System

Problem	Cause	Solution
Low brake pedal (excessive pedal travel required for braking action.)	· Excessive clearance between rear linings and drums caused by inoperative automatic adjusters	· Make 10 to 15 alternate forward and reverse brake stops to adjust brakes. If brake pedal does not come up, repair or replace adjuster parts as necessary.
	· Worn rear brakelining	· Inspect and replace lining if worn beyond minimum thickness specification
	· Bent, distorted brakeshoes, front or rear	· Replace brakeshoes in axle sets
	· Air in hydraulic system	· Remove air from system. Refer to Brake Bleeding.
Low brake pedal (pedal may go to floor with steady pressure applied.)	· Fluid leak in hydraulic system	· Fill master cylinder to fill line; have helper apply brakes and check calipers, wheel cylinders, differential valve tubes, hoses and fittings for leaks. Repair or replace as necessary.
	· Air in hydraulic system	· Remove air from system. Refer to Brake Bleeding.
	· Incorrect or non-recommended brake fluid (fluid evaporates at below normal temp).	· Flush hydraulic system with clean brake fluid. Refill with correct-type fluid.
	· Master cylinder piston seals worn, or master cylinder bore is scored, worn or corroded	· Repair or replace master cylinder
Low brake pedal (pedal goes to floor on first application—o.k. on subsequent applications.)	· Disc brake pads sticking on abutment surfaces of anchor plate. Caused by a build-up of dirt, rust, or corrosion on abutment surfaces	· Clean abutment surfaces
Fading brake pedal (pedal height decreases with steady pressure applied.)	· Fluid leak in hydraulic system	· Fill master cylinder reservoirs to fill mark, have helper apply brakes, check calipers, wheel cylinders, differential valve, tubes, hoses, and fittings for fluid leaks. Repair or replace parts as necessary.
	· Master cylinder piston seals worn, or master cylinder bore is scored, worn or corroded	· Repair or replace master cylinder
Decreasing brake pedal travel (pedal travel required for braking action decreases and may be accompanied by a hard pedal.)	· Caliper or wheel cylinder pistons sticking or seized	· Repair or replace the calipers, or wheel cylinders
	· Master cylinder compensator ports blocked (preventing fluid return to reservoirs) or pistons sticking or seized in master cylinder bore	· Repair or replace the master cylinder
	· Power brake unit binding internally	· Test unit according to the following procedure: (a) Shift transmission into neutral and start engine (b) Increase engine speed to 1500 rpm, close throttle and fully depress brake pedal (c) Slow release brake pedal and stop engine (d) Have helper remove vacuum check valve and hose from power unit. Observe for backward movement of brake pedal. (e) If the pedal moves backward, the power unit has an internal bind—replace power unit

TCCA9C01

10

BODY AND TRIM

EXTERIOR

Doors

REMOVAL & INSTALLATION

▶ **See Figures 1, 2 and 3**

1. Disconnect the negative battery cable.
2. If necessary, remove the door trim panel and water shield to unplug any/all wiring harness connectors. Slide the wiring harness out of the door.
3. Matchmark the hinge-to-door position.
4. Have an assistant support the door.
5. Using a pair of pliers, remove the door stop-to-pillar pin.
6. Remove the hinge-to-door bolts, catch the shims, and lift off the door.

To install:

7. Position the door and shims, then install, but do not tighten the bolts.
8. Perform the door adjustment procedure, as described below. Tighten the front door hinge bolts to 26 ft. lbs. (35 Nm). Tighten the rear door hinge bolts to 26 ft. lbs. (35 Nm) on Cherokee/Wagoneer and 21 ft. lbs. (28 Nm) on Grand Cherokee.
9. Install the door stop-to-pillar pin. Spray a white lubricant on the hinge pivot points to eliminate any binding conditions. Open and close the door several times to be sure that the lubricant is evenly and thoroughly distributed.
10. Install and connect any/all wiring.
11. Spray a white lubricant on the hinge pivot points to eliminate any binding conditions. Open and close the door several times to be sure that the lubri-

cant is evenly and thoroughly distributed.

12. If removed earlier, install the water shield and door trim panel.
13. Connect the negative battery cable.

ADJUSTMENT

Except Grand Cherokee

▶ **See Figure 4**

Door adjustment is made by means of shims located between the door and the hinge plate. The shims are placed in hinge plates. Add or remove shims as necessary to obtain proper door fit. When adjustment is complete, torque the mounting bolts to 26 ft. lbs. (35 Nm).

➡**Be sure to apply a general purpose sealant around the door hinge/face mating area.**

Grand Cherokee

Adjustment for proper door alignment is made by moving the latch striker.

1. Loosen the door latch striker.
2. Tap the latch striker in whatever direction will properly align the door character line to the character line on the body.
3. Inspect the door alignment. If correct, tighten the striker bolts to 21 ft. lbs. (28 Nm).

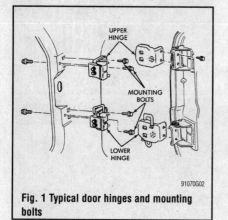

Fig. 1 Typical door hinges and mounting bolts

Fig. 2 Using a pair of pliers, pull out the door stop-to-pillar pin

Fig. 3 Lubricate the door stop-to-pillar strap mechanism

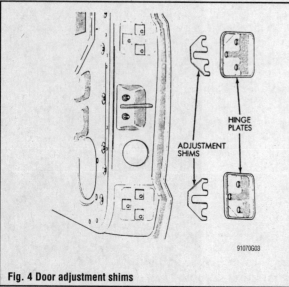

Fig. 4 Door adjustment shims

Hood

REMOVAL & INSTALLATION

▶ **See Figures 5, 6, 7, 8 and 9**

1. Raise the hood fully.
2. If the hood is properly aligned, prior to removal, matchmark the position of the hinges and hood reinforcement.
3. Disconnect the wiring and the release cable.
4. While your assistant supports the hood, remove the hood-to-hinge bolts and lift off the hood. Don't lose the shims, if used.
5. Installation is the reverse of removal. Tighten the bolts to 17 ft. lbs. (23 Nm).

ALIGNMENT

➡**Hood hinge mounting holes are oversized to permit movement for hood alignment. If the hood is to be moved to either side, the hood lock striker, hood lever lock and safety hook assembly must first be loosened.**

Fig. 5 Matchmark the position of the hood

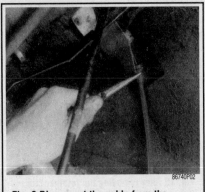

Fig. 6 Disconnect the cable from the bracket . . .

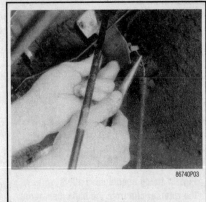

Fig. 7 . . . and the release rod

1. Loosen the hinge mounting bolts slightly on one side and tap the hinge in the direction opposite to that in which the hood is to be moved.
2. Tighten the bolts.
3. Repeat this procedure for the opposite hinge.
4. Check that the lock striker, lever lock and safety hook are properly adjusted to ensure positive locking. Tighten the lockbolts to 8 ft. lbs. (11 Nm).
5. If the rear edge of the hood is not flush with the cowl, add or subtract shims (caster and camber adjusting shims will work) or flat washers between the hinge and the hood at the rear bolt (hood too low) or front bolt (hood too high).
6. Adjust the hood-to-fender height using the front bumpers, located at the left and right front corners of the vehicle.

Tailgate

REMOVAL & INSTALLATION

Comanche

1. Lower the tailgate.
2. Pull each support up at the center and force the upper end forward, then inward, to disengage it from the retaining dowel.
3. Pull the right side of the tailgate rearward to disengage the hinge.
4. Move the tailgate to the right to disengage the left hinge.
5. Installation is the reverse of removal.

ALIGNMENT

The only adjustment possible to the Comanche's tailgate is the striker adjustment. This is performed by loosening the striker plate screws and moving the striker to properly position it.

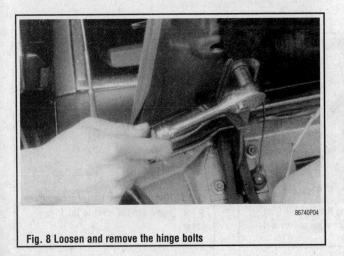

Fig. 8 Loosen and remove the hinge bolts

Fig. 9 Remove the shims and place them aside

Liftgate

REMOVAL & INSTALLATION

▶ See Figures 10, 11, 12 and 13

1. Open the liftgate.
2. Remove the trim panel.

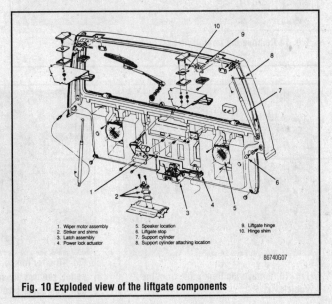

1. Wiper motor assembly
2. Striker and shims
3. Latch assembly
4. Power lock actuator
5. Speaker location
6. Liftgate stop
7. Support cylinder
8. Support cylinder attaching location
9. Liftgate hinge
10. Hinge shim

Fig. 10 Exploded view of the liftgate components

Fig. 11 Using needle nose pliers, remove the retainer clip from the ball studs at the end of the liftgate support cylinders

Fig. 12 After removing the retainer clip, firmly pull the support cylinder off of the stud

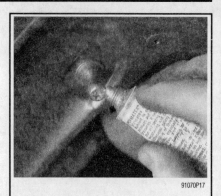

Fig. 13 Lubricate the ball stud with grease before installing the support cylinder

✳✳ CAUTION

Never attempt to remove a support cylinder with the liftgate closed. The cylinders contain gas under high pressure. Severe personal injury may occur if the cylinders are disconnect with the liftgate closed!

3. Remove the retainer clips from the ball studs at the ends of the liftgate support cylinders.
4. Pull the support cylinders off of the ball studs.
5. Disconnect and remove the wiring harness.
6. Have a helper support the liftgate and remove the liftgate hinge bolts.
7. Installation is the reverse of removal. Tighten fasteners to 7 ft. lbs. (10 Nm). Check alignment.

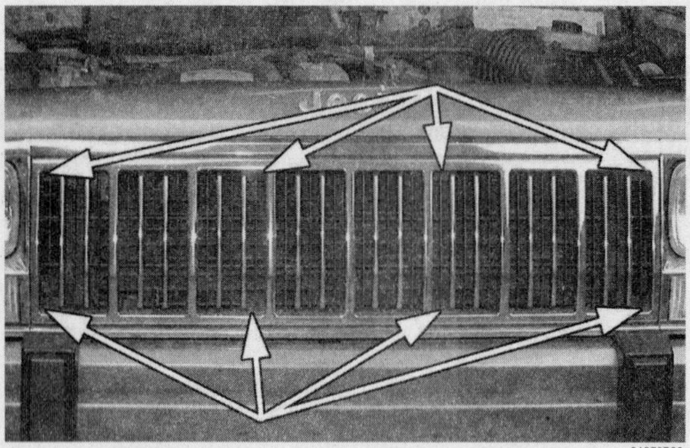

Fig. 14 Remove the front grille assembly mounting screws

ALIGNMENT

The position of the liftgate can be adjusted upward or downward, and inward or outward by use of hinge shims. Also, the hinge-to-body bolt holes are slotted to permit satisfactory alignment. Liftgate stop bumpers must also be adjusted if the hinges are adjusted. The bumpers are adjusted by shims.

Grille

REMOVAL & INSTALLATION

▶ **See Figures 14 and 15**

1. Remove the grille attaching screws and lift the grille from the grille panel.
2. Installation is the reverse of removal.

Outside Mirrors

REMOVAL & INSTALLATION

Regular
▶ **See Figures 16, 17, 18, 19 and 20**

1. Remove door interior trim panel.
2. Remove the screws holding the window trim cover and remove.
3. If equipped with remote mirror, use a small hex key tool to loosen the set screw which holds the toggle control. Remove the trim cover and gasket.
4. If equipped with power windows, disconnect the wire harness at the connector in the door. Pull the harness up through the door.
5. Remove the mirror retaining screws. Remove the mirror from the door.
6. Installation is the reverse of removal.

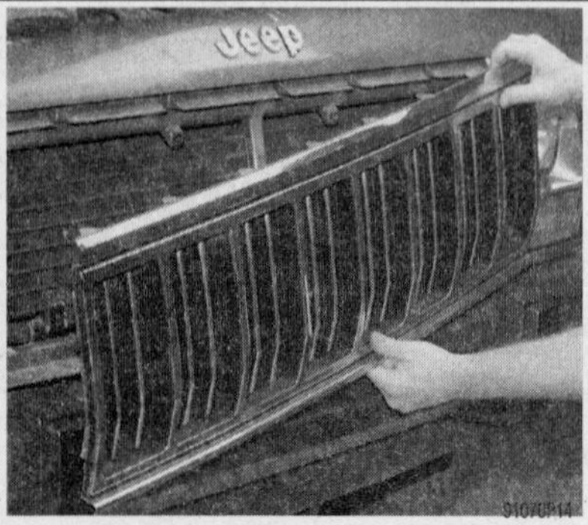

Fig. 15 Remove the front grille from the vehicle

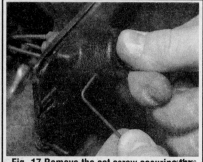

Fig. 16 After removing the interior door panel, remove the side view mirror window trim cover screw

Fig. 17 Remove the set screw securing the mirror toggle control lever to the trim cover

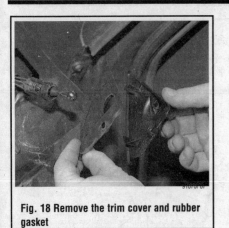
Fig. 18 Remove the trim cover and rubber gasket

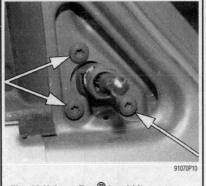
Fig. 19 Using a Torx® head bit, remove the 3 side view mirror retaining screws

Fig. 20 . . . then pull the side view mirror assembly out of the door

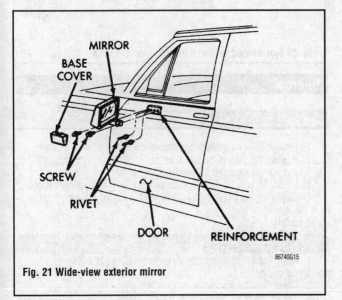
Fig. 21 Wide-view exterior mirror

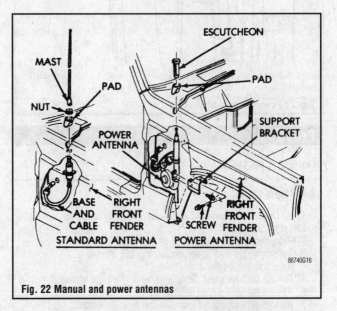
Fig. 22 Manual and power antennas

Wide—View

▶ See Figure 21

1. Remove the mirror base cover.
2. Remove the mirror base attaching screws. The mirror base reinforcement is attached to the inside of the door with rivets.
3. Remove the mirror from the door panel.
4. Installation is the reverse of removal.

Antenna

REPLACEMENT

▶ See Figures 22, 23 and 24

1. Remove the fender inner splash shield nuts and move the panel aside far enough to get at the antenna cable and base.
2. Unscrew the antenna mast and nut, then remove the antenna pad from the top of the fender.
3. Remove the passenger side kick panel.
4. If equipped with a power antenna:
   a. Disconnect the negative battery cable.
   b. Disconnect the harness from the relay. The relay is located behind the right hand side of the dash just above its lower edge.
   c. Remove the antenna mounting bolts and washers.
   d. Pull the antenna motor harness through the hole in the kick panel.
5. Disconnect the antenna lead by pull and twisting the metal connectors. NEVER pull on the cable!

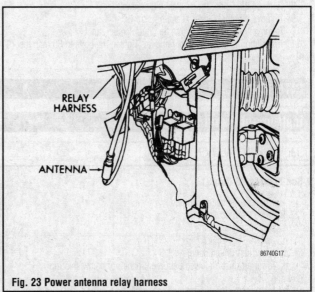
Fig. 23 Power antenna relay harness

6. Pull the rubber grommet out of the kick panel.
7. Remove the antenna assembly from the inside of the wheelhouse.
8. Installation is the reverse of removal.

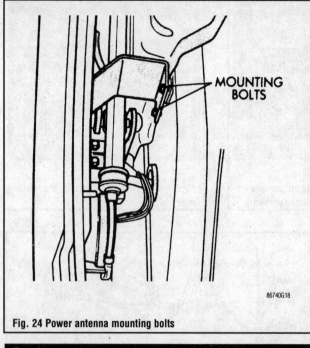

Fig. 24 Power antenna mounting bolts

Fenders

REMOVAL & INSTALLATION

▶ See Figure 25

1. On Grand Cherokee/Grand Wagoneer, remove the headlamp, side marker and turn signal lamp.
2. Remove the front bumper.
3. If removing the right fender, remove the radio antenna.
4. Raise and support the vehicle safely.
5. Remove the front wheel, fender liner, fender flare and retainers.
6. Remove the grille and air deflector.
7. Remove the rocker panel moulding and all fender braces.
8. Remove the fender lower attaching screws.
9. Remove all other fender attaching screws.
10. Remove the front fender from the inner fender panel.
11. Installation is the reverse of removal. Tighten the bolts to 80 inch lbs. (9 Nm).

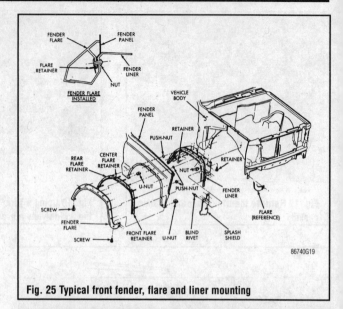

Fig. 25 Typical front fender, flare and liner mounting

Sunroof

REMOVAL & INSTALLATION

1. Remove the wind deflector mechanism covers.
2. Position the glass to the vent position.
3. Position the sunshade full rearward.
4. Loosen the nuts holding the glass panel to the side adjustment brackets.
5. Slide the glass panel rearward 0.50 in. (12mm) and separate the glass from the sunroof unit.

To install:

6. Position the glass panel in the opening with the logo rearward and slide the panel forward 0.50 in. (12mm).
7. Verify that the attaching nuts are below the top surface of the glass adjustment brackets.
8. Close the sunroof to center the glass in the opening.
9. Tighten the center screws to hold the adjustment.
10. Open the glass to the vent position and tighten the nuts to 71 inch lbs. (8 Nm).
11. Close the glass and check the alignment.
12. Install the mechanism covers.
13. Adjust the wind deflector if necessary.

INTERIOR

Instrument Panel and Pad

REMOVAL & INSTALLTION

▶ See Figures 26 thru 31

1. Disconnect the battery ground.
2. Remove the following:
   a. parking brake handle
   b. ash tray
   c. lower instrument panel
   d. lower air duct on lower instrument panel, or below steering column
   e. instrument cluster bezel and assembly
   f. clock
   g. radio and heater control panel
   h. instrument panel switches
   i. headlamp switch
   j. antenna connector
   k. blower motor resistors

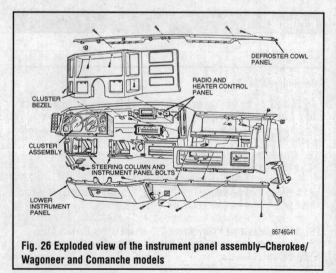

Fig. 26 Exploded view of the instrument panel assembly—Cherokee/Wagoneer and Comanche models

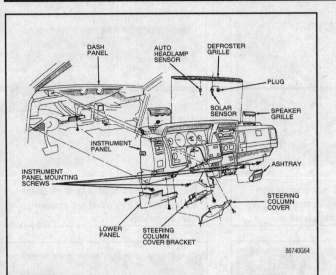

Fig. 27 Exploded view of the instrument panel assembly—Grand Cherokee/Grand Wagoneer models

l. ground lead
m. disconnect glove box light
n. defroster cowl panel
o. instrument panel attaching bolts
p. steering column attaching bolts
q. instrument panel assembly
3. Pull the panel out and disconnect the wiring harness.
4. Installation is the reverse of removal.

Console

REMOVAL & INSTALLATION

Center

▶ **See Figures 32 thru 41**

1. If equipped with an automatic transmission, remove the shift lever knob by pulling the knob straight up. Then carefully Carefully pry up and pull to remove the transmission shift indicator bezel.

2. If equipped with a manual transmission, remove the shift lever knob by loosening the locknut and then unthreading the knob from the shaft. Pull up the shift boot to remove.

3. Pry up and pull to remove the transfer case selector bezel.

4. If equipped, loosen the console trim panel retaining screws, then carefully pull up on the console trim panel and remove from the vehicle.

5. Open up the storage box lid on the console and remove the 2 retaining screws located at the bottom of the compartment.

6. Remove any other console housing retaining screws.

7. If necessary, disengage the wiring harness connector.

8. Carefully pull up on the console assembly and remove from the vehicle

9. If necessary after removing the console unit, remove the A/C-warm air duct from the center of the floor

10. Installation is the reverse of removal.

Overhead

1. Remove attaching screw located forward of compass.

2. Flex housing outward while pressing upward to disengage from rear bracket.

3. Slide console rearward until the console detaches from the front mounting bracket.

4. While pressing upwards on the rear of the console, slide it forward hold-

Fig. 28 Remove the ashtray from the dash board . . .

Fig. 29 . . . then remove the retaining screw located behind it

Fig. 30 Remove the lower dash panel retaining screws

Fig. 31 Disconnect the lower A/C duct hose from the outlet on the lower dash panel

Fig. 32 Firmly pull off the shift lever knob

Fig. 33 Carefully pry up and pull to remove the transmission shift indicator bezel

Fig. 34 Pry up and pull to remove the transfer case selector bezel

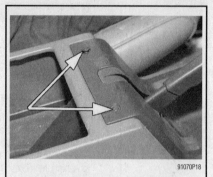

Fig. 35 Remove the 2 rear console trim panel retaining screws located just above the emergency handbrake lever . . .

Fig. 36 . . . then carefully pull up on the center console trim panel and remove from the vehicle

Fig. 37 Remove the screw that secures the transfer case selector light bulb socket housing

Fig. 38 After removing the transmission shift indicator bezel (automatic only), remove the 2 console housing retaining screws . . .

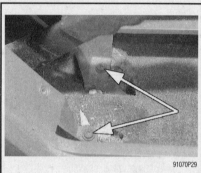

Fig. 39 . . . as well as the 2 retaining screws located under the emergency handbrake lever

Fig. 40 Open the storage box lid on the console and remove the 2 retaining screws located at the bottom of the compartment

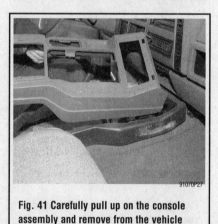

Fig. 41 Carefully pull up on the console assembly and remove from the vehicle

Fig. 42 Using a small flat bladed tool, disengage the small retaining clip for the interior door handle

ing the front away from the headliner, until the rear detaches from the headliner and becomes free.

5. Disconnect wire harness from console and remove.

6. Installation is the reverse of removal. Be sure to flex console outward near the rear allowing engagement with the rear mounting bracket.

Door Panels

REMOVAL & INSTALLATION

Front

▶ See Figures 42 thru 49

1. Unbolt and remove the inside door latch and remove the latch panel retaining screws.

2. Disconnect the door latch control linkage and, if equipped, wiring harness. Remove the control panel.

3. If equipped with manual windows, remove the window crank handles.

4. Remove the armrest lower retaining screws and swing the armrest downward to disengage the upper retaining clip. Pull the armrest straight out from the door panel.

5. Starting at the bottom of the door panel, use a flat tool, such as a wood spatula, pry out the panel-to-door frame retaining pins by levering right up against the pin. If a forked-end tool is available, use one. These pins are easy to rip out of the trim panel.

6. Installation is the reverse of removal. A firm hit with the heel of your palm is usually enough to drive the retainers into the holes in the door panel. Make sure that the retainer is directly over the hole before knocking it in, or it may be damaged.

Fig. 43 Using a small flat bladed tool, disengage the small retaining clip for the interior door lock button

91070P13

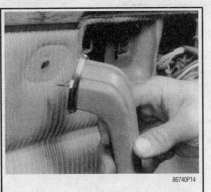

Fig. 44 . . . and wiring harness

86740P11

Fig. 45 Remove the armrest attaching screws . . .

86740P12

Fig. 46 . . . then swing it downwards . . .

86740P13

Fig. 47 . . . and pull it from the panel

86740P14

Fig. 48 A special tool is available to disengage the retaining clips

86740P15

Rear Door

1. Unbolt and remove the inside door latch. Remove the latch panel retaining screws.
2. Disconnect the door latch control linkage and, if equipped, wiring harness. Remove the control panel.
3. If equipped with manual windows, remove the window crank handles.
4. Remove the armrest retaining screws and lift off the armrest.
5. Starting at the bottom of the door panel, use a flat tool, such as a wood spatula, pry out the panel-to-door frame retaining pins by levering right up against the pin. If a forked-end tool is available, use one. These pins are easy to rip out of the trim panel.

6. Installation is the reverse of removal. A firm hit with the heel of your palm is usually enough to drive the retainers into the dooe panel holes. To prevent damage, make sure the retainer is directly over the hole before knocking it in.

Manual Door Locks

REMOVAL & INSTALLATION

Lock Cylinder

▶ See Figure 50

1. Remove the door trim panel and plastic waterproof sheet.
2. Working through an access hole, remove the lock cylinder retaining clip.

Fig. 49 Carefully pull away the interior door trim panel

91070P11

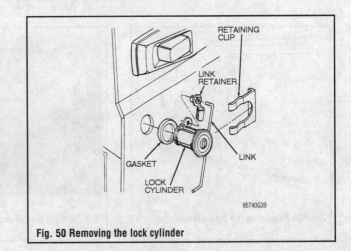

Fig. 50 Removing the lock cylinder

86740G39

3. Disconnect the lock control linkage.
4. Push the lock cylinder from the door.
5. Installation is the reverse of removal.

Latch and Linkage

▶ See Figure 51

1. Remove the door trim panel and plastic waterproof sheet.
2. Remove the latch retaining bolts from the rear edge of the door.
3. Disconnect the linkage from the lock cylinder and remove the latch and linkage.
4. Installation is the reverse of removal. Tighten the latch retaining bolts to 7 ft. lbs.

Power Door Locks

REMOVAL & INSTALLATION

Switch

1. Disconnect the battery ground.
2. Remove the door trim panel and watershield.
3. Remove the switch housing from the inner door panel.
4. Disconnect the wiring and pry up the switch retaining clips. Remove the switch.
5. Installation is the reverse of removal.

Actuator Motor

▶ See Figure 52

1. Disconnect the battery ground.
2. Remove the door trim panel and watershield.

3. Using a 1/4 in. drill bit, drill out the motor mounting rivets.
4. Disconnect the motor actuator rod from the bellcrank.
5. Disconnect the wires from the motor and lift the motor from the door.
6. Installation is the reverse of removal. Use 1/4 x 1/2 in. bolts and locknuts in place of the rivets.

Door Glass and Regulator

REMOVAL & INSTALLATION

Front Door

▶ See Figures 53 thru 60

1. Remove the trim panel and waterproof plastic sheet.
2. Remove the window frame trim molding.
3. Remove the glass channel bottom screw.
4. Remove the vent window frame screws.
5. Tilt the vent window and glass channel backward and remove it from the door frame.
6. Remove the door glass attaching stud nut and spring washer.
7. If equipped with electric windows, disconnect the wiring harness.
8. Drill or grind the heads off the regulator rivets and knock the rivets out with a hammer and punch.
9. Pull the glass upward and out of the door.
10. Remove the regulator.
11. Installation is the reverse of removal. The regulator must be attached with special regulator pop rivets (available at autobody supply stores) or bolts and nuts. Tighten the door glass stud nut to 48 inch lbs. (5 Nm); the vent window bottom screw to 84 inch lbs. (9 Nm); the upper vent window screws to 10 ft. lbs. (14 Nm).

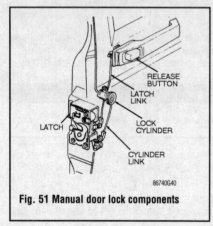

Fig. 51 Manual door lock components

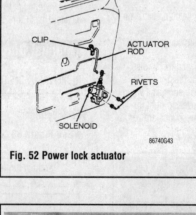

Fig. 52 Power lock actuator

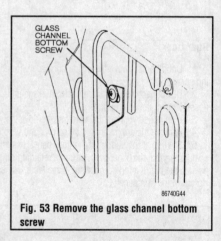

Fig. 53 Remove the glass channel bottom screw

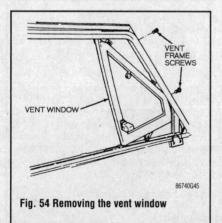

Fig. 54 Removing the vent window

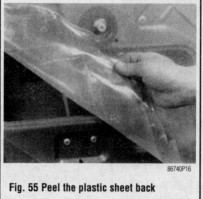

Fig. 55 Peel the plastic sheet back

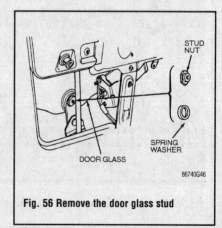

Fig. 56 Remove the door glass stud

Fig. 57 On power windows, unplug the wiring connector

Fig. 58 Manual window regulator rivet locations

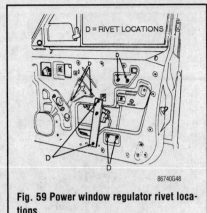

Fig. 59 Power window regulator rivet locations

Fig. 60 Drill the heads off the rivets. Don't forget your safety glasses

Rear Door

1. Remove the trim panel and waterproof plastic sheet.
2. Lower the door glass and remove the weatherstripping.
3. Remove the stationary glass frame screws.
4. Remove the glass channel upper screws.
5. Remove the glass channel lower screws.
6. Tilt the stationary glass and its channel forward and remove it.
7. Remove the door glass stud nut and lift the glass from the door.
8. Grind the heads off the regulator rivets and knock the rivets out with a hammer and punch.
9. Pull the glass upward and out of the door.
10. Installation is the reverse of removal. Torque the stud nut to 48 inch lbs. and the glass channel screws to 60-84 inch lbs. Use special regulator pop rivets (available at autobody supply stores) or nuts and bolts to install the regulator.

Electric Window Motor

REMOVAL & INSTALLATION

1. Remove the window glass and regulator.
2. Disconnect the wiring.
3. Unbolt and remove the motor.

Windshield and Fixed Glass

REMOVAL & INSTALLATION

If your windshield, or other fixed window, is cracked or chipped, you may decide to replace it with a new one yourself. However, there are two main reasons why replacement windshields and other window glass should be installed only by a professional automotive glass technician: safety and cost.

The most important reason a professional should install automotive glass is for safety. The glass in the vehicle, especially the windshield, is designed with safety in mind in case of a collision. The windshield is specially manufactured from two panes of specially-tempered glass with a thin layer of transparent plastic between them. This construction allows the glass to "give" in the event that a part of your body hits the windshield during the collision, and prevents the glass from shattering, which could cause lacerations, blinding and other harm to passengers of the vehicle. The other fixed windows are designed to be tempered so that if they break during a collision, they shatter in such a way that there are no large pointed glass pieces. The professional automotive glass technician knows how to install the glass in a vehicle so that it will function optimally during a collision. Without the proper experience, knowledge and tools, installing a piece of automotive glass yourself could lead to additional harm if an accident should ever occur.

Cost is also a factor when deciding to install automotive glass yourself. Performing this could cost you much more than a professional may charge for the same job. Since the windshield is designed to break under stress, an often life saving characteristic, windshields tend to break VERY easily when an inexperienced person attempts to install one. Do-it-yourselfers buying two, three or even four windshields from a salvage yard because they have broken them during installation are common stories. Also, since the automotive glass is designed to prevent the outside elements from entering your vehicle, improper installation can lead to water and air leaks. Annoying whining noises at highway speeds from air leaks or inside body panel rusting from water leaks can add to your stress level and subtract from your wallet. After buying two or three windshields, installing them and ending up with a leak that produces a noise while driving and water damage during rainstorms, the cost of having a professional do it correctly the first time may be much more alluring. We here at Chilton, therefore, advise that you have a professional automotive glass technician service any broken glass on your vehicle.

WINDSHIELD CHIP REPAIR

♦ **See Figures 61 and 62**

➥**Check with your state and local authorities on the laws for state safety inspection. Some states or municipalities may not allow chip repair as a viable option for correcting stone damage to your windshield.**

Although severely cracked or damaged windshields must be replaced, there is something that you can do to prolong or even prevent the need for replacement of a chipped windshield. There are many companies which offer windshield chip repair products, such as Loctite's ® Bullseye™ windshield repair kit. These kits usually consist of a syringe, pedestal and a sealing adhesive. The syringe is mounted on the pedestal and is used to create a vacuum which pulls the plastic layer against the glass. This helps make the chip transparent. The adhesive is then injected which seals the chip and helps to prevent further stress cracks from developing

➥**Always follow the specific manufacturer's instructions.**

TCCA0P00

Fig. 61 Small chips on your windshield can be fixed with an after-market repair kit, such as the one from Loctite®

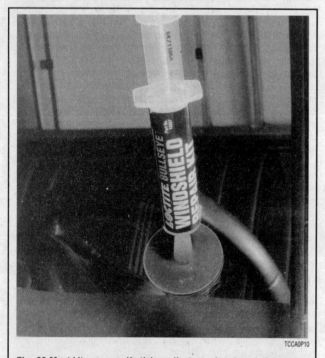

TCCA0P10

Fig. 62 Most kits use a self-stick applicator and syringe to inject the adhesive into the chip or crack

Inside Rear View Mirror

REPLACEMENT

To replace the rear view mirror, loosen the mirror set screw and slide the mirror base up and off the retaining bracket. Install the replacement mirror on to the retaining bracket and tighten the set screw. DO NOT overtighten the set screw as this will chip or break the windshield.

To replace the retaining bracket use the following procedure:

1. Mark installation reference position lines on the outside of the windshield glass with a grease pencil. Mark both horizontal and vertical reference marks.

2. If the vinyl pad remained on the windshield glass, soften and remove it with a heat gun.

3. Thoroughly clean the bracket contact surface area on the glass. Use a mild abrasive cleaning solution and final clean with isopropyl alcohol.

4. Lightly sand the contact area on the replacement bracket with fine grit sandpaper. Wipe the bracket clean with alcohol.

5. Follow the manufacturers instructions for preparing the adhesive.

6. Install the rear view mirror.

Seats

REMOVAL & INSTALLATION

Bucket Seats

Bucket seat platforms are attached to the floor panel with studs and nuts. The trim covers are attached to the platform with either push-on type fasteners or screws.

1. Remove the seat platform cover fasteners and platform cover.

2. For power seats, disconnect the wire harness connector.

3. Remove the seat retaining nuts and remove the seat from the floor panel.

4. Installation is the reverse of removal. Tighten the retaining nuts to 18 ft. lbs. (24 Nm).

Rear Seat

1. Disengage the seat cushion at the rear by pulling upward on the release strap.

2. Tilt the seat cushion forward and disengage the seat cushion latch with the release lever knob. Separate the right side latch and the left side seat bracket from the floor anchor bolts, then remove the cushion from the vehicle.

3. Remove the shoulder/lap belt buckles from the elastic straps. Release the seatback lock.

4. Remove the pivot bolts and the washers from the wheelhouse panel anchors.

5. Tilt the seatback forward, lift it upward and remove from the vehicle.

To install:

6. Position the seatback in the vehicle. Install the pivot bolts/washers and tighten to 38 ft. lbs. (52 Nm).

7. Lock the seatback in place. Insert the shoulder/lap belt buckles in the elastic straps.

8. Position the seat cushion in the vehicle. Insert the left pivot in the anchor grommet.

9. Force the tight side latch onto the anchor bolt and pivot the seat cushion to the horizontal position.

10. Lock the seat cushion in-place by pressing firmly on the center of the cushion until the latch engages.

Bench Seat (Comanche)

1. If equipped, disengage the seat frame trim cover retainers and remove the trim covers.

2. Detach the shoulder belt buckles and lap belts from the seat.

3. Remove the seat track platform retaining nuts from the studs and remove the seat.

4. Installation is the reverse of removal. Tighten the retaining nuts to 18 ft. lbs. (24 Nm).

GLOSSARY

AIR/FUEL RATIO: The ratio of air-to-gasoline by weight in the fuel mixture drawn into the engine.

AIR INJECTION: One method of reducing harmful exhaust emissions by injecting air into each of the exhaust ports of an engine. The fresh air entering the hot exhaust manifold causes any remaining fuel to be burned before it can exit the tailpipe.

ALTERNATOR: A device used for converting mechanical energy into electrical energy.

AMMETER: An instrument, calibrated in amperes, used to measure the flow of an electrical current in a circuit. Ammeters are always connected in series with the circuit being tested.

AMPERE: The rate of flow of electrical current present when one volt of electrical pressure is applied against one ohm of electrical resistance.

ANALOG COMPUTER: Any microprocessor that uses similar (analogous) electrical signals to make its calculations.

ARMATURE: A laminated, soft iron core wrapped by a wire that converts electrical energy to mechanical energy as in a motor or relay. When rotated in a magnetic field, it changes mechanical energy into electrical energy as in a generator.

ATMOSPHERIC PRESSURE: The pressure on the Earth's surface caused by the weight of the air in the atmosphere. At sea level, this pressure is 14.7 psi at 32°F (101 kPa at 0°C).

ATOMIZATION: The breaking down of a liquid into a fine mist that can be suspended in air.

AXIAL PLAY: Movement parallel to a shaft or bearing bore.

BACKFIRE: The sudden combustion of gases in the intake or exhaust system that results in a loud explosion.

BACKLASH: The clearance or play between two parts, such as meshed gears.

BACKPRESSURE: Restrictions in the exhaust system that slow the exit of exhaust gases from the combustion chamber.

BAKELITE: A heat resistant, plastic insulator material commonly used in printed circuit boards and transistorized components.

BALL BEARING: A bearing made up of hardened inner and outer races between which hardened steel balls roll.

BALLAST RESISTOR: A resistor in the primary ignition circuit that lowers voltage after the engine is started to reduce wear on ignition components.

BEARING: A friction reducing, supportive device usually located between a stationary part and a moving part.

BIMETAL TEMPERATURE SENSOR: Any sensor or switch made of two dissimilar types of metal that bend when heated or cooled due to the different expansion rates of the alloys. These types of sensors usually function as an on/off switch.

BLOWBY: Combustion gases, composed of water vapor and unburned fuel, that leak past the piston rings into the crankcase during normal engine operation. These gases are removed by the PCV system to prevent the buildup of harmful acids in the crankcase.

BRAKE PAD: A brake shoe and lining assembly used with disc brakes.

BRAKE SHOE: The backing for the brake lining. The term is, however, usually applied to the assembly of the brake backing and lining.

BUSHING: A liner, usually removable, for a bearing; an anti-friction liner used in place of a bearing.

CALIPER: A hydraulically activated device in a disc brake system, which is mounted straddling the brake rotor (disc). The caliper contains at least one piston and two brake pads. Hydraulic pressure on the piston(s) forces the pads against the rotor.

CAMSHAFT: A shaft in the engine on which are the lobes (cams) which operate the valves. The camshaft is driven by the crankshaft, via a belt, chain or gears, at one half the crankshaft speed.

CAPACITOR: A device which stores an electrical charge.

CARBON MONOXIDE (CO): A colorless, odorless gas given off as a normal byproduct of combustion. It is poisonous and extremely dangerous in confined areas, building up slowly to toxic levels without warning if adequate ventilation is not available.

CARBURETOR: A device, usually mounted on the intake manifold of an engine, which mixes the air and fuel in the proper proportion to allow even combustion.

CATALYTIC CONVERTER: A device installed in the exhaust system, like a muffler, that converts harmful byproducts of combustion into carbon dioxide and water vapor by means of a heat-producing chemical reaction.

CENTRIFUGAL ADVANCE: A mechanical method of advancing the spark timing by using flyweights in the distributor that react to centrifugal force generated by the distributor shaft rotation.

CHECK VALVE: Any one-way valve installed to permit the flow of air, fuel or vacuum in one direction only.

CHOKE: A device, usually a moveable valve, placed in the intake path of a carburetor to restrict the flow of air.

CIRCUIT: Any unbroken path through which an electrical current can flow. Also used to describe fuel flow in some instances.

CIRCUIT BREAKER: A switch which protects an electrical circuit from overload by opening the circuit when the current flow exceeds a predetermined level. Some circuit breakers must be reset manually, while most reset automatically.

COIL (IGNITION): A transformer in the ignition circuit which steps up the voltage provided to the spark plugs.

COMBINATION MANIFOLD: An assembly which includes both the intake and exhaust manifolds in one casting.

COMBINATION VALVE: A device used in some fuel systems that routes fuel vapors to a charcoal storage canister instead of venting them into the atmosphere. The valve relieves fuel tank pressure and allows fresh air into the tank as the fuel level drops to prevent a vapor lock situation.

COMPRESSION RATIO: The comparison of the total volume of the cylinder and combustion chamber with the piston at BDC and the piston at TDC.

CONDENSER: 1. An electrical device which acts to store an electrical charge, preventing voltage surges. 2. A radiator-like device in the air conditioning system in which refrigerant gas condenses into a liquid, giving off heat.

CONDUCTOR: Any material through which an electrical current can be transmitted easily.

CONTINUITY: Continuous or complete circuit. Can be checked with an ohmmeter.

COUNTERSHAFT: An intermediate shaft which is rotated by a mainshaft and transmits, in turn, that rotation to a working part.

CRANKCASE: The lower part of an engine in which the crankshaft and related parts operate.

CRANKSHAFT: The main driving shaft of an engine which receives reciprocating motion from the pistons and converts it to rotary motion.

CYLINDER: In an engine, the round hole in the engine block in which the piston(s) ride.

CYLINDER BLOCK: The main structural member of an engine in which is found the cylinders, crankshaft and other principal parts.

CYLINDER HEAD: The detachable portion of the engine, usually fastened to the top of the cylinder block and containing all or most of the combustion chambers. On overhead valve engines, it contains the valves and their operating parts. On overhead cam engines, it contains the camshaft as well.

DEAD CENTER: The extreme top or bottom of the piston stroke.

DETONATION: An unwanted explosion of the air/fuel mixture in the combustion chamber caused by excess heat and compression, advanced timing, or an overly lean mixture. Also referred to as "ping".

DIAPHRAGM: A thin, flexible wall separating two cavities, such as in a vacuum advance unit.

DIESELING: A condition in which hot spots in the combustion chamber cause the engine to run on after the key is turned off.

DIFFERENTIAL: A geared assembly which allows the transmission of motion between drive axles, giving one axle the ability to turn faster than the other.

DIODE: An electrical device that will allow current to flow in one direction only.

DISC BRAKE: A hydraulic braking assembly consisting of a brake disc, or rotor, mounted on an axle, and a caliper assembly containing, usually two brake pads which are activated by hydraulic pressure. The pads are forced against the sides of the disc, creating friction which slows the vehicle.

DISTRIBUTOR: A mechanically driven device on an engine which is responsible for electrically firing the spark plug at a predetermined point of the piston stroke.

DOWEL PIN: A pin, inserted in mating holes in two different parts allowing those parts to maintain a fixed relationship.

DRUM BRAKE: A braking system which consists of two brake shoes and one or two wheel cylinders, mounted on a fixed backing plate, and a brake drum, mounted on an axle, which revolves around the assembly.

DWELL: The rate, measured in degrees of shaft rotation, at which an electrical circuit cycles on and off.

ELECTRONIC CONTROL UNIT (ECU): Ignition module, module, amplifier or igniter. See Module for definition.

ELECTRONIC IGNITION: A system in which the timing and firing of the spark plugs is controlled by an electronic control unit, usually called a module. These systems have no points or condenser.

END-PLAY: The measured amount of axial movement in a shaft.

ENGINE: A device that converts heat into mechanical energy.

EXHAUST MANIFOLD: A set of cast passages or pipes which conduct exhaust gases from the engine.

FEELER GAUGE: A blade, usually metal, or precisely predetermined thickness, used to measure the clearance between two parts.

FIRING ORDER: The order in which combustion occurs in the cylinders of an engine. Also the order in which spark is distributed to the plugs by the distributor.

FLOODING: The presence of too much fuel in the intake manifold and combustion chamber which prevents the air/fuel mixture from firing, thereby causing a no-start situation.

FLYWHEEL: A disc shaped part bolted to the rear end of the crankshaft. Around the outer perimeter is affixed the ring gear. The starter drive engages the ring gear, turning the flywheel, which rotates the crankshaft, imparting the initial starting motion to the engine.

FOOT POUND (ft. lbs. or sometimes, ft.lb.): The amount of energy or work needed to raise an item weighing one pound, a distance of one foot.

FUSE: A protective device in a circuit which prevents circuit overload by breaking the circuit when a specific amperage is present. The device is constructed around a strip or wire of a lower amperage rating than the circuit it is designed to protect. When an amperage higher than that stamped on the fuse is present in the circuit, the strip or wire melts, opening the circuit.

GEAR RATIO: The ratio between the number of teeth on meshing gears.

GENERATOR: A device which converts mechanical energy into electrical energy.

HEAT RANGE: The measure of a spark plug's ability to dissipate heat from its firing end. The higher the heat range, the hotter the plug fires.

HUB: The center part of a wheel or gear.

HYDROCARBON (HC): Any chemical compound made up of hydrogen and carbon. A major pollutant formed by the engine as a byproduct of combustion.

HYDROMETER: An instrument used to measure the specific gravity of a solution.

INCH POUND (inch lbs.; sometimes in.lb. or in. lbs.): One twelfth of a foot pound.

INDUCTION: A means of transferring electrical energy in the form of a magnetic field. Principle used in the ignition coil to increase voltage.

INJECTOR: A device which receives metered fuel under relatively low pressure and is activated to inject the fuel into the engine under relatively high pressure at a predetermined time.

INPUT SHAFT: The shaft to which torque is applied, usually carrying the driving gear or gears.

INTAKE MANIFOLD: A casting of passages or pipes used to conduct air or a fuel/air mixture to the cylinders.

JOURNAL: The bearing surface within which a shaft operates.

KEY: A small block usually fitted in a notch between a shaft and a hub to prevent slippage of the two parts.

MANIFOLD: A casting of passages or set of pipes which connect the cylinders to an inlet or outlet source.

MANIFOLD VACUUM: Low pressure in an engine intake manifold formed just below the throttle plates. Manifold vacuum is highest at idle and drops under acceleration.

MASTER CYLINDER: The primary fluid pressurizing device in a hydraulic system. In automotive use, it is found in brake and hydraulic clutch systems and is pedal activated, either directly or, in a power brake system, through the power booster.

MODULE: Electronic control unit, amplifier or igniter of solid state or integrated design which controls the current flow in the ignition primary circuit based on input from the pick-up coil. When the module opens the primary circuit, high secondary voltage is induced in the coil.

NEEDLE BEARING: A bearing which consists of a number (usually a large number) of long, thin rollers.

OHM: (Ω) The unit used to measure the resistance of conductor-to-electrical flow. One ohm is the amount of resistance that limits current flow to one ampere in a circuit with one volt of pressure.

OHMMETER: An instrument used for measuring the resistance, in ohms, in an electrical circuit.

OUTPUT SHAFT: The shaft which transmits torque from a device, such as a transmission.

OVERDRIVE: A gear assembly which produces more shaft revolutions than that transmitted to it.

OVERHEAD CAMSHAFT (OHC): An engine configuration in which the camshaft is mounted on top of the cylinder head and operates the valve either directly or by means of rocker arms.

OVERHEAD VALVE (OHV): An engine configuration in which all of the valves are located in the cylinder head and the camshaft is located in the cylinder block. The camshaft operates the valves via lifters and push-rods.

OXIDES OF NITROGEN (NOx): Chemical compounds of nitrogen produced as a byproduct of combustion. They combine with hydrocarbons to produce smog.

OXYGEN SENSOR: Use with the feedback system to sense the presence of oxygen in the exhaust gas and signal the computer which can reference the voltage signal to an air/fuel ratio.

PINION: The smaller of two meshing gears.

PISTON RING: An open-ended ring with fits into a groove on the outer diameter of the piston. Its chief function is to form a seal between the piston and cylinder wall. Most automotive pistons have three rings: two for compression sealing; one for oil sealing.

PRELOAD: A predetermined load placed on a bearing during assembly or by adjustment.

PRIMARY CIRCUIT: the low voltage side of the ignition system which consists of the ignition switch, ballast resistor or resistance wire, bypass, coil, electronic control unit and pick-up coil as well as the connecting wires and harnesses.

PRESS FIT: The mating of two parts under pressure, due to the inner diameter of one being smaller than the outer diameter of the other, or vice versa; an interference fit.

RACE: The surface on the inner or outer ring of a bearing on which the balls, needles or rollers move.

REGULATOR: A device which maintains the amperage and/or voltage levels of a circuit at predetermined values.

RELAY: A switch which automatically opens and/or closes a circuit.

RESISTANCE: The opposition to the flow of current through a circuit or electrical device, and is measured in ohms. Resistance is equal to the voltage divided by the amperage.

RESISTOR: A device, usually made of wire, which offers a preset amount of resistance in an electrical circuit.

RING GEAR: The name given to a ring-shaped gear attached to a differential case, or affixed to a flywheel or as part of a planetary gear set.

ROLLER BEARING: A bearing made up of hardened inner and outer races between which hardened steel rollers move.

ROTOR: 1. The disc-shaped part of a disc brake assembly, upon which the brake pads bear; also called, brake disc. 2. The device mounted atop the distributor shaft, which passes current to the distributor cap tower contacts.

SECONDARY CIRCUIT: The high voltage side of the ignition system, usually above 20,000 volts. The secondary includes the ignition coil, coil wire, distributor cap and rotor, spark plug wires and spark plugs.

SENDING UNIT: A mechanical, electrical, hydraulic or electro-magnetic device which transmits information to a gauge.

SENSOR: Any device designed to measure engine operating conditions or ambient pressures and temperatures. Usually electronic in nature and designed to send a voltage signal to an on-board computer, some sensors may operate as a simple on/off switch or they may provide a variable voltage signal (like a potentiometer) as conditions or measured parameters change.

SHIM: Spacers of precise, predetermined thickness used between parts to establish a proper working relationship.

SLAVE CYLINDER: In automotive use, a device in the hydraulic clutch system which is activated by hydraulic force, disengaging the clutch.

SOLENOID: A coil used to produce a magnetic field, the effect of which is to produce work.

SPARK PLUG: A device screwed into the combustion chamber of a spark ignition engine. The basic construction is a conductive core inside of a ceramic insulator, mounted in an outer conductive base. An electrical charge from the spark plug wire travels along the conductive core and jumps a preset air gap to a grounding point or points at the end of the conductive base. The resultant spark ignites the fuel/air mixture in the combustion chamber.

SPLINES: Ridges machined or cast onto the outer diameter of a shaft or inner diameter of a bore to enable parts to mate without rotation.

TACHOMETER: A device used to measure the rotary speed of an engine, shaft, gear, etc., usually in rotations per minute.

THERMOSTAT: A valve, located in the cooling system of an engine, which is closed when cold and opens gradually in response to engine heating, controlling the temperature of the coolant and rate of coolant flow.

TOP DEAD CENTER (TDC): The point at which the piston reaches the top of its travel on the compression stroke.

TORQUE: The twisting force applied to an object.

TORQUE CONVERTER: A turbine used to transmit power from a driving member to a driven member via hydraulic action, providing changes in drive ratio and torque. In automotive use, it links the driveplate at the rear of the engine to the automatic transmission.

TRANSDUCER: A device used to change a force into an electrical signal.

TRANSISTOR: A semi-conductor component which can be actuated by a small voltage to perform an electrical switching function.

TUNE-UP: A regular maintenance function, usually associated with the replacement and adjustment of parts and components in the electrical and fuel systems of a vehicle for the purpose of attaining optimum performance.

TURBOCHARGER: An exhaust driven pump which compresses intake air and forces it into the combustion chambers at higher than atmospheric pressures. The increased air pressure allows more fuel to be burned and results in increased horsepower being produced.

VACUUM ADVANCE: A device which advances the ignition timing in response to increased engine vacuum.

VACUUM GAUGE: An instrument used to measure the presence of vacuum in a chamber.

VALVE: A device which control the pressure, direction of flow or rate of flow of a liquid or gas.

VALVE CLEARANCE: The measured gap between the end of the valve stem and the rocker arm, cam lobe or follower that activates the valve.

VISCOSITY: The rating of a liquid's internal resistance to flow.

VOLTMETER: An instrument used for measuring electrical force in units called volts. Voltmeters are always connected parallel with the circuit being tested.

WHEEL CYLINDER: Found in the automotive drum brake assembly, it is a device, actuated by hydraulic pressure, which, through internal pistons, pushes the brake shoes outward against the drums.

MASTER
INDEX